Random House Webster's Pocket Russian Dictionary

Richard RAPPAPORT

РИЧАРД РАППАПОРТ

3301 Bayshore Blvd

Tampa FL 33629

813 639-9221

Random House Webster's Pocket Russian Dictionary

Second Edition

Russian-English
English-Russian

Русско-английский
Англо-русский словарь

Edited by
I. Christina Sperrle
Ph.D., Slavic Languages and Literatures
COLUMBIA UNIVERSITY

RANDOM HOUSE
NEW YORK

Random House Webster's Pocket Russian Dictionary,
Second Edition

This book is available for special purchases in bulk by organizations and institutions, not for resale, at special discounts. Please direct your inquiries to the Random House Special Sales Department, toll-free 888-591-1200 or fax 212-572-4961.

Please address inquiries about electronic licensing of reference products, for use on a network or in software or on CD-ROM, to the Subsidiary Rights Department, Random House Reference & Information Publishing, fax 212-940-7370.

Library of Congress Catalog Card Number: 99-69324

Visit the Random House Reference & Information Publishing web site at www.randomwords.com

Typeset and printed in the United States of America.

Second Random House Edition
9 8 7 6 5 4 3 2 1
March 2000

ISBN: 0-375-70467-1
SAP Network: 10036536

New York Toronto London Sydney Auckland

Abbreviations Used in This Dictionary

abbr.	abbreviation	f.	feminine
A	accusative case	Fig.	figurative
adj.	adjective	FILL	fill vowel in
adv.	adverb		nominative
aero.	aeronautics		case
anat.	anatomy	fut.	future tense
archit.	architecture	G	genitive case
astr.	astronomy,	geog.	geography
	astrology	geol.	geology
attrib.	attributive	gram.	grammar
aux.	auxiliary	hist.	historical
biol.	biology	I	instrumental
bot.	botany		case
cap.	capital letter	impers.	impersonal
chem.	chemistry	impf.	imperfective
coll.	collective		verb
Colloq.	colloquial	indecl.	indeclinable
com.	commerce	indet.	indeterminate
comb.	combination,		verb of motion
	combining	infin.	infinitive
compar.	comparative	interj.	interjection
	degree of	ling.	linguistics
	adjective	lit.	literature
comput.	computers	loc.	location
conj.	conjunction	m.	masculine
cul.	culinary	math.	mathematics
D	dative case	mech.	mechanical
decl. f.	declined with	med.	medicine
	feminine	metal.	metallurgy
	endings	mil.	military
det.	determinate	mus.	music
	verb of motion	myth.	mythology
dim.	diminutive	n.	noun
dir.	direction	naut.	nautical
eccles.	ecclesiastic	neut.	neuter
econ.	economics	nom.	nominative
elec.	electricity,		case
	electrical	Obs.	obsolete

v

P	prepositional case	pres.	present tense
		pron.	pronoun
Pej.	pejorative	psychol.	psychology
pers.	personal	refl.	reflexive
pf.	perfective verb	relig.	religion
photog.	photography	sing.	singular
phys.	physics	superl.	superlative
physiol.	physiology	tech.	technical
pl.	plural	theat.	theater
poet.	poetic	usu.	usually
polit.	politics	v.	verb
poss.	possessive	v.i.	intransitive verb
pred.	predicate		
pref.	prefix	v.t.	transitive verb
prep.	preposition	zool.	zoology

Explanatory Notes

In both sections of this dictionary, all terms (including geographical names and abbreviations) are entered in a single alphabetical listing.

Many main entries contain compounds, phrases, and expressions that appear as boldface subentries. These subentries are preceded by a semicolon. If a main entry term is repeated, it is replaced by a swung dash (~).

Many main entries also contain run-on derived words that are formed by adding a prefix or suffix. If a main entry term is repeated as part of the run-on, it is replaced by a long dash (—) after the prefix or before the suffix.

Homographs (identically spelled terms that differ in derivation) are listed as separate entries and marked with a superscript number.

An explanatory note, gloss, or field label is given in parentheses if the sense that is being translated is not self-evident.

In the English-Russian section, definition numbers are used when there is more than one part of speech; semicolons are used to separate different senses of the English word. In the Russian-English section, definition numbers are used when the Russian word has more than one sense.

This dictionary shows the pronunciation of English headwords. The pronunciation system is a version of the International Phonetic Alphabet (IPA). Each Russian word is given in its basic form with the correct stress mark for that form. An explanation of Russian pronunciation begins on page ix. An explanation of English pronunciation begins on page xi.

In the English-Russian section, part of speech is indicated for every word. If grammatical or gender information remains the same for a series of words, it will be listed only for the last word in such a series.

In general, Russian nouns are given in the nominative singular case. Russian has three genders: masculine, feminine, and neuter. In the majority of cases, the determination of gender in Russian is quite straightforward and not indicated in this dictionary: nouns ending in a consonant are masculine, most nouns ending in -a or -я are feminine, and those ending in -o or -e are neuter. Nouns ending in the suffix -ость, -ность, -есть are always feminine, and those ending in the suffix -тель (usually indicating an agent or profession) are masculine. The gender of all nouns not covered by the basic rules are indicated in this dictionary. This includes, among others, all indeclinable nouns, as well as nouns ending in a soft sign in the nominative case (with the exception of the two instances mentioned above).

There are a number of Russian nouns that can indicate a person of either sex. Such nouns can be of masculine or feminine gender, depending on the person referred to; for example: сирота́ (orphan), уби́йца (murderer). These nouns in general follow a feminine declension. They are marked in this dictionary as: *m. & f.* As a rule, the masculine and feminine forms are given for nouns that indicate a profession. If the feminine form is formed by adding a suffix, a long dash is used, for example: учи́тель, —ница (teacher). In cases where the ending changes, a hyphen is used, for example: корми́лец, -лица (breadwinner).

Nouns marked **FILL** in this dictionary belong to the large group of nouns that have a fill vowel in part of their declension. In these nouns, the vowel in the final syllable disappears in some or all of the oblique cases (accusative, genitive, dative, instrumental, and prepositional). For example: замо́к (door lock), genitive замка́, dative замку́; оте́ц (father), genitive отца́, dative отцу́.

The aspect of all Russian verbs is indicated. In the Russian-English section, verbs are usually listed under the imperfective, followed immediately by the perfective form. Prefixed perfective verbs are hyphenated, for example: чита́ть *impf.*, про- *pf.* The perfective verb is cross-referenced to the imperfective, for example: взять *pf. of* брать. A perfective verb may also appear as an independent main entry if its corresponding imperfective is never or rarely used, or if its meaning is different in each aspect. The government of verbs is indicated in parentheses with the appropriate case in those instances where it differs significantly from the English equivalent, for example: избега́ть *impf.* (+ *G*) avoid.

Russian Alphabet and Pronunciation Guide

The Russian (or Cyrillic) alphabet consists of 33 letters: 21 consonants, 10 vowels, and 2 signs that provide information on the pronunciation of the preceding consonant.

Note: The pronunciation of several of the vowel letters changes when that vowel is unstressed. The values given in this guide are for stressed vowels only. (See below for the pronunciation of unstressed vowels.)

Letter	Russian Name	Closest Equivalent in English
А а	а	calm, father
Б б	бэ	bit, rob
В в	вэ	vest, love
Г г	гэ	get, bag
Д д	дэ	day, bad
Е е	е	yes, yet
Ё ё	ё	yo-yo
Ж ж	жэ	measure, azure
З з	зэ	zero, size
И и	и	machine
Й й	и краткое	boy, noise
К к	ка	kind, back
Л л	эль	lead, wool
М м	эм	man, am
Н н	эн	no, can
О о	о	hot, box
П п	пэ	pin, top
Р р	эр	Slightly to moderately trilled **r** (no English equivalent; similar to Spanish a**rr**iba!)
С с	эс	say, less
Т т	тэ	top, pot
У у	у	fool, ooze
Ф ф	эф	fine, off
Х х	ха	as in German Ba**ch**, or Scottish lo**ch**
Ц ц	цэ	hats, its
Ч ч	че	**ch**urch, whi**ch**
Ш ш	ша	sharp, mash
Щ щ	ща	Slightly longer than letter **ш**; similar to ha**sh**ish.

Letter	Russian Name	Closest Equivalent in English
Ъ ъ	твёрдый знак	(not pronounced)
Ы ы	ы	(approximately) bit, hit, still
Ь ь	мягкий знак	(not pronounced)
Э э	э оборотное	let, set
Ю ю	ю	you, yule
Я я	я	yarn, yard

Stress and Pronunciation of Vowels

Russian words have only *one* stress per word. Since stress (or accent) in Russian is mobile, the stress pattern of an individual word may change in the various inflected forms and must be memorized.

Pronunciation of Unstressed Vowels

Of the ten Russian vowels (а е ё и о у ы э ю я), three (е о я) change their pronunciation in an unstressed position. In the syllable immediately preceding a stressed syllable, **o** is pronounced like the **u** in **but** (/ʌ/ in the pronunciation guide). In other unstressed syllables **o** is pronounced like the **e** in **mother** (/ə/ in the pronunciation guide). For example: хорошо—/khərʌˈʃo/.

In unstressed syllables (with the exception of certain grammatical endings), **e** and **я** are pronounced close to a short **i** (/ɪ/ in the pronunciation guide). For example: теперь—/tɪpˈɛr/; прямой—/prɪˈmɔi/.

Pronunciation Guide for English
Краткое описание произношений английских
гласных и согласных

Phonetic Symbol	Example	Closest Equivalent in Russian
Фонетический символ	Английский пример	Приблизительное соответствие в русском языке

English Vowels
Английские гласные

/æ/	bat, hat	(нет соответствия)
/ɑ/	father	палка, мать
/ɒ/	pot	(нет соответствия)
/ɛ/	bet	эхо, поэт
/ɛə/ [fol. by /r/]	hair	эра
/i/	beat	или, рис
/ɪ/	sit	(нет прямого соответствия; краткое, очень открытое и)
/ɪə/ [fol. by /r/]	hear	ирис
/ɔ/	talk	(нет соответствия; краткое, очень открытое о)
/u/	food	ну, кухня
/ʊ/	book	ну-ну, кнут (краткое у)
/ɜ/	burn	(нет соответствия)
/ə/	mother	хорошо (безударный слабый звук)
/ᵊ/	fire (faiᵊr)	аэропорт
/ʌ/	but	хорошо (подобно на русское неударное о и а, но английский звук почти всегда под ударением)

English Diphthongs
Английские двугласные (дифтонги)

/ei/	take	музе́й
/ou/	boat	шоу-би́знес
/ai/	bite	рай, чай
/au/	now	фрау
/ɔi/	boy	домо́й

In all diphthongs stress falls on the fiirst vowel sound.
Ударение в двугласных падает на первый элемент.

English Consonants
Английские согласные

/p/	stop	па́па
/b/	back	брат
/t/	ten	так, тот
/d/	do	дом, дача
/k/	keep	как, крик
/g/	give	год, глаз
/f/	for	фильм
/v/	voice	ве́чер
/θ/	thin, path	(нет соответствия)
/ð/	that, other	(нет соответствия)
/s/	see	сила, нос
/z/	zeal, those	завод, зуб
/ʃ/	shoe	шум, ваш
/ʒ/	pleasure	жена
/h/	hat, help	(нет соответствия, звук-выдох)
/tʃ/	chest	час, врач
/dʒ/	just, gin	джинсы
/m/	my	мой, нам
/n/	now	нос, сон
/ŋ/	going, sing	(нет соответствия, задненебное н)
/l/	love	лук, класс
/r/	read	(нет соответствия; нераскатистое слабое р)
/w/	with, away	(нет прямого соответствия)
/y/	yes	иезуит, Йемен

Russian-English
Dictionary

а *conj.* but; and; **а то** otherwise; **а и́менно** that is

абажу́р lampshade

аббревиату́ра abbreviation

абза́ц paragraph

абитурие́нт university applicant

абонеме́нт subscription

абоне́нт subscriber

абориге́н aborigine

або́рт abortion

абрико́с apricot

абсолю́тно *adv.* absolutely

абсолю́тный absolute

абстра́ктный abstract

абсу́рд absurdity; **—ный** absurd

абсце́сс abscess

аванга́рд advance guard; avant-garde; **—ный** avant-garde

ава́нс advance (*of money*)

ава́нсом *adv.* in advance

авантю́ра adventure

авантюри́ст **—ка** adventurer

авантю́рный risky

авари́йный salvage; emergency

ава́рия accident, crash

а́вгуст; **—овский** August

авиа- *abbr. in comb.* aviation; air-; aero-

авиакомпа́ния airline

авиано́сец aircraft carrier

авиапо́чта airmail

авиацио́нный *attrib.* aviation

авиа́ция aviation

авока́до *neut. indecl.* avocado

авра́л *Colloq.* rush job

австрали́ец FILL, **-ли́йка** Australian; **Австра́лия** Australia

австри́ец FILL, **-ри́йка** Austrian; **А́встрия** Austria

авто- *abbr. in comb.* auto-, automatic, motor

автобиогра́фия autobiography

автобус bus

авто́граф autograph

авто́л motor oil

автомагистра́ль *f.* superhighway

автома́т 1. automatic weapon 2. public telephone 3. vending machine

автома́тика automation

автомати́ческий automatic

автомоби́ль *m.* automobile

автоно́мный autonomous

автопортре́т self-portrait

а́втор author

авторите́т authority; **—ный** authoritative

а́вторский author's; **а́вторское пра́во** copyright

авторучка pen, fountain pen

автостра́да expressway

аге́нт agent; **—ство** agency

аге́нтура intelligence agency

агита́тор agitator; propagandist

аго́ния agony

агра́рный agrarian

агре́ссия aggression

агроно́м agronomist; **—и́ческий** agricultural; **—ия** agriculture

ад hell

адвока́т lawyer; attorney

адвокату́ра the practice of law

администра́тор manager

администра́ция administration

адмира́л admiral

а́дрес address; **—а́нт** sender

а́дский hellish, of hell

ажиота́ж *Colloq.* hullabaloo

аза́рт excitement; passion

аза́ртный ardent; reckless

а́збука alphabet

Азербайджа́н Azerbaijan

азербайджа́нец FILL, **-ка** Azerbaijani

азиа́т, **—ка** Asian

азиа́тский Asiatic

А́зия Asia

азо́т nitrogen

а́ист stork

академи́ческий academic

акаде́мия academy

аквамари́н aquamarine

акваре́ль *f.* watercolor

аква́риум aquarium

аккомпанеме́нт accompaniment

акко́рд chord

аккордео́н accordion

акко́рдная рабо́та piecework

аккумуля́тор battery

аккура́тный 1. neat 2. accurate 3. punctual

акроба́т acrobat

аксессуа́р accessory

аксио́ма axiom

акт act; deed

актёр actor

акти́в (financial) assets

активи́ст, **—ка** activist

акти́вный active; energetic

а́ктовый зал assembly hall

актри́са actress

актуа́льный 1. urgent **2.** topical

аку́ла shark

аку́стика acoustics

акуше́р, —ка obstetrician; midwife

акце́нт accent; stress

акционе́р shareholder

а́кция share, stock; action

а́лгебра algebra

а́либи neut. indecl. (law) alibi

алиме́нты pl. alimony

алкоголи́зм alcoholism

алкого́лик, -ли́чка alcoholic

алкого́ль m. alcohol

Алла́х Allah

аллего́рия allegory

аллерги́я allergy

алле́я avenue; path

аллига́тор alligator

аллилу́йя interj. halleluia

алма́з diamond

алта́рь m. altar

алфави́т alphabet; **—ный** alphabetical

а́лый scarlet

алыча́ cherry plum

альбатро́с albatross

альбо́м album

альмана́х literary miscellany

альпи́йский alpine

альпини́зм mountain climbing

альт 1. alto **2.** viola

альтернати́ва alternative

альтруи́зм altruism

алья́нс alliance

алюми́ний aluminum

амба́р barn; silo

амби́ция arrogance; conceit

амбразу́ра loophole

амбулато́рия dispensary; outpatient clinic

амбулато́рный attrib. dispensary

Аме́рика America

америка́нец FILL, **-ка́нка** American

америка́нский American

ами́нь particle, interj. amen

аммиа́к ammonia

амни́стия amnesty

амора́льный amoral; immoral

амортиза́ция amortization

ампе́р ampere

амплуа́ neut. indecl. (theat.) a kind of role

ампута́ция amputation

амуле́т amulet; charm

амфи́бия amphibian

амфитеа́тр amphitheater

ана́лиз analysis

анализи́ровать impf., **про-** pf. analyze

анали́тик analyst

аналоги́чный analogous

анало́гия analogy

анало́й (church) lectern

ана́льный anal

анана́с pineapple

анархи́ст anarchist

анархи́стский anarchic

ана́рхия anarchy

анато́мия anatomy

ана́фема anathema

анахрони́зм anachronism

анга́р 1. hangar **2.** shed

а́нгел angel; **—ьский** angelic

анги́на tonsillitis

англи́йский English; **англи́йская була́вка** safety pin

англича́нин Englishman

англича́нка Englishwoman

А́нглия England

анекдо́т 1. anecdote **2.** joke

анеми́я anemia

анестезио́лог anesthesiologist

анестези́я anesthesia

ани́с anise; **—овый** anise

анке́та form; questionnaire

анкла́в enclave

анне́ксия annexation

анно́тация synopsis

аннули́ровать impf. & pf. annul; cancel

анома́лия anomaly

анони́м anonymous author

анони́мный anonymous

ано́нс 1. announcement **2.** notice

анса́мбль m. ensemble

антагони́зм antagonism

Анта́рктика Antarctica

анте́нна antenna

антибио́тик antibiotic

антивое́нный antiwar

антиква́р antique dealer

антило́па antelope

антипа́тия aversion; antipathy

антисанита́рный insanitary

антисемити́зм anti-Semitism

антисе́птик antiseptics

антите́за antithesis

антифри́з antifreeze

анти́христ Antichrist

анти́чный 1. antique **2.** ancient

антоло́гия anthology

антра́кт intermission

антраци́т anthracite

антреко́т entrecote; rib steak

антрепренёр impresario

антресо́ли pl. mezzanine

антропо́лог anthropologist
антрополо́гия anthropology
анфа́с adv. full-face
анфила́да suite of rooms
анчо́ус anchovy
аншла́г (theat.) full house
ао́рта aorta
апартеи́д apartheid
апати́чный apathetic
апа́тия apathy
апелли́ровать impf. & pf. appeal
апелля́ция appeal
апельси́н orange
аплоди́ровать impf. & pf. applaud
аплодисме́нты pl. applause
апло́мб self-assurance
апока́липсис apocalypse
апокрифи́ческий apocryphal
апоплекси́я apoplexy; apoplectic stroke
апо́стол apostle
апостро́ф apostrophe
аппара́т apparatus
аппарату́ра apparatus; equipment
аппара́тчик party functionary
аппе́ндикс (anat.) appendix
аппендици́т appendicitis
аппети́т appetite; **—ный** appetizing
апплика́ция appliqué work
апре́ль m.; **—ский** April
апте́ка pharmacy, drugstore
апте́карь m. pharmacist
апте́чка medicine chest
а́ра macaw
ара́б, **—ка** Arab; **—ский** Arab
арави́йский Arabian, Arabic
аранжиро́вка (mus.) arrangement
ара́хис peanut; peanut plant
арби́тр arbitrator
арбитра́ж arbitration
арбу́з watermelon
аргуме́нт argument
аргумента́ция argumentation
аре́на 1. arena, ring 2. scene
аре́нда lease
аренда́тор tenant; leaseholder
арендова́ть impf. & pf. rent (from)
аре́ст 1. arrest 2. custody
аресто́ванный person arrested
аресто́вывать impf., **арестова́ть** pf. arrest
аристокра́т, **—ка** aristocrat
арифме́тика arithmetic
арифмети́ческий arithmetical
а́рия aria
а́рка arch
арка́да arcade

арка́н lasso
А́рктика the Arctic
арлеки́н harlequin
армату́ра 1. fixtures; fittings 2. armature 3. steel framework
арме́йский attrib. army
а́рмия army
арома́т aroma, fragrance
арсена́л armory
арте́ль f. cooperative
артериа́льный arterial
арте́рия artery
арти́кль m. (gram.) article
артилле́рия artillery
арти́ст artist; **—и́ческий** artistic
артри́т arthritis
а́рфа harp
архаи́чный archaic
арха́нгел archangel
археоло́гия archeology
архи́в archive; **—ный** attrib. archive
архиепи́скоп archbishop
архиере́й bishop
архипела́г archipelago
архите́ктор architect
архитекту́ра architecture
асбе́ст asbestos
асимметри́чный asymmetric
асимметри́я asymmetry
аске́т ascetic
аскети́зм asceticism
аспира́нт, **—ка** postgraduate student
аспири́н aspirin
ассамбле́я assembly
асигна́ция banknote
ассимиля́ция assimilation
ассисте́нт, **—ка** assistant
ассортиме́нт assortment; selection
ассоциа́ция association
ассоции́ровать impf. & pf. associate
а́стма asthma
астроло́гия astrology
астрона́вт astronaut
астроно́м astronomer; **—ия** astronomy
асфа́льт asphalt
ата́ка attack
атакова́ть impf. & pf. attack
атама́н ataman (Cossack chieftain)
атеи́ст, **—ка** atheist
ателье́ neut. indecl. studio
а́тлас atlas
атла́с satin; **—ный** satin
атле́т athlete; **—ика** athletics
атлети́ческий athletic
атмосфе́ра atmosphere

атмосфе́рный atmospheric
а́том atom; **—ный** atomic
атрибу́т characteristic
атташе́ m. indecl. attaché
аттеста́т 1. certificate **2.** endorsement
аттеста́ция recommendation
аттестова́ть impf. & pf. **1.** certify **2.** recommend
аттракцио́ны pl. amusements; attractions (in a park)
аудие́нция formal interview
аудито́рия auditorium
аукцио́н auction
аул aul (village in the Caucasus)

афе́ра fraud; swindle
афи́ша placard, poster
афори́зм aphorism
афористи́чный aphoristic
А́фрика Africa
африка́нец, -а́нка African
аффе́кт 1. fit **2.** paroxysm
а́хать impf., **а́хнуть** pf. gasp
ацето́н acetone
аэровокза́л air terminal
аэродина́мика aerodynamics
аэродинами́ческий aerodynamic
аэродро́м aerodrome
аэрозо́ль m. aerosol
аэропо́рт airport

б

ба́ба[1] Colloq. woman; **снéжная ~** snow woman
ба́ба[2] (tech.) ram
ба́бочка[1] butterfly
ба́бочка[2] Colloq. bow tie
ба́бушка grandmother
ба́бье ле́то Indian summer
бага́ж luggage; baggage
бага́жник 1. trunk (of car) **2.** luggage carrier; rack
баго́р hook; boat hook
багро́вый crimson
бадминто́н badminton
ба́за 1. base; basis **2.** depot
база́р market, bazaar
базили́к basil
бази́ровать impf. & pf. base
ба́зис basis; base
байда́рка canoe; kayak
бак tank, cistern; boiler
бакала́вр bachelor (degree)
бакале́йный grocery
бакале́я Colloq. groceries
ба́кен buoy
бакенба́рды pl. side whiskers
баклажа́н eggplant
бал ball, dance
балага́н 1. booth; show **2.** farce
балала́йка balalaika
балала́ечник balalaika player
бала́нс balance; **—овый** balance
баланси́р balancing pole
балдахи́н canopy
балери́на ballerina
бале́т ballet; **—ный** ballet
балетме́йстер ballet master
ба́лка beam, girder
балко́н balcony

балл 1. (school) mark **2.** (sports) point
балла́да 1. ballad **2.** ballade
балла́ст ballast
балло́н 1. cylinder **2.** rubber tire
баллоти́ровать impf. vote; **—ся** be a candidate, run for office
ба́ловать impf. pamper; spoil; **—ся** Colloq. play pranks
баловство́ 1. spoiling **2.** mischief
бальза́м balsam
балюстра́да balustrade
бамбу́к bamboo; **—овый** bamboo
ба́мпер bumper
бана́льность banality
бана́льный banal, trite
бана́н banana
ба́нда gang
банда́ж 1. bandage **2.** truss, belt
бандеро́ль f. wrapper; small parcel
ба́нджо neut. indecl. banjo
банди́т thug, bandit
банк bank
ба́нка jar, pot
банке́т banquet
банки́р banker
банкно́т, банкно́та banknote
ба́нковский attrib. bank
банкро́т bankrupt; **—ство** bankruptcy
бант (ribbon) bow
ба́ня bath; bathhouse
бар bar
бараба́н drum; **—ить** impf. drum
бараба́нщик, -щица drummer
бара́к wooden barrack; hut
бара́н ram; **—ина** mutton
бара́нка bagel
барахло́ 1. junk **2.** old clothes
бара́шек lamb; lambskin

бара́шковый lambskin
бард bard; folk singer
ба́ржа barge
ба́рин gentleman; nobleman
баритóн baritone
ба́рка barge
барка́с 1. launch **2.** longboat
барóкко baroque
барóметр barometer
барóн baron
баронéсса baroness
ба́рочный *attrib.* barge
ба́ррель *m.* (*measure*) barrel
баррика́да barricade
барс snow leopard
барсу́к badger
барха́н sand dune
ба́рхат velvet; **—ный** velvet
ба́рыня mistress; noblewoman
ба́рышня young lady; miss
барьéр barrier; hurdle
бас bass; **—óвый** bass
баскетбóл basketball
баснослóвный 1. legendary **2.** *Fig.*
  incredible
ба́сня fable
бассéйн 1. pond; pool **2.** basin
бастова́ть *impf.* strike; go on
  strike
баталóн battalion
батарéйка (*elec.*) battery
батарéя 1. (*mil.*) battery **2.** radiator
бата́т sweet potato; yam
батóн long loaf of bread
бату́т trampoline
ба́тюшка 1. father **2.** priest
бах *interj.* bang!
бахрома́ fringe
бахча́ melon field
бац *interj.* bang! crack!
баци́лла bacillus
ба́шенка turret
башка́ *Colloq.* head
башлы́к hood
башма́к shoe
ба́шня tower
бая́н 1. accordion **2.** bard
бдéние vigil
бег *pl.* **—á 1.** race **2.** run, running
бéгать *indet.*, **бежа́ть** *det.* run
бегемóт hippopotamus
бегле́ц, —ля́нка fugitive
бéглый 1. fluent **2.** cursory **3.** fugitive
бегóния begonia
беготня́ *Colloq.* running about;
  scurrying about
бéгство flight; escape

бегу́н (*tech.*) runner
беда́ misfortune, trouble
бéдность poverty
бéдный poor
бедня́га, бедня́жка *m.* & *f. Colloq.*
  poor thing, poor creature
бедрó 1. thigh **2.** hip
бéдственный disastrous
бéдствие calamity; disaster
бéдствовать *impf.* live in poverty
бежа́ть *impf.*, **по—** *pf.* run; escape;
  flee
бéжевый beige
бéженец FILL, **-нка** refugee
без (бéзо) *prep.* (+ *G*) without
безалкогóльный nonalcoholic
безапелляциóнный peremptory;
  categorical
безбилéтный without a ticket
безбóжник, -ница atheist
безбóжный godless, atheistic
безболéзненный painless
безбоя́зненный fearless
безбра́чие celibacy
безвéтрие absence of wind
безвку́сица lack of taste
безвла́стие anarchy
безвозвра́тный irrevocable
безвозмéздный gratuitous
безвóлие weakness of will
безврéдный harmless, innocuous
безврéменный untimely
безвы́ездно *adv.* **1.** uninterrupt-
  edly **2.** without a break
безвы́ходный hopeless; desperate
безгла́зый without eyes
безголóсый voiceless
безгра́мотный 1. ungrammatical
  2. illiterate
безгрéшный sinless
безда́рный untalented
бездéйствие inaction, inertia
безделу́шка trinket; knickknack
бездéлье idleness
бездéльник, -ница idler, loafer
безденéжье lack of money
бездéтный childless
бéздна abyss, chasm
бездоказа́тельный unsupported
бездóмный homeless
бездóнный bottomless
бездорóжье time of bad roads
бездýшный callousness
безжа́лостный pitiless, merciless
безжи́зненный lifeless
беззабóтный carefree, careless
беззакóние lawlessness
беззакóнность lawlessness
беззасте́нчивый shameless

беззащи́тный unprotected
беззвёздный starless
беззву́чный soundless, noiseless
безземе́льный landless
беззло́бный good-natured
беззу́бый toothless
безлю́дный uninhabited; deserted
безмо́лвный speechless, silent
безмяте́жный serene, tranquil
безнадёжный hopeless
безнадзо́рный neglected
безнака́занно *adv.* with impunity
безнали́чный (*of transaction*) performed without cash
безно́гий legless; one-legged
безнра́вственный immoral
безоби́дный inoffensive
безо́блачный cloudless; serene
безобра́зие ugliness; deformity
безобра́зный 1. ugly; deformed **2.** disgraceful
безогля́дный headlong
безопа́сность safety
безопа́сный safe
безору́жный unarmed
безостано́вочный non-stop
безотве́тственный irresponsible
безотлага́тельный urgent
безоши́бочный unerring; correct
безрабо́тица unemployment
безрабо́тный unemployed
безразли́чие indifference
безразли́чно *adv.* indifferently
безразли́чный indifferent
безразме́рный one-size-fits-all
безрассу́дный thoughtless, rash
безро́потность resignation
безрука́вка sleeveless jacket
безуда́рный (*gram.*) unstressed
безуде́ржный unrestrained
безукори́зненный irreproachable
безу́мие folly; madness
безу́мный mad
безу́мство madness
безупре́чный irreproachable
безусло́вно *adv.* certainly; absolutely
безусло́вный unconditional
безуспе́шный unsuccessful
безуча́стный apathetic, indifferent
безъя́дерный nuclear-free
безымя́нный nameless
безынициати́вный unenterprising
безысхо́дный hopeless
бейсбо́л baseball
беко́н bacon
беле́ть *impf.*, **по-** *pf. v.i.* turn white, whiten
белизна́ whiteness

бе́лка squirrel
беллетри́ст fiction writer, novelist; **—ика** belles-lettres; fiction
белови́к clean copy
белово́й clean; final
белогварде́ец FILL White Guard
бело́к FILL egg white
белокро́вие leukemia
белоку́рый blond, fair, fair-haired
белору́с, —ка Belarussian
Белору́с, Белору́ссия Belarus
белу́га beluga; white sturgeon
бе́лый white
бельги́ец FILL, **-ги́йка** Belgian
Бе́льгия Belgium
бельё linen
бельэта́ж dress circle
бемо́ль *m.* (*mus.*) flat
бенефи́с benefit performance
бензи́н benzine; gasoline
бензоба́к gas tank
бензоколо́нка gasoline pump
бе́рег shore; coast
берегово́й coast; coastal
бережли́вый thrifty, economical
бе́режный careful; considerate
берёза birch
бере́менеть *impf.*, **за-** *pf.* become pregnant, be pregnant
бере́менная pregnant
бере́менность pregnancy
бере́чь *impf.* **1.** take care of **2.** cherish; **-ся** be careful; beware
берло́га den, lair
бес demon
бесе́да conversation, talk
бесе́дка gazebo
бесе́довать *impf.* talk
бесконе́чность infinity
бесконе́чный endless, infinite
бесконтро́льный unsupervised
бескоры́стный disinterested
бескульту́рье lack of culture
бесо́вский devilish; diabolical
беспа́мятство unconsciousness
беспате́нсый unlicensed
беспереб́ойный uninterrupted
бесперспекти́вный hopeless; without prospects
беспе́чный careless; carefree
беспла́тный free of charge
беспло́дие sterility, barrenness
беспло́дный sterile, barren; futile
беспозвоно́чный invertebrate
беспоко́ить *impf.* trouble; disturb; **-ся** worry; be anxious
беспоко́йный uneasy, troubled
беспоко́йство worry; anxiety
беспол́езный useless

беспо́лый sexless, asexual
беспомо́щный helpless
беспоро́чный irreproachable
беспоря́док FILL disorder
беспоса́дочный non-stop
беспо́шлинный duty-free
беспоща́дный merciless, ruthless
бесправный without any rights
беспреде́льный boundless, infinite
беспрепя́тственный unimpeded
беспреры́вный incessant
беспрецеде́нтный unprecedented
беспризо́рник, —ница homeless
  child
беспризо́рный neglected; homeless
беспринци́пный unscrupulous
беспристра́стный impartial
беспро́игрышный safe; risk-free
беспу́тный dissolute
бессвя́зный incoherent
бессерде́чие heartlessness
бессерде́чный heartless; callous
бесси́лие impotence; weakness
бесси́льный impotent; feeble
бессла́вный infamous
бессле́дно adv. without a trace
бессло́весный meek
бессме́ртие immortality
бессме́ртный immortal
бессмы́сленный senseless, foolish
бессо́вестный unscrupulous
бессозна́тельный unconscious
бессо́нница insomnia
бесспо́рный indisputable
бессро́чный indefinite; without
  time limit
бесстра́стный impassive
бесстра́шный fearless, intrepid
бессты́дный shameless
беста́ктность tactlessness
беста́ктный tactless
бестолко́вый stupid; incoherent
бестсе́ллер bestseller
бесфо́рменный shapeless
бесхара́ктерный weak-willed
бесхи́тростный artless; ingenuous
бесхозя́йственный inefficient
бесцве́тный colorless, drab
бесце́льный aimless
бесце́нный priceless
бесце́нок: за ~ for next to nothing
бесперемо́нный unceremonious
бесчелове́чный inhuman; brutal
бесчи́сленный innumerable
бесчу́вственный insensible; insensitive; unconscious
бесчу́вствие insensibility; insensitivity; unconsciousness
бесшу́мный noiseless

бето́н, —ный concrete
бечёвка string; twine
бе́шенство 1. rabies 2. fury
бе́шеный 1. rabid, mad 2. furious
библе́йский Biblical
библиогра́фия bibliography
библиоте́ка library
библиоте́карь m. librarian
Би́блия Bible
би́вень FILL m. tusk
бигуди́ pl. hair curlers
бидо́н large can
бие́ние beating, throbbing
биле́т, —ный ticket
билья́рд billiards
бино́кль m. binoculars
бинт bandage
бинтова́ть impf., за- pf. bandage
биогра́фия biography
биоло́гия biology
би́ржа exchange
биржево́й attrib. stock (market)
бирюза́ turquoise
би́сер beads; —ный adj. beaded
бисирова́ть impf. & pf. 1. repeat
  2. play encores
бискви́т sponge cake
битко́м наби́т filled to capacity
бить impf., за-, по- pf. 1. beat, hit
  2. break
бифште́кс steak; beefsteak
бич whip, lash
бичева́ть impf. 1. whip, lash 2.
  castigate
бла́го blessing, boon
благоволе́ние goodwill; kindness
благовоспи́танный courteous
благогове́йный reverent
благодари́ть impf. thank
благода́рность gratitude; thanks
благода́рный grateful, thankful
благодаря́ prep. (+ D) thanks to
благода́ть f. grace; blessing
благоде́тель, —ница benefactor
благоде́тельный beneficial
благоду́шный good-natured
благожела́тельный benevolent
благозву́чный melodious
благонадёжный trustworthy
благополу́чие welfare; well-being
благополу́чный favorable
благоразу́мие sense, prudence
благоразу́мный sensible; prudent
благоро́дный noble
благоро́дство nobility
благослове́ние blessing(s)

благословля́ть *impf.*, **-ви́ть** *pf.* bless
благосостоя́ние well-being
благотвори́тель, **—ница** philanthropist
благоустро́енный well-designed
благоуха́ть *impf.* smell sweet
блаже́нство bliss, beatitude
бланк blank; form
блат pull; connections
блатно́й thieves'
бле́дный pale, pallid; colorless
блёклый faded
блёкнуть, **по-** *pf.* fade
блеск brilliance, luster
блесну́ть *pf.* flash
блесте́ть *impf.* shine; sparkle
блёстки *pl.* 1. spangles 2. flashes
блестя́щий brilliant
блеф bluff
бле́ять *impf.* bleat
ближа́йший 1. nearest 2. next
бли́же *adv.* nearer, closer
бли́жний neighboring; n. neighbor
бли́зиться *impf.* draw near
бли́зкий near; similar; intimate
близне́ц twin
близору́кость nearsightedness
бли́зость nearness; proximity
блик patch of light
блин pancake
блиста́тельный brilliant, splendid
блиц flashbulb
блок (*tech.*) pulley
блока́да blockade
блоки́ровать *impf. & pf.* blockade
блокно́т notebook; writing pad
блонди́н, **-ка** blond(e)
блоха́ flea
блуд lechery; **—ли́вый** lascivious
блужда́ть *impf.* roam, wander
блу́за, **блу́зка** blouse
блю́до dish; course
блю́дце saucer
боб bean; **—о́вый** *attrib.* bean
бобр beaver
бобро́вый *adj. attrib.* beaver
бобсле́й bobsled
Бог God
богате́ть *impf.* grow rich
бога́тство wealth; riches
бога́тый rich; wealthy
богаты́рь *m.* bogatyr (*folk hero*)
бога́че *compar.* of **бога́тый**
боги́ня goddess
Богома́терь *f.* Mother of God
богомо́л praying mantis
богомо́лец FILL, **-лка** pilgrim
Богоро́дица Mother of God

богосло́в theologian
богосло́вие theology
богослуже́ние religious service
боготвори́ть *impf.* idolize
богоху́льство blasphemy
бо́дрость energy; vigor
бо́дрый brisk; cheerful
боеви́к *Colloq.* action movie
боево́й *attrib.* battle; combat
боеголо́вка warhead
боеприпа́сы *pl.* ammunition
бое́ц FILL fighter, warrior
бо́же *interj.* God!
боже́ственный divine
божество́ deity; idol
божи́ться *impf.*, **по-** *pf.* swear
бой battle, combat
бо́йкий brisk; lively; clever; glib
бойко́т boycott
бо́йня slaughterhouse
бок side
бока́л glass; wineglass; goblet
боково́й lateral; side
бокс boxing; **—ёр** boxer; **—и́ровать** *impf.* box
Болга́рия Bulgaria
бо́лее *adv.* more; ~ **и́ли ме́нее** more or less; **тем ~**, **что** especially as
боле́зненный sickly; morbid
боле́знь *f.* illness, disease
боле́льщик, **-щица** fan
боле́ть[1] *impf.* (*pres.* -ле́ю, -ле́ет) be ill
боле́ть[2] *impf.* (*pres.* -ли́т, -ля́т) ache, hurt
болеутоля́ющий pain-relieving
боло́то swamp, marsh, bog
болта́ть[1] *impf.* talk, chatter
болта́ть[2] *impf.* stir; shake; **-ся** dangle, swing
болтли́вый talkative
болту́н, **—ья** chatterbox
болту́нья scrambled eggs
боль *f.* pain, ache
больни́ца hospital
бо́льно *adv.* painfully; badly; *pred.* (It is) painful
больно́й sick, ill, diseased; *n.* patient, sick person
бо́льше bigger, greater; *adv.* more
бо́льший larger; greater
большинство́ majority
большо́й big, great; ~ **па́лец** thumb; large toe
бо́мба bomb
бомбардиро́вка bombing
бомбардиро́вщик bomber
бомби́ть *impf.* bomb
бомбоубе́жище bomb shelter

бомж vagrant; bum

бо́нза *Colloq.* bigwig, superior

бор coniferous forest

бордю́р border

боре́ц FILL **1.** fighter **2.** wrestler

бормаши́на (dentist's) drill

бормота́ть *impf.* mutter, mumble

борода́ beard; **—тый** bearded

борода́вка wart

борозда́ furrow; fissure

боро́ться *impf.* fight, struggle

борт side (of ship); **за ~о́м** (loc.), **за ~** (dir.) overboard

бортово́й on-board

бортпроводни́к, -ни́ца steward(ess)

борщ borscht

борьба́ struggle, fight; wrestling

босико́м *adv.* barefoot

босо́й barefoot

босоно́жки *pl.* sandals, mules

бота́ник botanist; **—а** botany

ботани́ческий botanical

боти́нки *pl.* boots

бо́цман boatswain

бо́чка barrel, cask

бочко́м *adv.* sideways

бочо́нок FILL keg, small barrel

боязли́вый timid, fearful

боя́знь *f.* dread, fear

боя́ться *impf.* (+ *G*) fear, be afraid (of)

брави́ровать *impf.* flaunt

брак[1] marriage

брак[2] defect; defective merchandise

бракова́ть *impf.*, **за-** *pf.* reject

браконье́р poacher

бракоразво́дный *attrib.* divorce

бракосочета́ние marriage

брани́ть *impf.* scold, reprove

бра́нный abusive; scolding

брань *f.* profanity, swearing

брасле́т bracelet

брат brother

бра́тия fraternity, brotherhood

братоуби́йство fratricide

брать *impf.*, **взять** *pf.* **1.** take, seize **2.** get **3.** charge (a price) **4.** clear (a hurdle); **—ся** grasp; (за + *A*) begin, take up; (+ *infin.*) undertake

бра́чный marital, conjugal

бреве́нчатый made of logs

бревно́ log

бред delirium; ravings

бре́день FILL *m.* dragnet

бре́дить *impf.* be delirious; rave

брезгли́вый squeamish; fastidious

брезе́нт tarpaulin

бре́зжить *impf.* glimmer; dawn

брело́к key ring

бре́мя *neut.* burden, load

бренча́ть *impf.* jingle, strum

брести́ *impf.* amble; stroll

брете́лька strap, shoulder strap

брешь *f.* breach; gap

брига́да 1. brigade **2.** team, crew

бри́джи *pl.* breeches

бриллиа́нт, —овый diamond

бри́тва razor

бри́твенный shaving

бри́тый shaved; clean-shaven

брить(ся) *impf. v.* shave (oneself)

бровь *f.* eyebrow, brow

брод ford

броди́ть *impf.* **1.** wander, roam **2.** ferment

бродя́га, -я́жка tramp

бродя́жничать *impf.* roam

бродя́жничество vagrancy

бродя́чий vagrant; itinerant

броже́ние fermentation; ferment

бронево́й armored

бронено́сец FILL **1.** battleship **2.** armadillo

бронетранспортёр armored personnel carrier

бро́нза bronze

бро́нзовый bronze

брониро́ванный armored

брони́ровать *impf. & pf.* reserve

бронхи́т bronchitis

бро́ня reservation

броня́ armor, armor plating

броса́ть *impf.*, **бро́сить** *pf.* throw, desert, give up; **—ся 1.** throw oneself **2.** rush

бросо́к FILL throw, heave

брошь *f.* brooch

брошю́ра brochure, pamphlet

брус beam; **бру́сья** *pl.* parallel bars

брусо́к FILL bar; ingot

брусча́тка paving stones

бру́тто *adv., adj. indecl.* gross

брызга́ть, -зжу, бры́знуть *pf.* **1.** splash **2.** spatter, sprinkle

бры́зги *pl.* spray; splashes

брыка́ть, брыкну́ть *pf.* kick

брюзга́ *m. & f.* grouch

брюзгли́вый peevish; grumbling

брюзжа́ть *impf.* grumble

брю́ки *pl.* trousers, pants

брюне́т, —ка brunette

брюшно́й abdominal

бря́цать *impf.* rattle; clang; clank

бубенцы́ *pl.* little bells

бу́блик bagel

бубно́вый (*cards*) of diamonds

бу́бны pl. (cards) diamonds

буго́р FILL 1. knoll; mound 2. lump; bump

буго́рчатый covered with lumps

бугри́стый bumpy

будди́зм Buddhism

бу́дет 3rd person sing. of **быть**

буди́льник alarm clock

буди́ть impf., **раз-** pf. wake, awaken; arouse

бу́дни pl. weekdays; **—й, —чный** everyday, humdrum

бу́дто conj. as if, as though

бу́дучи gerund being

бу́дущее n. future

бу́дущий future

бу́дущность future

будь(те) imperative of **быть**

бузина́ (bot.) elder

буй buoy

бу́йвол buffalo

бу́йный 1. violent 2. lush, thick

бу́йство uproar; **—вать** impf. behave violently

бук beech

бука́шка bug; insect

бу́ква letter (of the alphabet)

буква́льный literal

буква́рь m. primer

буке́т bouquet

букини́ст secondhand bookseller

букле́т booklet

букси́р tug, tugboat

буксирова́ть impf. tow

буксова́ть impf. spin around

була́вка pin

бу́лка roll, bun

бу́лочка small bun; small roll

бу́лочная n. bakery

булы́жник cobble, cobblestone

бульва́р boulevard, avenue

бульдо́г bulldog

бульдо́зер bulldozer

булька́ть impf. gurgle

бульо́н broth

бума́га paper

бума́жник wallet, pocketbook

бума́жный attrib. paper

бу́нкер bunker

бунт riot, mutiny, revolt; **—ова́ть** impf. revel, revolt; **—овщи́к, —овщи́ца** rebel, insurgent

бур auger; drill

бура́в auger; gimlet; **—ить** impf. drill

бура́н snowstorm

бурдю́к wineskin

буреве́стник stormy petrel

буроле́м storm-damaged trees

буржуа́ m. & f. indecl. bourgeois; **—зный** bourgeois

буржуази́я bourgeoisie

бури́льный drilling

бури́ть impf., **про-** pf. bore; drill

бурли́ть impf. seethe

бу́рный stormy; impetuous

бурово́й drilling

бурунду́к chipmunk

бурча́ть impf., **про-** pf. mutter

бу́рый brown

бурья́н tall weeds

бу́ря storm, tempest, gale

бу́сина bead

бу́сы pl. beads

бутафо́рия stage props

бутербро́д sandwich

буто́н bud

буты́лка bottle

буты́ль f. large bottle

буфе́т refreshment bar

буфе́тчик, —чица bartender

буха́нка loaf of bread

бухга́лтер accountant

бухгалте́рия 1. accounting 2. accounting department

бу́хта 1. bay 2. coil

бушева́ть impf. rage, storm

буя́н roughneck; ruffian

буя́нить impf. create an uproar

бы particle used with verbs in past tense to form the subjunctive or conditional

быва́лый 1. former 2. experienced

быва́ть impf. 1. frequent 2. happen 3. take place

бы́вший former; ex-

бык 1. bull, ox 2. pier

были́нка blade of grass

бы́ло particle just about to; nearly

было́й former, bygone, past

быль f. fact; true story

быстрота́ rapidity, speed

бы́стрый quick, rapid, swift

быт way of life

бытова́ть impf. exist; occur

бытово́й everyday; social

быть be

бычо́к FILL young ox, young bull

бюдже́т budget

бюллете́нь m. bulletin, report; **избира́тельный ~** ballot

бюро́ neut. indecl. office

бюрокра́т bureaucrat

бюрократи́зм bureaucracy

бюрокра́тия bureaucracy; **—ра́ть** impf.

бюст bust; **—га́льтер** bra

бязь f. heavy cloth

В

в, во *prep.* **1.** (+ *A*) (*dir.*) in, into, to **2.** (+ *P*) (*loc.*) in, at

ва-ба́нк *adv.*: **идти́ ~** go for broke

ваго́н 1. carriage; coach **2.** car

ва́жность importance; significance

ва́жный important; significant

ва́за 1. vase **2.** bowl

вазели́н Vaseline

вака́нсия vacancy

вакци́на vaccine

вакцини́ровать *impf.* vaccinate

вал 1. billow **2.** bank, rampart

ва́ленок FILL felt boot

вале́т (*cards*) jack

ва́лик roller

вали́ть *impf.*, **по-** *pf.* overturn

валово́й gross

валто́рна French horn

валу́н boulder

вальс waltz; **—и́ровать** *impf.* waltz

валю́та (foreign) currency

валя́ть *impf.* drag (along); roll; ~ **дурака́** play the fool; **-ся** wallow; lounge around; lie around

вам *pron.*, *D pl. of* **вы**

ва́ми *pron.*, *I pl. of* **вы**

вампи́р vampire

вани́ль *f.*, **—ный** vanilla

ва́нна 1. bath **2.** bathtub

ва́нная (ко́мната) bathroom

ва́рвар, **—ка** barbarian; **—ский** barbaric

ва́режка mitten

варе́ник curd *or* fruit dumpling

варёный boiled

варе́нье jam

вариа́нт version; alternative

вари́ть(ся) *impf.*, **с-** *pf.* boil; cook

варьете́ *neut. indecl.* variety show

вас *pron.*, *G, A, P of* **вы**

василёк FILL cornflower

ва́та cotton

ватерпа́с spirit level

ва́тник quilted jacket

ва́тный quilted; wadded

ватру́шка jam *or* cheese pastry

ватт watt

ва́фля waffle

ва́хта (*naut.*) watch

вахтёр watchman; janitor

ваш *pron.* your; yours

вбега́ть *impf.*, **вбежа́ть** *pf.* run in

вбива́ть *impf.*, **вбить** *pf.* drive in

вбира́ть *impf.*, **вобра́ть** *pf.* absorb; take in

вбок *adv.* to one side; to the side

вброд *adv.*: **переходи́ть ~** ford

введе́ние introduction; preface

ввезти́ *pf. of* **ввози́ть**

вверх *adv.* up, upwards; ~ **дном** upside down

вверя́ть *impf.*, **вве́рить** *pf.* entrust

ввиду́ *prep.* (+ *G*) in view of

вви́нчивать *impf.*, **ввинти́ть** *pf.* screw (in)

вводи́ть *impf.*, **ввести́** *pf.* introduce; bring in

ввоз importation; imports

ввози́ть *impf.*, **ввезти́** *pf.* import

вглубь *adv.* deep in(to)

вгля́дываться *impf.*, **вгляде́ться** *pf.* peer at; observe closely

вдалеке́, **вдали́** *adv.* in the distance

вдаль *adv.* into the distance

вдвое *adv.* double; twice; ~ **бо́льше** twice as much

вдвоём *adv.* two together

вдвойне́ *adv.* doubly, double

вдева́ть *impf.*, **вдеть** *pf.* put in

вдоба́вок *adv.* in addition

вдова́ widow

вдове́ц FILL widower

вдо́воль *adv.* enough, plenty

вдого́нку *adv.* in pursuit of; after

вдоль *prep.* (+ *G*) along; ~ **и попере́к** far and wide; thoroughly

вдох *adv.* (a single) breath

вдохнове́ние inspiration

вдохновля́ть *impf.*, **-ви́ть** *pf.* inspire; **-ся** become inspired

вдохну́ть *pf. of* **вдыха́ть**

вдре́безги *adv.* into smithereens

вдруг *adv.* suddenly

вду́мчивый thoughtful

вдыха́ние inhalation

вдыха́ть *impf.*, **вдохну́ть** *pf.* inhale

вегетариа́нец FILL, **-а́нка** vegetarian

ве́дение authority; competence

веде́ние conduct; direction

ве́домость list; register

ве́домственный departmental

ве́домство department

ведро́ bucket, pail

веду́щий 1. leading **2.** chief

ведь *particle* but; indeed, well

ве́дьма witch

ве́ер fan

ве́жливый polite, courteous

везде́ *adv.* everywhere
везе́ние *Colloq.* luck
везти́ *impf.*, **по-** *pf.* (*impers.* + *D*) be lucky
век century; age; lifetime
ве́ко eyelid
ве́ксель *m.* promissory note
веле́ние command
велика́н giant
вели́кий great
Великобрита́ния Great Britain
великоду́шный magnanimous
великоле́пно *adv.* magnificently
вели́чественный majestic; grand
вели́чие greatness; grandeur
величина́ size; quantity; magnitude
велосипе́д bicycle; **—и́ст** cyclist
вельве́т velveteen
ве́на vein
венге́рский Hungarian
венгр, венге́рка Hungarian
Ве́нгрия Hungary
венери́ческий venereal
вене́ц FILL crown; wreath
ве́ник twig broom; besom
ве́нтиль *m.* valve
вентиля́тор fan
вентиля́ция ventilation
венча́ние 1. wedding **2.** coronation
венча́ть *impf.*, **по-** *pf.* marry
ве́ра faith, belief; trust
вера́нда veranda
ве́рба pussy willow
верблю́д camel
вербо́вка recruitment
верёвка cord, rope; string
верени́ца line; row
ве́рить *impf.*, **по-** *pf.* **1.** (+ *D*) believe **2.** (в + *A*) believe (in); trust
верне́е *adv.* rather
ве́рно *particle* probably
ве́рность faithfulness, fidelity
верну́ть *pf. v.t.* return, give back; **—ся** *v.i.* return, come back
ве́рный correct; true; faithful
ве́рование belief
ве́ровать *impf.* (в + *A*) believe in
вероуче́ние dogma
вероя́тно *adv.* probably
вероя́тность probability
вероя́тный probable, likely
ве́рсия version
верте́ть *impf.* twirl, turn, twist; **—ся** spin, rotate; fidget
вертика́ль *f.* vertical line
вертика́льный vertical
вертолёт helicopter

верту́шка flirtatious woman
ве́рующий *n.* believer
верфь *f.* shipyard; dockyard
верх top, summit; height
ве́рхний upper; top
верхова́я езда́ horseback riding
верхо́м *adv.* (on) horseback
верши́на summit, peak; apex
вес weight; *Fig.* influence
весели́ть *impf.*, **раз-** *pf.* cheer; amuse; **—ся** enjoy oneself
ве́село *adv.* happily; merrily
весёлый merry; cheerful
весе́лье merriment, merry-making
весе́нний *attrib.* spring
ве́сить *impf.* weigh
весло́ oar, paddle
весна́ spring; **весно́й, весно́ю** *adv.* in the spring
весну́шка freckle
весо́мый weighty
вести́ себя́ *impf.* behave
вестибю́ль *m.* lobby
ве́стник herald; bulletin
весть *f.* news, word
весы́ *pl.* scale, scales
весь, f. вся, neut. всё, pl. все all; the whole
весьма́ *adv.* very; extraordinarily
ветвь *f.* branch, bough
ве́тер FILL wind; breeze
ветера́н veteran
ветерина́р veterinarian
ветеро́к FILL light breeze
ве́тка branch, twig
ве́то *neut. indecl.* veto
ве́тошь *f.* tatters; rags
ве́треный 1. windy **2.** frivolous
ветрово́й *attrib.* wind
ветря́нка chicken pox
ве́тхий decrepit; dilapidated;
Ве́тхий Заве́т the Old Testament
ветчина́ ham
ве́чер 1. evening **2.** party
вечери́нка (evening) party
вече́рний *attrib.* evening
вече́рня vespers
ве́чером *adv.* in the evening
вечнозелёный evergreen
ве́чность eternity
ве́чный eternal, everlasting
ве́шалка hanger; clothes rack
ве́шать *impf.*, **пове́сить** *pf.* hang (up); **—ся** hang oneself
веще́ственный material
вещество́ matter, substance
вещь *f.* thing; object; work
ве́яние 1. winnowing **2.** trend
вживля́ть *impf.* (*med.*) implant

взад и вперёд up and down, back and forth

взаимный mutual, reciprocal

взаимодействие interaction

взаимодействовать *impf.* interact; cooperate

взаимоотношение interrelation

взаимопомощь *f.* mutual aid

взаимосвязанный interconnected

взаймы *adv.:* брать ~ borrow; давать ~ lend

взамен *prep.* (+ *G*) in exchange for

взаперти *adv.* locked up

взбалмошный eccentric; erratic

взбалтывать *impf.* shake up

взбегать *impf.* run up

взбесить *pf.* enrage

взбивать *impf.* whip up

взбираться *impf.* climb up

взбитый beaten; whipped

взбунтоваться *pf.* revolt

взваливать *impf.*, взвалить *pf.* (на + *A*) load onto; saddle with

взвешивать(ся) *impf.*, взвесить(ся) *pf.* weigh (oneself)

взвинчивать *impf.* inflate

взволнованный agitated; anxious

взволновать *pf.* of волновать

взгляд glance, look; opinion

взглядывать *impf.*, взглянуть *pf.* (на + *A*) glance at, look at

взгорье hill

вздёргивать *impf.* jerk up

вздорный cantankerous

вздох sigh

вздохнуть *pf.* of вздыхать

вздрагивать *impf.*, вздрогнуть *pf.* shudder; wince

вздремнуть *pf.* nap

вздутый 1. inflated 2. swollen

вздыхать *impf.*, вздохнуть *pf.* sigh

взламывать *impf.*, взломать *pf.* break into

взлёт take-off

взлетать *impf.*, взлететь *pf.* 1. fly up 2. take off

взлом break-in

взломать *pf.* of взламывать

взломщик burglar

взмах stroke; movement; wave

взмахивать *impf.*, взмахнуть *pf.* flap; wave

взнос payment, fee

взойти *pf.* of всходить

взрослый adult; *n.* an adult

взрыв explosion

взрыватель fuse

взрывать *impf.*, взорвать *pf.* blow up; —ся explode

взрывчатка explosive

взрывчатый explosive

взъерошенный disheveled

взятие seizure, capture

взятка bribe; graft

взять(ся) *pf.* of брать(ся)

вибратор vibrator

вибрация vibration

вид 1. appearance, look 2. shape, form; view 3. (*gram.*) aspect

видать *impf.*, по- *pf. Colloq.* see

видение vision, apparition

видео *neut. indecl.* video recorder

видеозапись *f.* videotape

видеть *impf.*, у- *pf.* see

видимо *adv.* apparently, evidently

видимость visibility, appearance

видный 1. visible 2. prominent

видоизменение modification

видоискатель viewfinder

виза visa

визг squeal; yelp

визитка business card

вилка 1. fork 2. electric plug

вилы *pl.* pitchfork

вилять *impf.* wag

вина 1. guilt 2. fault

винегрет beet and potato salad

винительный (*gram.*) accusative

винить *impf.*, об- *pf.* accuse

винный *attrib.* wine

вино wine

виноватый guilty

виновник culprit

виновный guilty

виноград grapes; —ник vineyard

виноградный *attrib.* grape

винокур distiller

винт screw

винтовка rifle

винтовой spiral

виола viola

виолончелист, —ка cellist

виолончель *f.* cello

вираж turn; curve

виртуоз virtuoso; —ный masterful

вирус virus

виселица gallows; gibbet

висеть *impf.*, повиснуть *pf.* hang

виски *neut. indecl.* whiskey

висок FILL temple (*of head*)

високосный год leap year

висячий hanging; suspended

витамин vitamin

витиеватый ornate

витой twisted

виток FILL turn; coil; loop
витра́ж stained-glass window
витри́на display window
вить *impf.*, **с-** *pf.* weave; twist;
  —ся curl; wind
вихо́р FILL tuft (of hair)
вихрь *m.* whirlwind
вишнёвый *attrib.* cherry
ви́шня cherry; cherry tree
вка́лывать *impf.*, **вколо́ть** *pf.* (в
  + A) stick in(to)
вка́тывать *impf.*, **вкати́ть** *pf.* v.t.
  roll in, wheel in
вклад 1. deposit **2.** contribution
вкла́дка supplement; insert
вкладно́й лист inserted page
вкла́дчик depositor
вкла́дывать *impf.*, **вложи́ть** *pf.*
  put in; invest
вкле́ивать *impf.*, **вкле́ить** *pf.*
  paste in
включа́ть *impf.*, **-чи́ть** *pf.* **1.** include **2.** switch on
включа́я *prep.* (+ A) including
включи́тельно *adv.* inclusive
вкось *adv.* aslant
вкра́дчивый insinuating
вкра́тце *adv.* in brief, briefly
вкруту́ю *adv.* hard-boiled
вкус taste; **—ный** tasty
вла́га moisture, dampness
влага́лище vagina
владе́лец FILL, **-льца** owner
владе́ние property; possession
владе́ть *impf.* (+ I) own; control
вла́жность humidity; moisture
вла́жный moist
вла́стный commanding; imperious
власть *f.* power; authority
вле́во *adv.* to the left
влеза́ть *impf.*, **влезть** *pf.* climb in
влета́ть *impf.*, **влете́ть** *pf.* fly in
влече́ние inclination; bent
влечь *impf.* draw; attract
влива́ть *impf.*, **влить** *pf.* pour in
влия́ние influence
влия́тельный influential
влия́ть *impf.*, **по-** *pf.* influence
вложе́ние enclosure; investment
вложи́ть *pf.* of **вкла́дывать**
влюблённый in love
влюбля́ться *impf.*, **-би́ться** *pf.* fall
  in love
вменя́емый responsible; sane
вменя́ть *impf.*, **-ни́ть** *pf.* impute
вме́сте *adv.* together
вмести́мость capacity
вмести́тельный capacious
вме́сто *prep.* (+ G) instead of, in
  place of

вмеша́тельство interference
вме́шиваться *impf.*, **вмеша́ться**
  pf. interfere; intervene
вмиг *adv.* in an instant *or* moment
вмя́тина dent
внача́ле *adv.* 'at first
вне *prep.* (+ G) outside; beyond;
  ~ себя́ beside oneself
внедре́ние inculcation; adoption
внедря́ть *impf.*, **-ри́ть** *pf.* inculcate
внеза́пно *adv.* suddenly
внеза́пный sudden
внести́ *pf.* of **вноси́ть**
вне́шний external, outward
вне́шность external appearance
вниз *adv.* (dir.) down, downwards; **—у́** (loc.) below
вника́ть *impf.*, **вни́кнуть** *pf.* delve
  into; try to understand
внима́ние attention
внима́тельный attentive
вничью́ *adv.* in or to a draw
вновь *adv.* again, anew
вноси́ть *impf.*, **внести́** *pf.* carry in;
  bring in; insert
внук grandson; grandchild
вну́тренний inner, inside, internal
вну́тренности *pl.* internal organs
внутри́ *adv.*, *prep.* (+ G) inside
внутриве́нный intravenous
внутрь *adv.*, *prep.* (+ G) in(to);
  inside
вну́чка granddaughter
внуша́ть *impf.*, **-ши́ть** *pf.* instill;
  inspire
внуше́ние suggestion
внуши́тельный imposing
вня́тный 1. distinct **2.** audible
во see **в.**
вовлека́ть *impf.*, **вовле́чь** *pf.* v.t.
  involve; draw in
вовлече́ние involvement
во́время *adv.* in time
во́все *adv.* quite; ~ нет not at all
во-вторы́х *adv.* secondly
во́гнутый concave
вода́ water
водворя́ть *impf.*, **-ри́ть** *pf.* settle;
  install; establish
води́тель driver; **—ские права́** *pl.*
  driver's license
води́ть *indet.*, **вести́** *det.* v.t. **1.**
  conduct, lead **2.** drive
во́дка vodka
водножы́жный спорт water skiing
во́дный *attrib.* water
водобоя́знь *f.* hydrophobia
водоворо́т whirlpool, eddy

водоём reservoir
водока́чка pumping station
водола́з diver
водонепроница́емый waterproof
водопа́д waterfall
водопо́й watering place
водопрово́д water pipe
водопрово́дчик plumber
водоразбо́рный кран hydrant
водоразде́л watershed
водоро́д hydrogen
во́доросль f. water plant; seaweed
водоснабже́ние water supply
водосто́к water pipe; gutter
водохрани́лище reservoir; tank
во́дочный attrib. vodka
водружа́ть impf., **-зи́ть** pf. erect
водяно́й attrib. water, aquatic
воева́ть impf. wage war; quarrel
воеди́но adv. together
вое́нно-возду́шные си́лы pl. air force
вое́нно-морско́й флот navy
военнопле́нный prisoner of war
военнослу́жащий serviceman
вое́нный military; martial
вожа́к 1. leader 2. guide
вожделе́ние lust; desire
вождь m. leader
во́жжи pl. reins
воз cart; cartful
возбуди́тель m. agent; stimulus
возбужда́ть impf., **-буди́ть** pf. excite, arouse, stimulate
возбужде́ние excitement
возвра́т return; reimbursement
возвраща́ть impf., **-ти́ть, верну́ть** pf. return; repay; **—ся** v.i. return; recur
возвраще́ние return
возвыша́ть impf., **возвы́сить** pf. raise
возвыше́ние rise; elevation
возвы́шенность height; loftiness
возвы́шенный high; elevated
возглавля́ть impf., **возгла́вить** pf. be at the head (of); head
воздвига́ть impf., **-гнуть** pf. erect
возде́йствие influence
возде́йствовать impf. influence
воздержа́ние abstinence
возде́ржанность temperance
возде́рживаться impf., **воздержа́ться** pf. refrain; abstain
во́здух air
возду́шный air; aerial
вози́ть indet., **везти́** det. carry, convey; bring (by vehicle)
вози́ться impf. (c + I) fiddle around with; putter

возлага́ть impf., **возложи́ть** pf. v.t. lay, place; hand over
во́зле adv., prep. (+ G) by, near
возме́здие requital; retribution
возмеща́ть impf., **-сти́ть** pf. compensate; repay
возмеще́ние refund; compensation
возмо́жно pred. (it is) possible
возмо́жность possibility
возмо́жный possible
возмути́тельный outrageous
возмуще́ние indignation
вознагражда́ть impf., **вознагради́ть** pf. reward; recompense
вознагражде́ние reward
возненави́деть pf. come to hate
возника́ть impf., **возни́кнуть** pf. arise; originate
возникнове́ние rise; origin
возобновля́ть impf., **-ви́ть** pf. renew; resume
возража́ть impf., **-зи́ть** pf. object
возраже́ние objection
во́зраст age
возрожда́ть impf., **-роди́ть** pf. revive
возрожде́ние revival; regeneration
во́ин warrior; **—ский** military
во́инственный warlike; martial
вой howl; wail
во́йлок felt
война́ war
во́йско army; pl. forces, troops
войти́ pf. of входи́ть
вокза́л railroad station; terminal
вокру́г adv., prep. (+ G) round, around
вол ox
вола́н shuttlecock
волды́рь m. blister
волево́й strong-willed
волейбо́л volleyball
волк wolf
волна́ wave; breaker
волне́ние 1. agitation 2. alarm
волни́стый wavy
волнова́ть impf., **вз-** pf. agitate; disturb; **—ся** worry; be upset
волноло́м, волноре́з breakwater
волну́ющий troubling
волокно́ fiber; filament
во́лос hair; **—а́тый** hairy
волосо́к FILL filament; hairspring
волочи́ть impf. v.t. drag
во́лчий attrib. wolf, wolf's
волше́бник, -ница magician
волше́бный magical
волшебство́ magic
волы́нка 1. bagpipes 2. Colloq. delay; procrastination

вольéр enclosure (*for birds*)
вóльность freedom; liberty
вóльный free
вольт volt; **—áж** voltage
вольфрáм tungsten
вóля 1. will 2. liberty, freedom
вон *adv.* there, over there
вонь *f.* stench
вонзáть *impf.*, **-зи́ть** *pf. v.t.*
plunge, thrust; **—cя** *v.i.* pierce
вони́чий stinking; foul
воня́ть *impf.* stink
воображáть *impf.*, **-зи́ть** *pf.* imagine
воображéние imagination
вообщé *adv.* in general, generally
вооружáть *impf.*, **-жи́ть** *pf.* arm
вооружéние arms; armament
вооружённый armed
во-пéрвых *adv.* first, first of all
вопи́ть *impf.* howl; wail
вопию́щий crying, flagrant
воплощáть *impf.*, **-ти́ть** *pf.* embody, personify
воплощéние embodiment
вопль *m.* cry, wail
вопреки́ *prep.* (+ D) in spite of
вопрóс 1. question 2. issue
вопроси́тельный questioning; interrogative; ~ **знак** question mark
вопрóсник questionnaire
вор thief
ворвáться *pf. of* врывáться
воробéй sparrow
воровáть *impf.* steal
воровствó thievery; stealing
вóрон raven
ворóна crow
ворóнка 1. funnel 2. bomb crater
воронóй (*of horse*) black
вóрот 1. collar 2. windlass; **воротни́к, воротничóк** collar
ворóта *pl.* gate; gates
ворóчаться *impf. v.i.* turn, toss
ворс nap; pile
ворси́нка fiber; hair
ворчáть *impf.* growl; grumble
ворчли́вый grumbling; grumpy
восемнáдцатый eighteenth
восемнáдцать eighteen
вóсемь eight; **—десят** eighty; **—сóт** eight hundred
вóсемью *adv.* eight times
воск wax
воскли́кнуть *pf. of* восклицáть
восклицáние exclamation
восклицáтельный exclamatory; ~ **знак** exclamation mark
восклицáть *impf.*, **воскли́кнуть** *pf.* exclaim

воскресáть *impf.*, **воскрéснуть** *pf.*
rise from the dead; revive
воскресéние resurrection; revival
воскресéнье Sunday
воскрешéние resurrection; revival
воспалéние inflammation
воспалённый inflamed
воспитáние education, upbringing
воспи́танник, —ница pupil
воспи́танный well-bred
воспитáтель, —ница teacher, tutor
воспи́тывать *impf.*, **воспитáть** *pf.*
rear, bring up; educate
воспламеня́ть *impf.*, **-ни́ть** *pf.* inflame; ignite
воспóльзоваться *pf.* (+ I) 1. use 2. take advantage of
воспоминáние recollection; reminiscence; *pl.* memoirs
воспрещáть *impf.*, **-ти́ть** *pf.* prohibit
воспрещéние prohibition
восприи́мчивость susceptibility
воспринимáть *impf.*, **восприня́ть** *pf.* perceive
восприя́тие perception
воспроизведéние reproduction
воспроизводи́ть *impf.*, **-вести́** *pf.*
reproduce
воспроти́виться *pf.* oppose
воссоединéние reunification
восставáть *impf.*, **восстáть** *pf.* (прóтив + D) rise; revolt
восстанáвливать *impf.*, **восстанови́ть** *pf.* restore, reestablish
восстáние revolt, insurrection
восстановлéние restoration
востóк east
востóрг rapture; enthusiasm
востóрженный rapturous; ecstatic
востóчный east, eastern; oriental
востребóвание: до ~ general delivery; poste restante
восхваля́ть *impf.*, **-ли́ть** *pf.*
praise; eulogize
восхити́тельный delightful
восхищáть *impf.*, **-ти́ть** *pf.*
charm, delight; **—ся** (+ I) admire; be delighted
восхищéние admiration; delight
восхóд rise, rising
восхождéние ascent
восьмёрка (*cards*) eight
восьмидеся́тый eightieth
восьмисóтый eight hundredth
восьмóй eighth
вот *particle* there; there is
воткнýть *pf. of* втыкáть
вóтум vote

вошь *f.* louse
воюющий warring, belligerent
впадать *impf.*, **впасть** *pf.* fall in
впадина hollow; cavity
впалый hollow; caved in
впасть *pf. of* впадать
впервые *adv.* the first time; first
вперёд *adv.* forward; in the future
впереди *adv.* in front, before
вперемежку *adv.* pell-mell
впечатление impression
впечатлительный impressionable
вписывать *impf.*, **вписать** *pf.* register, enter
впитывать *impf.*, **впитать** *pf.* absorb
впихивать *impf.*, **впихнуть** *pf.* stuff in; cram in
вплавь *adv.* by swimming
вплоть *adv.*: ~ до (+ *G*) right up to
вполголоса *adv.* in a low voice
вползать *impf.*, **вползти** *pf.* crawl in, creep in
вполне *adv.* entirely, quite
вполоборота *adv.* half-turned
впопыхах *adv.* hastily, in a hurry
впорхнуть *pf.* fly in
впоследствии *adv.* consequently
впотьмах *adv.* in the dark
вправе *adv.* having a right
вправо *adv.* to the right of
впредь *adv.* in the future
впроголодь *adv.* half-starving
впрок *adv.* for future use
впрочем *adv.* however; though
впрыскивать *impf.*, **впрыснуть** *pf.* inject
впрямую *adv. Colloq.* directly
впускать *impf.*, **впустить** *pf.* admit
впутывать *impf.*, **впутать** *pf.* involve; entangle; —**ся** become entangled
враг enemy, foe
вражда enmity, hostility
враждебный hostile
высыпать *impf.*, **высыпать** *pf.* **1.** pour out **2.** (rash) break out
вразброд *adv.* separately, in disunity
вразброс *adv.* scattered around
вразрез *adv.* contrary (to)
вразумительный intelligible, clear
врасплох *adv.* unawares
вратарь *m.* goalkeeper
врать *impf.*, co— *pf.* lie, tell lies
врач doctor; —**ебный** medical
вращать(ся) *impf.* revolve, rotate
вращение rotation

вред harm; injury
вредить *impf.*, по— *pf.* harm, injure; damage
вредный harmful, injurious
временно *adv.* temporarily
временный 1. temporary **2.** provisional
время *neut.* (*pl.* времена) time; (*gram.*) tense; ~ года season
времяпрепровождение pastime
вровень *adv.* even; on a level
вроде *prep.* (+ *G*) like
врождённый innate, inborn
врозь *adv.* apart; separately
врун, —**ья** liar, fibber
вручать *impf.*, —**чить** *pf.* hand; award; deliver; entrust
вручную *adv.* by hand; manually
врываться *impf.*, **ворваться** *pf.* (в + *A*) burst in
вряд ли *particle* hardly
всадник, —**ница** rider
все *adj.*, *see* весь; *pron.* everyone, all
всё *adj.*, *see* весь; *pron.* all, everything; *adv.* always; still
всегда *adv.* always
всего *pron.*, *G of* весь; *adv.* in all; only
вселенная *n.* universe
вселенский universal; ecumenical
всемирная паутина World Wide Web (*abbr.* WWW)
всемирный worldwide
всемогущий omnipotent
всенародный nationwide
всенощная *n.* vespers
всеобщий general, universal
всерьёз *adv.* seriously; in earnest
всесторонний comprehensive
всё-таки *adv.* nevertheless; still
всеядный omnivorous
вскакивать *impf.*, **вскочить** *pf.* (на, в + *A*) jump on
вскапывать *impf.*, **вскопать** *pf.* dig
вскарабкаться *impf.*, **вскарабкаться** climb onto
вскачь *adv.* at a gallop
вскидывать *impf.*, **вскинуть** *pf.* throw up
вскипятить *pf. of* кипятить
всколыхнуть *pf.* stir up; agitate
вскользь *adv.* casually, in passing
вскоре *adv.* shortly or soon after
вскочить *pf. of* вскакивать
вскрикивать *impf.*, **вскрикнуть** *pf.* scream, shriek
вскрытие dissection
вслед *adv.* after; following

вследствие *prep.* (+ G) owing to, on account of

вслепую *adv.* blindly

вслух *adv.* out loud

всмятку *adv.* soft-boiled

вспоминать *impf.*, **вспомнить** *pf.* remember; recollect; recall

вспомогательный auxiliary

вспотеть *pf. of* потеть

вспухать *impf.*, **вспухнуть** *pf.* swell up

вспыльчивый hot-tempered

вспыхивать *impf.*, **вспыхнуть** *pf.* blaze up; flare up

вспышка 1. flash 2. outbreak

вставать *impf.*, **встать** *pf.* stand up; get up; (*of sun*) rise

вставка 1. mounting 2. insert

вставлять *impf.*, **вставить** *pf.* put in; insert; interpose

вставной inserted

встревоженный alarmed

встревожить *pf. of* тревожить

встреча 1. meeting 2. match

встречать *impf.*, **встретить** *pf.* meet, encounter

встречный 1. oncoming 2. counter

вступительный introductory

вступление entry; introduction; joining

всхлипывать *impf.*, **всхлипнуть** *pf.* sniffle; sob

всюду *adv.* everywhere

вся *adj., see* весь

всякий any; every; *pron.* anyone

всякое *n.* anything

всячески *adv.* in every possible way

втайне *adv.* secretly, in secret

втирать *impf.*, **втереть** *pf.* rub in

вторгаться *impf.*, **вторгнуться** *pf.* (в + A) invade; intrude

вторжение invasion; intrusion

вторичный second; secondary

вторник Tuesday

второе *n.* main course; entrée

второй second; the latter

второпях *adv.* hurriedly; hastily

второстепенный secondary, minor

в-третьих *adv.* thirdly; third

втрое, втройне *adv.* three times as much

втроём *adv.* three together

втыкать *impf.*, **воткнуть** *pf.* drive, stick, thrust in

втягивать *impf.*, **втянуть** *pf.* draw in; pull in

вуз (*abbr. of* высшее учебное заведение) institution of higher education

вулкан volcano

вульгарный vulgar

вундеркинд child prodigy

вход entrance, entry, admittance

входить *impf.*, **войти** *pf.* enter, go in, come in

входной entrance; admission

вчера *adv.* yesterday

вчерашний yesterday's

вчерне *adv.* in the rough

вчетвером *adv.* four together

въезд entry, entrance

въезжать *impf.*, **въехать** *pf.* (в + A) enter; drive in

вы *pron. pl.* you

выбегать *impf.*, **выбежать** *pf.* run out

выбирать *impf.*, **выбрать** *pf.* choose; elect; **—ся** (из + G) get out of

выбор choice, selection

выборы *pl.* election(s)

выбрасывать *impf.*, **выбросить** *pf.* throw out

выбрать(ся) *pf. of* выбирать(ся)

вываливать *impf.* throw out; **—ся** pour out

вывезти *pf. of* вывозить

вывернуть *pf. of* выворачивать

вывёртывать *impf.*, **вывернуть** *pf.* 1. unscrew 2. turn inside out

вывеска sign, signboard

вывести *pf. of* выводить

вывешивать *impf.*, **вывесить** *pf.* hang out

вывих dislocation

вывихнуть *pf.* dislocate, sprain

вывод 1. conclusion 2. withdrawal

выводить *impf.*, **вывести** *pf.* 1. lead out; remove 2. exterminate 3. conclude

вывоз export

вывозить *impf.*, **вывезти** *pf.* 1. remove 2. export

выворачивать *impf.*, **вывернуть** *pf.* unscrew

выгиб curve; bend

выгладить *pf. of* гладить

выглядывать *impf.*, **выглянуть** *pf.* look out, peep out

выгнать *pf. of* выгонять

выгнутый curved; convex

выговор 1. reprimand 2. pronunciation

выгода gain, profit; advantage

выгодный profitable; advantageous

вы́гоня́ть *impf.*, **вы́гнать** *pf.* drive out

выгружа́ть *impf.*, **вы́грузить** *pf.* unload

вы́грузка unloading

выдава́ть *impf.*, **вы́дать** *pf.* **1.** distribute, give out **2.** betray

выдаю́щийся outstanding; eminent, distinguished

выдвига́ть *impf.*, **вы́двинуть** *pf.* pull out; put forward

выделе́ние 1. allotment **2.** secretion; discharge

выделя́ть *impf.*, **вы́делить** *pf.* **1.** single out **2.** detach **3.** secrete; —ся stand out; exude

вы́держанность endurance, firmness, steadfastness

выде́рживать *impf.*, **вы́держать** *pf.* **1.** bear, endure **2.** sustain

вы́держка endurance; self control

вы́дох exhalation

вы́дра otter

вы́драть *pf.* thrash, flog

вы́думка invention

выду́мывать *impf.*, **вы́думать** *pf.* invent, make up

выдыха́ть *impf.*, **вы́дохнуть** *pf.* exhale; breathe out

вы́езд departure

выезжа́ть *impf.*, **вы́ехать** *pf.* leave, depart

вы́емка depression, hollow

выжива́ние survival

выжива́ть *impf.*, **вы́жить** *pf.* survive

выжима́ть *impf.*, **вы́жать** *pf.* wring out, squeeze out

вы́звать *pf.* of вызыва́ть

выздора́вливать *impf.*, **вы́здороветь** *pf.* recover, get well

выздоровле́ние convalescence, recovery

вы́зов summons; call; challenge

вызыва́ть *impf.*, **вы́звать** *pf.* **1.** call, summon; challenge **2.** cause

выи́грывать *impf.*, **вы́играть** *pf.* win; gain

вы́игрыш winnings, prize

вы́йти *pf.* of выходи́ть

вы́кидыш abortion; miscarriage

выкла́дывать *impf.*, **вы́ложить** *pf.* lay out, spread out

выключа́тель switch

выключа́ть *impf.*, **вы́ключить** *pf.* turn off; switch off

выкру́чивать *impf.*, **вы́крутить** *pf.* twist; unscrew; —ся extricate oneself

вы́куп redemption; ransom

выкупа́ть *impf.*, **вы́купить** *pf.* redeem; ransom

вы́купать *pf.* of купа́ть

выла́вливать *impf.*, **вы́ловить** *pf.* fish out

вы́лазка sortie; excursion

вылеза́ть *impf.*, **вы́лезть** *pf.* climb out; come out

вы́лет flight; takeoff

вылета́ть *impf.*, **вы́лететь** *pf.* fly, dash out; take off

выле́чивать *impf.*, **вы́лечить** *pf.* cure

вылива́ть *impf.*, **вы́лить** *pf.* pour out

вы́ложить *pf.* of выкла́дывать

выма́нивать *impf.*, **вы́манить** *pf.* lure out of

вы́мести *pf.* of мести́

вымира́ть *impf.*, **вы́мереть** *pf.* die out; become extinct

вымога́тельство extortion

вымога́ть *impf.* extort

вы́мпел pennant

вы́мысел fabrication, fiction

вы́мышленный fictitious

вы́мя *neut.* udder

вынима́ть *impf.*, **вы́нуть** *pf.* take out

выноси́ть *impf.*, **вы́нести** *pf.* carry, take, bring out; carry away; endure

выно́сливый hardy; enduring

вы́нужденный forced; constrained

вы́нуть *pf.* of вынима́ть

вы́пад 1. attack **2.** thrust

выпада́ть *impf.*, **вы́пасть** *pf.* fall, fall out, drop out; turn out

выпека́ть *impf.*, **вы́печь** *pf.* bake

вы́пить *pf.* of пить; have a drink

вы́пивка (drinking) spree; drinks

вы́писка certificate

выпи́сывать *impf.*, **вы́писать** *pf.* **1.** write out; copy **2.** order **3.** discharge

вы́плата payment

выпла́чивать *impf.*, **вы́платить** *pf.* pay (out), pay off

выплёвывать *impf.*, **вы́плюнуть** *pf.* spit out

выпола́скивать *impf.*, **вы́полоскать** *pf.* rinse out

выполне́ние execution; fulfillment

выполня́ть *impf.*, **вы́полнить** *pf.* execute, carry out; fulfill

вы́пуклый 1. bulging **2.** convex

вы́пуск issue, edition

выпуска́ть *impf.*, **вы́пустить** *pf.*

1. release **2.** issue **3.** publish **4.** omit

выпускни́к, -ни́ца graduate

выпускно́й attrib. **1.** (mech.) exhaust **2.** graduation

выража́ть impf., **вы́разить** pf. express

выраже́ние expression

вырази́тельный expressive

выраста́ть impf., **вы́расти** pf. grow; grow up

выра́щивать impf., **вы́растить** pf. bring up, grow

выреза́ть impf., **вы́резать** pf. cut out, carve out; engrave

вы́резка 1. cutting out **2.** fillet

вырожде́ние degeneration

вы́рубка cutting, chopping down

вы́ругать pf. of руга́ть

выруча́ть impf., **вы́ручить** pf. **1.** rescue **2.** help someone out **3.** make (money or a profit)

вы́ручка 1. Colloq. rescue **2.** proceeds; receipts; takings

вырыва́ть¹ impf., **вы́рвать** pf. pull out, tear out

вырыва́ть² impf., **вы́рыть** pf. dig up, dig out

вы́садка 1. debarkation **2.** transplanting **3.** (mil.) landing

выселе́ние eviction

выселя́ть impf., **вы́селить** pf. evict

выска́зывание 1. opinion, saying **2.** declaration

вы́скочка m. & f. Colloq. upstart

вы́слать pf. of высыла́ть

выслу́шивать impf., **вы́слушать** pf. hear, hear out; listen

вы́сморкаться pf. of сморка́ться

высо́вывать impf., **вы́сунуть** pf. stick out

высо́кий 1. high **2.** tall

высоко́ adv. high, high up

высокока́чественный high-quality

высокоме́рие haughtiness

высокоме́рный haughty

высокоопла́чиваемый high-paid

высота́ height; altitude

высо́тный 1. high-rise; tall **2.** high-altitude

вы́сохнуть pf. of высыха́ть

вы́ставка exhibition

выставля́ть impf., **вы́ставить** pf. exhibit; expose

вы́стрел shot

вы́ступ 1. projection **2.** ledge

выступа́ть impf., **вы́ступить** pf. come out; come forward

выступле́ние appearance

вы́сушить pf. of суши́ть

вы́сший 1. higher **2.** superior

высыла́ть impf., **вы́слать** pf. send out, forward; dispatch

вы́сылка dispatch; deportation

высыпа́ться¹ impf., **вы́спаться** pf. v.i. spill out

высыпа́ться² impf., **вы́спаться** pf. have a good night's sleep

высыха́ть impf., **вы́сохнуть** pf. dry out; wither

выта́скивать impf., **вы́тащить** pf. drag out; pull out

вытека́ть impf., **вы́течь** pf. flow out, leak out

вытира́ть impf., **вы́тереть** pf. dry; wipe

вытрезви́тель sobering-up station

вы́ть impf. howl

вытя́гивать impf., **вы́тянуть** pf. stretch (out)

вы́тяжка 1. drawing out **2.** extract

вы́хлоп (mech.) exhaust

вы́ход exit, outlet; issue

выходи́ть impf., **вы́йти** pf. **1.** go out **2.** look out on

вы́ходка trick; prank

выходно́й день m. day off

вычёркивать impf., **вы́черкнуть** pf. cross out; delete

вы́честь pf. of вычита́ть

вычисле́ние calculation

вычисля́ть impf., **вы́числить** pf. calculate

вычита́ть impf., **вы́честь** pf. deduct; subtract

вычища́ть impf., **вы́чистить** pf. clean; brush; polish

вы́чурный fancy; elaborate

вы́ше adv. higher

вышеска́занный aforesaid

вышеупомя́нутый above-mentioned

вышиба́ла m. & f. bouncer

вышиба́ть impf., **вы́шибить** pf. kick out; throw out

вышива́ть impf., **вы́шить** pf. embroider

вы́шивка embroidery

вы́шка tower

выявле́ние revelation; discovery

выявля́ть impf., **вы́явить** pf. reveal

выясне́ние clarification

выясня́ть impf., **вы́яснить** pf. elucidate

вью́чное живо́тное beast of burden

вью́щийся 1. curly **2.** climbing

вяз elm, elm tree

вяза́ние 1. knitting 2. crocheting
вяза́ть *impf.*, с- *pf.* 1. tie, bind 2. knit
вя́зка 1. binding; tying 2. bundle

вя́зкий 1. viscous 2. swampy
вя́лый 1. flabby 2. sluggish
вя́нуть *impf.*, за- *pf.* 1. wither, fade 2. droop

Г

габари́т dimensions; size
га́вань *f.* 1. harbor 2. haven
гад 1. reptile 2. *Colloq.* rat, louse
гада́лка fortuneteller
гада́ние fortunetelling; guesswork
гада́ть *impf.*, по- *pf.* tell fortunes; guess
га́дкий repulsive, vile, horrid
га́дость 1. filth 2. dirty trick
гадю́ка viper; adder
газ 1. gas 2. gauze, gossamer
газе́та newspaper
газиро́ванный carbonated
газо́н lawn; —окоси́лка lawn mower
газопрово́д gas pipeline
га́йка (*mech.*) nut
гала́ктика galaxy
галантере́я haberdashery
гала́нтный gallant
галере́я gallery
галиматья́ nonsense
галифе́ *pl. indecl.* riding breeches
галлюцина́ция hallucination
гало́п gallop
га́лочка check, mark
гало́ши *pl.* galoshes, rubbers
га́лстук tie, necktie
галу́шки *pl.* dumplings
гальвани́ческий galvanic
га́лька pebble
гама́к hammock
гама́ши *pl.* leggings
га́мма (*mus.*) scale; *Fig.* gamut
гангре́на gangrene
га́нгстер gangster
ганте́ль *f.* dumbbell
гара́ж garage
гаранти́ровать *impf. & pf.* guarantee; vouch
гара́нтия guarantee
гардеро́б wardrobe
гардеро́бщик, -щица cloakroom attendant
гарди́на window curtain
гаре́м harem
гармонизи́ровать *impf.* harmonize
гармо́ника accordion
гармони́ческий, гармони́чный harmonic; harmonious
гармо́ния harmony; concord

гармо́нь *f.* accordion
гарнизо́н garrison
гарни́р garnish
гарниту́р set; (*furniture*) suite
гаси́ть *impf.*, по- *pf.* extinguish
га́снуть *impf.*, у- *pf.* go out
гастри́т gastritis
гастро́ль *pl.* guest performance
гастроно́м gourmet; delicatessen
гастроно́мия gastronomy
гауптва́хта (*mil.*) guardhouse
гаши́ш hashish
гварде́ец FILL member
гва́рдия guard
гво́здик small nail; tack
гвозди́ка 1. carnation 2. clove
гвоздь *m.* nail
где *adv.* where; ~-либо, ~-нибудь, ~-то somewhere; anywhere
гекта́р hectare
гемоглоби́н hemoglobin
геморро́й hemorrhoids
гемофили́я hemophilia
ген gene
генера́л general
генера́льный general
гене́тика genetics
гениа́льный brilliant
ге́ний genius
геноци́д genocide
геогра́фия geography
геоло́гия geology
геоме́трия geometry
георги́н, георги́на dahlia
гепа́рд cheetah
гепати́т hepatitis
гера́нь *f.* geranium
герб coat of arms
ге́рбовый heraldic
Герма́ния Germany
гермафроди́т hermaphrodite
гермети́ческий airtight
герои́н heroin
герои́ня heroine
геро́йческий heroic; epic
геро́й hero; —ство heroism
ге́рцог duke; герцоги́ня duchess
ги́бель *f.* death; destruction; ruin; —ный ruinous
ги́бкий flexible; subtle; pliant
ги́бнуть *impf.*, по- *pf.* perish
гибри́д hybrid

гига́нт giant; —**ский** gigantic
гигие́на hygiene
гид guide
гидра́влика hydraulics
гидро- pref. hydro-
гидроэлектроста́нция hydroelectric station
гие́на hyena
ги́льза 1. cartridge case; shell **2.** cigarette wrapper
гимн anthem
гимна́зия high school
гимна́стика gymnastics
гимнасти́ческий gymnastic
гинеколо́гия gynecology
гипно́з hypnosis
гипнотизи́ровать impf., за- pf. hypnotize
гипо́теза hypothesis
гиппопота́м hippopotamus
гипс gypsum; plaster; **ги́псовый** plaster
гирля́нда garland
ги́ря 1. dumbbell **2.** weight
гита́ра guitar
глава́ 1. chapter **2.** head, chief
главнокома́ндующий n. commander in chief
гла́вный main, chief, principal; **гла́вным о́бразом** mainly
глаго́л verb; —**ный** verbal
гла́деть impf., вы́-, по- pf. **1.** iron **2.** stroke
гла́дкий smooth, even, sleek
гладь f. smooth surface
гла́женье ironing, pressing
глаз eye; **в** —**á** to one's face; **за** —**á** behind one's back
глази́рованный 1. glazed **2.** iced
глазно́й optic(al), attrib. eye
глазо́к Colloq. peephole
глазу́нья fried eggs
глазу́рь f. (ceramic) glaze; icing
гла́нды pl. tonsils
гла́сность openness; publicity
гли́на clay
гли́няный attrib. clay; earthenware
гли́ссер hydroplane
глист intestinal worm
глицери́н glycerine
глоба́льный global
гло́бус 1. globe **2.** sphere
глота́ть FILL gulp; swallow, gulp
гло́тка throat; gullet
глото́к FILL gulp; mouthful
гло́хнуть impf., о- pf. grow deaf
глубина́ depths; heart, interior
глубо́кий deep; profound
глубоко́ adv. deeply; profoundly

глупе́ц FILL fool, blockhead
глу́пость stupidity; dullness
глу́пый stupid; dull
глуха́рь m. **1.** wood grouse **2.** Colloq. deaf person
глухо́й deaf; n. deaf person
глухонемо́й deaf-mute; n. deaf-mute
глухота́ deafness
глуши́тель silencer; muffler
глушь f. wilderness; backwoods
глы́ба block; clod; lump
глюко́за glucose
гляде́ть impf., по- pf. (на + A) look at, stare at
гля́нец gloss; luster
гнать impf. drive (on); pursue; persecute
гнев anger; **гне́вный** angry
гнедо́й (of a horse) bay
гнездо́ 1. nest **2.** (tech.) socket
гнёт oppression
гнету́щий oppressive
гни́да nit
гние́ние decay, rotting
гнило́й rotten, decayed
гниль f. something decayed
гнить impf., с- pf. rot, decay
гное́ние festering
гной pus; **гно́йный** festering
гном gnome
гнус bloodsucking insects
гну́сный vile, foul
гнуть impf., со- pf. v.t. bend
гобеле́н tapestry
гобо́й oboe
гове́ть impf. fast
говори́ть impf. **1.** pf. сказа́ть say, tell **2.** pf. по- talk
говорли́вый talkative, loquacious
говя́дина beef
говя́жий attrib. beef
го́гот cackle (of a goose)
год year; —**а́ми** adv. for years on end
годи́ться impf. be fit or suitable
го́дность validity
го́дный fit; suitable; valid
годова́лый attrib. year-old
годово́й annual, yearly
годовщи́на anniversary
гол (sports) goal
го́лень f. shin
голла́ндец FILL, -**дка** Dutchman; Dutchwoman
Голла́ндия Holland
голла́ндский Dutch
голова́ head
голо́вка head; tip
головна́я боль f. headache

головно́й *attrib.* head; leading
головокруже́ние dizziness
головоло́мка *Colloq.* puzzle
головоре́з *Colloq.* cutthroat
го́лод hunger; starvation; —о́вка hunger strike
голода́ние starvation
голода́ть *impf.* starve
гололе́дица icy surface
го́лос 1. voice 2. vote
голосова́ние voting
голосова́ть *impf.*, про- *pf.* vote
голубе́ц FILL stuffed cabbage
голу́бка 1. pigeon 2. darling
голубо́й light blue; sky-blue
голу́бчик my dear
го́лубь *m.* pigeon, dove
голубя́тня dovecote
го́лый naked, bare
гольф golf
гомеопа́тия homeopathy
гомосексуали́ст homosexual
гони́тель, —ница persecutor
го́нки *pl.* 1. races 2. regatta
гонора́р fee
гоноре́я gonorrhea
го́ночный *attrib.* racing
гонча́р potter
го́нчая *n.* hound
го́нщик racer
гоня́ть *impf.* drive; send; hunt
гора́ mountain, hill
гора́здо *adv.* much, far
горб hump, hunch
горба́тый hunchbacked
горбу́шка end crust
горде́ли́вый proud
горди́ться *impf.* (+ *I*) be proud (of)
го́рдость pride
го́ре 1. grief 2. misfortune
горева́ть *impf.* grieve
горе́лка burner
горе́ние burning; combustion
горе́ть *impf.*, с- *pf.* burn
го́рец FILL, го́рянка mountaineer
го́речь *f.* bitterness; bitter taste
горизо́нт horizon
горизонта́ль *f.* horizontal line; —ный horizontal
го́рка hill; hillock
го́рло throat
гормо́н hormone
горн[1] furnace, forge
горн[2] bugle
горни́ло crucible
го́рничная *n.* maid, chambermaid
горноста́й ermine

го́рный mountainous; mining; mineral
горня́к miner
го́род city; town; —ско́й city, municipal, urban
городо́к small town
го́род-побрати́м sister city
горожа́нин, -нка town dweller
гороско́п horoscope
горо́х *coll.* peas
горо́шек polka dots
го́рсточка handful
горсть *f.* handful
горта́нь *f.* larynx
горчи́ца mustard
горшо́к FILL pot
го́рький bitter
горю́чее *n.* fuel
горя́чий 1. hot 2. passionate
горя́чка fever
горя́чность ardor, fervor
госдепарта́мент State Department
госпитализа́ция hospitalization
госпита́ль *m.* military hospital
Го́споди *interj.* Good heavens!
господи́н master; gentleman; Mr.
госпо́дство supremacy, reign
Госпо́дь *m.* the Lord; God
госпожа́ lady; Mrs.
гостеприи́мство hospitality
гости́ная *n.* living room
гости́ница hotel; inn
гости́ть *impf.* (у + *G*) be a guest
гость *m.* guest; visitor
госуда́рственный 1. *attrib.* state; government 2. national
госуда́рство state, nation, country
готи́ческий Gothic
гото́вить(ся) *impf.*, при- *pf.* prepare (oneself)
гото́вый ready; prepared
гофри́ровать *impf.* corrugate
грабёж plunder; robbery
граби́тель, —ница burglar
гра́бить *impf.*, о- *pf.* rob; pillage
гра́бли *pl.* rake
граве́р engraver; etcher
гра́вий gravel
гравиро́вка engraving
гравита́ция gravitation
гравю́ра engraving, print
град hail
гра́дус degree; —ник thermometer
граждани́н, -да́нка (*pl.* гра́ждане) citizen
гражда́нский civil; civilian
гражда́нство citizenship
грамм gram
грамма́тика grammar

граммати́ческий grammatical
граммофо́н phonograph
гра́мота 1. reading and writing **2.** charter **3.** document
гра́мотность literacy
гра́мотный literate; competent
грампласти́нка phonograph record
грана́т 1. pomegranate **2.** garnet
грана́та grenade
гранёный (of glass, gems) cut
грани́т, —**ный** granite
грани́ца boundary; border, limit; **за грани́цей** (loc.) abroad; **за грани́цу** (dir.) abroad
грани́чить impf. border
гра́нка proof; galley
грань f. border; verge; surface, side
граф count
графа́ (page) column
гра́фик[1] graph, chart; schedule
гра́фик[2] graphic artist
гра́фика graphic arts
графи́ня countess
графи́т graphite
грацио́зный graceful
гра́ция grace
грач (bird) rook
гре́бень m. comb; crest
гребе́ц FILL oarsman
гре́бля rowing
грек, греча́нка Greek
гре́лка hot-water bottle
греме́ть impf. thunder
грему́чая змея́ rattlesnake
грему́чий thunderous
гренки́ pl. croutons
грести́ impf. **1.** row **2.** rake
греть impf. warm; heat
грех sin
Гре́ция Greece
гре́цкий оре́х walnut
гре́ческий Greek
гре́чиха buckwheat
греши́ть impf., **co**- pf. sin
гре́шник, -ница sinner
грешно́ adv. pred. it's a sin (to)
гриб, —**но́й** mushroom
грибо́к FILL fungus
гри́ва mane
грим stage make-up
грипп flu, influenza; grippe
гриф[1] **1.** vulture **2.** griffin
гриф[2] (mus.) fingerboard
гри́фель m. slate pencil
гроб coffin; —**ни́ца** tomb
гробовщи́к coffin maker
гроза́ storm, thunderstorm

гроздь f. cluster; bunch
грози́ть impf., **при**- pf. threaten
гро́зный threatening; terrible
гром thunder
грома́дный vast; huge
громи́ть impf., **раз**- pf. smash, destroy; rout
гро́мкий 1. loud **2.** famous
гро́мкость loudness; volume
громо́здкий cumbersome
громоотво́д lightning rod
гроссме́йстер (chess) grandmaster
грот 1. grotto **2.** mainsail
гро́хот crash; rattle; rumble
грохота́ть impf., **про**- pf. rumble; crash; rattle
грош 1. half a kopeck **2.** penny
грошо́вый cheap
грубия́н boor
гру́бость rudeness; rude remark
гру́бый rude; coarse; rough
гру́динка brisket
грудь f. breast; chest
груз load; cargo; burden
грузи́ло (fishing) sinker
грузи́н, —ка Georgian
Гру́зия Georgia
грузови́к truck
гру́зчик stevedore, longshoreman
грунт 1. soil **2.** ground, base
гру́ппа group
группиро́вка group; grouping
группово́й attrib. group
гру́стный melancholy; sad
грусть f. sadness
гру́ша pear; pear tree
гры́жа (med.) rupture, hernia
грызть impf. gnaw; —**ся** fight, squabble
грызу́н rodent
гряда́ 1. bed **2.** bank
гря́дка (flower) bed
гря́зный dirty; filthy
грязь f. dirt; filth
гуа́шь f. gouache
губа́ lip
губерна́тор governor
губи́ть impf., **по**- pf. destroy; ruin
гу́бка sponge
губна́я пома́да lipstick
гуде́ть impf. buzz; honk; drone
гудо́к FILL whistle; horn
гудро́н tar
гул rumble; hum; din
гу́лкий hollow; resounding
гуля́ть impf. walk, take a walk
гуля́ш goulash
гуманита́рный humanitarian, humanistic; human

гума́нный humane; humanitarian

гурма́н, —ка gourmet

гу́сеница 1. caterpillar **2.** Caterpillar tractor

гуси́ный *attrib.* goose

густо́й thick; dense

густота́ thickness; denseness

гусь *m.* goose

гусько́м *adv.* (in) single file

гутали́н shoe polish

гу́ща 1. grounds, lees **2.** thicket

гу́ще thicker, denser

Д

да *particle* yes; *conj.* and; but

дава́й(те) *particle* let's; let us; come on!

дава́ть *impf.*, **дать** *pf.* give; let; grant

дави́ть *impf.*, **по—** *pf.* press; squeeze; crush; **—ся** choke

да́вка crowding together; crush

давле́ние pressure

да́вний old, ancient; bygone

давно́ *adv.* long ago; for a long time; **давны́м-давно́** long long ago

да́же *adv.* even

да́лее *adv.* further; **и так ~** and so on

далёкий distant, remote

далеко́ *adv.* far; **~ не** far from

да́льний 1. far-off; distant **2.** long; **Да́льний Восто́к** the Far East

да́льность distance; range

дальтони́зм color blindness

да́льше *adv.* **1.** then, next **2.** further; longer

да́ма 1. lady **2.** (*cards*) queen

да́мский lady's, ladies'

Да́ния Denmark

да́нные *pl.* data, facts

да́нный 1. given **2.** present

данти́ст dentist

дань *f.* tribute; contribution

дари́ть *impf.*, **по—** *pf.* give (a present)

да́ром *adv.* **1.** gratis, free **2.** in vain

да́та date

да́тельный (*gram.*) dative

да́тский Danish

датча́нин, датча́нка Dane

да́тчик sensor

дать *pf.* of **дава́ть**

да́ча country house; **на да́че** in the country

два *m. & neut.*, **две** two

двадцатиле́тний twenty-year-old

двадца́тый twentieth

два́дцать twenty

два́жды *adv.* twice

двена́дцатый twelfth

двена́дцать twelve

дверь *f.* door

две́сти two hundred

дви́гатель motor, engine

дви́гать(ся) *impf.*, **дви́нуть(ся)** *pf.* move; advance

движе́ние 1. motion, movement **2.** traffic

дви́жущий motive; driving

дво́е *coll.* two

двоебра́чие bigamy

двоежёнец FILL bigamist

двоето́чие (*punctuation*) colon

дво́йка 1. two **2.** (*cards*) deuce

двойни́к double; counterpart

двойно́й double, twofold

двойня́ twins

дво́йственный dual; two-faced

двор court, yard

дворе́ц FILL palace

дво́рник caretaker

дворня́га *m. & f.* mongrel

дворяни́н, -я́нка member of nobility

двою́родная сестра́ first cousin

двою́родный брат first cousin

двузна́чный two-digit

двукра́тный double, twofold

двули́кий two-faced

двули́чие duplicity

двупо́лый bisexual

двусмы́сленный ambiguous

двуспа́льный (*of bed*) double

двуство́лка double-barreled gun

двусторо́нний 1. double-sided **2.** two-way **3.** bilateral

двухко́мнатный *attrib.* two-room

двухле́тний two-year-old

двухме́стный for two; accomodating two persons

двухмото́рный *attrib.* twin-engine

двухсотле́тие bicentennial

двухсо́тый two-hundredth

двухфо́кусный bifocal

двухэта́жный two-story

двуязы́чие bilingualism

деба́ты pl. debate; discussion

деби́л *Slang* idiot; moron

дебо́ш brawl; fracas; row

дébри pl. jungle; the wilds
дебют debut
дéва Obs. maid; maiden
девáть impf., **деть** pf. put; do with; —**ся** disappear to
дéверь m. brother-in-law
дéвица unmarried woman
дéвочка girl, little girl
дéвственный virgin
дéвушка young girl
девянóсто ninety
девянóстый ninetieth
девятка nine; figure nine
девятнáдцатый nineteenth
девятнáдцать nineteen
девятый ninth
дéвять nine; —**сóт** nine hundred; —**сóтый** nine hundredth
дéготь m. tar
деградáция degeneration
дегустáтор taster
дед 1. grandfather 2. old man
дед-морóз Santa Claus
дéдушка grandpa, granddad
дееспосóбный 1. effective 2. able to function 3. (law) competent
дежýрный on duty; n. person on duty; —**ство** (being on) duty
дезертúр deserter
дезертúровать impf. & pf. desert
дезинфицúровать impf. & pf. disinfect
дезинформáция disinformation
дезодорáнт deodorant
дéйственный effective, efficacious
дéйствие action; act; operation
действúтельно adv. really; indeed
действúтельность 1. reality 2. validity; —**ный** real, actual; valid
действúтельный real, actual; valid
дéйствовать impf., **по—** pf. act; operate, work; have an effect
дéйствующий active, working; **дéйствующие лица** pl. cast of characters
дéка (mus.) sounding board
декáбрь m., —**ский** December
декáда decade
декáн dean
декларáция declaration
декольтé neut. indecl. decolletage
декоратúвный decorative
декорáтор decorator
декорáция scenery; display
декрéтный óтпуск maternity leave
дéланный artificial; affected
дéлать impf., **с—** pf. make; do; —**ся** become; happen
делегáт delegate

делегáция delegation
деликатéс delicacy
деликáтный delicate; tactful
делúть impf., **раз—**, **по—** pf. divide; share; —**ся** divide, be divisible; (+ I) share
дéло 1. affair, business, matter 2. deed; case; **в сáмом дéле** as a matter of fact; **на сáмом дéле** actually; in fact; **не в этом ~** that is not the point
деловúтый businesslike
деловóй attrib. business
дéльный efficient, effective
дéльта delta
дельфúн dolphin
демагóг demagogue
демисезóнный worn in the spring or fall
демобилизовáть impf. demobilize
демокрáт democrat
демократúческий democratic
демокрáтия democracy
дéмон demon
демонстрáнт demonstrator
демонстрáция demonstration
демонстрúровать impf. & pf. demonstrate
демонтáж dismantling
деморализовáть impf. demoralize
дéнежный attrib. money, monetary; —**перевóд** money order
день m. day; **на днях** the other day; **one of these days**
дéньги pl. money
департáмент department
депéша dispatch
депó neut. indecl. depot
депрéссия depression
депутáт deputy
депутáция deputation
дёргать impf., **дёрнуть** pf. pull, tug, jerk; —**ся** twitch
деревéнский rural; rustic
дерéвня 1. village 2. the country
дéрево 1. tree 2. wood
деревянный wooden
держáва 1. state 2. power
держáть impf. hold; keep; ~ **парú** bet; ~ **ся** hold (on); adhere
дéрзкий impudent; audacious
дéрзость impudence; audacity
дёрн turf, sod
дёрнуть pf. of **дёргать**
десáнт landing (of troops)
десéрт dessert
деснá (anat.) gum
дéспот despot
деснúца (poet.) hand; right hand
десятибóрье decathlon

десятилéтие 1. tenth anniversary **2.** decade

десятилéтний ten-year-old

десятка ten; figure ten; *Colloq.* a ten-ruble note

десяток FILL ten; *pl.* scores; dozens

десятый tenth

десять ten

детáль *f.* detail; **—ный** detailed

детдóм orphanage

детектив detective (story)

детёныш young one; *pl.* the young

дети *pl.* children

детонировать *impf.* detonate

деторóдные óрганы genitals

детсáд kindergarten

дéтская *n.* nursery

дéтский childish; children's

дéтство childhood

деть(ся) *pf. of* **девáть(ся)**

дефéкт defect

дефис hyphen

дефицит deficit; **—ный** scarce

деформировать *impf.* deform

дешевéть *impf.*, **по-** *pf.* become cheaper, cheaper

дешéвле *compar. of* **дешёвый**

дёшево *adv.* cheap, cheaply

дешёвый cheap

дешифрóвка deciphering

дéятель 1. worker **2.** activist

дéятельность activity; work

дéятельный active

джаз jazz

джем jam

джéмпер pullover; jersey

джентльмéн gentleman

джигит Caucasian horseman

джинсы *pl.* jeans

джип Jeep

джунгли *pl.* jungle

дзюдó *neut. indecl.* judo

диабéт diabetes

диáгноз diagnosis

диагонáль *f.* diagonal

диагрáмма diagram

диалéкт dialect; **—ика** dialectics

диалóг dialogue

диáметр diameter

диапазóн range; scope; band

диапозитив slide; transparency

диафрáгма (*anat.*) diaphragm

дивáн sofa

диверсáнт saboteur

диверсия (*mil.*) diversion

дивизия (*mil.*) division

дáво wonder, marvel

диéз (*mus.*) sharp

диéта diet

диетический dietary

дизáйн design

дизель *m.* diesel engine

дикáрь, дикáрка savage

дикий wild, savage; queer

дикобрáз porcupine

дикóвина *Colloq.* novelty

дикóвинный strange; bizarre

дикость savagery, savageness

диктáнт (classroom) dictation

диктáтор dictator

диктатýра dictatorship

диктóвка dictation

диктор (radio) announcer

диктофóн Dictaphone

дилетáнт, —ка dilettante

динáмика dynamics

динамит dynamite

динамический dynamic

динáстия dynasty

динозáвр dinosaur

диплóм diploma

дипломáт diplomat

дипломатический diplomatic

дипломатичный tactful

директор director

директорáт board of directors

дирéкция 1. top management **2.** director's office

дирижáбль *m.* dirigible

дирижёр (*mus.*) conductor

дирижировать *impf.* conduct

дисгармóния disharmony

диск disk, discus

дискáнт (*mus.*) treble

дисквалификáция disqualification

дискотéка discotheque

дискриминáция discrimination

дискýссия discussion

дискутировать *impf.* discuss

диспансéр dispensary

диспéтчер (traffic) controller

диспéтчерская *n.* control tower

диспýт dispute; debate

диссертáция dissertation; thesis

дистанцибнный remote; remote-control

дистáнция distance

дисциплина discipline

дитя child

дифтерия, дифтерит diphtheria

диффамáция defamation

дичáть *impf.*, **о-** *pf.* become wild

дичь *f.* game; wildfowl

длинá length; **в длинý** lengthwise

длинный long

длительный long, prolonged

дли́ться *impf.,* **про—** *pf.* last

для *prep.* (+ G) for; to

дневни́к diary; journal

дневно́й day; daily; ла́мпа дневно́го све́та fluorescent light

дневно́й спекта́кль *m.* matinee

днём *adv.* in the daytime; by day

дни́ще bottom

дно bottom; вверх —м upside down

до *prep.* (+ G) (up) to; until; as far as; before

добавле́ние addition; appendix

добавля́ть *impf.,* **доба́вить** *pf.* add

доба́вочный additional; extra

добива́ть *impf.,* **доби́ть** *pf.* finish off; **—ся** obtain; achieve

добира́ться *impf.,* **добра́ться** *pf.* (до + G) reach, get to

до́блесть *f.* valor

добро́ 1. good **2.** possessions

доброво́лец FILL volunteer

доброво́льный voluntary

доброде́тель *f.* virtue

доброде́тельный virtuous

доброду́шие good nature

доброка́чественный of high quality; (*med.*) benign

Добро́ пожа́ловать *interj.* Welcome!

добросерде́чный kindhearted

добросо́вестный conscientious

доброта́ goodness; kindness

добро́тный of high quality

до́брый good; kind

добыва́ть *impf.,* **добы́ть** *pf.* get, obtain; mine

добы́ча procurement; mining; loot

дове́ренность power of attorney

дове́ренный authorized; *n.* agent

дове́рие trust; confidence

дове́рчивый trustful, credulous

доверя́ть *impf.,* **дове́рить** *pf.* entrust; trust

до́вод reason; argument

доводи́ть *impf.,* **довести́** *pf.* bring to; drive to

дово́енный *attrib.* prewar

дово́льно *adv.* rather; fairly; quite

дово́льный content; satisfied

дог Great Dane

дога́дка guess; conjecture

дога́дываться *impf.,* **догада́ться** *pf.* guess, suspect

догна́ть *pf. of* догоня́ть

догова́риваться *impf.,* **договори́ться** *pf.* arrange; agree

догово́р agreement; contract; treaty

догово́рный contractual

догола́ *adv.* to the skin

догоня́ть *impf.,* **догна́ть** *pf.* overtake; catch up

доду́мываться *impf.,* **доду́маться** *pf.* think of

доезжа́ть *impf.,* **дое́хать** *pf.* reach; arrive (at)

дожда́ться *pf.* wait (for)

дождли́вый rainy

дождь *m.* rain; ~ идёт it's raining

дожива́ть *impf.,* **дожи́ть** *pf.* live (to see); live out (one's days)

до́за dose

дозапра́вка refueling

дозволя́ть *impf.,* **дозво́лить** *pf.* permit, allow

дозиро́вка dosage

дозна́ние (*law*) inquest; inquiry

доистори́ческий prehistoric

дои́ть *impf.,* **по—** *pf.* milk

дойти́ *pf. of* доходи́ть

док dock

доказа́тельство proof; evidence

дока́зывать *impf.,* **доказа́ть** *pf.* prove

докла́д lecture; paper; report

докла́дывать *impf.,* **доложи́ть** *pf.* report, make a report

до́ктор doctor

доктри́на doctrine

докуме́нт document

документа́льный documentary

долби́ть *impf.,* **про—** *pf.* **1.** hollow out **2.** *Colloq.* learn by rote

долг 1. debt **2.** duty

до́лгий long

долгове́чный long-lasting

долговре́менный of long duration

долгожда́нный long-awaited

долголе́тний of many years

долгосро́чный long-term

долгота́ length; longitude

до́лжен, —жна́; —жно́; *pl.* —жны́ must; should; owe

должни́к, —ни́ца debtor

до́лжность position; post

доли́на valley

до́ллар dollar

доложи́ть *pf. of* докла́дывать

до́лька lobule; section

до́льше *adv.* longer

до́ля 1. portion; share **2.** fate

дом house; home; до́ма at home

дома́шний domestic; home

домини́ровать *impf.* (над + I) (pre)dominate (over)

домкра́т jack (for lifting)

до́мна blast furnace

домовладе́лец FILL, **-льца** home-owner

домога́тельство solicitation; bid

домосе́д, —а homebody

домоуправле́ние building management

домохозя́йка housewife

домрабо́тница maid; housemaid

до́мысел FILL conjecture; guess

дона́шивать *impf.*, **доноси́ть** *pf.* wear out

доне́льзя *adv.* completely

донесе́ние report; dispatch

до́нop blood donor

доно́с denunciation; accusation

доноси́ть[1] *impf.*, **донести́** *pf.* denounce; inform; report

доноси́ть[2] *pf.* of **дона́шивать**.

допла́та surcharge

допла́чивать *impf.*, **доплати́ть** *pf.* pay in addition; pay in full

допо́длинный true; authentic

допоздна́ *adv.* till late at night

дополне́ние 1. supplement; addition **2.** (*gram.*) object

дополни́тельный supplementary

дополня́ть *impf.*, **допо́лнить** *pf.* supplement; add

допра́шивать *impf.*, **допроси́ть** *pf.* examine, question

допро́с examination; interrogation

допуска́ть *impf.*, **допусти́ть** *pf.* admit; permit; grant; assume

дореволюцио́нный prerevolutionary

доро́га road; way; journey

до́рого *adv.* expensive; dear; dearly

дорого́й dear; expensive

доро́же *compar.* of **дорого́й**

дорожи́ть *impf.* (+ *I*) value; treasure

доро́жка path; track; runner

доро́жный *attrib.* road; travel

доса́да nuisance; annoyance

доса́дный annoying

доса́довать *impf.* (**на** + *A*) be annoyed with

доска́ (black)board; plank

досло́вный literal; word for word

досмо́тр examination; inspection

досро́чно *adv.* ahead of schedule

достава́ть *impf.*, **доста́ть** *pf.* **1.** get; obtain **2.** (**до** + *G*) reach; touch

доставля́ть *impf.*, **доста́вить** *pf.* **1.** deliver; supply **2.** give; cause

доста́точно *adv.* enough; sufficiently

доста́точный sufficient

доста́ть *pf.* of **достава́ть**

достига́ть *impf.*, **дости́чь**, **дости́гнуть** *pf.* (+ *G*) achieve; reach

достиже́ние achievement

достове́рность authenticity

достове́рный trustworthy, reliable

досто́инство merit; virtue; dignity

досто́йный 1. worthy; deserving **2.** fitting; suitable

достопримеча́тельность object or place of interest; sight

достоя́ние property; holdings

до́ступ 1. access **2.** approach

досу́г leisure

до́суха *adv.* until completely dry

до́сыта *adv.* one's fill

досье́ *neut. indecl.* dossier

досяга́емость reach; (*mil.*) range

дота́ция subsidy; grant

дотла́ *adv.* to the ground

до́хнуть[1] *impf.*, **по-** *pf.* die

дохну́ть[2] *pf.* take a breath

дохо́д income; return

дохо́дный profitable

дохо́дчивый easy to understand

доце́нт university lecturer

до́чиста *adv.* clean

дочь *f.*, **до́чка** daughter

дошко́льный preschool

доща́тый made of boards

доще́чка small board

дра́га dredge

драгоце́нность jewel; precious stone; *pl.* valuables

драгоце́нный precious

драже́ *neut. indecl.* (*candy*) drops

дразни́ть *impf.* tease

дра́ка fight

драко́н dragon

дра́ма drama; **—ти́ческий** dramatic; **—ту́рг** playwright

драматурги́я dramaturgy

драп heavy woolen cloth

драпирова́ть *impf.* drape

драпиро́вка drapery

драть, вы-, co- *pf.* tear; flog; **—ся** *impf.*, **по-** *pf.* fight

драчу́н *Colloq.* brawler

древеси́на wood; timber

древе́сный *attrib.* wood

древнегре́ческий ancient Greek

древнеевре́йский Hebrew

древнеру́сский Old Russian

дре́вний ancient

дре́вность antiquity

дрейф (*ocean*) drift

дрейфова́ть *impf.* drift

дрель *f.* (*tool*) drill

дрема́ть *impf.* doze; nap

дремо́та drowsiness
дрему́чий dense, thick
дрессиро́ванный (animal) trained
дрессирова́ть impf., вы- pf. train; school
дрессиро́вщик (animal) trainer
дроби́на pellet
дроби́ть impf., раз- pf. split up; crush; smash
дро́бный fractional
дробови́к shotgun
дробь f. 1. shot; pellets 2. drumming 3. (math.) fraction
дрова́ pl. firewood
дро́гнуть pf. shake; flinch
дрожа́ние trembling; shivering
дрожа́ть impf. shiver; tremble
дро́жжи pl. yeast
дрожь f. trembling, quivering
дро́ссель m. throttle; choke
друг friend; ~ дру́га one another
друго́й other; another; next
дру́жба amity, friendship
дружелю́бный friendly; amicable
дру́жеский friendly
дружи́ть impf. be friends with
дру́жный amicable, friendly
дружо́к FILL Colloq. friend; pal
дры́гать impf. jerk, twitch; kick
дря́зги pl. Colloq. squabbles
дря́нной worthless; bad; trashy
дрянь f. rubbish; trash
дря́хлый 1. decrepit 2. senile
дуб oak; —о́вый oak
дуби́на club; bludgeon; blockhead
дубле́ние tanning
дублёный tanned
дублика́т duplicate
дубли́рование 1. duplication 2. dubbing
дубра́ва oak forest
дуга́ 1. arc; arch 2. shaft bow
ду́дка fife
ду́жка hoop
ду́ло muzzle (of gun)
ду́ма 1. thought 2. Duma
ду́мать impf., по- pf. think; (+ infin.) intend
дунове́ние puff; breath
дупло́ 1. hollow 2. cavity
ду́ра, дура́к fool

дура́чество prank
дурма́н narcotic; drug
ду́рно adv. badly; мне ~ I feel faint
дурно́й foul; bad; ugly
дурнота́ faintness; nausea
дуршла́г colander
ду́ть impf., вы-, по- pf. blow
ду́ться impf. pout; sulk
дух 1. spirit; heart 2. ghost
духи́ pl. perfume
духове́нство clergy
духо́вка oven
духо́вный 1. spiritual 2. ecclesiastical
духово́й wind; ~ орке́стр brass band
духота́ stuffiness, closeness
душ shower; shower bath
душа́ soul
душева́я n. shower; shower room
душе́вный sincere; cordial; mental
душераздира́ющий heart-rending
души́стый fragrant; scented
души́ть[1] impf., за- pf. strangle; stifle, smother
души́ть[2] impf., на- pf. perfume
ду́шный close; stuffy
ду́эт duet
ды́бом adv. (of hair) on end
дыбы́ pl. дыбы́: станови́ться на ~ impf. (of horses) rear
дым smoke; smoky
ды́мный smoky; muskmelon
дыми́ть impf., на- pf. fill with smoke; —ся v.i. smoke; steam
ды́мка haze
дымохо́д flue; stovepipe
ды́ня melon; muskmelon
дыра́, ды́рка hole
дыроко́л hole punch
дыря́вый full of holes
дыха́ние respiration; breathing
дыха́тельный respiratory
дыша́ть impf. breathe, respire
дья́вол devil; —ьский devilish
дья́кон deacon
дю́жина dozen
дюйм inch
дю́на dune
дя́дя m. uncle
дя́тел woodpecker

Ева́нгелие Gospel
евангели́ст Evangelist
евре́й, —ка Jew; Hebrew; **—ский** Jewish; Hebrew
Евро́па Europe
европе́ец FILL, **-пе́йка** European
европе́йский European
е́герь *m.* professional hunter
Еги́пет Egypt
еги́петский Egyptian
египтя́нин, -я́нка Egyptian
его́ *pron. G & A of* **он, оно́**
еда́ food; meal
едва́ *adv.* hardly; ~ **не** nearly
едине́ние unity
едини́ца unity; the numeral one
едини́чный single; isolated
единобра́чие monogamy
единовла́стие absolute rule
единогла́сие unanimity
единогла́сный unanimous
единоду́шие unanimity
единоду́шный unanimous
единомы́шленник like-minded person
единоро́г unicorn
еди́нственный sole, only
еди́нство unity
еди́ный united; single
е́дкий caustic
едо́к FILL mouth to feed; eater
её *pron. G & A of* **она́**
ёж hedgehog
ежего́дник yearbook; annual
ежего́дный annual
ежедне́вный daily
ежеме́сячный monthly
еженеде́льный weekly
ёжиться *impf.,* **съ-** *pf.* huddle up
езда́ ride; drive; driving, traveling
е́здить *indet.,* **е́хать** *det.* ride; drive, go; travel
ей *pron. D & I of* **она́**
ей-бо́гу *interj.* really; truly!
е́ле *adv.* scarcely
еле́й holy oil; unction; balm
ёлка fir tree; Christmas tree
ель *f.* spruce; **—ник** spruce grove
ёмкий capacious
ёмкость capacity, capaciousness
ему́ *pron. D of* **он, оно́**
ено́т raccoon
епи́скоп bishop
е́ресь *f.* heresy
ерети́к, ерети́чка heretic
ёрзать *impf. Colloq.* fidget

ерунда́ nonsense; rubbish
е́сли *conj.* if; ~ **бы** he were it not for
есте́ственный natural
естество́ nature; essence
естествозна́ние natural sciences
естествоиспыта́тель naturalist
есть[1] *impf.,* **съ-** *pf.* eat (away)
есть[2] *3rd person sing. pres. of* **быть** there is, there are; **у меня́ ~** I have
е́хать *impf.,* **по-** *pf.* go, ride, drive
ехи́дный malicious; venomous
ещё *adv.* still, yet; more; already
е́ю *pron. I of* **она́**

ж *see* **же**
жа́ба toad
жа́бры *pl.* gills
жа́воронок FILL lark
жа́дность greed; stinginess
жа́дный greedy; avid, covetous
жа́жда thirst
жаке́т jacket
жале́ть *impf.,* **по-** *pf.* feel sorry; regret
жа́лкий pitiful; pitiable; miserable
жа́лко *see* **жаль**
жа́ло (*zool.*) sting; stinger
жа́лоба complaint
жа́лобный plaintive; sorrowful
жа́ловаться *impf.,* **по-** *pf.* complain
жа́лость pity
жаль, жа́лко *impers. pred.* it's a pity; **мне его́ ~** I feel sorry for him
жалюзи́ *pl. indecl.* venetian blinds
жанр genre
жар 1. heat; ardor **2.** fever
жара́ heat
жарго́н jargon, slang
жа́реный fried; grilled; broiled
жа́рить(ся) *impf.,* **из-** *pf.* fry; roast; broil; grill
жа́ркий 1. hot, torrid **2.** ardent
жарко́е *n.* meat dish; roast
жаро́вня brazier
жар-пти́ца firebird
жасми́н jasmine; **—ный** jasmine
жа́тва harvest; reaping
жать *impf.* (*pres.* **жму, жмёшь,** **с-, по-** *pf.* press, squeeze; pinch
жва́чка 1. cud **2.** chewing gum
жгут twisted braid; tourniquet
жгу́чий burning

ждать *impf.,* **подо-** *pf.* wait, expect

же, ж *conj.* but; *particle* **1.** (*emphasis*) что — ты де́лаешь? What are you doing? **2.** (*identity*) так — in the same way

жева́ть *impf.* chew, ruminate

жела́ние wish, desire

жела́нный 1. desired **2.** welcome

жела́тельный desirable

жела́ть *impf.,* **по-** *pf.* wish, desire

желе́ *neut. indecl.* jelly

железа́ gland

желе́зная доро́га railway; railroad

железнодоро́жный railroad

желе́зный iron; ferrous

желе́зо iron

жёлоб gutter; chute

желтизна́ yellowness

желто́к FILL egg yolk

желту́ха jaundice

жёлтый yellow

желу́док FILL stomach

желу́дочный stomach; gastric

жёлудь *m.* acorn

жёлчность biliousness

жема́нный affected; unnatural

жёмчуг *coll.* pearls

жемчу́жина (single) pearl

жена́ wife

жена́тый (на + *P*) married

жени́ть *impf. & P.* marry; **—ся** (на + *P*) (*of a man*) marry, get married (to)

жени́тьба marriage

жени́х fiancé; bridegroom

женонави́стник misogynist

женоподо́бный effeminate

же́нский female; feminine

же́нственность femininity

же́нщина woman

женьше́нь *m.* ginseng

жердь *f.* rod, pole; long stick

жеребёнок FILL foal

жеребе́ц FILL stallion

жеребьёвка casting of lots

жерло́ 1. crater **2.** muzzle

же́ртва 1. sacrifice **2.** victim

же́ртвовать *impf.,* **по-** *pf.* donate, endow; sacrifice

жест gesture

жестикули́ровать *impf.* gesticulate

жёсткий hard; strong; firm; rigid

жёсткость hardness

жесто́кий cruel; fierce; harsh

жесто́кость cruelty; atrocity

жесть *f.* tin

жето́н 1. token **2.** medal

жечь *impf.,* **с-** *pf.* burn; sting

жже́ние burning sensation

жи́во *adv.* lively, animatedly

живода́р, —ка Colloq. hustler

живо́й lively; live; alive

живопи́сец FILL painter

живопи́сный picturesque

жи́вопись *f.* painting

жи́вость *f.* liveliness, animation

живо́т stomach; belly

животново́дство livestock breeding; animal husbandry

живо́тное *n.* animal; beast

живо́тный *attrib.* animal

живу́чий viable; tenacious of life

живчик FILL lively person

жи́дкий 1. liquid **2.** thin; watery

жи́дкость liquid; fluid

жи́жа swill; liquid; wash

жи́же *compar. of* жи́дкий

жи́зненный lifelike; vital

жизнера́достный cheerful, joyous

жизнеспосо́бный viable

жизнь *f.* life

жи́ла 1. vein **2.** sinew

жиле́т, —ка vest, waistcoat

жиле́ц FILL, **—ли́ца** tenant; lodger

жи́листый sinewy; stringy; wiry

жили́ще dwelling; abode

жило́й dwelling; habitable

жилпло́щадь *f.* floorspace

жильё dwelling; domicile

жир fat

жира́ф giraffe

жи́рный greasy; fat; rich

жите́йский worldly; mundane

жи́тель, —ница inhabitant

жить *impf.* live

жму́риться *impf.,* **за-** *pf.* squint

жонглёр juggler

жонгли́ровать *impf.* juggle

жра́ть *impf.,* **со-** *pf.* gobble

жре́бий lot; fate, destiny

жрец, жри́ца pagan priest(ess)

жужжа́ть *impf.* hum; buzz; drone

жук beetle

жу́лик crook; cheat; swindler

жу́льничать *impf.* Colloq. cheat

жура́вль *m.* (*bird*) crane

журна́л magazine, periodical

журнали́ст, —ка journalist

журнали́стика journalism

журча́ть *impf.* babble; murmur

жу́ткий horrible; terrible

жу́тко *adv.* frighteningly; terribly

жуть *f.* Colloq. horror

жюри́ *neut. indecl.* judges; jury

за 1. *prep.* (+ A) (dir.) behind; beyond; across, over; for, by **2.** (+ I) (loc.) behind, beyond; after

заатланти́ческий transatlantic

забавля́ть *impf.* amuse; entertain

заба́вный amusing

забастова́ть *pf. of* бастова́ть

забасто́вка strike

забе́г (sports) heat; round; race

забере́менеть *pf. of* бере́менеть

забива́ть *impf.*, **заби́ть** *pf.* **1.** drive, hammer in **2.** block up

забинтова́ть *pf. of* бинтова́ть

забира́ть *impf.*, **забра́ть** *pf.* take; **—ся** get into

заблаговре́менно *adv.* **1.** in good time **2.** in advance

заблуди́ться *pf.* get lost

заблужда́ться *impf.* be mistaken

заблужде́ние error

заболева́ние illness; disease

заболева́ть *impf.*, **заболе́ть** *pf.* get sick

забо́р fence

забо́та care; concern; trouble

забо́титься *impf.*, **по-** *pf.* (о + P) be concerned about; take care

забо́тливый thoughtful; concerned

забра́ть(ся) *pf. of* забира́ть(ся)

заброни́ровать *pf. of* брони́ровать

забро́шенный neglected; deserted

забыва́ть *impf.*, **забы́ть** *pf.* forget

забы́вчивый forgetful; absent-minded

забытьё drowsiness

зава́ливать *impf.*, **завали́ть** *pf.* pile up; encumber; overload

зава́ривать *impf.*, **завари́ть** *pf.* brew

заведе́ние establishment

заве́довать *impf.* (+ I) manage

заве́домо *adv.* knowingly

заве́дующий *n.* manager, director

завербова́ть *pf. of* вербова́ть

заве́ренный certified

завёртывать *impf.*, **заверну́ть** *pf.* wrap (up); turn; roll up

заверша́ть *impf.*, **-ши́ть** *pf.* complete, conclude

заве́са curtain; screen

завести́ *pf. of* заводи́ть

Заве́т: Ве́тхий (Но́вый) ~ Old (New) Testament

заве́тный cherished; secret

заве́шивать *impf.*, **заве́сить** *pf.* cover; curtain off

завеща́ние will; testament

завеща́ть *impf. & pf.* bequeath

завива́ть(ся) *impf.*, **зави́ть(ся)** *pf.* wave, curl

зави́вка curling; wave

зави́довать *impf.*, **по-** *pf.* (+ D) envy

завизжа́ть *pf. of* визжа́ть

зави́нчивать *impf.*, **завинти́ть** *pf.* tighten (a screw, nut)

зави́сеть *impf.* (от + G) depend on

зави́симость dependence

зави́симый dependent

зави́стник envious person

за́висть *f.* envy

зави́ть *pf. of* завива́ть

завладе́ть *pf. of* владе́ть

завлека́тельный enticing; alluring

завлека́ть *impf.*, **завле́чь** *pf.* entice; lure

заво́д factory; plant; works

заводи́ть *impf.*, **завести́** *pf.* **1.** bring; take to **2.** acquire **3.** establish **4.** introduce **5.** wind

заводно́й winding

заводско́й *attrib.* factory

завоева́тель conqueror

завоёвывать *impf.*, **завоева́ть** *pf.* conquer; win

заво́з delivery

завози́ть *impf.*, **завезти́** *pf.* deliver; bring

завора́живать *impf.*, **заворожи́ть** *pf.* bewitch; captivate

завора́чивать *impf.*, **заверну́ть**, **завороти́ть** *pf.* turn (around); roll up; wrap (up)

заворо́т sharp turn; bend

завсегда́тай habitué

за́втра *adv.* tomorrow

за́втрак breakfast

за́втракать *impf.*, **по-** *pf.* (eat) breakfast

за́втрашний tomorrow's

завыва́ть *impf.* howl; wail

завя́зка string; lace; beginning

завя́зывать *impf.*, **завяза́ть** *pf.* bind; fasten; tie

завя́нуть *pf. of* вя́нуть

зага́дка riddle; enigma, mystery

зага́дочный enigmatic; mysterious

зага́дывать *impf.*, **загада́ть** *pf.* ask a riddle; think of, tell fortunes

зага́р sunburn; tan

загаси́ть *pf.* extinguish

загиба́ть *impf.*, загну́ть *pf.* bend; turn up *or* down

загипнотизи́ровать *pf. of* гипнотизи́ровать

загла́вие title, heading

загла́вная бу́ква capital letter

загла́живать *impf.*, загла́дить *pf.* 1. press; iron 2. make up for

заглóхнуть *pf. of* глóхнуть

заглуша́ть *impf.*, -ши́ть *pf.* muffle; drown out; suppress

загля́дывать *impf.*, загляну́ть *pf.* look into; *Colloq.* drop in

загна́ть *pf. of* загоня́ть

загнива́ть *impf.*, загни́ть *pf.* rot

за́говор conspiracy; plot

заголóвок FILL title; headline

загоня́ть *impf.*, загна́ть *pf.* drive in *or* under; exhaust

загора́живать *impf.*, загороди́ть *pf.* enclose; block; obstruct

загора́ть *impf.*, -ре́ть *pf. v.i.* sunburn; —ся catch fire

за́городный suburban; rural

загото́вка (state) procurement, purchase; stockpiling

заготовля́ть *impf.*, загото́вить *pf.* prepare, store up

загражда́ть *impf.*, загради́ть *pf.* block

загражде́ние obstacle; barrier

грани́ца foreign countries

заграни́чный foreign

загреба́ть *impf.*, загрести́ *pf.* rake up; gather in

загромождáть *impf.*, -мозди́ть *pf.* encumber; block

загружа́ть *impf.*, загрузи́ть *pf.* load (up)

загру́зка load(ing); capacity

загрязне́ние pollution

загрязня́ть *impf.*, -ни́ть *pf.* soil; pollute

загс (*abbr. of* за́пись а́ктов гражда́нского состоя́ния) civilian registry office

зад back; buttocks; hind quarters

задава́ть *impf.*, зада́ть *pf.* set; pose; assign

зада́ние task

зада́ток FILL deposit; advance

зада́ча problem; task

задвига́ть *impf.*, задви́нуть *pf.* push (under); slide (shut)

задви́жка bolt; door bolt

задвижно́й sliding

задева́ть *impf.*, заде́ть *pf.* brush (against); (за + A) snag; offend

задёргать *pf.* bother; harass

задёргивать *impf.*, задёрнуть *pf.* pull, draw

заде́рживание detention; retention

заде́рживать *impf.*, задержа́ть *pf.* detain, delay; arrest

заде́ржка delay

заде́ть *pf. of* задева́ть

задира́ть *impf.*, задра́ть *pf.* 1. turn up; lift up 2. pick on

за́дний back; rear; ~ план background; ~ ход reverse gear

задо́лго *adv.* long before

задолжа́ть *pf.* (+ D) be in debt

задо́лженность indebtedness

задо́р fervor; enthusiasm

задра́ть *pf. of* задира́ть, драть

заду́мчивость pensiveness

заду́мчивый pensive; thoughtful

заду́мывать *impf.*, заду́мать *pf.* conceive; plan; intend; —ся become pensive; meditate

заду́шевный sincere; intimate

задуши́ть *pf. of* души́ть

заёзд 1. visit 2. horserace

заезжа́ть *impf.*, зае́хать *pf.* drop in on; (за + I) pick up

заём loan; —щик borrower

зажа́ть *pf. of* зажима́ть

заже́чь *pf. of* зажига́ть

зажива́ть *impf.*, зажи́ть *pf.* heal

за́живо *adv.* alive

зажига́лка cigarette lighter

зажига́ть *impf.*, заже́чь *pf.* set fire (to); light; —ся catch fire

зажи́м clamp

зажима́ть *impf.*, зажа́ть *pf.* squeeze; grip; suppress

заземле́ние (*elec.*) ground

зазу́бренный jagged; serrated

зазыва́ть *impf.*, зазва́ть *pf. Colloq.* urge to come

заи́грывать *impf.*, заигра́ть *pf. Colloq.* flirt

заика́ние stuttering; stutter

заика́ться *impf.*, заикну́ться *pf.* 1. stutter; stammer 2. *Colloq.* (o + P) mention

займствовать *impf.*, по- *pf.* adopt; borrow

заинтересо́ванность interest

заинтересова́ть *pf.* interest; —ся (+ I) become interested

заинтригова́ть *pf. of* интригова́ть

заи́скивать *impf.* (перед + I) ingratiate oneself

зайти́ *pf. of* заходи́ть

за́йчик 1. *dim. of* за́яц 2. spot of light

зака́з order

заказно́й made to order; заказно́е письмо́ registered letter

зака́зчик customer

зака́зывать *impf.*, заказа́ть *pf.* order

зака́лка tempering; *Fig.* toughness

зака́лывать *impf.*, заколо́ть *pf.* pin up; stab; slaughter

закаля́ть *impf.*, -ли́ть *pf.* temper; harden

зака́нчивать *impf.*, зако́нчить *pf.* finish (up); conclude

зака́пать *pf.* spot; begin to drip

зака́пывать *impf.*, закопа́ть *pf.* bury

зака́т **1.** sunset **2.** *Fig.* decline

зака́тывать[1] *impf.*, заката́ть *pf.* roll in, out, up

зака́тывать[2] *impf.*, закати́ть *pf.* roll; *Colloq.* make (a scene)

заква́ска ferment; leaven

закипа́ть *impf.*, -пе́ть *pf.* begin to boil; seethe with

закла́д pledge; pawn

закла́дка **1.** bookmark **2.** laying

закле́ивать *impf.*, закле́ить *pf.* glue

заклейми́ть *pf. of* клейми́ть

заклёпка rivet

заклина́ние incantation

заклина́ть *impf.* invoke; entreat

заключа́ть *impf.*, -чи́ть *pf.* conclude; infer; contain; confine

заключе́ние conclusion; inference; confinement

заключённый *n.* prisoner

заключи́тельный final; conclusive

зако́лка hairpin

заколо́ть *pf. of* зака́лывать

зако́н law

зако́нность legitimacy; legality

зако́нный legal; legitimate

законода́тель legislator

законода́тельный legislative

закономе́рный regular; natural

законослу́шный law-abiding

законопрое́кт (legislative) bill

зако́нченный complete; accomplished

зако́нчить *pf. of* зака́нчивать

закопа́ть *pf. of* зака́пывать

закостене́ть *pf.* become numb

закочене́лый frozen stiff; numb

закра́дываться *impf.*, закра́сться *pf.* steal into

закра́шивать *impf.*, закра́сить *pf.* paint over

закрепля́ть *impf.*, -пи́ть *pf.* fasten; secure

закрича́ть *pf.* (begin to) shout, yell

закружи́ть(ся) *pf.* begin to whirl; go round, spin

закру́чивать *impf.*, закрути́ть *pf.* twist, twirl

закрыва́ть(ся) *impf.*, закры́ть(ся) *pf.* close; shut off; shut down; cover (oneself)

закры́тие closing; close; end

закры́тый closed, shut; private

закупа́ть *impf.*, -пи́ть *pf.* buy up

заку́пка purchase

заку́порка plugging up; thrombosis

заку́пщик (wholesale) buyer

закури́ть *pf.* begin to smoke; light up (a cigarette)

заку́ска snack; hors d'oeuvres

заку́сочная *n.* snack bar

заку́сывать *impf.*, закуси́ть *pf.* have a snack

заку́тывать(ся) *impf.*, заку́тать(ся) *pf.* wrap (oneself) up, bundle up

зал hall; room

залата́ть *pf. of* лата́ть

залеза́ть *impf.*, зале́зть *pf.* climb (up); get in

залепля́ть *impf.*, -пи́ть *pf.* seal up

залета́ть *impf.*, -те́ть *pf.* fly into

зали́в (*geog.*) bay

залива́ть *impf.*, зали́ть *pf.* flood; inundate

заливно́е *n.* aspic

зало́г deposit; pledge; security

зало́жник hostage

залп volley

зама́лчивать *impf.*, замолча́ть *pf.* hush up; be silent about

зама́нивать *impf.*, замани́ть *pf.* tempt; lure

зама́нчивый tempting

замара́ть *pf. of* мара́ть

замаскиро́вывать *impf.*, замаскирова́ть *pf.* mask, disguise

зама́хиваться *impf.*, замахну́ться *pf.* brandish

зама́шки *pl.* ways; manner

замедля́ть(ся) *impf.*, заме́длить(ся) *pf.* slow down

заме́на substitution; substitute

заменя́ть substitute

заменя́ть *impf.*, -ни́ть *pf.* substitute; replace

замерза́ть *impf.*, замёрзнуть *pf. v.i.* freeze (to death); be freezing

замести́тель substitute; deputy

замести́ть *pf. of* замеща́ть

заме́тка note; notice; mark

заме́тный visible; outstanding

замеча́ние remark; reprimand

замеча́тельный remarkable

замеча́ть *impf.*, **заме́тить** *pf.* note; notice; remark

заме́шивать *impf.*, **замеша́ть** *pf.* (**в** *with acc.*) mix up in; implicate

замеща́ть *impf.*, **-сти́ть** *pf.* replace; substitute for

замеще́ние replacement; substitution

замира́ть *impf.*, **замере́ть** *pf.* stand still; die down

за́мкнутый closed; reserved

за́мок FILL castle

замо́к FILL lock; padlock

замолча́ть *pf.* fall silent; stop talking

замора́живать *impf.*, **заморо́зить** *pf. v.t.* freeze

заморо́женный frozen

за́морозки *pl.* light frost

за́муж *adv.*: **вы́йти ~** (**за** + *A*) (*of a woman*) marry

за́мужем *adv.* (**за** + *I*) married

заму́чить *pf.* torment; wear out

за́мша suede; chamois

замыка́ние: **коро́ткое ~** (*elec.*) short circuit

за́мысел FILL plan, intention

замышля́ть *impf.*, **замы́слить** *pf.* conceive; plan

за́навес, **занаве́ска** curtain

зана́шивать *impf.*, **заноси́ть** *pf.* (*of clothes*) wear out

занести́ *pf. of* **заноси́ть**

занима́тельный entertaining

занима́ть *impf.*, **заня́ть** *pf.* occupy; borrow; **—ся** (+ *I*) be occupied (with); be engaged (in); study

за́ново *adv.* over again, anew

зано́за splinter

зано́с 1. drift 2. skidding

заноси́ть[1] *impf.*, **занести́** *pf.* 1. bring, carry 2. enter (*on a list*)

заноси́ть[2] *pf. of* **зана́шивать**

заня́тие occupation; *pl.* studies

заня́той busy; occupied

за́нятый *short form* **за́нят**, **занята́**, **за́нято** 1. busy 2. occupied

заня́ть(ся) *pf. of* **занима́ть(ся)**

заодно́ *adv.* in unison, in concert

заостри́ть *impf.*, **-ри́ть** *pf.* sharpen; *Fig.* emphasize

зао́чно *adv.* in absentia

зао́чный курс correspondence course

за́пад west; **—ный** west, western

запа́здывать *impf.*, **запозда́ть** *pf.* be late

запа́л ignition; fuse

запа́льная свеча́ spark plug

запа́с supply, stock; reserve

запаса́ть *impf.*, **запасти́** *pf.* store, stock; **—ся** (+ *I*) stock up on

запа́сливый provident

запасно́й, **запа́сный** spare, reserve; (for an) emergency

за́пах smell, odor; scent

запека́нка baked dish

запина́ться *impf.*, **запну́ться** *pf.* stumble; hesitate

запира́ть *impf.*, **запере́ть** *pf.* lock; bolt

запи́ска note; memorandum

записна́я кни́жка notebook

запи́сывать *impf.*, **записа́ть** *pf.* note, jot down, enter; **—ся** register

за́пись *f.* entry; registration; recording

запи́хивать *impf.*, **запиха́ть**, **запихну́ть** *pf.* stuff into; cram into

запла́канный tearful; tear-stained

запла́та patch

заплати́ть *pf. of* **плати́ть**

запове́дник reserve; preserve

запове́дный forbidden; secret

за́поведь *f.* (*relig.*) commandment

запозда́ть *pf. of* **запа́здывать**

запо́й drinking bout

заполня́ть *impf.*, **запо́лнить** *pf.* fill (in, out, up)

запомина́ть *impf.*, **запо́мнить** *pf.* remember; memorize

запо́нка cuff link

запо́р 1. bolt 2. constipation

запоте́ть *pf. of* **поте́ть**

запра́вка 1. seasoning 2. refueling

заправля́ть *impf.*, **запра́вить** *pf.* 1. tuck in 2. season 3. refuel

запра́вочная ста́нция gas station

запра́шивать *impf.*, **запроси́ть** *pf.* 1. inquire 2. overcharge

запре́т prohibition

запре́тный forbidden

запреща́ть *impf.*, **-ти́ть** *pf.* prohibit

запреще́ние prohibition; ban

запро́с inquiry; demand

запру́да dam

запряга́ть *impf.*, **запря́чь** *pf.* harness

запу́гивать *impf.*, **запуга́ть** *pf.* intimidate

за́пуск 1. launching 2. starting

запуска́ть *impf.*, **-сти́ть** *pf.* launch; start

запусте́лый desolate; neglected

запусте́ние neglect; desolation

запу́тывать *impf.*, запу́тать *pf.* tangle; muddle; confuse

запу́щенный neglected

запыха́ться *pf.* pant; be out of breath

запя́стье wrist

запята́я *n.* comma

зараба́тывать *impf.*, зарабо́тать *pf.* earn

за́работок ᴼᴵᴸᴸ earnings

заража́ть *impf.*, зарази́ть *pf.* infect; —ся become infected with

зара́за contagion; infection

зарази́тельный, зара́зный infectious; contagious

зарази́ть(ся) *pf. of* заража́ть(ся)

зара́нее *adv.* beforehand

за́рево glow

зарегистри́ровать *pf. of* регистри́ровать

зарека́ться *impf.*, заре́чься *pf.* renounce

заржаве́ть *pf.* become rusty

зарисо́вка sketch; sketching

зарни́ца summer lightning

заро́дыш embryo

зарожда́ть *impf.*, зароди́ть *pf.* conceive; engender

зарожде́ние conception

за́росли *pl.* undergrowth

зарпла́та wages

зарубе́жный foreign

заря́ light; glow; dawn

заря́д charge; warhead; cartridge

заря́дка **1.** charging; loading **2.** exercise

заряжа́ть *impf.*, -ди́ть *pf.* charge; load

заса́харенный candied

засветло́ *adv.* before nightfall

засвиде́тельствовать *pf. of* свиде́тельствовать

заседа́ние meeting, conference

засека́ть *impf.*, засе́чь *pf.* notch

засекре́ченный secret; classified

заси́живаться *impf.*, засиде́ться *pf.* remain for a long time

заслоня́ть *impf.*, -ни́ть *pf.* screen, hide, shield

заслу́га merit; *pl.* achievements

заслу́женный **1.** deserved **2.** distinguished **3.** (*in title*) Honored

заслу́живать *impf.*, заслужи́ть *pf.* earn, merit, deserve

засма́триваться *impf.*, засмотре́ться *pf.* (на + *A*) be lost in contemplation

засмея́ться *pf.* (begin to) laugh

засне́женный snow-covered

засну́ть *pf. of* засыпа́ть

засо́в bolt; bar

засо́л salting; pickling

засоря́ть *impf.*, -ри́ть *pf.* litter; clog up

засо́хнуть *pf. of* засыха́ть

засо́хший dry, withered

застава́ть *impf.*, заста́ть *pf.* find

заставля́ть *impf.*, заста́вить *pf.* compel, force

застаре́лый inveterate; chronic

застёгивать *impf.*, застегну́ть *pf.* button (up); fasten; clasp

засте́нчивый shy, bashful; timid

застила́ть *impf.*, застла́ть *pf.* cover; cloud; obscure

засто́й stagnation, stagnancy

засто́лье **1.** meal **2.** feast

застрахова́ть *pf. of* страхова́ть

застрева́ть *impf.*, застря́ть *pf.* get stuck; stick

застрели́ть(ся) *pf.* shoot (oneself)

застря́ть *pf. of* застрева́ть

засту́пник, -ница intercessor; defender

застыва́ть *impf.*, засты́ть, засты́нуть *pf.* congeal; set; harden

за́суха drought

засыпа́ть[1] *impf.*, засну́ть *pf.* fall asleep

засыпа́ть[2] *impf.*, засы́пать *pf.* fill (up); cover; strew

засыха́ть *impf.*, засо́хнуть *pf.* dry (up), wither

зата́пливать *impf.*, затопи́ть *pf.* turn on heating

зата́птывать *impf.*, затопта́ть *pf.* trample down

затво́р lock; bolt; shutter

затворя́ть *impf.*, -ри́ть *pf.* shut

зате́вать *impf.*, зате́ять *pf.* venture; undertake

затека́ть *impf.*, зате́чь *pf.* **1.** leak into **2.** swell up; become numb

зате́м *adv.* then; next

за́темно *adv.* before dawn

затемня́ть *impf.*, -ни́ть *pf.* darken; obscure

затеря́ть *pf.* mislay; lose

зате́я undertaking; amusement

затиха́ть *impf.*, зати́хнуть *pf.* subside; abate

зати́шье calm, lull

затки́уть *pf. of* затыка́ть

затме́ние eclipse

зато́ *conj.* in return; but then

затону́ть *pf. v.i.* sink

затопи́ть[1] *pf. of* зата́пливать

затопи́ть[2] *pf. of* **затопля́ть**

затопле́ние flooding

затопля́ть *impf.*, **-пи́ть** *pf.* flood; inundate; submerge

зато́р jam; congestion

затра́гивать *impf.*, **затро́нуть** *pf.* affect; touch

затра́та expenditure, expense

затрудне́ние difficulty

затрудни́тельный difficult

затрудня́ть *impf.*, **-ни́ть** *pf.* render difficult; hamper; impede

за́тхлый musty

затыка́ть *impf.*, **заткну́ть** *pf.* stop up; cork up

заты́лок FILL back of the head

затя́гивать *impf.*, **затяну́ть** *pf.* **1.** tighten; cover **2.** delay

затя́жка 1. delaying **2.** puff; drag

затяжно́й 1. delaying **2.** lengthy

заура́дный mediocre; ordinary

заусе́ница 1. burr **2.** hangnail

зау́ченный studied; affected

зау́чивать *impf.*, **заучи́ть** *pf.* memorize; learn by heart

захва́т seizure, capture

захва́тчик invader

захва́тывать *impf.*, **захвати́ть** *pf.* seize; take; thrill

захлёбываться *impf.*, **захлебну́ться** *pf.* (+ *I*) choke (with)

захло́пывать *impf.*, **захло́пнуть** *pf.* slam

заходи́ть *impf.*, **зайти́** *pf.* **1.** set **2.** call on; drop in **3.** go behind

захо́д со́лнца sunset

захолу́стье out-of-the-way place

захорони́ть *pf.* bury

захоте́ть(ся) *pf. of* **хоте́ть(ся)**

заце́пка hook; connections

зачаро́ванный enchanted

зачасту́ю *adv.* often, frequently

зача́тие (*physiol.*) conception

зача́ть *pf.* (*physiol.*) conceive

заче́м *adv.* why, what for

заче́м-то *adv.* for some reason

зачёркивать *impf.*, **зачеркну́ть** *pf.* cross out; strike out

заче́рпывать *impf.*, **зачерпну́ть** *pf.* ladle; scoop up

зачёт test, examination

зачисля́ть *impf.*, **зачи́слить** *v.t.* include; enlist, enroll

зашива́ть *impf.*, **заши́ть** *pf.* sew up

защи́та defense; protection

защи́тник defender, protector

защи́тный protective

защища́ть *impf.*, **-ти́ть** *pf.* defend

за́явка claim; order; application

заявле́ние statement; application

заявля́ть *impf.*, **-ви́ть** *pf.* declare, announce; report

за́яц FILL **1.** hare **2.** stowaway; **éхать за́йцем** travel without ticket

зва́ние rank, title

звать *impf.*, **по-** *pf.* call; invite; **как вас зову́т?** what is your name?

звезда́ star

звёздный starry

звёздочка asterisk; little star

звене́ть *impf. v.i.* ring; jangle

звено́ 1. link **2.** team, group

звери́нец FILL menagerie

звери́ный *attrib.* animal; savage

зверобо́й St.-John's-wort

зве́рство bestiality; brutality

зверь *m.* wild animal; beast; brute

звон ringing; peal

звони́ть *impf.*, **по-** *pf.* ring; phone

зво́нкий ringing; clear

звоно́к FILL bell; phone call

звук sound; **—оизоляцио́нный** soundproof; **—ово́й** *attrib.* sound

звуча́ние sound

звуча́ть *impf.*, **про-** *pf.* sound; resound, be heard

зву́чный resounding, sonorous

звя́кать *impf.*, **звя́кнуть** *pf.* jingle

зда́ние building, edifice

здесь *adv.* here

зде́шний local

здоро́ваться *impf.*, **по-** *pf.* (с + *I*) greet, exchange greetings

здо́рово *adv.* well, excellently; very; *interj.* great! well done!

здоро́вый healthy

здоро́вье health

здравоохране́ние public health

здра́вствуй(те) how do you do? hello!

здра́вый sensible; ~ смысл common sense

зе́бра zebra

зева́ть *impf.*, **зевну́ть** *pf.* yawn

зево́та yawning

зек (*abbr. of* **заключённый**) prisoner; convict

зелёный green

зе́лень *f.* greens, fresh herbs

землевладе́лец FILL, **-льца** landowner

земледе́лец FILL farmer

земледе́лие agriculture

землетрясе́ние earthquake

земли́стый 1. earthy **2.** sallow

земля́ earth, soil; *cap.* the earth

земля́к, **земля́чка** compatriot

земляни́ка wild strawberries
земно́й terrestrial; earthly
зени́т zenith; —**ный** attrib. zenith; antiaircraft
зе́ркало mirror, looking glass
зерка́льный mirror; reflecting
зерни́стый grainy; granular
зерно́ grain; seed; kernel
зерново́й attrib. grain; cereal
зернохрани́лище granary
зефи́р marshmallow
зигза́г zigzag
зима́ winter
зи́мний winter, wintry
зимова́ть impf., **про-, от-** pf. hibernate; spend the winter
зимо́вка hibernation
зимо́й adv. in (the) winter
злак cereal
злить impf., **разо-** pf. anger; irritate
зло evil; harm; malice
зло́ба spite; malice
зло́бный malicious; spiteful
злободне́вный actual, topical
злоба́ствовать impf. (на + A) bear malice, bear a grudge
зловре́дный harmful, noxious
злой evil; malicious, vicious; bad-tempered
злока́чественный malignant
злопа́мятный unforgiving
злополу́чный ill-fated; hapless
злора́дный gloating
злора́дствовать impf. gloat
злосло́вие malicious gossip
зло́стный malicious
злость f. malice; rage, fury
злоупотребле́ние (+ I) misuse
злоупотребля́ть impf., **-би́ть** pf. (+ I) abuse
змеи́ный snake; snake's
змей 1. serpent, dragon **2.** kite
змея́ snake; serpent
знак sign, token, symbol, mark
знако́мить impf., **по-** pf. acquaint; introduce; —**ся** (с + I) become acquainted; meet; get to know
знако́мство acquaintance
знако́мый familiar; (с + I) acquainted with; n. acquaintance
знаме́ние sign
знамени́тость celebrity; fame
знамени́тый celebrated; famous
зна́мя neut. (pl. знамёна) banner; flag
зна́ние knowledge; erudition

знато́к authority, expert
значе́ние meaning; significance
значи́тельный significant
зна́чит so; well then
значи́тельный considerable; sizable, substantial
зна́чить impf. mean, signify
значо́к FILL mark; badge; pin
зноби́ть impf. impers.: меня́ зноби́т I feel shivery
зной intense heat
зно́йный burning hot; sultry
зоб 1. crop **2.** goiter
зодиа́к zodiac
зола́ (sing. only) ashes
золо́вка sister-in-law (husband's sister)
зо́лото gold
золото́й gold; golden
золочёный gilded; gilt
зо́на zone
зонд probing device
зонди́ровать impf. probe; sound out
зонт, зо́нтик umbrella
зоо́лог zoologist
зоологи́ческий zoological
зооло́гия zoology
зоопа́рк zoo
зрачо́к FILL pupil (of the eye)
зре́лище spectacle, sight
зре́лость ripeness; maturity
зре́ние sight, eyesight; vision; то́чка зре́ния point of view
зреть impf., **со-** pf. ripen
зри́тель, —**ница** spectator; —**ный** visual, optical
зря adv. in vain
зуб tooth
зубно́й attrib. tooth; dental; ~ врач dentist; зубна́я па́ста toothpaste
зубочи́стка toothpick
зубр (European) bison
зуб́ить impf. cram
зуд itch; —**е́ть** impf. itch
зу́ммер buzzer
зы́бкий unstable, unsteady
зы́бучий (sand) shifting
зыбь f. rippling; ripple (on water)
зюйд (naut.) south; south wind
зя́бкий chilly; sensitive to cold
зя́бнуть impf. suffer from cold
зябь f. land plowed in autumn for spring sowing
зять m. son-in-law; brother-in-law (sister's husband)

и *conj.* and; **и ... и ...** both ... and
...

и́бо *conj.* for

и́ва willow

и́вовый *attrib.* willow

иврит (*modern*) Hebrew

игла́ needle; thorn

иглотерапи́я acupuncture

игнори́ровать *impf. & pf.* ignore

и́го yoke

иго́лка needle

иго́рный *attrib.* gambling

игра́ 1. game 2. play; acting 3. performance

игра́-аттракцио́н video game

игра́ть *impf.*, **сыгра́ть** *pf.* play; act

игри́вый playful

игрово́й 1. *attrib.* acting 2. playing 3. full of action

игро́к player; gambler

игру́шка toy

идеа́л ideal; **—ьный** ideal

идеализи́ровать *impf. & pf.* idealize

идеали́зм idealism

иде́йный 1. ideological 2. lofty

идентифици́ровать *impf. & pf.* identify

иденти́чность identity

иде́я idea, notion, concept

иди́ллия idyll

идио́т idiot; **—ский** idiotic

и́диш Yiddish

и́дол idol

идолопокло́нничество idolatry

и др. (*abbr. of* **и други́е**) et al

идти́ *impf.*, **пойти́** *pf.* go; come; proceed; work

иера́рхия hierarchy

иеро́глиф hieroglyph

из, изо *prep.* (+ G) from, out (of); made of; consisting of

изба́ cottage, hut, hovel

избави́тель redeemer, savior

избавля́ть *impf.*, **изба́вить** *pf.* save; deliver; **—ся** (от + G) get rid of

избало́ванный spoiled

избега́ть *impf.*, **избежа́ть**, **избе́гнуть** *pf.* (+ G) avoid; escape; evade

избива́ть *impf.*, **изби́ть** *pf.* beat (up); slaughter; massacre

избира́тель voter; elector

избира́тельный electoral; election; **избира́тельная у́рна** ballot box

избира́ть *impf.*, **избра́ть** *pf.* elect; choose

избива́ть *pf. of* **избива́ть**

избра́ние election

избра́ть *pf. of* **избира́ть**

избы́ток FILL surplus

и́зверг monster; fiend

изверже́ние eruption; discharge, ejection; excretion

извести́ *pf. of* **изводи́ть**

изве́стие piece of news; *pl.* information

извести́ть *pf. of* **извеща́ть**

изве́стно *impers.* (it is) known

изве́стность fame, reputation

изве́стный famous, well-known

и́звесть f. lime

извеща́ть *impf.*, **—сти́ть** *pf.* inform, notify

извива́ться *impf.* coil; twist; wind

изви́лина curve, bend

извине́ние apology; excuse

извини́ть *impf.*, **—ни́ть** *pf.* excuse, pardon; **—ся** apologize

извлека́ть *impf.*, **извле́чь** *pf.* extract; elicit; derive

извне́ *adv.* from outside

изво́зчик coachman; driver

изворо́тливый resourceful; evasive

извраща́ть *impf.*, **—ти́ть** *pf.* pervert; distort

извраще́ние perversion; distortion

изги́б curve; bend

изгна́ние banishment; exile

изгна́нник, -ница exile

изголо́вье head of a bed

изгоня́ть *impf.*, **изгна́ть** *pf.* banish

и́згородь f. fence

изгота́вливать, изготовля́ть *impf.*, **изгото́вить** *pf.* make, manufacture

изготовле́ние manufacture

издава́ть *impf.*, **изда́ть** *pf.* publish; give off; produce

издалека́, и́здали *adv.* from afar

изда́ние publication; edition, issue

изда́тель publisher

изда́ть *pf. of* **издава́ть**

издева́тельство mockery; harassment

издева́ться *impf.* (над + I) mock; taunt; harass

изде́лие product; manufactured article

издыха́ть *impf.*, **издо́хнуть** *pf.* (of

animals, or in slang use, *of people*) die

изжо́га heartburn

из-за *prep.* (+ *G*) **1.** from behind **2.** because of

излага́ть *impf.*, **изложи́ть** *pf.* state, set forth; expound

излече́ние recovery, cure; treatment

изле́чивать *impf.*, **излечи́ть** *pf.* cure; **—ся** (**от** + *G*) be cured

излечи́мый curable

излия́ние outpouring

изложе́ние account; statement

изложи́ть *pf. of* **излага́ть**

изло́манный 1. fractured; broken **2.** bent

излуча́ть *impf.* radiate

излуче́ние radiation; emanation

изме́на treason; betrayal; infidelity

измене́ние change, alteration

изме́нник, -ница traitor

изменя́ть[1] *impf.*, **-ни́ть** *pf. v.t.* change, alter; **—ся** *v.i.* change

изменя́ть[2] *impf.*, **-ни́ть** *pf.* (+ *D*) be unfaithful

измере́ние measurement, measuring

измеря́ть *impf.*, **изме́рить** *pf.* measure, gauge

изму́чить *pf.* torture; exhaust

измя́тый 1. haggard **2.** crumpled

измя́ть *pf.* crumple

изна́нка reverse side; wrong side

изнаси́лование rape; violation

изнаси́ловать *pf. of* **наси́ловать**

изнача́льный primordial

изна́шивание wearing out

изнемога́ть *impf.*, **изнемо́чь** *pf.* be exhausted

изнеможе́ние extreme exhaustion

изно́с wear (and tear)

изно́шенный worn out; shabby

изнуря́ть *impf.*, **-ри́ть** *pf.* exhaust

изнутри́ *adv.* from inside

изныва́ть *impf.*, **изны́ть** *pf.* languish

изо *prep., see* **из**

изоби́лие abundance

изобража́ть *impf.*, **-зи́ть** *pf.* portray; represent

изображе́ние image; representation

изобрази́тельные иску́сства *pl.* fine arts

изобрета́тель inventor; **—ный** inventive

изобрета́ть *impf.*, **изобрести́** *pf.* invent; devise

изобрете́ние invention

изо́гнутый bent; curved

изоли́ровать *impf. & pf.* isolate; insulate

изоля́тор isolation ward; insulator

изоля́ция isolation; insulation

изорва́ть *pf.* rend; tear

изощрённый keen; acute

изощря́ть *impf.*, **-ри́ть** *pf.* refine (one's taste)

из-под *prep.* (+ *G*) from under

изразе́ц FILL glazed tile

Изра́иль *m.* Israel

изра́нить *pf.* wound severely

израсхо́довать *pf. of* **расхо́довать**

и́зредка *adv.* now and then

изрече́ние dictum; saying

изря́дно *adv.* rather, fairly

изря́дный quite a; handsome

изуве́р fanatic

изуве́чивать *impf.*, **изуве́чить** *pf.* maim

изуми́тельный amazing

изумле́ние amazement, wonder

изумля́ть *impf.*, **изуми́ть** *pf.* amaze

изумру́д emerald; **—ный** emerald

изуро́довать *pf. of* **уро́довать**

изуча́ть *impf.*, **-чи́ть** *pf.* study; learn

изуче́ние studying; study

изъе́здить *pf.* **1.** travel all over **2.** wear out

изъя́н defect; flaw

изъя́тие withdrawal, removal; exception

изыма́ть *impf.*, **изъя́ть** *pf.* withdraw, remove

изыска́ния *pl.* research; prospecting

изы́сканный exquisite; refined

изыска́тель prospector

изю́м (*sing. only*) raisins

изю́минка sparkle (*in a person*)

изя́щество refinement; elegance

изя́щный refined; elegant

ика́ть *impf.*, **икну́ть** *pf.* hiccup

ико́на icon

ико́та hiccups

икра́[1] roe; caviar

икра́[2] calf (of a leg)

ил silt

и́ли, иль *conj.* or; ~ ... ~ ... either ... or ...

иллю́зия illusion

иллюзо́рный illusory

иллюмина́тор porthole

иллюстра́тор illustrator

иллюстра́ция illustration

иллюстри́ровать *impf. & pf.* illustrate

им *pron.* I of **он**, **онó**; D of **они́**

име́ние estate

имени́нник, -ница person celebrating his/her name day

имени́ны *pl.* name day

имени́тельный nominative

и́менно *adv.* precisely; namely

именно́й nominal; inscribed

именова́ть *impf.*, **на-** *pf.* name

име́ть *impf.* have; ~ **в виду́** mean; bear in mind; ~ **ме́сто** take place; **—ся** be available, be

и́ми *pron.* I of **они́**

имита́ция imitation; mimicry

иммигра́нт, —ка immigrant

иммигра́ция immigration

иммигри́ровать *impf. & pf.* immigrate

иммуниза́ция immunization

иммуните́т immunity

импера́тор emperor

импе́рия empire

импи́чмент impeachment

импоза́нтный imposing

импони́ровать *impf.* (+ D) impress

и́мпорт import; importation

импортёр importer

импорти́ровать *impf. & pf.* import

и́мпортный imported

импоте́нция (*med.*) impotence

импровиза́ция improvisation

импровизи́ровать *impf.*, **сымпровизи́ровать** *pf.* improvise

и́мпульс impulse

иму́щество property; belongings

и́мя *neut.* name; first name; ~ **прилага́тельное** adjective; ~ **существи́тельное** noun; ~ **числи́тельное** numeral

инакомы́слие dissidence; dissent

инакомы́слящий *n. m. & f.* dissident

ина́че *adv.* differently; otherwise

инвали́д, —ка disabled person

инвали́дность disability

инвента́рь *m.* inventory

инвести́ровать *impf.*, **про-** *pf.* invest

инвести́ция investment

ингаля́тор (*med.*) inhaler

индеве́ть *impf.*, **за-** *pf.* become covered with frost

инде́ец FILL American Indian

инде́йка turkey

и́ндекс index

индиа́нка American Indian woman; woman from India

индивидуали́ст individualist

индивидуа́льный individual

индиви́ддуум individual

индие́ц FILL Indian (*Asian*)

инди́йский Indian

Индия India

индоевропе́йский Indo-European

индуи́зм Hinduism

индустриализа́ция industrialization

индустриализи́ровать *impf. & pf.* industrialize

индустриа́льный industrial

индустри́я, инду́стрия industry

индю́к, индю́шка turkey

и́ней hoarfrost; rime

ине́рция inertia

инжене́р engineer

инжи́р fig; fig tree

инициа́лы *pl.* initials

инициати́ва initiative

инкорпора́ция incorporation

инкруста́ция inlay; inlaid work

инкуба́тор incubator

иногда́ *adv.* sometimes

иногоро́дний from another city

ино́й another, other; different

иностра́нец FILL, **-а́нка** foreigner

иностра́нный foreign

и́ноходь *f.* amble; pace

иноязы́чный foreign; speaking another language

инсектици́д insecticide

инспе́ктор inspector

инспе́кция inspection

инста́нция (*law*) instance

инсти́нкт instinct

инстинкти́вный instinctive

институ́т institute; institution

инстру́ктор instructor

инстру́кция instructions

инструме́нт instrument; tool

инсули́н insulin

инсу́льт (*med.*) stroke

инсцени́ровать *impf. & pf.* stage

инсцениро́вка staging; dramatization

интелле́кт intellect

интеллектуа́льный intellectual

интеллиге́нт, —ка intellectual; **—ный** educated, cultured

интеллиге́нция intelligentsia

интенси́вность intensity

интенси́вный intense

интерва́л interval

интервью́ *neut. indecl.* interview

интервью́и́ровать *impf. & pf.* interview

интере́с interest; **—ный** interesting; attractive

интересова́ть *impf.* interest; **—ся** (+ I) be interested in

интернат boarding school
интернациональный international
интернировать *impf. & pf.* intern
интерпретация interpretation
интерпретировать *impf.* interpret
интерсеть *f.* Internet
интерьер interior (*of building*)
интимный intimate
интонация intonation
интрига intrigue
интриган, —ка schemer
интуиция intuition
инфаркт heart attack
инфекция infection, contagion
инфинитив infinitive
инфляция inflation
информация information
информировать *impf.,* про- *pf.* inform
инфракрасный infrared
инъекция injection
ипотека mortgage
ипохондрия hypochondria
ипподром racetrack
и пр. (*abbr. of* и прочее) and so on
Ирак Iraq; иракец FILL Iraqi
Иран Iran; иранец FILL, -нка Iranian
ирис toffee; taffy
ирландец FILL, -дка an Irish person
Ирландия Ireland
иронический ironic(al)
ирония irony
иррациональный irrational
иск legal action, suit
искажать *impf.,* -зить *pf.* distort; misrepresent
искажение distortion
искалечить *pf. of* калечить
искать *impf.* search; look (for)
исключать *impf.,* -чить *pf.* exclude; expel; eliminate
исключение exception; exclusion; expulsion
исключительно *adv.* exclusively; solely; exceptionally
исконный primordial; indigenous
ископаемое *n.* fossil; mineral
ископаемый fossil, fossilized
искоренять *impf.,* -нить *pf.* eradicate
искоса *adv.* askance
искра spark; glimmer
искренний sincere
искривление bend; distortion
искривлять *impf.,* -вить *pf.* bend; distort

искупать *impf.,* -пить *pf.* atone for
искупление atonement
искусный skillful
искусственный artificial
искусство art; skill
искусствовед art historian
искушение temptation; seduction
искушённый knowledgeable
испанец FILL, -нка Spaniard
Испания Spain
испанский Spanish
испарение evaporation
испарять(ся) *impf.,* -рить(ся) *pf.* evaporate
испачкать *pf. of* пачкать
испечь *pf. of* печь
исписывать *impf.,* исписать *pf.* cover with writing; use up
исповедание religious belief
исповедовать(ся) *impf. & pf.* confess
исповедь *f.* confession
исподволь *adv.* slowly; gradually
исполин giant
исполнение execution, fulfillment
исполнитель executor; performer
исполнительный executive
исполнять *impf.,* исполнить *pf.* fulfill, carry out; execute
использование use; utilization
использовать *impf. & pf.* utilize; make use of
испортить *pf. of* портить
испорченный spoiled; depraved
исправление correction; correcting
исправлять *impf.,* исправить *pf.* correct; repair; reform
исправный in good condition; in working order; meticulous
испражнение defecation
испуг fright; —анный frightened
испугать *pf. of* пугать
испытание trial; test; ordeal
испытательный *attrib.* test; trial
испытывать *impf.,* испытать *pf.* try, test; experience
исследование investigation; research
исследователь researcher; —ский *attrib.* research
исследовать *impf. & pf.* investigate; explore; examine
иссякать *impf.,* иссякнуть *pf.* dry up; be used up
истаптывать *impf.,* истоптать *pf.* trample down; wear out
истекать *impf.,* истечь *pf.* expire; elapse
истёкший past

истерза́ть pf. torment

исте́рика hysterics

истери́ческий hysterical

истери́чка hysterical woman

истёртый worn down or out

исте́ц FILL plaintiff

исте́чь pf. of истека́ть

и́стина truth

и́стинный veritable, true

истлева́ть impf., **истле́ть** pf. rot

исто́к source

исто́пник stoker; boilerman

исторга́ть impf., **исто́ргнуть** pf. wrest (from); throw out

исто́рик historian

истори́ческий historical

исто́рия history; event; story

исто́чник source, spring

исто́шный heart-rending

истоща́ть impf., **-щи́ть** pf. exhaust; emaciate

истоще́ние exhaustion; emaciation

истра́тить pf. of тра́тить

истреби́тель destroyer; fighter

истребля́ть impf., **-би́ть** pf. destroy; exterminate

истяза́ть impf. torture

исхо́д outcome, result; end

исходи́ть impf. (из, от + G) issue (from); proceed (from)

исхо́дный starting; initial

исхуда́ть pf. become emaciated

исцели́тель healer

исцеля́ть impf., **-ли́ть** pf. heal; cure

исчеза́ть impf., **исче́знуть** pf. disappear, vanish

исчезнове́ние disappearance

исче́рпывать impf., **исче́рпать** pf. exhaust

исче́рпывающий exhaustive; comprehensive

исчисля́ть impf., **исчи́слить** pf. calculate; **—ся** (в + P) amount to

ита́к conj. thus; so

Ита́лия Italy

италья́нец FILL, **-я́нка** Italian

италья́нский Italian

и т. д. (abbr. of и так да́лее) and so forth

ито́г sum, total; result

итого́ adv. in all, altogether

и т. п. (abbr. of и тому́ подо́бное) and the like

их pron. G, A of они́; poss. their, theirs

иша́к donkey

ишь particle FILL, look!; see!; oh!

ище́йка bloodhound; police dog

ию́ль m., **—ский** July

ию́нь m., **—ский** June

йог m.; **йо́га** yoga

йо́гурт yogurt

йод iodine

К

к, ко prep. (+ D) to, towards; by; for, of, to

каба́к tavern

каба́н wild boar; hog

кабаре́ neut. indecl. cabaret

кабачо́к FILL (vegetable) squash

ка́бель m. cable

ка́бельное телеви́дение cable television

каби́на booth; cockpit; cabin

кабине́т study; office; (polit.) cabinet

каблу́к heel (of shoe)

ка́бы conj. if; if only

кавале́р admirer; partner

кавале́рия cavalry

ка́верзный Colloq. intricate; tricky

каве́рна (med.) cavity

Кавка́з (mountains) Caucasus

кавка́зец FILL, **-зка** Caucasian

кавы́чки pl. quotation marks

кагебе́шник, кагеби́ст KGB policeman

кадр (film) frame; shot; scene

ка́дровый trained; skilled

ка́дры pl. personnel; cadres

кады́к Adam's apple

ка́ждый each, every; n. everyone

ка́жущийся seeming; imaginary

каза́к, каза́чка Cossack

каза́рма barracks

каза́ться impf., **по-** pf. seem, appear; **ка́жется** it seems

каза́х, каза́шка Kazakh

Казахста́н Kazakhstan

каза́чий attrib. Cossack

казённый fiscal; State; public

казино́ neut. indecl. casino

казнь f. execution; death penalty

кайма́ border; edging

кайф euphoria

как adv. how; what; conj. as; like; when

кака́о neut. indecl. cocoa; cacao

ка́к-либо, ка́к-нибудь adv. somehow; any which way

как-ника́к adv. still; after all

како́й *pron.* which?; what?; what kind of; what a …!

какой-либо, какой-нибудь *pron.* some, any; some kind of

какой-то *pron.* some; some kind of

ка́к-то *adv.* somehow; once

ка́ктус cactus

кал excrement

каламбу́р pun

каланча́ watchtower; fire tower

кала́ч white wheat bread

калейдоско́п kaleidoscope

кале́ка *m. & f* handicapped person

календа́рь *m.* calendar

кале́чить *impf.,* **ис-** *pf.* cripple, maim

кали́бр caliber; gauge

кали́тка gate

кали́ть *impf.* make red hot

каллигра́фия calligraphy

кало́рия calorie

кало́ши *pl.* galoshes

ка́лька tracing paper

кальки́ровать *impf.,* **с-** *pf.* trace

калькуля́тор *m.* calculator

кальма́р squid

кальсо́ны *pl.* long johns

ка́льций calcium

камбала́ flounder; plaice

камене́ть *impf.,* **о-** *pf.* petrify

камени́стый stony; rocky

ка́менный stone; stony; ~ век the Stone Age; ~ у́голь coal

ка́менщик bricklayer; mason

ка́мень *m.* FILL *m.* stone, rock

ка́мера 1. chamber; cell **2.** inner tube **3.** film camera

ка́мерный (*mus.*) chamber

камерто́н tuning fork

ка́мешек FILL small stone; pebble

ками́н fireplace

камо́рка closet; tiny room

кампа́ния campaign

камуфля́ж camouflage

ка́мфара camphor

камы́ш reed; rush; cane

кана́ва ditch

кана́дец FILL, -дка Canadian

кана́дский Canadian

кана́л canal; channel; —иза́ция sewerage

канаре́йка canary

кана́т cable; rope

канва́ canvas; background

кандида́т, —ка candidate

кандидату́ра candidacy

кани́кулы *pl.* vacation

каните́ль *f. Colloq.* long drawn-out proceedings

канони́ческий canonical

кано́э *neut. indecl.* canoe

кант edging; piping

кантова́ть *impf.,* **о-** *pf.* **1.** mount **2.** turn over; invert

ка́нтор cantor

кану́н eve

канцеля́рия office

канцеля́рский clerical; *attrib.* office

канцероге́н carcinogen

ка́нцлер chancellor

каню́к buzzard

ка́пать *impf.,* **ка́пнуть** *pf.* drip, dribble; spill

капе́лла choir; chapel

капелла́н chaplain

капельме́йстер (*mus.*) conductor

ка́пельница (medicine) dropper

капилля́р capillary

капита́л capital

капитали́зм capitalism

капитали́ст capitalist

капиталисти́ческий capitalistic

капиталовложе́ние capital investment

капита́н captain

капитули́ровать *impf. & pf.* capitulate

капитуля́ция capitulation

ка́пля drop

капо́т[1] woman's housecoat

капо́т[2] (*mech.*) hood

капра́л corporal

капри́з caprice; —ный capricious

капри́зничать *impf.,* **по-** *pf.* behave capriciously

ка́псула capsule

ка́псюль *m.* primer; percussion cap

капу́ста cabbage

капюшо́н hood

ка́ра retribution; punishment

карава́й (round) loaf of bread

карава́н caravan; convoy

кара́ковый (*of a horse*) dark bay

кара́кули *pl.* scribble; scrawl

кара́куль *m.* astrakhan; karakul

караме́ль *f.* caramel

караме́лька *Colloq.* caramel

каранда́ш pencil

каранти́н quarantine

кара́сь *m.* European carp

кара́т carat

кара́тельный punitive

кара́ть *impf.,* **по-** *pf.* punish

карау́лить *impf.* stand guard

карбюра́тор carburetor

кардина́л cardinal

кардиогра́мма cardiogram

кардиоло́гия cardiology

каре́л, —ка Karelian; —ьский Karelian

Каре́лия Karelia

каре́та carriage, coach

каре́тка (typewriter) carriage

ка́риес caries

ка́рий (of eyes) brown

карикату́ра caricature

карио́зный carious

ка́ркать *impf.*, ка́ркнуть *pf.* caw

ка́рлик, -лица dwarf; —овый miniature

карма́н pocket

карма́нник pickpocket

карнава́л carnival

карни́з cornice

карп carp

ка́рта 1. map 2. (playing) card

картёжник *Colloq.* cardplayer

карте́чь *f.* buckshot

карти́на picture; painting; scene

карти́нка illustration; picture

карти́нный picturesque; *attrib.* picture

картóграф cartographer

картóн cardboard; —ка cardboard box

картоте́ка card index; card file

картóфель *m.* (*sing. only*) potatoes; —ина *attrib.* potato; —оый

картóфельное пюре́ mashed potatoes

ка́рточка photograph; card; rationing card

картóшка *Colloq.* potato(es)

карусе́ль *f.* carousel

карье́р[1] full gallop

карье́р[2] quarry

карье́ра career

каса́ние contact; touch

каса́тельная *n.* (*math.*) tangent

каса́тик (flower) iris

каса́тка barn swallow

каса́ться *impf.*, косну́ться *pf.* (+ *G*) touch, touch on; concern; что каса́ется (+ *G*) as for

каса́ющийся *prep.* (+ *G*) concerning

ка́ска helmet

каска́д cascade

ка́сса box-office; cash register; cash box; cashier's desk

касса́ция (*law*) appeal

кассе́та cassette

касси́р cashier; teller

ка́ста caste

ка́стовый *attrib.* caste

ка́сторовое ма́сло castor oil

кастра́т eunuch

кастри́ровать *impf. & pf.* castrate

кастрю́ля saucepan; pot

катализа́тор catalyst

катало́г catalogue

ката́ние driving; rolling

катара́кта cataract (of eyes)

катастрóфа catastrophe

ката́ть *impf.*, по— *pf.* (take for a) drive; roll, wheel; —ся take a drive; roll

катафа́лк hearse

категори́ческий categorical

катего́рия category

ка́тер cutter; launch; boat

кати́ть *impf.*, по— *pf.* roll (along); wheel; —ся roll; flow; slide down

катóк skating rink; roller

катóлик, католи́чка Catholic

католи́ческий Catholic

ка́торга hard labor

ка́торжник convict

кату́шка 1. spool 2. reel; bobbin

катю́ша rocket launcher

каучу́к rubber

кафе́ *neut. indecl.* café

ка́федра 1. chair, rostrum 2. department, faculty

ка́фель *m.* tile

кафете́рий cafeteria

кача́лка rocking chair, rocker

кача́ть *impf.*, качну́ть *pf.* rock, swing; shake; —ся *v.i.* swing; rock; stagger

каче́ли *pl.* (child's) swing

ка́чественный of high quality

ка́чество quality

ка́чка rolling; tossing

ка́ша porridge; gruel; ма́нная ~ farina

кашалóт cachalot; sperm whale

ка́шель FILL *m.* cough

кашеми́р cashmere

ка́шлять *impf.*, ка́шлянуть *pf.* cough

кашне́ *neut. indecl.* muffler, scarf

кашта́н chestnut

кашта́новый chestnut (colored)

каю́та cabin; stateroom

ка́яться *impf.*, по— *pf.* repent; confess

квадра́т square; —ный square

ква́кать *impf.*, ква́кнуть *pf.* croak

квалифика́ция qualification

квалифици́рованный skilled

кварта́л quarter; city block

кварте́т (*mus.*) quartet

кварти́ра apartment; quarters

квартира́нт, —ка tenant

квартпла́та, кварти́рная пла́та rent

ква́рц quartz
квас kvass
ква́сить *impf.* pickle
ква́шеный pickled; fermented;
  ква́шеная капу́ста sauerkraut
кве́рху *adv.* upward(s), up
квита́нция receipt
кво́рум quorum
кво́та quota
КГБ (*abbr. of* **Комите́т госуда́рст-
венной безопа́сности**) KGB
кегельба́н bowling alley
кегль *m.* (*type*) point
ке́гля bowling pin
кедр, —о́вый cedar
ке́ды *pl.* sneakers
кекс biscuit; fruitcake
кем *pron. I of* **кто**
ке́мпинг campsite
кенгуру́ *m. indecl.* kangaroo
ке́пка cap
кера́мика ceramics
кероси́н kerosene
ке́сарево сече́ние Cesarean section
ке́та Siberian salmon
ке́товая икра́ red caviar
кефи́р (*yogurt-like drink*)
киберне́тика cybernetics
киберпростра́нство cyberspace
кива́ть *impf.,* **кивну́ть** *pf.*
  (+ *I,* на + *A*) nod; motion (to)
ки́ви *f. indecl.* kiwi
киво́к FILL nod
кида́ть *impf.,* **ки́нуть** *pf.* throw,
  fling; **—ся** throw oneself; rush
кий billiard cue
кило́ *neut. indecl. Colloq.* kilo
килова́тт kilowatt
килогра́мм kilogram
киломе́тр kilometer
киль *m.* keel
ки́лька sprat
кинжа́л dagger
кино́ *neut. indecl.* cinema
киноактри́са movie actress
киноарти́ст movie actor; **—ка**
  movie actress
кинозвезда́ movie star
кинока́мера movie camera
кинокарти́на film; movie; picture
киномеха́ник projectionist
кинооперато́р cameraman
киноплёнка movie film
кинорежиссёр film director
киносту́дия movie studio
кинотеа́тр cinema; movie theater
кинохро́ника newsreel
ки́нуть *pf. of* **кида́ть**

кио́ск stall, kiosk; newsstand
кипе́ние boiling
кипе́ть *impf.* boil; seethe
кипяти́льник heating coil
кипяти́ть(ся) *impf.,* **вс-** *pf.* boil
кипято́к FILL boiling water
кипячёный boiled
кирги́з, —ка Kyrgyz
Кыргызста́н Kyrgyzstan
кири́ллица Cyrillic alphabet
ки́рка Protestant church
кирка́ (*tool*) pickax; pick
кирпи́ч brick
кисе́т pouch, tobacco pouch
кисея́ muslin
кислоро́д oxygen
кислота́ acidity; acid
ки́слый sour
ки́снуть *impf.,* **про-** *pf.* **1.** turn
  sour **2.** (*of a person*) vegetate
киста́ cyst
ки́сточка paintbrush; tassel
кисть[1] *f.* **1.** cluster; bunch **2.**
  paintbrush
кисть[2] *f.* hand
кит whale
кита́ец FILL, **китая́нка** Chinese
Кита́й China
кита́йский Chinese
кичли́вый arrogant; conceited
кише́ть *impf.* (+ *I*) swarm
кише́чник intestines; bowels
кишка́ intestine
клавеси́н harpsichord
клавиату́ра keyboard
кла́виша (*piano, etc.*) key
клад (buried) treasure
кла́дбище cemetery
кла́дка laying (*masonry*)
кладова́я *n.* pantry; storeroom
кладовщи́к storekeeper
кла́няться *impf.,* **поклони́ться** *pf.*
  bow, greet
кла́пан valve; flap
кларне́т clarinet; **—и́ст** clarinetist
класс class; classroom
кла́ссик classic
кла́ссика the classics
классифици́ровать *impf. & pf.*
  classify
класси́ческий classic(al)
класть *impf.,* **положи́ть** *pf.* put
  (down); place; lay
клева́ть *impf.,* **клю́нуть** *pf.* peck;
  (*of fish*) bite
кле́вер clover
клевета́ slander
клевета́ть *impf.,* **на-** *pf.* (на + *A*)
  slander
клеёнка oilcloth

клеить *impf.,* **с-** *pf.* glue; paste; **—ся** stick

клеймо́ stamp; mark; brand

клейми́ть *impf.,* **за-** *pf.* brand

клён maple

клёпка riveting

клептома́н, —ка kleptomaniac

клерк clerk

кле́тка¹ 1. cage 2. check, square; **в кле́тку** checked

кле́тка² (*biol.*) cell

кле́точка cellule

кле́точный cell; cellular

клетча́тка cellulose

клещ tick; mite

клещи́ *pl.* pincers; nippers; tongs

клие́нт, —ка client, customer

кли́зма enema

кли́макс menopause

кли́мат climate; **—и́ческий** climatic

клин wedge

кли́ника clinic

клини́ческий clinical

кли́рос choir (*part of church*)

кли́тор clitoris

кли́чка nickname

клоа́ка sewer; cesspool

клок shred; tuft; wisp

клони́ть *impf.* bend; incline

клоп bedbug

клоун clown

клочо́к FILL scrap; shred; wisp

клуб¹ club; **—ный** *attrib.* club

клуб² cloud; puff

клубе́нь *m.* tuber

клуби́ть(ся) *impf.* swirl; curl

клубни́ка strawberry

клубо́к FILL ball

клу́мба flower bed

клык fang; tusk

клю́нуть *pf.* of **клева́ть**

ключ¹ clue; key; clef; **га́ечный ~** wrench

ключ² spring; source

ключево́й key; vital

ключи́ца collarbone; clavicle

кля́кса inkblot; smudge

кляп gag

клясть *impf.* curse; **—ся** swear

кля́тва oath

кля́твенный solemn; sworn

кни́га book

кни́га жа́лоб book of complaints

кни́жка: сберега́тельная ~ bankbook; **че́ковая ~** checkbook

кни́жник bibliophile

кни́жный *attrib.* book

кни́зу *adv.* down(wards)

кни́ксен curtsy

кно́пка button; knob; tack

кнут whip

княги́ня princess

княжеский prince's; princely

княжна́ princess (*prince's daughter*)

князь *m.* prince

ко *see* **к**

коали́ция coalition

кобе́ль *m.* male dog

кобура́ holster

кобы́ла mare

кова́рный perfidious; treacherous

ковбо́й cowboy

ковбо́йка *Colloq.* cowboy shirt

ковёр carpet; rug

коверка́ть *impf.,* **ис-** *pf.* mangle; wreck; distort

коври́жка gingerbread

ко́врик small rug; mat

ковш scoop; dipper

ковы́ль *m.* feather grass

ковыля́ть *impf.* hobble

когда́ *adv., conj.* when

когда́-либо, когда́-нибудь *adv.* sometime, someday; ever

когда́-то *adv.* once, at one time

кого́ *pron.* G, A *of* **кто**

ко́готь *m.* claw, talon

когти́стый with sharp claws

код code; postal code

кодеи́н codeine

ко́декс code

ко́е-где *adv.* here and there

ко́е-ка́к *adv.* any old way; somehow

ко́е-како́й *pron.* some

ко́е-кто́ *pron.* somebody

ко́е-что́ *pron.* something

ко́жа, —ный skin; leather

ко́жный *attrib.* skin

кожура́ rind; peel

коза́, козёл goat

козеро́г ibex

ко́зий goat, goat's

козлёнок FILL kid, young goat

ко́злы *pl.* 1. coachman's seat 2. sawhorse; trestle

козырёк peak; visor

ко́зырь *m.* trump

козыря́ть *impf.,* **козырну́ть** *pf.* 1. play a trump 2. flaunt

козыря́ть *impf.,* **козырну́ть** *pf.* salute

ко́йка cot, bunk; berth

кока́ин cocaine

коке́тка coquette

коке́тливый coquettish; flirtatious

ко́клюш whooping cough
коко́с, -овый coconut
кокте́йль *m.* cocktail; моло́чный ~ milkshake
ко́лба retort; flask
колбаса́ sausage
колба́сник sausage maker
колго́тки *pl.* pantyhose
колдо́бина rut; pothole
колдова́ть *impf.* practice witchcraft
колдовство́ *impf.* witchcraft
колду́н, -ья sorcerer; sorceress
колеба́ние oscillation; vacillation
колеба́ться *impf.*, по- *pf.* oscillate; fluctuate; hesitate
коленко́р buckram
коле́но knee; bend
коле́нчатый вал crankshaft
колесо́ wheel
коле́чко *dim. of* кольцо́
коле́й rut; track
коли́т colitis
коли́чество quantity; amount
ко́лкий prickly; biting
колле́га *m. & f.* colleague
колле́гия board; collegium
колле́дж college
колекти́в, -ный collective
коллекционе́р collector
коллекциони́ровать *impf.* collect
колле́кция collection
колобро́дить *impf.* drift
коло́да¹ (wood) log
коло́да² (cards) deck, pack
коло́дец FILL well
ко́локол bell
колоко́льный of bells
колоко́льня belfry
колоко́льчик small bell
колониа́льный colonial
колониза́тор colonialist; colonizer
колониза́ция colonization
коло́ния colony
коло́нка 1. hot-water heater 2. column; бензи́новая ~ gas pump
коло́нна column
колонна́да colonnade
колори́т coloring; color
колори́тный colorful
ко́лос ear (of corn)
колосса́льный colossal; huge
колоти́ть *impf.*, по- *pf.* pound, smash; —ся thump, shake
коло́ть *impf.* prick; stab; slaughter
колпа́к cap; cover; cowl
колхо́з (*abbr. of* коллекти́вное хозя́йство) collective farm
колхо́зник, -ница collective farmer

колыбе́ль *f.* cradle
колыбе́льная пе́сня lullaby
колыха́ть(ся) *impf.*, колыхну́ть(ся) *pf.* sway
колье́ *neut. indecl.* necklace
кольцева́я доро́га beltway
кольцо́ ring
колю́чая про́волока barbed wire
колю́чий prickly, thorny
колю́чка thorn; barb
ко́лющий stabbing
коля́ска carriage
ком¹ lump; ball; clod
ком² *pron. P of* кто
ко́ма coma
кома́нда command; team
команди́р commander
командиро́вка 1. assignment; mission 2. business trip
кома́ндный *attrib.* 1. command 2. team
кома́ндовать *impf.*, с- *pf.* order, command; be in command
кома́р mosquito; gnat
комба́йн 1. (*harvesting machine*) combine 2. food processor
комбина́ция combination
комбинезо́н overalls
комбини́ровать *impf.*, с- *pf.* combine
коме́дия comedy
коменда́нт 1. commandant 2. building superintendent
комендату́ра commandant's headquarters
коме́та comet
ко́мик comedian
ко́микс *usu. pl.* comic book; cartoons
комисса́р commissar
коми́ссия commission; committee
комите́т committee
коммента́рий commentary
коммента́тор commentator
комменти́ровать *impf. & pf.* 1. annotate 2. comment on
коммерса́нт merchant
комме́рция commerce
комме́рческий commercial
коммуна́лка communal apartment
коммуна́льный municipal; public; communal
коммуника́бельный communicative; easy to talk to
коммуника́ция communications
коммуни́ст, -ка communist
коммунисти́ческий communist
ко́мната room
ко́мнатный *attrib.* room
комо́д chest of drawers

комо́к fill lump; ball
компа́ктный compact; solid
компа́ктный диск compact disc
компа́ния company
компаньо́н, –ка companion
ко́мпас compass
компенса́ция compensation
компенси́ровать impf. & pf. compensate
компете́нтный 1. competent; qualified **2.** having jurisdiction
компете́нция jurisdiction
ко́мплекс complex; system
компле́кт 1. complete set **2.** full staff
компле́кция build; frame; figure
комплиме́нт compliment
компози́тор composer
компози́ция composition
компоне́нт component
компонова́ть impf., c- pf. group
компо́стер (ticket) punch
компости́ровать impf., про- pf. punch (a ticket)
компо́т stewed fruit
компре́сс compress
компромети́ровать impf., c- pf. compromise
компроми́сс compromise
компью́тер computer
компьютериза́ция computerization
кому́ pron. D of кто
комфо́рт comfort; с по́лным —ом with all amenities
комфорта́бельный comfortable
конве́йер conveyor
конве́нция convention
конве́рт envelope
конверти́руемый convertible
конво́й escort; armed guard
конвои́ровать impf. escort
конво́й armed escort
конгре́сс congress
конденса́тор condenser
конди́тер pastry chef
конди́терская n. pastry shop
кондиционе́р (air) conditioner
конево́дство horse breeding
конёк fill hobby horse
коне́ц fill end; в конце́ концо́в in the end; after all
коне́чно adv. of course
коне́чность extremity (of body)
коне́чный final; terminal
кони́на horsemeat
конкре́тный concrete
конкуре́нт, –ка competitor
конкуре́нция competition
конкури́ровать impf. compete

ко́нкурс competition; contest
ко́нник cavalryman
ко́нный attrib. horse
конопля́ hemp
консерва́нт preservative
консервати́вный conservative
консерва́тор conservative
консервато́рия conservatory
консерви́ровать impf., за- pf. preserve; can
консе́рвный canning
консе́рвный нож can opener
консе́рвы pl. canned food
конси́лиум consultation
ко́нский attrib. horse
консо́ль f. pedestal; stand
конспе́кт synopsis; summary
конста́ти́ровать impf. & pf. ascertain; state
конституцио́нный constitutional
конститу́ция constitution
констру́и́ровать impf., c- pf. construct; design
констру́ктор designer
констру́кция construction; design
ко́нсул consul; —ьство consulate
консульта́ция consultation
консульти́ровать impf., про- pf. advise; (c + I) consult
конта́кт contact
конта́ктные ли́нзы pl. contact lenses
конте́йнер container
контине́нт continent; mainland
конто́ра office
конто́рский attrib. office
контраба́нда smuggled goods
контрабанди́ст smuggler
контраба́с double bass
контраге́нт contractor
контра́кт contract; agreement
контра́льто neut. indecl. contralto
контрама́рка complimentary ticket
контрапу́нкт counterpoint
контра́ст contrast
контрибу́ция indemnity
контролёр inspector; ticket collector
контроли́ровать impf., про- pf. control
контро́ль m. control; inspection; —ный attrib. control; check
контрразве́дка counterintelligence
контрреволю́ция counterrevolution
конту́зия contusion
ко́нтур contour
конура́ kennel
ко́нус cone

конфедера́ция confederation
конферансье́ *m. indecl.* master of ceremonies
конфере́нция conference
конфе́та, конфе́тка piece of candy
конфиденциа́льный confidential
конфирма́ция (*relig.*) confirmation
конфискова́ть *impf. & pf.* confiscate
конфли́кт conflict
конфо́рка stove burner
конформи́зм conformism
конфу́з embarrassment
концентра́т concentrate
концентра́ция concentration
концентри́ровать *impf.*, с- *pf.* concentrate; —ся concentrate (on)
конце́пция conception
конце́рн business concern
конце́рт concert; recital
концертме́йстер concertmaster
конце́ртный *attrib.* concert
конце́ссия (*com.*) concession
концла́герь *m.* (*abbr. of* концентрацио́нный ла́герь) concentration camp
конча́ть *impf.*, **ко́нчить** *pf.* finish; end; (+ *infin.*) stop; —ся expire, end
ко́нчик tip; end
кончи́на death, demise
конъюнкту́ра state of affairs
конъюнкту́рный of the moment
конь 1. *m.* horse 2. (*chess*) knight
коньки́ *pl.* skates
конькобе́жец FILL skater
конья́к cognac
ко́нюх groom; stable hand
кооперати́в cooperative
кооперати́вный cooperative
коопера́ция cooperation
координа́ты *pl.* one's location
координа́ция coordination
координи́ровать *impf. & pf.* coordinate
копа́ть *impf.*, **копну́ть**, **вы-** *pf.* dig; dig out; dig up
копе́йка kopeck
копи́лка piggy bank
копи́ровать *impf.*, с- *pf.* copy; imitate
копиро́вка copying
копи́ть *impf.*, с- *pf.* accumulate, save (up)
ко́пия copy
ко́поть *f.* soot, lampblack
копти́ть *impf.* smoke; vegetate
копти́ть *impf.*, за-, на- *pf.* smoke, cure

копчёности *pl.* smoked products
копчёный smoked
копы́то hoof
кора́ bark; crust
кора́бельный *attrib.* ship; ship's
кораблекруше́ние shipwreck
кораблестрое́ние shipbuilding
кора́бль *m.* ship
кора́лл coral
коре́ец FILL, **коре́янка** Korean
коре́йка brisket (*pork or veal*)
коре́йский Korean
корена́стый stocky; heavyset
корённо́й radical; indigenous
ко́рень *m.* root
Коре́я Korea
ко́ржик cookie
корзи́на, корзи́нка basket
коридо́р corridor
кори́ца cinnamon
кори́чневый brown
ко́рка crust; rind
корм fodder
корма́ (*naut.*) stern
корми́лец FILL, **-лица** breadwinner
корми́ть *impf.*, на-, по- *pf.* feed
кормле́ние feeding
кормово́й[1] *attrib.* (*naut.*) stern
кормово́й[2] *attrib.* fodder; forage
корму́шка feeding trough
ко́рмчий helmsman
корнево́й *attrib.* root
корнишо́н gherkin
коро́бить *impf.*, по-, с- *pf.* 1. warp 2. grate on; —ся warp
коро́бка box
коро́бок FILL, **коро́бочка** small box
коро́ва cow
короле́ва queen
короле́вский royal
короле́вство kingdom
коро́ль *m.* king
коромы́сло *n.* yoke; rocking shaft
коро́на crown
корона́ция coronation
коро́нка (*dental*) crown
коро́ста sores; pustules
коро́ткий short; intimate
ко́ротко *adv.* short; briefly
коротково́лновый short-wave
коро́че *compar. of* коро́ткий
корпорати́вный corporate
корпора́ция corporation
ко́рпус trunk; body; corps; building; (*sports*) length
корре́ктность proper behavior
корре́ктный correct; proper
корре́ктор proofreader

корректу́ра proofs; proofreading

корреспонде́нт, –ка correspondent

корреспонде́нция correspondence

корро́зия corrosion

корру́пция corruption

корт tennis court

ко́рточки *pl.:* **сиде́ть на ко́рточках** *impf.* squat

корыстный mercenary

корыстолю́бие self-interest

ко́рысть *f.* self-interest

коры́то trough

корь *f.* measles

коря́вый twisted; gnarled

коса́[1] scythe

коса́[2] plait

коса́тка killer whale

ко́свенный indirect; oblique

коси́ть[1] *impf.,* **c–** *pf.* mow

коси́ть[2] *impf.,* **по–, c–** *pf.* twist; squint

коси́чка pigtail

косма́тый shaggy

косме́тика cosmetics; make-up

космети́чка *Colloq.* make-up bag

косми́ческий *attrib.* space; cosmic

космодро́м space center

космона́вт, –ка cosmonaut; astronaut

космополи́т, –ка cosmopolitan

ко́смос (outer) space; the cosmos

косну́ться *pf. of* каса́ться

ко́сный stagnant; inert

ко́со *adv.* obliquely; aslant

косо́й 1. slanting, oblique 2. squinting

костене́ть *impf.,* **о–** *pf.* become numb; stiffen

костёр bonfire; campfire

костля́вый bony; skinny

ко́сточка pit, stone (*of fruit*)

косты́ль *m.* crutch

кость *f.* bone; **игра́льные ко́сти** dice

костю́м costume; suit

костюме́р costume designer

костюмиро́ванный costumed

костя́к skeleton

костяно́й (made of) bone

косы́нка kerchief; scarf

кося́к[1] doorpost

кося́к[2] flock; school (*of fish*)

кот tomcat

котёл boiler

котело́к FILL kettle, pot

коте́льная *n.* boiler room

котёнок FILL kitten

котле́та cutlet; chop; burger

котлова́н foundation pit

кото́рый *pron.* which; what; who

ко́фе *m. indecl.* coffee

кофева́рка coffee maker

кофе́йник coffeepot

кофе́йница coffee mill

ко́фта woman's jacket

ко́фточка blouse

коча́н head of cabbage

кочева́ть *impf.* wander; migrate

кочево́й nomad's; nomadic

кочене́ть *impf.,* **о–, за–** *pf.* become numb

ко́чка hummock

коша́чий feline

кошелёк purse; wallet

ко́шка cat

кошма́р nightmare

кошма́рный nightmarish

кощу́нство sacrilege; blasphemy

кощу́нствовать *impf.* blaspheme

коэффицие́нт coefficient; ratio

краб crab

кра́деный stolen

краеве́дение study of region

краево́й regional

краеуго́льный ка́мень *m.* cornerstone

кра́жа theft

край edge; land; region

кра́йне *adv.* extremely

кра́йний extreme; last; utter; **по кра́йней ме́ре** at least

кра́йность extreme; extremity

кран[1] faucet; **водоразбо́рный ~** hydrant

кран[2] (*tech.*) crane

кра́пать *impf.* drizzle

крапи́ва nettle

кра́пинка spot; speck; dot

краса́вец FILL handsome man

краса́вица beautiful woman

краси́вый beautiful

краси́тель *m.* dye

кра́сить *impf.,* **по–** *pf.* color; dye; paint

кра́ска color; paint; dye

красне́ть *impf.,* **по–** *pf.* flush, blush

кра́сное де́рево mahogany

красноречи́вый eloquent

краснота́ redness; ruddiness

кра́сный red

красота́ beauty

красо́тка *Colloq.* pretty girl

красть *impf.,* **y–** *pf.* steal

кра́сящий *attrib.* dye; dyeing

крат: **во сто ~** *adv.* a hundredfold

кра́тер crater

кра́ткий brief; short

кратковре́менный transitory

краткосро́чный short-term

кра́ткость brevity

крах crash, bankruptcy; failure

крахма́л starch

кра́ше more beautiful

кра́шеный painted, dyed, colored

креве́тка shrimp

креди́т credit

креди́тная ка́рточка credit card

креди́тный attrib. credit

кредитова́ть impf. & pf. extend credit

кредитоспосо́бный solvent

кре́йсер cruiser

крем cream

кремато́рий crematorium

крема́ция cremation

креме́нь m. flint

кремлёвский attrib. Kremlin

кремль m. fortress, citadel

кре́мний silicon

кре́мовый attrib. cream

крен (naut.) list, heel

кре́ндель m. pretzel

крени́ть impf., на- pf. tip; tilt

креп crêpe

кре́пкий strong; firm, sturdy

крепле́ние strengthening; fastening

кре́пнуть impf., о-, pf. get stronger

крепостни́чество serfdom

крепостно́й attrib. serf

кре́пость f. fortress; strength

кре́пче compar. of кре́пкий

кре́сло armchair

крест, кресто́к cross

крести́ны pl. christening

крести́ть impf. 1. pf. пере- make the sign of the cross 2. pf. о- baptize

крест-на́крест adv. crisscross

крёстная n. godmother

кре́стник, -ница godchild

крёстное зна́мение sign of the cross

крёстный оте́ц godfather

крёстная мать f. godmother

кресто́вый похо́д crusade

крестоно́сец FILL crusader

крестья́нин, -я́нка peasant

крестья́нский attrib. peasant

крестья́нство peasantry

креще́ние christening; Epiphany

крещёный baptized

крива́я n. (math.) curve

кривизна́ crookedness; curvature

криво́й crooked; curved

кри́зис crisis; —ный attrib. crisis

крик shout, cry

крике́т (sports) cricket

крикли́вый loud; noisy; flashy

кри́кнуть pf. of крича́ть

кримина́л Colloq. crime

криминали́стика criminal law

криминальный criminal

криста́лл crystal

кристалли́ческий crystalline

криста́льный crystal-clear

крите́рий criterion

кри́тик critic

кри́тика criticism

критикова́ть impf. criticize

крити́ческий critical

крича́ть impf., кри́кнуть pf. shout, yell

кров roof; shelter; house

крова́вый bloody; murderous

крова́тка, крова́ть f. bed

кровено́сный circulatory, blood-

кро́вный attrib. blood

кровожа́дный bloodthirsty

кровоизлия́ние hemorrhage

кровообраще́ние blood circulation

кровоподтёк bruise

кровотече́ние bleeding

кровь f. blood

кровяно́й attrib. blood

крои́ть impf., с- pf. cut (out)

кро́йка cutting

крокоди́л crocodile

кро́лик rabbit

кроль m. (swimming) crawl

кро́ме prep. (+ G) except; besides

кро́мка selvage

кронци́ркуль m. calipers

кропи́ть impf. drizzle; sprinkle

кропотли́вый laborious; painstaking

кросс cross-country race

кроссво́рд crossword puzzle

кроссо́вка usu. pl. sneaker

крот mole; moleskin

кро́ткий gentle; meek

кро́тость gentleness; meekness

кро́ха, кро́шка crumb

кро́хотный, кро́шечный tiny

кроши́ть(ся) impf., ис-, рас- pf. crumble

круг circle; sphere

круглосу́точный round the clock

кру́глый round; ~ год all year round

кругозо́р prospect; outlook

круго́м adv. all around

кругосве́тный round-the-world

кру́жево lace

кружи́ть(ся) *impf.* spin (round), whirl
кру́жка mug
кружо́к FILL circle; club
круи́з cruise
крупа́ groats
крупи́ца 1. grain 2. fragment
крупноинформа́тивная электро́нная табли́ца (*abbr.* КЭТ) spreadsheet
крупномасшта́бный large-scale
кру́пный big, large; large-scale; ~ план closeup
крутизна́ steepness
крути́ть(ся) *impf.* turn; twist; whirl
кру́то *adv.* 1. steeply 2. sharply
круто́е яйцо́ hard-boiled egg
круто́й steep; sharp, severe
круше́ние crash; collapse; ruin
круши́ть *impf.* destroy; shatter
крыжо́вник gooseberry (bush)
крыла́тый winged
крыло́ wing; blade; vane
крыльцо́ porch
Крым Crimea
кры́са rat
крысоло́вка rattrap
крыть *impf.*, по- *pf.* cover; —ся lie beneath; be concealed
кры́ша roof
кры́шка cover; lid
крюк hook
крючо́к FILL hook; hitch; catch
крюшо́н wine punch
кря́кать *impf.*, кря́кнуть *pf.* quack
кряхте́ть *impf.* groan
ксерокопи́ровать *impf.*, от- *pf.* photocopy, xerox
ксероко́пия photocopy
ксе́рокс photocopier
ксилогра́фия wood engraving
ксилофо́н xylophone
кста́ти *adv.* by the way; apropos
кто *pron.* who; anyone
кто́-либо, кто́-нибудь *pron.* somebody; anyone
кто́-то *pron.* somebody
куб 1. (*math.*) cube 2. boiler
ку́бик brick, block
куби́нец FILL, куби́нка Cuban
ку́бок FILL goblet; cup
кувши́н pitcher; jug
кувырка́ться *impf.*, кувыркну́ться *pf.* turn somersaults
куда́ *adv.* where, whither
куда́-либо, куда́-нибудь *adv.* somewhere; anywhere
куда́-то *adv.* somewhere
ку́дри *pl.* curls

кудря́вый curly, curly-headed
кузне́ц FILL blacksmith
кузне́чик grasshopper
ку́зница blacksmith's shop; forge
ку́зов 1. body 2. basket
кукаре́кать *impf.* crow
ку́кла doll; puppet
кукова́ть *impf.* cuckoo
ку́колка 1. doll 2. chrysalis
ку́кольный *attrib.* doll; puppet
кукуру́за corn; воздушная ~ popcorn
куку́шка cuckoo
кула́к fist
кула́чный *attrib.* fist
кулина́рия cookery; cooking
кулина́рный culinary
кули́сы *pl.* (*theat.*) wings; за кули́сами behind the scenes
кули́ч Easter cake
кулуа́рный unofficial; secretive
кулуа́ры *pl.* corridors, lobby
куль *m.* sack
кульмина́ция culmination
культ cult
культу́ра culture; cultivation
культу́рный cultural; cultured; refined
кум, кума́ godparent
кума́ч red calico
куми́р idol
кумы́с kumiss (*fermented mare's milk*)
куни́ца marten
купа́льник bathing suit
купа́льщик, -щица bather
купа́ть(ся) *impf.*, вы- *pf.* bathe
купе́ *neut. indecl.* compartment
купе́ц FILL merchant
купи́ть *pf. of* покупа́ть
купле́т verse; stanza
ку́пол dome
купо́н coupon
купчи́ха female merchant
купю́ра 1. deletion 2. denomination
кура́нты *pl.* chimes
курга́н barrow; burial mound
куре́ние smoking
кури́льщик, -щица smoker
кури́ный *attrib.* chicken
кури́ть(ся) *impf.*, по- *pf.* smoke
ку́рица hen, chicken
куро́к cock; hammer (*of gun*)
куропа́тка partridge
куро́рт health resort
курс *m.*: exchange rate; policy; —овой *attrib.* course; term
курса́нт cadet

курси́в italics; **—ый** italic
курси́ровать *impf.* shuttle
ку́ртка (winter) jacket
ку́ры *pl. of* **ку́рица**
курье́р messenger
куря́тник chicken coop; henhouse
куря́щий *n.* smoker
куса́ть(ся) *impf.*, **укуси́ть** *pf.* bite
кусо́к FILL **1.** piece **2.** lump
кусо́чек FILL *dim. of* **кусо́к**
куст bush, shrub
куста́рник bushes; shrubs

ку́тать *impf.*, **за-** *pf.* wrap; bundle
кутёж drinking bout; spree; binge
ку́хня 1. kitchen **2.** cuisine
ку́хонный *attrib.* kitchen
ку́ча heap; pile
ку́чер coachman
ку́чка *dim. of* **ку́ча**
ку́шанье food; dish
ку́шать *impf.*, **по-** *pf.* eat
куше́тка couch

— Л —

лабири́нт labyrinth; maze
лабора́нт, —ка laboratory assistant
лаборато́рия laboratory
лава́нда lavender
лави́на avalanche
ла́вка¹ bench
ла́вка² shop
ла́вочка small bench
лавр laurel; **—о́вый лист** bay leaf
ла́вра monastery
ла́герь *m.* camp
лад 1. harmony **2.** manner, way
ла́дан incense
ла́дить *impf.* get along; be on good terms
ла́дно *adv.* well; all right
ладо́нь *f.* palm
ладья́ (*chess*) rook; castle
лазаре́т hospital; infirmary
лазе́йка small opening; loophole
ла́зер, —ный laser
ла́зерно-цифрово́й прои́грыватель CD (compact disc) player
ла́зить, ла́зать *impf.* climb
лазу́рный azure
лазу́рь *f.* azure
лай barking
ла́йка¹ Siberian husky
ла́йка² kidskin
ла́йнер (ocean, air) liner
лак varnish
лакиро́вка lacquering; varnishing
ла́кмус litmus
ла́ковый lacquered
ла́комство delicacy
ла́комый 1. tasty; dainty; luscious **2.** fond of
лакони́ческий laconic
лакони́чный laconic
лакри́ца licorice
ламанти́н manatee
Ла-Ма́нш проли́в English Channel

ла́мпа lamp
лампа́да icon lamp
ла́мпочка light bulb
ландша́фт landscape
ла́ндыш lily of the valley
лань *f.* doe; fallow deer
ла́па, ла́пка paw
лапта́ lapta (*ball game*)
лапша́ noodles; noodle dish
ларёк FILL stall
ларе́ц FILL small box
ларь *m.* bin
ла́ска¹ caress; kindness
ла́ска² weasel
ласка́ть *impf.* caress, pet
ла́сковый affectionate, tender
ла́стик eraser
ла́сточка (*bird*) swallow
латви́ец FILL, **латви́йка** Latvian
латви́йский Latvian
Ла́твия Latvia
лати́нский Latin
лату́к lettuce
лату́нь *f.* brass
ла́ты *pl.* armor
латы́нь *f.* Latin
латы́ш, —ка Latvian, Lett
лауреа́т laureate
ла́цкан lapel
ла́ять *impf.* bark
лгать *impf.*, **со-, на-** *pf.* lie
лгун, лгу́нья liar
лебёдка¹ female swan
лебёдка² (*mech.*) winch
ле́бедь *m.* swan
лев FILL lion
левша́ *m. & f.* left-hander
ле́вый left; left-wing
легализи́ровать *impf. & pf.* legalize
лега́льный legal
леге́нда legend
легенда́рный legendary
лёгкий light; easy; slight

легко́ adv. easily; lightly
легкоатле́т, —ка track-and-field athlete
легкове́рие gullibility; credulity
легково́й автомоби́ль m. passenger car
лёгкое n. lung
легкомы́слие frivolity
лёгкость lightness
лёгочный attrib. lung; pulmonary
ле́гче compar. of лёгкий, легко́
лёд FILL ice
ледене́ть impf., за-, о- pf. freeze
ледене́ц FILL hard candy
ледни́к glacier
леднико́вый glacial
ледо́вый attrib. ice
ледоко́л (ship) icebreaker
ледохо́д drifting of ice
ледяно́й icy
лёжа adv. in a lying position
лежа́ть impf. lie; be (situated)
лежа́чий lying, recumbent
ле́звие blade; edge
лезть impf., по-, за- pf. climb, clamber; (в + A) get in
лейбори́ст Labourite
ле́йка 1. watering can 2. funnel
лейтена́нт lieutenant
лека́ло French curve; template
лека́рственный medicinal
лека́рство medicine; drug
ле́карь m. Obs. doctor
ле́ксика vocabulary; lexicon
лексико́н lexicon
ле́ктор lecturer
ле́кция lecture
лён FILL flax
лени́вец FILL lazy person; sloth
лени́вый lazy
ле́нинский Leninist
лени́ться impf., по- pf. be lazy
ле́ность laziness
ле́нта ribbon, tape; band
лентя́й, —ка lazy person
лень f. laziness
лепесто́к FILL petal
ле́пет babble; prattle
лепета́ть impf., про- pf. babble
лепёшка 1. flat cake 2. tablet
лепи́ть impf., вы-, с- pf. model, fashion, shape
лес forest, wood; timber
леса́ pl. scaffold(ing)
лесбия́нка lesbian
лесни́к forester; forest ranger
лесни́чество forest district
лесни́чий n. forest warden
лесно́й attrib. forest

лесово́дство forestry
лесозаво́д lumber mill
ле́стница staircase, stairs; ladder
ле́стный flattering
лесть f. flattery
лёт flight; на лету́ in flight
лета́ pl. years; age
лета́тельный attrib. flying
лета́ть indet., лете́ть det., полете́ть pf. fly; rush
лета́ющая таре́лка flying saucer
ле́тний attrib. summer
лётный attrib. flying, flight
ле́то summer
летоисчисле́ние chronology
ле́том adv. in (the) summer
ле́топись f. chronicle; annal
летучий flying; летучая мышь f. (zool.) bat
лётчик, —чица flier, pilot
лече́бный curative; medicinal
лече́ние treatment; cure
лечи́ть impf. treat; cure
лечь pf. of ложи́ться
лещи́на hazel
лжесвиде́тельство false evidence
лжец liar
лжи́вый false; lying
ли conj. whether; if
либера́л, —ка liberal
ли́бо conj. or; ~ ... ~ ... either ... or ...
ли́вень m. downpour
ли́вер giblets; (cul.) liver
ливре́я livery
ли́га league
ли́дер leader; —ство leadership
лиди́ровать impf. be in the lead
лиза́ть impf., лизну́ть pf. lick
ликвида́ция liquidation
ликвиди́ровать impf. & pf. liquidate
ликви́дный (finance) liquid
ликёр cordial
ликова́ние rejoicing; exultation
ли́лия lily
лило́вый violet; purple
лими́т limit; quota
лимо́н lemon
лимона́д lemonade
лимо́нный lemon; citric
лимузи́н limousine
ли́мфа lymph
лингви́ст linguist
лингви́стика linguistics
лине́йка ruler; line; line-up
лине́йный linear
ли́нза lens
ли́ния line

линчева́ть *impf. & pf.* lynch
ли́нька molting
линя́ть *impf.*, по-, вы́- *pf.* fade; molt
ли́па linden tree; lime tree
ли́пкий sticky
ли́пнуть *impf.* stick
ли́повый **1.** *attrib.* linden **2.** fake
липу́чий sticky
ли́рика lyrics; lyric poetry
лири́ческий lyric(al)
лиса́, лиси́ца fox
лист[1] (*pl.* ли́стья) leaf
лист[2] (*pl.* листы́) sheet; page
листа́ть *impf.* leaf through
листва́ foliage
листопа́д falling of leaves
Литва́ Lithuania
литера́тор literary person
литерату́ра literature
литерату́рный literary
лито́вец FILL, -вка Lithuanian
лито́вский Lithuanian
литр liter
лить[1] *impf.* pour; spill; flow
лить[2] *impf.* cast; form
литьё founding; casting; molding
лифт elevator
ли́фчик brassiere
ли́хо misfortune; evil
лихо́й evil
лихора́дка fever
лихора́дочный feverish
лицева́я сторона́ front; facade
лицеме́р, —ка hypocrite
лицеме́рие hypocrisy
лицеме́рить *impf.* be hypocritical
лице́нзия license
лицо́ **1.** face **2.** person **3.** exterior
ли́чно *adv.* in person; personally
ли́чность personality
ли́чный personal, private
лиша́ть *impf.*, —ши́ть *pf.* (+ G) deprive of; —ся be deprived of
лише́ние deprivation; privation
ли́шнее *n.* extras
ли́шний surplus; superfluous
лишь *adv.* only; *conj.* ~ бы if only; ~ то́лько as soon as
лоб forehead; ло́бный, —ово́й frontal; front
лов catch (*of fish*)
ловела́с ladies' man
лови́ть *impf.*, пойма́ть *pf.* catch
ло́вкий adroit, dexterous
ло́вкость adroitness; dexterity
ло́вля catching; trapping
лову́шка snare, trap
ло́гика logic

логи́ческий, логи́чный logical
ло́дка boat
ло́дочный *attrib.* boat, boating
лоды́жка ankle
лодыри́чать *impf.* loaf
ло́дырь *m.* loafer; idler
ло́жа (*theat.*) box
ложи́ться *impf.*, лечь *pf.* lie down; ~ спать go to bed
ло́жка spoon
ло́жный false
ложь *f.* lie; falsehood
лоза́ vine
ло́зунг slogan
локализова́ть *impf. & pf.* localize
лока́льный local
лока́тор locator; radar
ло́кон curl, lock
ло́коть *m.* FILL elbow
лом[1] crowbar
лом[2] (*coll.*) scrap
лома́ть(ся) *impf.*, с-, по- *pf.* break
ломба́рд pawnshop
ло́мберный стол card table
ло́мка breaking
ло́мкий brittle; fragile
ломо́та dull ache
ломо́ть *m.* chunk; big piece
ло́мтик slice
ло́пасть *f.* blade; vane
лопа́та spade, shovel
лопа́тка shovel; trowel; blade
лопа́тка[2] shoulder blade
ло́паться *impf.*, ло́пнуть *pf.* snap, break, burst
лопу́х burdock
лоск luster, gloss
лоску́т scrap of cloth; shred
лоску́тный patchwork
лососи́на (*cul.*) salmon
ло́сось *m.* salmon
лось *m.* elk
лосьо́н face lotion
лотере́я lottery
лото́ *neut. indecl.* lotto
лото́к FILL **1.** tray, stand (*of street hawker*) **2.** chute
лохма́тый shaggy; tousled
лохмо́тья *pl.* rags
лошади́ный *attrib.* horse
ло́шадь *f.* horse
лоя́льный loyal, loial
луб bast
лубо́к FILL woodcut
луг meadow
лу́жа puddle
лужа́йка lawn; clearing
лужо́к FILL *dim. of* луг
лук[1] onion, onions

лук² bow
лука́вить *impf.* be cunning
лука́вство slyness, cunning
лука́вый sly, cunning
лу́ковица onion; bulb
лук-поре́й scallion; leek
луна́ moon
луна́-па́рк amusement park
луна́тик, лунати́чка sleepwalker
лу́нный lunar, moon
лу́па magnifying glass
луч ray, beam
лучево́й radial; *attrib.* radiation
лучи́ться *impf.* sparkle; radiate
лу́чше *adv.* better
лу́чший better; best
лы́жа *usu. pl.* ski; snowshoe
лы́жник, -ница skier
лы́жный *attrib.* ski; skiing
лысе́ть *impf.* об-, по- *pf.* grow bald
лы́сина baldness, bald spot
лы́сый bald
льви́ный lion's
льго́та privilege
льго́тный privileged; favorable; reduced
льди́на ice floe
льнуть *impf.* при- *pf.* (к + D) **1.** cling to **2.** have a weakness for
льстец flatterer
льстить *impf.*, по- *pf.* flatter
любе́зничать *impf. Colloq.* (с + I) say nice things to

любе́зность courtesy; kindness
любе́зный courteous, kind; polite
люби́мый beloved; favorite
люби́тель, —ница lover; amateur;
—ский amateur
люби́ть *impf.* love; like
любова́ться *impf.*, по- *pf.* (+ I, на + A) admire
любо́вник, -ница lover
любо́вный love, loving
любо́вь f. FILL love
любозна́тельный inquisitive
любо́й any; *n.* anyone
любопы́тный curious
любопы́тство curiosity
лю́бящий affectionate; loving
лю́ди *pl.* people
людое́д cannibal
люк hatch; trap door; manhole
люминесце́нтный luminescent
люминесце́нция luminescence
лю́стра chandelier
лютера́нский Lutheran
лю́тня lute
лю́тость ferocity
ляга́ть(ся) *impf.*, лягну́ть *pf.* kick
лягу́шка frog
ля́жка thigh; haunch
ля́згать *impf.*, ля́згнуть *pf.* clang; clank; (+ I) rattle
ля́мка shoulder strap
ля́пнуть *pf.* blurt out
ля́псус blunder

M

м *abbr. of* метр
мавзоле́й mausoleum
магази́н store, shop
маги́стр (holder of) master's degree
магистра́ль f. main (line); highway
маги́ческий magic
ма́гия magic
магнети́зм magnetism
магни́т magnet; —ный magnetic
магнитофо́н tape recorder
магомета́нин, -та́нка Mohammedan
магомета́нский Mohammedan
мае́вка spring picnic
мажо́р (*mus.*) major key
ма́зать *impf. Colloq.* oil, grease; smear; daub
мазня́ *Colloq.* poor painting
мазо́к FILL **1.** dab **2.** smear
мазохи́ст, —ка masochist

мазу́т fuel oil
мазь f. ointment; grease
май May; —ский *attrib.* May
ма́йка (sleeveless) T-shirt
майоне́з mayonnaise
майо́р major
мак poppy; poppy seed
макаро́ны *pl.* pasta
мака́ть *impf.*, макну́ть *pf.* dip
ма́клер broker
ма́клерство brokerage
ма́ковка 1. poppy head **2.** crown of head **3.** dome
максима́льный maximum
ма́ксимум maximum
макулату́ра 1. paper for recycling **2.** pulp fiction
маку́шка crown of head; top
малахи́т malachite
мале́йший smallest, least, slightest
ма́ленький small, little
мали́на raspberry; raspberries

мали́новый *attrib.* raspberry
ма́ло *adv.* (a) little; not enough
маловеро́ятный unlikely
малогабари́тный small-size
малогра́мотный semiliterate
малоду́шный fainthearted
малоиму́щий poor
малокро́вие anemia
малоле́тний underage; juvenile
малолитра́жный fuel-efficient
малолю́дный sparsely populated
ма́ло-ма́льски *adv.* the slightest bit
ма́ло-пома́лу *adv.* little by little
малоприбы́льный of little profit
малора́звитый underdeveloped
малоро́слый undersized
малосодержа́тельный lacking substance
малосо́льный lightly salted
малочи́сленный not numerous
ма́лый small, little
малы́ш small child
ма́льчик boy, lad
мальчи́шеский boyish; childish
мальчи́шка little boy
маля́р house painter
маля́рия malaria
ма́ма mother, mama
ма́мин mother's
ма́монт mammoth
мандари́н tangerine; mandarin
манёвр maneuver
маневри́ровать *impf.*, с- *pf.* maneuver
мане́ж riding school; circus area
манеке́н mannequin; dummy
манеке́нщик, -щица fashion model
мане́ра manner; style
мане́рный mannered; affected
манже́та cuff
маниака́льно-депресси́вный manic-depressive
маникю́р manicure
маникю́рша manicurist
манипули́ровать *impf.* manipulate
манипуля́ция manipulation
мани́ть *impf.*, по- *pf.* beckon; lure, attract
манифе́ст manifesto
манифеста́ция demonstration
ма́ния mania
ма́нная ка́ша farina
мано́метр pressure gauge
манса́рда attic; garret
ма́нтия mantle; cloak; robe
мануфакту́ра manufacturing
манья́к maniac

мара́ть *impf.* **1.** *pf.* за- soil; stain **2.** *pf.* на- daub
марафо́н marathon
ма́рганец FILL manganese
маргари́н margarine
маргари́тка daisy
ма́рево 1. mirage **2.** haze
мари́ец FILL *f.* **мари́йка** Mari
марина́д marinade
маринова́ть *impf.*, за- *pf.* marinate
марионе́тка puppet; marionette
марихуа́на marijuana
ма́рка 1. postage stamp **2.** brand; trademark
марки́за awning; marquee
маркирова́ть *impf.* & *pf.* mark
маркси́стский Marxist
ма́рля cheesecloth; gauze
мармела́д fruit jellies
мародёр marauder
Маро́кко Morocco
ма́рочный high-quality
Марс Mars
март, ма́ртовский March
марты́шка marmoset
марш march
марширова́ть *impf.* march
маршру́т itinerary; route
ма́ска mask
маскара́д masquerade
маскирова́ть *impf.*, за- *pf.* mask, disguise; camouflage
маскиро́вка masking; camouflage
Ма́сленица Shrovetide; carnival
маслёнка butter dish; oil can
ма́слёный oily; greasy
масли́на olive; olive tree
ма́сло 1. butter **2.** oil
ма́сляный *attrib.* oil; grease
масо́н Mason
ма́сса mass; pulp; (+ *G*) a lot
масса́ж massage
массажи́ст, —а masseur, masseuse
масси́вный massive
масси́ровать *impf.* & *pf.* massage
массо́вка (film) crowd scene
ма́ссовый mass; of the masses
ма́стер 1. foreman **2.** expert
мастери́ть *impf.*, с- *pf.* fashion; build; put together
мастерска́я *n.* workshop; studio
ма́стерски *adv.* masterfully
мастерство́ skill; craftsmanship
масть *f.* **1.** color **2.** (cards) suit
масшта́б scale
мат (chess) checkmate, mate
матема́тик mathematician

матема́тика mathematics
материа́л material
материали́ст, —ка materialist
материа́льный material; financial
матери́к mainland; continent
материко́вый continental
матери́нский maternal
матери́нство motherhood
мате́рия matter; subject
матёрый full-grown; inveterate
ма́тка 1. womb **2.** female, queen
ма́товый mat; dull
матра́с, матра́ц mattress
матрёшка set of wooden dolls
матриарха́льный matriarchal
ма́трица matrix
матро́с sailor, seaman
матч (*sports*) match
мать *f.* mother
мах stroke; swing
маха́ть *impf.*, **махну́ть** *pf.* (+ *I*)
  wave; wag; brandish
махина́ция machination
махови́к flywheel
махо́рка inferior tobacco
махро́вый *attrib.* **1.** terry cloth **2.**
  blatant
ма́чеха female stepmother
ма́чта mast
маши́на 1. machine **2.** car
маши́нальный mechanical
машини́ст machinist; operator
машини́стка typist
маши́нка 1. typewriter **2.** sewing
  machine
машинопи́сный typewritten
маши́нопись *f.* typing; typescript
машинострое́ние mechanical engineering
мая́к lighthouse
ма́ятник pendulum
ма́яться *impf.* toil; suffer
мгла mist, haze; gloom
мгнове́ние instant; moment
мгнове́нный instantaneous; momentary
ме́бель *f.* furniture
меблиро́ванный furnished
меблиро́вка furnishings, furniture
мега- *in combinations* mega-
мегафо́н megaphone
меге́ра shrew; termagant; virago
мёд honey
медали́ст, —ка medalist
меда́ль *f.* medal
медальо́н medallion
медве́дица female bear; **Больша́я
  Медве́дица** Big Dipper
медве́дь *m.* bear

медвежо́нок bear cub
ме́дик doctor; health provider;
  medical student
медикаме́нты *pl.* medicines
медици́на medicine
медици́нский medical
ме́дленный slow
ме́длить *impf.* linger; delay
ме́дный copper
медо́вый *attrib.* honey
медосмо́тр medical checkup
медпу́нкт first-aid station
медсестра́ female nurse
меду́за jellyfish; medusa
медь *f.* copper; **жёлтая ~** brass
меж *prep.* (+ *I*) between
междоме́тие (*gram.*) interjection
междоусо́бица internecine strife
ме́жду *prep.* (+ *I*) between;
  among; **~ тем** meanwhile;
  ~ про́чим by the way
междугоро́дный inter-city
междунаро́дный international
межконтинента́льный intercontinental
межплане́тный interplanetary
межсезо́нье off-season
мезони́н attic; mezzanine
Ме́ксика Mexico
мексика́нец FILL, **-нка** Mexican
мел chalk
меланхо́лия melancholy
мелиора́ция land reclamation
ме́лкий small; fine; shallow; petty
мелкобуржуа́зный petit-bourgeois
мелково́дье shallow water
мелоди́чный melodious
мело́дия melody
мелодра́ма melodrama
мелома́н music lover
ме́лочный petty; small-minded
ме́лочь *f.* **1.** trifle; trivia **2.**
  (*money*) change
мель *f.* shoal; (*sand*) bank
мелька́ть *impf.*, **мелькну́ть** *pf.* be
  glimpsed; flash by; glimmer
ме́льком *adv.* in passing
ме́льница mill
мельча́ть *impf.*, **из-** *pf.* become
  smaller; become shallow
мемора́ндум memorandum
мемориа́льный memorial
ме́нее *adv.* less; **тем не ~** nonetheless
менструа́ция menstruation
менто́л menthol
ме́ньше *adv.* smaller; less
ме́ньший lesser, smaller
меньшинство́ minority
меню́ *neut. indecl.* menu

меня́ pron. G, A of я.

меня́ть(ся) impf., по- pf. change; exchange

ме́ра measure

мерза́вец FILL, -вка vile person

ме́рзкий vile; disgusting

мерзлота́ frozen earth

мёрзнуть impf., за- pf. freeze

мёрзость f. abomination

меридиа́н meridian

мери́ло criterion; standard

ме́рить impf., по- pf. measure; try on

ме́рка measure; yardstick

ме́ркнуть impf., по- pf. grow dark

мерлу́шка lambskin

мероприя́тие 1. measure 2. social event

мертве́ть impf., по-, о- pf. grow numb

мертве́ц corpse

мёртвый dead; n. dead person

мерца́ть impf. shimmer; glimmer

меси́ть impf., вы- pf. knead

ме́сса (relig.) Mass

месте́чко small town

мести́ impf., вы- pf. sweep

ме́стность f. area; locality

ме́стный local

ме́сто 1. place 2. room 3. seat 4. job

местоиме́ние pronoun

местонахожде́ние location

месть f. vengeance; revenge

ме́сяц 1. month 2. moon

ме́сячный monthly; n.pl. menstrual period

мета́лл metal

металли́ческий metal; metallic

металлоло́м scrap metal

металлу́ргия metallurgy

метаморфо́за metamorphosis

мета́н methane

мета́ние throwing

метаста́з metastasis

мета́ть[1] impf., метну́ть pf. throw, fling; ~ икру́ spawn; —ся rush about; toss about

мета́ть[2] impf., с- pf. baste

метафи́зика metaphysics

мета́фора metaphor

мете́ль f. snowstorm

метео́р meteor

метеори́т meteorite

метеоро́лог meteorologist

метеороло́гия meteorology

мети́л methyl

ме́тить[1] impf., по-, на- pf. mark

ме́тить[2] impf., на- pf. (в + A) aim at; aspire to

ме́тка mark

ме́ткий well-aimed; accurate

ме́ткость accuracy

метла́ broom

метну́ть pf. of мета́ть[1]

ме́тод method

мето́дика method; methodology

методи́ческий methodical

методоло́гия methodology

метр meter

метра́ж (film) footage

метрдоте́ль maître d'hôtel

ме́трика birth certificate

метри́ческий metric

метро́ neut. indecl. subway

метрополите́н metro; subway

мех (pl. меха́) fur

механиза́ция mechanization

механи́зм mechanism

меха́ник mechanic

меха́ника mechanics

мехи́ pl. bellows

меховой fur

мецена́т patron of the arts

меч sword

мече́ть f. mosque

мечта́ (day)dream

мечта́тель, —ница dreamer

мечта́ть impf. dream

меша́лка mixer

мешани́на mishmash

меша́ть[1] impf., по- pf. (+ D) disturb; hinder; interfere

меша́ть[2] impf., по-, с- pf. stir; mix

мешкови́на sackcloth

мешо́к FILL bag; sack

меща́нин, меща́нка petit-bourgeois; narrow-minded person

меща́нский petit-bourgeois; narrow-minded

меща́нство petite bourgeoisie; narrow-mindedness

миг instant; moment

мига́лка Colloq. blinker

мига́ние winking; blinking

мига́ть impf., мигну́ть pf. blink; wink; twinkle

ми́гом adv. Colloq. in a flash

мигра́ция migration

мигре́нь f. migraine

ми́дия mussel

мизантро́п, —ка misanthrope

мизе́рный meager; paltry

мизи́нец FILL little finger

микро́б microbe; germ

микроко́см microcosm

микро́н micron

микрооргани́зм microorganism

микроско́п microscope

микросхе́ма microchip
микрофо́н microphone
ми́ксер mixer, blender
миксту́ра mixture
ми́лая n. darling; sweetheart
милитари́зм militarism
милиционе́р policeman
мили́ция 1. the police 2. militia
миллиа́рд billion
миллиме́тр millimeter
миллио́н million; —ный millionth
миллионе́р millionaire
ми́ловать impf., по- pf. pardon
милосе́рдие mercy; charity
ми́лостивый gracious
ми́лостыня alms
ми́лость f. favor; mercy
ми́лый pleasant; nice; dear
ми́ля mile
ми́мика facial expressions
мимикри́я (biol.) mimicry
ми́мо adv., prep. (+ G) past, by
мимохо́дом adv. in passing
ми́на (mil.) mine
минда́лина tonsil
минда́ль m. almond tree; almonds
минера́л mineral; —ьный mineral
миниатю́ра miniature
миниатю́рный miniature, tiny
минима́льный minimum
ми́нимум minimum
министе́рство ministry, department
мини́стр minister
минова́ть impf. & pf. pass (by)
миноиска́тель m. mine detector
миноме́т (mil.) mortar
миноно́сец FILL torpedo boat
мино́р minor (key)
мину́вший past
ми́нус minus; defect
мину́та minute
мину́тный attrib. minute; momentary
мир[1] peace
мир[2] world
мира́ж mirage
мири́ть impf., по-, при- pf. reconcile; —ся be reconciled
ми́рный peace; peaceful
мирова́я паути́на World Wide Web (abbr. WWW)
мировоззре́ние world view
мирово́й attrib. world
миролюби́вый peace-loving
миротво́рец FILL peacemaker
ми́рра myrrh
мирско́й secular; worldly
миря́нин, миря́нка Obs. layperson

ми́ска bowl; tureen
миссионе́р, —ка missionary
ми́ссия mission
ми́стик mystic
мистифика́ция hoax
ми́тинг rally; mass meeting
митка́ль m. calico
митрополи́т metropolitan
миф myth; —и́ческий mythical
мифологи́ческий mythological
мифоло́гия mythology
мише́нь f. target
мишура́ tinsel; ostentation
младе́нец FILL infant
младе́нчество infancy
мла́дший younger; junior
млекопита́ющее n. mammal
Мле́чный Путь the Milky Way
мне pron. D, P of я
мнемони́ческий mnemonic
мне́ние opinion
мни́мый imaginary
мно́гие adj., pron. many
мно́го adv. (+ G) much; a lot of
многобра́чие polygamy
многова́то adv. a bit much
многогра́нный many-sided; multifaceted; polyhedral
мно́гое n. much; a large amount
многожёнство polygamy
многозначи́тельный 1. significant 2. (of a glance or smile) knowing
многокра́тный repeated, frequent
многоле́тний 1. of many years 2. perennial 3. long-lasting
многолю́дный crowded
многонациона́льный multinational
многообра́зие variety; diversity
многосеме́йный with a large family
многосло́вный verbose
многосторо́нний 1. versatile 2. multilateral
многоступе́нчатый multistage
многото́мный multivolume
многото́чие dots; omission points
многоуважа́емый (in letter) Dear
многоуго́льник polygon
многоцве́тный multicolored
многочи́сленный numerous
многочле́нный polynomial
многоэта́жный multistoried
многоязы́чный multilingual
мно́жественный plural
мно́жество multitude
мно́жить impf., по- pf. multiply
мной, мно́ю pron., I of я
мобилиза́ция mobilization

мобилизова́ть *impf. & pf.* mobilize

моби́льность mobility

моги́ла grave

могу́чий powerful; mighty

могу́щественный powerful

могу́щество power; might

мо́да fashion

модели́ровать *impf. & pf.* design

моде́ль *f.* model; pattern

модельер fashion designer

мо́дем modem

модернизи́ровать *impf. & pf.* modernize

мо́дно *adv.* fashionably; stylishly

мо́дный fashionable; stylish

модули́ровать *impf.* modulate

мо́дуль *m.* module; modulus

мо́жет быть perhaps, maybe

можжеве́льник juniper

мо́жно *impers.* it is possible; one may, one can

моза́ика mosaic

мозг brain; marrow; **—ово́й** cerebral

мозо́ль *f.* callus; corn

мой *poss.* my; mine

мо́йка washing; washer

мо́кнуть *impf.* get wet; soak

мокрота́ humidity

мо́крый wet

мол 1. pier 2. breakwater, jetty

молдава́нин, -ва́нка Moldavian

Молда́вия, Молдо́ва Moldavia

молекула molecule

моле́ние 1. prayer service 2. supplication

моли́тва prayer

моли́твенник prayer book

моли́ть *impf.* entreat, implore; **—ся** (o + *P*) pray (for); (на + *A*) adore

моллю́ск mollusk

молниено́сный lightning-fast

мо́лния 1. lightning 2. zipper

молодёжь *f.* youth; the young

молоде́ц FILL good boy; good girl; *interj.* well done!

молодожёны *pl.* newlyweds

молодо́й young

мо́лодость youth

молоды́е *pl.* young couple

моло́же, *compar. of* молодо́й

молоко́ milk

моло́т FILL hammer

мо́лотый ground

моло́ть *impf.*, c- *pf.* grind; mill

моло́чная *n.* dairy; creamery

моло́чник milk pitcher; milkman

моло́чница yeast infection

моло́чный *attrib.* milk; dairy

молча́ *adv.* silently, in silence

молча́ние silence

молча́ть *impf.* be *or* keep silent

моль *f.* clothes moth

мольбе́рт easel

моме́нт moment; factor

момента́льный instantaneous

мона́рх monarch

мона́рхия monarchy

монасты́рь *m.* monastery; convent

мона́х monk

мона́хиня nun

монго́л, —ка Mongolian

Монго́лия Mongolia

моне́та coin

монограмма monogram

монографи́ческий monographic

моноли́тный monolithic

моноло́г monologue

монополизи́ровать *impf. & pf.* monopolize

монопо́лия monopoly

моното́нность monotony

моното́нный monotonous

монта́ж 1. installing 2. editing 3. montage

монти́ровать *impf.*, с- *pf.* assemble; mount

монуме́нт monument

монумента́льный monumental

мопе́д moped

мора́ль *f.* moral; morals

мора́льный moral

морг morgue

морга́ть *impf.*, моргну́ть *pf.* wink; blink

мо́рда muzzle

мордви́н, —ка Mordvin

мо́ре sea

морепла́вание navigation

морепла́ватель, —ница navigator

морж walrus

морко́вный *attrib.* carrot

морко́вь *f.* a carrot; carrots

моро́женое *n.* ice cream

моро́женый frozen

моро́з frost

морози́лка freezer; freezer compartment

моро́зить *impf.* freeze; be freezing

моро́зный frosty

мороси́ть *impf.* drizzle

морс fruit drink

морско́й sea; maritime; nautical

мо́рфий morphine
морщи́на wrinkle
мо́рщить *impf.*, на-, с- *pf.* wrinkle
моря́к seaman, sailor
москви́ч, —ка́ Muscovite
моски́т sand fly
моско́вский *attrib.* (of) Moscow
мост bridge; —ово́й *attrib.* bridge
мо́стик small bridge
мости́ть *impf.*, вы- *pf.* pave
мостова́я *n.* pavement
мота́ть *impf.*, на- *pf.* wind
моти́в 1. motive, reason 2. motif
мотиви́ровать *impf. & pf.* explain; justify
мотобо́л soccer played on motorcycles
мотого́нки *pl.* motorcycle races
мото́к FILL 1. skein 2. hank
мото́р motor, engine
моторо́ллер motor scooter
мотоци́кл motorcycle
моты́га hoe
мотылёк butterfly; moth
мох moss
мохе́р mohair
мохна́тый hairy; shaggy
моча́ urine; мочево́й urinary
моча́лка bath sponge; loofa
мочёный (*of food*) soaked
мочи́ть *impf.*, на-, за- *pf.* soak; wet; —ся *impf.*, по- *pf.* urinate
мо́чка у́ха ear lobe
мочь *impf.*, с- *pf.* be able to
моше́нник swindler
моше́нничать *impf.*, с- *pf.* swindle
мо́шка midge; gnat
мошо́нка scrotum
мо́щи *pl.* relics (of a saint)
мо́щность power; capacity
мощь *f.* power, might
мо́ющий cleansing
мрак gloom; darkness, blackness
мра́мор marble
мра́чный gloomy; dark, dreary
мсти́тель, —ница avenger
мсти́тельный vindictive
мстить *impf.*, ото- *pf.* avenge
мудрёный *Colloq.* complicated
мудре́ц wise man; sage
му́дрость wisdom
му́дрый wise, sage
муж husband
му́жественный courageous, manly
му́жество courage
мужи́к peasant; fellow
мужско́й masculine, male
мужчи́на *m.* man; male
му́за muse

музе́йный *attrib.* museum
му́зыка music
музыка́льный music; musical
музыка́нт musician
му́ка suffering, torment
мука́ flour; meal
мул mule
мультипликáция multiplication
мультфи́льм animated cartoon
му́мия mummy
мунди́р uniform
мундштук cigarette *or* cigar holder; mouthpiece
муниципалите́т municipality
муниципа́льный municipal
мураве́й FILL ant
муравейник anthill
муска́т nutmeg
му́скул muscle
мускули́стый muscular
мускулату́ра muscles
му́скус musk
мусли́н muslin
му́сор rubbish, trash
мусоропрово́д garbage chute
муссо́н monsoon
мусульма́нин, -ма́нка Muslim
мута́ция mutation
мути́ть *impf.*, вз- *pf.* make muddy; upset
мутне́ть *impf.*, по- *pf.* get muddy
му́тный cloudy; muddy; dull
муть *f.* 1. sediment; murk 2. haze; mist
му́фта muff
му́ха fly
мухомо́р fly agaric
муче́ние torture
му́ченик, -ница martyr
мучи́тель, -ница tormentor, torturer; —ный agonizing
му́чить(ся) *impf.* torture; torment (oneself)
мучно́й *attrib.* flour; meal
мча́ться *impf.*, по- *pf.* rush (along)
мще́ние vengeance
мы *pron.* we
мы́лить *impf.*, на- *pf.* soap, lather
мы́ло soap
мы́льница soap dish
мы́льный soapy
мыс (*geog.*) cape
мы́сленный mental
мы́слить *impf.* think; reason
мысль *f.* thought, idea
мыть(ся) *impf.*, по- *pf.* wash (oneself)
мытьё washing
мышело́вка mousetrap

мы́шечный muscular
мы́шка[1] dim. of **мышь**
мы́шка[2]: **под мы́шкой** (loc.), **под мы́шку** (dir.) under one's arm
мышле́ние, мы́шление thinking
мы́шца muscle
мышь f. mouse; **лету́чая ~** bat
мышья́к arsenic
мэр mayor; **мэ́рия** city hall
мюзи́кл musical
мюзи́к-хо́лл music hall
мя́гкий soft; mild, gentle
мягкосерде́чный tenderhearted
мя́гкость softness; mildness
мя́гче, compar. of **мя́гкий**

мя́коть f. **1.** fleshy part **2.** pulp
мя́млить impf., **про-** pf. mumble
мяси́стый fleshy; meaty
мясни́к butcher
мясно́й attrib. meat; meaty
мя́со meat
мясору́бка meat grinder
мя́та (bot.) mint
мяте́ж mutiny; revolt
мяте́жник rebel; insurgent
мя́тный attrib. mint, peppermint
мя́тый crushed; crumpled
мять impf., **по-, из-** pf. crumple, crush
мяч, мя́чик ball

Н

на[1] prep. **1.** (+ A) onto; to; till; for **2.** (+ P) in, at; on
на[2] particle. Colloq. here!
наба́т alarm; tocsin
набе́г raid
набекре́нь adv. Colloq. aslant
на́бело adv. without corrections
на́бережная n. embankment
набива́ть impf., **наби́ть** pf. stuff; fill; hammer
набира́ть impf., **набра́ть** pf. gather; compose; recruit
наблюда́тель, —ница observer; **—ный** observant
наблюда́ть impf. observe
на́божность piety
на́божный pious, devout
набо́к adv. to one side
набо́р 1. recruitment **2.** set; collection **3.** (typog.) typesetting
набра́ть pf. of **набира́ть**
набро́сок FILL sketch; outline
наважде́ние delusion
нава́ристый (of soup) rich
наведе́ние 1. aiming **2.** application **3.** guidance
наве́к, наве́ки adv. forever
наве́рно adv. probably
наверняка́ adv. Colloq. for sure
навёрстывать impf., **наверста́ть** pf. make up (for)
наве́рх adv. up(wards); upstairs
наверху́ adv. upstairs; above
наве́с 1. awning **2.** cover
навесе́ле adv. Colloq. tipsy
навеща́ть impf., **-сти́ть** pf. visit
на́взничь adv. on one's back
навзры́д adv.: **пла́кать ~** sob uncontrollably
навига́тор navigator
навига́ция navigation

нависа́ть impf., **нави́снуть** pf. (**над** + I) hang over; overhang
навлека́ть impf., **навле́чь** pf. (**на** + A) bring on; incur
наводи́ть impf., **навести́** pf. (**на** + A) **1.** direct (at) **2.** cover
наводне́ние flood
наво́з manure
на́волочка pillowcase
навсегда́ adv. for ever
навстре́чу adv. from the opposite direction; prep. (+ D) towards
навы́ворот adv. inside out
на́вык skill; knack; habit
навы́нос adv. (food) to go
навя́зчивый obtrusive
навя́зывать impf., **навяза́ть** pf. **1.** tie; fasten **2.** (+ D) force or thrust (on)
нагиба́ть(ся) impf., **нагну́ть** pf. bend (over)
нагишо́м adv. stark naked
нагле́ц impudent person
на́глость insolence; impudence
наглу́хо adv. tightly
на́глый impudent; insolent
нагля́дный visual; clear; graphic
нагова́ривать impf., **наговори́ть** pf. (**на** + A) calumniate; record
наго́й nude; bare
наго́рный attrib. mountain
нагота́ nakedness; nudity
награ́да reward; decoration
награжда́ть impf., **награди́ть** pf. reward; decorate
нагрева́тель m. heater
нагрева́ть impf., **нагре́ть** pf. warm (up); heat; **—ся** get hot
нагромождА́ть impf., **-зди́ть** pf. pile up
нагроможде́ние piling up

награбить pf. of **грубить**

нагружать impf., **-зить** pf. load

нагрузка load; workload

над, надо prep. (+ I) over, above

надвигающийся approaching

надвое adv. in two; in half

надгробие 1. tombstone **2.** epitaph

надевать impf., **надеть** pf. put on

надежда hope

надёжность dependability

надёжный dependable; reliable

наделать pf. make; cause; do

надеть pf. of **надевать**

надеяться impf. (на + A) hope for; rely on

надзор surveillance

надлежащий proper, suitable, fit

надлежит impers. it is required

надлом fracture, break

надменный haughty, arrogant

надо¹ prep., see **над**

надо² impers. (+ D) it is necessary

надобность need; necessity

надоедать impf., **надоесть** pf. **1.** bother, annoy **2.** impers. be tired of

надоедливый boring, tiresome

надолго adv. for a long time

надомник, -ница homeworker

надпись f. inscription

надрез incision, cut

надпочечник adrenal gland

надругательство outrage

надрыв tear; strain; outburst

надрывать impf., **надорвать** pf. overtax, strain; **—ся** strain oneself

надрывный heartrending; hysterical

надстройка 1. building onto **2.** superstructure

надстрочный знак superscript

надтреснутый cracked

надувать impf., **надуть** pf. **1.** inflate **2.** Colloq. cheat; **—ся** sulk

надувной inflatable

надутый inflated; pompous

надушить pf. of **душить**

наедаться impf., **наесться** pf. eat one's fill

наедине adv. in private, privately

наезд quick visit; raid, incursion

наездник, -ница rider (on horse)

наезжать impf., **наехать** pf. **1.** (на + A) collide **2.** visit from time to time

наёмник mercenary; hireling

нажать pf. of **нажимать**

наждак emery

наждачная бумага sandpaper

наживать impf., **нажить** pf. acquire; gain; **—ся** enrich oneself

нажим pressure; clamp

нажимать impf., **нажать** pf. press; push

назавтра adv. the next day

назад adv. back(wards); **тому ~** ago

название name; title

назвать pf. of **называть**

наземный attrib. ground; surface

назло adv. to spite; out of spite

назначать impf., **назначить** pf. appoint; fix; prescribe

назойливый importunate

назревать impf., **назреть** pf. ripen; mature

называемый: **так ~** so-called

называть impf., **назвать** pf. name; call

наиболее adv. the most

наивысший the highest; the greatest

наизнанку adv. inside out

наизусть adv. by heart

наилучший the best

наименее adv. the least

наименование name; title

наименовать pf. of **именовать**

наискосок adv. at an angle

найти inspiration; intuition

найти(сь) pf. of **находить(ся)**

наказание punishment, penalty

наказывать impf., **наказать** pf. punish

накал incandescence

накаливать impf., **накалить** pf. make red hot; inflame

накануне adv. the day before

накачивать impf., **накачать** pf. pump (up); inflate

накидывать impf., **накинуть** pf. throw on or over; slip on

накипь f. scum

накладная invoice; waybill

накладной false; paste-on

накладывать impf., **наложить** pf. impose; lay, put on

наклейка label; sticker

наклон incline; slope

наклонность inclination; tendency

наклонять impf., **-нить** pf. bend; incline; **—ся** stoop, bend

наколенник kneepad

наконец adv. finally, at last

накоплять(ся) impf., **-пить(ся)** pf. accumulate

накормить pf. of **кормить**

накрахмалить pf. of **крахмалить**

накрыва́ть *impf.*, накры́ть *pf.* **1.** cover (with) **2.** set a table

нала́живание adjustment

нала́живать *impf.*, нала́дить *pf.* adjust; repair

нале́во *adv.* to the left; on the left

налегке́ *adv.* with little baggage

налёт **1.** (air) raid **2.** thin coating

налётчик, -чица robber; assailant

налива́ть *impf.*, нали́ть *pf.* pour; spill; fill

нали́вка fruit liqueur

налицо́ *adv.* present; on hand

нали́чие presence

нали́чные *pl.* cash

нали́чный present; available

нало́г tax; *attrib.* tax

налогообложе́ние taxation

налогоплате́льщик, -щица taxpayer

нало́женным платежо́м cash on delivery (*abbr.* C.O.D.)

наложи́ть *pf.* of накла́дывать

на́лысо *adv.*: брить ~ *impf.* shave someone's head

нам *pron. D* of мы

намёк hint; allusion

намека́ть *impf.*, намекну́ть *pf.* (на + A) hint (at); allude (to)

намерева́ться *impf.* intend; mean

наме́рение intention

наме́ренный intentional

на́мертво *adv. Colloq.* firmly; fast

намеча́ть *impf.*, наме́тить *pf.* plan, outline; mark

на́ми *pron. I* of мы

намно́го *adv.* greatly; much

намо́рдник muzzle

намо́рщить *pf.* of мо́рщить

намы́лить *pf.* of мы́лить

нанима́тель, -ница **1.** employer **2.** tenant

нанима́ть *impf.*, наня́ть *pf.* rent; hire; engage

наоборо́т *adv.* on the contrary; vice versa

наобу́м *adv.* at random

наотма́шь *adv.* with full force

наотре́з *adv.* flatly; pointblank

напада́ть *impf.*, напа́сть *pf.* (на + A) attack

нападе́ние attack, assault

напа́рник partner; buddy

напа́сть¹ *pf.*

напа́сть² *f.* misfortune

напе́в tune, air

наперегонки́ *adv.* racing one another

напереко́р *prep.* (+ D) contrary to; in defiance of

наперере́з *prep.* (+ D) so as to intercept; so as to head off

напёрсток *fill.* thimble

напи́льник file

написа́ние **1.** writing **2.** spelling

написа́ть *pf.* of писа́ть

напи́ток *fill.* beverage, drink

напи́ться *pf.* **1.** drink one's fill **2.** get drunk

наплева́ть *pf.* (на + A) **1.** spit on **2.** *Colloq.* not give a damn

наплы́в **1.** influx **2.** canker; excrescence

напова́л *adv.* outright

напои́ть *pf.* of пои́ть

напока́з *adv.* for show

наполня́ть(ся) *impf.*, напо́лнить(ся) *pf.* fill

наполови́ну *adv.* half; by half

напомина́ние reminder; reminding

напомина́ть *impf.*, напо́мнить *pf.* (+ D) remind

напо́р pressure

напо́ристый aggressive; assertive

напосле́док *adv.* on parting

направле́ние direction

направля́ть *impf.*, напра́вить *pf.* direct; send; —ся head (towards or for)

напра́во *adv.* to, on the right

напра́сно *adv.* in vain; to no purpose

напра́сный vain; futile

наприме́р *adv.* for example

напрока́т *adv.* for hire

напро́тив *adv.* opposite; on the contrary; *prep.* (+ G) opposite

напряже́ние strain; tension; voltage

напряжённость tension

напряжённый **1.** strained **2.** tense

напуга́ть *pf.* frighten; scare

напускно́й affected; assumed

напу́тствие parting words

наравне́ *adv.* level (with); equally

нараспа́шку *adv.* unbuttoned

нараста́ть *impf.*, нарасти́ pf. grow

нара́схват *adv.* like hot cakes

нара́щивать *impf.*, нарасти́ть *pf.* increase; augment; grow

нарва́ть *pf.* gather; pluck

наре́зка cutting; thread (*of screw*)

наре́чие adverb

нарисова́ть *pf.* of рисова́ть.

наркоби́знес drug business

нарко́з anesthesia

наркома́н, —ка drug addict

нарко́тик narcotic; drug

наркоти́ческий narcotic

наро́д nation; people; **—ность** nationality; **—ный** national; folk

наро́ст growth; tumor

наро́чно adv. on purpose

на́рты pl. dog sled; reindeer sled

нару́жный external

нару́жу adv. out(side); outward

нару́чник usu. pl. handcuff

нару́чный attrib. wrist

наруша́ть impf., нару́шить pf. break; violate; disrupt

наруше́ние violation, breach

наруши́тель, **—ница** violator

на́ры pl. plank bed

нары́в abscess; boil

наря́д attire, dress; **—ный** smart, well-dressed; elegant

наряжа́ть(ся) impf., -ди́ть(ся) pf. dress (up)

нас pron. G, A of мы.

наса́дка 1. putting on 2. attachment (for a tool) 3. bait

насажде́ние planting

насе́дка brood hen

насеко́мое n. insect

населе́ние population

населённый populated

наси́лие violence; force

наси́ловать impf., из- pf. violate; rape; coerce

наси́льник rapist; aggressor

наси́льственный forcible; violent

наскво́зь adv. through(out)

наско́лько adv. as far as

на́скоро adv. in a hurry

наслажда́ться impf., наслади́ться pf. (+ I) enjoy

наслажде́ние enjoyment; pleasure

насле́дие legacy

насле́дник, **—ница** heir(ess)

насле́дственность heredity

насле́дственный hereditary

насле́дство inheritance

на́смерть adv. to (the) death

насме́шка mockery; mocking

на́сморк (head) cold

насори́ть pf. of сори́ть

насо́с pump

на́спех adv. hastily; in a hurry

наст thin crust of ice on snow

настава́ть impf., наста́ть pf. come

наставле́ние admonition

наста́вник mentor; tutor

наста́ивать impf., настоя́ть pf. (на + P) insist; persist (in)

на́стежь adv. wide open

насте́нный attrib. wall

насто́й extract

насто́йка 1. liqueur 2. tincture

насто́йчивый persistent

насто́лько adv. so, so much

насто́льный attrib. table; desk

настора́живать impf., насторожи́ть pf. put on one's guard

настоя́тель abbot; prior

настоя́тельница mother superior

настоя́тельный urgent, pressing

настоя́ть pf. of наста́ивать

настоя́щее n. the present

настоя́щий present; genuine, real

настра́ивать impf., настро́ить pf. tune; dispose

настрое́ние mood; humor

настро́йка tuning

настро́йщик tuner

наступле́ние 1. approach, coming 2. (mil.) offensive.

на́сухо adv. dry

насуши́ть pf. dry

насчёт adv., prep. (+ G) regarding

насчи́тывать impf., насчита́ть pf. count; number

насыпа́ть impf., насы́пать pf. 1. sprinkle 2. pour 3. fill

насыща́ть impf., насы́тить pf. satiate; saturate; **—ся** be full

ната́лкивать impf., натолкну́ться pf. (на + A) come across

нате́льный worn close to the body

натира́ть impf., натере́ть pf. 1. rub (on) 2. irritate 3. polish

на́тиск charge; onslaught

натоща́к adv. on an empty stomach

на́трий sodium

нату́жный strenuous

нату́ра nature; character

натурализа́ция naturalization

натурализова́ть impf. & pf. naturalize; grant citizenship (to)

натура́льный natural

нату́рщик, **—ица** (artist's) model

натюрмо́рт still life

натя́гивать impf., натяну́ть pf. stretch; draw or pull on

натя́жка stretching

натя́нутость strain; tension

натя́нутый strained; forced

науга́д adv. at random

нау́ка science

научи́ть(ся) pf. of учи́ть(ся)

нау́чный scientific

нау́шник usu. pl. earphone; earflap

нафтали́н naphthalene

наха́л, **—ка** insolent person

наха́льный impudent

наха́льство impertinence
нахле́бник parasite
нахму́риться *pf. of* хму́риться
находи́ть *impf.*, найти́ *pf.* find;
—ся turn up; be (situated)
Нахо́дка Nakhodka
нахо́дка find
нахо́дчивый resourceful; inventive
наце́нка price increase; markup
национализа́ция nationalization
национализи́ровать *impf. & pf.*
nationalize
национали́зм nationalism
националист, —ка nationalist
национа́льность nationality
национа́льный national
наци́ст, —ка Nazi
на́ция nation
нача́ло beginning; source; principle
нача́льник, -ница boss; head;
chief
нача́льство the authorities; command
нача́ть *pf. of* начина́ть
на́черно *adv.* in the rough
начина́ние project; undertaking
начина́ть(ся) *impf.*, нача́ть(ся) *pf.*
begin
начина́ющий *n.* beginner
начина́я *prep.* (c + G) beginning
with
начи́нка filling; stuffing
на́чисто *adv.* clean; openly
начистоту́ *adv.* frankly; straight
начи́танность erudition
наш *poss.* our, ours
нашаты́рный spirit ammonia
нашаты́рь *m.* ammonium chloride
наше́ствие invasion
наши́вка (*mil.*) chevron; stripe
нашуме́вший sensational
наяву́ *adv.* while awake
не *particle.* not
неаккура́тный sloppy; unpunctual
небезопа́сный unsafe
небезразли́чный concerned; not
indifferent
небезызве́стный well known
небе́сный celestial; heavenly
неблагода́рный ungrateful
неблагожела́тельный unfriendly
неблагозву́чие disharmony
неблагонадёжный unreliable
неблагополу́чие trouble(s)
неблагополу́чный unfavorable
неблагопристо́йный indecent
неблагоприя́тный unfavorable
неблагоразу́мный imprudent
неблагоскло́нный ill-disposed

неблагоустро́енный lacking con-
veniences (*house* or *apartment*)
не́бо sky; heaven
нёбо palate; нёбный palatal
небога́тый not rich
небольшо́й small; short
небосво́д firmament
небоскло́н horizon
небоскрёб skyscraper
небо́сь *particle.* probably
небре́жность carelessness
небре́жный careless; negligent
небри́тый unshaven
небыли́ца fable; tall story
небытие́ nonexistence
небью́щийся unbreakable
нева́жный unimportant
неве́дение ignorance
неве́домо *adv.* God (only) knows
неве́жа *m. & f.* boor; lout
неве́жда *m. & f.* ignoramus
неве́жественный ignorant
неве́жливый impolite; rude
невезе́ние bad luck
невели́кий not large
неве́рие unbelief; atheism
неве́рный incorrect; unfaithful
неве́роятность unbelievability
невероя́тный incredible
неве́рующий unbelieving; *n.* non-
believer
невесо́мость weightlessness
неве́ста bride; fiancée
неве́стка daughter-in-law; sister-
in-law (*brother's wife*)
невзнача́й *adv.* by chance
невида́нный unprecedented
неви́димка invisible
неви́димый invisible
неви́дный **1.** invisible **2.** insignificant **3.** *Colloq.* unattractive
невидя́щий unseeing; blind
неви́нность innocence; virginity
неви́нный innocent; naive
невино́вность innocence
невино́вный innocent; not guilty
невку́сный tasteless
невмеша́тельство nonintervention
невнима́тельный inattentive
невня́тный indistinct
невозвра́тный irrevocable
невозвраще́нец FILL, -нка defector
невозде́ржанность intemperance
невозмо́жный impossible
невозмути́мый imperturbable
нево́льник, -ница slave
нево́льно *adv.* unintentionally
нево́льный involuntary
необрази́мый inconceivable
невооружённый unarmed

невоспи́танный ill-mannered
невосприи́мчивый unreceptive; immune
невпопа́д adv. not to the point
невразуми́тельный unintelligible
невралги́я neuralgia
невреди́мый unharmed; safe
вре́дный harmless
невро́з neurosis
невро́лог neurologist
невроло́гия neurology
невы́года disadvantage
невы́годный 1. unprofitable **2.** unfavorable **3.** unattractive
невы́держанность lack of self-control
невыноси́мый unbearable; intolerable
невы́полненный unfulfilled
невыполни́мость impracticability
невырази́тельный inexpressive
невысо́кий low; short
не́га comfort; bliss
негати́в (*photog.*) negative
негати́вный negative
негашёный (*stamps*) uncanceled
не́где adv. (+ infin.) nowhere
неги́бкий inflexible
неглубо́кий shallow
неглу́пый rather intelligent
него́дный unfit; useless
негодова́ние indignation
негодова́ть *impf.* be indignant
негодя́й, —ка scoundrel; lowlife
негостеприи́мный inhospitable
негр, —ити́нка black person
негра́мотность illiteracy
негра́мотный illiterate
негритя́нский (*person*) black
негро́мкий low; not loud
неда́вно adv. recently
недалеко́, недалёко adv. not far
недальнови́дный shortsighted
неда́ром adv. not without reason; not in vain
недви́жимость real estate
недви́жимый motionless
недви́жимый immovable
недееспосо́бный unable to function
недействи́тельный invalid; ineffective
неделика́тный indelicate; tactless
недели́мый indivisible
неде́льный weekly
неде́ля week
недержа́ние (*med.*) incontinence
недёшево adv. not cheap
недо́брое *n.* trouble
недоброжела́тельный unfriendly

недоброка́чественный of poor quality
недобросо́вестный unscrupulous; careless
недо́брый malicious; bad
недове́рие distrust; mistrust
недове́рчивый distrustful
недово́льный discontented
недово́льство discontent
недога́дливый slow to grasp
недоеда́ние malnutrition
недозво́ленный unlawful
недока́занный unproved
недо́лго adv. not long
недолгове́чный short-lived
недомога́ние indisposition
недомо́лвка innuendo
недоно́шенный born prematurely
недооце́нивать *impf.*, **недооцени́ть** *pf.* underestimate
недооце́нка underestimation
недопечённый half-baked
недопусти́мый inadmissible
недора́звитый underdeveloped
недоразуме́ние misunderstanding
недо́рого adv. inexpensively
недорого́й inexpensive
недосмо́тр oversight
недоста́ток FILL lack; shortage
недоста́точный insufficient
недоста́ча *Colloq.* shortage
недостижи́мый unattainable
недостове́рный dubious
недосто́йный unworthy
недостро́енный unfinished
недосту́пный inaccessible
недосу́г lacking time
недосчи́тываться *impf.*, **недосчи-та́ться** *pf.* be short; be missing
недосыпа́ние lack of sleep
недосяга́емый unattainable
недотро́га *m.* & *f.* touchy person
недоуме́ние bewilderment
недочёт deficit; shortcoming
не́дра *pl. Fig.* depths; heart
не́друг enemy; foe
недружелю́бный unfriendly
неду́г ailment
недурно́й not bad (looking)
неесте́ственный unnatural
нежда́нный unexpected
нежела́ние unwillingness
нежела́тельный undesirable
нежи́зненный unrealistic
нежило́й (*house*) vacant
не́жность tenderness
не́жный tender; affectionate
незаброни́рованный unreserved
незабыва́емый unforgettable

незавершённый unfinished
незави́симость independence
незави́симый independent
незадо́лго *adv.* not long (before)
незако́нный illegal; illegitimate
незако́нченный unfinished
незамени́мый irreplaceable
незаме́тный imperceptible
незаня́тый unoccupied
незара́зный noncontagious
незаря́женный unloaded
незаслу́женный undeserved
не́зачем *adv.* there is no need to
незащищённый unprotected
незва́ный uninvited
зде́шний not of this place
нездоро́вый unhealthy
нездоро́вье ill health
незло́й good-natured
незлопа́мятный forgiving
незнако́мец fill, **-мка** stranger
незнако́мый unknown
незна́ние ignorance
незначи́тельный insignificant
незре́лый immature; unripe
незы́блемый firm; unshakable
неизбе́жность inevitability
неизбе́жный inevitable
неизве́стный unknown
неи́зданный unpublished
неизлечи́мый incurable
неизме́нный unchanging
неизмери́мый immeasurable
неиме́ние: за —м (+ *G*) due to
the lack of
неиму́щий poor; indigent
неинтере́сный uninteresting
неискорени́мый ineradicable
неи́скренний insincere; false
неиску́шённый unexperienced
неисполни́мый impracticable
неиспо́льзованный unused
неиспо́рченный unspoiled
неисправи́мый incorrigible
неиспра́вность malfunctioning
неисцели́мый incurable
неисчерпа́емый inexhaustible
нейло́н nylon
нейро́н neuron
нейрохиру́рг neurosurgeon
нейтрализа́ция neutralization
нейтрализова́ть *impf. & pf.* neutralize
нейтралите́т neutrality
нейтро́н neutron
неквалифици́рованный unskilled
не́кий *pron.* a certain
не́когда[1] *adv.* once; formerly
не́когда[2] *adv.* there is no time

некомпете́нтный incompetent
неконституцио́нный unconstitutional
не́который *pron.* some
некраси́вый ugly; not nice
некрити́ческий uncritical
некроло́г obituary
некста́ти *adv.* **1.** inopportunely **2.**
not to the point
не́кто *pron.* someone; a certain
не́куда *adv.* (there is) nowhere
некульту́рный uncivilized
неку́рящий *n.* nonsmoker
нела́дное *n.* something wrong
нела́сковый unfriendly; cold
нелега́льный illegal
нелёгкий not easy; difficult
неле́пый absurd; nonsensical
неле́стный unflattering
нело́вкий awkward
нелоги́чный illogical
нельзя́ *adv.* it's prohibited, it is
impossible
нелюби́мый unloved
нелюбо́вь *f.* (к + *D*) dislike (for)
нелюди́мый unsociable
нема́ло *adv.* (+ *G*) quite a lot
(of)
немалова́жный of no small importance
неме́дленно *adv.* immediately
не́мец fill, **не́мка** German
неме́цкий German
неми́лостивый *Obs.* ungracious
неминуе́мый unavoidable
немно́гие *pron. pl.* (a) few
немно́го *adv.* a little, not much
немногочи́сленный not numerous
немно́жко *adv. Colloq.* a little
немо́й dumb; mute
немота́ muteness
не́мощь *f.* feebleness
немы́слимый unthinkable
ненави́деть *impf.* hate; abhor
ненави́стник, -ница hostile person
не́нависть *f.* hatred
ненадёжный unreliable
ненадо́лго *adv.* for a short time
неназа́ванный unnamed
неназака́зуемый not punishable
нанападе́ние nonaggression
ненаро́ком *adv.* by chance
нена́стный inclement
нена́стье foul weather
ненасы́тный insatiable
ненатура́льный unnatural
ненау́чный unscientific
не́нец fill, **не́нка** Nenets
ненорма́льный abnormal

нену́жный unnecessary
необду́манный hasty; rash
необеспе́ченный without means
необита́емый uninhabited
необосно́ванный unfounded
необразо́ванный uneducated
необрати́мый irreversible
необходи́мость necessity
необходи́мый necessary
необщи́тельный unsociable
необъекти́вный biased
необъя́вленный undeclared
необъясни́мый inexplicable
необыкнове́нный unusual
необыча́йный extraordinary
необы́чный unusual
необяза́тельный optional
неограни́ченный unlimited
неоднокра́тный repeated
неодобри́тельный disapproving
неодушевлённый inanimate
неожи́данность unexpectedness
неожи́данный unexpected
неоконча́тельный not final
неоко́нченный unfinished
нео́н, —овый neon
неопа́сный not dangerous
неопера́бельный inoperable
неопла́тный that cannot be repaid
неопла́ченный unpaid
неопра́вданный unjustified
неопределённость vagueness
неопределённый indefinite; vague
неопровержи́мый irrefutable
неопря́тность untidiness
неопубликованный unpublished
нео́пытный inexperienced
неорганизо́ванный disorganized
неоргани́ческий inorganic
неосведомлённый uninformed
неосмотри́тельный careless
неоснова́тельный unfounded
неоспори́мый indisputable
неосторо́жный careless
неосуществи́мый impracticable
неотврати́мый inevitable
неотвя́зчивый nagging; annoying
неотдели́мый inseparable
нео́ткуда adv. there is nowhere
неотло́жка ambulance service
неотло́жный urgent
неотрази́мый irresistible
неотсту́пный persistent
неотчётливый indistinct
неотъе́млемый inalienable
неофициа́льный unofficial
неохо́та Colloq. reluctance
неохо́тно adv. reluctantly
неоцени́мый invaluable

неочи́щенный unrefined; crude
неощути́мый imperceptible
непарти́йный non-party
непереводи́мый untranslatable
неперспекти́вный unpromising
неплатёж nonpayment
неплатёжеспосо́бный insolvent
неплате́льщик, -щица person who has not paid; defaulter
непло́хо adv. not badly; rather well
неплохо́й not a bad; quite good
непобеди́мый invincible
непого́да bad weather
непогреши́мый infallible
неподалёку adv. not far (away)
неподви́жный immobile
неподгото́вленный unprepared
неподде́льный genuine
неподку́пный incorruptible
неподоба́ющий improper
неподража́емый inimitable
неподходя́щий unsuitable
неподчине́ние insubordination
непозволи́тельный impermissible
непоколеби́мый unshakable
непоко́рный recalcitrant; unruly
неполноце́нность inferiority
неполноце́нный inferior
непо́лный not full; incomplete
непоня́тный incomprehensible
непоправи́мый irreparable
непоро́чность chastity; purity
непо́ртящийся nonperishable
непоря́док FILL disorder
непоря́дочный dishonorable
непосле́довательный inconsistent
непослу́шный disobedient
непосре́дственность spontaneity
непосре́дственный direct
непостижи́мый incomprehensible
непостоя́нство inconstancy
непотопля́емый unsinkable
непотре́бный Obs. indecent
непохо́жий (на + A) unlike
непочти́тельность disrespect
непра́вда untruth
неправдоподо́бный improbable
непра́вильный incorrect; wrong
неправомо́чный not legally qualified
непракти́чный impractical
непревзойдённый unsurpassed
непредви́денный unforeseen
непреднаме́ренный unintentional
непредска́зуемый unpredictable
непредусмотри́тельный improvident; short-sighted
непреме́нно adv. without fail

непременный indispensable
непреодолимый insurmountable
непрерывный continuous
непрестанный incessant; continual
непривлекательный unattractive
непривычный unaccustomed
непригодность uselessness
непригодный unfit; useless
неприемлемый unacceptable
непризнанный unrecognized
неприкаянный Colloq. aimless
неприкосновенный inviolable
неприкрытый ajar; uncovered
неприличный indecent
непримиримый irreconcilable
непринуждённость ease; abandon
непринуждённый unconstrained; spontaneous
неприспособленный maladjusted
непристойный obscene
неприступный inaccessible
непритворный unfeigned; genuine
неприхотливый unpretentious
неприязнь f. hostility; enmity
приятель, —ница enemy
неприятность unpleasantness; nuisance, annoyance, trouble
неприятный unpleasant
непродолжительный short
непродуктивный unproductive
непродуманный not thought out
непроезжий impassable
непроизводительный unproductive
непроизвольный involuntary
непроизносимый unpronounceable
непроницаемый impenetrable
непросвещённый unenlightened
непростительный unforgivable
непроходимый impassable
непрочный not durable; flimsy
непьющий n. nondrinker
нерабочий nonworking
неравенство inequality
неравнодушный not indifferent
неравномерный uneven
неравноправие lack of equal rights
неравный unequal
неразбериха Colloq. confusion
неразборчивый 1. illegible 2. undiscriminating
неразведанный unexplored
неразвитый undeveloped
неразговорчивый uncommunicative
неразделимый indivisible
неразрешённый 1. unsolved 2. forbidden
неразрешимый insoluble

неразумный unwise; unreasonable
нерастворимый insoluble
нерасторопный sluggish; inert
нерасчётливый 1. wasteful; extravagant 2. improvident
нерациональный inefficient
нерв nerve; **—ный** nervous
нервничать impf. be nervous
нервозность nervousness
нервозный nervous; high-strung
нереальный unreal; unrealistic
нередкий not uncommon
нерентабельный unprofitable
нерешённый unresolved
нерешительность indecisiveness
нерешительный indecisive; irresolute
нержавеющий rust-resistant
неровный uneven
нерушимый inviolable
неряшливость sloppiness
неряшливый sloppy; slovenly
несведущий ignorant
несвежий stale
несвоевременный ill-timed
несговорчивый uncooperative
несгораемый fireproof
несдержанный unrestrained
несерьёзный not serious
несессер toilet case
нескладный awkward; incoherent
несклоняемый indeclinable
несколько several, a few; adv. somewhat
нескончаемый indeterminable
нескромный immodest
нескрываемый unconcealed
неслыханный unheard-of
неслышный inaudible
несмотря на prep. (+ A) in spite of
несносный unbearable
несоблюдение non-observance
несовершеннолетний underage; n. minor
несовершённый 1. imperfect; incomplete 2. imperfective
несовершенство imperfection
несовместимый incompatible
несогласие disagreement
несогласный disagreeing
несогласованный uncoordinated
несознательный unconscious
несоизмеримый incommensurable
несокрушимый indestructible
несомненный undoubted
несообразительный dense; dull
несообразный incongruous
несоответствие disparity

несоразме́рно adv. (c + I) disproportionately (to)

несоразме́рный disproportionate

несостоя́тельный of modest means; insolvent

неспе́лый unripe

неспе́шный unhurried

неспоко́йный restless

неспосо́бный incapable

несправедли́вость injustice

несправедли́вый unjust, unfair

нестерпи́мый unbearable

нести́[1] *impf.*, **по-** *pf.* carry; bring; suffer; **—сь** race, rush, be heard, float

нести́(сь)[2] *impf.*, **с-** *pf.* lay (eggs)

несто́ящий *Colloq.* worthless

несудохо́дный unnavigable

несхо́дство difference; disparity

несчастли́вый unhappy; unlucky

несча́стный unhappy; unfortunate; ~ **слу́чай** accident

несча́стье misfortune; disaster; **к несча́стью** unfortunately

несъедо́бный inedible

нет *particle.* no; not

нетакти́чный tactless

нетвёрдый unsteady; unsure

нетерпели́вый impatient

нетерпе́ние impatience

нетерпи́мый intolerable; intolerant

неторопли́вый leisurely

нето́чный inexact; inaccurate

нетре́бовательный undemanding

нетре́звый intoxicated; drunk

нетро́нутый untouched

нетрудоспосо́бный disabled; incapacitated

не́тто *indecl. adj., adv.* net

неубеди́тельный unconvincing

неу́бранный not cleaned; not straightened; not put away

неуваже́ние disrespect

неуважи́тельный disrespectful

неуве́ренный uncertain

неуда́ча failure

неуда́чник, -ница unlucky person

неуда́чный unsuccessful

неудо́бный uncomfortable; inconvenient

неудо́бство inconvenience

неудовлетворе́ние dissatisfaction

неудовлетворённый dissatisfied

неудово́льствие displeasure

неуже́ли *particle.* indeed?; really?

неужи́вчивый hard to get along

неузнава́емый unrecognizable

неукло́нный steady; unwavering

неуклю́жий awkward; clumsy

неукосни́тельный unfailing

неуме́лый clumsy; inept

неуме́ние inability

неуме́ренность immoderation

неуме́стный 1. inappropriate; out of place **2.** irrelevant

неумоли́мый implacable

неумы́шленный unintentional

неупла́та nonpayment

неупла́ченный unpaid

неупотребля́емый not in use

неуравнове́шенный unbalanced

неурегули́рованный unsettled

неурожа́й poor harvest

неусто́йка (*law*) forfeit

неусто́йчивый unsteady; unstable

неустро́енный unsettled

неуступчи́вый uncompromising

неутеши́тельный unencouraging

неутоли́мый unquenchable

неутоми́мый indefatigable

неу́ч ignoramus

неучти́вый discourteous

неуязви́мый invulnerable

нефри́т nephritis

нефтеперего́нный заво́д oil refinery

нефтепрово́д oil pipeline

нефть *f.* petroleum; oil

нефтяно́й *attrib.* oil; petroleum

нехва́тка *Colloq.* shortage

нехи́трый *Colloq.* ingenuous

неходово́й 1. not in working order **2.** not selling well

нехоро́ший bad

нехорошо́ *adv.* (it is) bad

нехотя *adv.* unwillingly

нецензу́рный unprintable

неча́янный unexpected; accidental

не́чего *pron.* (+ I) it is no good; (there is) nothing

нечелове́ческий inhuman

нече́стный dishonest; unfair

нечётный (*of a number*) odd

нечистопло́тный dirty; sloppy

нечи́стый unclean; impure

не́чисть *f.* **1.** evil spirits **2.** scum

нечленоразде́льный inarticulate

не́что *pron.* something

нечёткий insensitive

нешу́точный not to be taken lightly

неэконо́мный uneconomical

неэтили́рованный unleaded

неэффекти́вный inefficient; ineffective

нея́вка failure to appear

нея́ркий dim; faint

нея́сный vague; unclear

ни *particle.* not a; (*with adverbs*) -ever; ~ ... ~ ... neither ... nor ...

ни́ва field; cornfield

нивели́р (*instrument*) level

нигде́ *adv.* nowhere

нидерла́ндец FILL., **-дка** a Dutch person

Нидерла́нды *pl.* the Netherlands

ни́же *adv.* lower; below, beneath

нижеподписа́вшийся the undersigned

нижесле́дующий the following

ни́жний lower; under

низ bottom

низверга́ть *impf.*, **низве́ргнуть** *pf.* overthrow

низи́на low-lying area; hollow

ни́зкий low; base, mean

низкоопла́чиваемый low-paid

низкопро́бный low-grade

низкоро́слый undersized

низкосо́ртный low-quality

ни́зменность 1. lowland **2.** baseness

низово́й 1. low; close to the ground **2.** at the local level

ни́зость *f.* lowness; baseness

ника́к *adv.* in no way

никако́й not any; no ... whatever

ни́кель *m.* nickel

нике́м *pron. I of* никто́

никогда́ *adv.* never

никого́ *pron. G, A of* никто́

никому́ *pron. D of* никто́

никоти́н, —овый nicotine

никто́ *pron.* nobody, no one

никуда́ *adv.* (*dir.*) nowhere

никчёмный *Colloq.* useless

нима́ло *adv.* not in the least

ни́мб nimbus, halo

ни́мфа nymph

ниотку́да *adv.* from nowhere

ниско́лько *adv.* not at all

ни́тка, ни́точка thread

нитроглицери́н nitroglycerine

нить *f.* thread; filament

ничего́ *adv.* never mind

ничегонеде́ланье idleness

ниче́й *pron.* nobody's, no one's

ниче́м *pron. I of* ничто́

ничему́ *pron. D of* ничто́

ничко́м *adv.* face downwards

ничто́ *pron.* nothing

ничто́жество nonentity

ничто́жный insignificant; paltry

ничу́ть *adv.* not in the least

ничья́ draw, drawn game

ни́ша niche; recess

ни́щенка beggarwoman

ни́щенский beggarly

нищета́ poverty

ни́щий indigent; poor; *n.* beggar

но *conj.* but

Но́вая Зела́ндия New Zealand

нове́йший newest, latest

нове́лла novella; short story

новизна́ novelty

нови́нка something new

новичо́к FILL novice

новобра́нец FILL new recruit

новобра́чные *pl.* newlyweds

нововведе́ние innovation

нового́дний New Year's

новозаве́тный *attrib.* New Testament

новока́ин novocaine

новолу́ние new moon

новорождённый newborn

новосёл new settler

новосе́лье housewarming

но́вость *f.* **1.** news **2.** novelty

но́вшество innovation; novelty

но́вый new

новь *f.* virgin soil

нога́ foot; leg

но́готь FILL *m.* fingernail; toenail

нож knife; —**evó** *attrib.* knife

но́жик small knife

но́жка (*of furniture*) leg; stem

но́жницы *pl.* scissors

но́жны *pl.* scabbard; sheath

ноздря́ nostril

нолево́й zero

ноль *m.* zero; nil; nought

номенклату́ра 1. nomenclature **2.** top administrative positions

но́мер number; hotel room; size

номерно́й знак license plate

номеро́к FILL ticket; receipt

номина́льный nominal

нора́ hole; den, burrow

Норве́гия Norway

норве́жец FILL, **-жка** Norwegian

норве́жский Norwegian

но́рка mink

но́рма norm, standard; rate

нормализа́ция normalization

норма́льно *Colloq.* all right; O.K.

норма́льный normal; standard

нормати́в standard

норми́рова́ть *impf. & pf.* standardize

нра́в *Colloq.* character; temperament

нос *nose;* —**ово́й** *attrib.* nose, nasal

носи́к 1. *dim. of* нос **2.** spout

носи́лки *pl.* stretcher

носи́льщик porter

носи́тель, —ница bearer; carrier; speaker (of a certain language)
носи́ть *indet.*, **нести́** *det.* **1.** carry, bear **2.** wear; **—ся 3.** rush about **4.** be carried *or* worn **5.** (с + *I*) fuss over
носово́й плато́к handkerchief
носо́к FILL sock
носоро́г rhinoceros
ностальги́я nostalgia
но́та note; **но́ты** *pl.* sheet music
нота́риус notary; notary public
ночева́ть *impf.*, **пере—** *pf.* spend the night
ночёвка spending the night
ночле́г lodging for the night
ночле́жка *Colloq.* flophouse
ночни́к night light
ночно́й attrib. night
ночь *f.* night
но́чью *adv.* at night
но́ша load; burden
но́ющий gnawing; nagging
ноя́брь *m.*, **—ский** November
нрав disposition; temper
нра́виться *impf.*, **по—** *pf.* (+ *D*) please
нра́вственность morality, morals
нра́вственный moral

нра́вы *pl.* customs; ways
ну *interj.* well
ну́дный tedious; tiresome
нужда́ need
нужда́ться *impf.* (в + *P*) need; be in need (of)
нужда́ющийся indigent; needy
ну́жно *adv. pred.* (it is) necessary; one must; one should
ну́жный necessary
нулево́й attrib. zero
нуль *m.* nought; zero
нумера́ция numbering
нумерова́ть *impf.*, **про—, за—** *pf.* number
ны́не *adv.* now, at present
ны́нешний present; today's
ныря́льщик diver
ныря́ть *impf.*, **нырну́ть** *pf.* dive
ны́тик *Colloq.* whiner
ныть *impf.* ache; whine
нытьё whining; complaining
н.э. (*abbr. of* на́шей э́ры) A.D.
нюа́нс nuance
нюх sense of smell
ню́хать *impf.*, **по—** *pf.* smell; sniff
ня́нчить *impf.* nurse
ня́нька *Colloq.* nurse
ня́ня nurse, nursemaid

O

о, об, о́бо *prep.* **1.** (+ *P*) of, about **2.** (+ *A*) against
оа́зис oasis
о́ба *m. & neut.* **о́бе** *f.* both
обанкро́титься *pf.* go bankrupt
обая́ние attraction; charm
обая́тельный charming
обва́л fall, collapse, landslide
обва́ливаться *impf.*, **обвали́ться** *pf.* fall; collapse
обва́ривать *impf.*, **обвари́ть** *pf.* scald; pour boiling water over
обве́тренный weather-beaten
обветша́лый decrepit; decayed
обвине́ние accusation
обвини́тель prosecutor
обвини́тельный accusatory
обвиня́емый *n.* defendant; accused person
обвиня́ть *impf.*, **-ни́ть** *pf.* (в + *P*) accuse (of)
обворожи́тельный enchanting
обгоня́ть *impf.*, **обогна́ть** *pf.* pass; surpass; excel
обгора́ть *impf.*, **-ре́ть** *pf.* get a (bad) sunburn
обгоре́лый charred; burned

обде́лывать *impf.*, **обде́лать** *pf.* **1.** finish **2.** arrange; manage; handle
обделя́ть *impf.*, **-ли́ть** *pf.* cheat (someone) out of his share
обду́манный well thought out
обду́мывать *impf.*, **обду́мать** *pf.* consider carefully
о́бе *see* о́ба
обе́д dinner; midday meal
обе́дать *impf.*, **по—** *pf.* dine; have dinner; have lunch
обе́денный attrib. dinner; lunch
обезбо́ливание anesthetization
обезбо́ливающее *n.* painkiller
обездо́ленный destitute; indigent
обеззара́живание disinfection
обезобра́живание disfigurement
обезопа́сить *pf.* secure against
обезору́живать *impf.*, **обезору́жить** *pf.* disarm
обезья́на monkey; ape
оберега́ть *impf.*, **обере́чь** *pf* guard against; protect
обёртка wrapper; bookcover
обёрточная бума́га wrapping paper

обескура́женность discouragement

обескура́живать *impf.*, обескура́жить *pf.* discourage

обеспе́ченный well-to-do

обеспе́чивать *impf.*, обеспе́чить *pf.* ensure; supply with; provide for

обеспоко́ить *pf.* worry; disturb

обесси́леть *pf.* grow weak

обесси́ливать *impf.*, обесси́лить *pf.* weaken

обеща́ние promise

обеща́ть *impf. & pf.* promise

обжа́лование (*law*) appeal

обжига́ть *impf.*, обже́чь *pf.* burn; bake

обжо́рство gluttony

обзо́р survey

оби́вка upholstering; upholstery

оби́да offense; insult

оби́дчивый touchy; sensitive

оби́дчик, -чица offender

обижа́ть *impf.*, оби́деть *pf.* offend

оби́женный offended

оби́лие abundance

оби́льный abundant, plentiful

обита́тель, -ница inhabitant

обита́ть *impf.* inhabit

оби́тый upholstered

обихо́д (general) use

обихо́дный everyday

обкла́дывать *impf.*, обложи́ть *pf.* surround; face; assess

обкра́дывать *impf.*, обокра́сть *pf.* rob

обла́ва police raid *or* roundup

облада́ть *impf.* (+ *I*) possess

о́блако, облачко cloud.

о́бласть *f.* region; district

о́блачный cloudy

облегча́ть *impf.*, облегчи́ть *pf.* lighten; relieve; facilitate

облегче́ние relief

облегчённо *adv.* with relief

обледене́ние icing up

обледене́ть *pf.* become coated with ice

облива́ть *impf.*, обли́ть *pf.* to pour; spill; soil

облига́ция (*econ.*) bond

о́блик appearance; look

облицо́вка facing; revetment

обличи́тельный exposing

обложе́ние taxation; levying

обложи́ть *pf.* face; cover

обло́жка cover

обло́мок FILL fragment

облупи́ть *pf. of* лупи́ть

облуче́ние irradiation

обма́н fraud; deception

обма́нчивый deceptive

обма́нщик, -щица liar; cheat

обма́нывать *impf.*, обману́ть *pf.* deceive; cheat

обме́н exchange

обме́нивать *impf.*, обмени́ть *pf.* exchange

обмо́лвка slip of the tongue

обморо́женный frostbitten

о́бморок faint; fainting spell

обмундирова́ть *pf.* outfit (with a uniform)

обмяка́ть *impf.*, обмя́кнуть *pf. Colloq.* become soft *or* flabby

обнадёживать *impf.*, обнадёжить *pf.* reassure; give hope

обнажа́ть *impf.*, -жи́ть *pf.* bare; uncover; reveal

обнажённый naked; nude; bare

обнаро́довать *impf. & pf.* promulgate

обнару́живать *impf.*, обнару́жить *pf.* discover; reveal

обнима́ть *impf.*, обня́ть *pf.* embrace

обни́мка *Colloq.*: в обни́мку in each other's embrace

обнища́лый impoverished

обнища́ть *pf.* become impoverished

обновле́ние renovation

обновля́ть *impf.*, -ви́ть *pf.* renovate; renew

обня́ть *pf. of* обнима́ть

о́бо *see* о

обобща́ть *impf.*, -щи́ть *pf.* generalize

обобще́ние generalization

обогаща́ть *impf.*, -ти́ть *pf.* enrich

обогаще́ние enrichment

обоготворе́ние deification

обогрева́тель heater

обогрева́ть *impf.*, обогре́ть *pf.* warm, heat

ободре́ние encouragement

ободря́ть *impf.*, -ри́ть *pf.* encourage

обожа́ть *impf.* admire; worship

обожествля́ть *impf.*, -ви́ть *pf.* deify

обознача́ть *impf.*, обозна́чить *pf.* mean; designate; mark

обозначе́ние designation

обозре́ние review; survey

обо́и *pl.* wallpaper

обо́йма cartridge clip

обойти́(сь) *pf. of* обходи́ть(ся)

оболо́чка shell; casing; membrane

обольсти́тельный seductive

обольща́ть *impf.*, -сти́ть *pf.* seduce

обольще́ние seduction

обоня́ние sense of smell

обо́рванный torn; ragged

оборва́ть(ся) *pf. of* обрыва́ть(ся)

обо́рка ruffle; flounce; frill

оборо́на defense

оборони́тельный defensive

оборо́нный *attrib.* defense

обороня́ть *impf.*, -ни́ть *pf.* defend

оборо́т revolution; turn

оборо́тный 1. (*econ.*) circulating; working 2. reverse

обору́дование equipment

обору́довать *impf. & pf.* equip

обоснова́ние basis

обосно́ванный well-founded

обосно́вывать *impf.*, обоснова́ть *pf.* base; ground; —ся settle down

обосо́бленный solitary; isolated

обострённый tense; sharp

обостря́ть *impf.*, -ри́ть *pf.* sharpen; aggravate; strain

обо́чина curb; shoulder

обою́дный mutual

обрабо́тка processing; cultivation

обра́довать *pf. of* ра́довать

о́браз¹ form, image; manner

о́браз² (*pl.* образа́) icon

образе́ц FILL model; specimen

о́бразный vivid; graphic

образова́ние education; formation

образо́ванный educated

образо́вывать *impf.*, образова́ть *pf.* form; —ся turn out, form

образчик specimen; sample

обра́тно *adv.* back(wards); conversely

обра́тный reverse; opposite; return

обраща́ть *impf.*, -ти́ть *pf.* turn; direct; —ся 1. (к + *D*) appeal; turn to 2. (в + *A*) turn into.

обраще́ние 1. appeal; address 2. (c + *I*) treatment; use (of)

обре́зание circumcision

обре́зание trimming; cutting

обреза́ть *impf.*, обреза́ть *pf.* cut (off), clip, pare

обре́зок FILL *usu. pl.* scrap

обремени́тельный burdensome

обременя́ть *impf.*, -ни́ть *pf.* burden

обречённый doomed

обруба́ть *impf.*, -би́ть *pf.* chop off

обру́бок FILL stump

о́бруч hoop

обруча́льный *attrib.* engagement

обруче́ние engagement

обры́в precipice

обрыва́ть(ся) *impf.*, оборва́ть(ся) *pf.* break (off); snap

обры́вок FILL scrap; fragment

обры́згивать *impf.*, обры́згать *pf.* splash; sprinkle

обря́д rite, ritual, ceremony; —ный, —овый ritual

обсле́довать *impf. & pf.* inspect

обслу́живание service

обслу́живать *impf.*, обслужи́ть *pf.* attend; serve; service

обставля́ть *impf.*, обста́вить *pf.* surround; furnish; arrange

обстано́вка 1. furniture 2. (*theat.*) set 3. situation

обстоя́тельный detailed; thorough

обстоя́тельство circumstance

обстре́л shelling; firing; fire

обстре́лянный battle-hardened

обстру́кция obstruction

обступа́ть *impf.*, -пи́ть *pf.* surround

обсужда́ть *impf.*, обсуди́ть *pf.* discuss

обсужде́ние discussion

обсчи́тываться *impf.*, обсчита́ться *pf.* miscount; miscalculate

обтека́емый streamlined

обтира́ние rubdown

обува́ть(ся) *impf.*, обу́ть(ся) *pf.* put on (one's) shoes

обувно́й *attrib.* shoe

о́бувь *f.* footwear; shoes

обу́за burden; chore

обусло́вливать *impf.*, обусло́вить *pf.* 1. stipulate 2. cause

обуча́ть *impf.*, -чи́ть *pf.* instruct; teach; —ся (+ *D*) learn

обуче́ние teaching; training

обходи́тельный polite; courteous

обходи́ть *impf.*, обойти́ *pf.* go around; pass (over); avoid; —ся manage; make do; cost; (c + *I*) treat

обходно́й roundabout

обши́вка 1. trimming; bordering 2. panelling; plating

обши́рный vast, extensive

обшла́г cuff

обща́ться *impf.* associate (with)

общедосту́пный generally accessible *or* available

общежи́тие dormitory; hostel

общеизве́стный generally known

обще́ние intercourse; contact

общеобразова́тельный (*school or subject*) general; not specialized

общепри́нятый generally accepted
обще́ственность the public
обще́ственный public; social
о́бщество society; company
о́бщий common; general
общи́тельный sociable; outgoing
о́бщность commonality
объеде́ние overeating
объедине́ние unification
объединённый united; Организа́ция Объединённых На́ций United Nations
объединя́ть *impf.*, **-ни́ть** *pf.* unite
объе́кт object; objective
объекти́в lens
объекти́вность objectivity
объекти́вный objective
объём scope; volume
объёмный by volume
объявле́ние declaration; announcement; advertisement
объявля́ть *impf.*, **-ви́ть** *pf.* declare; announce
объясне́ние explanation
объясни́мый explainable
объясня́ть *impf.*, **-ни́ть** *pf.* explain
объя́тие embrace
обыва́тель, —ница philistine
обыва́тельский narrow(-minded)
обыкнове́нный usual; ordinary
о́быск search
обы́скивать *impf.*, **обыска́ть** *pf.* search
обы́чай custom
обы́чный usual; ordinary
обя́занность duty
обя́занный obliged (to); indebted to
обяза́тельно *adv.* without fail
обяза́тельный obligatory
обя́зывать *impf.*, **обяза́ть** *pf.* oblige; obligate; bind
ова́л oval; **—ьный** oval
ова́ция ovation
ове́с FILL oats
ове́чка *dim.* of овца́
ОВИ́Р (abbr. of отде́л виз и регистра́ции) visa and registration department; OVIR
овладева́ть *impf.*, **овладе́ть** *pf.* (+ I) seize; capture; master
о́вощ vegetable
овощно́й *attrib.* vegetable
овра́г ravine
овся́ный *attrib.* oat
овуля́ция ovulation
овца́ sheep; ewe
овча́рка sheepdog; неме́цкая ~ German shepherd
овчи́на sheepskin

ога́рок FILL candle end
оглавле́ние table of contents
огло́хнуть *pf.* of гло́хнуть
оглуша́ть *impf.*, **-ши́ть** *pf.* deafen; stun
оглуши́тельный deafening
огля́дываться *impf.*, **огляде́ться, огляну́ться** *pf.* look around; look back
огнемёт flame thrower
о́гненный fiery
огнеопа́сный inflammable
огнесто́йкий fireproof
огнестре́льное ору́жие firearms
огнетуши́тель fire extinguisher
огнеупо́рный fire-resistant
ого́нёк FILL (point of) light; zest
ого́нь *m.* FILL fire; light
огоро́д vegetable garden
огорче́ние distress; grief
огорчи́тельный distressing
огра́бить *pf.* of гра́бить
ограбле́ние robbery
огра́да fence; wall
огражда́ть *impf.*, **огради́ть** *pf.* guard; protect against
ограниче́ние limitation; restriction
ограни́чивать *impf.*, **ограни́чить** *pf.* limit; restrict
ограничи́тельный restrictive
огро́мный enormous
огрубе́ть *pf.* of грубе́ть
огры́зок FILL bit; end; stub
огуре́ц FILL cucumber
ода́лживать *impf.*, **одолжи́ть** *pf.* lend
одарённый gifted
одева́ть *impf.*, **оде́ть** *pf.* dress; **—ся** get dressed
оде́жда clothes
одеколо́н eau de Cologne
одержи́мый obsessed
одея́ло blanket
оди́н, одна́, одно́ one; *adj.* a; a certain; alone
одина́ковый identical; equal
оди́ннадцатый eleventh
оди́ннадцать eleven
одино́кий lonely; solitary
одино́чество solitude; loneliness
одино́чка *m. & f.* lone person
одича́лый wild
одна́жды *adv.* once
одна́ко *conj.* however; yet
однобо́кий lopsided; one-sided
однобо́ртный single-breasted
одновреме́нно *adv.* simultaneously
одного́дичный *attrib.* one-year

однозна́чный synonymous; one-digit

одноимённый of the same name

однокла́ссник, -ница classmate

однокле́точный one-celled

однокомнатный *attrib.* one-room

однокра́тный single

однокурсник, -ница (*college*) classmate

одноле́тний *attrib.* one-year

одноме́стный *attrib.* single-seat

однообра́зный monotonous

одноро́дный homogeneous; similar; uniform

односторо́нний one-sided

однофами́лец FILL, **-льца** person with the same last name

одноцве́тный monochrome

одноэта́жный one-story

одобре́ние approval

одобри́тельный approving

одобря́ть *impf.*, **одо́брить** *pf.* approve (of)

одолева́ть *impf.*, **одоле́ть** *pf.* overcome; master

одолже́ние favor

одряхле́вший decrepit; enfeebled

одува́нчик dandelion

одурма́нить *pf. of* дурма́нить.

о́дурь *f. Colloq.* trance; stupor

одутлова́тый puffy

одушевлённый animated

одушевля́ть *impf.*, **-ви́ть** *pf.* animate

оды́шка shortness of breath

ожере́лье necklace

ожесточе́ние bitterness

ожесточённый embittered; fierce

ожива́ть *impf.*, **ожи́ть** *pf.* revive

оживле́ние animation

оживлённый animated; lively

ожида́ние expectation

ожида́ть *impf.* (+ *G*) expect; wait for

ожире́ние obesity

ожо́г burn

озабо́ченность preoccupation

озабо́ченный preoccupied

озвере́лый crazed

оздорови́тельный sanitary; *attrib.* health

озеленя́ть *impf.*, **-ни́ть** *pf.* plant trees

о́зеро lake

о́зимь *f.* winter crops

озлобле́ние animosity

ознакомля́ться *impf.*, **ознако́миться** *pf.* (с + *I*) familiarize oneself (with)

означа́ть *impf.* mean; signify

озно́б chill; shivering

озо́н, —овый ozone

озорно́й mischievous

озорство́ mischief

ока́зия opportunity

ока́зывать *impf.*, **оказа́ть** *pf.* render; show; **—ся** (+ *I*) prove; turn out (to be)

окамене́лый petrified

окамене́ть *pf. of* камене́ть.

ока́нчивать(ся) *impf.*, **око́нчить(ся)** *pf.* finish; end

ока́янный damned; cursed

океа́н ocean; **—ский** oceanic

о́кисел FILL oxide

окисле́ние oxidation

о́кись *f.* oxide

окку́льтный occult

оккупа́ция military occupation

оккупи́ровать *impf. & pf.* occupy

окла́д salary; wages

о́клик call; challenge

окно́ window

око́вы *pl.* shackles; fetters

о́коло *prep.* (+ *G*) by, near, around; about, nearly

око́льный roundabout

оконча́ние termination; end

оконча́тельный final; definitive

око́нчить *pf. of* ока́нчивать

око́п, —ный trench

око́рок ham; leg

окочене́лый numb

окра́ина outskirts

окра́ска painting; dyeing; coloration

окре́пнуть *pf.* get stronger

окрести́ть *pf. of* крести́ть.

окре́стность environs

окре́стный neighboring

о́крик shout; cry

окру́га *Colloq.* neighborhood

окру́глый round; rounded

окружа́ть *impf.*, **-жи́ть** *pf.* surround

окружа́ющий surrounding

окруже́ние encirclement

окружно́й *attrib.* district

окру́жность circumference

октя́брь, —ский October

окули́ст oculist

окуна́ть(ся) *impf.*, **-ну́ть(ся)** *pf.* (в + *A*) dip

о́кунь *m.* (*fish*) perch

оку́рок FILL cigarette butt

ола́дья fritter; pancake

оледене́лый frozen

оле́ний *attrib.* deer

оле́нь *m.* deer; reindeer

оли́ва olive (tree)

оли́вковый *attrib.* olive

олимпиа́да Olympiad; Olympics

олимпи́йский Olympic

оли́фа drying oil

олицетворе́ние personification

олицетворя́ть *impf.,* -ри́ть *pf.* personify

о́лово tin; оловя́нный *attrib.* tin

ом ohm

ома́р lobster

омерзе́ние loathing

омерзи́тельный loathsome

омертве́лый dead

омле́т omelet

омове́ние ablution

омоложе́ние rejuvenation

омо́ним homonym

о́мут whirlpool; maelstrom

он *pron.* he

она́ *pron.* she

онда́тра muskrat

онеме́лый numb; stiff

онеме́ть *pf.* become numb

они́ *pron.* they

оно́ *pron.* it

опа́здывать *impf.,* опозда́ть *pf.* be late

опаса́ться *impf.* (+ *G*) fear; avoid

опасе́ние fear, apprehension

опа́сность danger

опа́сный dangerous

опе́ка guardianship; trusteeship

опеку́н, —ша guardian

опеку́нство guardianship

о́пера opera

операти́вный operative; surgical

опера́тор operator

операцио́нная *n.* operating room

операцио́нный (*med.*) operating

опера́ция operation

опере́ние plumage

опере́тта operetta

опере́ться *pf. of* опира́ться

опери́ровать *impf. & pf.* operate

о́перный operatic, opera

опеча́ленный sad; sorrowful

опеча́тка misprint

опира́ться *impf.,* опере́ться *pf.* lean on; be based on

описа́ние description

опи́сывать *impf.,* описа́ть *pf.* describe

о́пись *f.* list; inventory

о́пиум, —ный opium

опла́кивать *impf.,* опла́кать *pf.* mourn

опла́та payment

опла́чивать *impf.,* оплати́ть *pf.* pay

оплодотворя́ть *impf.,* -ри́ть *pf.* impregnate; fertilize

оповеще́ние notification

опозда́ние delay; lateness

опозда́ть *pf. of* опа́здывать

опознава́тельный identifying; *attrib.* identification

опозна́ние identification

опо́мниться *pf.* come to one's senses

опо́ра support

опо́рный supporting

опошля́ть *impf.,* опо́шлить *pf.* vulgarize; debase

оппози́ция opposition

оппоне́нт, —ка opponent

оппони́ровать *impf.* oppose

оппортуни́ст, —ка opportunist

опра́ва setting; mounting

оправда́ние justification; excuse

опра́вдывать *impf.,* оправда́ть *pf.* justify; acquit; vindicate

определе́ние definition

определённый definite; certain

определя́ть *impf.,* -ли́ть *pf.* define; determine

опроверга́ть *impf.,* опрове́ргнуть *pf.* refute

опроверже́ние refutation

опроки́дывать(ся) *impf.,* опроки́нуть(ся) *pf.* overturn; topple

опроме́тчивый rash; imprudent

опро́с inquest; interrogation; poll

опро́сный *attrib.* questionnaire

опти́ка optics

оптима́льный optimal

оптими́зм optimism

оптими́ст, —ка optimist

опти́ческий optic(al)

опто́вый wholesale

опубликова́ть *pf. of* публикова́ть

опуска́ть *impf.,* -сти́ть *pf.* lower; omit; —ся lower oneself; sink

опусте́лый deserted

опусте́ть *pf. of* пусте́ть.

опустоша́ть *impf.,* -ши́ть *pf.* devastate

опустоше́ние devastation

опустоши́тельный devastating

опуха́ть *impf.,* опу́хнуть *pf.* swell

о́пухоль *f.* swelling; tumor

опу́шка 1. edge of the forest 2. (*fur*) trimming

о́пыт experiment; experience

о́пытный 1. experienced 2. experimental

опьяне́ние intoxication

опьяне́ть *pf. of* пьяне́ть

опя́ть *adv.* again

ора́нжевый orange
оранжере́я hothouse; greenhouse
ора́тор orator; speaker
ора́торский oratorical
ора́ть *impf.* yell; scream
орби́та orbit
о́рган organ
орга́н *(mus.)* organ
организа́тор organizer
организа́ция organization
органи́зм organism
организо́ванный (well-)organized
организова́ть *impf.* & *pf.* organize
органи́ст, —ка organist
органи́ческий organic
о́ргия orgy
о́рден order, decoration
орёл FILL eagle; ~ и́ли ре́шка heads or tails
орео́л halo; aureole; aura
оре́х, —овый nut
оре́шник hazel tree
оригина́л original; eccentric
оригина́льный original
ориента́льный oriental
ориенти́р reference point; landmark
ориентиро́вка orientation
орке́стр orchestra
орла́н sea eagle; bald eagle
орли́ный *attrib.* eagle
орна́мент ornament
ороше́ние irrigation
ортодокса́льный orthodox
ортодо́ксия orthodoxy
ортопе́д orthopedist
ору́дие instrument; tool
оруже́йный *attrib.* gun; arms
ору́жие weapon
орфогра́фия orthography
орхиде́я orchid
оса́ wasp
оса́да siege
оса́дный *attrib.* siege
оса́док FILL sediment
оса́нка bearing; carriage
осва́ивать *impf.*, осво́ить *pf.* master, become familiar; —ся familiarize oneself
осведоми́тель informant
осведомле́ние notification
осведомлённый informed; knowledgeable
освежа́ющий refreshing
освежи́тельный refreshing
освеща́ть *impf.*, -ти́ть *pf.* illuminate, elucidate
освеще́ние light, lighting
освиде́тельствовать *pf.* examine; inspect.

освободи́тель, —ница liberator
освобожда́ть *impf.*, освободи́ть *pf.* liberate; release; exempt
освобожде́ние liberation; release
освое́ние mastering
освои́ть(ся) *pf. of* осва́ивать(ся)
освяще́ние sanctification; consecration
освящённый sanctified; honored
оседа́ть *impf.*, осе́сть *pf.* settle
осёл FILL donkey; ass
осе́нний *attrib.* autumn
о́сень *f.* autumn, fall
о́сенью *adv.* in the fall
осётр, осетри́на sturgeon
осе́чка misfire
оси́пнуть *pf.* become hoarse
осироте́ть *pf.* be orphaned
оскверне́ние desecration
оскверня́ть *impf.*, -ни́ть *pf.* defile; profane
оско́лок FILL splinter
оско́лочный *(mil.)* fragmentation
оскорби́тельный insulting; offensive
оскорбле́ние insult; offense
оскорбля́ть *impf.*, -би́ть *pf.* insult; offend
ослабева́ть *impf.*, ослабе́ть *pf.* weaken
ослабле́ние weakening
ослепи́тельный blinding; dazzling
осле́пнуть *pf. of* сле́пнуть
осложне́ние complication
осложня́ть *impf.*, -ни́ть *pf.* complicate
ослы́шаться *pf.* mishear
осма́тривать *impf.*, осмотре́ть *pf.* examine; survey; —ся look around
осме́ивать *impf.*, осмея́ть *pf.* ridicule
осме́ливаться *impf.*, осме́литься *pf.* dare
осмо́тр examination, checkup
осмотри́тельный circumspect
осмы́сленный sensible
оснаще́ние equipment
осно́ва base; basis; *(gram.)* stem; *pl.* fundamentals
основа́ние 1. founding 2. foundation, basis
основа́тель, —ница founder
основа́тельный well-founded; solid; thorough
основно́й fundamental, basic
осно́вывать *impf.*, основа́ть *pf.* found; (на + *P*) base (on)
осо́ба person
осо́бенность peculiarity; feature

осо́бенный especial; particular

особня́к private mansion

осо́бый special; separate

о́собь f. individual; specimen

осознава́ть impf., осозна́ть pf. realize

о́спа smallpox

оспори́мый debatable

остава́ться impf., оста́ться pf. remain; stay

оставля́ть impf., оста́вить pf. **1.** leave; abandon **2.** retain

остально́е n. the rest

остально́й the remaining

остальны́е pl. the others; the rest

остана́вливать impf., останови́ть pf. stop, restrain; —ся stop; stay

остано́вка stop, halt; station

оста́ток FILL rest; remainder; pl. remains

оста́точный remaining; residual

оста́ться pf. of остава́ться

остервене́ть become enraged

остерега́ть impf., остере́чь pf. warn; —ся (+ G) beware (of)

осторо́жно adv. carefully; interj. watch out!

осторо́жность care; caution

осторо́жный careful; cautious

острига́ть impf., остри́чь pf. cut; clip

острие́ point; edge

остри́чься pf. of стри́чься

о́стров island, isle

острови́тянин, -я́нка islander

остро́та witticism

острота́ sharpness; keenness

остроу́мие wit

остроу́мный witty; clever

о́стрый sharp; acute; keen

остыва́ть impf., осты́ть pf. v.i. cool off

осужда́ть impf., осуди́ть pf. blame; condemn; convict

осужде́ние condemnation; conviction

осуждённый n. convict

осуше́ние drainage

осуществи́мый feasible

осуществле́ние realization; implementation

осуществля́ть impf., -ви́ть pf. realize; accomplish; —ся come true

ось f. axis; axle

осьмино́г octopus

осяза́ние touch

осяза́тельный tactile; tangible

осяза́ть feel

от, о́то prep. (+ G) (away) from

отбивна́я котле́та chop; cutlet

отбира́ть impf., отобра́ть pf. take away; select

отбо́йный молото́к jackhammer

отбо́р selection; —ный select; choice

отбра́сывать impf., отбро́сить pf. throw away or off; reject

отбро́сы pl. garbage; waste

отбыва́ть impf., отбы́ть pf. **1.** depart **2.** serve (time)

отбы́тие departure

отва́га courage; bravery

отва́жный brave; courageous

отвезти́ pf. of отвози́ть

отверга́ть impf., отве́ргнуть pf. reject

отве́рстие opening; slot

отвёртка screwdriver

отве́с **1.** precipice **2.** plumb

отвести́ pf. of отводи́ть

отве́т reply, answer

отве́тить pf. of отвеча́ть

отве́тный retaliatory

отве́тственность responsibility

отве́тственный responsible

отвеча́ть impf., отве́тить pf. (на + A) answer; (за + A) be responsible for

отви́нчивать impf., отвинти́ть pf. unscrew

отви́слый loose-hanging; flaccid

отвлека́ть impf., отвле́чь pf. distract; divert; —ся be distracted

отвлечённый abstract

отводи́ть impf., отвести́ pf. lead or draw aside; ward off

отвози́ть impf., отвезти́ pf. take or drive away

отвора́чивать impf., отверну́ть pf. turn (aside, away, down); unscrew; —ся turn away

отворо́т lapel; cuff

отворя́ть(ся) impf., -ри́ть(ся) pf. open

отврати́тельный disgusting

отвраще́ние aversion; disgust

отвыка́ть impf., отвы́кнуть pf. get out of a habit

отвя́зывать impf., отвяза́ть pf. untie; —ся get rid of

отга́дка answer, solution

отга́дывать impf., отгада́ть pf. guess

отгова́ривать impf., отговори́ть pf. (от + G) dissuade

отгово́рка excuse; pretext

отгора́живать impf., отгороди́ть pf. fence off; isolate

отдава́ть impf., отда́ть pf. return, give (back, up, away)

отдалённый remote; distant

отдаля́ть *impf.*, -ли́ть *pf.* remove; —ся (от + *G*) move away

отда́ча return; payment; output

отде́л section; department; —е́ние separation; section; department; —ьный separate

отделя́ть(ся) *impf.*, -ли́ть(ся) *pf.* separate, detach (oneself)

о́тдых rest

отдыха́ть *impf.*, отдохну́ть *pf.* rest; take a rest

отдыша́ться *pf.* catch one's breath

отёк swelling

оте́ль *m.* hotel

оте́ц FILL father

оте́чество fatherland

о́тзыв reference, opinion; review

отзыва́ться *impf.*, отозва́ться *pf.* 1. (на + *A*) answer 2. (о + *P*) comment on

отка́з refusal; rejection

отка́зывать *impf.*, отказа́ть *pf.* refuse; deny; —ся decline; renounce

откла́дывать *impf.*, отложи́ть *pf.* put aside; postpone

о́тклик response; echo

отклоне́ние deflection; deviation; rejection

отклоня́ть *impf.*, -ни́ть *pf.* deflect; decline

отко́с slope

открове́ние revelation

открове́нный frank, outspoken

открыва́ть *impf.*, откры́ть *pf.* open; reveal; discover

откры́тие discovery; opening

откры́тка postcard

откры́тый open

отку́да *adv.* from where

отку́да-нибудь *adv.* from somewhere or other

отку́да-то *adv.* from somewhere

отку́сывать *impf.*, откуси́ть *pf.* bite off

отлёт takeoff

отлича́ть *impf.*, -чи́ть *pf.* distinguish; —ся differ; distinguish oneself

отли́чие difference

отли́чный different; excellent

отложи́ть *pf.* of откла́дывать

отме́на abolition; cancellation

отменя́ть *impf.*, -ни́ть *pf.* cancel; abolish; abrogate

отме́тка note; mark, grade

отмеча́ть *impf.*, отме́тить *pf.* mark; note; celebrate

отморо́жение frostbite

отмы́чка master key

отнека́ться *impf.* refuse

отнести́(сь) *pf.* of относи́ть(ся)

отнима́ть *impf.*, отня́ть *pf.* take off or away; amputate

относи́тельно *adv.* relatively; *prep.* (+ *G*) concerning

относи́тельность relativity

относи́тельный relative

относи́ть *impf.*, отнести́ *pf.* carry away; attribute; —ся (к + *D*) treat; regard; concern

отноше́ние attitude; relation

отня́ть *pf.* of отнима́ть

отобра́ть *pf.* of отбира́ть

отовсю́ду *adv.* from everywhere

отодвига́ть *impf.*, отодви́нуть *pf.* move aside; postpone

отозва́ть(ся) *pf.* of отзыва́ть(ся)

отойти́ *pf.* of отходи́ть

отомсти́ть *pf.* of мстить

отопле́ние heating; heat

оторва́ть *pf.* of отрыва́ть

отосла́ть *pf.* of отсыла́ть

отпеча́ток FILL imprint

отпла́та repayment

отплыва́ть *impf.*, отплы́ть *pf.* swim away; sail

отплы́тие sailing; departure

отпо́р rebuff

отпра́вка dispatch

отправле́ние sending; departure

отправля́ть *impf.*, отпра́вить *pf.* send, forward; —ся set out, depart

отпра́здновать *pf.* of пра́здновать

о́тпуск leave; vacation

отпуска́ть *impf.*, отпусти́ть *pf.* release; free; slacken

отра́ва poison

отравле́ние poisoning

отравля́ть *impf.*, -ви́ть *pf.* poison

отража́ть *impf.*, -зи́ть *pf.* reflect

отраже́ние reflection

о́трасль *f.* branch

отреза́ть *impf.*, отре́зать *pf.* cut off

отре́зок FILL segment; section

отрека́ться *impf.*, отре́чься *pf.* renounce; repudiate

отрица́ние negation; denial

отрица́тельный negative

отрица́ть *impf.* deny; refute

отрыва́ть *impf.*, оторва́ть *pf. v.t.* tear off or away

отры́вок FILL fragment

отры́жка belch

отря́д detachment

отсве́т reflection

отсекáть *impf.*, отсéчь *pf.* cut off
отсрóчивать *impf.*, отсрóчить *pf.* postpone
отсрóчка postponement
отставáние lag
отставáть *impf.*, отстáть *pf.* fall behind; be slow
отстáвка resignation; retirement
отстáивать *impf.*, отстоáть *pf.* stand up for; defend
отстáлость backwardness
отстáлый backward
отстáть *pf.* of отставáть.
отступáть *impf.*, -пúть *pf.* retreat; recede; deviate
отступлéние retreat; deviation
отсýтствие absence
отсýтствовать *impf.* be absent
отсýтствующий absent; *n.* absentee
отчёт counting out; reading
отсылáть *impf.*, отослáть *pf.* send (away)
отсюда *adv.* from here
оттéнок FILL shade; hue
óттепель *f.* thaw
óттиск impression; reprint
оттогó that is why
оттýда *adv.* from there
отупéние daze; torpor; stupor
отхóд departure; deviation
отходúть *impf.*, отойтú *pf.* depart
отцóвский paternal
отчáсти *adv.* partly, in part
отчáяние despair
отчáянный desperate
отчегó *adv.* why
отчегó-нибудь *adv.* for some reason or other
отчегó-то *adv.* for some reason
отчекáнить *pf.* of чекáнить
óтчество patronymic
отчёт account; report
отчётливый distinct; clear
отчúзна *Obs.* fatherland
óтчим stepfather
отчислáть *impf.*, отчúслить *pf.* deduct; dismiss
отчуждéние alienation; estrangement
отшéльник, -ница hermit
отъéзд departure
отъезжáть *impf.*, отъéхать *pf.* depart; drive off
отыскивать *impf.*, отыскáть *pf.* find; search for
офицéр officer; —ский officer's
официáльный official

официáнт waiter
официáнтка waitress
оформлéние mounting; processing; design
охáпка armful
охвáтывать *impf.*, охватúть *pf.* embrace; seize; overcome
охлаждéние cooling
охмелéть *pf.* become intoxicated
охóта[1] hunt, hunting
охóта[2] wish; desire
охóтиться *impf.* hunt
охóтник[1] hunter
охóтник[2], -ница amateur, lover
охóтно *adv.* willingly, gladly
охрáна guard; guarding
охранáть *impf.*, -нúть *pf.* guard; protect
охрúпнуть *pf.* become hoarse
охрúпший hoarse
оценáть *impf.*, оценúть *pf.* evaluate; estimate; value
оцéнка estimate, appraisal
оцепенéние stupor; torpor
оцеплáть *impf.*, -пúть *pf.* surround; seal off
очáг hearth; center
очаровáние charm; fascination
очаровáтельный charming
очарóвывать *impf.*, очаровáть *pf.* charm; fascinate
очевúдец FILL, -дица eyewitness
очевúдный obvious
óчень *adv.* very; very much
очереднóй next in turn; usual
óчередь *f.* 1. turn 2. line 3. order
óчерк sketch; outline
очертáние outline
очéрчивать *impf.*, очертúть *pf.* outline
очищéние 1. cleansing 2. purification 3. clearing
очкú *pl.* eyeglasses, spectacles
очкó (*in games*) point
очнýться *pf.* come to; regain consciousness
очутúться *pf.* find oneself
ошеломлáтельный stunning
ошибáться *impf.*, -бúться *pf.* make a mistake; be wrong
ошúбка error, mistake
ошúбочный erroneous; mistaken
оштрафовáть *pf.* of штрафовáть
óщупь *f.* touch
óщупью *adv.* gropingly
ощутúмый perceptible; tangible
ощущáть *impf.*, -тúть *pf.* feel
ощущéние feeling; sensation

павильо́н pavilion
павли́н peacock
па́губный pernicious; disastrous
па́даль f. carrion
па́дать impf., упа́сть, пасть pf. fall
паде́ж (gram.) case
паде́ние fall; downfall
па́дкий susceptible to
па́дчерица stepdaughter
па́дший fallen
паёк FILL ration
па́зуха bosom; sinus; axil
пай share
па́йщик, -щица shareholder
паке́т package; paper bag
Пакиста́н Pakistan
пакиста́нец FILL, **-та́нка** Pakistani
пакова́ть impf., за-, у- pf. pack
па́кость dirty trick; obscenity
пакт pact
пала́та¹ (polit.) house; chamber
пала́та² (polit.) house; chamber
пала́тка tent; booth; stall
пала́ч executioner; hangman
па́лец FILL finger; toe
палиса́дник small garden
пали́тра palette
пали́ть impf., о-, с- pf. singe; burn
па́лка stick; cane
пало́мник, -ница pilgrim
пало́мничество pilgrimage
па́лочка 1. (drum)stick **2.** baton; wand **3.** bacillus
па́луба (naut.) deck
пальто́ neut. indecl. (over)coat
па́льчик dim. of па́лец
па́мятник monument
па́мятный memorable; commemorative
па́мять f. memory
пана́ма Panama hat
панаце́я panacea
пане́ль f. 1. paneling **2.** sidewalk
па́ника panic
паникёр, —ша alarmist
панихи́да requiem
пани́ческий panic-stricken
панора́ма panorama
пансио́н boarding house
пансиона́т 1. resort hotel **2.** boarding school
пансионе́р, —ка boarder
пантало́ны pl. leggings
панте́ра panther; leopard

пантоми́ма pantomime
па́нцирь m. coat of mail; armor
па́па¹ papa, daddy
па́па² Pope
папа́ха tall fur hat
па́перть f. church portico
папиро́са cigarette
па́пка file; folder
па́поротник fern
па́пство papacy
пар steam
па́ра pair, couple
пара́граф paragraph
пара́д parade; review
пара́дное n. front door
пара́дный attrib. parade; gala
парадо́кс paradox
парадокса́льный paradoxical
парази́т parasite
парализова́ть impf. & pf. paralyze
парали́тик, -ли́чка paralytic
парали́ч paralysis
паралле́ль f. parallel
паралле́льный parallel
парано́йя paranoia
парафи́н paraffin
парашю́т parachute
парашюти́ст, —ка parachutist
па́рень m. young lad; fellow
пари́ neut. indecl. bet, wager
пари́к wig
парикма́хер hairdresser
парикма́херская n. hairdresser's
парите́т parity; —ный equal
па́рить impf. steam; stew; impers. be sultry
пари́ть impf. soar; glide
па́рия pariah; outcast
парк¹ park
парк² (of vehicles) depot; fleet
парла́мент parliament
парламента́рий n. member of parliament
парламентёр envoy; bearer of a flag of truce
парни́к hothouse; greenhouse
парнико́вый attrib. greenhouse
па́рный paired; paired off
парово́з locomotive, engine
паро́дия parody
паро́ль m. password
паро́м ferry; raft
паро́мщик ferryman
парохо́д steamship; steamer
па́рта school desk
парте́р (theat.) orchestra

партиза́н, —ка guerrilla
партиза́нский attrib. guerrilla
парти́йный attrib. Party
па́ртия 1. party 2. game, set 3. score
партнёр, —ша partner
па́рус sail; —ный attrib. sail
паруси́на canvas; sailcloth
па́русник sailboat
парфюме́рия perfumes
парча́ brocade
парша́ mange
пас pass (in cards or in sports)
па́сека apiary; bee garden
па́сечник beekeeper
па́сквиль m. lampoon; libel
па́смурный cloudy; gloomy
пасова́ть impf., с- pf. retreat; (cards, sports) pass
па́спорт passport
пасса́ж arcade
пассажи́р, —ка passenger
пассажи́рский attrib. passenger
пасси́вный passive
па́ста paste; зубна́я ~ toothpaste
па́стбище pasture
па́ства parishioners; flock
пасте́ль f., —ный pastel
пастериза́ция pasteurization
пасти́ impf. tend; graze; —сь graze
пасту́х shepherd
пасть[1] f. (of animal) mouth
пасть[2] pf. of па́дать
Па́сха Easter
па́сынок FILL stepson
пасья́нс (cards) solitaire
пат (chess) stalemate
пате́нт patent
патентова́ть impf., за- pf. patent
патети́ческий passionate
па́тока molasses; treacle
патологи́ческий pathological
патоло́гия pathology
патриа́рх patriarch
патрио́т, —ка patriot
патро́н 1. cartridge 2. (mech.) chuck 3. lamp socket
патрули́ровать impf. patrol
патру́ль m. patrol
па́уза pause
пау́к spider
паути́на spider web
па́фос fervor; zeal
пах groin
паха́ть impf. plow; work hard
па́хнуть impf. v.i. smell
пахну́ть pf. impers. blow in
паху́чий strong-smelling

пацие́нт, —ка patient
пацифи́ст, —ка pacifist
пацифи́стский pacifist
па́чка 1. bundle; batch 2. tutu
па́чкать impf., за-, ис- pf. soil
па́шня plowed land
паште́т pâté
па́юсная икра́ pressed caviar
пая́льник soldering iron
пая́льный attrib. soldering
пая́ть solder
певе́ц FILL, певи́ца singer
певу́чий melodious
пе́гий piebald
педаго́г pedagogue; teacher
педаго́гика pedagogy
педагоги́ческий pedagogical
педа́ль f. pedal
педанти́чный pedantic
педиа́тр pediatrician
педикю́р pedicure; chiropody
пейза́ж landscape (painting)
пека́рня bakery
пе́карь m. baker
пекло́ scorching heat
пелена́ cover; veil
пелена́ть impf., с-, за- pf. diaper; swaddle
пеленга́тор direction finder
пеленгова́ть impf., за- pf. take the bearing of
пелёнка diaper
пельме́ни pl. meat dumplings
пе́на foam; lather
пена́л pencil case
пе́ние singing
пе́нистый foamy
пеницилли́н penicillin
пе́нный foamy
пенопла́ст foam plastic
пенсионе́р, —ка pensioner
пе́нсия pension
пень FILL m. stump
пе́ня penalty
пе́пел FILL ashes
пепели́ще site of a fire
пе́пельница ashtray
пе́пельный ash-colored
перве́нец FILL first-born
пе́рвенство first place; championship
пе́рвенствовать impf. come in first
пе́рвое n. first course
первоисто́чник original source
первокла́ссный first-class
первоку́рсник, -ница freshman
первома́йский attrib. May-Day
первонача́льный original

первоочередно́й primary
перворазря́дный first-rate
первосо́ртный best quality
пе́рвый first
перга́мент parchment
перебази́ровать *pf.* relocate
перебега́ть *impf.*, **-бежа́ть** *pf.* run across, cross; defect
перебинтова́ть *pf.* rebandage
перебира́ть *impf.*, **-бра́ть** *pf.* sort out; go through; **-ся** cross
перебра́нка hassle; squabble
перева́л mountain pass
перева́ривать *impf.*, **-вари́ть** *pf.* recook; overcook; digest
переверну́ть *impf.*, **-верну́ть** *pf.* turn (over, inside out); upset
перево́д 1. transfer 2. translation; **—чик**, **—чица** translator, interpreter.
переводи́ть *impf.*, **-вести́** *pf.* 1. transfer 2. translate
перевози́ть *impf.*, **-везти́** *pf.* transport (across)
перево́зка transportation
перевооруже́ние rearmament
переворо́т revolution; overturn
перевя́зка bandage, dressing
перевя́зывать *impf.*, **-вяза́ть** *pf.* tie (up); bandage, dress
пе́ревязь *f.* sling
перегля́дываться *impf.*, **-гляну́ться** *pf.* exchange glances
перегно́й humus
перегово́ры *pl.* negotiations
перегоро́дка partition
перегре́в overheating
перегру́зка 1. transfer of cargo 2. overloading
пе́ред, пе́редо *prep.* (+ *I*) before; in front of
передава́ть *impf.*, **-да́ть** *pf.* pass, hand; transmit; broadcast; tell
переда́ча 1. transmission 2. transfer 3. broadcast
передвиже́ние movement; transportation
передёргивать *impf.*, **-дёрнуть** *pf.* 1. pull (aside, over) 2. *Colloq.* cheat
пере́дний front
пере́дник apron
пере́дняя *n.* entry hall
передови́ца, передова́я статья́ editorial, leading article
переду́мывать *impf.*, **-ду́мать** *pf.* change one's mind
переды́шка respite; rest
перее́зд crossing; move, moving

переезжа́ть *impf.*, **-éхать** *pf.* 1. cross (over) 2. move
пережива́ние experience
пережива́ть *impf.*, **-жи́ть** *pf.* experience; endure
пережи́тое *n.* past experiences
переизбра́ние reelection
переиздава́ть *impf.*, **-изда́ть** *pf.* republish; reissue
переизда́ние republication
переимено́вывать *impf.* rename
перейти́ *pf.* of **переходи́ть**
переквалифика́ция retraining
переквалифици́ровать *impf. & pf.* retrain
пе́рекись *f.* peroxide
перекла́дина crossbar; crossbeam
перекла́дывать *impf.*, **-ложи́ть** *pf.* transfer; shift; (+ *I*) interlay
переключа́тель switch
перекрёсток FILL crossroad
переку́р cigarette break
перелёт flight; migration
перелета́ть *impf.*, **-лете́ть** *pf.* fly over
перелётный (of bird) migratory
перелива́ние 1. pouring 2. transfusion
перели́стывать *impf.*, **-листа́ть** *pf.* leaf through
перелицо́вывать *impf.*, **-лицева́ть** *pf.* turn (inside out)
перелага́ть *pf.* of **перекла́дывать**
перело́м 1. fracture 2. crisis
перело́мный crucial; critical
переме́на change; break
переме́нный variable; alternating
перемеще́ние shift; displacement
переми́рие truce; armistice
перенаселе́ние overpopulation
перенаселённый overpopulated
перено́с moving; transferring
переноси́ть *impf.*, **-нести́** *pf.* 1. transfer; carry over 2. postpone 3. endure
перено́сица bridge of the nose
переночева́ть *pf.* of **ночева́ть**
переоце́нка overestimation
пе́репел quail
перепи́ска correspondence
перепи́сываться *impf.* (c + *I*) correspond with
пе́репись *f.* census
переплёт 1. binding 2. *Colloq.* scrape
перепо́лох commotion
перепо́нка membrane; web
перепра́ва crossing; ford
перепроизво́дство overproduction
перепу́г fright

перепугáть *pf.* frighten; terrify

перепýтье crossroads

переработка 1. processing **2.** reworking **3.** overtime work

перераспределéние redistribution

перерождéние regeneration

перерыв recess; break

пересáдка 1. change (*of bus, plane etc.*) **2.** transplantation

пересáживать *impf.*, **-садить** *pf.* **1.** transplant; graft **2.** move somebody to another seat

пересáживаться *impf.*, **пересéсть** *pf.* **1.** move to another seat **2.** change (*trains, etc.*)

переселéнец FILL, **-лéнка** migrant

переселéние migration

пересечéние crossing; intersection

пересмóтр review; revision

переставáть *impf.*, **-стáть** *pf.* stop, cease

перестанóвка rearrangement

перестрáивать *impf.*, **-стрóить** *pf.* rebuild; reorganize

перестрахóвка reinsurance

перестрахóвщик, -щица overcautious person

перестрéлка exchange of gunfire

перестрóйка reorganization

пересылка sending; forwarding

перетасóвка reshuffle; shuffling

переýлок side street; alley

переутомлéние overwork; exhaustion

перехвáтчик interceptor

перехóд crossing; passage

переходить *impf.*, **перейти** *pf.* **1.** cross **2.** (в + *A*) turn into

перехóдный transitional

пéрец FILL pepper

пéречень FILL *f.* list, listing

перечёркивать *impf.*, **-черкнýть** *pf.* cross out

перечислéние enumeration

пéречница pepper shaker

перешéек isthmus

перила *pl.* banister; railing

перио́д period

перио́дика periodicals

периоди́ческий, периоди́чный periodic

пéристый feathered

перифери́я periphery

перламýтр mother-of-pearl

перло́вая крупá pearl barley

перлюстрáция secret opening of mail

перманéнт permanent wave

перманéнтный permanent

пернáтый feathered

перó[1] feather, plume

перó[2] pen

перочи́нный но́жик penknife

перпендикуля́р perpendicular

перрóн platform

перс, -ня́нка Persian

пéрсик peach

персонáж personage; character

персонáл personnel

персонáльный personal; ~ код personal identification number (*abbr.* P.I.N.); ~ компью́тер personal computer (*abbr.* P.C.)

перспекти́ва perspective

перспекти́вный perspective; promising; long-term

пéрстень FILL *m.* ring

пертурбáция perturbation

перфорáция perforation

пéрхоть *f.* dandruff

перцóвка pepper brandy

перчáтка glove

пёс FILL dog

песéц FILL polar fox

пéсня song

песóк FILL sand; **песóчный** sandy

песóчница sandbox

пессими́ст, -ка pessimist

пессимисти́ческий pessimistic

пестротá diversity of colors

пёстрый multicolored; diverse

песчáный вездехóд beach buggy

песчи́нка grain of sand

петéлька *dim. of* **пéтля**

пéтля loop; noose

петрýшка parsley

петýх rooster

петуши́ный *attrib.* rooster

петь *impf.* **1.** sing **2.** crow

пехóта infantry; **морскáя** ~ the marines

печáль *f.* sorrow; **—ный** sad

печáтать *impf.*, **на-** *pf.* **1.** print **2.** type

печáтный *attrib.* printing; printed

печáть *f.* **1.** seal; stamp **2.** press; print, printing

печёнка (*cul.*) liver

печёный baked

пéчень *f.* (*anat.*) liver

печéнье pastry; cookies

пéчка stove

печнóй *attrib.* stove

печь[1] *f.* stove; oven

печь[2] *impf.*, **ис-** *pf.* bake

пешехóд pedestrian

пéший pedestrian

пéшка (*chess*) pawn

пешкóм *adv.* on foot

пещéра cave

пещёрный *attrib.* cave

пианино *neut. indecl.* piano

пианист, —ка pianist

пивная *n.* tavern; pub; bar

пиво beer

пивовар brewer

пигмей pygmy

пиджак jacket; coat

пижама pajamas

пижон *Slang* fop; dandy

пик peak; **час ~** rush hour

пика lance, pike

пикантность piquancy

пикантный 1. spicy **2.** pungent

пикап pickup truck

пикет picket line

пикетировать *impf.* picket

пики *pl.* (cards) spades

пикировка bickering; squabbling

пикировщик dive bomber

пикник picnic

пикнуть *pf.* squeak

пиковый (cards) of spades

пила saw

пилигрим, —ка pilgrim

пилить *impf.* **1.** saw **2.** *Fig.* nag

пилот pilot

пилотаж piloting; flying

пилотировать *impf.* pilot

пилюля pill

пинать *impf.,* **пнуть** *pf.* kick

пингвин penguin

пинок FILL *Colloq.* kick

пинцет tweezers

пионер, —ка pioneer

пипетка eye dropper

пир banquet; feast

пирамида pyramid

пират pirate; **—ский** pirate

пировать *impf.* feast

пирог pie

пирожное *n.* pastry

пирожок FILL small pie; pastry

пирс pier

пируэт pirouette

писание writing; **Священное Писание** Holy Scripture

писаный handwritten

писатель, —ница writer

писать *impf.,* **на—** *pf.* write; paint

писк peep; chirp

пискливый squeaky

писсуар urinal

пистолет pistol

письменность literature

письменный written

письмо letter

питание feeding; diet

питательный nourishing

питать *impf.* feed; nourish

питомник (plant) nursery

пить *impf.,* **вы—** *pf.* drink

питьё drink; drinking

питьевой *attrib.* drinking

пихта fir

пишущая машинка typewriter

пища food

пищать *impf.,* **пискнуть** *pf.* cheep

пищеварение digestion

пиявка leech

плавание swimming; navigation

плавать *indet.,* **плыть** *det.* swim; float; sail

плавить *impf.* melt; smelt

плавки *pl.* swimming trunks

плавник¹ fin; flipper

плавник² driftwood

плавный fluent; smooth

плагиат plagiarism

плакат poster, placard

плакать *impf.* cry; weep

пламя *neut.* flame; blaze

план plan; **учёбный ~** curriculum

планёр (aero.) glider

планета planet

планировать *impf.,* **за—** *pf.* plan

плановый planned

пласт layer; stratum

пластинка 1. phonograph record **2.** (metal) plate

пластырь *m.* plaster

плата payment; fee; fare

платан plane tree

платёж payment

платина platinum

платить *impf.,* **за—** *pf.* pay

платный 1. paying **2.** paid **3.** requiring payment

платок FILL shawl; **носовой ~** handkerchief

платье dress; clothes, clothing

плацкарта reserved seat ticket

плач weeping

плащ cloak; raincoat

плева membrane; film

плевать *impf.,* **плюнуть** *pf.* spit

плевок FILL spit; spittle

плед rug; plaid

племя (*pl.* племена) *neut.* tribe

племянник nephew

племянница niece

плен captivity

пленарный plenary

пленительный captivating

плёнка 1. film **2.** tape

пленник, —ница prisoner; captive

плесень *f.* mold

плеск splash

плете́ние weaving
плеть f. lash
плечо́ shoulder
плешь f. bald spot
плита́ 1. slab 2. stove; cooker
пли́тка 1. thin slab; tile 2. bar (of chocolate) 3. small stove
плов pilaf
плове́ц FILL, пловчи́ха swimmer
плод fruit
плодови́тый fruitful; prolific
плодоро́дный fertile
пло́мба (dental) filling
пломби́р ice cream
пло́ский flat
пло́скость flatness; platitude
плот raft
плоти́на dam
пло́тник carpenter
пло́тный dense; tight; solid
плотоя́дный carnivorous
плоть f. flesh
пло́хо adv. badly
плохо́й bad; inferior
площа́дка 1. ground; site 2. (sports) court 3. landing
пло́щадь f. 1. area 2. square
плуг plow
плыть det. of пла́вать
плю́нуть pf. of плева́ть
плюс plus; advantage
плющ ivy
пляж beach
пля́ска dance
по prep. 1. (+ D) on, along; according to; over. 2. (+ A) to, up to; (with time expressions) through 3. (+ P) upon; after
по-англи́йски adv. in English
побе́г[1] escape
побе́г[2] (bot.) sprout; shoot
побе́да victory
победи́тель, —ница winner
победи́ть pf. of бежа́ть
побежда́ть impf., победи́ть pf. conquer; be victorious
побере́жье shore, coast
побледне́ть pf. turn pale
побли́зости adv. nearby
побо́и pl. beating
побо́чный secondary; collateral
по-бра́тски adv. in a brotherly fashion
побыва́ть pf. visit
пова́дка habit; mannerism
повали́ть pf. of вали́ть
пова́льный general, mass
по́вар, повари́ха cook
по-ва́шему adv. in your opinion
поведе́ние behavior; conduct

повезти́ pf. of везти́
повеле́ние command
повели́тельный imperative
повенча́ть pf. of венча́ть
пове́ренный n. attorney; confidant
пове́рнуть pf. of повора́чивать
пове́рх prep. (+ G) over; —ност-ный superficial; —ность surface
пове́сить(ся) pf. of ве́шать(ся)
повествова́ние narration
повести́ pf. of вести́
пове́стка notice; summons
по́весть f. story; tale
по-ви́димому adv. apparently
повидло jam
пови́нность duty
повинова́ться impf. & pf. (+ D) obey
повлия́ть pf. of влия́ть
по́вод[1] occasion, reason
по́вод[2] bridle, rein
поводо́к FILL leash
повора́чивать(ся) impf., поверну́ть(ся) pf. turn
поворо́т turn; turning point
повреди́ть pf. of вреди́ть, повре-жда́ть
поврежда́ть impf., повреди́ть pf. damage; harm
повсю́ду adv. everywhere
повторе́ние repetition
повторя́ть impf., -ри́ть pf. repeat
повыша́ть impf., повы́сить pf. raise, increase
повя́зка bandage
пога́нка toadstool
пога́ный 1. inedible 2. vile
погаси́ть pf. of гаси́ть
погиба́ть impf., поги́бнуть pf. per-ish
погла́дить pf. of гла́дить
поглоща́ть impf., -ти́ть pf. absorb; swallow up
погово́рка proverb; saying
пого́да weather
пого́ст village cemetery
пограни́чный attrib. border
по́греб cellar
погребе́ние burial, internment
погро́м pogrom; massacre
погружа́ть impf., -зи́ть pf. immerse
погру́зка loading
погуби́ть pf. of губи́ть
под, подо prep. (+ A) under; towards; (+ I) under; near, by
подава́ть impf., пода́ть pf. give; serve
подави́ться pf. of дави́ться
пода́вленный depressed

пода́гра gout
подари́ть pf. of дари́ть
пода́рок FILL gift
пода́ть pf. of подава́ть
подая́ние Obs. alms
подбо́рка selection
подборо́док FILL chin
подва́л basement, cellar
подверга́ть impf., подве́ргнуть pf. (+ D) subject (to); expose (to)
подве́рженный subject to; liable
подвести́ pf. of подводи́ть
по́двиг feat; exploit
подви́д subspecies
подви́жный agile; lively
подводи́ть impf., подвести́ pf. lead up
подво́дный attrib. submarine
подвы́пивший Colloq. tipsy
подгоре́лый slightly burnt
подготови́тельный preparatory
подгото́вка preparation
поддава́ться impf., подда́ться pf. (+ D) yield (to)
по́дданный n. subject; citizen
по́дданство citizenship
подде́лка counterfeit; forgery
подде́лывать impf., подде́лать pf. counterfeit; forge
подде́ржка support
подде́йствовать pf. of де́йствовать
подели́ть(ся) pf. of дели́ть(ся)
поде́ржанный used, second-hand
поджига́ть impf., подже́чь pf. set fire (to)
поджима́ть impf., поджа́ть pf. draw in, under
поджо́г arson
подзаголо́вок FILL subtitle
подзе́мный underground
подки́дыш foundling
подкла́дка lining
подко́ва horseshoe
подкра́дываться impf., подкра́сться pf. steal up (to)
по́дкуп bribery
по́дле prep. (+ G) near; beside
подлежа́ть impf. (+ D) be subject to
подлежа́щее n. (gram.) subject
подле́сок FILL undergrowth
подле́ц scoundrel
подли́вка gravy; sauce
по́длинник original
по́длинный original
подло́г forgery
по́длость meanness; baseness
по́длый mean, base
подме́на substitution
подмётка sole (of a shoe)

подмы́шка armpit
поднима́ть impf., подня́ть pf. lift, raise; —ся rise; climb (up)
подно́с tray
подо́бие likeness; similarity
подо́бный similar; и тому́ подо́бное and the like; ничего́ подо́бного nothing of the sort
подогрева́ть impf., подогре́ть pf. v.t. warm up
пододе́яльник blanket cover
подожда́ть pf. of ждать
подозрева́ть impf. (в + P) suspect
подозре́ние suspicion
подозри́тельный suspicious
подойти́ pf. of подходи́ть
подоко́нник windowsill
подо́л hem
подоплёка underlying cause
подо́пытный experimental
подорва́ть pf. of подрыва́ть
подорожа́ть pf. become more expensive
подохо́дный нало́г income tax
подо́шва sole; (mountain) foot
подпева́ть impf. sing along
подпи́ска subscription
подпи́сывать impf., подписа́ть pf. sign; —ся sign; (на + A) subscribe (to)
по́дпись f. signature
подпо́лье underground
подпо́рка prop
подража́ть impf. imitate
подразумева́ть impf. imply
подро́бность detail
подру́га (girl)friend
по-дру́жески adv. friendly
подрыва́ть impf., подорва́ть pf. sap; undermine
подсве́чник candlestick
подслу́шивать impf., подслу́шать pf. eavesdrop; overhear
подсозна́ние the subconscious
подста́вка support; stand
подстерега́ть impf., подстере́чь pf. lie in wait for
по́дступ approach
подсуди́мый n. defendant
подсчёт count; calculations
подтвержда́ть impf., подтверди́ть pf. confirm
подтёк streak; bruise
подте́кст subtext
подтя́жки pl. suspenders
подтя́нутый smart; neat; fresh
поду́шка pillow; cushion
подходи́ть impf., подойти́ pf. approach

подходя́щий suitable

подчёркивать *impf.*, подчеркну́ть *pf.* underline; emphasize

подчинённый *n.* subordinate

подчиня́ть *impf.*, -ни́ть *pf.* subordinate; (-ся *v* + *D*) submit to

подъе́зд driveway; entrance

подъезжа́ть *impf.*, подъе́хать *pf.* drive up to

подъём ascent; lifting (up)

поеди́нок FILL MALE duel

по́езд train

пое́здка trip, journey

пое́хать take off; leave

пожале́ть *pf.* of жале́ть

пожа́ловаться *pf.* of жа́ловаться

пожа́луйста *particle.* please; certainly!, don't mention it

пожа́р fire

пожела́ть *pf.* of жела́ть

поже́ртвовать *pf.* of же́ртвовать

пожива́ть *impf.* get along, get on

пожило́й elderly

по́за pose

позабо́титься *pf.* of забо́титься

позави́довать *pf.* of зави́довать

позавчера́ *adv.* the day before yesterday

позади́ *adv.*, *prep.* (+ *G*) behind

позва́ть *pf.* of звать

позволя́ть *impf.*, позво́лить *pf.* allow; permit

позвони́ть *pf.* of звони́ть

позвоно́чник spine

по́здний late

поздоро́ваться *pf.* of здоро́ваться

поздравля́ть *impf.*, поздра́вить *pf.* congratulate

по́зже *adv.* later, later on

познако́мить(ся) *pf.* of знако́мить(ся)

позо́р disgrace; shame

пои́ть *impf.*, на- *pf.* give someone a drink; (*animal*) water

пойма́ть *pf.* of лови́ть

пойти́ *pf.* of идти́ go; take off

пока́ *conj.* while; ~ не until; *adv.* for the present; *interj.* take care!

пока́з demonstration; show

показа́ться *pf.* of каза́ться

пока́зывать *impf.*, показа́ть *pf.* show

покая́ние repentance

пока́яться *pf.* confess; repent

поки́нутый abandoned

покло́н 1. bow 2. regards

поклоне́ние worship

поклони́ться *pf.* of кла́няться

покло́нник, -ница admirer

поко́й rest

поко́йник, -ница deceased

поколе́ние generation

поко́нчить *pf.* (с + *I*) finish

поко́рный submissive; obedient

покра́сить *pf.* of кра́сить

покрасне́ть *pf.* of красне́ть

покрови́тель, —ница patron

покупа́тель, —ница customer

покупа́ть *impf.*, купи́ть *pf.* buy

поку́пка purchase

поку́шать *pf.* of ку́шать

покуше́ние assasination attempt

пол¹ floor

пол² gender, sex

полага́ть *impf.* think, suppose; —ся (на + *A*) rely (on)

полго́да *adv.* half a year

по́лдень FILL MALE *m.* noon

по́ле field; *pl.* margin; brim

поле́зный useful

полете́ть *pf.* of лете́ть take off

по́лзать *indet.*, ползти́ *det.* crawl

поли́тика politics

полити́ческий political

поли́ция police

полк regiment

по́лка shelf

полнолу́ние full moon

по́лностью *adv.* completely

по́лночь *f.* midnight

по́лный full

полови́на half

полово́й sexual

положе́ние position; condition

положи́тельный affirmative,

положи́ть *pf.* of класть

полоса́ strip; stripe; region

полоска́ть *impf.* rinse; gargle

полоте́нце towel

полотно́ linen

полтора́ one and a half

полукру́г semicircle

полуо́стров peninsula

получа́ть *impf.*, -чи́ть *pf.* receive; —ся result; turn out

полуша́рие hemisphere

полчаса́ *m.* half an hour

по́льза use; benefit

по́льзоваться *impf.*, вос- *pf.* (+ *I*) 1. make use of; profit by 2. *impf.* only enjoy

по́льский Polish

польсти́ть *pf.* of льсти́ть

По́льша Poland

полюби́ть *pf.* fall in love with

по́люс (*geog.*) pole

поля́к, по́лька Pole

поменя́ть *pf.* of меня́ть

поме́тка mark; note

помеща́ть *impf.*, -сти́ть *pf.* **1.** place; accommodate **2.** invest
помеще́ние location; investment
помидо́р tomato
помири́ть(ся) *pf. of* мири́ть(ся)
по́мнить remember; recall
помога́ть *impf.*, помо́чь *pf.* (+ *D*) help
по-мо́ему *adv.* in my opinion
помо́щник, -ница assistant
по́мощь *f.* help; assistance
понеде́льник Monday
понести́(сь) *pf. of* нести́(сь)
понижа́ть *impf.*, пони́зить *pf.* lower; reduce
понима́ние understanding
понима́ть *impf.*, поня́ть *pf.* understand; comprehend
понра́виться *pf. of* нра́виться
поня́тие idea; notion; conception
пообе́дать *pf. of* обе́дать
попере́к *adv.*, *prep.* (+ *G*) across
поплы́ть *pf. of* плыть
попола́м *adv.* in half
попра́вка correction; recovery
поправля́ть *impf.*, попра́вить *pf.* repair; correct; —ся recover; improve
по-пре́жнему *adv.* as before
попрёк reproach
попро́бовать *pf. of* про́бовать
попроси́ть *pf. of* проси́ть
попро́сту simply
попуга́й parrot
популя́рный popular
попу́тно *adv.* in passing
попы́тка attempt
пора́ time; it is time
порази́тельный striking
поро́г threshold; *pl.* rapids
поро́да breed; species
поро́дистый pedigreed
по́рознь *adv.* separately
поро́к **1.** vice **2.** defect
по́рох powder
поро́чный vicious; depraved
порошо́к FILL powder
порт port; harbor
по́ртить *impf.*, ис- *pf. v.t.* spoil, damage; corrupt
портни́ха (female) dressmaker
портно́й *n.* tailor
портре́т portrait
Португа́лия Portugal
портфе́ль *m.* briefcase
по-ру́сски *adv.* (in) Russian
поруче́ние commission; message
поручи́ться *pf. of* руча́ться
по́рция portion
поры́в gust; —истый gusty

поря́док FILL order; sequence
поря́дочный decent, honest
посади́ть *pf.* plant; imprison
по-сво́ему *adv.* in one's own way
посвяща́ть *impf.*, -ти́ть *pf.* devote; dedicate
посети́тель, —ница visitor
посеща́ть *impf.*, -ти́ть *pf.* visit
посе́ять *pf. of* се́ять
поско́льку *conj.* so far as
посла́ть *pf. of* посыла́ть
по́сле *adv.*, *prep.* (+ *G*) after(wards)
после́дний last; latter; the latest
после́дствие consequence
после́дующий following, next
послеза́втра *adv.* the day after tomorrow
посло́вица proverb
послужи́ть *pf. of* служи́ть
послу́шать(ся) *pf. of* слу́шать(ся)
посме́ртный posthumous
посмотре́ть *pf. of* смотре́ть
посо́бие **1.** textbook **2.** allowance **3.** aid
посо́льство embassy
посреди́ *adv.*, *prep.* (+ *G*) in the middle (of)
посре́дник, -ница mediator
поста́вить *pf. of* поставля́ть, ста́вить
поставля́ть *impf.*, поста́вить *pf.* supply
постано́вка (*theat.*) production
постара́ться *pf. of* стара́ться
посте́ль *f.* bed
постепе́нный gradual
постига́ть *impf.*, пости́гнуть, пости́чь *pf.* **1.** comprehend **2.** befall
посто́льку *conj.* insofar as
посторо́нний strange, foreign; *n.* outsider
постоя́нный constant, permanent
постро́ить *pf. of* стро́ить
поступа́ть *impf.*, -пи́ть *pf.* **1.** act **2.** (с + *I*) treat **3.** (на, в + *A*) join
посту́пок action, deed
посу́да dishes; utensils
посыла́ть *impf.*, посла́ть *pf.* send
посяга́ть *impf.*, посягну́ть *pf.* (на + *A*) encroach on
пот sweat, perspiration
поте́ря **1.** loss **2.** waste
потеря́ть(ся) *pf. of* теря́ть(ся)
поте́ть *impf.*, вс- *pf.* sweat
пото́к stream, torrent; flow
потоло́к FILL ceiling

пото́м *adv.* afterwards; then; —ок descendant; —ство posterity

потому́ *adv.* for this reason; ~ что *conj.* because; for

пото́п flood, deluge

потреби́тель consumer

потребля́ть *impf.*, -би́ть *pf.* consume; use

потре́бовать *pf.* of тре́бовать

потряса́ть *impf.* потрясти́ *pf.* shake; shock

поучи́тельный instructive

похвала́ praise

похвали́ть(ся) *pf.* of хвали́ть(ся)

похища́ть *impf.*, похи́тить *pf.* kidnap; steal; hijack

похо́д hike; —ка gait

похо́жий (на + *A*) similar

похорони́ть *pf.* of хорони́ть

по́хороны *pl.* burial, funeral

по́хоть *f.* lust

поцелова́ть *pf.* of целова́ть

поцелу́й kiss

по́чва soil; ground

почему́ *adv.* why; ~-либо for some reason or other

по́черк handwriting

почёт honor; —ный honorary, honorable

почини́ть *pf.* of чини́ть

по́чта mail; —льон postman.

почта́мт post office

почте́ние respect

почти́ *adv.* almost, nearly

по́шлина duty; customs

по́шлый vulgar

поща́да mercy

поэ́зия poetry

поэ́ма poem

поэ́т poet; —и́ческий poetic

поэ́тому *adv.* therefore

появле́ние appearance

появля́ться *impf.*, -ви́ться *pf.* appear

по́яс 1. belt 2. zone

пра́вда truth

пра́вило rule

пра́вильный right, correct

пра́вить, —ница ruler

прави́тельство government

пра́вить *impf.* (+ *I*) govern, rule

пра́вка correcting

правле́ние government; management

пра́внук great-grandson

пра́во right; law

правонаруши́тель, —ница lawbreaker; offender

правописа́ние spelling

правосла́вие Orthodoxy

правосла́вный Orthodox

правосу́дие justice

пра́вый 1. right 2. correct, just

пра́вящий ruling

пра́здник holiday

пра́здновать *impf.*, от- *pf.* celebrate

пра́здный idle

пра́ктика practice

практи́ческий, практи́чный practical

прах (*poet.*) dust

пра́чечная *n.* laundry

пребыва́ние stay; tenure

пребыва́ть *impf.*, -бы́ть *pf.* stay

превосходи́ть *impf.*, превзойти́ *pf.* surpass

превосхо́дный excellent

превраща́ть *impf.*, -ти́ть *pf.* (в + *A*) turn (into)

прегра́да bar; obstacle

прегражда́ть *impf.*, прегради́ть *pf.* bar; block

предава́ть *impf.*, -да́ть *pf.* betray

пре́данный devoted

преда́тель, —ница traitor; —ство treason; betrayal

предвари́тельный preliminary

предви́деть *impf.* foresee

предвкуше́ние anticipation

преде́л limit; boundary; —ьный maximum; extreme

предисло́вие preface

предлага́ть *impf.*, предложи́ть *pf.* offer; propose

предло́г¹ (*gram.*) preposition

предло́г² pretext

предложе́ние¹ offer; proposal

предложе́ние² (*gram.*) sentence

предме́т object, subject; topic

предназнача́ть *impf.*, -зна́чить *pf.* (pre)destine; earmark

преднаме́ренный premeditated; deliberate; intentional

пре́док FILL ancestor

предоставля́ть *impf.*, -ста́вить *pf.* grant; give; leave (to do)

предостерега́ть *impf.*, -сте́речь *pf.* (от + *G*) warn against

предостереже́ние warning

предосуди́тельный reprehensible

предохране́ние protection

предохрани́тельный precautionary; *attrib.* safety

предполага́ть *impf.*, -положи́ть *pf.* assume; propose

предположе́ние 1. supposition, assumption 2. plan

предпосле́дний next to last

предпосы́лка prerequisite; premise

предпочита́ть *impf.*, **-поч́есть** *pf.* prefer

предпочте́ние preference

предприи́мчивый enterprising

предпринима́тель entrepreneur; businessman

предпринима́ть *impf.*, **-приня́ть** *pf.* undertake

предприя́тие undertaking; venture

предрасполо́женный (к + *D*) predisposed to

предрассу́док FILL prejudice

председа́тель, —ница chairperson

предска́зывать *impf.*, **-сказа́ть** *pf.* foretell; predict

представи́тель, —ница representative; spokesperson

представле́ние 1. performance **2.** presentation **3.** idea; notion

представля́ть *impf.*, **-ста́вить** *pf.* **1.** (re)present; introduce; **—ся** *pf.* occur, present itself

предстоя́щий impending; forthcoming

предупреди́тельный preventive

предупрежда́ть *impf.*, **-упреди́ть** *pf.* warn; prevent; let know

предусма́тривать *impf.*, **-усмотре́ть** *pf.* foresee

предчу́вствие presentiment

предчу́вствовать *impf.* have a presentiment *or* foreboding

предше́ственник, -ница predecessor

предъявля́ть *impf.*, **-ви́ть** *pf.* show; produce

предыду́щий previous

прее́мник, -ница successor

преждевре́менный premature

пре́жний previous; former

презерва́тив condom

презира́ть *impf.*, **презре́ть** *pf.* **1.** *impf. only* despise **2.** disregard

презри́тельный contemptuous

преиму́щественный principal

преиму́щество advantage

прейскура́нт price list

преклоне́ние reverence (for)

прекра́сный beautiful; excellent

прекраща́ть *impf.*, **-ти́ть** *pf.* stop, discontinue; **—ся** end

прекраще́ние cessation

пре́лесть *f.* charm; delight

прелюбодея́ние adultery

пре́мия *f.* prize; premium; bonus

премье́р prime minister

премье́ра première

пренебрега́ть *impf.*, **-бре́чь** *pf.* (+ *I*) neglect; disregard

пренебреже́ние neglect; disregard

преоблада́ть *impf.* predominate

преображе́ние 1. transformation **2.** *cap.* Transfiguration

преобразова́ние transformation

преодолева́ть *impf.*, **-доле́ть** *pf.* overcome; surmount

препина́ние: знак препина́ния punctuation mark

преподава́тель, —ница teacher

преподава́ть *impf.* teach

препя́тствие obstacle

препя́тствовать *impf.*, **вос-** *pf.* (+ *D*) hinder; impede

прерыва́ть *impf.*, **прерва́ть** *pf.* interrupt; break off

пресека́ть *impf.*, **пресе́чь** *pf.* put a stop to; cut short

пресле́довать *impf.* persecute; pursue, haunt

пресмыка́ющееся *n.* reptile

пре́сный bland; (*water*) fresh

пресс press; (*machine*) punch

пре́сса the press

пресс-конфере́нция press-conference

престаре́лый aged

престо́л throne

преступле́ние crime; offense

престу́пник, -ница criminal

претендова́ть *impf.* (на + *A*) lay claim to

прете́нзия pretension; claim

преувели́чивать *impf.*, **преувели́чить** *pf.* exaggerate

при *prep.* (+ *P*) **1.** by, at **2.** in the presence of **3.** in the time of **4.** attached to

прибавля́ть *impf.*, **приба́вить** *pf.* increase; add

прибалти́йский Baltic

прибе́жище refuge

приближа́ться *impf.*, **прибли́зиться** *pf.* (к + *D*) approach

приблизи́тельный approximate

прибо́й surf; breakers

прибо́р device; instrument; set

прибыва́ть *impf.*, **прибы́ть** *pf.* **1.** arrive **2.** increase

при́быль *f.* profit; increase; gain

прибы́тие arrival

приве́т greeting(s)

приве́тствовать *impf.*, **по-** *pf.* welcome; greet

приви́вка inoculation

при́вкус aftertaste; flavor

привлека́ть *impf.*, **привле́чь** *pf.* attract

приво́д drive; driving gear

привози́ть *impf.*, **привезти́** *pf.* bring (by vehicle)

привыка́ть *impf.*, **привы́кнуть** *pf.* (**к** + *D*) get used to

привы́чка habit

привы́чный usual; customary

привя́занность attachment

привя́зывать *impf.*, **привяза́ть** *pf.* tie; attach; **—ся** become attached; bother

приглаша́ть *impf.*, **—си́ть** *pf.* invite

приглаше́ние invitation

пригова́ривать *impf.*, **приговори́ть** *pf.* sentence; condemn

пригово́р sentence

приго́дный suitable; fit

при́город suburb

приготовля́ть *impf.*, **пригото́вить** *pf. v.t.* prepare

пригрози́ть *pf.* of **грози́ть**

придава́ть *impf.*, **прида́ть** *pf.* give; impart; attach

прида́вливать *impf.*, **придави́ть** *pf.* press (down); weigh down

прида́ное *n.* dowry

прида́ток FILL appendage

придоро́жный roadside

приду́мывать *impf.*, **приду́мать** *pf.* dream up; invent

прие́зд arrival

приезжа́ть *impf.*, **прие́хать** *pf.* arrive (by vehicle)

прие́зжий visiting; *n.* newcomer

прие́м 1. reception **2.** (*med.*) dose **3.** method, way; **—ная** *n.* reception room; **—ник** receiver

прие́млемый acceptable

прижима́ть *impf.*, **прижа́ть** *pf.* (**к** + *D*) press (against)

приз prize

призва́ние vocation, calling

приземля́ть *impf.*, **-ли́ть** *pf.* land

призёр prizewinner

признава́ть *impf.*, **призна́ть** *pf.* acknowledge, recognize; **—ся** (**в** + *P*) confess, admit

при́знак sign

призна́ние 1. acknowledgement **2.** recognition **3.** confession

призна́тельный grateful

призна́ть(ся) *pf.* of **признава́ть(ся)**

при́зрак ghost; apparition

призыва́ть *impf.*, **призва́ть** *pf.* call (up, upon); summon

прийти́(сь) *pf.* of **приходи́ть(ся)**

прика́з order, command

прика́зывать *impf.*, **приказа́ть** *pf.* order; command

прикаса́ться *impf.*, **прикосну́ться** *pf.* (**к** + *D*) touch

прикладно́й applied

прикла́дывать *impf.*, **приложи́ть** *pf.* add; enclose; apply

приключе́ние adventure

прикоснове́ние touch, contact

прикрепля́ть *impf.*, **-пи́ть** *pf.* fasten; attach

прилага́тельное *n.* adjective

прилага́ть *impf.*, **приложи́ть** *pf.* attach; apply

прила́скать *pf.* pet; caress

прилета́ть *impf.*, **-те́ть** *pf.* arrive (by air)

прили́в high tide; *Fig.* surge

прили́чие decency; decorum

прили́чный decent

приложе́ние supplement; enclosure; appendix

приложи́ть *pf.* of **прикла́дывать**, **прилага́ть**

прима́нка bait; lure

примене́ние application; use

применя́ть *impf.*, **-ни́ть** *pf.* apply, adapt; use

приме́р example; **—ный** exemplary; approximate

примеря́ть *impf.*, **приме́рить** *pf.* try on

приме́та sign, token, mark

примеча́ние (foot)note; comment

примире́ние reconciliation

примиря́ть *impf.*, **-ри́ть** *pf.* reconcile; conciliate

примо́рье seaside

принадлежа́ть *impf.* (+ *D*) belong

принадле́жность belonging; affiliation; *pl.* accessories

принима́ть *impf.*, **приня́ть** *pf.* take; receive; accept; adopt

приноси́ть *impf.*, **принести́** *pf.* bring; yield

принужда́ть *impf.*, **прину́дить** *pf.* compel, force

при́нцип principle

приобрета́ть *impf.*, **приобрести́** *pf.* acquire; gain

приобрете́ние acquisition

приорите́т priority

припа́док FILL attack; fit

припа́с supply, store

припе́в (*mus.*) refrain

припи́ска postscript

приписывать *impf.*, **приписать** *pf.* add (*in writing*); attribute

приподнятый exultant; elated

припоминать *impf.*, **припомнить** *pf.* remember, recollect

приправа seasoning; flavoring

природа nature

природный natural; inborn

прирост increase

присваивать *impf.*, **присвоить** *pf.* appropriate

приседать *impf.*, **присесть** *pf.* squat

прислать *pf. of* присылать

прислоняться *impf.*, **-ниться** *pf.* lean (against); rest

прислуга crew; servant

присмотр supervision

присниться *pf. of* сниться

присоединять(ся) *impf.*, **-нить(ся)** *pf.* join

приспособление adaptation; device; appliance

приспособлять *impf.*, **приспособить** *pf.* adapt; adjust

приставать *impf.*, **пристать** *pf.* stick (to); pester, nag

приставка (*gram.*) prefix

приставлять *impf.*, **приставить** *pf.* (к + D) put *or* lean against

пристальный (*of look*) fixed

пристань *f.* pier, dock, wharf

пристать *pf. of* приставать

пристойный proper; decorous

пристрастие (к + D) weakness; predilection; bias

приступ attack, fit

приступать *impf.*, **-пить** *pf.* (к + D) begin, start

присутствие presence

присутствовать *impf.* be present

присылать *impf.*, **прислать** *pf.* send

присяга oath

притворяться *impf.*, **-риться** *pf.* (+ I) feign

притеснять *impf.*, **-нить** *pf.* oppress

приток tributary

притом *conj.* besides

притон den (*e.g. gambling*)

притча parable

притягивать *impf.*, **притянуть** *pf.* attract

притязание claim; pretension

приучать *impf.*, **-чить** *pf.* train

прихлынуть *pf.* rush; surge

приход 1. arrival 2. receipts

приходить *impf.*, **прийти** *pf.*

come, arrive; **—ся** *impers.* (+ *infin.*) have to

приходо-расходный *attrib.* receipts and disbursements

прихожая *n.* hall; lobby

прихотливый whimsical

прихоть *f.* caprice, whim

прицел sight (*on a gun*)

прицеп trailer

причал mooring (line)

причаливать *impf.*, **причалить** *pf.* moor; (к + D) tie up

причём *conj.* moreover; and

причёска haircut

причёсывать(ся) *impf.*, **причесать(ся)** *pf.* comb; brush

причина cause; reason

причинять *impf.*, **-нить** *pf.* cause

пришивать *impf.*, **пришить** *pf.* sew on

приют shelter, refuge

приятель, **-ница** friend

приятный pleasant

про *prep.* (+ A) about; for

проанализировать *pf. of* анализировать

проба 1. trial, test 2. sample

пробег run; race

пробел gap; flaw

пробивать *impf.*, **пробить** *pf.* pierce; punch; **—ся** force one's way through

пробирка test tube

пробка 1. cork; stopper 2. (*elec.*) fuse 3. traffic jam

проблема problem

проблеск gleam; flash

пробовать *impf.*, **по-** *pf.* try

пробуждать *impf.*, **пробудить** *pf.* awaken; arouse

провал collapse; failure

проваливаться *impf.*, **провалиться** *pf.* fail; fall through

провезти *pf. of* провозить

проверка check (up); control

проверять *impf.*, **проверить** *pf.* check; verify; inspect

провести *pf. of* проводить

проветривать *impf.*, **проветрить** *pf.* air, ventilate

провод wire

проводить[1] *pf. of* провожать

проводить[2] *impf.*, **провести** *pf.* lead; take; pass; carry out

проводник[1], **-ница** guide

проводник[2] conductor

проводы *pl.* seeing off

провожать *impf.*, **-дить** *pf.* accompany; see off

провоз transport

провозглаша́ть *impf.*, -си́ть *pf.* proclaim

провози́ть *impf.*, провезти́ *pf.* transport; convey

про́волока wire; колю́чая ~ barbed wire

провоци́ровать *impf. & pf.* provoke

прогно́з forecast

проголосова́ть *pf. of* голосова́ть

прогоня́ть *impf.*, прогна́ть *pf.* drive away *or* off

програ́мма program; schedule

программи́ст programmer

прогресси́ровать *impf.* progress

прогу́лка walk, stroll

продава́ть *impf.*, прода́ть *pf.* sell

продаве́ц FILL salesman

продавщи́ца saleswoman

прода́жа sale; selling

продвиже́ние advancement

продлева́ть *impf.*, продли́ть *pf.* prolong; extend

продово́льствие food; foodstuffs

продолжа́ть *impf.*, продо́лжить *pf. v.t.* continue; prolong

продолже́ние continuation

проду́кт product; проду́кты groceries; —о́вый магази́н grocery store

продукти́вность productivity

проду́кция production; output

прое́зд passage; thoroughfare

проездно́й биле́т monthly ticket

проезжа́ть *impf.*, прое́хать *pf.* pass by *or* through

прое́зжий *n.* (passing) traveler

прое́кт project; design

проекти́ровать *impf.*, за- *pf.* project; plan, design

проже́ктор searchlight

прожива́ть *impf.*, прожи́ть *pf.* 1. live through 2. *impf.* live, reside

прожо́рливый voracious

про́за prose

про́звище nickname

прозра́чный transparent

прои́грыватель record player

прои́грывать *impf.*, проигра́ть *pf.* lose

про́игрыш loss

произведе́ние work; product

производи́ть *impf.*, произвести́ *pf.* produce; make; carry put

произво́дный derivative

произво́дственный industrial

произво́дство production; manufacture

произво́льный arbitrary

произноси́ть *impf.*, произнести́ *pf.* pronounce

произноше́ние pronunciation

происходи́ть *impf.*, произойти́ *pf.* 1. happen 2. result

происхожде́ние origin

происше́ствие event; occurrence

пройти́ *pf. of* проходи́ть

прока́за leprosy

прока́лывать *impf.*, проколо́ть *pf.* pierce

прока́т hire

прокла́дка 1. laying; building 2. washer; gasket

проклина́ть *impf.*, прокля́сть *pf.* damn; curse

прокля́тие curse; damnation

проко́л puncture

проколо́ть *pf. of* прока́лывать

прокуро́р prosecutor

прокути́ть *pf.* squander

проле́т 1. flight 2. bridge span

пролета́рий *n.*, -а́рка proletarian

проли́в (*geog.*) strait

пролива́ть *impf.*, проли́ть *pf.* spill; shed

про́мах miss; blunder

промедле́ние delay

проме́жность crotch

промежу́ток FILL interval

проме́нивать *impf.*, променя́ть *pf.* exchange; barter

промока́ть *impf.*, промо́кнуть *pf.* get wet; be drenched

промолча́ть *pf.* keep silent

промы́шленник manufacturer

промы́шленность industry

пронза́ть *impf.*, -зи́ть *pf.* pierce

пронзи́тельный piercing

проника́ть *impf.*, прони́кнуть *pf.* penetrate

проница́тельный perspicacious

пропада́ть *impf.*, пропа́сть *pf.* disappear; perish

пропа́жа loss

про́пасть *f.* chasm; abyss

пропи́ска 1. residence permit 2. registration

прописна́я бу́ква capital letter

пропи́сывать *impf.*, прописа́ть *pf.* 1. prescribe 2. register

пропита́ние subsistence

пропи́тывать *impf.*, пропита́ть *pf.* saturate

пропове́довать *impf.* preach

про́поведь *f.* sermon

пропо́рция proportion

про́пуск 1. omission 2. pass

пропуска́ть *impf.*, -сти́ть *pf.* 1. let pass, admit 2. omit; miss

прораста́ть *impf.*, **прорасти́** *pf.* germinate; sprout

про́резь *f.* slit; opening; cut

проро́к, -ро́чица prophet

проро́чество prophecy

про́рубь *f.* ice hole

прорыва́ть *impf.*, **прорва́ть** *pf.* break through; **—ся** burst open

просвети́тельный instructive

просветле́ние brightening

просве́чивать *impf.*, **просвети́ть** *pf.* x-ray; be translucent

просвеща́ть *impf.*, **-ти́ть** *pf.* enlighten

просвеще́ние enlightenment

про́сека cleared path in forest

просёлок FILL country road

проси́ть *impf.*, **по-** *pf.* ask; request

прославля́ть *impf.*, **просла́вить** *pf.* glorify; make famous

просле́живать *impf.*, **проследи́ть** *pf.* trace; track (down)

просло́йка layer; stratum

просма́тривать *impf.*, **просмотре́ть** *pf.* look through; overlook

просну́ться *pf. of* **просыпа́ться**

про́со millet

проспа́ть *pf. of* **просыпа́ть**

проспе́кт avenue

просро́ченный overdue

просро́чивать *impf.*, **просро́чить** *pf.* exceed a time limit

просро́чка 1. delinquency (*in paying a bill*) 2. expiration

простира́ть *pf.* wash (out)

прости́тельный pardonable

прости́ть(ся) *pf. of* **проща́ть(ся)**

про́сто *adv.* simply; **—ду́шие** artlessness; **—ре́чие** popular speech; **—серде́чный** simple-hearted

просто́й[1] simple; plain; ordinary

просто́й[2] downtime; idle time

простоква́ша thick sour milk

просто́р spaciousness; scope

просто́рный spacious; roomy

простота́ simplicity

простра́нство space

просту́да cold; chill

простужа́ться *impf.*, **-ди́ться** *pf.* catch a cold

просту́пок FILL misconduct

простыня́ bedsheet

просчёт miscalculation

просыпа́ть[1] *impf.*, **проспа́ть** *pf.* oversleep

просыпа́ть[2] *impf.*, **просы́пать** *pf. v.t.* spill; **—ся** *v.i.* spill

просыпа́ться *impf.*, **просну́ться** *pf.* wake up, awake

про́сьба request

проте́з prosthetic device; artificial limb

протека́ть *impf.*, **проте́чь** *pf.* leak; elapse

протере́ть *pf. of* **протира́ть**

протестова́ть *impf.* protest

про́тив *prep.* (+ *G*) against; opposite

про́тивень FILL *m.* baking sheet

проти́вник, -ница opponent

проти́вный 1. opposite, contrary 2. disgusting

противо- *in compounds* anti-, counter-

противозако́нный illegal

противозача́точный contraceptive

противополо́жный contrary; opposite

противопоставля́ть *impf.*, **-ста́вить** *pf.* oppose

противоре́чить *impf.* contradict

противостоя́ть *impf.* resist; withstand

противоя́дие antidote

протира́ть *impf.*, **-тере́ть** *pf.* 1. wear through 2. wipe (dry)

протоко́л minutes; record

протя́гивать *impf.*, **протяну́ть** *pf.* stretch (out); reach out

протяже́ние extent; stretch

профессиона́л professional; **—ьный** professional

профе́ссия profession

профе́ссор professor

про́филь *m.* profile; type

профсою́з trade union

прохла́да coolness

прохла́дный cool, chilly

прохо́д passage(way)

проходи́ть *impf.*, **пройти́** *pf.* pass; elapse; go through; study

прохо́жий *n.* passer-by

процвета́ть *impf.* prosper

проце́нт percentage; interest

проце́сс 1. process 2. lawsuit

проче́сть *pf. of* **чита́ть**

про́чий other; **и про́чее** and so on; **ме́жду про́чим** by the way

прочита́ть *pf. of* **чита́ть**

про́чный firm, solid; lasting

прочь *adv.* away; off

проше́дшее, про́шлое *n.* the past

проше́дший past

про́шлый past; last

проща́й(те) *interj.* good-bye!

проща́ние farewell, parting

проща́ть *impf.*, **-сти́ть** *pf.* forgive; excuse; **—ся** take leave

про́ще, *adv.* simpler, easier

проще́ние forgiveness; pardon

проявля́ть *impf.*, -яви́ть *pf.* display, show; (*photog.*) develop

пруд pond

пружи́на spring

прут twig; rod

пры́гать *impf.*, пры́гнуть *pf.* jump; leap; hop

прыжо́к FILL jump, leap; ~ в во́ду dive

прыщ, пры́щик pimple

прядь *f.* lock (of hair)

пря́жа thread, yarn

пря́жка buckle, clasp

пря́мо *adv.* straight; frankly

прямо́й straight; direct; frank

прямота́ uprightness

прямоуго́льник rectangle

пря́ник spice cake; gingerbread

пря́ность spice

пря́тать(ся) *impf.*, с- *pf.* hide (oneself)

пря́тки *pl.* hide-and-seek

Псалты́рь *m.* & *f.* Psalter

психиа́тр psychiatrist

психоана́лиз psychoanalysis

психо́лог psychologist

птене́ц FILL fledgling

пти́ца bird

пти́чий *attrib.* bird; poultry

публи́ка public; audience

публикова́ть *impf.*, о- *pf.* publish

публи́чный public

пу́гало scarecrow

пуга́ть *impf.*, ис-, пугну́ть *pf.* frighten; scare

пугли́вый timid; fearful

пу́говица button

пу́дра powder

пузырёк FILL 1. bubble 2. small bottle

пузы́рь *m.* 1. bubble; blister 2. bladder

пулемёт machine gun

пуло́вер pullover; sweater

пульс pulse

пульт console; control panel

пу́ля bullet

пункт point; item

пупо́к FILL navel

пурга́ blizzard; snowstorm

пурпу́рный purple

пуска́ть *impf.*, пусти́ть *pf.* let (go; in); start; permit

пусте́ть *impf.*, о- *pf.* become empty

пусто́й empty, hollow; vacant

пустота́ emptiness; vacuum

пусты́ня desert

пусты́рь *m.* abandoned lot

пусть *particle.* let; ~ он идёт let him go

пустя́к trifle

пу́таница confusion

пу́тать *impf.* confuse; mix up

путёвка 1. (travel) voucher 2. place in a tourist group

путеводи́тель guidebook

путём *prep.* (+ G) by means of

путеше́ственник, -ница traveler

путеше́ствие trip, journey

путеше́ствовать *impf.* travel

путь *m.* road; way; means

пух down; пу́хлый chubby

пу́хнуть *impf.*, вс-, о- *pf.* swell

пучо́к FILL bunch; tuft

пуши́стый fluffy; downy

пу́шка cannon; gun

пчела́ bee

пшени́ца wheat

пшено́ millet

пыл ardor, passion; fervor

пыла́ть *impf.* flame; blaze; glow

пылесо́с vacuum cleaner

пы́лкий ardent; passionate

пыль *f.* dust; пы́льный dusty

пыльца́ pollen

пыта́ть *impf.* torture

пыта́ться *impf.*, по- *pf.* try, endeavor

пы́тка torture; agony

пы́шный magnificent; luxuriant

пье́са (*theat.*) play

пьяне́ть *impf.*, о- *pf.* get drunk

пья́ница *m.* & *f.* drunkard

пья́ный drunk(en)

пядь *f.* span

пятёрка five-ruble note

пятидеся́тый fiftieth

пя́тка (*anat.*) heel

пятна́дцатый fifteenth

пятна́дцать fifteen

пятна́шки *pl.* (game) tag

пятни́стый spotty, spotted

пя́тница Friday

пятно́ stain, spot

пя́тый fifth

пять five; —деся́т fifty; —со́т five hundred

раб, раба́ slave
рабо́та work
рабо́тать *impf.*, по- *pf.* work
рабо́тник, -ница worker
работода́тель employer
рабо́чий worker's; *n.* worker
ра́бство slavery
ра́венство equality
равни́на (*geog.*) plain
равнове́сие equilibrium; balance
равноду́шный indifferent
равнопра́вие equal rights
ра́вный equal
рад *pred.* glad; pleased
ра́ди *prep.* (+ *G*) for the sake of
радиа́ция radiation
ра́дио *neut. indecl.* radio;
—веща́ние broadcasting;
—переда́ча broadcast; —приёмник radio receiver
ра́довать *impf.*, об- *pf.* gladden
ра́достный joyous; joyful
ра́дость joy; delight
ра́дуга rainbow
ра́дужный iridescent; bright
раз (one) time; *conj.* since
разбавля́ть *impf.*, разба́вить *pf.*
dilute
разбива́ть *impf.*, разби́ть *pf. v.t.*
break; smash; defeat; divide (up)
разбира́ть *impf.*, разобра́ть *pf.*
dismantle; take apart; investigate;
sort out; —ся (в + *P*) understand; sort out
разбогате́ть *pf.* get rich
разбо́й robbery
разбо́р analysis; —чивый 1. legible 2. fastidious
разбра́сывать *impf.*, разброса́ть
pf. scatter
разбро́д confusion; discord
разбуди́ть *pf.* wake
разва́лина wreck; *pl.* ruins
ра́зве *particle.* really?
разведе́ние 1. breeding 2. cultivation
разве́дка reconnaisance; intelligence (service)
развёртывать *impf.*, разверну́ть
pf. unfold, open; spread out
развести́(сь) *pf. of* разводи́ть(ся)
разветвле́ние branching
развива́ть(ся) *impf.*, разви́ть(ся)
pf. develop
разви́тие development
развлека́ть *impf.*, развле́чь *pf.*
amuse

развлече́ние amusement
разво́д divorce
разводи́ть *impf.*, развести́ *pf.* 1.
divorce 2. breed 3. dilute; —ся
(с + *I*) get divorced; multiply
разводно́й мост drawbridge
разворо́т turn; U-turn; development
развра́т depravity
развраща́ть *impf.*, -ти́ть *pf.* corrupt; deprave
развя́зка outcome; climax
развя́зывать *impf.*, развяза́ть *pf.*
untie; unleash
разга́дывать *impf.*, разгада́ть *pf.*
solve; guess
разгляде́ть *pf.* discern
разгова́ривать *impf.* talk, converse
разгово́р conversation
разгово́рник phrase book
разгово́рный colloquial
разгово́рчивый talkative
разгоня́ть *impf.*, разогна́ть *pf. v.t.*
disperse
разгро́м defeat, rout
разгроми́ть *pf. of* громи́ть
разгружа́ть *impf.*, -зи́ть *pf.* unload
раздава́ть *impf.*, разда́ть *pf.* distribute; —ся resound; ring out
раздави́ть *pf.* crush; smash
разда́ча distribution
раздева́лка *Colloq.* coatroom;
checkroom
раздева́ть(ся) *impf.*, разде́ть(ся)
pf. undress
разде́л division; section; —е́ние
division; —ьный separate.
разделя́ть(ся) *pf. of* дели́ть(ся),
разделя́ть
разделя́ть *impf.*, -ли́ть *pf.* separate; divide
раздо́лье expanse; liberty
раздо́р discord
раздража́ть *impf.*, -жи́ть *pf.* irritate
раздражи́тельный irritable
разду́мывать *impf.* deliberate
разду́мье meditation
разду́тый swollen; excessive
разева́ть *impf.*, рази́нуть *pf. Colloq.* open one's mouth wide
разжига́ть *impf.*, разже́чь *pf.* kindle; stir up
разжима́ть *impf.*, разжа́ть *pf.* release; relax

разлага́ться *impf.*, разложи́ть *pf.* decompose, decay

разла́д discord

разли́в flood; overflow

разлива́ть *impf.*, разли́ть *pf.* spill; pour out

разливно́й (*of beer*) draft; on tap

различа́ть *impf.*, -чи́ть *pf.* distinguish; —ся *pf.* only differ

разли́чие difference; distinction

разли́чный different; diverse

разложи́ться *pf. of* разлага́ться

разло́м breaking up; break

разлу́ка separation

разлуча́ть *impf.*, -чи́ть *pf.* separate

разлюби́ть *pf.* cease to love

разма́х sweep; scope, range

разма́хивать *impf.*, размахну́ть *pf.* (+ *I*) brandish; swing

разме́н exchange

разме́нивать *impf.*, разменя́ть *pf.* change (money)

разме́р dimension, size; scale

размеща́ть *impf.*, -сти́ть *pf.* place; accommodate

разми́нка warm-up

размножа́ть *impf.*, размно́жить *pf.* multiply

размо́лвка spat; disagreement

размышле́ние reflection

размышля́ть *impf.*, разми́слить *pf.* reflect; ponder

разнести́ *pf. of* разноси́ть

ра́зница difference

разнови́дность variety

разногла́сие difference; disagreement

разнообра́зный diverse; varied

разноро́дный heterogeneous

разноси́ть *impf.*, разнести́ *pf.* 1. carry; deliver 2. spread

разносторо́нний many-sided, versatile

разну́зданный unruly; rowdy

ра́зный different; diverse

разоблача́ть *impf.*, -чи́ть *pf.* expose

разобра́ть *pf. of* разбира́ть

ра́зовый valid for one time

разогна́ть *pf. of* разгоня́ть

разозли́ть *pf.* anger, enrage

разойти́сь *pf. of* расходи́ться

разорва́ться *pf. of* разрыва́ться

разоре́ние destruction; ruin

разоружа́ть *impf.*, -жи́ть *pf.* disarm

разоря́ть *impf.*, -ри́ть *pf.* ruin

разоча́ровывать *impf.*, разочаро-ва́ть *pf.* disappoint

разраба́тывать *impf.*, -рабо́тать *pf.* work out; elaborate; (*mine*) exploit

разреза́ть *impf.*, разре́зать *pf.* cut; slit; section

разреша́ть *impf.*, -ши́ть *pf.* 1. permit, allow 2. solve

разреше́ние permission; solution

разру́ха ruin, devastation

разруша́ть *impf.*, разру́шить *pf.* destroy; raze; demolish

разруши́тельный destructive

разры́в break, rupture

разрыва́ться *impf.*, разорва́ться *pf.* burst; explode

разря́д¹ category; class

разря́д² (*elec.*) (*weapon, etc.*) discharge

разря́дка détente; unloading

разряжа́ть *impf.*, -дя́ть *pf.* unload; discharge

ра́зум reason; mind, intellect

разуме́ется *impers.* of course; it goes without saying

разу́мный reasonable

разъединя́ть *impf.*, -ни́ть *pf.* disconnect

разъясня́ть *impf.*, -ни́ть *pf.* explain

разы́скивать *impf.*, разыска́ть *pf.* search for; *pf.* find

рай paradise

райо́н region; district

рак¹ crayfish

рак² (*med.*) cancer

раке́та rocket; missile

раке́тка (*sports*) tennis racket

ра́ковина 1. shell 2. sink

раку́шка shell; seashell

ра́ма frame

ра́на wound

ра́неный *n.* wounded person

ра́нец FILL knapsack

ра́нить *impf. & pf.* wound

ра́нний early; ра́но *adv.* early

ра́ньше *adv.* earlier

ра́са race

раска́иваться *impf.*, раска́яться *pf.* be sorry; repent

раскалённый red-hot; scorching

раска́яние remorse; repentance

раскладу́шка cot

раскла́дывать *impf.*, разложи́ть *pf.* lay out; spread

раско́л split; schism

раско́пки *pl.* excavations

раско́сый (*eyes*) slanting

раскра́шивать *impf.*, раскра́сить *pf.* color; paint

раскритикова́ть pf. criticize severely

раскрыва́ть impf., **раскры́ть** pf. uncover; open; disclose

раскупо́ривать impf., **раскупо́рить** pf. uncork

ра́совый racial

распада́ться impf., **распа́сться** pf. disintegrate; break apart

распако́вывать impf., **распакова́ть** pf. unpack

распа́хивать impf., **распахну́ть** pf. open wide; throw open

распеча́тка printout

распеча́тывать impf., **распеча́тать** pf. unseal; open

расписа́ние schedule; timetable

распи́ска receipt

распла́вленный molten

распла́каться pf. burst into tears

распла́та payment; retribution

распла́чиваться impf., **расплати́ться** pf. pay off; get even

располага́ть impf., **расположи́ть** pf. dispose (of); win over; arrange; **—ся** settle (down)

расположе́ние 1. disposition; inclination **2.** arrangement **3.** location

располо́женный 1. located **2.** (к + D) fond of; disposed toward

распоряди́тель, —ница manager

распоря́док FILL order; routine

распоряжа́ться impf., **-ди́ться** pf. order; be in command; manage

распоряже́ние order; instruction

распра́ва reprisal

распределя́ть impf., **-ли́ть** pf. distribute

распрода́жа clearance sale

распространённый widespread; widely disseminated

распространя́ть impf., **-ни́ть** pf. spread; disseminate

ра́спря 1. discord **2.** strife

распуска́ть impf., **-сти́ть** pf. dismiss, disband; let out; **—ся** open; come undone; let oneself go; get out of hand

распу́тный dissolute

распу́тывать impf., **распу́тать** pf. disentangle

распу́щенный dissolute

распыли́тель sprayer; atomizer

распя́тие crucifixion; crucifix

рассве́т dawn, daybreak

рассе́янный scattered; absent-minded

расска́з story; tale; **—чик, —чица** storyteller

расска́зывать impf., **рассказа́ть** pf. recount; tell

рассла́бленный weak; unsteady

рассле́довать impf. & pf. investigate

расслое́ние stratification

рассма́тривать impf., **рассмотре́ть** pf. consider; examine; pf. only discern

расспра́шивать impf., **расспроси́ть** pf. question; make inquiries

рассро́чка installment

расстава́ться impf., **расста́ться** pf. v.i. part; separate

расстано́вка placement; arrangement

расстёгивать impf., **расстегну́ть** pf. undo; unbutton; unhook

расстоя́ние distance

расстра́ивать impf., **расстро́ить** pf. disturb; unsettle; upset

расстре́л execution (by shooting)

расстро́йство disorder

рассуди́тельный reasonable; sensible

рассу́док FILL reason; common sense

рассужда́ть impf. discuss; reason

рассчи́тывать impf., **рассчита́ть** pf. calculate; reckon; intend

рассыпа́ть impf., **рассы́пать** pf. spill; strew; scatter

растая́ть pf. of **та́ять**

раство́р solution

раствори́мый soluble

растворя́ть(ся) impf., **-ри́ть(ся)** pf. dissolve

расте́ние plant

растёрянный confused; dismayed

растеря́ть pf. lose

расти́ impf., **вы́-** pf. v.i. grow (up)

растира́ние grinding; rubbing

расти́тельность vegetation

расти́ть impf., **вы́-** pf. raise; grow

растле́нный decadent; corrupt

расторга́ть impf., **расто́ргнуть** pf. dissolve; cancel

расторо́пный efficient; quick

растра́та waste; embezzlement

растра́чивать impf., **растра́тить** pf. squander; embezzle

растрёпанный tattered; tousled

растро́гать pf. move; touch

расти́гивать impf., **растяну́ть** pf. stretch; prolong; strain

расхва́ливать impf., **расхвали́ть** pf. extol; rave about

расхи́титель, —ница embezzler

расхища́ть impf., **расхи́тить** pf. plunder

расхо́д expenditure
расходи́ться *impf.*, разойти́сь *pf.* break up; disperse; diverge
расхо́довать *impf.*, из- *pf.* spend
расхожде́ние divergence
расхоте́ть *pf.* want no longer
расцве́т bloom; flowering
расцвета́ть *impf.*, расцвести́ *pf.* blossom out; flourish
расцве́тка color scheme
расце́нка evaluation; price
расчёт calculation; —ливый thrifty; prudent
распа́танный wobbly; rickety
расширя́ть *impf.*, расши́рить *pf.* widen; enlarge; extend
расшифро́вывать *impf.*, расшифрова́ть *pf.* decipher
расще́лина cleft; fissure; crevice
ра́товать *impf.* fight (for: за + *A*; against: про́тив + *G*)
ра́ция walkie-talkie
ра́шпер gridiron; grill
рва́ный torn; full of holes
рвать *impf. v.t.* tear; rend; pick; pull out *or* off; —ся burst; break (+ *infin.*) be dying to
рве́ние zeal; ardor
рво́та vomiting
реаги́ровать *impf.* react; respond
реакти́вный 1. reactive 2. *attrib.* jet 3. jet propelled
реа́льность reality
ребёнок FILL *m.* baby
ребро́ 1. rib 2. edge
ребя́та *pl.* children; boys
рёв roar; bellow; howl
реве́ранс curtsy
реви́зия inspection; revision
ревизо́р inspector
ревмати́зм rheumatism
ревни́вый jealous
ревнова́ть *impf.* be jealous
ре́вность jealousy
револьве́р revolver
революционе́р, —ка revolutionary
револю́ция revolution
регистри́ровать *impf.*, за- *pf.* register
регла́мент agenda; allotted time
регули́ровать *impf.* regulate
редакти́ровать *impf.*, от- *pf.* edit.
реда́ктор editor
реда́кция 1. editing 2. editorial offices
реди́ска radish
ре́дкий rare
ре́дкость rarity; sparseness
ре́же *compar.* of ре́дкий, ре́дко
режи́м regime; routine

режиссёр director; producer
ре́зать *impf.* cut; carve
резви́ться *impf.* frolic; romp
ре́звый playful, frisky
резе́рв reserve
рези́на rubber
рези́нка 1. elastic 2. eraser
ре́зкий harsh; biting, sharp
резня́ slaughter
резона́нс response; reaction
результа́т result
резь *f.* sharp pain; colic
резьба́ carving; fretwork
рейс trip, voyage; flight
рейту́зы *pl.* leggings
река́ river
реквизи́т (*theat.*) stage prop
рекла́ма advertisement; publicity
рекомендова́ть *impf. & pf. also* по- *pf.* recommend
реко́рд record
рели́гия religion
рели́кт relic; ancient artifact
релье́ф relief
рельс rail
реме́нь FILL *m.* strap; belt
ремесло́ trade; handicraft
ремо́нт repair; overhaul
ремонти́ровать *impf.*, от- *pf.* repair; overhaul
ре́нта rent; income
рентге́н X-ray (machine)
ре́па turnip
репети́тор 1. tutor 2. coach
репети́ция rehearsal
ре́плика retort; rejoinder; cue
репорта́ж reporting; news report
репортёр reporter
репроду́ктор loudspeaker
репута́ция reputation
ресни́ца eyelash
респу́блика republic
рессо́ра (*mech.*) spring
рестора́н restaurant
ресу́рсы *pl.* resources
рефера́т essay, paper; abstract
рефо́рма reform
рецензе́нт reviewer; critic
реце́нзия review; criticism
реце́пт 1. prescription 2. recipe
рециди́в recurrence; relapse; (*law*) second offense.
речь *f.* speech
реша́ть *impf.*, реши́ть *pf.* decide; solve
реше́ние decision; solution
решётка grating; lattice
реши́тельный decisive; resolute
ржаве́ть *impf.* rust

ржа́вчина rust
ржать *impf.* neigh
ри́за (*eccles.*) chasuble
ри́млянин, -ля́нка Roman
ри́мский Roman
рис rice
риск risk
рискова́ть *impf.*, рискну́ть *pf.* risk
рисова́ть *impf.*, на- *pf.* draw; depict
рису́нок drawing
ритм rhythm
ри́фма rhyme
робе́ть *impf.* be timid; be shy
ро́бкий timid; shy
ро́бот robot
ров ditch
рове́сник, -ница agemate
ро́вный flat; even; equal
ровня́ть *impf.*, с- *pf.* even; level
рог horn, antler; —а́тый horned
рога́тка slingshot
род 1. kin; family; kind 2. (*gram.*) gender
роди́льный *attrib.* maternity
ро́дина homeland
роди́нка mole; birthmark
роди́тели *pl.* parents
роди́ть(ся) *pf. of* рожда́ть(ся)
родни́к spring
родно́й own; native
родня́ *coll.* relatives
ро́дственник, -ница relative
ро́дственный kindred, related
ро́ды *pl.* childbirth
рожа́ть *impf.*, роди́ть *pf.* give birth; have a child
рожда́ть *impf.*, роди́ть *pf.* give birth (to); —ся be born
рожде́ние birth
Рождество́ Christmas
рожь *f.* rye
ро́за rose; ро́зовый pink; rosy
ро́зга rod (*for whipping*)
розе́тка (*elec.*) socket
розма́рин rosemary
ро́зничный retail
ро́зыгрыш 1. (lottery) drawing 2. (*sports*) playoffs
ро́зыск search; investigation
рок fate; —ово́й fatal
ро́лик 1. roller; caster 2. (*film*) reel; *pl.* roller skates
ро́ликовая доска́ skateboard
роль *f.* role, part
ром rum
рома́н novel; love affair
рома́нс (*mus.*) romance
рома́шка camomile

роня́ть *impf.*, урони́ть *pf.* drop
ро́пот murmur; grumble
ропта́ть *impf.* murmur
роса́ dew
роско́шный luxurious
ро́скошь *f.* luxury
ро́спись *f.* painting; mural
росси́йский Russian
Росси́я Russia
рост growth; increase; height
ро́стбиф roast beef
росто́к FILL sprout; shoot
рот FILL mouth
ро́та (*mil.*) company
ро́ща grove
роя́ль *f.* (grand) piano
ртуть *f.* mercury
руба́шка shirt
рубе́ж boundary, border; за рубежо́м abroad
рубе́ц FILL 1. scar; welt 2. hem
руби́н ruby
руби́ть *impf.* fell; chop
рубль *m.* ruble
ру́брика heading
руга́нь *f.* verbal abuse; swearing
руга́тельство swearword
руга́ть *impf.*, вы́- *pf.* scold; swear at; curse out
руда́ ore; рудни́к mine; pit
ружьё gun; arms
руи́ны ruins
рука́ hand; arm; —в sleeve
рука́вица mitten
руководи́ть *impf.* (+ *I*) manage; lead
руково́дство guidance, leadership
рукоде́лие needlework
ру́копись *f.* manuscript
рукопожа́тие handshake
рулево́й *attrib.* steering
руле́т meatloaf or potato loaf
руле́тка tape measure
руль *m.* 1. rudder; helm 2. steering wheel
румы́н, —ка Romanian
Румы́ния Romania
румя́на *pl.* rouge
румя́нец FILL flush; blush
румя́ный rosy, ruddy
ру́пор megaphone; mouthpiece
руса́лка mermaid
ру́сло channel; riverbed
ру́сский, ру́сская *adj., n.* Russian
ру́сый light brown
ру́хнуть *pf.* crash; collapse
руча́тельство guarantee
руче́й brook; stream
ру́чка handle; knob; (*chair*) arm

ручнóй *attrib.* hand; manual

рýшить *impf.* tear down; **—ся** collapse

рыба fish

рыбáк, рыбáчка fisherman

рывóк FILL jerk; spurt; dash

рыдáть *impf.* sob

рыжий red; red-haired

рынок FILL market(place)

рысь¹ lynx

рысь² *f.* trot; **рысью** at a trot

рыть *impf.* dig; **рыться** rummage

рыхлить *impf.,* вз- *pf.* loosen

рыхлый loose; crumbly; friable

рыцарь *m.* knight

рычáг lever

рычáть *impf.* growl; snarl

рюкзáк knapsack; backpack

рюмка liqueur glass

рябина mountain ash

рябить *impf.* ripple

рябóй pitted, pock-marked

рявкать *impf.,* ря́вкнуть *pf.* roar

ряд row; line; series; **—овóй** ordinary, common; n. (mil.) private

рядом *adv.* side by side; ~ с (+ I) next (to)

С

с, со *prep.* **1.** (+ I) with **2.** (+ G) from; since; off; down from **3.** (+ A) about

сáбля saber

саботáж sabotage

саботировать *impf. & pf.* sabotage

сáван shroud; cover

сад garden; **детский ~** kindergarten

садиться *impf.,* сесть *pf.* sit down; land; set; shrink

сáднить *impf.* smart; burn

садóвник, -ница gardener

садóвый *attrib.* garden

сáжа soot

сажáть *impf.,* посадить *pf.* plant; seat

салáт lettuce, salad

сáло fat; suet

салóн salon

салфéтка napkin

сáльный greasy; *attrib.* tallow

салю́т salute

салютовáть *impf. & pf.* salute

сам *pron.* **—á, —ó,** *pl.* **сáми** -self; **~ по себé** by itself

самéц FILL (zool.) male

самиздáт underground publication

сáмка (zool.) female

само- *pref.* self-, auto-

самобы́тный original; distinctive

самовáр samovar

самовлюблённый conceited

самовозгорáние spontaneous combustion

самогóн homemade vodka

самодéльный homemade

самодержáвие autocracy

самодéржец FILL, **-жица** autocrat

самодéятельность amateur work; personal initiative

самодовóльный self-satisfied

самодýр petty tyrant

самодýрство high-handedness

самозащита self-defense

самозвáнец FILL, **-áнка** impostor

самозвáный self-styled

самокáт scooter

самолёт airplane

самолю́бие pride; self-respect

самомнéние conceit, self-importance

самонадéянный presumptuous

самооблáдание self-control

самообмáн self-deception

самооборóна self-defense

самообслýживание self-service

самоотвéрженный selfless

самопожéртвование self-sacrifice

самородок FILL **1.** nugget **2.** person with natural talent

самосáд home-grown tobacco

самосвáл dump truck

самосознáние consciousness

самосохранéние self-preservation

самостоя́тельный independent

самосýд lynching

самотёк drift

самоубийство (act) suicide

самоубийца *m. & f.* (person) suicide

самоувéренный self-confident

самоуправлéние self-government

самоучитель self-study guide

самоýчка *m. & f.* self-taught person

самоходный self-propelled

самоцвéт semiprecious stone

сáмый *pron., adj.* (the) very; (the) most

сан rank; title; office

санатóрий sanitorium

сандáлия sandal

са́ни *pl.* sleigh

санита́р hospital attendant

санита́рия sanitation

санита́рный sanitary; medical

са́нкция sanction(s)

санте́хник plumber

сантиме́тр centimeter

сапёр (*mil.*) sapper

сапо́г boot

сапо́жник shoemaker

сара́й shed; barn

сарде́лька short, thick sausage

сарди́на, сарди́нка sardine

саркофа́г sarcophagus

сати́ра satire; **сати́рик** satirist.

сати́рический satirical

Сау́довская Ара́вия Saudi Arabia

са́хар sugar; **—ница** sugar bowl; **—ный** *attrib.* sugar, sugary

сачо́к FILL net

сбавля́ть *impf.*, **сба́вить** *pf.* reduce

сбаланси́ровать *pf.* regain one's balance

сберега́тельный *attrib.* savings

сберега́ть *impf.*, **сбере́чь** *pf.* save; preserve

сберка́сса savings bank

сберкни́жка bankbook

сбива́ть *impf.*, **сбить** *pf.* knock or bring down; distract

сближа́ть *impf.*, **сбли́зить** *pf.* draw *or* bring together; **—ся** approach; draw near

сбо́ку *adv.* from one side; on one side

сбор collection; dues; duty

сбо́рище *Colloq.* gathering; crowd

сбо́рник collection; anthology

сбо́рщик, —щица collector; assembler

сбра́сывать *impf.*, **сбро́сить** *pf.* throw off; overthrow; discard

сбыт sale; market

сва́дьба wedding

сва́ливать *impf.*, **свали́ть** *pf.* knock down; heap up

сва́лка dump; scuffle

сва́ривать *impf.*, **свари́ть** *pf.* weld

свари́ть *pf. of* вари́ть, сва́ривать

сварли́вый cantankerous

сват, сва́ха matchmaker

сватовство́ matchmaking

све́дения *pl.* information; intelligence; knowledge

све́дущий knowledgeable; well-versed

све́жий fresh

свекла́ beet

свёкор FILL father-in-law (*husband's father*)

свекро́вь *f.* mother-in-law (*husband's mother*)

сверже́ние overthrow

сверка́ть *impf.*, **сверкну́ть** *pf.* sparkle; twinkle

сверли́ть *impf.*, **про-** *pf.* drill

сверло́ (*tool*) drill, borer

све́рстник, -ница person of one's own age

свёрток package; bundle

сверх *prep.* (+ *G*) beyond; above; over; ~ того́ moreover

сверхпри́быль *f.* excess profits

све́рху *adv.* from above

сверхуро́чные *n. pl.* overtime

сверхъесте́ственный supernatural

свести́ *pf. of* своди́ть

свет[1] light

свет[2] 1. world 2. society

света́ть *impf. impers.* dawn

свети́ло luminary

свети́льник (oil) lamp

свети́ть(ся) *impf.* shine

светле́ть *impf.*, **по-, про-** *pf.* brighten (up)

све́тлый bright; light; clear

светлячо́к FILL firefly

светонепроница́емый lightproof

светопреставле́ние end of the world

светофо́р traffic light

све́тский fashionable; refined; secular

свеча́, све́чка 1. candle 2. suppository

свида́ние appointment; до свида́ния! goodbye!

свиде́тель, —ница witness

свиде́тельство 1. testimony; evidence 2. license; certificate

свиде́тельствовать *impf.*, **за-, о-** *pf.* witness; testify (to); be evidence of

свине́ц FILL (*metal*) lead

свини́на pork

сви́нство squalor; filth

свинья́ pig

свире́пость ferocity

свире́пый fierce, ferocious

свист (*sound*) whistle

свиста́ть, свисте́ть *impf.* whistle

свисто́к FILL whistle

сви́та suite; retinue

сви́тер sweater

свия́зь *f.* (*duck*) widgeon

свобо́да freedom; liberty

свобо́дный 1. free; vacant 2. loose; spare

свод 1. arch, vault **2.** code
своди́ть *impf.*, **свести́** *pf.* bring together; take (down, away); reduce
сво́дка summary; report
сво́дный *attrib.* summary; step-
своево́льный strong-willed
своевре́менный timely
своенра́вный arbitrary; capricious
своеобра́зный original; distinctive
свой, своя́, своё, *pl.* **свои́** one's (own)
сво́йственный (+ *D*) characteristic
сво́лочь *Colloq. f.* swine; bastard; riffraff
сво́ра pack; gang
высо́ка́ *adv.* with disdain
свы́ше *adv.* from above; *prep.* (+ *G*) over; beyond
свя́занный 1. related **2.** connected **3.** (*chem.*) combined
связа́ть *pf.* of **вяза́ть, свя́зывать**
свя́зка 1. bunch **2.** ligament
свя́зный connected; coherent
свя́зывать *impf.*, **связа́ть** *pf.* tie, bind, connect
связь *f.* tie; bond; connection
Свя́тки *pl.* yuletide
свято́й holy, sacred; *n.* saint
свя́тость holiness; sanctity
святота́тственный sacrilegious
святы́ня sacred object *or* place
свяще́нник priest; clergyman
свяще́нный sacred
гиба́ть *impf.*, **согну́ть** *pf.* bend
сгла́зить *pf.* jinx
сгни́ть *pf.* of **гнить**
сгова́риваться *impf.*, **сговори́ться** *pf.* arrange; agree; conspire
сго́вор conspiracy; collusion
сгора́ть *impf.*, **сгоре́ть** *pf. v.i.* burn (down); be consumed
сго́рбленный hunched; stooped
сгоряча́ *adv.* in a fit of temper
сгуща́ть *impf.*, **-сти́ть** *pf.* thicken; condense; clot
сгущёнка *Colloq.* condensed milk
сдава́ть *impf.*, **сдать** *pf.* pass *or* hand in; yield; rent; lease; **—ся** surrender
сда́ча 1. surrender **2.** letting in (money) change
сдвиг change; improvement
сде́лать(ся) *pf.* of **де́лать(ся)**
сде́лка deal; transaction
сде́льный by the piece
сде́ржанный reserved; restrained
сде́рживать *impf.*, **держа́ть** *pf.*

restrain, hold in, keep back; **—ся** control oneself
сдо́ба 1. shortening **2.** sweet roll; bun(s)
сеа́нс 1. session **2.** performance
себе́ *pron.*, *D, P* of **себя́**
себесто́имость cost, price
себя́ *refl. pron.* oneself
се́вер north; **—ный** North, northern; **—я́нин, —я́нка** northerner
се́веро-восто́к northeast
се́веро-за́пад northwest
сего́дня *adv.* today
сего́дняшний today's
сегрега́ция segregation
седе́ть *impf.*, **по-** *pf.* turn gray
седина́ gray hair
седло́ saddle
седлови́на (*geog.*) depression
седо́й (of hair) gray
седо́к 1. rider **2.** passenger
седьмо́й seventh
сезо́н season; **—ный** seasonal
сейф safe
сейча́с *adv.* now; at once
сека́ч (*tool*) chopper
секре́т secret; **—ный** secret
секрета́рский secretarial
секрета́рь *m.*, **-та́рша** secretary
секре́тер desk
секре́ция secretion
секс sex; **—уа́льность** sexuality; **—уа́льный** sexual
се́кта sect
секта́нт, —ка sectarian
секта́нтский sectarian
се́ктор sector
секу́нда second
секундоме́р stopwatch
се́кция section
селёдка herring
селезёнка (*anat.*) spleen
се́лезень FILL M. drake
селе́кция selection
сели́тра saltpeter; niter
село́ village
сельдере́й celery
сельдь *f.* herring
се́льский 1. rural **2.** *attrib.* village
сельскохозя́йственный agricultural
семафо́р semaphore
сёмга salmon
семе́йный domestic; family
семе́йство family
семени́к 1. seed plant **2.** testicle
семёрка seven; the number seven
семе́стр semester
сѐмечко *dim.* of **сѐмя**

семидеся́тый seventieth

семина́р seminar

семинари́ст seminary student

семина́рия seminary

семисо́тый seven-hundredth

семна́дцатый seventeenth

семна́дцать seventeen

семь seven; —деся́т seventy; —со́т seven hundred

семья́нин family man

семья́ family

се́мя neut. (pl. семена́) seed; semen

сена́т senate; —ор senator

се́но hay; —ва́л hayloft; —ко́с haymaking

сенсацио́нный sensational

сенса́ция sensation

сенте́нция maxim; saying

сентимента́льный sentimental

сентя́брь m., —ский September

сень f. Obs. cover; canopy

се́псис sepsis

се́ра 1. sulfur 2. ear wax

серафи́м seraph

серб, се́рбка Serb

серви́з set (of dishes)

сервиро́вка setting (of table)

серде́чно-сосу́дистый cardiovascular

серде́чный 1. attrib. heart; cardiac 2. tender, cordial

серди́тый angry

серди́ть impf., рас- pf. anger

се́рдце heart; —биéние palpitation; —ви́дный heart-shaped; —ви́на core

серебро́ silver

сере́бряный silver

середи́на middle

сере́динный middle

сери́йный mass-produced

се́рия series; part

се́рна chamois

серп sickle

серпанти́н (paper) streamer

сертифика́т certificate

се́рфинг surfing

се́рый gray

серьга́ earring

серьёзный serious; earnest

се́ссия session

сестра́ sister; медици́нская ~ nurse

сесть pf. of сади́ться

се́тка net; netting; grid; system

се́тчатый netted; reticular

сеть f. 1. net 2. system

се́ять impf., по- pf. sow

сжа́литься pf. (над + I) take pity on

сжа́тый concise; clenched; compressed

сжать[1] pf. of сжима́ть

сжать[2] pf. of жать

сжечь pf. of жечь

сжи́женный liquefied

сжима́ть impf., сжать pf. press, squeeze; condense

сза́ди adv. from behind; prep. (+ G) behind

сиби́рский Siberian

Сиби́рь f. Siberia

сибиря́к, -ря́чка Siberian

си́вый gray; grayish

сига́ра cigar

сигаре́та cigarette

сигна́л signal; —ьный attrib. signal

сигнализа́ция alarm system

сиде́лка nurse; home attendant

сиде́нье seat

сиде́ть impf. sit, be seated

сидр cider

сидя́чий 1. sitting 2. sedentary

си́зый blue-gray

си́ла strength; power; force

сила́ч, -ка́ strong person

силико́н silicone

си́лос silo

силуэ́т silhouette

си́льный strong

симбио́з symbiosis

си́мвол symbol; character

символизи́ровать impf. symbolize

симметри́ческий, симметри́чный symmetrical

симпати́чный likable; nice

симпа́тия (к + D) liking for

симпто́м symptom

симули́ровать impf. & pf. simulate; feign

симуля́ция simulation

симфони́ческий attrib. symphony; symphonic

синаго́га synagogue

синдро́м syndrome

синева́ blue expanse

синегла́зый blue-eyed

си́ний dark blue

сини́ца titmouse

си́ний dark blue

сино́ним synonym

сино́птик weather forecaster

сино́птика weather forecasting

синта́ксис syntax

си́нтез synthesis

синтети́ческий synthetic

синхрониза́ция synchronization

си́нька blueing

синя́к bruise

сиони́ст, —ка Zionist

сип griffon vulture

си́плый hoarse

сире́нь f. lilac

Си́рия Syria

сиро́п syrup

сирота́ m. & f. orphan

систе́ма system

систематизи́ровать impf. & pf. systematize

системати́ческий systematic

си́тец FILL cotton (print)

си́течко filter; strainer

си́то sieve

ситуа́ция situation

си́тцевый made of printed cotton

сифи́лис syphilis

сифо́н siphon

сия́ние glow; radiance

сия́ть impf. shine; beam

скабрёзный indecent

сказа́ние tale; legend

сказа́ть pf. of говори́ть

ска́зка fairy tale; tale, story

сказу́емое n. (gram.) predicate

скака́ть impf., по- pf. skip; jump; gallop

скала́ rock

ска́лка rolling pin

ска́льпель m. scalpel

скаме́йка skamья́, скамья́ f. bench

сканда́л scandal

сканда́лить impf., на- pf. brawl

сканда́льный scandalous

скарабе́й scarab

скарб household belongings

скарлати́на scarlet fever

скат slope; ramp

ска́терть f. tablecloth

ска́тывать impf., скати́ть pf. roll or slide down

скафа́ндр diving or space suit

ска́чки pl. the races

скачо́к FILL jump; leap

сква́жина chink; slit; well; замо́чная ~ keyhole

сквалы́га m. & f. Colloq. cheap-skate

сквер public garden

скверносло́вие foul language

скве́рный nasty; foul

сквозня́к draft

сквозь prep. (+ A) through

скворе́ц FILL starling

скворе́чник bird house

скеле́т skeleton

скепти́ческий skeptical

ски́дка discount; reduction

скипида́р turpentine

склад[1] storehouse

склад[2] mold; mode; coherence

скла́дка fold, crease, pleat

складно́й folding; collapsible

скла́дывать impf., сложи́ть pf. put (together); fold (up); pack up; compose; —ся turn out; take shape

скле́ить pf. of кле́ить

склеп crypt; burial vault

склеро́з sclerosis

склероти́ческий sclerotic

скло́ка squabble; row

склоне́ние declension

скло́нность (к + D) inclination; tendency

скло́нный (к + D) inclined to; disposed toward

склоня́ть impf., -ни́ть pf. incline; bend

скло́чный Colloq. argumentative

ско́бка bracket, parenthesis

ско́ванный awkward; constrained

сковорода́ frying pan

ско́вывать impf., скова́ть pf. forge (together)

скользи́ть impf., скользну́ть pf. slip; slide

ско́льзкий slippery

ско́лько adv. how much, how many

ско́лько-нибудь adv. any … at all

скомпромети́ровать pf. of компромети́ровать.

сконфу́зить pf. of конфу́зить

сконча́ться pf. pass away; die

скопле́ние accumulation

ско́рбный sorrowful, sad

скорбь f. sorrow; grief

скорлупа́ shell

ско́ро adv. quickly; soon

скорогово́рка tongue twister

скоропости́жный sudden

ско́рость 1. speed 2. (motor) gear

скоросшива́тель binder

скорпио́н scorpion

ско́рый quick, fast

скот cattle; livestock

скоти́на 1. cattle 2. Fig. beast

скотобо́йня slaughterhouse

скотово́дство cattle breeding

скребо́к FILL scraper

скре́жет grinding; gnashing

скре́пка paper clip; staple

скрепля́ть impf., -пи́ть pf. fasten (together); countersign

скре́щивание crossbreeding

скрипа́ч, —ка violinist

скрипе́ть *impf.*, про- *pf.* squeak
скри́пка violin
скрои́ть *pf. of* крои́ть
скро́мничать *impf.* be excessively modest
скро́мность modesty
скро́мный modest
скрупулёзный scrupulous
скрыва́ть(ся) *impf.*, скры́ть(ся) *pf.* hide (oneself)
скры́тный reserved; secretive
ску́дный scanty; sparse
ску́ка boredom; tedium
скула́ cheekbone
скули́ть *impf.* whine; whimper
ску́льптор sculptor
скульпту́ра sculpture
скупо́й stingy
ску́пщик, -щица buyer
скуча́ть *impf.* be bored; (по + *D*) miss
ску́чный boring; tedious
слабе́ть *impf.*, о- *pf.* weaken
слаби́тельное *n.* laxative, purgative
слабово́льный weak-willed
слаборазви́тый underdeveloped
сла́бость weakness
сла́бый weak; faint; poor
сла́ва fame; glory
слави́ст Slavist; Slavicist
слави́стика Slavic studies
сла́вный glorious; famous; nice
славяни́н, славя́нка Slav
славя́нский Slavic; Slavonic
сла́дкий sweet
сла́дкое *n.* **1.** sweets **2.** dessert
сладостра́стный voluptuous
сла́дость sweetness
сла́женность harmony
сластёна *m. & f.* person with a sweet tooth
слаща́вый sugary; honeyed
сле́ва *adv.* from *or* on the left
слегка́ *adv.* somewhat; a little
след trace; track; sign
следи́ть *impf.* (за + *I*) watch; follow; shadow
сле́дователь investigator
сле́довательно *adv.* consequently
сле́довать *impf.*, по- *pf.* (за + *I*) **1.** follow **2.** *impers.* (+ *D*) ought, should; be owed
сле́дом *adv.* close behind
сле́дствие consequence
сле́дующий next; following
слеже́ние monitoring; tracking
слеза́ tear; сле́зный tearful

слеза́ть *impf.*, слезть *pf.* get down
слепи́ть *pf. of* лепи́ть
сле́пнуть *impf.*, о- *pf.* become blind
слепо́й blind; *n.* blind person
слепота́ blindness
слеса́рный attrib. metalworking
сле́сарь *m.* plumber; locksmith
слива́ть(ся) *impf.*, слить *pf.* pour out *or* off; fuse
сли́вки *pl.* cream
сли́зистый slimy; mucous
слизь *f.* mucus; slime; mucilage
сли́ток FILL ingot; bar
сли́шком *adv.* too (much)
слия́ние confluence; blending
Слова́кия Slovakia
слова́рь *m.* dictionary; vocabulary
Слове́ния Slovenia
слове́сность literature; philology
сло́вно *conj.* as if; as; like
сло́во word; ~ в ~ word for word; —м in short; —сочета́ние word combination
слог[1] syllable
слог[2] style
сло́ёный attrib. puff; flaky
сложе́ние composition; build
сложи́ть *pf. of* скла́дывать
сло́жность complexity
сло́жный complicated; compound
сло́истый stratified; laminated
слой layer
слома́ть *pf. of* лома́ть
слон elephant; (*chess*) bishop; —о́вая кость *f.* ivory
слоня́ться *impf.* loiter
слуга́, служа́нка servant
служа́щий serving; *n.* employee
слу́жба service; work
служе́бный **1.** attrib. service; office **2.** auxiliary
служи́ть *impf.*, по- *pf.* serve
слух hearing; rumor
слухово́й attrib. hearing; auditory
слу́чай case; occasion; incident; opportunity
случа́йный chance; accidental; incidental
случа́ться *impf.*, —чи́ться *pf.* happen
слу́шатель, —ница listener; student
слу́шать *impf.*, по-, про- *pf.* listen (to); hear; attend a lecture; —ся obey
слы́шать *impf.*, у- *pf.* hear (of)
слы́шимость audibility
слы́шный audible

слюна́ saliva

сля́коть f. slush

сма́зка grease; lubrication

сма́зывать impf., сма́зать pf. oil; grease; smudge

сма́тывать impf., смота́ть pf. wind (in); reel

сма́хивать impf., смахну́ть pf. brush off; brush away

сма́чивать impf., смочи́ть pf. moisten

сме́жный adjacent; adjoining

смека́лка shrewdness

сме́лость audacity; boldness

сме́лый bold; daring

сме́на change; replacement; shift; relief

сменя́ть impf., -ни́ть pf. change; replace; relieve

смерте́льный deadly; mortal

сме́ртность mortality; death rate

сме́ртный attrib. death; n. mortal

смерть f. death

смерч 1. tornado 2. waterspout

смеси́тель mixer; blender

смести́ть pf. of смеща́ть

смесь f. mixture; blend

смета́на sour cream

сметь impf., по- pf. dare

смех laughter; laugh

сме́шанный mixed; hybrid

сме́шивать impf., смеша́ть pf. v.t. mix, blend; confuse

смеши́ть impf., на- pf. make (someone) laugh

смешно́й funny; ridiculous

смеща́ть impf., -сти́ть pf. displace; remove

смея́ться impf. (над + I) laugh (at)

смире́ние humility; meekness

смире́нный humble; meek

сми́рный 1. quiet 2. mild

смиря́ть impf., -ри́ть pf. restrain; —ся resign oneself; submit

смо́ква fig

смо́кинг tuxedo; dinner jacket

смола́ 1. resin 2. tar

смолка́ть impf., смо́лкнуть pf. become or grow silent

сморка́ться impf., вы- pf. blow one's nose

сморо́дина currant(s)

смо́рщить pf. of мо́рщить

смотр review

смотре́ть impf., по- pf. look (at, after, through); watch

смочь pf. of мочь

смрад stench

сму́глый swarthy

сму́тный vague; dim; troubled

смуща́ть impf., -ти́ть pf. confuse; embarrass; trouble

смуще́ние embarrassment

смыва́ть impf., смыть pf. wash off

смысл sense, meaning; point

смы́чка joining; linking

смычо́к FILL (mus.) bow

смягча́ть(ся) impf., -чи́ть(ся) pf. soften

смяте́ние 1. confusion 2. panic

смять pf. crush, crumple

снабжа́ть impf., -ди́ть pf. supply

снайпер sniper

снару́жи adv. from the outside

снаря́д 1. shell; missile 2. device; apparatus

снаряжа́ть impf., -ди́ть pf. equip; outfit

снасть f. tackle

снача́ла adv. at first; all over again

сна́шивать impf., сноси́ть pf. wear out

снег snow; —оочисти́тель snow-plow; —опа́д snowfall

снегу́рочка snow maiden

снежи́нка snowflake

сне́жный attrib. snow, snowy

снести́ pf. of сноси́ть

снижа́ть impf., сни́зить pf. lower; reduce; decrease

сни́зу adv. from below

снима́ть impf., снять pf. 1. take away or off or down 2. photograph 3. rent

сни́мок FILL photograph

снисходи́тельный condescending; lenient

сни́ться impf., при- pf. impers. (+ D) dream

сно́ва adv. anew; again

сноп sheaf

сноро́вка skill; knack

снос 1. demolition 2. wear 3. drift

сноси́ть¹ impf., снести́ pf. 1. take down; demolish 2. bear; endure 3. bring together

сноси́ть² pf. of сна́шивать

сно́сный tolerable

снотво́рный soporific

сноха́ daughter-in-law

сноше́ния pl. intercourse, dealings

снять pf. of снима́ть

со prep., see с

соба́ка dog; соба́чий dog's

собесе́дник, -ница interlocutor

собесе́дование conversation

собира́ть impf., собра́ть pf.

gather; collect; assemble; **—ся** gather; (+ *infin.*) prepare, intend

соблазн temptation

соблазнительный seductive

соблазнять *impf.*, **-нить** *pf.* tempt; seduce

соблюдать *impf.*, **соблюсти** *pf.* observe

собой, собою *pron.*, I of **себя**

соболезнование condolence(s)

соболь *m.* sable

собор cathedral

собрание 1. meeting, assembly **2.** collection

собрать *pf.* of **собирать**

собственно *adv.* properly; in fact

собственноручный handwritten

собственность property

собственный own; proper

событие event

сова́ owl

совать *impf.*, **су́нуть** *pf.* stick; thrust

совершать *impf.*, **-шить** *pf.* accomplish; commit

совершеннолетний of age

совершенный absolute; perfect

совершенство perfection

совершить *pf.* of **совершать**

совесть *f.* conscience

совет 1. advice; counsel **2.** council **3.** soviet; **—ский** Soviet

советник, -ница advisor

советовать *impf.*, **по-** *pf.* advise; **—ся** (*c* + *I*) consult

совещание conference

совещаться *impf.* deliberate

совладелец FILL, **-лица** joint owner

совместимый compatible

совместный joint; combined; **совместное предприятие** (*abbr.* **СП**) joint venture

совмещать *impf.*, **-стить** *pf.* combine

совок FILL scoop; dustpan

совокупление copulation

совокупный aggregate, total

совпадать *impf.*, **совпасть** *pf.* coincide

соврать *pf.* of **врать**

совращать *impf.*, **-тить** *pf.* pervert; seduce

современник, -ница contemporary

современный contemporary; modern

совсем *adv.* completely; quite; **~ не** not at all

согласие agreement; consent

согласно *adv.* in agreement; *prep.* (*c* + *I*) according to

согласный¹ agreeable (to)

согласный² *n.* consonant

согласовывать *impf.*, **согласовать** *pf.* coordinate; make agree

соглашаться *impf.*, **-ситься** *pf.* agree

соглашение agreement

согнутый bent; stooped

согнуть *pf.* of **гнуть**, **гибать**

согревать *impf.*, **согреть** *pf.* warm (up); heat (up)

сода soda

содействовать *impf.*, **по-** *pf.* (+ *D*) assist

содержание 1. support; maintenance **2.** content(s); matter

содержать *impf.* contain **2.** maintain, keep, support

содружество 1. concord **2.** community; commonwealth

Соединённые Штаты *pl.* United States

соединённый united

соединять(ся) *impf.*, **-нить(ся)** *pf.* join, unite

сожаление regret; pity

сожалеть *impf.* (*o* + *P*) regret; be sorry (for)

сожжение cremation; burning

сожительство cohabitation

созваниваться *impf.*, **созвониться** *pf.* get in touch (by phone)

созвать *pf.* of **созывать**

созвездие constellation

создавать *impf.*, **создать** *pf.* create

создание creation

создатель, —ница creator; founder

созерцательный contemplative

сознавать *impf.*, **сознать** *pf.* be aware of; realize; **—ся** confess

сознание consciousness

сознательный conscious; deliberate

созревать *impf.*, **созреть** *pf.* ripen

созывать *impf.*, **созвать** *pf.* convoke; summon

соискатель, —ница competitor

сойти(сь) *pf.* of **сходить(ся)**

сок juice; sap

соковыжималка juicer

сокол falcon

сокращать *impf.*, **-тить** *pf.* shorten; abbreviate; reduce

сокращение reduction; abbreviation; shortening

сокровище treasure

сокрушáть *impf.*, -шúть *pf.* destroy; distress

сокрушúтельный crushing

солгáть *pf. of* лгать

солдáт soldier

солёный salty, salt(ed); pickled

солéнье pickled foods

солидáрность solidarity

солúдный solid; reliable

солúст, —ка soloist

солúть *impf.*, за-, по- *pf.* salt; pickle

сóлнечный solar, sun; sunny

сóлнце sun; —стоя́ние solstice

сóло *neut. indecl.* solo

соловéй FILL nightingale

солóма straw

солóменный *attrib.* straw; thatched

солóминка a straw

солонúна corned beef

солóнка salt shaker

соль *f.* salt

соля́рий solarium

сóмкнутый close

сомневáться *impf.* doubt

сомнéние doubt

сомнúтельный doubtful; dubious

сон 1. sleep 2. dream

сóнный sleepy; drowsy

соображáть *impf.*, -зúть *pf.* consider; understand

сообразúтельный quick-witted

сообрáзный (с + *I*) consistent (with)

сообщá *adv.* jointly

сообщáть *impf.*, -щúть *pf.* announce; inform; communicate

сообщéние report; message; communication(s)

сообщество association

сооружéние structure; building

соотвéтствовать *impf.* (+ *D*) correspond (to)

соотвéтствующий corresponding; suitable; appropriate

соотéчественник, -ница compatriot

соотношéние correlation

сопéрник, -ница rival; competitor

сопéрничать *impf.* compete (with)

сóпка knoll; mound; hill

соплó nozzle

сопоставля́ть *impf.*, -стáвить *pf.* compare; confront

соприкасáться *impf.*, -коснýться *pf.* touch (on); adjoin

сопровождáющий accompanying

сопровождáть *impf.*, сопроводúть *pf.* accompany; escort

сопротивлéние resistance

сопротивля́ться *impf.* (+ *D*) resist

сопýтствовать *impf.* accompany

сор garbage; litter

соразмéрный commensurate; proportionate

сорвáть(ся) *pf. of* срывáть(ся)

соревновáние competition; contest

соревновáться *impf.* compete

сорúнка speck of dust

сорúть *impf.*, на- *pf.* litter

сорня́к weed

сóрок forty; —овóй fortieth

сорóка magpie

сорóчка shirt; blouse; shift

сорт sort, kind; quality

сортировáть *impf.*, рас- *pf.* sort

сосáть *impf.* suck

сосéд, —ка neighbor; —ний neighboring; —ский neighborly; —ство neighborhood, proximity

сосúска sausage

сослáть(ся) *pf. of* ссылáть(ся)

сослóвие estate; class

соснá pine; pine tree

сосредотóчивать(ся) *impf.*, -тóчить(ся) *pf.* concentrate

состáв 1. composition; structure 2. staff; —úтель, —úтельница compiler; —лéние compilation

составля́ть *impf.*, состáвить *pf.* compose; put together; form

составнóй compound; component

состáриться *pf. of* стáриться

состоя́ние condition; state

состоя́тельный well-off; sound

состоя́ть *impf.* 1. be 2. (из + *G*) consist (of)

состоя́ться *pf.* take place

сострадáние compassion

сострадáтельный compassionate

состязáние contest; competition

сосýд vessel; —úстый vascular

сосуществовáние coexistence

сотворéние creation

сотворúть *pf. of* творúть

сóтня *coll.* a hundred

сóтовый of a honeycomb; (telephone) cellular

сотрýдник, —ница colleague; associate; collaborator

сотрýдничать *impf.* collaborate; contribute (to)

сотрýдничество cooperation

сотрясéние vibration; impact

сóты *pl.* honeycomb

сóтый hundredth

сóус sauce

соуча́стник, -ница accomplice; participant

со́хнуть *impf.*, вы́- *pf.* dry

сохране́ние preservation; conservation

сохраня́ть *impf.*, -ни́ть *pf.* preserve; maintain; keep

социа́льный social

социо́лог sociologist

социоло́гия sociology

Соче́льник Christmas Eve

сочета́ние combination

сочета́ть *impf. & pf.* combine; —ся combine; match

сочине́ние work(s); composition

сочиня́ть *impf.*, -ни́ть *pf.* write; compose; invent

со́чный juicy; succulent

сочу́вствие (к + D) sympathy

сочу́вствовать *impf.* sympathize

сою́з¹ union; alliance; —ник, —ница ally; —ный allied

сою́з² (*gram.*) conjunction

со́я soy

спад decline; recession

спада́ть *impf.*, спасть *pf.* fall (down); abate

спазм, спа́зма spasm

спали́ть *pf. of* пали́ть

спа́льный for sleeping

спа́льня bedroom

спаса́тель, —ница rescue worker; lifeguard

спаса́тельный *attrib.* rescue

спаса́ть *impf.*, спасти́ *pf.* save; rescue

спасе́ние rescue

спаси́бо *particle.* thank you

спаси́тель, —ница rescuer; *cap.* the Savior

спасти́ *pf. of* спаса́ть

спасть *pf. of* спада́ть

спать *impf.* sleep; be asleep

спекта́кль *m.* performance

спектр spectrum

спекули́ровать *impf.* speculate

спекуля́ция speculation

спе́лый ripe

спе́реди *adv.* at or from the front

спесь *f.* haughtiness; conceit

специализа́ция specialization

специализи́ровать *impf. & pf.* specialize

специали́ст, —ка specialist

специа́льность specialty; profession

специа́льный special

специ́фика characteristic

специфи́ческий specific

спе́ция spice

спецоде́жда working clothes

спеши́ть *impf.*, по- *pf.* hurry; be in a hurry; be fast

спе́шка rush; haste

спе́шный 1. urgent 2. hasty

СПИД AIDS

спина́ (*anat.*) back

спи́нка (*furniture, etc.*) back

спира́ль *f.* spiral

спирт alcohol; spirit(s)

спиртно́й alcoholic

спирто́вка spirit lamp

спи́сок FILL list; roll

спи́сывать *impf.*, списа́ть *pf.* copy (from); write off

спи́чечный *attrib.* match

спи́чка match

сплав 1. alloy; fusion 2. floating

сплетни́чать *impf.*, на- *pf.* gossip

спле́тня gossip

сплочённый united

сплошно́й continuous; solid; sheer

сплю́щивать *impf.*, сплю́щить *pf.* flatten

споко́йной но́чи *interj.* good night!

споко́йный quiet; calm

споко́йствие tranquility; calm(ness); composure

спола́скивать *impf.* rinse out

спо́нсор sponsor; promoter

спонта́нный spontaneous

спор argument; controversy

спо́рить *impf.*, по- *pf.* argue

спо́рный controversial

спорт sport; —и́вный *attrib.* sports

спортсме́н, —ка athlete

спо́соб way; method

спосо́бность ability; capacity

спосо́бный able; clever; capable

спосо́бствовать *impf.* further; assist

спотыка́ться *impf.*, споткну́ться *pf.* stumble; trip

спра́ва *adv.* from or on the right

справедли́вость justice; fairness

справедли́вый just; fair; true

спра́вка information; certificate

справля́ться *impf.*, спра́виться *pf.* (с + *I*) cope with, manage

спра́вочник reference book

спра́вочный *attrib.* reference

спра́шивать *impf.*, спроси́ть *pf.* ask

спринцо́вка syringe

спрос (на + *A*) demand (for)

спряже́ние (*gram.*) conjugation

спря́тать *pf. of* пря́тать

спуск descent; slope; landing

спуска́ть *impf.*, -сти́ть *pf.* let

down; lower; let go; squander;
—ся go down, descend
спустя́ prep. (+ A) after
спу́танный tangled; muddled
спу́тник 1. ~, спу́тница (traveling)
companion 2. satellite
сравне́ние comparison
сра́внивать[1] impf., сравни́ть pf.
compare
сра́внивать[2] impf., сравня́ть pf.
level out; make even
сравни́тельный comparative
сража́ть impf., —зи́ть pf. strike;
overwhelm; —ся fight
сраже́ние battle
сра́зу adv. at once
среда́[1] Wednesday
среда́[2] environment, surroundings
среди́ prep. (+ G) among; amidst
средне- pref. Central; Middle
средневеко́вый medieval
средневеко́вье the Middle Ages
сре́днее n. average; the average
сре́дний average; middle; neuter
сре́дство means; remedy
срез slice; cut; section
среза́ть impf., сре́зать pf. cut off
сровня́ть pf. of ровня́ть
срок date; time; period
сро́чный urgent; of fixed date
срыв collapse; failure
срыва́ть[1] impf., сорва́ть pf. tear
off; pick; pluck; —ся break off;
fall (through)
срыва́ть[2] impf., срыть pf. level to
the ground, raze
сса́дина scratch; abrasion
ссо́ра quarrel
ссо́риться impf., по— pf. quarrel
ссу́да loan
ссыла́ться impf., сосла́ться pf.
(на + A) refer to; cite
ссы́лка[1] exile
ссы́лка[2] (cross) reference
стабилиза́тор stabilizer
стаби́льность stability
стаби́льный stable
ста́вить impf., по— pf. 1. put;
place; set 2. stage
ста́вка 1. rate 2. (cards) stake
стадио́н stadium
ста́дия stage
ста́до herd, flock
стаж length of service
стажёр, —ка trainee; intern
стажиро́вка practical training
ста́йка dim. of стая
стака́н (drinking) glass
ста́лкивать impf., столкну́ть pf.
push off; —ся (с + I) collide

сталь f. steel; —нóй steel
станда́рт standard
стандартизи́ровать impf. & pf.
standardize
станда́ртный standard
стани́ца large Cossack village
станови́ться impf., стать pf.
stand; (+ I) become
становле́ние formation
стано́к FILL machine (tool)
станцио́нный attrib. station
ста́нция station; base
стара́ние endeavor, effort
стара́тельный diligent
стара́ться impf., по— pf. endeavor;
try
старе́ть impf., по— pf. grow old
стари́к old man
старина́ antiquity; olden times
стари́нный ancient; old
ста́риться impf., со— pf. grow old
старове́р, —ка Old Believer
старомо́дный old-fashioned
ста́рость old age
старт (sports) start
стартова́ть impf. & pf. start
стару́ха, стару́шка old woman
ста́рческий senile
ста́рше adv. compar. of ста́рый
ста́рший older; elder; oldest; eldest; senior
ста́рый old
стати́ст, —ка (theat.) extra
стати́стика statistics
ста́тус status
стату́этка statuette; figurine
ста́туя statue
стать 1. pf. of станови́ться 2.
(+ I) begin, commence
статья́ article; item; clause
стациона́р permanent establishment; hospital
стациона́рный permanent; stationary; ~ больно́й n. in-patient
ста́я flock; pack; school
ствол 1. (tree) trunk 2. (gun) barrel
ство́рка leaf; fold; valve
стеари́н stearin
сте́бель FILL m. stem, stalk
стёганый quilted
стега́ть impf., стегну́ть pf. whip
стезя́ Obs. way; road; path
стека́ть impf., стечь pf. flow
down
стекло́ glass; lens; (window) pane
стеклоочисти́тель windshield
wiper
стекля́нный attrib. glass
стелла́ж shelves; rack

сте́лька insole; inner sole

стена́ wall

сте́нка wall; side

стенографи́ст, —ка stenographer

стеногра́фия shorthand

стенокарди́я angina pectoris

сте́пень f. degree; extent

степь f. steppe; **степно́й** steppe

стереоти́п stereotype

стере́ть pf. of **стира́ть**

стере́чь impf. watch, guard

сте́ржень FILL m. rod; pivot; core

стерилиза́ция sterilization

стери́льный sterile

стёртый worn; effaced

стесни́тельный 1. shy **2.** restrictive

стесня́ть impf., **по-** pf. constrain; inhibit; **—ся** feel shy, feel awkward

стечь pf. of **стека́ть**

стилисти́ческий stylistic

стиль m. style

сти́мул stimulus; incentive

стимули́ровать impf. & pf. stimulate

стипе́ндия grant; scholarship

стира́льный attrib. washing

стира́ть¹ impf., **стере́ть** pf. wipe off; erase; rub sore

стира́ть² impf., **вы-**, **по-** pf. wash

сти́рка washing, laundry

стих verse; pl. poetry; poems

стихи́йный elemental; spontaneous

стихи́я element

стихотворе́ние poem

сто hundred

сто́имость cost; value

сто́ить impf. cost; be worth(while); deserve

сто́йка counter; bar

сто́йкий firm; stable

сто́йло stall

сток gutter; drainage

стол table; desk; board

столб pillar, post

столбе́ц (typog.) column

столбня́к tetanus

столе́тие century; centenary

столе́тний attrib. hundred-year

столи́ца capital; metropolis

столкнове́ние collision, clash

столкну́ть(ся) pf. of **ста́лкивать(ся)**

столо́вая n. dining room

столо́вый attrib. table; dining

сто́лько adv. so much; so many

столя́р cabinetmaker; joiner

стомато́лог dentist

стон groan; moan

стона́ть impf. moan, groan

стоп interj. stop!

стопа́ foot, step

сто́пка¹ pile; heap

сто́пка² small glass (for vodka)

сто́пор (mech.) stop; catch

стоп-сигна́л stoplight; brake light

сто́рож watchman; guard

сторожи́ть impf. guard, watch

сторона́ side; part; direction

сторони́ться impf., **по-** pf. **1.** stand aside **2.** (+ G) avoid

сторо́нник, -ница supporter

сто́чный attrib. drainage

стошни́ть impf. impers. vomit

стоя́нка parking; parking (place)

стоя́ть impf. stand; stay; be

страда́ние suffering

страда́ть impf., **по-** pf. suffer

страна́ country; land

страни́ца page

стра́нник, -ница wanderer

стра́нный strange; odd

стра́нствовать impf. wander

стра́стный passionate

страсть f. passion

стратеги́ческий strategic

страте́гия strategy

стра́ус ostrich

страх fear

страхова́ние insurance

страхова́ть impf., **за-** pf. insure

страхо́вка insurance

страхо́вщик insurer

страши́ть impf. frighten

стра́шный terrible; awful

стрела́ arrow

Стреле́ц Sagittarius

стре́лка arrow, pointer, hand

стрело́к FILL marksman; gunner

стрельба́ shooting

стреми́тельный swift; impetuous

стреми́ться impf. (к + D) strive

стремле́ние aspiration

стремя́нка stepladder

стресс (emotional) stress

стри́жка haircut

стри́чься impf., **о-**, **об-** pf. have one's hair cut; get a haircut

стро́гий strict; severe

строи́тель builder

строи́тельный attrib. building; construction

стро́ить impf., **по-** pf. build, construct

строй system; order

стро́йка building; construction

стро́йный shapely; harmonious

строкá line of text
строфá stanza
стрóчная бýква lower case letter
структýра structure
структýрный structural
струнá (*mus.*) string
стрýнный *attrib.* string; stringed
стручóк FILL pod
струя́ stream, jet; current
студéнт, —ка student; —ческий *attrib.* student; student's
стýдень *m.* aspic
студи́ть *impf.*, о- *pf.* cool
стýдия studio
стýжа severe cold
стук knock, tap; thump
стул chair
ступáть *impf.*, ступи́ть *pf.* step
ступéнчатый stepped; graded
ступéнь *f.* step; stage
ступня́ foot
стучáть *impf.*, по- *pf.* knock; bang; strike
стыд shame
стыди́ться *impf.*, по- *pf.* (+ *G*) be ashamed (of)
стыдли́вый modest; bashful; shy
сты́дно *pred.* мне ~ I am ashamed
стык joint; junction
стыкóвка docking
сты́нуть, стыть *impf.*, о- *pf.* v.i. cool off
стю́ард steward
стюардéсса air hostess
стя́гивать *impf.*, стяну́ть *pf.* tighten; pull together; assemble
суббóта Saturday
сублимáция sublimation
субси́дия subsidy
субстáнция substance
субти́тр (*movies*) subtitle
субтрóпики *pl.* subtropics
субъéкт subject; person; character
субъекти́вный subjective
сувени́р souvenir
суверените́т sovereignty
суверéнный sovereign
сугрóб snowdrift
сугýбо *adv.* especially
суд court; trial; —éбный legal; judicial; —и́мость previous convictions
судáрыня *Obs.* madam
сýдарь *m. Obs.* sir
суди́ть *impf.* try, judge; umpire, referee
сýдно ship, vessel
судовóй *attrib.* ship; ship's
судопроизвóдство legal proceedings

сýдорога cramp; convulsion
сýдорожный convulsive
судострое́ние shipbuilding
судохóдный navigable
судьбá fate, destiny
судья́ *m.* judge; (*sports*) umpire
суевéрие superstition
суевéрный superstitious
суетá fuss; bustle
суетли́вый restless; bustling
суждéние judgment
суже́ние narrowing; contraction
сук bough
сýка bitch
сукнó cloth
сульфáт sulfate
сумасбрóдный wild; extravagant
сумасшéдший mad; *n.* madman
сумато́ха commotion; tumult
суматóшный hectic; bustling
сýмерки *pl.* twilight
сумéть *pf.* (+ *infin.*) be able (to)
сýмка bag; handbag
сýмма sum
сумми́ровать *impf. & pf.* sum up
сýмрак dusk, twilight
сундýк trunk; chest
суп soup; —овóй *attrib.* soup
суперобло́жка dust jacket
супрýг, супрýга spouse
супрýжеский marital; spousal
сурóвый severe; stern
суррогáт substitute
суррогáтный substitute; ersatz
сусáльное зóлото gold leaf
сýслик gopher
сустáв (*anat.*) joint
сýтки *pl.* twenty-four hours; a day
сýточные *n.pl.* per diem
сýточный a day's, daily
сутýлый round-shouldered
суть *f.* essence; main point
суфлé *neut. indecl.* soufflé
суфлёр (*theat.*) prompter
суфли́ровать *impf.* prompt
сухáрь *m.* zwieback; rusk
сухожи́лие tendon
сухóй dry
сухощáвый lean; skinny
сучóк twig
сýша land; dry land
сушёный dried; dry
суши́лка dryer; drying room
суши́ть(ся) *impf.*, вы́- *pf.* dry
сýшка small, round cracker
сушь *f.* dry spell
существенный essential
существи́тельное *n.* noun; и́мя существи́тельное proper noun

существо́ being; creature; essence
существова́ние existence
существова́ть *impf.* exist
су́щий existing; real
су́щность essence; nature
сфе́ра sphere
сфотографи́ровать *pf. of* **фотографи́ровать**
схвати́ть(ся) *pf. of* **схва́тывать(ся), хвата́ть(ся)**
схва́тка fight; skirmish; *pl.* cramps
схва́тывать *impf.*, **схвати́ть** *pf.* grasp; catch; **—ся (за + A)** seize
схе́ма diagram; outline
сход 1. descent **2.** meeting
сходи́ть¹ *impf.*, **сойти́** *pf.* go down; get off; leave; **~ с ума́** go mad; **—ся** meet; agree; become intimate
сходи́ть² *pf.* **(за + I)** go and get
схо́дни *pl.* gangway, gangplank
схо́дный similar
схо́дство similarity
схорони́ть *pf. of* **хорони́ть**
сцежива́ть *impf.*, **сцеди́ть** *pf.* strain off
сце́на *(theat.)* stage; scene
сцена́рий scenario; script
сценари́ст, —ка script writer
сцепле́ние coupling; clutch
счастли́вец FILL, **-вица** lucky person
счастли́вый happy; fortunate
сча́стье happiness; luck
счесть *pf. of* **счита́ть**
счёт calculation; account; bill
счётчик meter; counter
счёты *pl.* abacus
счисле́ние *(math.)* numbering
счита́ть *impf.* **1.** *pf.* **счесть (+ I)** consider **2.** *pf.* со- count; **—ся**

(с + I) reckon with; be considered; settle accounts
США *pl. (abbr. of* **Соединённые Шта́ты Аме́рики)** USA
сшить *pf. of* **шить**
съеда́ть *impf.*, **съесть** *pf.* eat up
съедо́бный edible
съёживаться *impf.*, **съёжиться** *pf.* shrivel; shrink; huddle up
съезд congress, convention
съезжа́ться *impf.*, **съе́хаться** *pf.* assemble
съёмка 1. survey **2.** *(film)* shooting; photographing
съёмный removable
съесть *pf. of* **съеда́ть**
сы́воротка 1. whey **2.** serum
сыгра́ть *pf. of* **игра́ть**
сын son; **—о́вний** filial
сы́пать *impf.* strew; pour; **—ся** pour out; rain down
сыпу́чий crumbly; loose
сыпь *f.* skin eruption; rash
сыр cheese; **сы́рный** cheesy
сыре́ц FILL raw product
сы́рник cheese pancake
сыро́й 1. damp **2.** raw
сы́рость *f.* dampness
сырьё raw material(s)
сы́тный nourishing; filling
сы́тость satiety
сы́тый satiated; full
сы́щик, сы́щица detective
сэр sir
сюда́ *adv. (dir.)* here
сюже́т subject matter; plot
сюрпри́з surprise
сюрреалисти́ческий surrealistic
сюрту́к frock coat
сям *adv.*: **там и сям** here and there

Т

та *pron., see* **тот**
табака tobacco
таба́чный *attrib.* tobacco
та́бель *m.* table; chart
табле́тка tablet; pill
табли́ца table; list
табло́ *neut. indecl.* **1.** scoreboard **2.** electronic indicator panel
та́бор gypsy band
табу́н herd; flock
табуре́т, табуре́тка stool
тага́н trivet
таджи́к, таджи́чка Tajik
Таджикиста́н Tajikistan

таёжный of the taiga
таз¹ wash basin
таз² pelvis
таи́нственный mysterious
таи́ть *impf.* conceal, hide
Тайва́нь *m.* Taiwan
тайга́ *(geog.)* taiga
Таила́нд Thailand
тайм period *(of a game)*
та́йна mystery; secret
та́йный secret
так *adv.* so, thus; like this; *conj.* then; so; **~ как** since
та́кже *adv.* also, too

тако́й *pron., adj.* such (a); что э́то тако́е? what is this?

тако́й-то *pron.* so-and-so; such and such

та́кса tariff, price

такси́ *neut. indecl.* taxi; cab

такси́ст cabdriver

такт[1] tact

такт[2] (*mus.*) time; measure

та́ктика tactics

такти́ческий tactical

такти́чный tactful

тала́нт talent; —ливый talented

та́лия waist

тало́н coupon

та́лый melting; melted

тальк talc; talcum powder

там *adv.* there

тамада́ toastmaster

та́мбур 1. vestibule 2. platform

тамо́женник customs official

тамо́женный *attrib.* customs

тамо́жня customs; custom house

тампо́н tampon

та́нец FILL dance

танк[1] (*mil.*) tank

танк[2] tank; cistern

та́нкер tanker

танки́ст member of a tank crew

танцева́ть *impf.* dance

танцо́вщик, -щица ballet dancer

танцо́р dancer

та́почки *pl.* slippers

та́ра 1. (shipping) container 2. packing material 3. (*com.*) tare

тарака́н cockroach

тарато́рить *impf.* chatter

таре́лка plate; satellite dish; летáющая ~ flying saucer

тари́ф tariff; rate

таска́ть *impf.* drag; pull

тасова́ть *impf.*, c- *pf.* shuffle

тата́рин, тата́рка Tatar

тата́рский Tatar

Татарста́н Tatarstan

татуиро́вка tatooing; tattoo

та́хта ottoman; divan

та́чка wheelbarrow

тащи́ть *impf.*, по- *pf.* pull; tow; drag 2. *pf.* вы́- pull out 3. *pf.* c- swipe; —ся drag oneself along

та́ять *impf.*, рас- *pf.* thaw; melt

тварь *f.* 1. creature 2. bastard

тверде́ть *impf.*, за- *pf. v.i.* harden

тверди́ть *impf.* reiterate

твёрдый hard, solid; firm

тверды́ня stronghold

твой *pron.*, *f.* твоя́, *neut.* твоё, *pl.* твои́ your, yours

творе́ние creation

творе́ц FILL creator; maker

твори́ть *impf.*, co- *pf.* create

творо́г cottage cheese; curds

тво́рческий creative

тво́рчество (creative) works

те *pron.*, *see* тот.

т. е. (*abbr.* of то есть) i.e.; that is

теа́тр theater

театра́л, —ка theatergoer

театра́льный *attrib.* theatrical

тебе́ *pron.* D of ты

те́зис thesis

тёзка *m. & f.* namesake

текст text; libretto; lyrics

тексти́льный textile

те́кстовая обрабо́тка (*comput.*) word processing

текстово́й textual; ~ реда́ктор (*comput.*) text editor

теку́чий fluid; fluctuating

теку́щий flowing; current

телеви́дение television

телеви́зор television set

теле́га cart

телегра́мма telegram

телегра́ф telegraph

теле́жка (luggage) cart

телезри́тель, —ница television viewer

телека́мера television camera

телёнок FILL (*pl.* теля́та) calf

телепа́тия telepathy

телепереда́ча television broadcast

телеско́п telescope

те́лесный corporeal; bodily

телесту́дия television studio

телефо́н telephone; ~ автома́т public telephone

телефони́ст, —ка telephone operator

телефо́нный *attrib.* telephone

те́ло body

телогре́йка padded jacket

телодвиже́ние body movement

телосложе́ние build; frame

телохрани́тель bodyguard

теля́тина veal

тем *pron.* I of тот.; *conj.* (so much) the; ~ не ме́нее nevertheless

те́ма subject, topic; theme

тембр timbre

темне́ть *impf.*, по- *pf.* grow dark

тёмно- *pf.* (of colors) dark

темноволо́сый dark-haired

темнота́ darkness, dark

тёмный dark; obscure

темп rate; pace; tempo

темпера́ментный temperamental

температу́ра temperature

тёмя neut. crown, top of the head

тенде́нция tendency

тени́стый shady

те́ннис tennis

тенниси́ст, —ка tennis player

те́нор tenor

тент awning

тень f. shade; shadow

теоло́гия theology

тео́рия theory

тепе́рь adv. now

тепли́ца hothouse

тепло́ warmth; heat; adv. warmly; pred. (it is) warm; **—во́й** thermal; attrib. heat

теплокро́вный warm-blooded

теплосто́йкий heat-resistant

теплота́ warmth, heat

теплохо́д motor ship

тёплый warm

терапевти́ческий therapeutic

терапи́я internal medicine

тереби́ть impf. pull at; pester

тере́ть impf. rub; grate

терза́ть impf. tear apart; torment

тёрка grater

те́рмин term

термина́л (computer) terminal

терминоло́гия terminology

терми́ческий thermal

термо́метр thermometer

те́рмос thermos (bottle)

термоя́дерный thermonuclear

терпели́вый patient

терпе́ние patience

терпе́ть impf. endure, suffer; have patience; tolerate

терпи́мость tolerance

терпи́мый tolerant; tolerable

те́рпкий tart

терра́са terrace

террито́рия territory

терро́р terror

террризи́ровать impf. & pf. terrorize

террори́ст, —ка terrorist

тёртый 1. grated 2. experienced

теря́ть impf., по— pf. lose; **—ся** be or get lost

теса́ть impf. cut; hew

тесёмка ribbon; braid

теснота́ crowdedness; crush

те́сный tight; close; crowded

те́сто dough

тесть m. father-in-law (wife's father)

тесьма́ ribbon; braid

тетра́дь f. notebook

тётя, тётка aunt

те́хник technician

те́хника technology; technique

те́хникум technical school

техни́ческий technical

технологи́ческий technological

техноло́гия technology

тече́ние flow; course; **в ~** prep. (+ G) during

те́чка heat (in animals)

течь impf. flow; run; leak

тёща mother-in-law (wife's mother)

тигр tiger; **—о́вый** tiger's

ти́кать impf. (of a clock) tick

ти́на slime

ти́нистый slimy

тип type; **—и́чный** typical

типа́ж model; prototype

типогра́фия printing house

типогра́фский typographical

тир shooting range or gallery

тира́ж (typog.) edition; circulation

тира́н tyrant

тира́нить impf. tyrannize

тире́ neut. indecl. (typog.) dash

тиски́ pl. (mech.) vise

тиснёный embossed; stamped

тита́н titan; boiler

титр (film) subtitle

ти́тул title (page); **—ьный** attrib. title

тиф typhus; typhoid

ти́хий quiet; still; gentle, soft

Ти́хий океа́н Pacific Ocean

ти́хо interj. quiet!

тишина́ quiet; stillness; silence

ткань f. cloth; fabric; (biol.) tissue

ткать impf., co— pf. weave

тка́цкий attrib. weaving

ткач, —и́ха weaver

ткнуть pf. of **ты́кать**

тлеть impf. smolder; rot, decay

тмин caraway

то pron., see **тот**; conj. then; **то́ есть** that is (to say); **а не то́** or else; otherwise

тобо́й, тобо́ю pron. I of **ты**

това́р goods; commodity

това́рищ comrade; buddy

това́рищеский comradely

това́рищество comradeship

товарообме́н barter

товарооборо́т turnover of goods

тогда́ adv. then; **~ как** whereas

того́ G of **тот**

тожде́ственный identical

то́же adv. also, too, as well

ток (also elec.) current

то́карь m. turner; lathe operator

токси́н toxin

токси́ческий toxic

толк sense; use

толка́ть *impf.*, **толкну́ть** *pf.* push

толкова́ть *impf.* interpret

толко́вый 1. intelligent **2.** explanatory **3.** intelligible

то́лком *adv.* clearly; seriously

толку́чка *Colloq.* flea market

толо́чь *impf.*, **ис-**, **рас-** *pf.* pound; crush

толпа́ crowd

толпи́ться *impf.* crowd, throng

толсте́ть *impf.*, **по-** *pf.* grow fat; put on weight

то́лстый fat, stout; thick

толчёный ground

толчея́ crowd; crush

толчо́к FILL, push; shove; jolt

толщина́ thickness

то́лько *adv.* only; **~ что** just now

том[1] *adj.* P of **тот**

том[2] (*book*) volume

тома́т tomato; **—ный** tomato

томи́тельный tiring; tedious

томи́ть *impf.* tire; wear out; **—ся** (**по** + *D*) languish (for); be tormented

то́мный languid

тому́ *D* of **тот**; **~ наза́д** ago

тон tone; **—а́льный** tonal

то́нкий fine; thin; slim; subtle

то́нна ton

тонне́ль, тунне́ль *m.* tunnel

то́нус (*physiol.*) tone

тону́ть *impf.*, **у-** *pf. v.i.* drown; sink

то́пать *impf.*, **то́пнуть** *pf.* stamp

топи́ть[1] *impf.* **1.** heat **2.** melt

топи́ть[2] *impf.*, **по-** *pf. v.t.* drown, sink

то́пливо fuel

топогра́фия topography

то́поль *m.* poplar

топо́р ax

то́пот tramp(ing); clatter

топта́ть *impf.* trample (down)

топь *f.* marsh; swamp; bog

торг trade; bargaining; *pl.* auction

торгова́ть *impf.* trade; deal (in); **—ся** bargain

торго́вец FILL, **торго́вка** merchant, dealer, trader

торго́вля trade; commerce

торго́вый *attrib.* trade; commercial

торже́ственный solemn

торжество́ celebration; triumph

торжествова́ть *impf.* triumph

то́рмоз brake; **—но́й** *attrib.* brake

тормози́ть *impf.*, **за-** *pf.* brake; hinder, hamper

тормоши́ть *impf.* pester; bother

торопи́ть *impf.*, **по-** *pf. v.t.* hurry, hasten; **—ся** be in a hurry

торопли́вый hasty

торпе́да torpedo

торт cake

торф peat; **—яно́й** peat

торча́ть *impf.* protrude; stick out

торше́р floor lamp

тоска́ 1. melancholy; anguish **2.** boredom **3.** yearning

тоскли́вый dull; dreary

тоскова́ть *impf.* be melancholy; long for; (**по** + *D*) miss

тост toast; **то́стер** toaster

тот *pron.*, *adj.*, *f.* **та**, *neut.* **то**, *pl.* **те** that; the other

тота́льный total

то́тчас *adv.* immediately

точи́лка (pencil) sharpener

точи́ть *impf.*, **на-** *pf.* sharpen; hone

то́чка point; dot; period

то́чно *adv.* exactly; *conj.* as if, as though

то́чность accuracy; punctuality

то́чный exact; precise; accurate

точь-в-то́чь *adv.* exactly

тошни́ть *impf. impers.*: **меня́ тошни́т** I feel nauseous

тошнота́ nausea

то́шный nauseating; tiresome

трава́ grass; herb

трави́нка blade of grass

трави́ть *impf.*, **вы-**, **за-** *pf.* **1.** exterminate; poison **2.** persecute

тра́вля hunting; persecution

тра́вма trauma; injury

травматоло́гия traumatology

травми́ровать *impf. & pf.* damage; injure

траге́дия tragedy

траги́ческий, траги́чный tragic

традицио́нный traditional

тради́ция tradition

тракт canal; tract

тракта́т treatise; treaty

трактова́ть interpretation

тра́ктор tractor

трамбова́ть *impf.*, **у-** *pf.* beat down

трамва́й streetcar; tram

трампли́н springboard

транзи́стор transistor (radio)

транзи́т transit; **—ный** transit

трансатланти́ческий transatlantic

трансконтинента́льный transcontinental

транслировать *impf. & pf.* broadcast; transmit

трансляция broadcast

транспорт transport(ation)

транспортабельный transportable

транспортёр conveyor

транспортир protractor

транспортировка transporting

трансформатор transformer

трансформировать *impf. & pf.* transform

траншея trench

трап boarding ramp

трасса route; highway

трата expense; waste

тратить *impf.,* ис-, по- *pf.* spend; waste

траулер trawler

траур mourning; **—ный** *attrib.* mourning; funeral

трафарет stencil; stereotype

трафаретный stereotyped

требование demand; request; requirement; requisition; order

требовательный demanding

требовать *impf.,* по- *pf.* demand; require

тревога alarm; anxiety

тревожить *impf.* **1.** *pf.* по- disturb **2.** *pf.* вс- worry, trouble

тревожный anxious; alarming

трезвость sobriety

трезвый sober

трек track, racetrack

трель *f.* trill; warble

трельяж trellis

тренер (*sports*) coach

трение friction

тренировать *impf.,* на- *pf.* train; coach

тренировка training; workout

треножник tripod

трепать *impf.,* по- *pf.* **1.** dishevel; fray; wear out **2.** *Colloq.* chatter

трепет trembling, quivering

трепетать *impf.* quiver, tremble

трепетный 1. quivering; flickering **2.** trembling **3.** timid

треск crackle, crack

треска cod

трескаться *impf.,* по- *pf.* crack

треснуть *pf.* crack; burst

трест (*econ.*) trust

третий third

третировать *impf.* slight; snub

треть *f.* a third

третье *n.* a third course; dessert

треугольник triangle

треугольный triangular

трефы *pl.* (*cards*) clubs

трёх- *in compounds* three-, tri-

трёхгранный trihedral

трёхколёсный three-wheeled

трёхкомнатный three-room

трёхлетний *attrib.* three-year

трёхмерный three-dimensional

трёхсотый three hundredth

трёхсторонний three-sided

трёхцветный tricolored

трёхэтажный three-story

трещать *impf.* crack, crackle; creak; chatter

трещина crack; split; fissure

трещотка rattle

три three

трибуна rostrum; grandstand

трибунал tribunal

тривиальный trite; banal

тридцатый thirtieth

тридцать thirty

трижды *adv.* thrice

трико *neut. indecl.* tricot

трикотаж knitted fabric; knitwear

тринадцатый thirteenth

тринадцать thirteen

триста three hundred

триумфальный triumphal

трогательный touching

трогать *impf.,* тронуть *pf.* touch; affect; **—ся** start, set out

трое *coll.* three

троекратный three-time

Троица Trinity

тройка three; numeral three; troika

тройной triple; treble

тройня triplets

тройственный triple

троллейбус trolley bus

тромб blood clot

трон throne

тронуть(ся) *pf. of* трогать(ся)

тропа, тропинка path

тропики *pl.* tropics

тропический tropical

трос rope; cable

тростник reed

трость *f.* cane, walking stick

тротуар pavement; sidewalk

трофей trophy

труба 1. pipe **2.** chimney **3.** (*mus.*) trumpet

трубач trumpet player

трубить *impf.,* про- *pf.* blow; sound; blare

трубка 1. tube **2.** (telephone) receiver **3.** (tobacco) pipe

трубопровод pipe; pipeline

труд labor, work; effort

труди́ться *impf.* work, toil
тру́дный difficult
трудово́й *attrib.* labor; working
трудолюби́вый hard-working
трудоспосо́бный able to work
трудоустро́йство job placement
трудя́щийся *n.* worker
труп corpse; dead body
тру́ппа troupe, company
трус, **—и́ха** coward
тру́сить *impf.*, **с-** *pf.* get cold feet
трусли́вый cowardly
труси́ца jogging
трусы́ *pl.* panties; trunks; shorts
труха́ dust; flakes; trash
трухля́вый rotten
трущо́ба out-of-the-way place;
slum
трюк trick; stunt
трюм hold of a ship
трю́фель *m.* truffle
тря́пка rag
тряпьё rags
тряси́на quagmire
тря́ска shaking
трясти́ *impf.*, **тряхну́ть** *pf.* shake
(out); **—ся** shake, tremble
ту *adj.*, *A of* **тот**
туале́т toilet
туберкулёз tuberculosis
туви́нец FILL, *f.* **туви́нка** Tuvinian
ту́го *adv.* tight(ly); with difficulty
туго́й tight; taut
туда́ *adv.* (over) there
туз (*cards*) ace
ту́ловище (*anat.*) trunk; torso
тулу́п sheepskin coat
тума́н fog, mist; **—ный** foggy
ту́мба post; stand; pedestal
ту́мбочка night table
ту́ндра tundra
туне́ц FILL tuna
тунне́ль *m.* tunnel
тупе́ть *impf.* become dull
тупи́к dead end; deadlock
тупо́й dull; blunt; slow-witted
тур round; turn
тура́ (*chess*) castle; rook
турба́за tourist center; campsite
туре́цкий Turkish
тури́зм tourism
тури́ст, **—ка** tourist
туристи́ческий *attrib.* tourist
туркме́н, **—ка** Turkmen
Туркмениста́н Turkmenistan
турне́ *neut. indecl.* tour
турнике́т turnstile

турни́р tournament, contest
ту́рок FILL, **турча́нка** Turk
Ту́рция Turkey
ту́склый dim; dull
тут *adv.* here
ту́фля slipper, shoe
ту́хлый rotten
ту́ча cloud; storm cloud
ту́чный obese, fat; (*of soil*) rich
туш (*mus.*) flourish
ту́ша carcass
тушёный stewed
туши́ть[1] *impf.*, **по-** *pf.* extinguish
туши́ть[2] *impf.*, **с-** *pf.* stew
тушь *f.* India ink
тща́тельный careful
тщеду́шный frail; feeble
тщесла́вный vain
тще́тный vain; futile
ты *pers. pron.* you
ты́кать *impf.*, **ткнуть** *pf.* poke
ты́ква pumpkin
тыл rear; **ты́льный** rear
ты́сяча a thousand
тысячеле́тие millennium
ты́сячный thousandth
тычи́нка stamen
тьма dark(ness); *Colloq.* lots (of)
тю́бик (*toothpaste, etc.*) tube
тюк bale; package; bundle
тюле́нь *m.* (*zool.*) seal
тюль *m.* tulle
тюльпа́н tulip
тюре́мный *attrib.* prison
тюрьма́ prison
тюфя́к straw mattress
тя́вкать *impf.*, **тя́вкнуть** *pf.* yap;
yelp
тя́га thrust; traction; pull; *Fig.*
bent
тяга́ч tractor
тя́гостный burdensome; painful
тяготе́ние gravitation; inclination
тяготе́ть (**к** + *D*) gravitate
тяготи́ть *impf.* be a burden
тягу́чий stretchable; ductile; viscous; *Fig.* slow
тя́жба *Obs.* lawsuit
тяжело́ *adv.* heavily; seriously;
pred. (it is) difficult; painful
тяжелоатле́т weightlifter
тяжелове́с (*sports*) heavyweight
тяжёлый heavy; serious; painful
тя́жесть weight; gravity; burden
тяну́ть *impf.*, **по-** *pf.* pull, draw,
tow; **—ся** stretch (out); drag on;
last

у *prep.* (+ *G*) at; by; with; from; of; (*possession*): **у меня́ (есть)** I have

убавля́ть *impf.*, **уба́вить** *pf.* reduce

убега́ть *impf.*, **убежа́ть** *pf.* run away; escape

убеди́тельный convincing, persuasive

убежда́ть *impf.*, **-ди́ть** *pf.* (**в** + *P*) convince (of); persuade

убежде́ние conviction; persuasion

убеждённый convinced; confirmed

убе́жище refuge; asylum

убива́ть *impf.*, **уби́ть** *pf.* kill, murder

уби́йство murder

уби́йца *m.* & *f.* murderer

убира́ть *impf.*, **убра́ть** *pf.* remove; harvest; clean *or* tidy up

уби́тый killed; crushed

уби́ть *pf. of* **убива́ть**

убо́гий wretched; squalid

убо́рка 1. harvesting **2.** cleaning

убо́рная *n.* bathroom; toilet

убо́рщик janitor

убо́рщица cleaning woman

убыва́ть *impf.*, **убы́ть** *pf.* subside

убы́ток FILL loss

убы́точный losing, unprofitable

уважа́емый respected, esteemed

уважа́ть *impf.* respect, esteem

уваже́ние respect

уважи́тельный respectful; valid

уведомле́ние notification

уведомля́ть *impf.*, **уве́домить** *pf.* notify; inform

увезти́ *pf. of* **увози́ть**

увели́чивать(ся) *impf.*, **увели́чить(ся)** *pf.* increase, enlarge

уве́ренность confidence

уве́ренный assured, certain; confident

увернуться *pf.* (**от** + *G*) evade

увертю́ра overture

уверя́ть *impf.*, **уве́рить** *pf.* assure; **—ся** become convinced

увесели́тельный *attrib.* amusement

увести́ *pf. of* **уводи́ть**

уве́чить *impf.* mutilate; cripple

уве́чье mutilation

увещева́ть, увеща́ть *impf.* admonish

уви́деть *pf.* see; **—ся** meet; get together

уви́деть *pf. of* **ви́деть**

увлека́тельный fascinating

увлека́ть *impf.*, **увле́чь** *pf.* fascinate; carry away; **—ся** be carried away

увлече́ние animation; (+ *I*) passion (for)

увлечённый enthusiastic

уводи́ть *impf.*, **увести́** *pf.* take away; steal

увози́ть *impf.*, **увезти́** *pf.* drive *or* take away

увольне́ние dismissal

увольня́ть *impf.*, **уво́лить** *pf.* discharge; dismiss; **—ся** be discharged; be dismissed; retire

увы́ *interj.* alas!

увяда́ть *impf.*, **увя́нуть** *pf.* fade; wither

уга́дывать *impf.*, **угада́ть** *pf.* guess

уга́р carbon-monoxide (poisoning); *Fig.* ecstasy

уга́рный газ carbon monoxide

угаса́ть *impf.*, **уга́снуть** *pf.* fade, die away

угле- *in compounds* coal; carbon

углево́д carbohydrate

углеро́д carbon

углово́й *attrib.* corner; angular

углублённый deepened; absorbed

углубля́ть *impf.* **-би́ть** *pf.* deepen; **—ся** deepen; become absorbed (in); delve (in)

угнета́ть *impf.* oppress; depress

угнетённый oppressed; depressed

угова́ривать *impf.*, **уговори́ть** *pf.* persuade

угово́р persuasion; agreement

угоди́ть *pf. of* **угожда́ть**

угодливый obsequious; officious

уго́дно *pred.* (+ *D*): **как вам ~** as you please; **кто ~** anybody

угожда́ть *impf.*, **угоди́ть** *pf.* please

у́гол FILL corner; angle

уголо́вник, -ница criminal

уголо́вный criminal; penal

уголо́к FILL corner, nook

у́голь FILL *m.* coal; **—ный** coal

уго́н driving away; stealing

угоня́ть *impf.*, **угна́ть** *pf.* drive away; (*car*) steal; (*plane*) hijack

угора́здить *pf.* urge; make

угоща́ть *impf.*, **угости́ть** *pf.* entertain, treat

угоще́ние food; refreshments

угрожа́ть *impf.* threaten

угро́за threat; menace

угрызе́ния со́вести *pl.* pangs of conscience

угрю́мый sullen; morose

уда́в boa; boa constrictor

удава́ться *impf.*, уда́ться *pf.* turn out well; *impers.* (+ D *and infin.*) succeed

удави́ть *pf.* strangle

удалённый remote

удаля́ть *impf.*, -ли́ть *pf.* remove; extract

уда́р 1. blow 2. (*med.*) stroke

ударе́ние stress; accent

ударя́ть *impf.*, уда́рить *pf.* strike; hit; —ся bump into, hit

уда́ться *pf.* of удава́ться

уда́ча success

уда́чник, -ница lucky person

уда́чный successful; lucky

уделя́ть *impf.*, -ли́ть *pf.* spare; give

удержа́ние deduction; retention

уде́рживать *impf.*, удержа́ть *pf.* restrain; retain; hold (back); —ся refrain (from); hold out

удиви́тельный surprising; amazing

удивле́ние surprise

удивля́ть *impf.*, -ви́ть *pf.* amaze; surprise; —ся be surprised

удила́ *pl.* bit

удира́ть *impf.*, удра́ть *pf.* make off

удлини́тель extension cord

удлиня́ть *impf.*, -ни́ть *pf.* lengthen

удо́бный comfortable; convenient

удобре́ние fertilization

удо́бство comfort; convenience

удовлетворе́ние satisfaction

удовлетвори́тельный satisfactory

удовлетворя́ть *impf.*, -ри́ть *pf.* satisfy

удово́льствие pleasure

удостовере́ние certificate; ~ ли́чности identity card

удостоверя́ть *impf.*, -ве́рить *pf.* certify; attest

у́дочка fishing rod

удруча́ть *impf.*, -чи́ть *pf.* depress

удручённый depressed

удуша́ть *impf.*, удуши́ть *pf.* suffocate; stifle

удушье difficulty in breathing

уедине́ние solitude

уединённый solitary

уезжа́ть *impf.*, уе́хать *pf.* leave; depart

уж[1] *adv.*, *see* уже́

уж[2] grass snake

ужа́лить *pf.* of жа́лить

у́жас horror; terror

ужаса́ть *impf.*, ужасну́ть *pf.* terrify; horrify; awe

ужа́сный horrible; terrible

уже́ *adv.* already; ~ не no longer

у́жин supper

у́жинать *impf.*, по- *pf.* have supper

узаконе́ние legalization

узбе́к, узбе́чка Uzbek

узда́ bridle

у́зел FILL knot.; junction; hub

у́зкий narrow; tight

узнава́ть *impf.*, узна́ть *pf.* learn; find out; recognize

у́зник, у́зница prisoner

узо́р pattern; design

у́зость narrowness

узурпа́ция usurpation

уйти́ *pf.* of уходи́ть

указа́ние indication; instruction; direction

указа́тель indicator; index

ука́зка pointer

ука́зывать *impf.*, указа́ть *pf.* indicate; point to *or* out

ука́чивать *impf.*, укача́ть *pf.* rock to sleep

укла́д structure; style

укла́дывать *impf.*, уложи́ть *pf.* lay; pack; put to bed; —ся pack up

укло́н slope; deviation; bias

уклоне́ние deviation; evasion

уклоня́ть *impf.*, -ни́ться *pf.* (от + G) deviate; evade

уко́л prick; injection

уко́р reproach

укора́чивать *impf.*, укороти́ть *pf.* shorten

укори́зненный reproachful

укоря́ть *impf.*, -ри́ть *pf.* (в + P) reproach (for)

укра́дкой *adv.* stealthily

Украи́на Ukraine

украи́нец, FILL -и́нка Ukrainian

укра́сть *pf.* of красть

украша́ть *impf.*, укра́сить *pf.* adorn, decorate

украше́ние decoration

укрепля́ть *impf.*, -пи́ть *pf.* strengthen

укро́п dill

укроти́тель, —ница tamer

укроща́ть *impf.*, -ти́ть *pf.* tame

укрыва́ть *impf.*, укры́ть *pf.*

cover; conceal; **—ся** cover oneself; take cover

у́ксус vinegar

уку́с bite; (insect) sting

укуси́ть pf. of **куса́ть**

ула́живать impf., **ула́дить** pf. arrange; settle

у́лей FILL beehive

улета́ть impf., **-те́ть** pf. fly away

ули́ка (piece of) evidence

ули́тка snail

у́лица street; **у́личный** street

уло́в catch (quantity caught)

уложи́ть(ся) pf. of **укла́дывать(ся)**

улучша́ть impf., **улу́чшить** pf. improve; better

улыба́ться impf., **улыбну́ться** pf. smile

улы́бка smile

ультима́тум ultimatum

ультра- pref. ultra-

ультразвуково́й ultrasonic

ультрафиоле́товый ultraviolet

ум mind; intellect

ума́лчивать impf., **умолча́ть** pf. pass over in silence

умаля́ть impf., **-ли́ть** pf. belittle

уме́лец FILL, **-льца** skilled craftsman

уме́лый skillful; able

уменьша́ть(ся) impf., **уме́ньшить(ся)** pf. decrease, diminish

уме́ренность moderation

умере́ть pf. of **умира́ть**

уме́рший dead; n. the deceased

умерщвля́ть impf., **умертви́ть** pf. kill

меря́ть impf., **уме́рить** pf. moderate

уме́стный appropriate; pertinent

уме́ть impf., **с-** pf. know (how to)

умили́тельный touching; moving

умира́ть impf., **умере́ть** pf. die

умне́ть impf., **по-** pf. grow wiser

умножа́ть(ся) impf., **умно́жить(ся)** pf. increase; multiply

умноже́ние multiplication

у́мный clever, intelligent

умозри́тельный speculative

умолка́ть impf., **умо́лкнуть** pf. fall silent; stop

умолча́ть pf. of **ума́лчивать**

умоля́ть impf. entreat; implore

умонастрое́ние frame of mind

умори́ть pf. kill; exhaust

у́мственный mental, intellectual

умыва́льник washstand

умыва́ние washing

умыва́ть impf., **умы́ть** pf. wash; **—ся** wash oneself

у́мысел design; intent(ion)

умы́шленный intentional

унести́ pf. of **уноси́ть**

универма́г (abbr. of **универса́льный магази́н**) department store

универса́льный universal; versatile; all-purpose

универса́м supermarket

университе́т university; **—ский** attrib. university

унижа́ть impf., **уни́зить** pf. humiliate; **—ся** degrade oneself

унизи́тельный humiliating

уника́льный unique

у́никум unique person or object

унима́ть impf., **-ня́ть** pf. calm; pacify

унита́з toilet (bowl)

унифици́ровать impf. & pf. standardize

уничтожа́ть impf., **уничто́жить** pf. destroy; annihilate

уничтожа́ющий devastating

уноси́ть impf., **унести́** pf. take or carry away; carry off

у́нция ounce

унbeforéть impf. lose heart

уны́лый dejected; downcast

упа́док FILL decline; decay

упа́дочный decadent; depressive

упако́вка packing (material)

упако́вывать impf., **упакова́ть** pf. pack (up)

упа́сть pf. of **па́дать** fall

упира́ться impf., **упере́ться** pf. rest or lean (against); resist

упи́танный well-fed; plump

упла́та payment

упла́чивать impf., **уплати́ть** pf. pay

уплотня́ть impf., **-ни́ть** pf. compress

уподобле́ние likening

уполномо́ченный n. representative; authorized agent

уполномо́чивать impf., **-мо́чить** pf. authorize, empower

упомина́ть impf., **упомяну́ть** pf. mention; refer to

упо́р support; prop; **в ~** point-blank; **упо́рный** stubborn; persistent

упо́рствовать impf. persist; be stubborn

употреби́тельный in common use

употребле́ние use; usage

употребля́ть impf., **-би́ть** pf. use; apply

управле́ние management, administration; control

управле́нческий administrative

управля́емый guided

управля́ть *impf.* (+ *I*) manage, govern; control; (*mus.*) conduct

упражне́ние exercise

упражня́ться *impf.* practice

упраздня́ть *impf.*, **-ни́ть** *pf.* abolish

упра́шивать *impf.*, **упроси́ть** *pf.* prevail upon; entreat

упрёк reproach; rebuke

упрека́ть *impf.*, **упрекну́ть** *pf.* reproach

упро́чивать *impf.*, **упро́чить** *pf. v.t.* strengthen; consolidate

упроща́ть *impf.*, **-сти́ть** *pf.* (over)simplify

упрощённый (over)simplified

упру́гий elastic; resilient

у́пряжь *f.* harness

упря́мство obstinacy

упря́мый stubborn; obstinate

упуска́ть *impf.*, **-сти́ть** *pf.* miss; let go (by); overlook

упуще́ние omission

упы́рь *m.* vampire

ура́ *interj.* hurrah!

уравне́ние equation; equation

ура́внивать[1] *impf.*, **уровня́ть** *pf.* make even; level

ура́внивать[2] *impf.*, **уравня́ть** *pf.* equalize

уравнове́шенный balanced; composed

урага́н hurricane

ура́н uranium

урегули́рование regulation; settlement

уре́зывать *impf.*, **уре́зать** *pf.* cut off; shorten

у́рна urn

у́ровень *m.* level; standard

уровня́ть *pf. of* ура́внивать

уро́д freak; monster

уро́дливый ugly; hideous

уро́довать *impf.*, **из-** *pf.* disfigure, deform

урожа́й harvest; yield

уро́к lesson

уро́лог urologist

уро́н damage; losses

урони́ть *pf. of* роня́ть

урча́ть *impf.* rumble

уса́дьба country estate; farmstead

уса́живать *impf.*, **усади́ть** *pf.* seat; offer a seat; plant

уса́тый mustached; whiskered

усва́ивать *impf.*, **усво́ить** *pf.* master, learn; assimilate

усе́рдный zealous; diligent

усе́рдствовать *impf.* show great zeal

уси́дчивый assiduous

у́сик 1. small mustache **2.** feeler; tendril

уси́ленный increased; intense; earnest

уси́ливать *impf.*, **уси́лить** *pf.* strengthen; intensify; amplify

уси́лие effort

усили́тель amplifier; booster

ускольза́ть *impf.*, **ускользну́ть** *pf.* slip away *or* off; steal away

ускоря́ть *impf.*, **ускори́ть** *pf.* hasten, quicken; accelerate

усло́вие condition

усло́вный conditional; conventional

усложне́ние complication

усложня́ть *impf.*, **-ни́ть** *pf.* complicate

услу́га service; favor

услу́живать *impf.*, **услужи́ть** *pf.* render a service; serve

услыха́ть *pf. of* слы́шать

усме́шка (ironical) smile; grin

усмиря́ть *impf.*, **-ри́ть** *pf.* pacify

усмотре́ние discretion; judgment

усну́ть *pf.* fall asleep

успева́ть *impf.*, **успе́ть** *pf.* manage (to); have time (to); succeed

успе́х success; *pl.* progress

успе́шный successful

успока́ивать *impf.*, **успоко́ить** *pf.* calm; soothe; assuage

успокои́тельный calming; reassuring

уста́в regulations; statute

устава́ть *impf.*, **уста́ть** *pf.* get tired

уста́лость fatigue

уста́лый fatigued, weary, tired

устана́вливать *impf.*, **установи́ть** *pf.* install; mount; establish

устано́вка installation; establishment; mounting; setting

устаре́лый outdated; obsolete

уста́ть *pf. of* устава́ть

у́стный oral; verbal

усто́й foundation; abutment

усто́йчивость stability

усто́йчивый steady; firm; stable

устра́ивать *impf.*, **устро́ить** *pf.* arrange; establish; make; **—ся** settle (down); work out

устраня́ть *impf.*, **-ни́ть** *pf.* remove; eliminate

устраша́ть *impf.*, -ши́ть *pf.* frighten

устремля́ть *impf.*, -ми́ть *pf.* direct; —ся rush

устро́ить *pf. of* устра́ивать

устро́йство arrangement; structure; system

усту́п ledge; projection

уступа́ть *impf.*, -пи́ть *pf.* yield; cede

усту́пка concession

усту́пчивый pliant; compliant

у́стье estuary, mouth

усугубля́ть *impf.*, -би́ть *pf.* increase; aggravate

усы́ *pl.* mustache; whiskers

усыновля́ть *impf.*, -ви́ть *pf.* adopt

усыпа́льница crypt; burial vault

усыпля́ть *impf.*, усыпи́ть *pf.* lull *or* put to sleep

усыпля́ющий soporific

усыха́ть *impf.*, усо́хнуть *pf.* wither; dry up; dry out

ута́ивать *impf.*, утаи́ть *pf.* conceal; withhold

у́тварь *f.* utensils

утверди́тельный affirmative

утвержда́ть *impf.*, утверди́ть *pf.* confirm; assert; approve

утека́ть *impf.*, уте́чь *pf.* leak

утёс rock; cliff; crag

уте́чка loss; leakage; drain

утеша́ть *impf.*, уте́шить *pf.* comfort; console

утеше́ние consolation; comfort

утеши́тельный comforting

утилиза́ция utilization

утилита́рный utilitarian

утира́ть *impf.*, утере́ть *pf.* wipe (dry)

утиха́ть *impf.*, ути́хнуть *pf.* quiet down

у́тка duck

утолще́ние thickening; bulge

утоля́ть *impf.*, -ли́ть *pf.* quench; appease

утоми́тельный tiresome; tiring

утомля́ть *impf.*, -ми́ть *pf.* tire; exhaust

утончённый refined; cultivated

утопа́ющий *n.* drowning person

утопи́ть *pf. of* топи́ть

уто́пия utopia

уто́пленник, -ница drowned person.

уточне́ние clarification

уточня́ть *impf.*, -ни́ть *pf.* clarify; amplify; specify

утра́та loss

у́тренний *attrib.* morning

утри́ровать *impf. & pf.* exaggerate

у́тро morning; по утра́м in the morning(s); —м in the morning

утро́ба womb

утружда́ть *impf.*, утруди́ть *pf.* trouble

утю́г (*appliance*) iron

уха́ fish soup

уха́живать *impf.* (за + *I*) care for; tend; court

хвата́ть *impf.*, ухвати́ть *pf.* catch, grasp

ухитря́ться *impf.*, -ри́ться *pf.* contrive

ухмы́лка grin; smirk

у́хо (*pl.* у́ши) ear

уходи́ть *impf.*, уйти́ *pf.* leave; go away

ухудша́ть *impf.*, уху́дшить *pf.* worsen, make worse

уцеле́ть *pf.* survive

уцепи́ть *pf.* grab

уча́ствовать *impf.* (в + *P*) participate

уча́стие participation; share

уча́стник, —ница participant

уча́сток FILL plot; part; section

уча́сть *f.* lot, fate

уча́щийся *n.* student

учёба studies; training

уче́бник textbook, manual

уче́бный educational; school

учени́к, учени́ца pupil

учёный learned; *n.* scholar; scientist

уче́сть *pf. of* учи́тывать

учёт stock-taking; registration

учи́лище vocational school

учи́тель, —ница teacher

учи́тельский teacher's

учи́тывать *impf.*, уче́сть *pf.* take into account; allow for

учи́ть *impf.*, вы́-, на- *pf.* **1.** learn **2.** teach; —ся learn; study

учреди́тель, —ница founder

учреди́тельный constituent

учрежда́ть *impf.*, учреди́ть *pf.* found; establish

учрежде́ние establishment; (social) institution; founding

учти́вый polite; courteous

уша́нка cap with earflaps

у́ши *pl. of* у́хо

уши́б injury; bruise

ушиба́ться *impf.*, -би́ться *pf.* hurt oneself

ушно́й aural; *attrib.* ear

уще́лье ravine, gorge

ущемля́ть *impf.*, -ми́ть *pf.* jam; catch; pinch; limit; hurt

уще́рб damage, loss; detriment
уще́рбный waning
ущипну́ть pf. pinch
ую́т comfort; —ный comfortable

уязви́мость vulnerability
уязви́мый vulnerable
уясня́ть impf., —ни́ть pf. understand; make out; size up

Ф

фа́брика factory; mill
фабрикова́ть impf., с- pf. fabricate
фабри́чный attrib. factory; manufactured
фа́була plot (of a story)
фавори́т, —ка favorite
фаго́т bassoon
фа́за phase
фаза́н pheasant
файл (comput.) file
фа́кел torch
факс fax
факси́миле neut. indecl. facsimile
фа́кт fact
факти́ческий virtual; factual
факту́ра texture; style
факультати́вный optional
факульте́т faculty, department
фальсифика́ция falsification
фальсифици́ровать impf. & pf. falsify
фальши́вить impf., с- pf. be insincere; sing off key
фальшивомоне́тчик, -щица counterfeiter
фальши́вый false; forged
фальшь f. deception; falseness
фами́лия surname
фами́льярный unceremonious
фана́тик, -ти́чка fanatic
фанати́чный fanatical
фане́ра veneer; plywood
фантазёр, —ка visionary; dreamer
фантази́ровать impf., за- pf. dream (up); improvise
фанта́зия fantasy; imagination
фанта́стика fiction; fantasy
фантасти́ческий fantastic
фа́ра headlight
Фаренге́йт Fahrenheit
фармаколо́гия pharmacology
фармаце́вт pharmacist
фарс farce
фа́ртук apron
фарфо́р porcelain; china
фарш stuffing; chopped meat
фарширова́ть impf., за- pf. stuff
фас front (of one's face)
фаса́д facade
фасова́ть impf., рас- pf. package
фасо́вка packaging

фасо́ль f. (kidney) bean(s)
фасо́н fashion, mode, style
фата́ bridal veil
фата́льный fatal
фа́янс glazed earthenware
февра́ль m., —ский February
федера́льный federal
федерати́вный federative
федера́ция federation
фейерве́рк fireworks
фельдма́ршал field marshal
фе́льдшер medical assistant
фельето́н satirical article
фемини́ст, —ка feminist; —и́ческий, —ский feminist
фен hair dryer
фено́мен phenomenon
феномена́льный phenomenal
ферзь m. (chess) queen
фе́рма[1] farm
фе́рма[2] girder; truss
фе́рмер farmer; —ство farming; —ский farmer's
фе́ска fez
фестива́ль m. festival
фети́ш fetish
фетр felt; фе́тровый felt
фехтова́льный attrib. fencing
фехтова́ть impf. fence
фешене́бельный fashionable
фе́я fairy
фиа́лка (bot.) violet
фигу́ра figure; shape; (chess) piece
фигура́льный figurative; metaphorical
фигури́ровать impf. figure or appear (as)
фигури́ст, —ка figure skater
фи́зик physicist; —а physics
физионо́мия face; expression
физиотерапе́вт physical therapist
физиотерапи́я physical therapy
физи́ческий physical
физкульту́ра (abbr. of физи́ческая культу́ра) physical education; gymnastic
физкульту́рник, -ница gymnast
фикти́вный fictitious
филантро́п, —ка philanthropist
филатели́я philately
филе́ neut. indecl. filet; sirloin

филёнка panel
филиа́л branch
филигра́нь f. filigree
фило́лог philologist
филологи́ческий philological
фило́соф philosopher
филосо́фия philosophy
филосо́фский philosophical
фильм film; movie
фильмоте́ка film library
фи́льтр filter
фильтрова́ть impf., от-, про- pf. filter
фимиа́м incense
фина́л finale; final; —ьный final
финанси́ровать impf. & pf. finance
фина́нсовый financial
фина́нсы pl. finances
фи́ник (fruit) date
фи́ниш (sports) finish (line)
фи́нишная n. home stretch
Финля́ндия Finland
финн, фи́нка Finn
фи́нно-уго́рский Finno-Ugric
фи́нский Finnish
фиоле́товый violet
фи́рма firm, company
фи́рменный attrib. company; brand name; house
фити́ль m. wick; fuse
фи́шка chip (used in games)
флаг flag, banner
флагшто́к flagpole
флажо́к FILL small flag
фланг (mil.) flank; wing
фране́ль f. flannel
флани́ровать impf. Obs. stroll
флегма́тик phlegmatic person
флегмати́ческий, флегмати́чный phlegmatic
фле́йта flute
флёр crepe
фли́гель m. wing
флирт flirting
флома́стер soft-tip pen; marker
флот fleet; вое́нно-морско́й ~ navy; возду́шный ~ air force
флю́гер weather vane
флюс¹ (metals) flux
флюс² gumboil; abscess
фля́га, фля́жка flask
фойе́ neut. indecl. foyer
фо́кус¹ focus
фо́кус² trick; —ник conjurer
фокуси́ровать impf. & pf. focus
фо́льга foil
фолькло́р folklore

фон background
фона́рик flashlight; lamp
фона́рный attrib. lamp; lantern
фона́рь m. 1. lantern, (street) lamp 2. flashlight
фонд fund; stock; reserves
фо́ндовый attrib. stock; фо́ндовая би́ржа stock exchange
фонети́ческий phonetic
фоноте́ка record library
фонта́н fountain
форе́ль f. trout
фо́рма 1. form, shape; mold 2. uniform
форма́льность formality
форма́льный formal
форма́т size; format
фо́рменный attrib. uniform
формирова́ть impf., с- pf. form; organize
фо́рмула formula
формулиро́вка 1. formulation 2. formula
форси́ровать impf. & pf. force
форсу́нка sprayer; injector
форте́ль m. trick; stunt
фортепья́но neut. indecl. piano
фо́рточка small hinged window pane for ventilation
фо́сфор phosphorus
фо́то neut. indecl. photo
фотоаппара́т camera
фото́граф photographer
фотографи́ровать impf., с- pf. photograph
фотогра́фия photograph
фотока́рточка photograph
фотоко́пия photocopy
фотолюби́тель, —ница amateur photographer
фрагме́нт fragment
фра́за sentence; phrase
фрак tails; tailcoat
фра́кция political faction; group
фраму́га transom
Фра́нция France
францу́з, -цуже́нка a French person
францу́зский French
фрахт freight
фрезерова́ть impf. & pf. cut (metal); mill (metal)
френч military jacket
фре́ска fresco
фриво́льный ribald
фрикаде́лька meatball
фронт front; —а́льный frontal
фронто́н pediment; gable
фрукт piece of fruit

фрукто́вый *attrib.* fruit; **~ сад** orchard

фтор fluorine

фуже́р tall wine glass

фунда́мент foundation; **—а́льный** main; solid; thorough; basic

фунду́к filbert

функциона́льный functional

фу́нкция function

фунт pound

фура́жка peak-cap; service cap

фурго́н van

фуру́нкул (*med.*) boil

фут (*measurement*) foot

футбо́л soccer; **—и́ст, —и́стка** soccer player; **—ьный** *attrib.* soccer

футбо́лка T-shirt

футля́р case

фы́ркать *impf.*, **-кнуть** *pf.* snort

фюзеля́ж fuselage

Х

хала́т dressing gown; smock

хала́тность indifference; negligence

халту́ра hack work

хам 1. boor **2. ~,** **ха́мка** crude person; **—ский** crude, vulgar

хамелео́н chameleon

ха́мство boorishness

хандра́ depression; melancholy

ханжа́ hypocrite

ха́ос chaos

хара́ктер character; nature

характери́стика 1. character reference **2.** characterization

характе́рный characteristic; typical

ха́ртия charter

харчо́ *neut. indecl.* mutton soup

ха́та hut

хвала́ praise

хвали́ть *impf.*, **по-** *pf.* praise; **—ся** boast

хва́статься *impf.*, **по-** *pf.* boast

хвастли́вый boastful

хвасту́н, —ья braggart

хвата́ть[1] *impf.*, **схвати́ть** *pf.* grab, seize; **—ся** snatch (at); catch

хвата́ть[2] *impf.*, **хвати́ть** *pf. impers.* (+ *G*) suffice; be enough

хва́тка 1. grasp; grip **2.** skill

хво́йный coniferous

хвора́ть *impf.* be ill

хво́рост brushwood

хвост tail; **—ово́й** *attrib.* tail

хво́я (*bot.*) needles

хи́лый feeble, sickly

химе́ра chimera

хи́мик chemist; **—а́лии** *pl.* chemicals

хими́ческий chemical

хи́мия chemistry

химчи́стка dry cleaning

хирома́нт palm reader

хиру́рг surgeon; **—и́ческий** surgical; **—и́я** surgery

хитре́ц cunning person

хитре́ть *impf.*, **с-** *pf.* use cunning

хи́трость cunning; guile

хи́трый cunning; intricate

хихи́кать *impf.* giggle; snigger

хище́ние theft; embezzlement

хи́щник beast *or* bird of prey

хи́щный predatory; rapacious

хладнокро́вие coolness; composure; sang-froid

хладнокро́вный composed, cool

хлам garbage; trash; rubbish

хлеб bread; corn, grain

хлеба́ть *impf.*, **хлебну́ть** *pf.* gulp down

хле́бница breadbasket

хле́бный *attrib.* bread; grain

хлебосо́льный hospitable

хлев barn

хлёсткий biting; sharp; scathing

хло́пать *impf.*, **хло́пнуть** *pf.* bang

хлопково́дство cotton growing

хло́пковый cotton

хло́пок FILL cotton

хлопо́к FILL bang; slap; pat

хлопота́ть *impf.*, **по-** *pf.* **1.** *impf.* bustle about **2.** solicit; intercede for

хлопотли́вый busy; bustling

хло́потный troublesome

хло́поты *pl.* trouble; efforts

хлопу́шка fly swatter

хлопчатобума́жный cotton

хло́пья *pl.* flakes

хлор chlorine

хло́ристый, хло́рный chlorine

хло́рка bleach

хлорофи́лл chlorophyll

хлорофо́рм chloroform

хлы́нуть *pf.* gush; pour

хмеле́ть *impf.* get intoxicated

хмель[1] *m.* hops

хмель[2] *m.* intoxication; **—но́й** intoxicating

хму́риться *impf.*, **на-** *pf.* frown

хму́рый gloomy

хо́бби *neut. indecl.* hobby

хо́бот (*zool.*) trunk, proboscis

ход motion, speed; course, turn; move, stroke; lead

хода́тайство petition(ing)

хода́тайствовать *impf.*, по- *pf.* (o + *P*) petition for

ходи́ть[1] *indet.*, идти́ *det.* go; walk; run

ходи́ть[2] *impf* (в + *P*) wear

ходово́й 1. working **2.** fast-selling

ходо́к FILL (*person*) walker

ходьба́ walking

хожде́ние walking; circulation

хозрасчёт self-supporting system

хозя́ин owner; landlord; host

хозя́йка landlady; proprietress; mistress; hostess

хозя́йничать *impf.* keep house

хозя́йственный 1. economic **2.** *attrib.* household **3.** economical

хозя́йство economy; household

хокке́й (ice) hockey

хо́леный well-groomed

холе́ра cholera

холе́рик high-strung person

холестери́н cholesterol

холл 1. meeting hall **2.** lobby

холм hill; —и́стый hilly

хо́лод cold

холоде́н FILL aspic

холоди́льник refrigerator

хо́лодно *adv.* coldly; *pred.* cold

холо́дный cold

холосто́й[1] unmarried; single

холосто́й[2] 1. (*tech.*) idle **2.** blank

холостя́к bachelor

холст canvas; linen

хор chorus, choir

хорва́т, —ка Croat

Хорва́тия Croatia

хореогра́фия choreography

хори́ст, —ка member of a choir

хорово́д round dance

хорони́ть *impf.*, по-, с- *pf.* bury

хоро́ший good; fine

хорошо́ *adv.* well; *pred.* all right

хоте́ть *impf.*, за- *pf.* want, wish; —ся *impers.* (+ *D*) feel like; мне хо́чется I want

хоть, хотя́ *conj.* although; at least; ~ бы if only

хохо́л crest; topknot

хо́хот loud laughter

хохота́ть *impf.* roar with laughter

хра́брость bravery; valor

хра́брый brave, courageous

храм temple; church

хране́ние keeping; storage

храни́лище storage; warehouse

храни́ть *impf.* store; preserve

храп snoring

храпе́ть *impf.* snore

хребе́т FILL **1.** (*anat.*) spine **2.** mountain ridge

хрен horseradish

хризанте́ма chrysanthemum

хрип wheeze; —лый hoarse

христиани́н, -а́нка Christian

Христиа́нство Christianity

Христо́с (G Христа́) Christ

хром chromium

хрома́ть *impf.* limp

хромо́й lame; *n.* lame person

хромосо́ма chromosome

хромота́ lameness

хро́ника chronicle; newsreel

хрони́ческий chronic

хронологи́ческий chronological

хру́пкий fragile; frail; delicate

хруст crackle; crunch

хруста́ль *m.* crystal; —ный crystal

хрусте́ть *impf.*, хру́стнуть *pf.* crackle, crunch

хрю́кать *impf.*, хрю́кнуть *pf.* grunt

хрящ[1] (*anat.*) cartilage

хрящ[2] gravel

худе́ть *impf.*, по- *pf.* lose weight

ху́до[1] harm, evil

ху́до[2] *adv.* badly; ill

худо́жественный *attrib.* art; artistic; худо́жественная литерату́ра fiction

худо́жник, -ница artist; painter

худо́й lean; thin; bad

худоща́вый skinny; lean; thin

ху́дший worse; worst

ху́же *adv.* worse

хулига́н, —ка hooligan

хулига́нить *impf.* behave like a hoodlum

хэ́кер hacker

ца́пля heron
цара́пать(ся) *impf.* scratch
цара́пина scratch
цари́ть *impf.* reign
цари́ца czarina; queen
ца́рский czar's; royal
ца́рственный majestic; regal
царь *m.* czar; emperor
цвести́ *impf.* bloom, flower
цвет¹ (*pl.* —á) color
цвет² (*pl.* —ы́) flower(s); blossom
цвете́ние blooming; blossoming
цветна́я капу́ста cauliflower
цветно́й colored
цветово́дство floriculture
цвето́к (*pl.* цветы́) flower; blossom
цвету́щий flowering; flourishing
цеди́ть *impf.* strain; filter
целе́бный medicinal, curative
целесообра́зный expedient
целеустремлённый purposeful
целико́м *adv.* entirely, whole
целина́ virgin soil
це́лить(ся) *impf.* aim
целлофа́н cellophane
целова́ть(ся) *impf.*, по- *pf.* kiss
це́лое *n.* whole
целому́дрие chastity
це́лый whole; solid; intact
цель *f.* aim, purpose; target
Це́льсий Centigrade; **10 гра́дусов по Це́льсию** ten degrees Celsius
цеме́нт cement
цементи́ровать *impf. & pf.* cement
цена́ price; cost; value
цензу́ра censorship
цени́тель, —ница judge; connoisseur
цени́ть *impf.* value; estimate
це́нность value; *pl.* valuables
це́нный valuable
цент cent
це́нтнер centner (100 kilograms)
центр center; —**а́льный** central
центробе́жный centrifugal
це́пкий obstinate; tenacious
цепля́ться *impf.* (за + A) cling to
цепо́чка small chain
цепь *f.* chain; (*elec.*) circuit
церебра́льный парали́ч cerebral palsy
церемо́ниться *impf.*, по- *pf.* stand on ceremony
церемо́ния ceremony

церковнославя́нский Church Slavonic
церко́вный *attrib.* church
це́рковь *f.* church
цех factory shop; section; guild
циани́д cyanide
цивилиза́ция civilization
цивилизо́ванный civilized
цикл cycle
цикло́н cyclone
цико́рий chicory
цили́ндр cylinder; —**и́ческий** cylindrical
цинга́ scurvy
ци́ник cynic
цинк zinc; **ци́нковый** *attrib.* zinc
цино́вка mat
цирк circus; —**ово́й** *attrib.* circus
цирка́ч, —ка circus performer
циркули́ровать *impf.* circulate
ци́ркуль *m.* pair of compasses; dividers
цисте́рна cistern; tank
цита́та quotation
цити́ровать *impf.*, про- *pf.* quote
ци́трус citrus
цифербла́т dial; (clock) face
ци́фра number; figure
цифрово́й numerical; ~ **про́игрыватель** CD player
цука́т candied fruit
цыга́н, —ка Romany (*formerly:* Gypsy); —**ский** Romany
цыплёнок FILL chick
цы́почки *pl.:* **на цы́почках** on tiptoe
ча́вкать *impf.* munch
чад fumes; smoke
чадра́ veil
чаевы́е *n.* tip; gratuity
чай tea
ча́йка seagull
ча́йная ло́жка teaspoon
ча́йник teapot; tea kettle
чалма́ turban
чару́ющий charming; enchanting
час hour; o'clock; кото́рый ~? what time is it?; ~ **пик** rush hour
часо́вня chapel
часово́й 1. hour-long **2.** *attrib.* clock; watch; time; *n.* sentry
часовщи́к watchmaker
части́ца (*gram.*) particle
части́чный partial
ча́стность particular(ity); detail
ча́стный private; particular

ча́сто *adv.* frequently
частота́ frequency
часту́шка ditty; jingle
ча́стый frequent
часть *f.* part; department; unit
ча́стью *adv.* partly; in part
часы́ *pl.* clock, watch
ча́хлый **1.** sickly **2.** withered
ча́шка cup
ча́ща thicket; dense forest
ча́ще *adv.* more often
чего́ *pron. G of* что
чей *indef. pron., f.* чья, *neut.* чьё, *pl.* чьи whose; чей-либо, ~-нибудь anyone's; чей-то someone's
чек check; bill; receipt
чека́нить *impf.,* от- *pf.* coin, mint
чека́нка coining, minting
чека́нный **1.** embossed; engraved **2.** crisp; precise
че́ковый *attrib.* check; checking
челно́чный *attrib.* shuttle; ~ кора́бль *m.* space shuttle
челове́к human being; person; man
челове́ческий human; humane
челове́чество humanity
челове́чность humaneness
челове́чный humane
че́люсть *f.* jaw; вставны́е ~ denture
чем *pron. I of* что; *conj.* than
чём *pron. P of* что
чемода́н suitcase
чемпио́н, —ка champion
чемпиона́т championship
чему́ *pron. D of* что
чепуха́ nonsense
че́рви *pl.* (*cards*) hearts
черви́вый worm-eaten
черво́нец FILL ten-ruble note
черво́нный[1] (*cards*) of hearts
черво́нный[2] red; scarlet
червь *m.,* червя́к worm
черда́к attic; garret
чередова́ть(ся) *impf.* alternate
че́рез, чрез *prep.* (+ A) across, over; through; (*time*) in; after; ~ день every other day
черёмуха bird cherry
чере́нок FILL handle; graft; cutting
че́реп skull
черепа́ха tortoise, turtle
черепи́ца tile
чересчу́р *adv.* too (much)
чере́шня cherry; cherry tree
черке́с, черке́шенка Circassian
черни́ка blueberries
черни́ла *pl.* ink

чёрно-бе́лый black and white
чернови́к draft; rough copy
чернобо́й rough; draft
чернозём rich black topsoil
черносли́в *coll.* prunes
чернота́ blackness
чёрный black; ~ ход back entrance
черстве́ть *impf.* become stale
чёрствый stale
чёрт devil
черта́ trait; feature; line
чертёж blueprint; plan
чертёжник, —ница draftsman
чертёнок FILL little devil
черти́ть *impf.,* на- *pf.* draw
чёртовский devilish
чертополо́х thistle
чёрточка line; hyphen
черче́ние drawing
чеса́ть *impf.,* по- *pf.* scratch; comb; —ся scratch oneself; itch
чесно́к garlic
че́ствовать *impf.* celebrate
че́стность honesty
че́стный honest; fair
честолю́бие ambition
честь *f.* honor
чета́ pair; couple
четве́рг Thursday
четвере́ньки *pl.*: на четвере́ньках on all fours
четвёрка *f.* numeral 4; No. 4
че́тверо *coll.* four
четверости́шие quatrain
четвёртый fourth
че́тверть *f.* quarter; (one) fourth
чётки *pl.* rosary (*string of beads*)
чёткий clear; legible; accurate
чётный (*of a number*) even
четы́ре four; —ста four hundred
четы́рех- in compounds four-
четырёхнеде́льный *attrib.* four-week
четырёхсторо́нний four-sided
четырёхуго́льный quadrangular
четырёхэта́жный four-story
четы́рнадцатый fourteenth
четы́рнадцать fourteen
чех, че́шка Czech
чехо́л FILL (slip)cover; case
чечеви́ца lentil
чече́нец, —нка Chechen
че́шский Czech
чешуя́ (*zool.*) scales
чин grade; rank
чини́ть[1] *impf.,* по- *pf.* repair
чини́ть[2] *impf.,* о- *pf.* sharpen
чино́вник official; bureaucrat

чино́вничий official's; official
чи́сленность number, quantity
чи́сленный numerical
числи́тельное *n.*, **и́мя числи́тельное** *neut.* numeral
число́ 1. number **2.** date
числово́й numerical
чисти́лище purgatory
чи́стить *impf.* clean; brush; peel
чи́стка cleaning; purge
чистово́й final, clean
чистокро́вный thoroughbred
чистопло́тный neat; clean
чистопоро́дный thoroughbred
чистосерде́чный frank, sincere
чистота́ cleanliness; purity
чи́стый clean; pure; clear
чита́льный зал reading room
чита́тель, —ница reader
чита́ть *impf.*, **про-** *pf.* read
чиха́ть *impf.*, **чихну́ть** *pf.* sneeze
чи́ще *adv. compar.* **чи́стый**
член member; limb
член-корреспонде́нт associate (*or*) corresponding member
членовреди́тельство (deliberate) mutilation
членоразде́льный articulate
чле́нский *attrib.* membership
чле́нство membership
чмо́кать *impf.*, **чмо́кнуть** *pf.* smack one's lips
чо́порный prim; stiff
чрезвыча́йный extraordinary
чрезме́рный excessive
чте́ние reading; **~ ле́кций** lecturing
что *pron.* what; *conj.* that
что́бы *conj.* in order to, so that

что́-либо, что́-нибудь *pron.* something; anything
что́-то *indef. pron.* something
чува́ш, —ка Chuvash
Чува́шия Chuvashia
чу́вственный sensual
чувстви́тельный sensitive; sentimental
чу́вство sense; feeling
чу́вствовать *impf.*, **по-** *pf.* feel
чугу́н cast iron
чуда́к, чуда́чка eccentric
чуда́чество eccentricity
чудеса́ *pl. of* **чу́до**
чуде́сный wonderful, miraculous
чудно́ *adv. Colloq.* oddly
чу́дно *adv.* wonderfully; marvelously; *interj.* wonderful!
чудно́й odd; strange
чу́до wonder; miracle
чудо́вище monster
чудо́вищный monstrous
чудотво́рец FILL miracle worker
чудотво́рный wonder-working
чужда́ться alien
чужезе́мный *Obs.* foreign
чужестра́нный *Obs.* foreign
чужо́й strange; someone else's
чуло́к FILL stocking; hose
чума́ plague
чу́ткий sensitive; delicate, considerate
чуть *adv.* **1.** slightly **2.** hardly; **~ не** almost; **~-чуть** a tiny bit
чутьё scent; intuition
чу́чело scarecrow; stuffed animal
чушь *f.* nonsense; rubbish
чу́ять *impf.*, **по-** *pf.* feel
чьё, чьи, чья *pron.*, *see* **чей**

Ш

шабло́н template; pattern; mold
шабло́нный *Fig.* stereotyped; trite
шаг step; pace
шага́ть *impf.*, **шагну́ть** *pf.* step; pace; stride
ша́йба 1. (*sports*) puck **2.** (*tool*) washer
шака́л jackal
шала́ш hut
ша́лость trick; prank
шалу́н, —ья mischievous child
шалфе́й (*plant*) sage
шаль *f.* shawl
шально́й 1. crazy; mad **2.** stray
шампа́нское *n.* champagne
шампу́нь *m.* shampoo
шанс chance

шанта́ж blackmail
шантажи́ровать *impf.* blackmail
ша́пка cap
шар ball; sphere; **возду́шный ~** balloon
шарж cartoon; caricature
ша́рик marble; small ball; globule
ша́ркать *impf.* shuffle one's feet
шарма́нка barrel organ
шарма́нщик organ grinder
шарни́р hinge; joint
шарова́ры *pl.* wide trousers
шарф scarf
шасси́ *neut. indecl.* chassis
шата́ть *impf.* rock; shake; **—ся** be(come) loose; stagger; reel
ша́ткий unsteady; shaky

шáфер best man (at wedding)
шафрáн saffron
шах (chess) check; ~ и мат check-mate; —матист, —матистка chess player
шáхматный attrib. chess
шáхматы pl. chess
шáхта mine; pit
шахтёр miner
шáшки pl. (game) checkers
шашлык shashlik; kebab
швед, —ка Swede; —ский Swed-ish
швéйный attrib. sewing
швейцáр porter; doorman
швейцáрец FILL. -áрка Swiss
Швейцáрия Switzerland
Швéция Sweden
швея́ seamstress
швыря́ть impf., швырну́ть pf. toss; fling; hurl
шевели́ть(ся) impf., по- pf. move, stir
шевелю́ра (head of) hair
шедéвр masterpiece
шéйный attrib. neck
шéлест rustle, rustling
шёлк silk; —овый silk(en)
шелкови́ца mulberry
шелохну́ть pf. move slightly
шелухá peel; husk; hull
шелуши́ть impf. shell, husk
шéльма m. rascal; scoundrel
шёпот whisper; —ом in a whisper
шептáть impf., шепну́ть pf. whis-per
шерохова́тый rough; rugged
шерсть f. (zool.) hair; wool
шерстяно́й woollen
шершáвый rough
шéршень FILL m. hornet
шест pole
шéствовать impf. parade; march
шестёрка the numeral six; No. 6
шестидеся́тый sixtieth
шестисóтый six-hundredth
шестиуго́льный hexagonal
шестна́дцатый sixteenth
шестна́дцать sixteen
шесто́й sixth
шесть six; —деся́т sixty; —сóт six hundred
шеф chief; chef; boss
шеф-пóвар (cul.) chef
шéфствовать impf. sponsor
шéя neck
шúворот m.: за ~ by the scruff of the neck
шизофрéник, -ни́чка schizo-phrenic

шизофрéния schizophrenia
шика́рный chic, smart; splendid
шúло awl
шúна 1. tire 2. (med.) splint
шинéль f. overcoat
шип thorn
шипéть impf. hiss; sizzle
шипóвник wild rose, rosehip
шипу́чий sparkling; fizzy
шúре compar. широ́кий
ширинá width; breadth
шири́нка fly (on trousers)
шúрить impf. widen; expand
шúрма screen; cover
широ́кий wide
широтá width; breadth; (geog.) latitude
ширь f. expanse
шить impf., с- pf. sew
шитьё sewing; embroidery
шúфер slate
шифр cipher; code
шифро́ванный coded
шифровáть impf., за- pf. encipher
шúшка bump, lump (bot.) cone
шкалá scale
шкату́лка box, case; casket
шкаф cupboard; wardrobe
шквал squall
шко́ла school; schoolhouse
шко́льник schoolboy
шко́льница schoolgirl
шко́льный attrib. school
шку́ра skin; hide
шлагбáум barrier; gate
шлак slag
шланг hose
шлейф train of a dress
шлем helmet
шлёпанцы pl. slippers
шлёпать impf., шлёпнуть pf. smack; shuffle; tramp
шлифовáть impf., от- pf. grind; polish
шлюз lock; sluice
шля́па hat
шмель m. bumblebee
шни́цель m. schnitzel
шнур string; cord
шнуровáть impf., за-, про- pf. string; lace (up); tie
шнурóк FILL lace; shoelace
шов seam; (med.) suture
шовини́стический chauvinist
шок (med.) shock
шоки́ровать impf. shock
шокола́д chocolate
шóрох rustle
шóрты pl. shorts

шоссе́ *neut. indecl.* highway

шотла́ндец FILL, **-ндка** Scot

Шотла́ндия Scotland

шотла́ндский Scotch, Scottish

шофёр chauffeur, driver

шпа́га sword, épée

шпага́т 1. string; cord **2.** a split

шпа́ла railroad tie

шпале́ра trellis; rows; columns

шпиго́вать *impf.*, **на-** *pf.* lard

шпиль *m.* spire; capstan

шпи́лька hairpin; tack; stiletto heel

шпина́т spinach

шпингале́т catch; latch; bolt

шпио́н, —ка spy; **—а́ж** espionage

шпио́нить *impf.* spy

шпо́ра spur

шприц syringe

шпро́ты *pl.* sprats

шрам scar

шрапне́ль *f.* shrapnel

шрифт print; type; font

штаб staff; headquarters

шта́бель *m.* pile; stack

штаке́тник picket fence

штамп stamp; *Fig.* cliché

штампо́ванный pressed; trite

штампова́ть *impf.*, **от-** *pf.* stamp; punch; *Fig.* grind out

шта́нга (*sports*) bar; barbell

штанги́ст weightlifter

штаны́ *pl.* pants; trousers

штат[1] (*administrative unit*) state

штат[2] staff; personnel

шта́тный staff; permanent

шта́тский civil; civilian

штемпель *m.* rubber stamp

штепсель *m.* (*elec.*) plug; socket

штибле́ты *pl.* boots; shoes

штопать *impf.*, **за-** *pf.* darn

што́пор corkscrew

што́ра windowshade; blind

шторм storm; **—ово́й** storm

штраф fine; penalty

штрафова́ть *impf.*, **о-** *pf.* fine

штрейкбре́хер strikebreaker

штрих stroke; trait; feature

штрихова́ть *impf.*, **за-** *pf.* shade; hatch

шту́ка piece; thing; item

штукату́рка plaster(ing)

штурва́л steering wheel; helm

штурм storm; assault

штурма́н navigator

штурмово́й *attrib.* assault

шту́цер carbine

шту́чный by the piece

штык bayonet

штырь *m.* dowel; pin

шу́ба fur coat

шу́лер cardsharp; cheat

шум noise; uproar

шуме́ть *impf.* make a noise; roar

шу́мный noisy; loud; tumultuous

шу́рин brother-in-law (*wife's brother*)

шуру́п screw

шурша́ть *impf.* rustle

шу́стрый sharp; bright; smart

шут, шута́ха jester; fool

шу́тка joke; jest

шутли́вый playful; joking

шутни́к, -ни́ца joker; jokester

шутя́ *adv.* in jest; for fun

Щ

ща́вель *m.* sorrel

щади́ть *impf.*, **по-** *pf.* spare

ще́бень FILL *m.* road metal; crushed stone

щебета́ть *impf.* chirp

щёголь *m.* fop; dandy

щегольско́й handsome; dashing

щеголя́ть *impf.*, **щегольну́ть** *pf.* dress fancily; (+ *I*) show off; flaunt

ще́дрый generous

щека́ cheek

щеко́лда door latch

щекота́ть *impf.*, **по-** *pf.* tickle

щекотли́вый ticklish; delicate

щёлкать *impf.*, **щёлкнуть** *pf.* click; smack; crack

щёлок lye

щёлочь *f.* alkali

щелчо́к FILL flick; slight; snub

щель *f.* crack, chink

щеми́ть *impf.* constrict; ache; *Fig.* weigh on

щено́к FILL pup; puppy

щепети́льный fussy; scrupulous

ще́пка (wooden) chip

щепо́тка pinch

щерби́на gap; hole; chip

щети́на bristle

щётка brush

щи *pl.* cabbage soup

щи́колотка ankle

щипа́ть *impf.*, **щипну́ть** *pf.* pinch

щипцы́ *pl.* tongs; pincers

щит shield; board; panel

щитови́дный thyroid

щу́ка (*fish*) pike

щуп probe

щу́пальце tentacle; feeler

щу́пать *impf.*, по- *pf.* feel; touch

щу́рить *impf.*, co- *pf.*: ~ глаза́ squint

Э

эвакуа́ция evacuation

эвакуи́ровать *impf. & pf.* evacuate

ЭВМ (*abbr. of* электро́нная вычисли́тельная маши́на) computer

эволю́ция evolution

эгалита́рный egalitarian

эго́ист, —ка egoist

эгоисти́ческий, эгоисти́чный egoistic; selfish

эйфори́я euphoria

эква́тор equator

эквивале́нт equivalent

эквилибри́ст, —ка tightrope walker

экзальта́ция exaltation

экза́мен examination

экзаменова́ть *impf.*, про- *pf.* examine; —ся take an examination

экземпля́р copy; specimen

экзо́тика exotic things

экипа́ж carriage; crew

экипиро́вка equipping; equipment

экле́р éclair

эко́лог ecologist

экологи́ческий ecological

эколо́гия ecology

эконо́мика economics

экономи́ст economist

эконо́мить *impf.*, c- *pf.* economize

экономи́ческий economic

эконо́мия economy

экра́н screen

экраниза́ция filming

экскава́тор excavator

э́кскурс digression

экскурса́нт, —ка tourist

экску́рсия excursion

экскурсово́д tour guide

экспанси́вный expansive

экспатри́ровать *impf. & pf.* expatriate

экспеди́ция expedition

экспериме́нт experiment; —а́льный experimental

экспе́рт expert; —ный expert

эксперти́за (expert) examination

эксплуата́ция exploitation

экспози́ция layout; display; exposition

экспона́т exhibit

э́кспорт export(s); —ный export

экспорти́ровать *impf. & pf.* export

экспре́сс express

экспро́мт impromptu; —ом *adv.* impromptu

экспроприи́ровать *impf. & pf.* expropriate

экста́з ecstasy

экстрава́гантный eccentric; bizarre

экстра́кт extract

экстраордина́рный extraordinary

экстреми́стский extremist

э́кстренный urgent; emergency; special

эксцентри́чный eccentric

эласти́чный elastic; supple

элева́тор grain elevator; hoist

элега́нтный elegant

электризова́ть *impf.*, на- *pf.* electrify

эле́ктрик electrician

электри́ческий electric(al)

электри́чество electricity

электри́чка suburban electric train

электро- *pref.* electrical

электродви́гатель electric motor

электромонтёр electrician

электро́ника electronics

электро́нная по́чта e-mail

электро́нная табли́ца spreadsheet

электро́нный electronic

электропита́ние power supply

электроста́нция power station

электроте́хник electrical engineer

электроте́хника electrical engineering

электроэне́ргия electrical energy

элеме́нт element; —а́рный elementary

эмалиро́ванный enameled

эма́ль *f.* enamel

эмансипа́ция emancipation

эмба́рго *neut. indecl.* embargo

эмбле́ма emblem

эмбрио́н embryo

эмигра́нт, —ка emigrant; émigré

эмигра́ция emigration

эмигри́ровать *impf. & pf.* emigrate

эмо́ция emotion

эму́льсия emulsion
энерге́тика power engineering
энерги́чный energetic
эне́ргия energy
энтузиа́зм enthusiasm
энцефали́т encephalitis
энциклопе́дия encyclopedia
эпигра́мма epigram
эпи́граф epigraph
эпиде́мия epidemic
эпизо́д episode
эпиле́псия epilepsy
эпистоля́рный epistolary
эпопе́я epic work
эпо́ха epoch
э́ра era; до на́шей э́ры B.C.; на́шей э́ры A.D.
эро́тика 1. erotic literature 2. sensuality
эруди́т erudite person
эруди́ция erudition
эскала́тор escalator
эски́з sketch
эскимо́ neut. indecl. ice cream
эскимо́с, —ка Eskimo; —ский Eskimo
эско́рт (mil.) escort

эскорти́ровать impf. escort
эстафе́та relay race; relays
эсте́тика esthetics
эстети́ческий esthetic
эсто́нец FILL, -нка Estonian
Эсто́ния Estonia
эстра́да platform; variety
эта́ж floor, story
этаже́рка bookcase
этало́н standard
эта́п stage; phase
э́тика ethics
этике́т etiquette
этике́тка label
этимоло́гия etymology
эти́ческий, эти́чный ethical
этни́ческий ethnic
этногра́фия ethnography
э́то pron. this, that; it; see э́тот
э́тот pron., f. э́та, neut. э́то, pl. э́ти this; these
этю́д study; sketch
эфи́р ether; air
эффе́кт effect; —и́вный effective; —ный effective, spectacular
э́хо echo

Ю Я

юбиле́й jubilee; anniversary
юбиле́йный attrib. anniversary
ю́бка skirt
ювели́р jeweler; —ный jewelry
юг south
югосла́в, —ка Yugoslav
Югосла́вия Yugoslavia
югосла́вский Yugoslav
южа́нин, южа́нка southerner
ю́жный south, southern
ю́мор humor
юмористи́ческий humorous
ю́ность youth
ю́ноша m. youth; young man
ю́ношество youth; young people
ю́ный young; youthful
юриди́ческий juridical, legal
юрисди́кция jurisdiction
юрисконсу́льт legal adviser
юриспруде́нция jurisprudence
юри́ст lawyer
ю́ркий brisk; nimble
юсти́ция justice
юти́ться impf. huddle (together)
я pron. I
я́беда m. & f. tattler
я́блоко apple; глазно́е ~ eyeball
я́блоня appletree
я́блочный attrib. apple

яви́ться pf. of явля́ться.
я́вка appearance; secret meeting
явле́ние appearance; phenomenon; occurrence; (theat.) scene
явля́ться impf., яви́ться pf. appear; (+ I) be
я́вный evident; obvious
явь f. reality
ягнёнок FILL lamb
я́года berry
яд poison
я́дерный nuclear
ядови́тый poisonous, venomous
ядохимика́т pesticide
ядро́ nucleus; толка́ние ядра́ (sports) shot put
я́зва ulcer
язви́тельный biting; caustic
язы́к[1] tongue
язы́к[2] language
языкове́д linguist; —ение linguistics
языкозна́ние linguistics
язы́ческий pagan
язы́чник, -ница pagan, heathen
яи́чко egg; testicle
яи́чник ovary
яи́чница scrambled eggs; omelet
яйцекле́тка (biol.) ovule

яйцо́ egg
я́кобы *conj.* as if; as though
я́корь *m.* anchor
Яку́тия Yakutia
яку́т, —ка Yakut
я́ма pit, hole
я́мка 1. *dim. of* **я́ма 2.** dimple
ямщи́к coach driver
янва́рь *m.*, **янва́рский** January
янта́рь *m.* amber
япо́нец FILL, **япо́нка** Japanese
Япо́ния Japan
япо́нский Japanese
яра́нга reindeer tent
я́ркий bright; clear; vivid
я́рко- *pref.* (*of colors*) bright

ярлы́к label; tag
я́рмарка fair
яровой (*of crops*) *attrib.* spring
я́ростный fierce, furious
я́рость fury, rage
я́сень *m.* (*tree*) ash
я́сли *pl.* **1.** manger **2.** day nursery
я́сность clarity; clearness
я́сный clear; bright; distinct
я́рус (*theat.*) tier, circle
я́хта yacht
яче́йка cell
ячме́нь *m.* barley
я́щерица lizard
я́щик box; drawer

English-Russian
Dictionary

A

a /ə, eɪ/ *indefinite article usu. not translated: once a year* раз в году

aback /ə'bæk/ *adv.:* take ~ *v.* поражать *impf.*

abacus /'æbəkəs/ *n.* счёты *pl.*

abandon /ə'bændən/ *v.* покидать *impf.*, покинуть *pf.*; оставлять *impf.*, оставить *pf.*

abandoned /ə'bændənd/ *adj.* покинутый, оставленный

abase /ə'beɪs/ *v.* унижать *impf.*; —ment *n.* унижение

abate /ə'beɪt/ *v.* уменьшать(ся) *impf.*, уменьшить(ся) *pf.*; затихать *impf.*, затихнуть *pf.*

abbey /'æbi/ *n.* аббатство

abbreviate /ə'briːvɪ,eɪt/ *v.* сокращать *impf.*, сократить *pf.*

abbreviation /ə,briːvɪ'eɪʃən/ *n.* аббревиатура, сокращение

abdicate /'æbdɪ,keɪt/ *v.* отрекаться *impf.*

abdication /,æbdɪ'keɪʃən/ *n.* отречение (от престола)

abdomen /'æbdəmən/ *n.* брюшная полость *f.*; живот

abdominal /æb'dɒmənl/ *adj.* брюшной

abduct /æb'dʌkt/ *v.* похитить *pf.*; —ion *n.* похищение

aberration /,æbə'reɪʃən/ *n.* отклонение

abet /ə'bet/ *v.* подстрекать *impf.*

abhor /æb'hɔːr/ *v.* ненавидеть *impf.*

abide /ə'baɪd/ *v.* (*tolerate*) терпеть *impf.*; ~ by соблюдать *impf.*

ability /ə'bɪlɪti/ *n.* способность

abject /'æbdʒekt/ *adj.* жалкий

ablaze /ə'bleɪz/ *adv.* в пламени

able /'eɪbl/ *adj.* способный; умелый; be ~ to *v.* мочь *impf.*, с- *pf.*; (*know how to*) уметь *impf.*, с- *pf.*

abnormal /æb'nɔːməl/ *adj.* ненормальный

abnormality /,æbnɔːr'mælɪti/ *n.* ненормальность, неправильность

aboard /ə'bɔːrd/ *adv.* на борт(у), в вагон(е)

abode /ə'boʊd/ *n.* жилище

abolish /ə'bɒlɪʃ/ *v.* отменять *impf.*, отменить *pf.*

abolition /,æbə'lɪʃən/ *n.* отмена

abominable /ə'bɒmənəbəl/ *adj.* отвратительный

abomination /ə,bɒmə'neɪʃən/ *n.* отвращение; мерзость

aboriginal /,æbə'rɪdʒənl/ *adj.* исконный, туземный

aborigine /,æbə'rɪdʒəni/ *n.* туземец; абориген

abort /ə'bɔːrt/ *v.* (*med.*) выкидывать плод *impf.*, выкинуть *pf.*; (*terminate*) прекращать *impf.*; —ion *n.* аборт, выкидыш; have an —ion сделать аборт *pf.*

abortive /ə'bɔːrtɪv/ *adj.* неудавшийся, бесплодный

abound /ə'baʊnd/ *v.:* ~ in изобиловать *impf.* (+ *I*)

about /ə'baʊt/ *adv., prep.* кругом; около (+ *G*); по (+ *D*); о, об (+ *P*); be ~ to *v.* собираться *impf.*

above /ə'bʌv/ 1. *adv.* выше; наверху; from ~ сверху 2. *prep.* над (+ *I*); выше, свыше (+ *G*); ~ all больше всего

abrasion /ə'breɪʒən/ *n.* истирание; (*med.*) ссадина

abrasive /ə'breɪsɪv/ 1. *adj.* абразивный 2. *n.* абразивный материал

abreast /ə'brest/ *adv.* в ряд; keep ~ of идти в ногу (с + *I*)

abridge /ə'brɪdʒ/ *v.* сокращать *impf.*, -тить *pf.*; —ment *n.* сокращение

abroad /ə'brɔːd/ *adv.* за границей; за границу; from ~ из-за границы

abrupt /ə'brʌpt/ *adj.* (*steep*) обрывистый; (*sudden*) внезапный; (*curt*) резкий

abscess /'æbses/ *n.* абсцесс

abscond /æb'skɒnd/ *v.* скрываться *impf.*, скрыться *pf.*

absence /'æbsəns/ *n.* отсутствие

absent /'æbsənt/ *adj.* отсутствующий; be ~ *v.* отсутствовать *impf.*

absenteeism /,æbsən'tiːɪzəm/ *n.* абсентеизм; (*from work*) прогул

absent-minded /,æbsənt'maɪndɪd/ *adj.* рассеянный; —ness *n.* рассеянность

absolute /'æbsə,luːt/ *adj.* полный; безусловный; абсолютный

absolution /,æbsə'luːʃən/ *n.* прощение; отпущение грехов

absolutism /'æbsəlu,tızəm/ n. абсолютизм

absolve /æb'zɒlv/ v. прощать impf., простить pf.

absorb /æb'sɔrb/ v. впитывать impf.; впитать pf.

absorbent /æb'sɔrbənt/ adj. поглощающий; всасывающий

absorbing /æb'sɔrbıŋ/ adj. захватывающий

absorption /æb'sɔrpʃən/ n. поглощение; (mind) погружённость

abstain /æb'stein/ v. воздерживаться impf., воздержаться pf.

abstemious /æb'stimiəs/ adj. воздержанный

abstention /æb'stenʃən/ n. воздержание (от + G)

abstinence /'æbstənəns/ n. воздержанность; воздержание

abstract / adj., v. æb'strækt; n. 'æbstrækt/ 1. adj. отвлечённый 2. n. резюме; конспект 3. v. отвлекать impf., отвлечь pf.

absurd /æb'sɜrd/ adj. абсурдный

absurdity /æb'sɜrdıti/ n. абсурд

abundance /ə'bʌndəns/ n. изобилие

abundant /ə'bʌndənt/ adj. обильный, изобильный

abuse / n. ə'byus; v. ə'byuz/ 1. n. (misuse) злоупотребление; (language) ругань f. 2. v. злоупотреблять impf., -бить pf.; оскорблять impf., -бить pf.

abusive /ə'byusıv/ adj. оскорбительный, ругательный

abut /ə'bʌt/ v. примыкать impf.

abysmal /ə'bızməl/ adj. бездонный; (horrible) ужасный

abyss /ə'bıs/ n. бездна, пропасть f.

academic /,ækə'demık/ adj. академический

academy /ə'kædəmi/ n. академия

accede /æk'sid/ v. (agree) соглашаться (на + A) impf.

accelerate /æk'selə,reit/ v. ускорять(ся) impf., ускорить(ся) pf.

acceleration /æk,selə'reiʃən/ n. ускорение

accelerator /æk'selə,reitər/ n. ускоритель, акселератор

accent /'æksent/ n. (stress) ударение, (speech) акцент

accentuate /æk'sentʃu,eit/ v. подчёркивать impf., подчеркнуть pf.

accept /æk'sept/ v. принимать impf., принять pf.; допускать impf., допустить pf.

acceptable /æk'septəbəl/ adj. приемлемый, допустимый

acceptance /æk'septəns/ n. принятие; признание, приём

access /'ækses/ n. доступ

accessible /æk'sesəbəl/ adj. доступный

accessory /æk'sesəri/ 1. adj. добавочный 2. n. (law) соучастник, -ница

accident /'æksıdənt/ n. несчастный случай; авария; (chance) случайность

accidental /,æksı'dentl/ adj. случайный; —ly adv. случайно

accident-prone adj. невезучий

acclaim /ə'kleim/ v. провозглашать impf., провозгласить pf.

acclimate /'æklə,meit/ v. акклиматизировать(ся) impf. & pf.

accommodate /ə'kɒmə,deit/ v. (adapt) приспособлять impf., приспособить pf.; (lodge) помещать impf., поместить pf.

accommodating /ə'kɒmə,deitıŋ/ adj. услужливый

accommodations /ə,kɒmə'deiʃənz/ n.pl. помещение, жильё

accompaniment /ə'kʌmpənimənt/ n. (mus.) аккомпанемент

accompanist /ə'kʌmpənist/ n. аккомпаниатор

accompany /ə'kʌmpəni/ v. сопровождать impf., сопроводить pf.; (mus.) аккомпанировать impf. & pf.

accomplice /ə'kɒmplıs/ n. соучастник, сообщник, -ница

accomplish /ə'kɒmplıʃ/ v. совершать impf., совершить pf.

accomplished /ə'kɒmplıʃt/ adj. законченный, совершённый

accomplishment /ə'kɒmplıʃmənt/ n. выполнение, достижение

accord /ə'kord/ 1. n. согласие; of one's own ~ добровольно 2. v. (grant) предоставлять impf.; —ance n. соответствие

according to /ə'kordıŋ/ prep. соответствии с (+ I)

accordion /ə'kordiən/ n. аккордеон

accost /ə'kɒst/ v. (pester) приставать (к + D) impf.

account /ə'kaunt/ 1. n. счёт, от-

чёт; **on ~ of** *prep.* из-за (+ G);
on no ~ *adv.* ни в ко́ем слу́чае
2. *v.* отчи́тываться (в + P)
impf.

accountability /ə,kauntə'bılıti/
n. отве́тственность

accountable /ə'kauntəbəl/ *adj.*
отве́тственный; подотчётный

accountant /ə'kauntət/ *n.*
бухга́лтер

accounting /ə'kauntıŋ/ *n.* бух-
галте́рия

accrue /ə'kru/ *v.* нараста́ть *impf.*

accumulate /ə'kyumyə,leıt/ *v.*
нака́пливать(ся) *impf.*, нако-
пи́ть(ся) *pf.*

accumulation /ə,kyumyə'leıʃən/
n. накопле́ние; скопле́ние

accuracy /'ækyərəsi/ *n.* то́чность

accurate /'ækyərıt/ *adj.* то́чный

accusation /,ækyu'zeıʃən/ *n.*
обвине́ние

accusative /ə'kyuzətıv/ *n.*
вини́тельный паде́ж

accuse /ə'kyuz/ *v.* обвиня́ть
impf., обвини́ть *pf.*

accused /ə'kyuzd/ *adj.*, *n.*
обвиня́емый

accustomed /ə'kʌstəmd/ *adj.*
привы́кший, привы́чный; **become ~** *v.* привыка́ть *impf.*,
привы́кнуть *pf.*

ace /eıs/ *n.* (*cards*) туз; (*pilot*) ас

ache /eık/ **1.** *n.* боль *f.* **2.** *v.*
боле́ть *impf.*

achieve /ə'tʃiv/ *v.* достига́ть
impf., дости́гнуть *pf.*; —**ment** *n.*
достиже́ние

acid /'æsıd/ **1.** *n.* кислота́ **2.** *adj.*
ки́слый, кисло́тный

acidity /ə'sıdıti/ *n.* кисло́тность

acknowledge /æk'nɒlıdʒ/ *v.*
признава́ть *impf.*, призна́ть *pf.*;
~ receipt *v.* подтвержда́ть
получе́ние *impf.*

acknowledgment
/æk'nɒlıdʒmənt/ *n.* призна́ние,
подтвержде́ние

acne /'ækni/ *n.* угри́ *pl.*

acorn /'eıkɔrn/ *n.* жёлудь *m.*

acoustics /ə'kustıks/ *n.* аку́стика

acquaint /ə'kweint/ *v.* знако́-
мить *impf.*, по- *pf.*; **~ oneself
with** ознако́мляться с (+ I)
impf., ознако́миться *pf.*

acquaintance /ə'kweintəns/ *n.*
знако́мство; (*person*) знако́мый

acquainted /ə'kweintıd/ *adj.*
знако́мый (с + I)

acquiesce /,ækwi'ɛs/ *v.* согла-
ша́ться *impf.*, согласи́ться *pf.*

acquiescence /,ækwi'ɛsəns/ *n.*
(молчали́вое) согла́сие

acquire /ə'kwaıər/ *v.* приобре-
та́ть *impf.*, приобрести́ *pf.*

acquisition /,ækwə'zıʃən/ *n.*
приобрете́ние

acquisitive /ə'kwızıtıv/ *adj.*
со́бственнический; стяжа́-
тельский

acquit /ə'kwıt/ *v.* опра́вдывать
impf., оправда́ть *pf.*

acquittal /ə'kwıtl/ *n.* оправда́ние

acre /'eıkər/ *n.* акр

acrid /'ækrıd/ *adj.* е́дкий; ре́зкий

acrimonious /,ækrə'mouniəs/
adj. язви́тельный; жёлчный

acrobat /'ækrə,bæt/ *n.* акроба́т

acrobatic /,ækrə'bætık/ *adj.*
акробати́ческий

across /ə'krɒs/ *adv.*, *prep.* че́рез
(+ A), поперёк (+ G); по ту
сто́рону (+ G)

acrylic /ə'krılık/ *adj.* акри́ловый

act /ækt/ **1.** *n.* посту́пок; (*theat.*)
де́йствие; акт; (*law*) зако́н **2.** *v.*
поступа́ть *impf.*, -пи́ть *pf.*; (*behave*) вести́ себя́ *impf.*; де́йство-
вать *impf.*, по- *pf.*

acting /'æktıŋ/ **1.** *n.* игра́ **2.** *adj.*
де́йствующий

action /'ækʃən/ *n.* де́йствие,
посту́пок; (*law*) иск; проце́сс;
(*mil.*) бой

activate /'æktə,veıt/ *v.* приво-
ди́ть в де́йствие *impf.*

active /'æktıv/ *adj.* де́ятельный

activity /æk'tıvıti/ *n.* де́ятель-
ность; *pl.* мероприя́тия *pl.*

actor /'æktər/ *n.* актёр

actress /'æktrıs/ *n.* актри́са

actual /'æktʃuəl/ *adj.* действи́-
тельный, настоя́щий

actuality /,æktʃu'ælıti/ *n.* действи́-
тельность

actually /'æktʃuəli/ *adv.*
факти́чески; на са́мом де́ле

acumen /ə'kyumən/ *n.* прони-
ца́тельность

acupuncture /'ækyu,pʌŋktʃər/ *n.*
акупункту́ра

acute /ə'kyut/ *adj.* о́стрый

A.D. *abbr.* на́шей э́ры; н.э.

adamant /'ædəmənt/ *adj.*
непрекло́нный

Adam's apple /'ædəmz/ *n.*
кады́к

adapt /ə'dæpt/ *v.* приспоса́бли-
вать(ся) *impf.*, приспосо́бить

(-ся) pf.; (theat.) инсцени́ровать impf. & pf.

adaptable /ə'dæptəbəl/ adj. (легко́) приспособля́ющийся

adaptation /,ædəp'teɪʃən/ n. приспособле́ние, (theat.) инсцени́ровка

adapter /ə'dæptər/ n. ада́птер

add /æd/ v. добавля́ть impf., доба́вить pf.; прибавля́ть impf., приба́вить pf.

addendum /ə'dɛndəm/ n. приложе́ние; дополне́ние

addict /'ædɪkt/ n. наркома́н, —ка

addicted /ə'dɪktɪd/ adj. скло́нный (к + D); предаю́щийся (+ D)

addiction /ə'dɪkʃən/ n. пристра́стие; (drugs) наркома́ния

addition /ə'dɪʃən/ n. прибавле́ние, дополне́ние; (math.) сложе́ние; in ~ вдоба́вок; кро́ме того́

address /ə'dres/ 1. n. а́дрес; (speech) обраще́ние 2. v.t. адресова́ть impf. & pf.; (speak to) обраща́ться (к + D) impf., обрати́ться pf.

addressee /,ædre'si/ n. адреса́т

adept /ə'dept/ adj. све́дущий

adequate /'ædɪkwɪt/ adj. отвеча́ющий тре́бованиям; доста́точный

adhere /æd'hɪər/ v. прилипа́ть (к + D) impf., Fig. приде́рживаться (+ G) impf.

adherence /æd'hɪərəns/ n. приве́рженность

adherent /æd'hɪərənt/ n. приве́рженец, сторо́нник

adhesive /æd'hisɪv/ 1. adj. ли́пкий 2. n. клей

adhesive tape n. кле́йкая ле́нта

adjacent /ə'dʒeɪsənt/ adj. сосе́дний, сме́жный

adjective /'ædʒɪktɪv/ n. и́мя прилага́тельное neut.

adjoin /ə'dʒɔɪn/ v.t. прилега́ть (к + D) impf.

adjourn /ə'dʒɜːn/ v.t. откла́дывать impf., отложи́ть pf.; v.i. объяви́ть переры́в pf.

adjudicate /ə'dʒudɪˌkeɪt/ v. суди́ть, выноси́ть пригово́р impf.

adjust /ə'dʒʌst/ v. прила́живать impf., регули́ровать impf. отпf.; приспосо́биться pf.

adjustable /ə'dʒʌstəbəl/ adj. регули́руемый; (movable) передвижно́й

adjustment /ə'dʒʌstmənt/ n. регулиро́вка; попра́вка

ad-lib /'æd'lɪb/ (theat.) 1. n. экспро́мт 2. v. импровизи́ровать impf.

administer /əd'mɪnəstər/ v. (manage) управля́ть (+ I) impf.; (give) дава́ть impf.

administration /əd,mɪnə'streɪʃən/ n. администра́ция, управле́ние

administrative /æd'mɪnəˌstreɪtɪv/ adj. администрати́вный

administrator /æd'mɪnəˌstreɪtər/ n. администра́тор, управля́ющий

admirable /'ædmərəbəl/ adj. восхити́тельный

admiral /'ædmərəl/ n. адмира́л

admiration /,ædmə'reɪʃən/ n. восхище́ние, восто́рг

admire /æd'maɪər/ v. любова́ться impf., по- pf.; восхища́ться impf., восхити́ться pf.

admirer /æd'maɪərər/ n. покло́нник, покло́нница

admissible /æd'mɪsəbəl/ adj. допусти́мый, прие́млемый

admission /æd'mɪʃən/ n. до́ступ, вход; (confession) призна́ние

admission fee n. входна́я пла́та

admit /æd'mɪt/ v. впуска́ть impf., впусти́ть pf.; (confess) признава́ть impf., призна́ть pf.

admonition /,ædmə'nɪʃən/ n. упрёк

adolescence /,ædl'ɛsəns/ n. о́трочество

adolescent /,ædl'ɛsənt/ 1. adj. о́троческий 2. n. подро́сток

adopt /ə'dɒpt/ v. принима́ть impf., приня́ть pf.; усыновля́ть impf., -ви́ть pf.; удочеря́ть impf., -ри́ть pf.

adopted /ə'dɒptɪd/ adj. (child) приёмный

adoption /ə'dɒpʃən/ n. усыновле́ние, приня́тие

adorable /ə'dɔrəbəl/ adj. восхити́тельный; преле́стный

adoration /,ædə'reɪʃən/ n. обожа́ние, поклоне́ние

adore /ə'dɔr/ v. обожа́ть impf.

adorn /ə'dɔrn/ v. украша́ть impf.; укра́сить pf.

adornment /ə'dɔrnmənt/ n. украше́ние

adrenalin /ə'drenəlɪn/ n. адренали́н

adulation /ˌædʒə'leiʃən/ n. преклонéние; низкопоклóнство

adult /ə'dʌlt, 'ædʌlt/ adj. n. взрóслый; совершеннолéтний

adulterate /ə'dʌltəˌreit/ v. фальсифицировать impf. & pf.

adulterous /ə'dʌltərəs/ adj. прелюбодéйский

adultery /ə'dʌltəri/ n. супружеская изменá; адюльтéр

advance /æd'væns/ **1.** n. продвижéние; прогрéсс; (of pay) авáнс; (progress) прогрéсс; **in** ~ зарáнее **2.** v. продвигáться вперёд; (a theory, etc.) выдвигáть impf.

advanced /æd'vænst/ adj. передовóй; продвинутый

advancement /æd'vænsmənt/ n. продвижéние, выдвижéние

advantage /æd'væntidʒ/ n. преимущество; выгода; польза; **take** ~ **of** воспóльзоваться pf.

advantageous /ˌædvən'teidʒəs/ adj. выгодный, благоприятный

adventure /æd'ventʃər/ n. приключéние

adventurer /æd'ventʃərər/ n. авантюрист, —ка

adventurous /æd'ventʃərəs/ adj. смéлый; предприимчивый

adverb /'ædvɜrb/ n. нарéчие

adversary /'ædvərˌseri/ n. противник

adverse /æd'vɜrs/ adj. враждéбный; неблагоприятный

adversity /æd'vɜrsiti/ n. несчáстье

advertise /'ædvərˌtaiz/ v. объявлять impf.; рекламировать impf. & pf.

advertisement /ˌæd'vɜrtismənt/ n. объявлéние, реклáма

advice /æd'vais/ n. совéт

advisable /æd'vaizəbəl/ adj. рекомендуемый, желáтельный

advise /æd'vaiz/ v. совéтовать impf.; (notify) уведомлять impf.

adviser /æd'vaizər/ n. совéтник

advisory /æd'vaizəri/ adj. совещáтельный

advocate / n. 'ædvəkit; v. 'ædvəˌkeit/ **1.** n. сторóнник **2.** v. выступáть (за + A) impf.

aegis /'idʒis/ n. эгида

aerial /'eəriəl/ **1.** adj. воздушный **2.** n. антéнна

aerobics /eə'roubiks/ n. аэрóбика

aerodynamics

/ˌeəroudai'næmiks/ n. аэродинáмика

aerosol /'eərəˌsɔl/ n. аэрозóль m.

aesthetic /es'θetik/ adj. эстетический

aesthetics /es'θetiks/ n. эстéтика

afar /ə'fɑr/ adv.: **from** ~ издалекá

affable /'æfəbəl/ adj. любéзный

affair /ə'feər/ n. дéло; (love) ромáн

affect /ə'fekt/ v. дéйствовать (на + A) impf.; (emotionally) трóгать, волновáть impf.

affectation /ˌæfek'teiʃən/ n. аффектáция

affected /ə'fektid/ adj. жемáнный; притвóрный

affection /ə'fekʃən/ n. привязанность

affectionate /ə'fekʃənit/ adj. любящий, нéжный

affiliated /ə'filiˌeitid/ adj. филиáльный, свя́занный

affinity /ə'finiti/ n. родствó; схóдство

affirm /ə'fɜrm/ v. утверждáть impf.

affirmation /ˌæfər'meiʃən/ n. утверждéние, подтверждéние

affirmative /ə'fɜrmətiv/ adj. утвердительный

affix /ə'fiks/ v. прикреплять impf.

afflict /ə'flikt/ v. причинять страдáние impf.

affliction /ə'flikʃən/ n. болéзнь f.

affluence /'æfluəns/ n. богáтство

affluent /'æfluənt/ adj. богáтый

afford /ə'fɔrd/ v. позвóлить себé pf.

affront /ə'frʌnt/ **1.** n. оскорблéние **2.** v. оскорблять impf., -бить pf.

Afghanistan /æf'gænəˌstæn/ n. Афганистáн

afloat /ə'flout/ adv. на плаву́

aforementioned /ə'fɔrˌmenʃənd/ adj. вышеупомя́нутый

afraid /ə'freid/ adj. испуганный; **be** ~ боя́ться impf.

afresh /ə'freʃ/ adv. снóва

Africa /'æfrikə/ n. Африка

African /'æfrikən/ **1.** adj. африкáнский **2.** n. африкáнец, африкáнка

after /'æftər/ **1.** prep. пóсле

(+ *G*); (*time*) через (+ *A*); (*behind*) за (+ *I*) **2.** *conj.* после того как **3.** *adv.* потом

aftereffect /'æftərɪˌfɛkt/ *n.* последствие

afternoon /ˌæftər'nun/ *n.* время&yacy *neut.*; после полудня; — днём

afterthought /'æftərˌθɔt/ *n.* запоздалая мысль

afterwards /'æftərwərdz/ *adv.* потом

again /ə'gɛn/ *adv.* опять, снова

against /ə'gɛnst/ *prep.* против (+ *G*); о (+ *A*); на фоне (+ *G*)

age /eidʒ/ **1.** *n.* возраст; (*era*) век, эпоха; **old age** старость *f.* **2.** *v.i.* стареть *impf.*, по- *pf.*

aged /'eidʒɪd/ *adj.* старый

agency /'eidʒənsi/ *n.* агентство

agenda /ə'dʒɛndə/ *n.* повестка дня

agent /'eidʒənt/ *n.* агент

aggrandize /ə'grændaiz/ *v.* увеличивать *impf.*

aggravate /'ægrəˌveit/ *v.* ухудшать *impf.*, ухудшить *pf.*

aggregate /'ægrɪgɪt/ **1.** *adj.* совокупный **2.** *n.* совокупность

aggression /ə'grɛʃən/ *n.* агрессия, нападение

aggressive /ə'grɛsɪv/ *adj.* агрессивный

aggressiveness /ə'grɛsɪvnɪs/ *n.* агрессивность

aggressor /ə'grɛsər/ *n.* агрессор

aggrieve /ə'griv/ *v.* огорчать *impf.*

aghast /ə'gæst/ *adj.* в ужасе (от + *G*); ошеломлённый

agile /'ædʒəl/ *adj.* проворный

agility /ə'dʒɪlɪti/ *n.* подвижность

agitate /'ædʒɪˌteit/ *v.* волновать *impf.*; агитировать *impf.* & *pf.*

agitation /ˌædʒɪ'teiʃən/ *n.* волнение; агитация

agnostic /æg'nɒstɪk/ *n.* агностик

agnosticism /æg'nɒstəˌsizəm/ *n.* агностицизм

ago /ə'gou/ *adv.* (тому) назад; **long ago** давно

agonize /'ægəˌnaiz/ *v.* мучиться *impf.*

agonizing /'ægəˌnaizɪŋ/ *adj.* мучительный

agony /'ægəni/ *n.* мука; агония

agrarian /ə'grɛəriən/ *adj.* аграрный

agree /ə'gri/ *v.* соглашаться

impf., -ситься *pf.*; (*arrange*) договариваться *impf.*

agreeable /ə'griəbəl/ *adj.* приятный; согласный

agreement /ə'grimənt/ *n.* соглашение, согласие; договор

agricultural /ˌægrɪ'kʌltʃərəl/ *adj.* сельскохозяйственный

agriculture /'ægrɪˌkʌltʃər/ *n.* сельское хозяйство; земледелие

aground /ə'graund/ *adv.* на мели; **run, go** — садиться на мель *impf.*

ahead /ə'hɛd/ *adv.* (*dir.*) вперёд; (*loc.*) впереди

aid /eid/ **1.** *n.* помощь *f.* **2.** *v.* помогать *impf.*, помочь *pf.*

AIDS /eidz/ *n.* СПИД

ailing /'eilɪŋ/ *adj.* больной

ailment /'eilmənt/ *n.* недуг

aim /eim/ **1.** *n.* цель *f.* **2.** *v.* прицеливаться (в + *A*) *impf.*, прицелиться (в + *A*) *impf.*; стремиться (к + *D*) *impf.*

aimless /'eimlɪs/ *adj.* бесцельный

air /ɛər/ **1.** *n.* воздух; (*look*) вид **2.** *v.* проветривать *impf.*, проветрить *pf.*

airborne /'ɛərˌbɔrn/ *adj.* авиационный, воздушный

air conditioner *n.* кондиционер

air conditioning *n.* кондиционирование воздуха

aircraft /'ɛərˌkræft/ *n.* самолёт

aircraft carrier *n.* авианосец

airfield /'ɛərˌfild/ *n.* аэродром

Air Force *n.* военно-воздушные силы *pl.* (*abbr.* ВВС)

airless /'ɛərlɪs/ *adj.* душный

airline /'ɛərˌlain/ *n.* авиалиния, авиакомпания

airliner /'ɛərˌlainər/ *n.* пассажирский самолёт

airmail /'ɛərˌmeil/ *n.* авиапочта

airplane /'ɛərˌplein/ *n.* самолёт

airport /'ɛərˌpɔrt/ *n.* аэропорт

air raid *n.* воздушный налёт

airsickness /'ɛərˌsɪknɪs/ *n.* воздушная болезнь *f.*

airstrip /'ɛərˌstrɪp/ *n.* взлётно-посадочная полоса

airtight /'ɛərˌtait/ *adj.* герметический, герметичный

airy /'ɛəri/ *adj.* (*light*) воздушный; (*spacious*) просторный

aisle /ail/ *n.* проход

ajar /ə'dʒɑr/ *adj.* приоткрытый

akin /ə'kin/ **1.** *adj.* родственный, похожий **2.** *adv.* сродни (+ *D*) alabaster /ˈæləˌbæstər/ **1.** n. алебáстр **2.** adj. алебáстровый

alacrity /əˈlækrɪtɪ/ n. быстротá

alarm /əˈlɑrm/ **1.** n. тревóга **2.** v. тревóжить impf., вс- pf.

alarm clock n. будúльник

alarming /əˈlɑrmɪŋ/ adj. тревóжный, волнýющий

alarmist /əˈlɑrmɪst/ n. паникёр

alas /əˈlæs/ interj. увы́

albeit /ɔlˈbiɪt/ conj. хотя́ (и)

albino /ælˈbaɪnou/ n. альбинóс

album /ˈælbəm/ n. альбóм

albumen /ælˈbyumən/ n. белóк

alchemist /ˈælkəmɪst/ n. алхúмик

alcohol /ˈælkəˌhɔl/ n. алкогóль m.; спирт

alcoholic /ˌælkəˈhɔlɪk/ **1.** adj. алкогóльный, алкоголúческий **2.** n. алкогóлик, алкоголúчка

alcove /ˈælkouv/ n. алькóв, нúша

alder /ˈɔldər/ n. ольхá

ale /eil/ n. пúво, эль m.

alert /əˈlɜrt/ **1.** adj. насторожённый, бдúтельный **2.** n. тревóга

alertness /əˈlɜrtnɪs/ n. бдúтельность

alfalfa /ælˈfælfə/ n. люцéрна

algebra /ˈældʒəbrə/ n. áлгебра

alias /ˈeiliəs/ n. клúчка, прóзвище

alibi /ˈæləˌbai/ n. áлиби neut. indecl.

alien /ˈeilyən/ **1.** adj. чужóй; чýждый **2.** n. инострáнец, -áнка

alienate /ˈeilyəˌneit/ v. отчуждáть impf., -дúть pf.

alienation /ˌeilyəˈneiʃən/ n. отчуждéние

alight /əˈlait/ v. сходúть; выходúть; садúться; приземля́ться impf.

align /əˈlain/ v. выра́внивать(ся) impf.

alignment /əˈlainmənt/ n. (leveling) выра́внивание; (arrangement) расстанóвка

alike /əˈlaik/ **1.** adj. похóжий, подóбный **2.** adv. одинáково

alimentary /ˌæləˈmentəri/ adj. пищевóй; ~ canal n. пищеварúтельный тракт

alimony /ˈæləˌmouni/ n. алимéнты pl.

alive /əˈlaiv/ adj. живóй

alkali /ˈælkəˌlai/ n. щёлочь f.

alkaline /ˈælkəˌlain/ adj. щелочнóй

all /ɔl/ adj. весь, вся, всё; ~ the more тем бóлее что; not at ~ совсéм не (нет); нискóлько

allay /əˈlei/ v. успокáивать impf., успокóить pf.

allegation /ˌæləˈgeiʃən/ n. утверждéние

allege /əˈledʒ/ v. утверждáть impf., утвердúть pf.

allegedly /əˈledʒɪdli/ adv. я́кобы

allegiance /əˈlidʒəns/ n. вéрность, прéданность (+ D)

allegorical /ˌæləˈgɔrɪkəl/ adj. аллегорúческий

allegory /ˈæləˌgɔri/ n. аллегóрия

allergy /ˈælərdʒi/ n. аллергúя

alleviate /əˈliviˌeit/ v. облегчáть impf., -чúть pf.

alleviation /əˌliviˈeiʃən/ n. облегчéние

alley /ˈæli/ n. ýзкий переýлок

alliance /əˈlaiəns/ n. сою́з

allied /əˈlaid, ˈælaid/ adj. сою́зный (c + I)

alligator /ˈæliˌgeitər/ n. аллигáтор

alliteration /əˌlɪtəˈreiʃən/ n. аллитерáция

allocate /ˈæləˌkeit/ v. распределя́ть; предназначáть (на + A) impf.

allocation /ˌæləˈkeiʃən/ n. распределéние, назначéние

allot /əˈlɒt/ v. раздавáть, распределя́ть impf.

allotment /əˈlɒtmənt/ n. распределéние, дóля

allow /əˈlau/ v. позволя́ть impf., позвóлить pf.; разрешáть; допускáть impf.

allowance /əˈlauəns/ n. (deduction) скúдка; (money) пособие; make ~ for учúтывать; учéсть pf.

alloy /ˈæləi/ n. сплав

all right adv. хорошó; лáдно

allude /əˈlud/ v. намекáть impf.; намекнýть (на + A) pf.

allure /əˈlur/ v. замáнивать impf., заманúть pf.

alluring /əˈlurɪŋ/ adj. замáнчивый; соблазнúтельный

allusion /əˈluʒən/ n. намёк; ссы́лка

ally /v. əˈlai; n. ˈælai/ **1.** v. соединя́ться impf., -нúться pf. **2.** n. сою́зник

almanac /ˈɔlməˌnæk/ n. альмана́х

almighty /ɔl'maiti/ *adj.* всемогущий

almond /'amənd/ *n.* миндаль *m.*

almost /'ɔlmoust/ *adv.* почти; едва не, чуть не

alms /amz/ *n.* милостыня

aloft /ə'lɔft/ *adv.* наверх; наверху

alone /ə'loun/ **1.** *adj.* один; одинокий **2.** *adv.* только

along /ə'lɔŋ/ *prep.* вдоль (+ G); по (+ D); **all** ~ *adv.* всё время; ~ **with** *prep.* вместе с (+ I)

alongside /ə'lɔŋ'said/ *adv.* рядом

aloof /ə'luf/ *adj.* сдержанный

aloud /ə'laud/ *adv.* вслух

alphabet /'ælfə,bet/ *n.* алфавит

alphabetical /,ælfə'betikəl/ *adj.* алфавитный

alpine /'ælpain/ *adj.* альпийский

already /ɔl'redi/ *adv.* уже

also /'ɔlsou/ *adv.* также, тоже

altar /'ɔltər/ *n.* алтарь *m.*

alter /'ɔltər/ *v.* изменять(ся) *impf.,* -нить(ся) *pf.*; переделывать *impf.,* переделать *pf.*

alteration /,ɔltə'reiʃən/ *n.* изменение; переделка

altercation /,ɔltər'keiʃən/ *n.* перебранка

alternate /*adj., n.* 'ɔltərnit; *v.* 'ɔltər,neit/ **1.** *adj.* чередующийся **2.** *v.* чередовать(ся) *impf.* **3.** *n.* заместитель

alternating current *n.* переменный ток

alternation /,ɔltər'neiʃən/ *n.* чередование

alternative /ɔl'tɜrnətɪv/ **1.** *adj.* альтернативный **2.** *n.* альтернатива

although /ɔl'ðou/ *conj.* хотя

altitude /'ælti,tud/ *n.* высота

alto /'æltou/ *n.* альт

altogether /,ɔltə'geðər/ *adv.* всего, вполне; совсем

altruistic /,æltru'istik/ *adj.* альтруистический

aluminum /ə'lumənəm/ *n.* алюминий

always /'ɔlweiz/ *adv.* всегда

a.m. *abbr.* утра́; ночи

amalgam /ə'mælgəm/ *n.* амальгама, смесь *f.*

amalgamation /ə,mælgə'meiʃən/ *n.* объединение, слияние

amass /ə'mæs/ *v.* копить *impf.*

amateur /'æmə,tʃur/ **1.** *n.* любитель, —ница **2.** *adj.* любительский

amateurish /,æmə'tʃuriʃ/ *adj.* любительский, дилетантский

amaze /ə'meiz/ *v.* изумлять *impf.,* -мить *pf.*

amazement /ə'meizmənt/ *n.* изумление

amazing /ə'meizɪŋ/ *adj.* удивительный

ambassador /æm'bæsədər/ *n.* посол

amber /'æmbər/ **1.** *adj.* янтарный **2.** *n.* янтарь *m.*

ambiance /'æmbiəns/ *n.* атмосфера; (*milieu*) среда

ambiguity /,æmbı'gyuiti/ *n.* двусмысленность

ambiguous /æm'bigyuəs/ *adj.* двусмысленный

ambition /æm'biʃən/ *n.* амбиция

ambitious /æm'biʃəs/ *adj.* честолюбивый

ambivalent /æm'bivələnt/ *adj.* раздвоенный; противоречивый

amble /'æmbəl/ *v.* идти не спеша *impf.*

ambulance /'æmbyələns/ *n.* скорая помощь *f.*

ambush /'æmbuʃ/ *n.* засада

ameliorate /ə'milyə,reit/ *v.* улучшать(ся) *impf.,* улучшить(ся) *pf.*

amelioration /ə,milyə'reiʃən/ *n.* улучшение

amen /'ei'men/ *interj.* аминь!

amenable /ə'minəbəl/ *adj.* уступчивый; сговорчивый

amend /ə'mend/ **1.** *v.* исправлять *impf.,* исправить *pf.* **2.** *n.pl.:* **make** —**s** компенсировать (за + A) *impf.*

amendment /ə'mendmənt/ *n.* поправка, исправление

amenities /ə'menitiz/ *n.* удобства *pl.*

America /ə'merikə/ *n.* Америка

American /ə'merikən/ **1.** *adj.* американский **2.** *n.* американец, американка

amiable /'eimiəbəl/ *adj.* любезный

amicable /'æmikəbəl/ *adj.* дружеский, дружный

amid /ə'mid/ *prep.* среди, посреди (+ G)

amino acid /ə'minou/ *n.* аминокислота

ammonia /ə'mounyə/ *n.* аммиак, нашатырный спирт

ammunition /ˌæmjəˈnɪʃən/ *n.* боеприпа́сы *pl.*; патро́ны *pl.*

amnesia /æmˈniːʒə/ *n.* амне́зия

amnesty /ˈæmnəsti/ *n.* амни́стия

among /əˈmʌŋ/ *prep.* ме́жду (+ *I*); среди́ (+ *G*)

amoral /eɪˈmɔːrəl/ *adj.* амора́льный

amorous /ˈæmərəs/ *adj.* любо́вный

amorphous /əˈmɔːrfəs/ *adj.* бесфо́рменный, амо́рфный

amortization /ˌæmɔːrtəˈzeɪʃən/ *n.* амортиза́ция

amount /əˈmaʊnt/ *n.* коли́чество

ampere /ˈæmpɪər/ *n.* ампе́р

amphetamine /æmˈfetəˌmiːn/ *n.* амфетами́н

amphibian /æmˈfɪbiən/ **1.** *adj.* земново́дный **2.** *n.* амфи́бия

amphibious /æmˈfɪbiəs/ *adj.* земново́дный

amphitheater /ˈæmfəˌθiːətər/ *n.* амфитеа́тр

ample /ˈæmpəl/ *adj.* оби́льный; доста́точный

amplification /ˌæmpləfɪˈkeɪʃən/ *n.* усиле́ние, увеличе́ние

amplifier /ˈæmpləˌfaɪər/ *n.* усили́тель

amplify /ˈæmpləˌfaɪ/ *v.* расширя́ть, усили́вать *impf.*, усили́ть *pf.*

amputate /ˈæmpjuˌteɪt/ *v.* ампути́ровать *impf.* & *pf.*

amputation /ˌæmpjuˈteɪʃən/ *n.* ампута́ция

amuse /əˈmjuːz/ *v.* забавля́ть *impf.*; ~ oneself развлека́ться, забавля́ться *impf.*

amusement /əˈmjuːzmənt/ *n.* развлече́ние

amusing /əˈmjuːzɪŋ/ *adj.* занима́тельный; заба́вный

anachronism /əˈnækrəˌnɪzəm/ *n.* анахрони́зм

anachronistic /əˌnækrəˈnɪstɪk/ *adj.* анахрони́ческий

analgesic /ˌænlˈdʒiːzɪk/ *n.* болеутоля́ющее сре́дство

analogous /əˈnæləgəs/ *adj.* аналоги́чный

analogy /əˈnælədʒi/ *n.* анало́гия

analysis /əˈnæləsɪs/ *n.* ана́лиз

analyst /ˈænlɪst/ *n.* анали́тик

analytical /ˌænlˈɪtɪkəl/ *adj.* аналити́ческий

analyze /ˈænlˌaɪz/ *v.* анализи́ровать *impf.*, про- *pf.*

anarchism /ˈænərˌkɪzəm/ *n.* анархи́зм

anarchist /ˈænərkɪst/ *n.* анархи́ст, —ка

anarchy /ˈænərki/ *n.* ана́рхия

anatomical /ˌænəˈtɒmɪkəl/ *adj.* анатоми́ческий

anatomy /əˈnætəmi/ *n.* анато́мия

ancestor /ˈænsestər/ *n.* пре́док

ancestral /ænˈsestrəl/ *adj.* родово́й; насле́дственный

ancestry /ˈænsestri/ *n.* происхожде́ние

anchor /ˈæŋkər/ **1.** *n.* я́корь *m.* **2.** *v.* стать на я́корь *pf.*

anchorage /ˈæŋkərɪdʒ/ *n.* я́корная стоя́нка

anchovy /ˈæntʃoʊvi/ *n.* анчо́ус

ancient /ˈeɪnʃənt/ *adj.* стари́нный; дре́вний

ancillary /ˈænsəˌleri/ *adj.* вспомога́тельный

and /ænd/ *conj.* и; а

androgynous /ænˈdrɒdʒənəs/ *adj.* двупо́лый; гермафроди́тный

anecdote /ˈænɪkˌdaʊt/ *n.* анекдо́т

anemia /əˈniːmiə/ *n.* анеми́я

anemic /əˈniːmɪk/ *adj.* анеми́ческий

anesthesia /ˌænəsˈθiːʒə/ *n.* анестези́я; нарко́з

anesthetic /ˌænəsˈθetɪk/ *n.* анестези́рующее сре́дство, анесте́тик

anesthetize /əˈnesθəˌtaɪz/ *v.* анестези́ровать *impf.* & *pf.*

anew /əˈnuː/ *adv.* сно́ва, за́ново

angel /ˈeɪndʒəl/ *n.* а́нгел

angelic /ænˈdʒelɪk/ *adj.* а́нгельский

anger /ˈæŋgər/ **1.** *n.* гнев **2.** *v.t.* серди́ть *impf.*, рас- *pf.*

angina /ænˈdʒaɪnə/ *n.* анги́на

angle /ˈæŋgəl/ *n.* у́гол; *Fig.* то́чка зре́ния

angler /ˈæŋglər/ *n.* рыболо́в

angry /ˈæŋgri/ *adj.* серди́тый

anguish /ˈæŋgwɪʃ/ *n.* му́ка, боль *f.*

anguished /ˈæŋgwɪʃt/ *adj.* мучи́тельный; отча́янный

angular /ˈæŋgjələr/ *adj.* углова́тый, углово́й

animal /ˈænəməl/ **1.** *n.* живо́тное **2.** *adj.* живо́тный

animate /ˈænəmɪt/ *v.* /ˈænəmeɪt/ **1.** *adj.* одушевлённый

2. v. одушевля́ть impf., -ви́ть pf.

animated /'ænə,meitid/ adj. оживлённый; ~ **cartoon** n. мультфи́льм

animation /,ænə'meiʃən/ n. оживле́ние, жи́вость

animosity /,ænə'mɒsiti/ n. враждéбность

ankle /'æŋkəl/ n. лоды́жка

annals /'ænlz/ n.pl. лéтопись f., хрóника

annex /'æneks/ n. пристрóйка

annexation /,ænik'seiʃən/ n. присоединéние, анне́ксия

annihilate /ə'naiə,leit/ v. уничтожа́ть impf., уничтóжить pf.

anniversary /,ænə'vɜrsəri/ n. годовщи́на

annotate /'ænə,teit/ v. анноти́ровать impf. & pf.

annotation /,ænə'teiʃən/ n. аннота́ция, коммента́рий

announce /ə'nauns/ v. объявля́ть impf., объяви́ть pf.

announcement /ə'naunsmənt/ n. объявле́ние, сообщéние

announcer /ə'naunsər/ n. ди́ктор

annoy /ə'nɔi/ v. досажда́ть impf., досади́ть pf.; надоеда́ть impf., надое́сть pf.

annoyance /ə'nɔiəns/ n. раздраже́ние

annoying /ə'nɔiiŋ/ adj. доса́дный

annual /'ænyuəl/ **1.** adj. ежегóдный, годовóй **2.** n. ежегóдник; (bot.) однолéтник

annuity /ə'nuiti/ n. ежегóдная рéнта, аннуите́т

annul /ə'nʌl/ v. аннули́ровать impf. & pf.

annulment /ə'nʌlmənt/ n. отмéна; аннули́рование

anoint /ə'nɔint/ v. (relig.) дéлать пома́зание impf.

anomalous /ə'nɒmələs/ adj. анома́льный; непра́вильный

anomaly /ə'nɒməli/ n. анома́лия

anonymity /,ænə'nimiti/ n. анони́мность

anonymous /ə'nɒnəməs/ adj. анони́мный

anorexia nervosa /,ænə'reksiə nɜr'vousə/ n. нéрвная аноре́ксия

anorexic /,ænə'reksik/ adj. больнóй анорекси́ей

another /ə'nʌðər/ pron. другóй; ~ **one** n. ещё (оди́н)

answer /'ænsər/ **1.** n. отвéт **2.** v. отвеча́ть impf., отвéтить pf.

answerable /'ænsərəbəl/ adj. отвéтственный

answering machine n. автоотвéтчик

ant /ænt/ n. мураве́й

antagonism /æn'tægə,nizəm/ n. антагони́зм, вражда́

antagonistic /æn,tægə'nistik/ adj. враждéбный, антагонисти́ческий

antagonize /æn'tægə,naiz/ v. вызыва́ть антагони́зм

Antarctic /æn'ɑrktik/ n. Анта́рктика

anteater /'ænt,itər/ n. муравьéд

antecedent /,æntə'sidnt/ adj. предшéствующий

antelope /'ænt|,oup/ n. антилóпа

antenna /æn'tenə/ n. анте́нна; (insects) щу́пальце pl.

anthem /'ænθəm/ n. гимн

anthill /'ænt,hil/ n. мураве́йник

anthology /æn'θɒlədʒi/ n. антолóгия

anthracite /'ænθrə,sait/ n. антраци́т

anthropologist /,ænθrə'pɒlədʒist/ n. антропóлог

anthropology /,ænθrə'pɒlədʒi/ n. антрополóгия

anti- pref. анти-, прóтиво-

antiaircraft /,ænti'eər,kræft, ,æntai-/ adj. противовозду́шный

antibiotic /,æntibai'ɒtik/ n. антибиóтик

antibody /'ænti,bɒdi/ n. анти-тéло

anticipate /æn'tisə,peit/ v. ожида́ть, предчу́вствовать impf.

anticipation /æn,tisə'peiʃən/ n. предвкушéние

anticipatory /æn'tisəpə,tɔri/ adj. предвари́тельный

anticlimax /,ænti'klaimæks/ n. разочарова́ние

antidepressant /,æntidi'presənt, ,æntai-/ n. антидепресса́нт

antidote /'ænti,dout/ n. противоя́дие

antifreeze /'ænti,friz/ n. антифри́з

antipathy /æn'tipəθi/ n. антипа́тия

antiperspirant /,ænti'pɜrspərənt/ n. срéдство от потéния

antiquarian /ˌæntɪˈkweəriən/ *adj.* антиква́рный; ~ **bookseller** букини́ст

antiquated /ˈæntɪˌkweitɪd/ *adj.* устаре́лый, старомо́дный

antique /ænˈtik/ **1.** *adj.* стари́нный; антиква́рный **2.** *n.* анти́к

antiquity /ænˈtɪkwɪtɪ/ *n.* дре́вность, старина́

anti-Semitism /ˈæntiˈsemɪˌtɪzəm, ˌæntai-/ *n.* антисемити́зм

antiseptic /ˌæntiˈseptɪk/ **1.** *adj.* антисепти́ческий **2.** *n.* антисепти́ческое сре́дство

antisocial /ˌæntiˈsouʃəl, ˌæntai-/ *adj.* необщи́тельный

antitank /ˌæntiˈtæŋk, ˌæntai-/ *adj.* противота́нковый

antithesis /ænˈtɪθəsɪs/ *n.* анти́теза, противопо́ложность

antler /ˈæntlər/ *n.* оле́ний рог

anus /ˈeinəs/ *n.* за́дний прохо́д

anvil /ˈænvɪl/ *n.* накова́льня

anxiety /æŋˈzaiɪti/ *n.* беспоко́йство

anxious /ˈæŋkʃəs/ *adj.* беспоко́йный; **be ~** *v.* беспоко́иться *impf.*

anxiously /ˈæŋkʃəsli/ *adv.* с трево́гой; с нетерпе́нием

any /ˈeni/ **1.** *adj., pron.* како́й-нибудь; любо́й; вся́кий; кто́-нибудь; что́-нибудь; (*with negative*) никако́й; ни оди́н; никто́ **2.** *adv.* ско́лько-нибудь; (*with negative*) ниско́лько

anybody /ˈeniˌbɒdi/ *pron.* вся́кий; кто́-нибудь; любо́й

anyhow /ˈeniˌhau/ **1.** *adv.* ка́к-нибудь, кое-ка́к **2.** *conj.* во вся́ком слу́чае

anything /ˈeniˌθiŋ/ *pron.* всё (что уго́дно)

anywhere /ˈeniˌweər/ *adv.* где́-нибудь; куда́-нибудь; где, куда́ уго́дно

apart /əˈpɑrt/ *adv.* в сто́рону; в стороне́; по́рознь; на части; ~ **from** кро́ме (+ *G*); **take ~** *v.* разбира́ть *impf.*

apartheid /əˈpɑrtheit, -hait/ *n.* апарте́ид

apartment /əˈpɑrtmənt/ *n.* кварти́ра

apathetic /ˌæpəˈθetɪk/ *adj.* равноду́шный, апати́чный

apathy /ˈæpəθi/ *n.* апа́тия

ape /eip/ **1.** *n.* обезья́на **2.** *v.* подража́ть *impf.*

aperture /ˈæpərtʃər/ *n.* отве́рстие

apex /ˈeipeks/ *n.* верши́на

aphorism /ˈæfəˌrizəm/ *n.* афори́зм

aphrodisiac /ˌæfrəˈdizɪˌæk/ *adj.* возбужда́ющий

apiary /ˈeipiˌeri/ *n.* па́сека

apiece /əˈpis/ *adv.* (*per thing*) за шту́ку, (*per person*) на ка́ждого

aplomb /əˈplɒm/ *n.* апло́мб

apocalyptic /əˌpɒkəˈliptɪk/ *adj.* апокалипти́ческий

apolitical /ˌeipəˈlɪtɪkəl/ *adj.* аполити́чный

apologetic /əˌpɒləˈdʒetɪk/ *adj.* извиня́ющийся

apologize /əˈpɒləˌdʒaiz/ *v.* извиня́ться *impf.*, -ни́ться *pf.*

apology /əˈpɒlədʒi/ *n.* извине́ние

apostate /əˈposteit/ *n.* отсту́пник

apostle /əˈpɒsəl/ *n.* апо́стол

apostrophe /əˈpɒstrəfi/ *n.* апостро́ф

appall /əˈpɔl/ *v.* шоки́ровать *impf.*

appalling /əˈpɔliŋ/ *adj.* ужа́сный

apparatus /ˌæpəˈrætəs/ *n.* аппара́т, прибо́р

apparel /əˈpærəl/ *n.* оде́жда

apparent /əˈpærənt/ *adj.* я́вный, очеви́дный

apparently /əˈpærəntli/ *adv.* очеви́дно; ка́жется

apparition /ˌæpəˈriʃən/ *n.* виде́ние; привиде́ние; при́зрак

appeal /əˈpil/ **1.** *n.* апелля́ция; призы́в, обраще́ние **2.** *v.* обраща́ться (к + *D*); апелли́ровать *impf.* & *pf.*

appealing /əˈpiliŋ/ *adj.* (*beseeching*) умоля́ющий; (*attractive*) привлека́тельный

appear /əˈpiər/ *v.* появля́ться *impf.*, -ви́ться *pf.*; (*seem*) каза́ться *impf.*, по- *pf.*

appearance /əˈpiərəns/ *n.* появле́ние; (вне́шний) вид

appease /əˈpiz/ *v.* умиротворя́ть *impf.*, -ри́ть *pf.* успока́ивать *impf.*, успоко́ить *pf.*

append /əˈpend/ *v.* прилага́ть *impf.*, приложи́ть *pf.*

appendicitis /əˌpendəˈsaitɪs/ *n.* аппендици́т

appendix /əˈpendɪks/ *n.* приложе́ние; (*anat.*) аппе́ндикс

appetite /ˈæpɪˌtait/ *n.* аппети́т

appetizer /ˈæpɪˌtaizər/ *n.* заку́ска

applaud /ə'plɔd/ *v.* аплодировать (+ *D*) *impf.* & *pf.*

applause /ə'plɔz/ *n.* аплодисменты *pl.*

apple /'æpəl/ **1.** *adj.* яблочный **2.** *n.* яблоко; ~ **tree** яблоня

appliance /ə'plaɪəns/ *n.* прибор

applicable /'æplɪkəbəl, ə'plɪkə-/ *adj.* применимый

applicant /'æplɪkənt/ *n.* кандидат, заявитель

application /,æplɪ'keɪʃən/ *n.* применение, заявление; просьба

applied /ə'plaɪd/ *adj.* прикладной

apply /ə'plaɪ/ *v.t.* прикладывать *impf.*, приложить *pf.*; применять *impf.*, -нить *pf.*; *v.i.* обращаться; подавать заявление *impf.*

appoint /ə'pɔɪnt/ *v.* назначать *impf.*, назначить *pf.*

appointment /ə'pɔɪntmənt/ *n.* назначение; (*rendezvous*) свидание; (*office*) должность

apportion /ə'pɔrʃən/ *v.* распределять *impf.*, -лить *pf.*

appraisal /ə'preɪzəl/ *n.* оценка

appraise /ə'preɪz/ *v.* оценивать *impf.*, оценить *pf.*

appreciable /ə'priʃiəbəl/ *adj.* значительный; ощутимый

appreciate /ə'priʃi,eɪt/ *v.* ценить *impf.*, о- *pf.*

appreciation /ə,priʃi'eɪʃən/ *n.* оценка, признательность

apprehend /,æprɪ'hɛnd/ *v.* арестовать *pf.*

apprehension /,æprɪ'hɛnʃən/ *n.* арест; (*fear*) опасение

apprehensive /,æprɪ'hɛnsɪv/ *adj.* озабоченный; опасающийся

apprentice /ə'prɛntɪs/ *n.* ученик

apprenticeship /ə'prɛntɪs,ʃɪp/ *n.* (*period*) срок учения; (*job*) учёба

approach /ə'proutʃ/ **1.** *n.* приближение; подход **2.** *v.* приближаться *impf.*, приблизиться *pf.*; подходить *impf.*, подойти *pf.*

approachable /ə'proutʃəbəl/ *adj.* доступный

approbation /,æprə'beɪʃən/ *n.* одобрение; апробация

appropriate /ə'proutʃ/ **1.** *adj.* ə'proupriɪt; v. ə'proupri,eɪt/ **1.** *adj.* подходящий **2.** *v.* присваивать *impf.*, присвоить *pf.*

appropriation /ə,proupri'eɪʃən/ *n.* присвоение, ассигнование

approval /ə'pruvəl/ *n.* одобрение

approve /ə'pruv/ *v.* одобрять *impf.*, одобрить *pf.*

approximate /adj. ə'prɒksəmɪt; v. -,meɪt/ **1.** *adj.* приблизительный **2.** *v.* приближаться (к + *D*) *impf.*

approximation /ə,prɒksə'meɪʃən/ *n.* приближение

apricot /'æprɪ,kɒt/ *n.* абрикос

April /'eɪprəl/ **1.** *n.* апрель *m.* **2.** *adj.* апрельский

apron /'eɪprən/ *n.* передник, фартук

apropos /,æprə'pou/ *adv.* кстати; относительно (+ *G*)

apt /æpt/ *adj.* удачный; склонный

aptitude /'æptɪ,tud/ *n.* способность, склонность

aquarium /ə'kwɛəriəm/ *n.* аквариум

aquatic /ə'kwætɪk/ *adj.* водный; водяной

aqueduct /'ækwɪ,dʌkt/ *n.* акведук

aquiline /'ækwə,laɪn/ *adj.* орлиный

Arab /'ærəb/ **1.** *n.* араб, —ка **2.** *adj.* арабский, аравийский

Arabia /ə'reɪbiə/ *n.* Аравия

arable /'ærəbəl/ *adj.* пахотный

arbitrariness /'ɑrbɪ,trɛrɪnɪs/ *n.* произвол

arbitrary /'ɑrbɪ,trɛri/ *adj.* произвольный

arbitrate /'ɑrbɪ,treɪt/ *v.* решать третейским судом *impf.*

arbitration /,ɑrbɪ'treɪʃən/ *n.* третейский суд; арбитраж

arbitrator /'ɑrbɪ,treɪtər/ *n.* третейский судья *m.*; арбитр

arbor /'ɑrbər/ *n.* беседка

arc /ɑrk/ *n.* дуга

arcade /ɑr'keɪd/ *n.* аркада; (*com.*) пассаж

arch[1] /ɑrtʃ/ *n.* арка, свод; дуга

arch[2] /ɑrtʃ/ *adj.* лукавый; главный

archaeologist /,ɑrki'ɒlədʒɪst/ *n.* археолог

archaeology /,ɑrki'ɒlədʒi/ *n.* археология

archaic /ɑr'keiɪk/ *adj.* архаический

archangel /'ɑrk,eɪndʒəl/ *n.* архангел

archbishop /'ɑrtʃ'bɪʃəp/ *n.* архиепископ

arched /ɑrtʃt/ *adj.* сводчатый

archenemy /ˈɑrtʃˈenəmi/ *n.* заклятый враг

archer /ˈɑrtʃər/ *n.* стрелок; **—y** *n.* стрельба из лука

archetypal /ˈɑrkɪˌtaɪpəl/ *adj.* архетипический

archipelago /ˌɑrkəˈpeləˌgou/ *n.* архипелаг

architect /ˈɑrkɪˌtekt/ *n.* архитектор

architectural /ˌɑrkɪˈtektʃərəl/ *adj.* архитектурный

architecture /ˈɑrkɪˌtektʃər/ *n.* архитектура, зодчество

archival /ɑrˈkaɪvəl/ *adj.* архивный

archive /ˈɑrkaɪv/ *n.* архив

archway /ˈɑrtʃˌweɪ/ *n.* арка

Arctic /ˈɑrktɪk/ *adj.* арктический; полярный

ardent /ˈɑrdnt/ *adj.* горячий

ardor /ˈɑrdər/ *n.* рвение, пыл

arduous /ˈɑrdʒuəs/ *adj.* трудный

area /ˈeəriə/ *n.* площадь *f.*; район

arena /əˈrinə/ *n.* арена

arguable /ˈɑrgyuəbəl/ *adj.* спорный

argue /ˈɑrgyu/ *v.* спорить *impf.*; (*maintain*) утверждать *impf.*

argument /ˈɑrgyəmənt/ *n.* спор; (*reason*) довод; аргумент

aria /ˈɑriə/ *n.* ария

arid /ˈærɪd/ *adj.* сухой

arise /əˈraɪz/ *v.* возникать *impf.*, возникнуть *pf.*

aristocracy /ˌærəˈstɔkrəsi/ *n.* аристократия

aristocrat /əˈrɪstəˌkræt/ *n.* аристократ, —а

aristocratic /əˌrɪstəˈkrætɪk/ *adj.* аристократический

arithmetic /əˈrɪθmətɪk/ *n.* арифметика

arithmetical /ˌærɪθˈmetɪkəl/ *adj.* арифметический

ark /ɑrk/ *n.* ковчег

arm¹ /ɑrm/ *n.* рука; (*of chair*) ручка

arm² /ɑrm/ **1.** *arms n.pl.* (*weapons*) оружие **2.** *v.* вооружать(ся) *impf.*, -жить(ся) *pf.*

armadillo /ˌɑrməˈdɪlou/ *n.* броненосец

armament /ˈɑrməmənt/ *n.* вооружение

armchair /ˈɑrmˌtʃeər/ *n.* кресло

Armenia /ɑrˈminiə/ *n.* Армения

Armenian /ɑrˈminiən/ **1.** *adj.*

армянский **2.** *n.* армянин, -мянка

armistice /ˈɑrməstɪs/ *n.* перемирие

armor /ˈɑrmər/ *n.* (*warrior*) доспехи *pl.*; (*tank, ship*) броня

armored /ˈɑrmərd/ *adj.* бронированный

armory /ˈɑrməri/ *n.* арсенал

armpit /ˈɑrmˌpɪt/ *n.* подмышка

army /ˈɑrmi/ **1.** *adj.* армейский **2.** *n.* армия, войско

aroma /əˈroumə/ *n.* аромат

aromatic /ˌærəˈmætɪk/ *adj.* ароматический, благовонный

around /əˈraund/ **1.** *prep.* вокруг (+ *G*) **2.** *adv.* кругом, в окрестностях; **all ~** повсюду

arouse /əˈrauz/ *v.* будить *impf.*, раз- *pf*; возбуждать *impf.*

arraign /əˈrein/ *v.* привлекать к суду *impf.*; **—ment** *n.* привлечение к суду

arrange /əˈreindʒ/ *v.* устраивать *impf.*, устроить *pf.*; (*mus.*) аранжировать *impf.* & *pf.*

arrangement /əˈreindʒmənt/ *n.* расположение; (*agreement*) соглашение; (*mus.*) аранжировка

array /əˈrei/ *n.* (*quantity*) множество; (*finery*) наряд

arrears /əˈrirz/ *n.* задолженность (по + *D*)

arrest /əˈrest/ **1.** *n.* арест **2.** *v.* арестовать; задержать *pf.*

arresting /əˈrestɪŋ/ *adj.* захватывающий

arrival /əˈraivəl/ *n.* прибытие, появление

arrive /əˈraiv/ *v.* приходить *impf.*; приезжать *impf.* приехать *pf.*; прибывать *impf.*, прибыть *pf.*

arrogance /ˈærəgəns/ *n.* высокомерие; надменность

arrogant /ˈærəgənt/ *adj.* высокомерный, надменный

arrow /ˈærou/ *n.* стрела; (*pointer, etc.*) стрелка

arsenal /ˈɑrsənl/ *n.* арсенал

arsenic /ˈɑrsənɪk/ *n.* мышьяк

arson /ˈɑrsən/ *n.* поджог

arsonist /ˈɑrsənɪst/ *n.* поджигатель

art /ɑrt/ **1.** *adj.* художественный **2.** *n.* искусство; **the arts** гуманитарные науки *pl.*

artery /ˈɑrtəri/ *n.* артерия

artful /ˈɑrtfəl/ *adj.* хитрый

arthritic /ɑr'θrɪtɪk/ adj. артри́тический

arthritis /ɑr'θraɪtɪs/ n. артри́т

article /'ɑrtɪkəl/ n. (thing) предме́т; (lit.) статья́; (gram.) арти́кль m.

articulate / adj. ɑr'tɪkyəlɪt; v. ɑr'tɪkyə,leɪt/ **1.** adj. отчётливый **2.** v. произноси́ть impf.

artifact /'ɑrtə,fækt/ n. изде́лие

artifice /'ɑrtəfɪs/ n. хи́трость

artificial /,ɑrtə'fɪʃəl/ adj. иску́сственный

artificial intelligence n. иску́сственный интелле́кт

artillery /ɑr'tɪləri/ n. артилле́рия

artisan /'ɑrtəzən/ n. реме́сленник

artist /'ɑrtɪst/ n. худо́жник

artistic /ɑr'tɪstɪk/ adj. худо́жественный, артисти́ческий

artless /'ɑrtlɪs/ adj. безыску́сный

artwork /'ɑrt,wɜrk/ n. (typog.) оформле́ние

as /æz/ **1.** adv. как **2.** conj. когда́, в то вре́мя как; **as for** что каса́ется (+ G)

asbestos /æs'bɛstəs/ n. асбе́ст

ascend /ə'sɛnd/ v. всходи́ть impf., взойти́ pf.; поднима́ться impf., подня́ться pf. (по + D)

ascendancy /ə'sɛndənsi/ n. госпо́дство, власть f.

ascent /ə'sɛnt/ n. восхожде́ние

ascertain /,æsər'teɪn/ v. установи́ть; удостове́риться pf.

ascetic /ə'sɛtɪk/ **1.** adj. аскети́ческий **2.** n. аске́т

ascribe /ə'skraɪb/ v. припи́сывать (+ D) impf., -пи́са́ть pf.

asexual /eɪ'sɛkʃuəl/ adj. беспо́лый

ash¹ /æʃ/ n. (tree) я́сень m.

ash² /æʃ/ n. usu. pl. пе́пел; зола́

ashamed /ə'ʃeɪmd/ adj.: **feel ~** стыди́ться (+ G) impf., по- pf.

ashore /ə'ʃɔr/ adv. на берегу́; **go ~** v. сходи́ть на бе́рег impf.

ashtray /'æʃ,treɪ/ n. пе́пельница

Asia /'eɪʒə/ n. А́зия

Asian /'eɪʒən/, **Asiatic** /,eɪʒi'ætɪk/ **1.** adj. азиа́тский **2.** n. азиа́т, -ка

aside /ə'saɪd/ adv. в сто́рону

ask /æsk/ v. спра́шивать impf., спроси́ть pf.; (request) проси́ть impf., по- pf.; **~ a question** зада́ть вопро́с pf.

askew /ə'skyu/ adv. кри́во, ко́со

asleep /ə'slip/ adj.: **be ~** спать impf.

asparagus /ə'spærəgəs/ n. спа́ржа

aspect /'æspɛkt/ n. вид; сторона́

aspen /'æspən/ **1.** n. оси́новый **2.** n. оси́на

aspersion /ə'spɜrʒən/ n. клевета́

asphalt /'æsfɔlt/ n. асфа́льт

asphyxiate /æs'fɪksi,eɪt/ v. удуши́ть pf.

aspiration /,æspə'reɪʃən/ n. стремле́ние, жела́ние

aspire /ə'spaɪər/ v. стреми́ться (к + D)

aspirin /'æspərɪn/ n. аспири́н

assail /ə'seɪl/ v. напада́ть impf., напа́сть pf.

assailant /ə'seɪlənt/ n. налётчик

assassin /ə'sæsɪn/ n. уби́йца m. & f.

assassinate /ə'sæsə,neɪt/ v. убива́ть impf., уби́ть pf.

assassination /ə,sæsə'neɪʃən/ n. уби́йство

assault /ə'sɔlt/ **1.** n. нападе́ние **2.** v. напада́ть impf., напа́сть pf.

assemblage /ə'sɛmblɪdʒ/ n. собра́ние; монта́ж, сбо́рка

assemble /ə'sɛmbəl/ v. собира́ть(ся) impf., собра́ть(ся) pf.

assembly /ə'sɛmbli/ n. собра́ние; монта́ж

assent /ə'sɛnt/ v. соглаша́ться (на + A) impf., -си́ться pf.

assert /ə'sɜrt/ v. утвержда́ть impf.; **~ oneself** отста́ивать свои́ права́ impf.

assertion /ə'sɜrʃən/ n. утвержде́ние

assertive /ə'sɜrtɪv/ adj. напо́ристый

assess /ə'sɛs/ v. оце́нивать impf., оцени́ть pf.; **—ment** n. оце́нка

asset /'æsɛt/ n. це́нное ка́чество; **—s and liabilities** акти́в и пасси́в

assiduous /ə'sɪdʒuəs/ adj. усе́рдный, приле́жный

assign /ə'saɪn/ v. назнача́ть impf., назна́чить pf.

assignment /ə'saɪnmənt/ n. зада́ние

assimilate /ə'sɪmə,leɪt/ v. ассимили́ровать(ся), усва́ивать impf.

assimilation /ə,sɪmə'leɪʃən/ n. усвое́ние; ассимиля́ция

assist /ə'sɪst/ v. помога́ть impf., помо́чь pf.

assistance /əˈsɪstəns/ n. по́мощь f.

assistant /əˈsɪstənt/ n. помо́щник, ассисте́нт

associate / n. əˈsouʃit, v. -si,eit/ **1.** n. колле́га m. & f.; сотру́дник **2.** v. ассоции́ровать impf. & pf.; обща́ться (+ I) impf.

association /ə,sousiˈeiʃən/ n. о́бщество, ассоциа́ция

assorted /əˈsɔrtid/ adj. подо́бранный

assortment /əˈsɔrtmənt/ n. подбо́р, ассортиме́нт

assuage /əˈsweidʒ/ v. смягча́ть; утоля́ть impf.

assume /əˈsum/ v. предполага́ть impf., -ложи́ть pf.; принима́ть impf.

assumption /əˈsʌmpʃən/ n. приня́тие, предположе́ние

assurance /əˈʃurəns/ n. самоуве́ренность; завере́ние

assure /əˈʃur/ v. уверя́ть impf., уве́рить pf.

asterisk /ˈæstərisk/ n. звёздочка

asthma /ˈæzmə/ n. а́стма

astonish /əˈstɒniʃ/ v. удивля́ть impf., -ви́ть pf.

astonishing /əˈstɒniʃiŋ/ adj. удиви́тельный, порази́тельный

astonishment /əˈstɒniʃmənt/ n. удивле́ние, изумле́ние

astound /əˈstaund/ v. изумля́ть impf., -ми́ть pf.; поража́ть impf., -зи́ть pf.

astounding /əˈstaundiŋ/ adj. порази́тельный

astray /əˈstrei/ adv.: **go ~** заблуди́ться pf.; **lead ~** сбива́ть impf., сбить с пути́ pf.

astride /əˈstraid/ adv. верхо́м (на + P)

astringent /əˈstrindʒənt/ **1.** adj. вя́жущий **2.** n. вя́жущее сре́дство

astrologer /əˈstrɒlədʒər/ n. астро́лог

astrology /əˈstrɒlədʒi/ n. астроло́гия

astronaut /ˈæstrə,nɔt/ n. астрона́вт

astronomer /əˈstrɒnəmər/ n. астроно́м

astronomy /əˈstrɒnəmi/ n. астроно́мия

astute /əˈstut/ adj. проница́тельный; хи́трый

asunder /əˈsʌndər/ adv. по́рознь

asylum /əˈsailəm/ n. убе́жище;

(institution) психиатри́ческая больни́ца

asymmetric /,eisəˈmetrik/ adj. асимметри́чный

asymmetry /eiˈsimitri/ n. асимметри́я

at /æt/ prep. у; во́зле; о́коло (+ G); при (+ P); (time) в, на (+ A); **at home** до́ма; **at my place** у меня́

atelier /ˈætl,yei/ n. мастерска́я

atheism /ˈeiθi,izəm/ n. атеи́зм

atheist /ˈeiθiist/ n. атеи́ст, —ка

athlete /ˈæθlit/ n. атле́т, —ка

athletic /æˈθletik/ adj. атлети́ческий

athletics /æˈθletiks/ n. атле́тика, физкульту́ра

atlas /ˈætləs/ n. а́тлас

atmosphere /ˈætməs,fiər/ n. атмосфе́ра

atmospheric /,ætməsˈferik/ adj. атмосфе́рный

atom /ˈætəm/ n. а́том

atomic /əˈtɒmik/ adj. а́томный

atomizer /ˈætə,maizər/ n. (spray) пульвериза́тор

atone /əˈtoun/ v. искупа́ть impf., -пи́ть pf.; **—ment** n. искупле́ние

atrocious /əˈtrouʃəs/ adj. зве́рский; ужа́сный

atrocity /əˈtrɒsiti/ n. зве́рство

atrophied /ˈætrəfid/ adj. исто́щенный

attach /əˈtætʃ/ v. прикрепля́ть impf., -пи́ть pf.; (attribute) придава́ть impf., прида́ть pf.; **—ment** n. прикрепле́ние; (emotional) привя́занность

attack /əˈtæk/ **1.** n. нападе́ние; (med.) припа́док, при́ступ **2.** v. напада́ть (на + A) impf., напа́сть pf.

attain /əˈtein/ v. достига́ть impf., дости́гнуть pf., доби́ться pf.

attainable /əˈteinəbəl/ adj. дости́жимый

attainment /əˈteinmənt/ n. достиже́ние

attempt /əˈtempt/ **1.** n. попы́тка **2.** v. пыта́ться impf., по- pf.; про́бовать impf., по- pf.

attend /əˈtend/ v. прису́тствовать (на + P); посеща́ть impf., -ти́ть pf.; **—ance** n. прису́тствие; посеща́емость

attendant /əˈtendənt/ **1.** n. провожа́тый **2.** adj. сопровожда́ющий

attention /əˈtenʃən/ n. внима́ние; **pay** ~ обраща́ть внима́ние pf.

attentive /əˈtentɪv/ adj. внима́тельный; забо́тливый

attest /əˈtest/ v. свиде́тельствовать impf., за- pf.; удостоверя́ть impf., -ве́рить pf.

attestation /ˌæteˈsteiʃən/ n. свиде́тельство

attic /ˈætik/ n. манса́рда, черда́к

attire /əˈtaiʳr/ 1. n. наря́д 2. v. наряжа́ть impf., -ди́ть pf.

attitude /ˈæti,tud/ n. отноше́ние; по́за

attorney /əˈtɜrni/ n. адвока́т

attract /əˈtrækt/ v. привлека́ть impf., привле́чь pf.

attraction /əˈtrækʃən/ n. привлека́тельность; (show) аттракцио́н

attractive /əˈtræktɪv/ adj. привлека́тельный, притяга́тельный

attribute / n. ˈætrə,byut/ v. əˈtribyut/ 1. n. сво́йство 2. v. припи́сывать impf., приписа́ть pf.

attribution /ˌætrəˈbyuʃən/ n. приписывание

attrition /əˈtriʃən/ n. истира́ние

attune /əˈtun/ v. настра́ивать impf., настро́ить pf.

auburn /ˈɔbərn/ adj. кашта́новый

auction /ˈɔkʃən/ 1. n. аукцио́н 2. v. продава́ть на аукцио́не impf.

auctioneer /ˌɔkʃəˈniər/ n. аукциони́ст

audacious /ɔˈdeiʃəs/ adj. сме́лый; де́рзкий

audacity /ɔˈdæsiti/ n. де́рзость

audible /ˈɔdəbəl/ adj. слы́шный

audience /ˈɔdiəns/ n. аудито́рия, слу́шатели pl., пу́блика; (interview) аудие́нция

audit /ˈɔdit/ n. реви́зия, прове́рка

audition /ɔˈdiʃən/ n. про́ба

auditor /ˈɔditər/ n. ревизо́р

auditorium /ˌɔdiˈtɔriəm/ n. зри́тельный зал, аудито́рия

augment /ɔgˈment/ v. прибавля́ть impf.; —**ation** n. увеличе́ние

augur /ˈɔgər/ v. предвеща́ть impf.

August /ˈɔgəst/ 1. n. а́вгуст 2. adj. а́вгустовский

aunt /ænt, ɑnt/ n. тётя, тётка

aura /ˈɔrə/ n. а́ура

auspicious /ɔˈspiʃəs/ adj. благоприя́тный

austere /ɔˈstiər/ adj. суро́вый; стро́гий

austerity /ɔˈsteriti/ n. стро́гость

Australia /ɔˈstreilyə/ n. Австра́лия

Australian /ɔˈstreilyən/ 1. adj. австрали́йский 2. n. австрали́ец, австрали́йка

Austria /ˈɔstriə/ n. А́встрия

Austrian /ˈɔstriən/ 1. adj. австри́йский 2. n. австри́ец, -ри́йка

authentic /ɔˈθentik/ adj. по́длинный, достове́рный

authenticate /ɔˈθenti,keit/ v. устана́вливать по́длинность impf.

authenticity /ˌɔθenˈtisiti/ n. по́длинность, достове́рность

author /ˈɔθər/ n. а́втор

authoritarian /əˌθɔriˈteəriən/ adj. авторита́рный

authoritative /əˈθɔri,teitiv/ adj. авторите́тный; повели́тельный

authority /əˈθɔriti/ n. авторите́т; (power) власть f., полномо́чие

authorization /ˌɔθərəˈzeiʃən/ n. уполномо́чивание, разреше́ние

authorize /ˈɔθə,raiz/ v. уполномо́чивать impf., -мо́чить pf.

authorship /ˈɔθər,ʃip/ n. а́вторство

auto- pref. авто-, само-

autobiographical /ˌɔtə,baiəˈgræfikəl/ adj. автобиографи́ческий

autobiography /ˌɔtəbaiˈɒgrəfi/ n. автобиогра́фия

autocracy /ɔˈtɒkrəsi/ n. самодержа́вие; автокра́тия

autocrat /ˈɔtə,kræt/ n. автокра́т

autocratic /ˌɔtəˈkrætik/ adj. автократи́ческий

autograph /ˈɔtə,græf/ n. авто́граф, оригина́л ру́кописи

automatic /ˌɔtəˈmætik/ adj. автомати́ческий

automatic pilot n. автопило́т

automation /ˌɔtəˈmeiʃən/ n. автоматиза́ция

automaton /ɔˈtɒmə,tɒn/ n. автома́т

automobile /ˌɔtəməˈbil/ n. автомоби́ль m., маши́на

autonomous /ɔˈtɒnəməs/ adj. автоно́мный

autonomy /ɔˈtɒnəmi/ n. автоно́мия

autopsy /'ɔtɒpsi/ n. вскрытие
autumn /'ɔtəm/ **1.** n. осень f.; in ~ осенью **2.** adj. осенний
auxiliary /ɔg'zɪljəri/ adj. вспомогательный
avail /ə'veil/ n.: to no ~ adv. напрасно; ~ oneself of пользоваться (+ I) impf.
availability /ə,veilə'bilɪti/ n. доступность
available /ə'veiləbəl/ adj. имеющийся в распоряжении
avalanche /'ævə,lænt∫/ n. лавина
avant-garde /ə,vant'gard/ **1.** n. авангард **2.** adj. авангардный
avarice /'ævərɪs/ n. скупость
avaricious /,ævə'rɪ∫əs/ adj. скупой
avenge /ə'vendʒ/ v. мстить (за + A) impf., отомстить pf.
avenger /ə'vendʒər/ n. мститель
avenue /'ævə,nyu/ n. проспект; авеню f. indecl.
average /'ævərɪdʒ/ **1.** adj. средний **2.** n. среднее число; on the ~ adv. в среднем **3.** v. брать среднее число impf.
averse /ə'vɜrs/ adj.: not ~ to не прочь (+ infin.)
aversion /ə'vɜrʒən/ n. отвращение, антипатия
avert /ə'vɜrt/ v. отводить impf., отвести pf.
aviary /'eivi,eri/ n. птичник
aviation /,eivi'ei∫ən/ n. авиация
avid /'ævɪd/ adj. жадный
avocado /,ævə'kadou/ n. авокадо neut. indecl.

avoid /ə'vɔid/ v. избегать (+ G) impf., избежать pf.
avoidance /ə'vɔidns/ n. избегание
avowed /ə'vaud/ adj. признанный; общепризнанный
await /ə'weit/ v. ожидать impf.
awake /ə'weik/ **1.** v. просыпаться impf., проснуться pf. **2.** adj. бодрствующий
awakening /ə'weikəniŋ/ n. пробуждение
award /ə'wɔrd/ **1.** n. награда **2.** v. награждать impf., наградить pf.
aware /ə'wɛər/ pred.: be ~ of сознавать impf.; **—ness** n. сознание
away /ə'wei/ adv. прочь
awe /ɔ/ n. благоговение, страх
awful /'ɔfəl/ adj. ужасный
awfully /'ɔfəli/ adv. страшно
awhile /ə'wail/ adv. ненадолго
awkward /'ɔkwərd/ adj. неуклюжий, неловкий; **—ness** n. неловкость, неуклюжесть
awl /ɔl/ n. шило
awning /'ɔniŋ/ n. навес, тент
awry /ə'rai/ adj. косой
ax /æks/ n. топор
axiom /'æksiəm/ n. аксиома
axis /'æksis/, **axle** /'æksəl/ n. ось f.
azalea /ə'zeilyə/ n. азалия
Azerbaijan /,azərbai'dʒan/ n. Азербайджан
Azerbaijani /,azərbai'dʒani/ n. азербайджанец, -джанка
azure /'æʒər/ **1.** adj. лазурный **2.** n. лазурь f.

B

babble /'bæbəl/ n. лепет
baboon /bæ'bun/ n. бабуин
baby /'beibi/ **1.** adj. детский **2.** n. маленький ребёнок, младенец
baby carriage n. (детская) коляска
babyish /'beibii∫/ adj. ребячиский
baby-sit v. присматривать за чужим ребёнком impf.
baby-sitter /'beibi,sɪtər/ n. приходящая няня f.
baby talk n. (child) детский лепет; (adult to child) сюсюканье
bachelor /'bæt∫ələr/ **1.** adj. хо-

лостой **2.** n. холостяк; (university) бакалавр
bacillus /bə'sɪləs/ n. бацилла
back /bæk/ **1.** adv. назад, обратно **2.** adj. спинной; задний **3.** n. оборотная сторона; (spine) спина; (rear) задняя часть; (chair) спинка
backbiting /'bæk,baitiŋ/ n. злословие
backbone /'bæk,boun/ n. хребет, позвоночник
backbreaking /'bæk,breikiŋ/ adj. изнурительный
backdrop /'bæk,drɒp/ n. (theat.) задник; Fig. фон
backer /'bækər/ n. спонсор

backfire /'bæk,faiər/ v. давáть осéчку impf.

backgammon /'bæk,gæmən/ n. триктрáк

background /'bæk,graund/ n. фон, зáдний план

backhand /'bæk,hænd/ n. (sports) удáр слéва

backing /'bækiŋ/ n. поддéржка

backlog /'bæk,lɔg/ n. скоплéние

backpack /'bæk,pæk/ n. рюкзáк

backrest /'bæk,rɛst/ n. опóра для спины

backslide /'bæk,slaid/ v. отступáть impf.

backstage /'bæk'steidʒ/ adj. закулисный

back-to-back adv. спинóй к спинé

backtrack /'bæk,træk/ v. идти на попятный

backup /'bæk,ʌp/ **1.** adj. запаснóй **2.** n. дублировáние

backward /'bækwərd/ **1.** adj. обрáтный; отстáлый **2.** adv. назáд; наоборóт; —ness n. отстáлость

backwater /'bæk,wɔtər/ n. зáводь f.

bacon /'beikən/ n. бекóн

bacterial /bæk'tiəriəl/ adj. бактериáльный

bacterium /bæk'tiəriəm/ n. бактéрия

bad /bæd/ adj. плохóй, дурнóй, врéдный; (language) грýбый

badge /bædʒ/ n. значóк

badger /'bædʒər/ n. барсýк

badly /'bædli/ adv. плóхо; (very much) óчень, сильно

badminton /'bædmintn/ n. бадминтóн

baffle /'bæfəl/ v. озадáчивать; сбивáть с тóлку impf.

bag /bæg/ **1.** n. сýмка, мешóк; (paper) пакéт **2.** v. схватить pf.

baggage /'bægidʒ/ **1.** adj. багáжный **2.** n. багáж

baggy /'bægi/ adj. мешковáтый

bagpipe /'bæg,paip/ n. волынка

bail /beil/ n. поручительство

bailiff /'beilif/ n. (law) судéбный пристав

bait /beit/ **1.** n. примáнка **2.** v. примáнивать impf.

bake /beik/ v. печь impf., с- pf.

baked /beikt/ adj. печёный

baker /'beikər/ n. пéкарь m.

bakery /'beikəri/ n. (store) бýлочная; пекáрня

balalaika /,bælə'laikə/ n. балалáйка

balance /'bæləns/ **1.** n. равновéсие; балáнс **2.** v. балансировать impf., с- pf.

balance sheet n. балáнс

balcony /'bælkəni/ n. балкóн

bald /bɔld/ adj. лысый

balding /'bɔldiŋ/ adj. лысéющий

baldness /'bɔldnis/ n. плешивость, облысéние

bale /beil/ n. кипа, тюк

baleful /'beilfəl/ adj. зловéщий

balk /bɔk/ v. упрямиться impf.

ball¹ /bɔl/ n. шар; мяч

ball² /bɔl/ n. (dance) бал

ballad /'bæləd/ n. баллáда

ballast /'bæləst/ n. баллáст

ballerina /,bælə'rinə/ n. балерина

ballet /bæ'lei/ **1.** adj. балéтный. **2.** n. балéт; ~ dancer артист, —ка балéта

balloon /bə'lun/ n. воздýшный шар

ballot /'bælət/ **1.** n. баллотирóвка **2.** v. баллотировать impf.

ballpoint pen /'bɔl,pɔint/ n. шáриковая рýчка

ballroom /'bɔl,rum/ n. танцевáльный зал

balm /bɑm/ n. бальзáм

balmy /'bɑmi/ adj. аромáтный; (air) мягкий, нéжный

balustrade /,bælə,streid/ n. балюстрáда

bamboo /bæm'bu/ n. бамбýк

bamboozle /bæm'buzəl/ v. обмáнывать, надувáть impf.

ban /bæn/ **1.** n. запрéт **2.** v. запрещáть impf., -тить pf.

banal /bə'næl/ adj. банáльный

banality /bə'næliti/ n. банáльность

banana /bə'nænə/ n. банáн

band /bænd/ **1.** n. (strip) полосá; (of people) грýппа; (mus.) оркéстр; (ribbon) лéнта **2.** v. ~ together объединиться pf.

bandage /'bændidʒ/ **1.** n. бинт **2.** v. перевязывать impf., перевязáть pf.; бинтовáть impf., за- pf.

bandit /'bændit/ n. бандит

bandstand /'bænd,stænd/ n. эстрáда для оркéстра

bandy-legged /'bændi,legid/ adj. кривонóгий

bane /bein/ n. отрáва

baneful /ˈbeinfəl/ *adj.*
ги́бельный

bang /bæŋ/ **1.** *n.* хлопо́к, уда́р **2.** *v.* хло́пать *impf.*, хло́пнуть *pf.*; ударя́ть *impf.*, уда́рить *pf.*

bangle /ˈbæŋɡəl/ *n.* брасле́т

banish /ˈbæniʃ/ *v.* изгоня́ть *impf.*, изгна́ть *pf.*; **—ment** *n.* изгна́ние

banister /ˈbænəstər/ *n.* пери́ла *pl.*

banjo /ˈbændʒou/ *n.* ба́нджо *neut. indecl.*

bank[1] /bæŋk/ **1.** *n.* (money) банк **2.** *v.* класть де́ньги в банк *impf.*

bank[2] /bæŋk/ **1.** *n.* (river) бе́рег; (slope) на́сыпь *f.* **2.** *v.* (embank) де́лать на́сыпь *impf.*

bankbook /ˈbæŋkˌbuk/ *n.* ба́нковская кни́жка

banker /ˈbæŋkər/ *n.* банки́р

banknote /ˈbæŋkˌnout/ *n.* банкно́та

bankrupt /ˈbæŋkrəpt/ **1.** *adj.* несостоя́тельный **2.** *n.* банкро́т

bankruptcy /ˈbæŋkrəptsi/ *n.* банкро́тство

banner /ˈbænər/ *n.* зна́мя

banquet /ˈbæŋkwit/ *n.* банке́тный *p.* банке́т

banter /ˈbæntər/ **1.** *n.* подшу́чивание **2.** *v.* подшу́чивать *impf.*

baptism /ˈbæptizəm/ *n.* креще́ние

baptismal /bæpˈtizməl/ *adj.* крести́льный

baptize /bæpˈtaiz/ *v.* крести́ть *impf.*; **be —d** крести́ться *impf.*

bar /bar/ **1.** *n.* полоса́, брусо́к; (tavern) бар; (of soap) кусо́к; (of chocolate) пли́тка; (law) адвокату́ра **2.** *v.* прегражда́ть *impf.*, прегради́ть *pf.*; (forbid) запреща́ть *impf.*

barbarian /barˈbeəriən/ **1.** *adj.* ва́рварский **2.** *n.* ва́рвар

barbaric /barˈbærik/, **barbarous** /ˈbarbərəs/ *adj.* ва́рварский

barbarity /barˈbæriti/ *n.* ва́рварство, жесто́кость

barbecue /ˈbarbiˌkyu/ *n.* поджа́ривание еды́, барбекю́ на откры́том огне́ *neut. indecl.*

barbed wire *n.* колю́чая про́волока

barbell /ˈbarˌbel/ *n.* гимнасти́ческая ги́ря

barber /ˈbarbər/ *n.* парикма́хер

bar code *n.* штрихово́й код

bard /bard/ *n.* бард, бая́н

bare /beər/ **1.** *adj.* го́лый **2.** *v.* обнажа́ть *impf.*, -жи́ть *pf.*

barefaced /ˈbeərˌfeist/ *adj.* бессты́дный

barefoot /ˈbeərˌfut/ *adj.* босоно́гий

bareheaded /ˈbeərˌhedid/ *adj.* с непокры́той голово́й

barely /ˈbeərli/ *adv.* едва́, е́ле

bargain /ˈbargən/ **1.** *n.* торго́вая сде́лка; уда́чная поку́пка **2.** *v.* торгова́ться *impf.*, с- *pf.*

barge /bardʒ/ *n.* ба́ржа, ба́рка

baritone /ˈbæriˌtoun/ *n.* барито́н

barium /ˈbæriəm/ *n.* ба́рий

bark[1] /bark/ *n.* (of tree) кора́

bark[2] /bark/ **1.** *n.* (of dog) лай **2.** *v.* ла́ять; га́вкать *impf.*

barley /ˈbarli/ *n.* ячме́нь *m.*

barn /barn/ *n.* амба́р, сара́й

barnacle /ˈbarnəkəl/ *n.* морско́й жёлудь *m.*

barometer /bəˈromitər/ *n.* баро́метр

baron /ˈbærən/ *n.* баро́н

baroness /ˈbærənis/ *n.* бароне́сса

baronet /ˈbærənit/ *n.* бароне́т

baroque /bəˈrouk/ *n.* баро́кко *neut. indecl.*

barracks /ˈbærəks/ *n.* бара́к, каза́рма

barrage /bəˈraʒ/ *n.* плоти́на; загражде́ние

barrel /ˈbærəl/ *n.* бо́чка; (of gun) ствол, ду́ло

barrel-chested *adj.* груда́стый

barrel organ *n.* шарма́нка

barren /ˈbærən/ *adj.* беспло́дный; **—ness** *n.* беспло́дие

barricade /ˈbæriˌkeid/ *n.* баррика́да

barrier /ˈbæriər/ *n.* барье́р

barring /ˈbariŋ/ *prep.* за исключе́нием (+ G), кро́ме (+ G)

barrow[1] /ˈbærou/ *n.* (cart) та́чка

barrow[2] /ˈbærou/ *n.* (tumulus) курга́н

bartender /ˈbarˌtendər/ *n.* буфе́тчик

barter /ˈbartər/ **1.** *n.* ба́ртер **2.** *v.* обме́нивать *impf.*, обменя́ть *pf.*

basalt /bəˈsolt/ **1.** *n.* база́льтовый **2.** *adj.* база́льт

base /beis/ **1.** *adj.* ни́зкий, по́длый **2.** *n.* осно́ва, ба́за **3.** *v.* осно́вывать *impf.*, основа́ть *pf.*

baseball /ˈbeisˌbol/ *n.* бейсбо́л

baseless /'beɪsləs/ *adj.* необосно́ванный

basement /'beɪsmənt/ *n.* подва́л

baseness /'beɪsnɪs/ *n.* по́длость

bash /bæʃ/ *v.* лупи́ть *impf.*

bashful /'bæʃfəl/ *adj.* засте́нчивый, ро́бкий

basic /'beɪsɪk/ *adj.* основно́й

basically /'beɪsɪkli/ *adv.* в основно́м

basil /'bæzəl, 'beɪzəl/ *n.* базили́к

basin /'beɪsən/ *n.* таз; (*geol.*) бассе́йн

basis /'beɪsɪs/ *n.* осно́ва, ба́зис

bask /bæsk/ *v.* гре́ться *impf.*

basket /'bæskɪt/ *n.* корзи́на

basketball /'bæskɪt,bɔl/ *n.* баскетбо́л

bass¹ /bæs/ *n.* (*fish*) о́кунь *m.*

bass² /beɪs/ **1.** *n.* (*mus.*) бас **2.** *adj.* басо́вый

bassoon /bæ'sun/ *n.* фаго́т

bastard /'bæstərd/ *n. Slang.* сво́лочь *m.* (*decl. f.*)

baste /beɪst/ *v.* (*cul.*) полива́ть (жи́ром) *impf.*

bastion /'bæstʃən/ *n.* бастио́н

bat¹ /bæt/ *n.* (*fish*) летучая мышь *f.*

bat² /bæt/ (*baseball*) би́та

batch /bætʃ/ *n.* ку́чка, па́чка

bath /bæθ/ *n.* ва́нна, купа́ние

bathe /beɪð/ *v.* купа́ть(ся) *impf.*

bather /'beɪðər/ *n.* купа́льщик, купа́льщица

bathhouse /'bæθ,haus/ *n.* ба́ня

bathing suit *n.* купа́льник

bathroom /'bæθ,rum/ *n.* ва́нная

bathtub /'bæθ,tʌb/ *n.* ва́нна

baton /bə'tɑn/ *n.* дуби́нка; (*mus.*) дирижёрская па́лочка; (*sports*) эстафе́тная па́лочка

battalion /bə'tælyən/ *n.* батальо́н

batter /'bætər/ **1.** *n.* взби́тое те́сто **2.** *v.* колоти́ть *impf.*

battery /'bætəri/ *n.* батаре́я; (*household battery*) батаре́йка

battle /'bætəl/ **1.** *n.* бой, би́тва, борьба́ **3.** *v.* боро́ться *impf.*

battlefield /'bætl,fild/ *n.* по́ле бо́я

bawdy /'bɔdi/ *adj.* непристо́йный

bawl /bɔl/ *v.* ора́ть *impf.*

bay¹ /beɪ/ *adj.* (*color*) гнедо́й

bay² /beɪ/ *n.* (*geog.*) бу́хта, зали́в

bay³ /beɪ/ **1.** *n.* (*of dog*) лай **2.** *v.* ла́ять *impf.*

bayonet /'beɪənɪt/ *n.* штык

bazaar /bə'zɑr/ *n.* ры́нок, база́р

B.C *abbr.* до на́шей э́ры

be /bi/ *v.* быть; находи́ться *impf.*

beach /bitʃ/ *n.* пляж

beacon /'bikən/ *n.* ба́кен, мая́к

bead /bid/ *n.* бу́синка, ка́пля; **—s** бу́сы *pl.*

beaded /'bidɪd/ *adj.* би́серный

beak /bik/ *n.* клюв

beaker /'bikər/ *n.* ку́бок

beam /bim/ *n.* (*light*) луч; (*wood*) ба́лка

bean /bin/ *n.* боб; фасо́ль *f.*

bear¹ /beər/ *n.* медве́дь *m.*

bear² /beər/ *v.* (*give birth*) рожда́ть *impf.*, роди́ть *impf. & pf.*; (*endure*) терпе́ть *impf.*; (*carry*) носи́ть *indet.*, нести́ *det.*

bearable /'beərəbəl/ *adj.* сно́сный, терпи́мый

beard /bɪərd/ *n.* борода́; **—ed** *adj.* борода́тый

bearer /'beərər/ *n.* носи́тель, предъяви́тель

bearing /'beərɪŋ/ *n.* поведе́ние, отноше́ние; (*tech.*) подши́пник

beast /bist/ *n.* зверь *m.*

beat /bit/ *v.* би́ть(ся) *impf.*, по-*pf.*; (*defeat*) побежда́ть *impf.*, победи́ть *pf.*

beating /'bitɪŋ/ *n.* битьё, бие́ние; (*defeat*) пораже́ние

beautician /byu'tɪʃən/ *n.* косме-то́лог

beautification /,byutəfɪ'keɪʃən/ *n.* украше́ние

beautiful /'byutəfəl/ *adj.* краси́вый, прекра́сный

beautify /'byutə,faɪ/ *v.* украша́ть *impf.*, укра́сить *pf.*

beauty /'byuti/ *n.* красота́; (*person*) краса́вец, краса́вица

beaver /'bivər/ **1.** *adj.* бобро́вый **2.** *n.* бобр

because /bɪ'kɔz/ **1.** *conj.* потому́ что; так как **2.** **~ of** *prep.* из-за (+ *G*)

beckon /'bekən/ *v.* мани́ть *impf.*

become /bɪ'kʌm/ *v.* станови́ться *impf.*, стать *pf.*; (*of dress*) быть к лицу́ (+ *D*) *impf.*

becoming /bɪ'kʌmɪŋ/ *adj.* к лицу́ (+ *D*)

bed /bed/ *n.* крова́ть, посте́ль *f.*; (*river*) дно; **go to ~** ложи́ться спать *impf.*, лечь *pf.*

bedclothes /'bed,klouz/ *n.* посте́льное бельё

bedlam /'bedləm/ *n.* бедла́м

bedraggle /bɪ'dræɡəl/ v.
запа́чкать, замара́ть impf.

bedridden /'bed,rɪdn/ adj.
прико́ванный к посте́ли

bedroom /'bed,rum/ n. спа́льня

bedspread /'bed,spred/ n.
посте́льное покрыва́ло

bee /bi/ n. пчела́

beech /bitʃ/ n. бук

beef /bif/ n. говя́дина

beefburger /'bif,bзrɡər/ n.
ру́бленая котле́та

beefsteak /'bif,steik/ n.
бифште́кс

beehive /'bi,haiv/ n. у́лей

beekeeper /'bi,kipər/ n. пчело-
во́д

beep /bip/ v. сигна́лить impf.

beer /bɪər/ n. пи́во

beet /bit/ n. свекла́

beetle /'bitl/ n. жук

befall /bɪ'fɔl/ v. случа́ться impf.,
-чи́ться pf.

befit /bɪ'fɪt/ v. подоба́ть impf.

before /bɪ'fɔr/ 1. prep. пе́ред
(+ I); до (+ G) 2. adv. ра́ньше;
—**hand** adv. зара́нее

befriend /bɪ'frend/ v. дружи́ться
impf., по- pf.

beg /beɡ/ v. проси́ть impf., поpf.; (entreat) умоля́ть impf.

beggar /'beɡər/ n. ни́щий; —**ly**
adj. ни́щенский, жа́лкий

begin /bɪ'ɡɪn/ v. начина́ть(ся)
impf., нача́ть(ся) pf.

beginner /bɪ'ɡɪnər/ n. начина́ю-
щий

beginning /bɪ'ɡɪnɪŋ/ n. нача́ло

begonia /bɪ'ɡounjə/ n. бего́ния

begrudge /bɪ'ɡrʌdʒ/ v.
зави́довать impf.

beguile /bɪ'ɡail/ v. (charm)
очаро́вывать impf., очарова́ть
pf.

beguiling /bɪ'ɡailɪŋ/ adj.
зама́нчивый

behalf /bɪ'hæf/ n.: **on ~ of** от
и́мени; в интере́сах (+ G)

behave /bɪ'heiv/ v. вести́ себя́,
поступа́ть impf.

behavior /bɪ'heivjər/ n.
поведе́ние

behest /bɪ'hest/ n.: **at the ~ of**
по веле́нию (+ G)

behind /bɪ'haind/ 1. adv. сза́ди,
позади́ 2. prep. за (+ A, I), по-
зади́ (+ G) 3. n. зад

behold /bɪ'hould/ v. ви́деть
impf.

beholden /bɪ'houldən/ pred.
обя́зан (+ D)

beige /beiʒ/ adj. бе́жевый

being /'biɪŋ/ n. (existence)
бытие́, существова́ние; (creature) существо́ f.

Belarus /,byelə'rus/ n. Белару́сь
f.

Belarussian /,byelou'rʌʃən/ 1. n.
(person) белору́с, —ка; (language) белору́сский язы́к 2. adj.
белору́сский

belated /bɪ'leitid/ adj. запо-
зда́лый

belch /beltʃ/ 1. n. отры́жка 2. v.
рыга́ть impf., рыгну́ть pf.

beleaguer /bɪ'liɡər/ v. осажда́ть
impf., осади́ть pf.

belfry /'belfri/ n. колоко́льня

Belgian /'beldʒən/ 1. adj.
бельги́йский 2. n. бельги́ец,
-ги́йка

Belgium /'beldʒəm/ n. Бе́льгия

belie /bɪ'lai/ v. противоре́чить
(+ D) impf.

belief /bɪ'lif/ n. ве́ра; (opinion)
убежде́ние

believable /bɪ'livəbəl/ adj.
вероя́тный; правдоподо́бный

believe /bɪ'liv/ v. ве́рить impf.;
(suppose) полага́ть, ду́мать
impf.

believer /bɪ'livər/ n. ве́рующий

belittle /bɪ'lɪtl/ v. умаля́ть impf.

bell /bel/ n. ко́локол; (doorbell)
звоно́к

belles-lettres /bel'letr/ n. белле-
три́стика

bellhop /'bel,hɒp/ n. посы́льный

bellicose /'beli,kous/ adj.
вои́нственный

bellicosity /,beli'kɒsiti/ n.
вои́нственность, драчли́вость

belligerent /bə'lidʒərənt/ adj.
вою́ющий

bellow /'belou/ v. мыча́ть impf.

bellows /'belouz/ n. мехи́ pl.

belly /'beli/ n. живо́т

belong /bɪ'lɔŋ/ v. принадлежа́ть
((к) + D) impf.

belongings /bɪ'lɔŋiŋz/ n. ве́щи,
принадле́жности pl.

beloved /bɪ'lʌvid, -'lʌvd/ adj.
люби́мый

below /bɪ'lou/ 1. adv. ни́же,
внизу́, вниз 2. prep. под (+ A,
I), ни́же (+ G)

belt /belt/ n. по́яс, реме́нь m.

bemoan /bɪ'moun/ v. опла́ки-
вать impf.

bemuse /bɪ'myuz/ v. смущать *impf.*

bench /bentʃ/ n. скамейка

bend /bend/ 1. n. изгиб; сгиб 2. v. сгибать(ся) *impf.*, согнуть(ся) *pf.*

beneath /bɪ'niθ/ prep. под (*dir.:* + A; *loc.:* + I)

benediction /,benɪ'dɪkʃən/ n. благословение

benefactor /'benə,fæktər/ n. благодетель

benefactress /'benə,fæktrɪs/ n. благодетельница

beneficial /,benə'fɪʃəl/ adj. полезный; выгодный

beneficiary /,benə'fɪʃi,eri/ n. наследник по завещанию

benefit /'benɪfɪt/ 1. n. выгода, польза, (*allowance*) пособие 2. v.t. приносить пользу *impf.*; v.i. извлекать выгоду *impf.*

benevolence /bə'nevələns/ n. благожелательность, щедрость

benevolent /bə'nevələnt/ adj. благотворительный

benign /bɪ'nain/ adj. милостивый; (*med.*) доброкачественный

bent /bent/ n. склонность, наклонность

bequeath /bɪ'kwið/ v. завещать *impf.* & *pf.*

bequest /bɪ'kwest/ n. наследство

berate /bɪ'reit/ v. бранить *impf.*

bereave /bɪ'riv/ v. лишать *impf.*

bereavement /bɪ'rivmənt/ n. тяжёлая утрата

berry /'beri/ n. ягода

berth /bɜrθ/ n. спальное место; (*on ship*) койка

beseech /bɪ'sitʃ/ v. умолять *impf.*

beset /bɪ'set/ v. осаждать *impf.*

beside /bɪ'said/ prep. рядом с (+ I), возле (+ G); ~ oneself вне себя (от + I)

besides /bɪ'saidz/ 1. prep. кроме (+ G) 2. adv. кроме того; к тому же

besiege /bɪ'sidʒ/ v. осаждать *impf.*, осадить *pf.*

besmirch /bɪ'smɜrtʃ/ v. пачкать, чернить *impf.*

besom /'bizəm/ n. веник

best /best/ 1. adj. лучший, самый лучший 2. adv. лучше всего; at ~ в лучшем случае

bestial /'bestʃəl/ adj. зверский

bestiality /,bestʃi'æliti/ n. скотство; зверство

bestow /bɪ'stou/ v. дарить *impf.*, даровать *impf.* & *pf.*

bestseller /'best'selər/ n. бестселлер

bet /bet/ 1. n. пари *neut. indecl.* 2. v.i. держать пари *impf.*

betray /bɪ'trei/ v. предавать *impf.*, предать *pf.*; изменять *impf.*, -нить *pf.*

betrayal /bɪ'treiəl/ n. измена

betroth /bɪ'trouð/ v. обручать *impf.*, -чить *pf.*; —al n. обручение

better /'betər/ 1. adj. лучший 2. adv. лучше 3. v. улучшать *impf.*, улучшить *pf.*; ~ oneself улучшаться *impf.*, улучшиться *pf.*; get ~ поправляться *impf.*, поправиться *pf.*

betterment /'betərmənt/ n. улучшение

between /bɪ'twin/ prep. между (+ I)

bevel /'bevəl/ n. скос

beverage /'bevərɪdʒ/ n. напиток

bevy /'bevi/ n. (*birds*) стая

beware /bɪ'wear/ v. остерегаться *impf.*, остеречься *pf.*

bewilder /bɪ'wildər/ v. сбивать с толку *impf.*, сбить *pf.*

bewilderment /bɪ'wildərmənt/ n. смущение, замешательство

bewitch /bɪ'witʃ/ v. заколдовать; очаровать *impf.*

beyond /bɪ'ɒnd/ prep. за (+ A, I); по ту сторону (+ G)

bezel /'bezəl/ n. остриё

bi- pref. дву(х)-

bias /'baiəs/ n. (*slant*) уклон; (*prejudice*) предубеждение

biased /'baiəst/ adj. (*for*) пристрастный; (*against*) предубеждённый

bib /bib/ n. (*детский*) нагрудник

Bible /'baibəl/ n. Библия

Biblical /'biblɪkəl/ adj. библейский

bibliographer /,bibli'ɒgrəfər/ n. библиограф

bibliography /,bibli'ɒgrəfi/ n. библиография

bicentennial /,baisen'teniəl/ 1. adj. двухсотлетний 2. n. двухсотлетие

biceps /'baiseps/ n. бицепс

bicker /'bikər/ v. спорить, пререкаться *impf.*

bickering /'bɪkərɪŋ/ n. перебра́нка

bicycle /'baisikəl/ n. велосипе́д

bid /bɪd/ 1. n. предложе́ние 2. v. предлага́ть (це́ну) impf.

bidder /'bɪdər/ n. покупщи́к

bidding /'bɪdɪŋ/ n. предложе́ние цены́

bide /baid/ v.: ~ one's time ждать благоприя́тного слу́чая impf.

biennial /bai'ɛniəl/ adj. дву(х)ле́тний

bier /bɪər/ n. катафа́лк

bifocals /bai'foukəlz/ n. бифока́льные очки́

big /bɪg/ adj. большо́й, кру́пный

bigamist /'bɪgəmɪst/ n. двоежёнец, двумужница

bigamy /'bɪgəmi/ n. (of man) двоежёнство; (of woman) двоему́жие

bigmouth /'bɪg,mauθ/ n. Colloq. болту́н

bigot /'bɪgət/ n. фана́тик, изуве́р

bigotry /'bɪgətri/ n. фанати́зм

bigwig /'bɪg,wɪg/ n. Colloq. больша́я ши́шка

bike /baik/ n. велосипе́д

biker /'baikər/ n. велосипеди́ст; мотоцикли́ст

bikini /bɪ'kini/ n. бики́ни neut. indecl.

bilateral /bai'lætərəl/ adj. двусторо́нний

bile /bail/ n. желчь f.

bilingual /bai'lɪŋgwəl/ adj. двуязы́чный

bill[1] /bɪl/ n. (account) счёт; (money) банкно́та

bill[2] /bɪl/ n. (bird) клюв

billboard /'bɪl,bɔrd/ n. доска́ для афи́ш

billet /'bɪlɪt/ 1. n. кварти́ра 2. v. расквartíровать pf.

billiards /'bɪlyərdz/ n. билья́рд

billion /'bɪlyən/ n. миллиа́рд

billow /'bɪlou/ 1. n. вал 2. v. вздыма́ться impf.

billy goat /'bɪli/ n. козёл

bimonthly /bai'mʌnθli/ 1. adj. двухмеся́чный 2. adv. раз в два ме́сяца

bin /bɪn/ n. я́щик; за́кром

binary /'bainəri/ adj. двойно́й, сдво́енный

bind /baind/ v. свя́зывать impf., связа́ть pf.; (book) переплета́ть impf., переплести́ pf.

binding /'baindɪŋ/ n. переплёт

binge /bɪndʒ/ n. кутёж

binoculars /bə'nɒkyələrz/ n. бино́кль pl.

biodegradable /ˌbaioudɪ'greidəbəl/ adj. разлага́емый микроорганизмами

biographer /bai'ɒgrəfər/ n. био́граф

biographical /ˌbaiə'græfikəl/ adj. биографи́ческий

biography /bai'ɒgrəfi/ n. биогра́фия

biological /ˌbaiə'lɒdʒikəl/ adj. биологи́ческий

biologist /bai'ɒlədʒist/ n. био́лог

biology /bai'ɒlədʒi/ n. биоло́гия

biopsy /'baiɒpsi/ n. биопсия

bipartisan /bai'partəzən/ adj. двупарти́йный

bipartite /bai'partait/ adj. двусторо́нний

birch /bɜrtʃ/ 1. adj. берёзовый 2. n. берёза

bird /bɜrd/ n. пти́ца

bird lover n. люби́тель птиц

bird of prey n. хи́щная пти́ца

bird's-eye view n. вид с пти́чьего полёта

birth /bɜrθ/ n. рожде́ние; (giving birth) ро́ды pl. **give** ~ **to** v. рожда́ть impf., роди́ть pf.

birth certificate n. ме́трика

birth control n. противоза́ча́точные ме́ры pl.

birthday /'bɜrθ,dei/ n. день рожде́ния m.

birthmark /'bɜrθ,mark/ n. роди́мое пятно́, ро́динка

birthright /'bɜrθ,rait/ n. пра́во по рожде́нию

biscuit /'bɪskɪt/ n. кекс

bisexual /bai'sɛkʃuəl/ adj. двупо́лый; бисексуа́льный

bishop /'bɪʃəp/ n. епи́скоп; (chess) слон

bit[1] /bɪt/ n. кусо́чек

bit[2] /bɪt/ n. (mech.) сверло́; (horse) удила́ pl.

bitch /bɪtʃ/ n. су́ка

bite /bait/ 1. n. уку́с; (morsel) кусо́чек 2. v. куса́ть impf., укуси́ть pf.

biting /'baitɪŋ/ adj. е́дкий

bitter /'bɪtər/ adj. го́рький

bitterness /'bɪtərnɪs/ n. го́речь f.

bitumen /'baitumən/ n. би́тум

biweekly /bai'wikli/ adj. двухнеде́льный

bizarre /bɪ'zar/ adj. стра́нный

black /blæk/ adj. чёрный

blackberry /'blæk,beri/ *n.* ежевика

blackbird /'blæk,bɜrd/ *n.* (чёрный) дрозд

blackboard /'blæk,bɔrd/ *n.* доска

black currant *n.* чёрная смородина

blacken /'blækən/ *v.t.* чернить *impf.*, за- *pf.*; *v.i.* чернеть *impf.*, за- *pf.*

blackguard /'blægɑrd/ *n.* мерзавец

blackhead /'blæk,hed/ *n.* угорь *m.*

blacklist /'blæk,lɪst/ *n.* чёрный список

blackmail /'blæk,meil/ **1.** *n.* шантаж **2.** *v.* шантажировать *impf.*

black market *n.* чёрный рынок

blackout /'blæk,aut/ *n.* потеря сознания

blacksmith /'blæk,smɪθ/ *n.* кузнец

bladder /'blædər/ *n.* пузырь *m.*

blade /bleid/ *n.* лезвие; (*of grass*) травинка; (*oar*) лопасть *f.*

blame /bleim/ **1.** *v.* порицать, винить (в + P) *impf.* **2.** *n.* порицание; вина

blameless /'bleimlɪs/ *adj.* невинный; безупречный

blanch /blæntʃ/ *v.t.* белить *impf.*; *v.i.* бледнеть *impf.*, по- *pf.*

bland /blænd/ *adj.* бесцветный

blandishment /'blændɪʃmənt/ *n.* уговаривание

blank /blæŋk/ **1.** *adj.* пустой, чистый; (*wall*) глухой; (*cartridge*) холостой **2.** *n.* (*form*) бланк

blanket /'blæŋkɪt/ *n.* одеяло

blare /bleər/ **1.** *n.* рёв **2.** *v.* громко трубить *impf.*

blaspheme /blæs'fim/ *v.* богохульствовать *impf.*

blasphemous /'blæsfəməs/ *adj.* богохульный

blasphemy /'blæsfəmi/ *n.* богохульство

blast /blæst/ **1.** *n.* порыв ветра; взрыв **2.** *v.* взрывать *impf.*, взорвать *pf.*

blast furnace *n.* домна

blatant /'bleitnt/ *adj.* явный

blaze /bleiz/ **1.** *n.* пламя; блеск **2.** *v.* гореть; пылать *impf.*

blazer /'bleizər/ *n.* блейзер

bleach /blitʃ/ **1.** *v.* отбеливать

(-ся) *impf.*, отбелить(ся) *pf.* **2.** *n.* хлорка

bleak /blik/ *adj.* унылый

bleary-eyed /'bliəri,aid/ *adj.* (*with sleep*) с заспанными глазами

bleat /blit/ *v.* блеять *impf.*

bleed /blid/ *v.* истекать кровью *impf.*; (*wound*) кровоточить *impf.*

bleeding /'blidɪŋ/ *n.* кровотечение

blemish /'blemɪʃ/ *n.* пятно

blend /blend/ **1.** *n.* смесь *f.* **2.** *v.* смешивать(ся) *impf.*, смешать(ся) *pf.*

blender /'blendər/ *n.* (*cul.*) кухонный комбайн

bless /bles/ *v.* благословлять *impf.*, -вить *pf.*; **—ed** *adj.* священный; (*blissful*) блаженный; **—ing** *n.* благословение; (*benefit*) благо

blight /blait/ *n.* гибель *f.*

blind /blaind/ **1.** *adj.* слепой **2.** *v.* ослеплять *impf.*, -пить *pf.*

blinders /'blaindərz/ *n.* шоры *pl.*

blindfold /'blaind,fould/ *v.* завязывать глаза *impf.*

blindness /'blaindnɪs/ *n.* слепота

blink /blɪŋk/ *v.* мигать *impf.*, мигнуть *pf.*; мерцать *impf.*

blinker /'blɪŋkər/ *n.* мигалка

bliss /blɪs/ *n.* блаженство

blissful /'blɪsfəl/ *adj.* блаженный

blithe /blaið/ *adj.* весёлый, жизнерадостный

blitz /blɪts/ *n.* бомбёжка

blizzard /'blɪzərd/ *n.* метель *f.*

bloat /blout/ *v.* раздуваться *impf.*, -дуться *pf.*; **—ed** *adj.* вздутый

blob /blɒb/ *n.* капля

bloc /blɒk/ *n.* (*polit.*) блок

block /blɒk/ **1.** *n.* глыба; (*wood*) чурбан; (*street*) квартал **2.** *v.* загородить *pf.*

blockade /blɒ'keid/ **1.** *n.* блокада; **2.** *v.* блокировать *impf.*

blockage /'blɒkidʒ/ *n.* затор; засорение

blockhead /'blɒk,hed/ *n.* болван

blond(e) /blɒnd/ **1.** *adj.* белокурый **2.** *n.* блондин, —ка

blood /blʌd/ *n.* кровь *f.*

bloodbath /'blʌd,bæθ/ *n.* резня

blood donor *n.* донор

bloodhound /'blʌd,haund/ *n.* бладхаунд

blood poisoning *n.* заражéние крóви

blood pressure *n.* кровянóе давлéние

blood relation *n.* крóвный рóдственник

bloodshed /'blʌd,ʃed/ *n.* кровопролúтие

bloodthirsty /'blʌd,θɜrsti/ *adj.* кровожáдный

bloody /'blʌdi/ *adj.* кровáвый

bloom /blum/ **1.** *n.* расцвéт **2.** *v.* цвестú *impf.*

blossom /'blɒsəm/ *n.* цветóк

blot /blɒt/ *n.* пятнó; кля́кса

blotch /blɒtʃ/ *n.* пятнó

blotting paper /'blɒtɪŋ/ промокáтельная бумáга

blouse /blaʊs/ *n.* блýза; кóфточка

blow¹ /bloʊ/ *n.* удáр; **with one ~** однúм удáром; срáзу

blow² /bloʊ/ *v.* дуть *impf.*; **~ out** тушúть *impf.*, по- *pf.*; **~ up** взрывáть(ся) *impf.*, взорвáть(ся) *pf.*

blow-dry *v.* сушúть фéном *impf.*

blowtorch /'bloʊ,tɔrtʃ/ *n.* пая́льная лáмпа

blubber /'blʌbər/ *n.* вóрвань *f.*

bludgeon /'blʌdʒən/ *n.* дубúнка

blue /blu/ *adj.* сúний, голубóй

bluebell /'blu,bel/ *n.* колокóльчик

blueberry /'blu,beri/ *n.* чернúка

bluebird /'blu,bɜrd/ *n.* слáвка

blueprint /'blu,prɪnt/ *n.* сúнька

bluff¹ /blʌf/ **1.** *n.* блеф, обмáн **2.** *v.* блефовáть *impf.*

bluff² /blʌf/ *n.* (cliff) отвéсный бéрег

blunder /'blʌndər/ **1.** *n.* прóмах **2.** *v.* промахнýться *pf.*

blunt /blʌnt/ *adj.* тупóй; (frank) прямóй

blurred /blɜrd/ *adj.* расплы́вчатый

blurt /blɜrt/ *v.* выбáлтывать *impf.*

blush /blʌʃ/ *v.* краснéть *impf.*, по- *pf.*

bluster /'blʌstər/ *n.* рёв, шум

boar /bɔr/ *n.* бóров; (wild) кабáн

board /bɔrd/ **1.** *n.* доскá; (meals) стол; (administrative) совéт **2.** *v.* сесть (в, на + A) *pf.*

boarder /'bɔrdər/ *n.* пансионéр, —ка; квартирáнт, —ка

boarding house /'bɔrdɪŋ/ *n.* пансиóн

boarding school *n.* шкóла-интернáт

boast /boʊst/ *v.* хвáстаться *impf.*, по- *pf.*

boaster /'boʊstər/ *n.* хвастýн, —ья

boastful /'boʊstfəl/ *adj.* хвастлúвый

boat /boʊt/ *n.* лóдка; (ship) сýдно, корáбль *m.*

boatswain /'boʊsən/ *n.* бóцман

bob /bɒb/ *v.* подпрýгивать *impf.*; кóротко стричь *impf.*

bobbin /'bɒbɪn/ *n.* катýшка

bobsled /'bɒb,sled/ *n.* бобслéй

bode /boʊd/ *v.* предвещáть, сулúть *impf.*

bodice /'bɒdɪs/ *n.* корсáж, лиф

bodily /'bɒdɪli/ *adj.* телéсный, физúческий

body /'bɒdi/ *n.* тéло; (corpse) труп; (of car) кýзов

bodybuilder /'bɒdi,bɪldər/ *n.* (sport) культурúст, —ка

bodyguard /'bɒdi,gɑrd/ *n.* лúчная охрáна; телохранúтель

bog /bɒg/ *n.* болóто

boggy /'bɒgi/ *adj.* болóтистый

bogus /'boʊgəs/ *adj.* поддéльный

boil¹ /bɔɪl/ *v.t.* кипятúть; варúть *impf.*; *v.i.* кипéть; варúться *impf.*

boil² /bɔɪl/ *n.* (med.) фурýнкул

boiled /bɔɪld/ *adj.* (food) варёный; **~ water** кипятóк

boiler /'bɔɪlər/ *n.* котёл

boiler room *n.* котéльная

boisterous /'bɔɪstərəs/ *adj.* бýйный; шумлúвый

bold /boʊld/ *adj.* смéлый; **—ness** *n.* смéлость

bold type *n.* жúрный шрифт

Bolshevik /'boʊlʃəvɪk/ **1.** *adj.* большевúстский **2.** *n.* большевúк

bolster /'boʊlstər/ **1.** *n.* вáлик **2.** *v.* подпирáть *impf.*, —перéть *pf.*

bolt /boʊlt/ **1.** *n.* засóв; (lightning) удáр мóлнии **2.** *v.* запирáть на засóв *impf.*; (flee) брóситься *pf.*

bomb /bɒm/ **1.** *n.* бóмба **2.** *v.* бомбúть *impf.*

bombard /bɒm'bɑrd/ *v.* (mil., phys.) бомбардировáть *impf.*

bombardment /bɒm'bɑrdmənt/ *n.* бомбардирóвка

bombastic /bɒm'bæstik/ adj. напы́щенный, велеречи́вый

bomber /'bɒmər/ n. (aircraft) бомбардиро́вщик

bomb shelter n. бомбоубе́жище

bond /bɒnd/ n. связь f.; pl. (econ.) облига́ция; (shackles) око́вы

bondage /'bɒndidʒ/ n. ра́бство

bondholder /'bɒnd,houldər/ n. владе́лец облига́ций

bone /boun/ n. кость f.

bonfire /'bɒn,faiər/ n. костёр

bonnet /'bɒnit/ n. чёпчик

bonus /'bounəs/ n. пре́мия

bony /'bouni/ adj. кости́стый; костля́вый

boo /bu/ v. осви́стывать impf.

booby trap /'bubi/ n. лову́шка

book /buk/ 1. adj. кни́жный 2. n. кни́га 3. v. (reserve) брони́ровать; зака́зывать impf.

bookbinder /'buk,baindər/ n. переплётчик

bookcase /'buk,keis/ n. кни́жный шкаф

booking /'bukiŋ/ n. бро́ня

bookish /'bukiʃ/ adj. кни́жный

bookkeeper /'buk,kipər/ n. бухга́лтер

bookkeeping /'buk,kipiŋ/ n. бухга́лтерия

booklet /'buklit/ n. брошю́ра

bookmaker /'buk,meikər/ n. (sports) букме́кер

bookseller /'buk,selər/ n. продаве́ц книг; (old books) букини́ст

bookstore /'buk,stor/ n. кни́жный магази́н

boom /bum/ 1. n. (sound) гул 2. v. греме́ть impf.; (econ.) бы́стро расти́ impf.

boon /bun/ n. бла́го, сча́стье

boor /bor/ n. хам

boorish /'buriʃ/ adj. грубый

boost /bust/ v. повыша́ть impf.

boot /but/ n. сапо́г

bootee /'buti/ n. (baby's) пине́тка

booth /buθ/ n. бу́дка, кио́ск

booty /'buti/ n. добы́ча

booze /buz/ n. Colloq. спиртно́е

border /'bordər/ 1. n. грани́ца 2. v. грани́чить (c + I) impf.

borderline /'bordər,lain/ n. грани́ца

bore¹ /bor/ 1. n. (hole) дыра́; (gun) кана́л ствола́ 2. v. сверли́ть impf.; про- pf.

bore² /bor/ n. (thing) ску́ка; (person) ску́чный челове́к

bored /bord/ pred.: **I am ~** мне ску́чно, мне надое́ло

boredom /'bordəm/ n. ску́ка

boring /'boriŋ/ adj. ску́чный

born /born/ adj. прирождённый; **be ~** роди́ться impf. & pf.

borough /'bərou/ n. райо́н

borrow /'bɒrou/ v. (adopt) заи́мствовать impf.; (receive as loan) занима́ть impf., заня́ть pf.

borrower /'bɒrouər/ n. заёмщик; (in library) абоне́нт, чита́тель

borscht /borʃt/ n. борщ

bosom /'buzəm/ n. грудь f.; па́зуха

boss /bos/ 1. n. нача́льник 2. v. кома́ндовать, управля́ть impf.

bossy /'bosi/ adj. нача́льственный

botanical /bə'tænikəl/ adj. ботани́ческий

botanist /'bɒtnist/ n. бота́ник

botany /'bɒtni/ n. бота́ника

both /bouθ/ pron., adj. о́ба m. & neut., о́бе f.; **~ ... and...** и... и...

bother /'bɒðər/ v. (worry) беспоко́ить impf.; (pester) меша́ть impf.

bothersome /'bɒðərsəm/ adj. надое́дливый

bottle /'bɒtl/ 1. n. буты́лка 2. v. разлива́ть по буты́лкам impf.

bottleneck /'bɒtl,nek/ n. го́рлышко; Fig. у́зкий прохо́д

bottom /'bɒtəm/ n. дно, ни́жняя часть f.; **—less** adj. безцо́нный

boudoir /'budwar/ n. будуа́р

bough /bau/ n. сук

boulder /'bouldər/ n. валу́н

bounce /bauns/ v. отска́кивать impf., отскочи́ть pf.

bouncer /'baunsər/ n. Colloq. вышиба́ла m. & f.

bouncy /'baunsi/ adj. упру́гий

bound¹ /baund/ 1. n.pl. грани́ца, преде́л 2. v. ограни́чивать impf., ограни́чить pf.

bound² /baund/ adj. pred.: **be ~ for** направля́ться impf., напра́виться pf.

boundary /'baundəri/ n. грани́ца

boundless /'baundlis/ adj. безграни́чный; беспреде́льный

bountiful /'bauntəfəl/ adj. (person) ще́дрый; (ample) оби́льный

bounty /'baunti/ n. щедрость; (reward) награда

bouquet /bou'kei, bu-/ n. букет

bourgeois /bur'ʒwa/ **1.** adj. буржуазный **2.** n. буржуа neut. indecl.

bourgeoisie /,burʒwa'zi/ n. буржуазия

bout /baut/ n. схватка; (of illness) приступ

boutique /bu'tik/ n. модная лавка

bow¹ /bau/ **1.** n. поклон **2.** v. кланяться impf., поклониться pf.

bow² /bou/ n. (archery) лук; (ribbon) бант; (mus.) смычок

bow³ /bau/ n. (ship) нос

bowels /'bauəlz/ n. кишки, внутренности, недра pl.

bower /'bauər/ n. (arbor) беседка

bowl¹ /boul/ n. миска, (sport) кубок

bowl² /boul/ v. играть в шары or в кегли impf.

bowlegged /'bou,legid/ adj. кривоногий

bowling /'bouliŋ/ n. кегли pl.

box¹ /bɒks/ n. коробка, ящик; (theat.) ложа; ~ **office** касса

box² /bɒks/ v.n. боксировать impf.

boxer /'bɒksər/ n. боксёр

boxing /'bɒksiŋ/ n. бокс

boy /bɔi/ n. мальчик

boycott /'bɔikɒt/ **1.** n. бойкот **2.** v. бойкотировать impf. & pf.

boyfriend /'bɔi,frend/ n. приятель

boyhood /'bɔihud/ n. отрочество

boyish /'bɔiiʃ/ adj. мальчишеский

bra /bra/ n. Colloq. лифчик

brace /breis/ **1.** n. скрепа **2.** v. скреплять impf., -пить pf.

bracelet /'breislit/ n. браслет

bracket /'brækit/ n. (printing) скобка; (support) кронштейн

brag /bræg/ v. хвастаться impf.

braggart /'brægərt/ n. хвастун

braid /breid/ **1.** n. коса **2.** v. заплетать impf., заплести pf.

Braille /breil/ n. шрифт Брайля

brain /brein/ n. мозг; рассудок

brainstorm /'brein,stɔrm/ n. блестящая идея

brainwash /'brein,wɒʃ/ v. забивать мозги impf.; **—ing** n. забивание мозгов

braise /breiz/ v. тушить impf.

brake /breik/ **1.** n. тормоз **2.** v. тормозить impf.; за- pf.

bramble /'bræmbəl/ n. ежевика

bran /bræn/ n. отруби pl.

branch /bræntʃ/ **1.** n. ветка; (subject) отрасль f.; (department) отделение **2.** adj. филиальный **3.** v. разветвляться impf., -виться pf.

brand /brænd/ **1.** n. (trademark) фабричная марка; (mus.) клеймо **2.** v. клеймить impf., за- pf.

brandish /'brændiʃ/ v. махать, размахивать (+ I) impf.

brand-name adj. фирменный

brandy /'brændi/ n. коньяк

brass /bræs/ n. латунь, жёлтая медь f.

brass band n. духовой оркестр

brassiere /brə'zɪər/ n. бюстгальтер

brat /bræt/ n. озорник

bravado /brə'vadou/ n. бравада

brave /breiv/ adj. храбрый

bravery /'breivəri/ n. храбрость

bravo /'bravou/ interj. браво!

brawl /brɔl/ **1.** n. шумная ссора, скандал **2.** v. скандалить impf.

brawn /brɔn/ n. мускулы pl.

bray /brei/ n. крик осла

brazen /'breizən/ adj. медный, латунный; Fig. бесстыдный

brazier /'breizər/ n. жаровня

breach /britʃ/ n. (break) пролом, (of law, etiquette, etc.) нарушение

bread /bred/ **1.** n. хлеб **2.** adj. хлебный

breadcrumb /'bred,krʌm/ n. крошка хлеба; pl. сухари

breadth /bredθ/ n. ширина

breadwinner /'bred,winər/ n. кормилец, -лица

break /breik/ **1.** n. разрыв, (pause) перерыв; пауза **2.** v. ломать(ся) impf., с- pf.; разбивать impf.; (violate) нарушать impf.; ~ **into** вламываться impf., вломиться pf.; ~ **through** прорываться impf., прорваться pf.

breakable /'breikəbəl/ adj. ломкий

breakage /'breikidʒ/ n. поломка

breakdown /'breik,daun/ n. (mech.) поломка; (med.) нервный срыв

breaker /'breikər/ n. бурун; (elec.) прерыватель

breakers /'breikərz/ n. прибой

breakfast /'brekfəst/ **1.** n. завтрак **2.** v. завтракать impf., по- pf.

break-in n. взлом

breakneck /'breik,nek/ adj.: **at ~ speed** adv. сломя голову

breakthrough /'breik,θru:/ n. (mil.) прорыв; (tech.) шаг вперёд

breakup /'breik,ʌp/ n. распад

breakwater /'breik,wɔtər/ n. волнорез

breast /brest/ n. грудь f.

breath /breθ/ n. дыхание

breathe /bri:ð/ v. дышать impf.

breathing /'bri:ðiŋ/ n. дыхание

breathless /'breθlis/ adj. запыхавшийся

breeches /'brit ʃiz/ n. бриджи pl.

breed /bri:d/ **1.** n. порода **2.** v.t. выводить, разводить impf.; v.i. размножаться impf.

breeder /'bri:dər/ n. животновод

breeding /'bri:diŋ/ n. разведение

breeze /bri:z/ n. лёгкий ветерок

breezy /'bri:zi/ adj. свежий; живой

brethren /'breðrin/ n. братья, собратья pl.

brevity /'breviti/ n. краткость

brew /bru:/ v. варить impf.

brewer /'bru:ər/ n. пивовар

brewery /'bru:əri/ n. пивзавод

bribable /'braibəbəl/ adj. подкупный, продажный

bribe /braib/ **1.** n. взятка, подкуп **2.** v. подкупать impf., -пить pf.

bribery /'braibəri/ n. взяточничество; подкуп

bric-a-brac /'brikə,bræk/ n. безделушки pl.

brick /brik/ **1.** n. кирпич **2.** adj. кирпичный

bricklayer /'brik,leiər/ n. каменщик

bridal /'braidl/ adj. свадебный

bride /braid/ n. невеста

bridegroom /'braid,grum/ n. жених

bridge¹ /bridʒ/ n. мост

bridge² /bridʒ/ n. (cards) бридж

bridle /'braidl/ **1.** n. узда **2.** v.t. обуздывать impf.

brief /bri:f/ **1.** adj. короткий; (concise) краткий **2.** n. инструкция

briefcase /'bri:f,keis/ n. портфель m.

briefing /'bri:fiŋ/ n. инструктаж

briefness /'bri:fnis/ n. краткость

brier /braiər/ n. (rose) шиповник

brigade /bri'geid/ n. бригада

brigadier /,brigə'diər/ n. бригадир

brigand /'brigənd/ n. разбойник

bright /brait/ adj. яркий

brighten /'braitn/ v. проясняться impf., -ниться pf.

brightness /'braitnis/ n. яркость

brilliance /'briliəns/ n. блеск

brilliant /'briliənt/ adj. блестящий

brim /brim/ n. край; (hat) поля pl.

brine /brain/ n. рассол

bring /briŋ/ v. (carry) приносить impf., принести pf.; (lead) приводить impf.; **~ up** воспитывать impf.

brink /briŋk/ n. край

brisk /brisk/ adj. живой, проворный; (air) свежий

brisket /'briskit/ n. грудинка

bristle /'brisəl/ **1.** n. щетина **2.** v. щетиниться impf., о- pf.

British /'britiʃ/ adj. английский; британский

Britisher /'britiʃər/ n. британец, -танка; англичанин, -чанка

brittle /'britl/ adj. хрупкий

broad /brɔ:d/ adj. широкий

broadcast /'brɔ:d,kæst/ **1.** n. передача **2.** v. передавать по радио (по телевидению) impf.

broaden /'brɔ:dn/ v. расширять(ся) impf., расширить(ся) pf.

broad-minded adj. с широкими взглядами

brocade /brou'keid/ n. парча

broccoli /'brɔkəli/ n. брокколи pl. indecl.

brochure /brou'ʃur/ n. брошюра

broil /brɔil/ v. жарить(ся) impf.

broiler /'brɔilər/ n. бройлер

broke /brouk/ pred. разорённый

broken /'broukən/ adj. разбитый

broker /'broukər/ n. маклер

brokerage /'broukəridʒ/ n. (fee) комиссия; (business) маклерство

bronchitis /brɔŋ'kaitis/ n. бронхит

bronze /brɔnz/ **1.** n. бронза **2.** adj. бронзовый

brooch /brout ʃ, brut ʃ/ n. брошь f.

brood /bru:d/ n. выводок

broody /'brudi/ *adj.* уны́лый

brook¹ /bruk/ *n.* ручеёк

brook² /bruk/ *v.* терпе́ть *impf.*

broom /brum/ *n.* метла́

broth /brɔθ/ *n.* бульо́н

brothel /'brɔθəl/ *n.* дом терпи́мости

brother /'brʌðər/ *n.* брат

brotherhood /'brʌðər,hud/ *n.* бра́тство

brother-in-law *n.* (*husband's brother*) де́верь *m.*; (*sister's husband*) зять *m.*; (*wife's brother*) шу́рин

brotherly /'brʌðərli/ *adj.* бра́тский

brow /brau/ *n.* бровь *f.*; лоб

brown /braun/ *adj.* кори́чневый

browse /brauz/ *v.* (*in a book*) листа́ть (кни́гу) *impf.*

bruise /bruz/ **1.** *n.* синя́к **2.** *v.* ушиба́ть *impf.,* -би́ть *pf.*

brunet(te) /bru'net/ *n.* брюне́т, —ка

brunt /brʌnt/ *n.* гла́вный уда́р; (*weight*) основна́я тя́жесть

brush /brʌʃ/ **1.** *n.* щётка; (*paint*) кисть *f.* **2.** *v.* чи́стить щёткой *impf.*

brushwood /'brʌʃ,wud/ *n.* за́росли *pl.*; (*dry branches*) хво́рост

brusque /brʌsk/ *adj.* ре́зкий

Brussels sprouts /'brʌsəlz/ *n.* брюссе́льская капуста

brutal /'brutḷ/ *adj.* жесто́кий

brutality /bru'tæliti/ *n.* жесто́кость

brute /brut/ *n.* ското́ина *m. & f.*

bubble /'bʌbəl/ *n.* пузы́рь *m.*

bubbly /'bʌbli/ *adj.* пе́нящийся

buck¹ /bʌk/ *n.* саме́ц

buck² /bʌk/ *v.* брыка́ться *impf.*

bucket /'bʌkit/ *n.* ведро́

buckle /'bʌkəl/ **1.** *n.* пря́жка **2.** *v.* застёгивать пря́жку *impf.*

buckwheat /'bʌk,wit/ *n.* гречи́ха; (*cul.*) гре́чневая крупа́

bud /bʌd/ *n.* по́чка

Buddha /'budə/ *n.* Бу́дда

Buddhism /'budizəm/ *n.* будди́зм

Buddhist /'budist/ **1.** *n.* будди́ст **2.** *adj.* будди́йский

budge /bʌdʒ/ *v.* шевели́ть(ся) *impf.,* по- *pf.*

budget /'bʌdʒit/ *n.* бюдже́т

buffalo /'bʌfə,lou/ *n.* буйвол

buffer /'bʌfər/ *n.* буфер

buffet¹ /bə'fei/ *n.* буфе́т

buffet² /'bʌfit/ *n.* (*blow*) уда́р

buffoon /bə'fun/ *n.* фигля́р

bug /bʌg/ *n.* бука́шка; (*virus*) ви́рус

bugle /'byugəl/ *n.* горн, рог

build /bild/ **1.** *v.* стро́ить *impf.,* по- *pf.* **2.** *n.* телосложе́ние

builder /'bildər/ *n.* строи́тель

building /'bildiŋ/ *n.* зда́ние; (*construction*) построе́ние **2.** *adj.* строи́тельный

build-up *n.* наро́ст; (*preparation*) подгото́вка

bulb /bʌlb/ *n.* лу́ковица; (*lamp*) электри́ческая ла́мпочка

bulbous /'bʌlbəs/ *adj.* лу́ковичный

Bulgaria /bʌl'geəriə/ *n.* Болга́рия

Bulgarian /bʌl'geəriən/ **1.** *adj.* болга́рский **2.** *n.* болга́рин; -га́рка

bulge /bʌldʒ/ **1.** *n.* вы́пуклость **2.** *v.* выпя́чиваться *impf.*

bulging /'bʌldʒiŋ/ *adj.* разбу́хший; вы́пуклый

bulk /bʌlk/ *n.* объём; ма́сса; бо́льшая часть *f.*

bulky /'bʌlki/ *adj.* объёмистый

bull /bul/ *n.* бык **2.** *adj.* бы́чий

bulldog /'bul,dɔg/ *n.* бульдо́г

bulldozer /'bul,douzər/ *n.* бульдо́зер

bullet /'bulit/ *n.* пу́ля

bulletin /'bulitṇ/ *n.* бюллете́нь *m.*

bulletin board *n.* доска́ объявле́ний

bulletproof /'bulit,pruf/ *adj.* пуленепробива́емый

bullfinch /'bul,fintʃ/ *n.* снеги́рь *m.*

bullion /'bulyən/ *n.* сли́ток зо́лота *or* серебра́

bullock /'bulək/ *n.* вол

bully /'buli/ *n.* зади́ра *m. & f.*

bulrush /'bul,rʌʃ/ *n.* камы́ш

bum /bʌm/ *n.* безде́льник

bumblebee /'bʌmbəl,bi/ *n.* шмель *m.*

bump /bʌmp/ **1.** *n.* (*collision*) столкнове́ние; (*swelling*) ши́шка **2.** *v.* сту́кнуть(ся) *pf.*

bumper /'bʌmpər/ *n.* ба́мпер

bumpkin /'bʌmpkin/ *n.* дереве́нщина *m. & f.*

bumpy /'bʌmpi/ *adj.* неро́вный

bun /bʌn/ *n.* бу́лочка

bunch /bʌntʃ/ **1.** *n.* свя́зка,

пучóк **2.** *v.* собирáть в пучóк *impf.*

bungalow /ˈbʌŋgəˌlou/ *n.* бýнгало *neut. indecl.*

bungle /ˈbʌŋgəl/ *v.t.* напýтать *pf.*

bunk /bʌŋk/ *n.* кóйка

bunker /ˈbʌŋkər/ *n.* бýнкер

bunting /ˈbʌntɪŋ/ *n.* флáги *pl.*

buoy /ˈbui/ *n.* бáкен, буй

buoyancy /ˈbɔiənsi/ *n.* плавýчесть

buoyant /ˈbɔiənt/ *adj.* плавýчий; *Fig.* бóдрый

burden /ˈbɜrdn/ **1.** *n.* брéмя *neut.* **2.** *v.* обременять *impf.*, -нить *pf.*

burdock /ˈbɜrdɒk/ *n.* лопýх

bureau /ˈbyurou/ *n.* бюрó *neut. indecl.*, контóра; (*furniture*) комóд

bureaucracy /byuˈrɒkrəsi/ *n.* бюрократия

burglar /ˈbɜrglər/ *n.* взлóмщик

burglary /ˈbɜrgləri/ *n.* крáжа со взлóмом

burial /ˈberiəl/ *n.* погребéние

burlap /ˈbɜrlæp/ *n.* холстина

burlesque /bərˈlesk/ *n.* бурлéск

burn /bɜrn/ *v.t.* жечь; сжигáть *impf.*, сжечь *pf.*; *v.i.* гореть *impf.*, с- *pf.*

burner /ˈbɜrnər/ *n.* горéлка

burning /ˈbɜrnɪŋ/ *adj.* горящий

burnish /ˈbɜrnɪʃ/ *v.* полировáть *impf.*; от- *pf.*

burp /bɜrp/ *v. Colloq.* рыгáть *impf.*

burrow /ˈbɜrou/ **1.** *n.* норá **2.** *v.* рыться *impf.*

bursar /ˈbɜrsər/ *n.* казначéй

burst /bɜrst/ *v.* взорвáться *pf.*

bury /ˈberi/ *v.* хоронить *impf.*, по- *pf.*; (*hide*) зарывáть *impf.*

Buryat /ˈbur'yat/ *n.* бурят, —ка

bus /bʌs/ **1.** *n.* автóбус **2.** *adj.* автóбусный

bush /buʃ/ *n.* кустáрник

bushy /ˈbuʃi/ *adj.* пушистый

business /ˈbɪznɪs/ *n.* дéло; делá *pl.*; **on ~** по дéлу

businesslike /ˈbɪznɪsˌlaik/ *adj.* деловóй

businessman /ˈbɪznɪsˌmæn/ *n.* делéц, бизнесмéн

bust /bʌst/ *n.* бюст

bus terminal *n.* автовокзáл

bustle /ˈbʌsəl/ **1.** *n.* суматóха; суетá **2.** *v.* суетиться *impf.*

bustling /ˈbʌslɪŋ/ *adj.* суетливый

busy /ˈbɪzi/ **1.** *adj.* занятóй, занятый **2.** *v.* ~ **oneself** занимáться (+ *I*) *impf.*

but /bʌt/ **1.** *conj.* но, а **2.** *adv.* тóлько, лишь

butcher /ˈbutʃər/ *n.* мясник

butler /ˈbʌtlər/ *n.* дворéцкий

butt¹ /bʌt/ *n.* (*target*) мишéнь *f.*

butt² /bʌt/ *n.* (*remainder*) остáток; (*rifle*) приклáд; (*cigarette*) окýрок

butt³ /bʌt/ *v.* бодáть(ся) *impf.*

butter /ˈbʌtər/ *n.* (*slivochnoe*) (сли́вочное) мáсло

butterfly /ˈbʌtərˌflai/ *n.* бáбочка

buttermilk /ˈbʌtərˌmɪlk/ *n.* простоквáша

butterscotch /ˈbʌtərˌskɒtʃ/ *n.* карамéль *f.*

buttock /ˈbʌtək/ *n.* ягодица

button /ˈbʌtn/ *n.* пýговица; (*elec.*) кнóпка

buttonhole /ˈbʌtnˌhoul/ *n.* петля

buttress /ˈbʌtrɪs/ *n.* подпóра; (*bridge*) бык; (*building*) контрфóрс; *Fig.* опóра, поддéржка

buxom /ˈbʌksəm/ *adj.* пышная

buy /bai/ **1.** *n.* покýпка **2.** *v.* покупáть *impf.*, купить *pf.*

buyer /ˈbaiər/ *n.* покупáтель

buzz /bʌz/ **1.** *n.* жужжáние **2.** *v.* жужжáть *impf.*

buzzard /ˈbʌzərd/ *n.* каню́к

buzzer /ˈbʌzər/ *n.* (*tech.*) зýммер

by /bai/ **1.** *prep.* к (+ *D*); за (+ *A*); (*place*) вóзле, óколо, мимо (+ *G*) **2.** *adv.* мимо; **~ the way** кстáти, мéжду прóчим

bygone /ˈbaiˌgɒn/ *adj.* прóшлый

bylaw /ˈbaiˌlɔ/ *n.* постановлéние

bypass /ˈbaiˌpæs/ **1.** *v.* обходить *impf.*, обойти *pf.* **2.** *n.* обхóд

by-product *n.* побóчный продýкт

bystander /ˈbaiˌstændər/ *n.* свидéтель

byte /bait/ *n.* байт

C

cab /kæb/ *n.* такси́ *neut. indecl.*

cabaret /ˌkæbəˈrei/ **1.** *n.* кабаре́ *neut. indecl.* **2.** *adj.* эстра́дный

cabbage /ˈkæbɪdʒ/ *n.* капу́ста

cabin /ˈkæbɪn/ *n.* хи́жина; *(ship)* каби́на, каю́та

cabinet /ˈkæbənɪt/ *n.* шкаф; *(polit.)* кабине́т

cabinetmaker /ˈkæbənɪtˌmeikər/ *n.* краснодере́вщик; столя́р

cable /ˈkeibəl/ *n.* ка́бель *m.*; кана́т

cable television *n.* ка́бельное телеви́дение

cache /kæʃ/ *n.* тайни́к; *(of weapons)* та́йный склад ору́жия

cackle /ˈkækəl/ *n.* куда́хтанье

cacophonous /kəˈkɒfənəs/ *adj.* неблагозву́чный

cactus /ˈkæktəs/ *n.* ка́ктус

cadaver /kəˈdævər/ *n.* труп

caddy /ˈkædi/ *n.* *(tea)* ча́йница

cadence /ˈkeidns/ *n.* ритм; темп

cadet /kəˈdet/ *n.* *(mil.)* каде́т

cadge /kædʒ/ *v.* попроша́йничать *impf.*

cadre /ˈkɑdrei/ *n.* кадр

Caesarean section /sɪˈzeəriən/ *n.* ке́сарево сече́ние

café /kæˈfei/ *n.* кафе́ *neut. indecl.*

cafeteria /ˌkæfɪˈtiəriə/ *n.* кафете́рий

caffeine /ˈkæfin/ *n.* кофеи́н

cage /keidʒ/ *n.* кле́тка

cajole /kəˈdʒoul/ *v.* угова́ривать *impf.*

cake /keik/ *n.* торт, кекс; пиро́жное

calamitous /kəˈlæmɪtəs/ *adj.* па́губный

calamity /kəˈlæmɪti/ *n.* бе́дствие

calcium /ˈkælsiəm/ *n.* ка́льций

calculate /ˈkælkyə,leit/ *v.* расчи́тывать *impf.*, вычи́слить *impf.*, вычи́слить *pf.*

calculated /ˈkælkyə,leitɪd/ *adj.* рассчи́танный

calculation /ˌkælkyəˈleiʃən/ *n.* вычисле́ние, расчёт

calculator /ˈkælkyə,leitər/ *n.* калькуля́тор

calendar /ˈkæləndər/ *n.* календа́рь *m.*

calf[1] /kæf/ *n.* телёнок

calf[2] /kæf/ *n.* *(leg)* икра́

caliber /ˈkæləbər/ *n.* кали́бр

calibrate /ˈkælə,breit/ *v.* градуи́ровать; калиброва́ть *impf.*

calico /ˈkæli,kou/ *n.* коленко́р; *(printed cotton)* набивно́й си́тец

calisthenics /ˌkæləsˈθeniks/ *n.* худо́жественная гимна́стика

call /kɔl/ **1.** *n.* крик; призы́в; *(visit)* визи́т **2.** *v.* звать *impf.*; *(name)* называ́ть *impf.*, назва́ть *pf.*; *(phone)* звони́ть *impf.*, по-*pf.*

calligraphy /kəˈlɪgrəfi/ *n.* каллигра́фия

calling /ˈkɔlɪŋ/ *n.* *(vocation)* призва́ние; *(profession)* профе́ссия

callous /ˈkæləs/ *adj.* *(skin)* мозо́листый; *(person)* чёрствый

callus /ˈkæləs/ *n.* мозо́ль *f.*

calm /kɑm/ **1.** *adj.* споко́йный **2.** *n.* тишина́, споко́йствие **3.** *v.* успока́ивать *impf.*, успоко́ить *pf.*; ~ **down** успока́иваться *impf.*, успоко́иться *pf.*

caloric /kəˈlɔrɪk/ *adj.* калори́йный

calorie /ˈkæləri/ *n.* кало́рия

calumny /ˈkæləmni/ *n.* клевета́

camaraderie /ˌkɑməˈrɑdəri/ *n.* това́рищество

camel /ˈkæməl/ *n.* верблю́д

camera /ˈkæmərə/ *n.* фотоаппара́т; **movie** ~ кинока́мера

cameraman /ˈkæmərə,mæn/ *n.* киноопера́тор

camomile /ˈkæmə,mil/ *n.* рома́шка

camouflage /ˈkæmə,flɑʒ/ **1.** *n.* маскиро́вка **2.** *v.* маскирова́ть *impf.*, за-*pf.*

camp /kæmp/ **1.** *n.* ла́герь *m.* **2.** *v.* распола́гаться ла́герем *impf.*

campaign /kæmˈpein/ *n.* кампа́ния

campfire /ˈkæmp,faiᵊr/ *n.* костёр

camphor /ˈkæmfər/ *n.* ка́мфора

campsite /ˈkæmp,sait/ *n.* ла́герь *m.*; ке́мпинг, туристи́ческая ба́за

campus /ˈkæmpəs/ *n.* университе́тский городо́к

can[1] /kæn/ *v.* мочь *impf.*, с-*pf.*; *(know how)* уме́ть *impf.*, с-*pf.*

can[2] /kæn/ **1.** *n.* банди́он; *(tin)* ба́нка **2.** *v.* консерви́ровать *impf.*, за-*pf.*

Canadian /kəˈneidiən/ **1.** *adj.* кана́дский **2.** *n.* кана́дец, -дка

canal /kəˈnæl/ n. кана́л

canary /kəˈneərı/ n. канаре́йка

cancel /ˈkænsəl/ v. вычёркивать impf., вы́черкнуть pf.; аннули́ровать impf. & pf.

cancellation /ˌkænsəˈleıʃən/ n. аннули́рование, вычёркивание

cancer /ˈkænsər/ n. рак

cancerous /ˈkænsərəs/ adj. ра́ковый

candelabra /ˌkændıˈlɑːbrə/ n. канделя́бр

candid /ˈkændıd/ adj. открове́нный; и́скренний

candidacy /ˈkændıdəsı/; n. кандидату́ра

candidate /ˈkændıˌdeıt/ n. кандида́т

candied /ˈkændıd/ adj. заса́харенный

candle /ˈkændl/ n. свеча́

candlestick /ˈkændlˌstık/ n. подсве́чник

candor /ˈkændər/ n. открове́нность; и́скренность

candy /ˈkændı/ n. конфе́та; (hard candy) ледене́ц

cane /keın/ n. па́лка; (walking) трость f.

canine /ˈkeınaın/ adj. соба́чий

canister /ˈkænəstər/ n. жестяна́я коро́бка; ба́нка

canker /ˈkæŋkər/ n. (med.) я́зва

canned /kænd/ adj. консерви́рованный; ~ food n. консе́рвы pl.

cannibal /ˈkænəbəl/ n. людое́д

cannibalism /ˈkænəbəˌlızəm/ n. людое́дство, каннибали́зм

cannon /ˈkænən/ n. пу́шка

canoe /kəˈnuː/ n. кано́э neut. indecl., байда́рка

canon /ˈkænən/ n. кано́н; (person) кано́ник

canonicals /kəˈnɒnıkəlz/ n. церко́вное облаче́ние

canonize /ˈkænəˌnaız/ v. канонизи́ровать impf. & pf.

can opener n. консе́рвный нож

canopy /ˈkænəpı/ n. балдахи́н

cantaloupe /ˈkæntəˌloup/ n. ды́ня

cantankerous /kænˈtæŋkərəs/ adj. вздо́рный

cantata /kənˈtɑːtə/ n. канта́та

canteen /kænˈtiːn/ n. (flask) фля́га; (in factory, etc.) столо́вая

canter /ˈkæntər/ n. лёгкий гало́п

canvas /ˈkænvəs/ n. холст; паруси́на

canvass /ˈkænvəs/ v. опра́шивать impf.

canyon /ˈkænyən/ n. каньо́н

cap /kæp/ n. ша́пка, ке́пка, фура́жка; (lid) кры́шка

capability /ˌkeıpəˈbılıtı/ n. спосо́бность

capable /ˈkeıpəbəl/ adj. спосо́бный

capacious /kəˈpeıʃəs/ adj. просто́рный, объёмистый

capacity /kəˈpæsıtı/ n. ёмкость; объём; (ability to contain) вмести́мость; (ability) спосо́бность

cape /keıp/ n. (geog.) мыс; (cloak) наки́дка

caper /ˈkeıpər/ n. (jump) прыжо́к; (prank) ша́лость

capers /ˈkeıpər/ n. ка́персы pl.

capillary /ˈkæpəˌlerı/ n. капилля́р

capital /ˈkæpıtl/ **1.** n. (money) капита́л; (city) столи́ца **2.** adj. (law) кара́емый сме́ртью; ~ letter прописна́я бу́ква; ~ punishment сме́ртная казнь f.

capitalism /ˈkæpıtlˌızəm/ n. капитали́зм

capitalist /ˈkæpıtlıst/ n. капитали́ст

capitalize /ˈkæpıtlˌaız/ v. капитализи́ровать impf. & pf.

capitulate /kəˈpıtʃəˌleıt/ v. сдава́ться impf., сда́ться pf.

capitulation /kəˌpıtʃəˈleıʃən/ n. капитуля́ция

caprice /kəˈpriːs/ n. капри́з

capricious /kəˈprıʃəs/ adj. капри́зный

capsize /ˈkæpsaız/ v. опроки́дывать(ся) impf., опроки́нуть(ся) pf.

capsule /ˈkæpsəl/ n. ка́псула

captain /ˈkæptən/ n. капита́н

caption /ˈkæpʃən/ n. заголо́вок

captious /ˈkæpʃəs/ adj. приди́рчивый

captivate /ˈkæptəˌveıt/ v. пленя́ть impf. -ни́ть pf.; очаро́вывать impf., очарова́ть pf.

captivating /ˈkæptəˌveıtıŋ/ adj. очарова́тельный

captive /ˈkæptıv/ n. пле́нный

captivity /kæpˈtıvıtı/ n. плен; нево́ля

capture /ˈkæptʃər/ **1.** n. захва́т, взя́тие **2.** v. захвати́ть pf.; взять в плен pf.

car /kar/ n. маши́на; (*train*) ваго́н

carafe /kəˈræf/ n. графи́н

caramel /ˈkærəməl/ n. караме́ль f.

carat /ˈkærət/ n. кара́т

caravan /ˈkærəˌvæn/ n. карава́н

caraway /ˈkærəˌweɪ/ n. тмин

carbohydrate /ˌkarbouˈhaɪdreɪt/ n. углево́д

carbon /ˈkarbən/ n. углеро́д

carbonated /ˈkarbəˌneɪtɪd/ adj. газиро́ванный

carbon paper n. копирова́льная бума́га

carburetor /ˈkarbəˌreɪtər/ n. карбюра́тор

carcass /ˈkarkəs/ n. труп; ту́ша

card /kard/ n. ка́рта, ка́рточка; (*ticket*) биле́т

cardboard /ˈkardˌbord/ **1.** adj. карто́нный **2.** n. карто́н

cardiac /ˈkardiˌæk/ adj. серде́чный

cardinal /ˈkardnl/ **1.** adj. основно́й, гла́вный **2.** n. кардина́л

card index n. картоте́ка

cardiologist /ˌkardiˈɑlədʒɪst/ n. кардио́лог

cardiology /ˌkardiˈɑlədʒi/ n. кардиоло́гия

cardsharp /ˈkardˌʃarp/ n. шу́лер

card table n. ломбе́рный стол

care /kɛər/ **1.** n. забо́та; ухо́д; попече́ние **2.** v. забо́титься impf., по- pf.; **I don't ~** мне всё равно́

career /kəˈrɪər/ n. карье́ра

carefree /ˈkɛərˌfri/ adj. беззабо́тный, беспе́чный

careful /ˈkɛərfəl/ adj. осторо́жный, тща́тельный

careless /ˈkɛərlɪs/ adj. небре́жный, невнима́тельный

caress /kəˈrɛs/ **1.** n. ла́ска **2.** v. ласка́ть impf.

caret /ˈkærɪt/ n. знак вста́вки

caretaker /ˈkɛərˌteɪkər/ n. смотри́тель, —ница

cargo /ˈkargou/ n. груз

caricature /ˈkærɪkətʃər/ **1.** n. карикату́ра **2.** v. изобража́ть в карикату́рном ви́де impf.

caries /ˈkɛəriz/ n. (*med.*) карио́з

carious /ˈkɛəriəs/ adj. карио́зный

carnage /ˈkarnɪdʒ/ n. резня́, бо́йня

carnal /ˈkarnl/ adj. пло́тский

carnation /karˈneɪʃən/ n. гвозди́ка

carnival /ˈkarnəvəl/ n. карнава́л

carnivore /ˈkarnəˌvɔr/ n. плотоя́дное живо́тное

carnivorous /karˈnɪvərəs/ adj. плотоя́дный

carol /ˈkærəl/ n. гимн

carousal /kəˈrauzəl/ n. попо́йка

carouse /kəˈrauz/ v. пирова́ть impf.

carousel /ˌkærəˈsɛl/ n. карусе́ль f.

car owner n. автовладе́лец

carp[1] /karp/ n. (*fish*) карп

carp[2] /karp/ v. придира́ться impf.

carpenter /ˈkarpəntər/ n. пло́тник

carpentry /ˈkarpəntri/ n. столя́рная рабо́та; пло́тницкое де́ло

carpet /ˈkarpɪt/ n. ковёр

carping /ˈkarpɪŋ/ adj. приди́рчивый

carriage /ˈkærɪdʒ/ n. (*conveying*) перево́зка; (*deportment*) оса́нка; (*vehicle*) коля́ска; **baby ~** де́тская коля́ска

carrier /ˈkæriər/ n. перено́счик; (*med.*) носи́тель

carrier pigeon n. почто́вый го́лубь m.

carrion /ˈkæriən/ n. па́даль f.

carrot /ˈkærət/ n. морко́вь f.

carry /ˈkæri/ v. носи́ть indet., нести́ det., понести́ pf.; (*convey*) вози́ть indet., везти́ det., повезти́ pf.; **~ in** вноси́ть impf., внести́ pf.; **~ out** выноси́ть impf., вы́нести pf.; (*execute*) выполня́ть impf.

cart /kart/ n. теле́га, теле́жка

cartel /karˈtɛl/ n. (*econ.*) карте́ль m.

cartilage /ˈkartlɪdʒ/ n. хрящ

cartographer /karˈtɒgrəfər/ n. карто́граф

carton /ˈkartn/ n. карто́нка

cartoon /karˈtun/ n. карикату́ра; (*film*) мультфи́льм

cartoonist /karˈtunɪst/ n. карикату́рист

cartridge /ˈkartrɪdʒ/ n. патро́н; **blank ~** холосто́й патро́н

carve /karv/ v. ре́зать impf., вы́резать pf.; (*in stone*) высека́ть impf., вы́сечь pf.; (*meat*) нареза́ть impf., наре́зать pf.

carver /ˈkarvər/ n. ре́зчик

carving /ˈkarvɪŋ/ n. резьба́

cascade /kæsˈkeɪd/ n. каска́д

case /keɪs/ n. (instance) слу́чай; (law) де́ло; (box) я́щик; (cover) чехо́л; (gram.) паде́ж

cash /kæʃ/ n. нали́чные де́ньги pl.; **pay** ~ v. плати́ть нали́чными impf.

cashew /'kæʃu/ n. анака́рдия

cashier /kæ'ʃɪər/ n. касси́р

cashmere /'kæʒmɪər/ 1. n. кашеми́р 2. adj. кашеми́ровый

cash register n. ка́сса

casing /'keɪsɪŋ/ n. оболо́чка; обши́вка; (tech.) кожу́х, ка́ртер

casino /kə'sinou/ n. казино́ neut. indecl.

cask /kæsk/ n. бо́чка, бочо́нок

casket /'kæskɪt/ n. шкату́лка

casserole /'kæsə,roul/ n. (pot) кастрю́ля; (food) запека́нка

cassette /kə'set/ n. кассе́та

cassette deck n. кассе́тная де́ка

cassette player n. магнитофо́н

cassock /'kæsək/ n. (Catholic) сута́на; (Orthodox) ря́са

cast /kæst/ 1. n. (mold) фо́рма; (theat.) соста́в исполни́телей; (med.) гипс; (of mind) склад 2. v. броса́ть impf., бро́сить pf.; отлива́ть impf., отли́ть pf.; (theat.) распределя́ть ро́ли (+ D) impf.

caste /kæst/ n. ка́ста

caster /'kæstər/ n. (wheel) ро́лик

castigate /'kæstɪ,geɪt/ v. бичева́ть; нака́зывать impf., наказа́ть pf.

cast-iron adj. чугу́нный

castle /'kæsəl/ n. за́мок; (chess) ладья́

cast-off adj. него́дный

castor oil /'kæstər/ n. касто́рка

castrate /'kæstreɪt/ v. кастри́ровать impf. & pf.

castration /kæ'streɪʃən/ n. кастра́ция

casual /'kæʒuəl/ adj. случа́йный; (informal) непринуждённый

casualty /'kæʒuəlti/ n. пострада́вший; (wounded) ра́неный; (killed) уби́тый

cat /kæt/ n. ко́шка; (male) кот

catalog /'kætl,ɔg/ 1. n. катало́г 2. v. каталоги́зи́ровать impf. & pf.

catalyst /'kætlɪst/ n. катализа́тор

catapult /'kætə,pʌlt/ 1. n. катапу́льта 2. v.i. взлета́ть impf.

cataract /'kætə,rækt/ n. водопа́д; (med.) катара́кта

catarrh /kə'tɑr/ n. ката́р

catastrophe /kə'tæstrəfi/ n. катастро́фа

catastrophic /,kætə'strɒfɪk/ adj. катастрофи́ческий

catcall /'kæt,kɔl/ n. свист

catch /kætʃ/ 1. v. лови́ть impf., пойма́ть pf.; (be on time for) успе́ть (на + A) pf.; (disease) зарази́ться (+ I) pf.; ~ **up** догна́ть pf.; (action) пойма́ть; (trick) уло́вка

catcher /'kætʃər/ n. лове́ц

catching /'kætʃɪŋ/ adj. зара́зный

catchword /'kætʃ,wɜrd/ n. мо́дное словечко́; (slogan) ло́зунг

catchy /'kætʃi/ adj. (pleasing) привлека́тельный

catechism /'kætɪ,kɪzəm/ n. катехи́зис

categorical /,kætɪ'gɔrɪkəl/ adj. категори́ческий, безусло́вный

categorize /'kætɪgə,raɪz/ v. распределя́ть по катего́риям impf.

category /'kætɪ,gɔri/ n. катего́рия

cater /'keɪtər/ v. снабжа́ть прови́зией impf.; ~ **to** угожда́ть impf.

caterer /'keɪtərər/ n. поставщи́к прови́зии

catering /'keɪtərɪŋ/ n. поста́вка проду́ктов

caterpillar /'kætə,pɪlər/ n. гу́сеница

catfish /'kæt,fɪʃ/ n. со́мик

cathedral /kə'θidrəl/ n. собо́р

catheter /'kæθɪtər/ n. катете́р

cathode /'kæθoud/ n. като́д

catholic /'kæθəlɪk/ adj. всеобъе́млющий; (eccles.) вселе́нский

Catholic /'kæθəlɪk/ 1. adj. католи́ческий 2. n. като́лик, -и́чка

Catholicism /kə'θɒlə,sɪzəm/ n. католи́чество, католици́зм

cat lover n. коша́тник

catnip /'kætnɪp/ n. коша́чья мя́та

cattle /'kætl/ n. скот

catty /'kæti/ adj. коша́чий; (spiteful) ехи́дный, язви́тельный

Caucasus /'kɔkəsəs/ n. Кавка́з

caucus /'kɔkəs/ n. парти́йный комите́т

cauldron /'kɔldrən/ n. котёл

cauliflower /'kɔlə,flauər/ n. цветна́я капу́ста

caulk /kɔk/ v. конопа́тить impf.

causal /ˈkɔzəl/ adj. причи́нный

cause /kɔz/ 1. n. причи́на; (law) де́ло 2. v. причиня́ть impf., -ни́ть pf.; вызыва́ть impf., вы́звать pf.

caustic /ˈkɔstɪk/ adj. е́дкий; язви́тельный

cauterize /ˈkɔtə,raɪz/ v. прижига́ть impf., прижечь pf.

caution /ˈkɔʃən/ n. осторо́жность

cautionary /ˈkɔʃə,neri/ adj. предупрежда́ющий, предостерега́ющий

cautious /ˈkɔʃəs/ adj. осторо́жный

cavalcade /ˌkævəlˈkeid/ n. кавалька́да

cavalry /ˈkævəlri/ n. кавале́рия

cave /keiv/ 1. n. пеще́ра 2. v. ~ **in** ру́хнуть pf.

caveman /ˈkeiv,mæn/ n. троглоди́т, пеще́рный челове́к

cavern /ˈkævərn/ n. пеще́ра

cavernous /ˈkævərnəs/ adj. пещери́стый

caviar /ˈkævi,ar/ n. икра́

cavity /ˈkævɪti/ n. по́лость; впа́дина

cavort /kəˈvɔrt/ v. скака́ть impf.

caw /kɔ/ v. ка́ркать impf.

CD-ROM /ˌsi,diˈrɒm/ n. компа́кт диск — постоя́нное запомина́ющее устро́йство (abbr.: КД-ПЗУ)

cease /sis/ v. прекраща́ть(ся) impf., прекрати́ть(ся) pf.; переставать impf., переста́ть pf.

cease-fire n. прекраще́ние огня́; (truce) переми́рие

ceaseless /ˈsislɪs/ adj. непреста́нный, непреры́вный

cedar /ˈsidər/ n. кедр

cede /sid/ v. сдава́ть impf., сдать pf.

ceiling /ˈsiliŋ/ n. потоло́к

celebrate /ˈselə,breit/ v. пра́здновать impf., от- pf.

celebrated /ˈselə,breitɪd/ adj. знамени́тый, просла́вленный

celebration /ˌseləˈbreiʃən/ n. пра́зднование

celebrity /səˈlebrɪti/ n. знамени́тость

celery /ˈseləri/ n. сельдере́й

celestial /səˈlestʃəl/ adj. небе́сный

celibacy /ˈseləbəsi/ n. безбра́чие

celibate /ˈseləbɪt/ adj. холосто́й

cell /sel/ n. (room) ке́лья; (prison) ка́мера; (biol.) кле́тка

cellar /ˈselər/ n. по́греб; подва́л

cello /ˈtʃelou/ n. виолонче́ль f.

cellophane /ˈselə,fein/ 1. n. целлофа́н 2. adj. целлофа́новый

cellular /ˈselyələr/ adj. кле́точный

cement /sɪˈment/ 1. n. цеме́нт 2. v. цементи́ровать impf.

cemetery /ˈsemɪ,teri/ n. кла́дбище

censor /ˈsensər/ 1. n. це́нзор 2. v. подверга́ть цензу́ре impf.

censorious /senˈsɔriəs/ adj. крити́ческий

censorship /ˈsensər,ʃip/ n. цензу́ра

censure /ˈsenʃər/ 1. n. осужде́ние 2. v. порица́ть; осужда́ть impf.

census /ˈsensəs/ n. пе́репись f.

cent /sent/ n. цент

centenary /senˈtenəri/ n. столе́тие

centennial /senˈteniəl/ adj. столе́тний

center /ˈsentər/ 1. n. центр 2. v. сосредото́чивать(ся) impf.

Centigrade /ˈsenti,greid/ adj.: **10 degrees** ~ 10 гра́дусов по Це́льсию

centimeter /ˈsentə,mitər/ n. сантиме́тр

centipede /ˈsentə,pid/ n. сороконо́жка

central /ˈsentrəl/ adj. центра́льный

centralization /ˌsentrələˈzeiʃən/ n. централиза́ция

centralize /ˈsentrə,laiz/ v. централизова́ть impf. & pf.

centrifugal /senˈtrifyəgəl/ adj. центробе́жный

century /ˈsentʃəri/ n. век, столе́тие

ceramic /səˈræmɪk/ adj. керами́ческий

ceramics /səˈræmɪks/ n. кера́мика

cereal /ˈsiriəl/ n. (хле́бные) зла́ки pl.; **breakfast** ~ хле́бные хло́пья pl.

cerebral /səˈribrəl/ adj. мозгово́й

cerebrum /səˈribrəm/ n. головно́й мозг

ceremonial /ˌserəˈmouniəl/ adj. церемониа́льный

ceremonious /ˌserəˈmounias/

adj. церемониа́льный; церемо́нный

ceremony /'sɛrə,mouni/ *n.* церемо́ния

certain /'sɜrtn/ *adj.* (fixed) определённый; (indefinite) не́кий, не́который; **be ~** быть уве́ренным

certainly /'sɜrtnli/ *adv.* коне́чно

certainty /'sɜrtnti/ *n.* уве́ренность

certificate /sər'tıfıkıt/ *n.* удостовере́ние; свиде́тельство

certify /'sɜrtə,faı/ *v.* свиде́тельствовать *impf.*, за- *pf.*

cervical /'sɜrvıkəl/ *adj.* ше́йный

cervix /'sɜrvıks/ *n.* ше́йка ма́тки

cessation /se'seıʃən/ *n.* прекраще́ние

cesspool /'ses,pul/ выгребна́я я́ма, помо́йная я́ма

chafe /tʃeıf/ *v.* тере́ть; натира́ть *impf.*, натере́ть *pf.*

chaff /tʃæf/ *n.* (grain husks) мяки́на; (cut straw) сечка

chaffinch /'tʃæfıntʃ/ *n.* зя́блик

chagrin /ʃə'grın/ *n.* огорче́ние

chain /tʃeın/ **1.** *n.* цепь *f.*; цепо́чка **2.** *v.* ско́вывать *impf.*, скова́ть *pf.* **3.** *adj.* цепно́й

chain reaction *n.* цепна́я реа́кция

chain smoker *n.* зая́длый кури́льщик

chair /tʃeər/ **1.** *n.* стул; (university) ка́федра **2.** *v.* председа́тельствовать (на + P) *impf.*

chairman /'tʃeərmən/ *n.* председа́тель

chairwoman /'tʃeər,wumən/ *n.* председа́тельница

chalice /'tʃælıs/ *n.* (eccles.) ча́ша

chalk /tʃɔk/ *n.* мел

chalky /'tʃɔki/ *adj.* мелово́й

challenge /'tʃælındʒ/ **1.** *n.* вы́зов **2.** *v.* вызыва́ть *impf.*, вы́звать *pf.*

challenger /'tʃælındʒər/ *n.* претенде́нт

challenging /'tʃælındʒıŋ/ *adj.* вызыва́ющий; тре́бовательный

chamber /'tʃeımbər/ *n.* (polit.) пала́та; (judge's) кабине́т

chambermaid /'tʃeımbər,meıd/ *n.* го́рничная

chamber music *n.* ка́мерная му́зыка

chamber pot *n.* ночно́й горшо́к

chameleon /kə'miliən/ *n.* хамелео́н

chamois /'ʃæmi/ **1.** *n.* (leather) за́мша **2.** *adj.* за́мшевый

champagne /ʃæm'peın/ *n.* шампа́нское

champion /'tʃæmpiən/ **1.** *n.* чемпио́н, —ка **2.** *v.* защища́ть *impf.*, -ти́ть *pf.*; подде́рживать *impf.*, -держа́ть *pf.*

championship /'tʃæmpiən,ʃıp/ *n.* чемпиона́т, пе́рвенство

chance /tʃæns/ *n.* слу́чай; возмо́жность; **by ~** случа́йно; **take a ~** рискова́ть *impf.*;

chancy *adj.* риско́ванный

chancellery /'tʃænsələri/ *n.* канцеля́рия

chancellor /'tʃænsələr/ *n.* ка́нцлер

chandelier /,ʃændl'ıər/ *n.* лю́стра

change /tʃeındʒ/ **1.** *n.* измене́ние, переме́на; (of clothes, e.g.) сме́на; (money) сда́ча; (of trains, e.g.) переса́дка **2.** *v.* меня́ть(ся) *impf.*

changeable /'tʃeındʒəbəl/ *adj.* изме́нчивый

channel /'tʃænl/ *n.* проли́в, кана́л; путь *m.*

chant /tʃænt/ **1.** *n.* (eccles.) песнопе́ние **2.** *v.* петь *impf.*

chaos /'keıɑs/ *n.* ха́ос

chaotic /keı'ɑtık/ *adj.* хаоти́ческий

chap[1] /tʃæp/ *n.* (fellow) па́рень *m.*; мужи́к

chap[2] /tʃæp/ *n.* (skin) тре́щина, сса́дина

chapel /'tʃæpəl/ *n.* часо́вня

chaperon /'ʃæpə,roun/ *n.* компаньо́н, —ка

chaplain /'tʃæplın/ *n.* капелла́н

chapter /'tʃæptər/ *n.* глава́

char /tʃɑr/ *v.* обу́гливать(ся) *impf.*

character /'kærıktər/ *n.* хара́ктер; (theat.) де́йствующее лицо́; (letter) бу́ква

characteristic /,kærıktə'rıstık/ **1.** *adj.* характе́рный **2.** *n.* характе́рная осо́бенность

characterization /,kærıktərə'zeıʃən/ *n.* характери́стика

characterize /'kærıktə,raız/ *v.* характеризова́ть *impf.* & *pf.*

charade /ʃə'reıd/ *n.* шара́да

charcoal /'tʃɑr,koul/ *n.* древе́сный у́голь *m.*

charge /tʃɑrdʒ/ **1.** *n.* (elec.)

заря́д; (fee) пла́та; (care) попече́ние; (accusation) обвине́ние; (order) поруче́ние **2.** v. (entrust) поруча́ть impf., -чи́ть pf.; (accuse) обвиня́ть impf., -ни́ть pf.; (elec.) заряжа́ть impf., -ди́ть pf.

charger /'tʃɑrdʒər/ n.: battery ~ заря́дный выпрями́тель

chariot /'tʃærɪət/ n. колесни́ца

charisma /kə'rɪzmə/ n. обая́ние

charismatic /,kærɪz'mætɪk/ adj. обая́тельный

charitable /'tʃærɪtəbəl/ adj. милосе́рдный

charity /'tʃærɪti/ n. милосе́рдие; (foundation) благотвори́тельное о́бщество

charlatan /'ʃɑrlətn/ n. шарлата́н

charm /tʃɑrm/ **1.** n. обая́ние, ча́ры pl.; (amulet) талисма́н **2.** v. очаро́вывать impf., очарова́ть pf.; **—ing** adj. очарова́тельный; snake **—er** n. заклина́тель змей

chart /tʃɑrt/ **1.** n. гра́фик; схе́ма; (naut.) морска́я ка́рта **2.** v. наноси́ть на гра́фик impf.

charter /'tʃɑrtər/ **1.** n. (document) ха́ртия, гра́мота; (constitution) уста́в; (hire) ча́ртер **2.** v. нанима́ть impf.

chase /tʃeɪs/ **1.** n. пресле́дование, пого́ня **2.** v. гна́ться (за + I) impf.

chasm /'kæzəm/ n. бе́здна

chassis /'tʃæsi/ n. шасси́ neut. indecl.

chaste /tʃeɪst/ adj. целому́дренный

chasten /'tʃeɪsən/ v. кара́ть impf.

chastise /tʃæs'taɪz/ v. нака́зывать impf., наказа́ть pf.

chastity /'tʃæstɪti/ n. целому́дрие

chat /tʃæt/ **1.** n. бесе́да **2.** v. бесе́довать impf.

chatter /'tʃætər/ v. болта́ть impf.; (of teeth) стуча́ть impf.

chatterbox /'tʃæt,ərbɒks/ n. болту́н, —ья

chatty /'tʃæti/ adj. болтли́вый

chauffeur /'ʃoufər/ n. шофёр

chauvinism /'ʃouvə,nɪzəm/ n. шовини́зм; male ~ женонена́вистничество

chauvinist /'ʃouvənɪst/ **1.** n. шовини́ст **2.** adj. шовинисти́ческий

cheap /tʃip/ adj. дешёвый

cheapen /'tʃipən/ v. обесце́нивать(ся) impf., -це́нить(ся) pf.

cheaply /'tʃipli/ adv. дёшево

cheat /tʃit/ **1.** v. обма́нывать impf., обману́ть pf. **2.** n. обма́нщик, -щица

check /tʃɛk/ **1.** n. контро́ль m., прове́рка; (bank) чек; (chess) шах; cash a ~ v. получа́ть де́ньги по че́ку **2.** v. проверя́ть impf., прове́рить pf.

checked /tʃɛkt/ adj. кле́тчатый

check list n. контро́льный спи́сок

checkmate /'tʃɛk,meɪt/ n. мат

checkout /'tʃɛk,aut/ n. ка́сса

checkpoint /'tʃɛk,pɔɪnt/ n. контро́льно-пропускно́й пункт

checkup /'tʃɛkʌp/ n. прове́рка

cheek /tʃik/ n. щека́

cheekbone /'tʃik,boun/ n. скула́

cheeky /'tʃiki/ adj. наха́льный

cheep /tʃip/ n. писк

cheer /tʃɪər/ **1.** n. ободре́ние **2.** v. ободря́ть impf., -ри́ть pf.; аплоди́ровать impf.

cheerful /'tʃɪərfəl/ adj. весёлый

cheerless /'tʃɪərlɪs/ adj. мра́чный

cheers /tʃɪərz/ interj. за ва́ше здоро́вье!

cheese /tʃiz/ n. сыр

cheetah /'tʃitə/ n. гепа́рд

chef /ʃɛf/ n. гла́вный по́вар

chemical /'kɛmɪkəl/ **1.** adj. хими́ческий **2.** n. химика́т

chemist /'kɛmɪst/ n. хи́мик

chemistry /'kɛməstri/ n. хи́мия

cherish /'tʃɛrɪʃ/ v. леле́ять, дорожи́ть impf.

cherry /'tʃɛri/ **1.** n. ви́шня **2.** adj. вишнёвый

cherub /'tʃɛrəb/ n. херуви́м

chess /tʃɛs/ n. ша́хматы pl.

chessboard /'tʃɛs,bɔrd/ n. ша́хматная доска́

chess player n. шахмати́ст

chest /tʃɛst/ **1.** n. (trunk) сунду́к; (anat.) грудь f. **2.** adj. грудно́й

chestnut /'tʃɛs,nʌt/ **1.** n. кашта́н **2.** adj. (horse) гнедо́й

chew /tʃu/ v. жева́ть impf.

chewing gum /'tʃuɪŋ/ n. жва́чка

chic /ʃik/ adj. шика́рный

chick /tʃik/ n. цыплёнок

chicken /'tʃikən/ **1.** n. ку́рица, цыплёнок **2.** adj. кури́ный

chickenpox /'tʃɪkən,pɒks/ n. ветряная óспа

chickpea /'tʃɪk,pi/ n. турéцкий горóх

chicory /'tʃɪkəri/ n. цикóрий

chide /tʃaɪd/ v. упрекáть impf.

chief /tʃif/ **1.** adj. глáвный **2.** n. глава, начáльник

chiefly /'tʃifli/ adv. в основнóм

chieftain /'tʃiftən/ n. вождь m.

chiffon /'ʃɪfɒn/ n. шифóн

child /tʃaɪld/ n. ребёнок

childbearing /'tʃaɪld,beərɪŋ/ n. деторождéние

childbirth /'tʃaɪldbɜrθ/ n. рóды pl.

childhood /'tʃaɪldhʊd/ n. дéтство

childish /'tʃaɪldɪʃ/, **childlike** /'tʃaɪldlaɪk/ adj. дéтский

childless /'tʃaɪldlɪs/ adj. бездéтный

chili /'tʃɪli/ n. стручкóвый пéрец

chill /tʃɪl/ **1.** n. хóлод; (ailment) простýда **2.** v. охлаждáть impf., охладúть pf.

chilly /'tʃɪli/ adj. прохлáдный

chime /tʃaɪm/ n. (bell) перезвóн, звон; (clock) бой; (set of bells) набóр колоколóв

chimney /'tʃɪmni/ n. трубá

chimpanzee /,tʃɪmpæn'zi/ n. шимпанзé m. indecl.

chin /tʃɪn/ n. подбородóк

china /'tʃaɪnə/ n. фарфóр

China /'tʃaɪnə/ n. Китáй

Chinese /tʃaɪ'niz/ **1.** adj. китáйский **2.** n. китáец, -тáянка

chink[1] /tʃɪŋk/ n. (crack) щель f.

chink[2] /tʃɪŋk/ n. (sound) звяканье

chintz /tʃɪnts/ n. сúтец

chip /tʃɪp/ n. (wood) щéпка; (glass, metal) оскóлок; (porcelain) щербúнка; (comput.) чип

chipmunk /'tʃɪpmʌŋk/ n. бурундýк

chirp /tʃɜrp/ v. чирúкать impf.

chisel /'tʃɪzəl/ **1.** n. резéц, долотó **2.** v. высекáть impf., высечь pf.

chivalrous /'ʃɪvəlrəs/ adj. рýцарский

chivalry /'ʃɪvəlri/ n. рýцарство

chive /tʃaɪv/ n. шнитт-лук

chlorinated /'klɔrə,neɪtɪd/ adj. хлорúрованный

chlorine /'klɔrin/ n. хлор

chloroform /'klɔrə,fɔrm/ n. хлорофóрм

chlorophyll /'klɔrəfɪl/ n. хлорофúлл

chocolate /'tʃɒkəlɪt/ **1.** n. шоколáд **2.** adj. шоколáдный

choice /tʃɔɪs/ **1.** adj. отбóрный **2.** n. выбор

choir /kwaɪər/ n. хор; клúрос

choirboy /'kwaɪər,bɔɪ/ n. пéвчий

choke /tʃoʊk/ v.t. душúть impf.; v.i. давúться; задыхáться impf.

cholera /'kɒlərə/ n. холéра

cholesterol /kə'lestə,roʊl/ n. холестерúн

choose /tʃuz/ v. выбирáть impf., выбрать pf.

choosy /'tʃuzi/ adj. приверéдливый

chop /tʃɒp/ **1.** n. отбивнáя котлéта **2.** v. рубúть; колóть impf.

chopped meat /tʃɒpt/ n. фарш

chopper /'tʃɒpər/ n. (ax) колýн

choppy /'tʃɒpi/ adj. неспокóйный

choral /'kɔrəl/ adj. хоровóй

chorale /kə'ræl/ n. хорáл

chord /kɔrd/ n. (mus.) аккóрд

choreographer /,kɔri'ɒgrəfər/ n. балетмéйстер

choreography /,kɔri'ɒgrəfi/ n. хореогрáфия

chorister /'kɔrəstər/ n. хорúст, —ка

chorus /'kɔrəs/ n. хор

chosen /'tʃoʊzən/ adj. úзбранный

Christ /kraɪst/ n. Христóс

christen /'krɪsən/ v. крестúть impf.; **—ing** n. крещéние

Christian /'krɪstʃən/ **1.** adj. христиáнский **2.** n. христианúн, -áнка

Christianity /,krɪstʃi'ænɪti/ n. Христиáнство

Christmas /'krɪsməs/ n. Рождествó; **~ tree** ёлка

chromatic /kroʊ'mætɪk/ adj. хроматúческий

chrome /kroʊm/ n. хром

chromium /'kroʊmiəm/ n. хром

chromosome /'kroʊmə,soʊm/ n. хромосóма

chronic /'krɒnɪk/ adj. хронúческий

chronicle /'krɒnɪkəl/ n. хрóника, лéтопись f.

chronological /,krɒn'ɒdʒɪkəl/ adj. хронологúческий

chronology /krə'nɒlədʒi/ n. хронолóгия

chrysalis /'krɪsəlɪs/ n. ку́колка

chrysanthemum /krɪ'sænθəməm/ n. хризанте́ма

chubby /'tʃʌbi/ adj. щека́стый

chuck /tʃʌk/ **1.** v. швыря́ть impf. **2.** n. лопа́тка

chuckle /'tʃʌkəl/ v. хихи́кать; посме́иваться impf.

chum /tʃʌm/ n. това́рищ

chummy /'tʃʌmi/ adj. общи́тельный

chunk /tʃʌŋk/ n. ло́моть f.

church /tʃɜːtʃ/ **1.** n. це́рковь f. **2.** adj. церко́вный

churlish /'tʃɜːlɪʃ/ adj. гру́бый

churn /tʃɜːn/ **1.** n. маслобо́йка **2.** v. сбива́ть impf.

chute /ʃuːt/ n. скат; жёлоб

Chuvash /tʃu'vɑʃ/ n. чува́ш, —ка

cider /'saɪdər/ n. сидр

cigar /sɪ'gɑr/ n. сига́ра

cigarette /ˌsɪgə'ret/ n. папиро́са, сигаре́та; ~ **lighter** зажига́лка

cinder /'sɪndər/ n. шлак; pl. пе́пел m.

Cinderella /ˌsɪndə'relə/ n. Зо́лушка

cine- pref. ки́но-

cinema /'sɪnəmə/ n. кино́ neut. indecl., кинотеа́тр

cinematography /ˌsɪnəmə'tɒgrəfi/ n. кинемато-гра́фия

cinnamon /'sɪnəmən/ n. кори́ца

cipher /'saɪfər/ n. (zero) ноль m.; (code) шифр

circle /'sɜːkəl/ n. круг, кружо́к

circuit /'sɜːkɪt/ n. оборо́т; **short** ~ коро́ткое замыка́ние; ~ **breaker** контáктный прерыва́тель

circuitous /sɜr'kyuːtəs/ adj. кру́жный, око́льный

circular /'sɜːkyələr/ adj. кру́глый

circulate /'sɜːkyə,leɪt/ v. циркули́ровать impf.

circulation /ˌsɜːkyə'leɪʃən/ n. циркуля́ция; (newspaper) тира́ж

circumcise /'sɜːkəm,saɪz/ v. обреза́ть impf., обре́зать pf.

circumcision /ˌsɜːkəm'sɪʒən/ n. обреза́ние

circumference /sər'kʌmfərəns/ n. окру́жность

circumscribe /'sɜːkəm,skraɪb/ v. ограни́чивать impf., ограни́чить pf.

circumspect /'sɜːkəm,spekt/ adj. осмотри́тельный

circumstance /'sɜːkəm,stæns/ n. обстоя́тельство; **under the —s** при да́нных обстоя́тельствах

circumstantial /ˌsɜːkəm'stænʃəl/ adj. обстоя́тельный; ~ **evidence** ко́свенные доказа́тельства pl.

circumvent /ˌsɜːkəm'vent/ v. обходи́ть pf.

circus /'sɜːkəs/ n. цирк

cirrhosis /sɪ'roʊsɪs/ n. цирро́з

cistern /'sɪstərn/ n. цисте́рна

citadel /'sɪtədl/ n. цитаде́ль f.

citation /sai'teɪʃən/ n. ссы́лка

cite /saɪt/ v. ссыла́ться impf., сосла́ться (на + A) pf.

citizen /'sɪtəzən/ n. граждани́н, -да́нка

citizenship /'sɪtəzən,ʃɪp/ n. гражда́нство

citrus /'sɪtrəs/ **1.** n. ци́трус **2.** adj. ци́трусовый

city /'sɪti/ **1.** n. го́род **2.** adj. городско́й

civic /'sɪvɪk/ adj. гражда́нский

civilian /sɪ'vɪlyən/ adj. шта́тский

civility /sɪ'vɪlɪti/ n. ве́жливость

civilization /ˌsɪvələ'zeɪʃən/ n. цивилиза́ция

civilize /'sɪvə,laɪz/ v. цивилизо-ва́ть impf. & pf.

civilized /'sɪvə,laɪzd/ adj. цивилизо́ванный; культу́рный

clad /klæd/ adj. оде́тый (в + A)

claim /kleɪm/ **1.** n. прете́нзия, тре́бование **2.** v. тре́бовать impf., по- pf.

claimant /'kleɪmənt/ n. предъявля́ющий права́

clairvoyant /kleər'vɔɪənt/ adj. яснови́дящий

clam /klæm/ n. моллю́ск

clamber /'klæmbər/ v. кара́бкаться impf., вс- pf.

clammy /'klæmi/ adj. холо́дный и вла́жный на о́щупь

clamor /'klæmər/ n. шум

clamorous /'klæmərəs/ adj. шу́мный; (shouting) крикли́вый

clamp /klæmp/ **1.** n. зажи́м **2.** v. скрепля́ть impf., -пи́ть pf.; зажима́ть impf., зажа́ть pf.

clan /klæn/ n. род, клан

clandestine /klæn'destɪn/ adj. та́йный, скры́тый

clang /klæŋ/, **clank** /klæŋk/ **1.** n. лязг **2.** v. ля́згать impf., ля́згнуть pf.

clap /klæp/ v. аплоди́ровать impf.; хло́пать impf., хло́пнуть pf.

clarification /ˌklærəfɪ'keɪʃən/ n. разъяснение

clarify /'klærə,faɪ/ v. выяснить pf.

clarinet /ˌklærə'net/ n. кларнет

clarity /'klærɪtɪ/ n. ясность

clasp /klæsp/ **1.** n. застёжка; (hand) рукопожатие **2.** v. застёгивать impf., застегнуть pf.; (hand) сжимать impf.

class /klæs/ n. класс

classic /'klæsɪk/ **1.** n. классик **2.** adj. классический

classical /'klæsɪkəl/ adj. классический

classification /ˌklæsəfɪ'keɪʃən/ n. классификация

classified /'klæsə,faɪd/ adj. секретный, засекреченный

classify /'klæsə,faɪ/ v. классифицировать impf. & pf.

classmate /'klæs,meɪt/ n. однокласник

classroom /'klæs,rum/ n. аудитория; класс

classy /'klæsɪ/ adj. классный

clatter /'klætər/ n. стук; грохот

clause /klɔz/ n. (law) статья; клаузула; (gram.) предложение

claw /klɔ/ n. коготь r., (of crustacean) клешня

clay /kleɪ/ **1.** n. глина **2.** adj. глиняный

clean /klin/ **1.** adj. чистый **2.** v. чистить impf., по- pf.; ~ up убирать impf.

cleaner /'klinər/ n. (product) очиститель; (dry cleaner) химчистка

cleaning /'klinɪŋ/ n. чистка

cleaning lady n. уборщица

cleanliness /'klenlɪnɪs/ n. чистота

cleanse /klenz/ v. очищать impf., очистить pf.

cleanser /'klenzər/ n. очистительное средство

clean-shaven adj. чисто выбритый

clear /klɪər/ **1.** adj. ясный **2.** v. очищать(ся) impf., очистить(ся) pf.; (acquit) оправдывать impf., оправдать pf.

clearance /'klɪərəns/ n. зазор; (sale) распродажа

clearing /'klɪərɪŋ/ n. (in forest) вырубка; (open area) поляна

clearly /'klɪərlɪ/ adv. (of course) конечно, явно

cleavage /'klivɪdʒ/ n. (splitting) расщепление, раскалывание

cleaver /'klivər/ n. тесак; сечка

clef /klef/ n. ключ

cleft /kleft/ n. трещина

clemency /'klemənsɪ/ n. милосердие

clement /'klemənt/ adj. милосердный; (weather) мягкий

clench /klentʃ/ v. сжимать impf., сжать pf.

clergy /'klɜrdʒɪ/ n. духовенство

clergyman /'klɜrdʒɪmən/ n. священник

clerical /'klerɪkəl/ adj. клерикальный, канцелярский

clerk /klɜrk/ n. клерк, служащий, чиновник; (salesperson) продавец

clever /'klevər/ adj. умный

cleverness /'klevərnɪs/ n. ловкость, сообразительность

cliché /kli'ʃeɪ/ n. клише neut. indecl.

click /klɪk/ **1.** n. щелчок **2.** v. щёлкать impf., щёлкнуть pf.

client /'klaɪənt/ n. клиент

clientele /ˌklaɪən'tel/ n. клиентура

cliff /klɪf/ n. утёс

climate /'klaɪmɪt/ n. климат

climax /'klaɪmæks/ n. кульминационный пункт

climb /klaɪm/ v. лазить indet., лезть det.; взбираться impf., взобраться pf.; Colloq. карабкаться impf.; ~ stairs подниматься по лестнице impf.

climber /'klaɪmər/ n. альпинист, —ка; (plant) вьющееся растение

climbing /'klaɪmɪŋ/ n. альпинизм

cling /klɪŋ/ v. цепляться (за + A) impf., цепиться pf.

clingy /'klɪŋɪ/ adj. (sticky) липкий; (clothes) облегающий

clinic /'klɪnɪk/ n. клиника

clinical /'klɪnɪkəl/ adj. клинический

clink /klɪŋk/ **1.** n. звон **2.** v. звенеть impf.; ~ glasses чокаться impf.

clip /klɪp/ **1.** n. скоба; скрепка **2.** v. скреплять impf., -пить pf.; зажимать impf., зажать pf.; (trim) стричь impf.

clippers /'klɪpərz/ n. ножницы pl.

clipping /'klɪpɪŋ/ n. вырезка

clique /klik/ *n.* кли́ка

cloak /klouk/ *n.* плащ

cloakroom /'klouk,rum/ *n.* гардеро́б, *Colloq.* раздева́лка

clock /klɒk/ *n.* часы́ *pl.*

clock face *n.* цифербла́т

clockwise /'klɒk,waiz/ *adv.* по часово́й стре́лке

clockwork /'klɒk,wɜrk/ *n.* часово́й механи́зм

clod /klɒd/ *n.* ком

clog /klɒg/ *v.* засоря́ть(ся) *impf.*, -ри́ть(ся) *pf.*

cloister /'klɔistər/ *n.* монасты́рь *m.*

cloning /'klouniŋ/ *n.* клони́рование

close /*adj., adv.* klous; *v.* klouz/ **1.** *adj.* бли́зкий **2.** *adv.* бли́зко **3.** *v.* закрыва́ть(ся) *impf.*, закры́ть(ся) *pf.*; (*conclude*) заключа́ть *impf.*, -чи́ть *pf.*

closed /klouzd/ *adj.* закры́тый

close-fitting *adj.* те́сный; облега́ющий те́ло

closeness /'klousnis/ *n.* (*nearness*) бли́зость; (*intimacy*) инти́мность

closet /'klɒzit/ *n.* шкаф

closeup /'klousʌp/ *n.* кру́пный план

closure /'klouʒər/ *n.* закры́тие; (*conclusion*) заключе́ние

clot /klɒt/ **1.** *n.* комо́к; тромб **2.** *v.* сгуща́ться *impf.*, сгусти́ться *pf.*

cloth /klɔθ/ *n.* сукно́, ткань *f.*

clothe /klouð/ *v.* покрыва́ть *impf.*, покры́ть *pf.*

clothes /klouz/ *n.* оде́жда; пла́тье

cloud /klaud/ *n.* о́блако, ту́ча

cloudiness /'klaudinis/ *n.* о́блачность

cloudy /'klaudi/ *adj.* о́блачный

clout /klaut/ *n.* тума́к

clove /klouv/ *n.* гвозди́ка

cloven /'klouvən/ *adj.* раздво́енный

clover /'klouvər/ *n.* кле́вер

clown /klaun/ *n.* кло́ун

cloying /'klɔiiŋ/ *adj.* слаща́вый, при́торный

club /klʌb/ *n.* клуб

cluck /klʌk/ *v.* куда́хтать *impf.*

clue /klu/ *n.* ключ к разга́дке

clumsiness /'klʌmzinis/ *n.* неуклю́жесть

clumsy /'klʌmzi/ *adj.* неуклю́жий

cluster /'klʌstər/ *n.* гроздь *f.*

clutch /klʌtʃ/ *v.* схва́тывать *impf.*; ~ **at** хвата́ться за (+ *A*) *impf.*

clutter /'klʌtər/ **1.** *v.* загроможда́ть *impf.* **2.** *n.* беспоря́док

coach /koutʃ/ **1.** *n.* каре́та; (*sports*) тре́нер **2.** *v.* тренирова́ть *impf.*

coagulant /kou'ægjulənt/ *n.* сгуща́ющее сре́дство

coagulate /kou'ægjə,leit/ *v.* свора́живаться *impf.*, створо́житься *pf.*

coal /koul/ *n.* у́голь *m.*

coalesce /,kouə'les/ *v.* сраста́ться *pf.*

coalition /,kouə'lɪʃən/ **1.** *n.* коали́ция **2.** *adj.* коалицио́нный

coal mine *n.* у́гольная ша́хта

coal miner *n.* шахтёр

coarse /kɔrs/ *adj.* гру́бый

coast /koust/ *n.* (*seashore*) бе́рег

coastal /'koustl/ *adj.* берегово́й

coaster /'koustər/ *n.* подста́вка

coast guard *n.* берегова́я охра́на

coastline /'koust,lain/ *n.* побере́жье

coat /kout/ **1.** *n.* пальто́ *neut. indecl.*, (*fur coat*) шу́ба; (*fur*) шерсть *f.*; (*paint*) слой **2.** *v.* покрыва́ть *impf.*, покры́ть *pf.*; ~ **of arms** герб

coax /kouks/ *v.* угова́ривать; выпра́шивать *impf.*, вы́просить *pf.*

cob /kɒb/ *n.* поча́ток кукуру́зы

cobbled /'kɒbəld/ *adj.* булы́жный

cobweb /'kɒb,web/ *n.* паути́на

cocaine /kou'kein/ *n.* кокаи́н

cock /kɒk/ *n.* (*rooster*) пету́х; (*faucet*) кран; (*of a gun*) куро́к

cocked /kɒkt/ *adj.* за́дранный

cocker spaniel /'kɒkər/ *n.* ко́кер-спание́ль *m.*

cockeyed /'kɒk,aid/ *adj.* косо́й

cockpit /'kɒk,pit/ *n.* каби́на (самолёта)

cockroach /'kɒk,routʃ/ *n.* тарака́н

cockscomb /'kɒks,koum/ *n.* петуши́ный гре́бень *m.*

cocktail /'kɒk,teil/ *n.* кокте́йль *m.*

cocky /'kɒki/ *adj.* наха́льный

cocoa /'koukou/ *n.* кака́о *neut. indecl.*

coconut /'koukə,nʌt/ *n.* коко́с

cocoon /kə'kun/ *n.* ко́кон

cod /kɒd/ n. треска

coddle /'kɒdl/ v. баловать impf.

code /koud/ n. (body of laws) кодекс; (communication) шифр

codify /'kɒdə,faɪ/ v. кодифицировать impf. & pf.

cod-liver oil n. рыбий жир

coeducation /,kouedʒʊ'keɪʃən/ n. совместное обучение

coefficient /,kouə'fɪʃənt/ n. коэффициент

coerce /kou'zrs/ v. принуждать impf., принудить pf.

coercion /kou'zrʃən/ n. принуждение

coexist /,kouɪg'zɪst/ v. сосуществовать impf.

coexistence /,kouɪg'zɪstəns/ n. сосуществование

coffee /'kɒfi/ n. кофе m. indecl.

coffee table n. журнальный столик

coffers /'kɒfərz/ n. казна pl.

coffin /'kɒfɪn/ n. гроб

cog /kɒg/ n. зубец

cogent /'koudʒənt/ adj. убедительный

cogged /kɒgd/ adj. зубчатый

cogitate /'kɒdʒɪ,teɪt/ v. обдумывать impf., обдумать pf.

cognac /'kounyæk/ n. коньяк

cognizance /'kɒgnəzəns/ n. знание; (law) подсудность

cohabit /kou'hæbɪt/ v. сожительствовать impf.

coherence /kou'hɪərəns/ n. последовательность

coherent /kou'hɪərənt/ adj. связный

cohesion /kou'hiʒən/ n. сцепление

cohesive /kou'hisɪv/ adj. сплочённый

coil /kɔɪl/ 1. n. (elec.) катушка; кольцо 2. v. свёртывать(ся) спирально impf.

coin /kɔɪn/ 1. n. монета 2. v. чеканить impf., от- pf.

coincide /,kouɪn'saɪd/ v. совпадать impf., совпасть pf.

coincidence /kou'ɪnsɪdəns/ n. совпадение

coincidental /kou,ɪnsɪ'dentl/ adj. случайный; совпадающий

coitus /'kouɪtəs/ n. совокупление

coke /kouk/ n. кокс

cola /'koulə/ n. кола

colander /'kʌləndər/ n. дуршлаг

cold /kould/ 1. adj. холодный 2. n. холод; (med.) простуда

cold-blooded adj. хладнокровный

coleslaw /'koul,slɔ/ n. салат из капусты

colic /'kɒlɪk/ n. колика

collaborate /kə'læbə,reɪt/ v. сотрудничать impf.

collaboration /kə,læbə'reɪʃən/ n. сотрудничество

collaborator /kə'læbə,reɪtər/ n. сотрудник, -ница

collapse /kə'læps/ 1. n. разрушение, крушение 2. v. рушиться impf., раз- pf.

collapsible /kə'læpsəbəl/ adj. складной; откидной

collar /'kɒlər/ n. воротник; (for dog) ошейник

collarbone /'kɒlər,boun/ n. ключица

collateral /kə'lætərəl/ n. дополнительное обеспечение

collation /kə'leɪʃən/ n. сличение

colleague /'kɒlig/ n. коллега m. & f.

collect /kə'lekt/ v. собирать(ся) impf., собрать(ся) pf.

collected /kə'lektɪd/ adj. собранный

collection /kə'lekʃən/ n. коллекция, сбор, скопление

collective /kə'lektɪv/ 1. n. коллектив 2. adj. коллективный

collective farm n. колхоз

collector /kə'lektər/ n. сборщик, коллекционер

college /'kɒlɪdʒ/ n. колледж

collide /kə'laɪd/ v. сталкиваться impf., столкнуться pf.

collision /kə'lɪʒən/ n. столкновение

colloquial /kə'loukwiəl/ adj. разговорный

colloquialism /kə'loukwiə,lɪzəm/ n. разговорное выражение

collude /kə'lud/ v. тайно сговариваться impf.

collusion /kə'luʒən/ n. сговор

cologne, **eau de Cologne** /'ou də kə'loun/ n. одеколон

colon¹ /'koulən/ n. (punctuation) двоеточие

colon² /'koulən/ n. (anat.) толстая кишка

colonel /'kзrnl/ n. полковник

colonial /kə'louniəl/ adj. колониальный

colonialism /kə'louniə,lɪzəm/ n. колониализм

colonization /ˌkɒlənə'zeiʃən/ n. колониза́ция

colonize /'kɒlə,naiz/ v. колонизи́ровать impf. & pf.

colony /'kɒləni/ n. коло́ния

color /'kʌlər/ 1. n. цвет; (paint) кра́ска 2. v.t. кра́сить impf., по- pf.

colorblind /'kʌlər,blaind/ adj. страда́ющий дальтони́змом

colored /'kʌlərd/ adj. цветной

colorfast /'kʌlər,fæst/ adj. цветосто́йкий

colorful /'kʌlərfəl/ adj. я́ркий

coloring /'kʌləriŋ/ n. раскра́ска

colossal /kə'lɒsəl/ adj. колосса́льный

colt /koult/ n. жеребёнок

column /'kɒləm/ n. коло́нка; столбе́ц, столб

columnist /'kɒləmnist/ n. фельето́нист

coma /'koumə/ n. ко́ма

comb /koum/ 1. n. расчёска 2. v. причёсывать impf., причеса́ть pf.

combat /n. 'kɒmbæt; v. kəm'bæt/ 1. n. бой, сраже́ние 2. v. боро́ться (про́тив + G) impf.

combative /kəm'bætiv/ adj. вои́нственный; драчли́вый

combination /ˌkɒmbə'neiʃən/ n. сочета́ние, комбина́ция

combine /kəm'bain/ v. объединя́ть impf.; сочета́ть impf. & pf.; **—d** adj. совме́стный

combustible /kəm'bʌstəbəl/ adj. горю́чий

combustion /kəm'bʌstʃən/ n. сгора́ние

come /kʌm/ v. (on foot) приходи́ть impf., прийти́ pf.; (by vehicle) приезжа́ть impf., прие́хать pf.; ~ **back** возвраща́ться impf., возврати́ться pf.

comeback /'kʌm,bæk/ n. возвраще́ние

comedian /kə'midiən/ n. ко́мик

comedy /'kɒmidi/ n. коме́дия

comely /'kʌmli/ adj. милови́дный

comet /'kɒmit/ n. коме́та

comfort /'kʌmfərt/ 1. n. комфо́рт; (consolation) утеше́ние 2. v. утеша́ть impf., уте́шить pf.

comfortable /'kʌmftəbəl/ adj. удо́бный

comic /'kɒmik/ adj. коми́ческий

coming /'kʌmiŋ/ 1. n. прие́зд, прихо́д 2. adj. наступа́ющий

comma /'kɒmə/ n. запята́я

command /kə'mænd/ 1. n. прика́з, распоряже́ние 2. v. прика́зывать impf., приказа́ть pf.

commandant /ˌkɒmən'dænt/ n. команди́р; коменда́нт

commander /kə'mændər/ n. команди́р; кома́ндующий (+ I)

commander in chief n. главнокома́ндующий

commandment /kə'mændmənt/ n. за́поведь f.

commando /kə'mændou/ n. деса́нтно-диверсио́нная гру́ппа

commemorate /kə'memə,reit/ v. пра́здновать impf., от- pf.

commemoration /kə,memə'reiʃən/ n. пра́зднование

commemorative /kə'memərətiv/ adj. мемориа́льный

commence /kə'mens/ v. начина́ть(ся) impf., нача́ть(ся) pf.

commend /kə'mend/ v. хвали́ть impf., по- pf.; **—ation** adj. похва́льный; **—ation** n. похвала́

commensurate /kə'mensərit/ adj. соотве́тственный

comment /'kɒment/ 1. n. замеча́ние; примеча́ние 2. v. комменти́ровать impf., про- pf.

commentary /'kɒmən,teri/ n. коммента́рий

commerce /'kɒmərs/ n. торго́вля

commercial /kə'mərʃəl/ 1. n. рекла́ма 2. adj. комме́рческий

commiserate /kə'mizə,reit/ v. сочу́вствовать (+ D) impf.

commiseration /kə,mizə'reiʃən/ n. сочу́вствие, соболе́знование

commission /kə'miʃən/ 1. n. поруче́ние, полномо́чие 2. v. дава́ть поруче́ние impf.

commissioner /kə'miʃənər/ n. комисса́р

commit /kə'mit/ v. соверша́ть impf., -ши́ть pf.; **—ment** n. обяза́тельство

committee /kə'miti/ n. комите́т

commodity /kə'mɒditi/ n. това́р

common /'kɒmən/ adj. о́бщий, обыкнове́нный

commonplace /'kɒmən,pleis/ adj. бана́льный

common sense n. здра́вый смысл

commonwealth /'kɒmənˌwelθ/ n. (state) государство; содружество

commotion /kə'məʊʃən/ n. волнение, суматоха

communal /kə'mjuːnl/ adj. общинный, коммунальный

commune /'kɒmjuːn/ n. община, коммуна

communicate /kə'mjuːnɪˌkeɪt/ v. сообщать impf., -щить pf.

communication /kəˌmjuːnɪ'keɪʃən/ n. связь f.; сообщение

communicative /kə'mjuːnɪkətɪv/ adj. разговорчивый

communion /kə'mjuːnjən/ n. (rite) причастие

communiqué /kəˌmjuːnɪ'keɪ/ neut. indecl. коммюнике

Communism /'kɒmjəˌnɪzəm/ n. коммунизм

Communist /'kɒmjənɪst/ **1.** n. коммунист, —ка **2.** adj. коммунистический

community /kə'mjuːnɪti/ n. (place) район; (people) община

commute /kə'mjuːt/ v. заменять impf.; (travel) ездить ежедневно impf.

commuter /kə'mjuːtər/ n. регулярный пассажир

compact /kəm'pækt, 'kɒmpækt/ adj. компактный, сжатый

compact disk n. компакт-диск

companion /kəm'pænjən/ n. компаньон; товарищ; спутник

companionship /kəm'pænjənˌʃɪp/ n. товарищество

company /'kʌmpəni/ n. компания, общество

comparable /'kɒmpərəbəl/ adj. сравнимый

comparative /kəm'pærətɪv/ adj. сравнительный

compare /kəm'peər/ v. сравнивать(ся) impf., сравнить(ся) pf.

comparison /kəm'pærəsən/ n. сравнение

compartment /kəm'pɑːtmənt/ n. отделение; (train) купе neut. indecl.

compass /'kʌmpəs/ n. компас

compassion /kəm'pæʃən/ n. сострадание

compassionate /kəm'pæʃənɪt/ adj. сострадательный

compatibility /kəmˌpætə'bɪlɪti/ n. совместимость

compatible /kəm'pætəbəl/ adj. совместимый

compatriot /kəm'peɪtrɪət/ n. соотечественник, -ница

compel /kəm'pel/ v. вынуждать impf., вынудить pf.

compelling /kəm'pelɪŋ/ adj. убедительный, неотразимый

compensate /'kɒmpənˌseɪt/ v. компенсировать impf. & pf.

compensation /ˌkɒmpən'seɪʃən/ n. возмещение; компенсация

compete /kəm'piːt/ v. состязаться, соревноваться impf.

competence /'kɒmpɪtəns/ n. умение; компетентность

competent /'kɒmpɪtənt/ adj. компетентный; правомочный

competition /ˌkɒmpɪ'tɪʃən/ n. конкуренция; соревнование

competitive /kəm'petɪtɪv/ adj. соперничающий; конкурсный

competitor /kəm'petɪtər/ n. конкурент, —ка

compilation /ˌkɒmpə'leɪʃən/ n. компилирование; составление

compile /kəm'paɪl/ v. составлять impf., составить pf.

complacence /kəm'pleɪsəns/ n. самодовольство

complacent /kəm'pleɪsənt/ adj. самодовольный

complain /kəm'pleɪn/ v. жаловаться impf., по- pf.

complaint /kəm'pleɪnt/ n. жалоба; недомогание

complement /'kɒmpləmənt/ n. дополнение; комплект

complementary /ˌkɒmplə'mentəri/ adj. дополнительный

complete /kəm'pliːt/ **1.** adj. полный, законченный **2.** v. заканчивать impf., закончить pf.

completely /kəm'pliːtli/ adv. совершенно

completion /kəm'pliːʃən/ n. окончание; завершение

complex /'kɒmpleks/ adj. сложный, составной

complexity /kəm'pleksɪti/ n. сложность

compliance /kəm'plaɪəns/ n. согласие

compliant /kəm'plaɪənt/ adj. податливый; угодливый

complicate /'komplı,keit/ v.
усложня́ть *impf.*, -ни́ть *pf.*

complicated /'komplı,keitıd/ *adj.*
сло́жный; запу́танный

complication /,komplı'keiʃən/ *n.*
сло́жность; запу́танность

complicity /kəm'plısıtı/ *n.*
соуча́стие (в + *P*)

compliment /'kompləmənt/ *n.*
комплиме́нт; *pl.* приве́т

complimentary
/,komplə'mentəri/ *adj.* ле́стный;
(free) беспла́тный

comply /kəm'plai/ v. подчиня́ть-
ся пра́вилам *impf.*

component /kəm'pounənt/ **1.**
adj. составно́й **2.** *n.* дета́ль *P*

compose /kəm'pouz/ v. сочи-
ня́ть *impf.*, -ни́ть *pf.*; состав-
ля́ть *impf.*, соста́вить *pf.*

composed /kəm'pouzd/ *adj.*
(calm) споко́йный

composer /kəm'pouzər/ *n.* ком-
пози́тор

composition /,kompə'zıʃən/ *n.*
сочине́ние

compost /'kompoust/ *n.*
компо́ст

composure /kəm'pouʒər/ *n.*
споко́йствие

compound /'kompaund/ **1.** *adj.*
сло́жный **2.** *n.* соста́в

comprehend /,komprı'hend/ v.
понима́ть *impf.*, поня́ть *pf.*

comprehension
/,komprı'henʃən/ *n.* понима́ние

comprehensive /,komprı'hensıv/
adj. всесторо́нний

compress /kəm'pres/ v. сжима́ть
impf., сжать *pf.*

comprise /kəm'praiz/ v. содер-
жа́ть *impf.*

compromise /'komprə,maiz/ **1.**
n. компроми́сс **2.** v. компроме-
ти́ровать *impf.*, с- *pf.*

compulsion /kəm'pʌlʃən/ *n.*
принужде́ние

compulsive /kəm'pʌlsıv/ *adj.*
принуди́тельный

compulsory /kəm'pʌlsəri/ *adj.*
обяза́тельный

compunction /kəm'pʌŋkʃən/ *n.*
угрызе́ние со́вести; сожале́ние

compute /kəm'pyut/ v. под-
счи́тывать *impf.*, подсчита́ть *pf.*

computer /kəm'pyutər/ *n.* ком-
пью́тер

computerized /kəm'pyutə,raizd/
adj. автоматизи́рованный

computer science *n.*
киберне́тика; информа́тика

computer screen *n.* диспле́й

comrade /'komræd/ *n.* това́рищ

comradeship /'komræd,ʃip/ *n.*
това́рищеские отноше́ния *pl.*

concave /kon'keiv/ *adj.*
во́гнутый

conceal /kən'sil/ v. скрыва́ть
impf., скрыть *pf.*

concede /kən'sid/ v. уступа́ть
impf., -пи́ть *pf.*; признава́ть
impf., призна́ть *pf.*

conceit /kən'sit/ *n.* самомне́ние
—ed *adj.* тщесла́вный

conceivable /kən'sivəbəl/ *adj.*
мысли́мый

conceive /kən'siv/ v. заду́мы-
вать *impf.*, заду́мать *pf.*; *(physiol.)* зачина́ть *impf.*, зача́ть *pf.*

concentrate /'konsən,treit/ v.
сосредото́чивать(ся) *impf.*,
сосредото́чить(ся) *pf.*

concentration /,konsən'treiʃən/
n. концентра́ция

concept /'konsept/ *n.* поня́тие

conception /kən'sepʃən/ *n.*
поня́тие; *(physiol.)* зача́тие

concern /kən'sɜrn/ **1.** *n.* забо́та,
интере́с **2.** v. каса́ться *impf.*;
—ed *adj.* озабо́ченный

concerning /kən'sɜrnıŋ/ *prep.*
относи́тельно (+ *G*)

concert /'konsɜrt/ *n.* конце́рт

concerted /kən'sɜrtıd/ *adj.* со-
гласо́ванный

concession /kən'seʃən/ *n.*
усту́пка

concessionaire /kən,seʃə'neər/
n. концессионе́р

conciliation /kən,sılı'eiʃən/ *n.*
примире́ние

conciliatory /kən'sılıə,tori/ *adj.*
примири́тельный

concise /kən'sais/ *adj.* сжа́тый

conciseness /kən'saisnıs/ *n.*
кра́ткость; сжа́тость

conclude /kən'klud/ v. заклю-
ча́ть *impf.*, -чи́ть *pf.*

conclusion /kən'kluʒən/ *n.*
заключе́ние; вы́вод

conclusive /kən'klusıv/ *adj.*
заключи́тельный

concoct /kon'kokt/ v. состря-
па́ть; приду́мать *pf.*

concordant /kon'kordnt/ *adj.*
согласу́ющийся

concrete /'konkrit/ **1.** *adj.* *(specific)* конкре́тный; *(made of concrete)* бето́нный **2.** *n.* бето́н

concur /kən'kɜr/ v. соглашаться impf., согласиться pf.

concurrently /kən'kɜrəntli/ adv. одновременно

concussion /kən'kʌʃən/ n. сотрясение мозга

condemn /kən'dem/ v. осуждать impf., -дить pf.; **~ation** —n. осуждение

condensation /ˌkɒndən'seiʃən/ n. сгущение; конденсация

condensed /kən'denst/ adj. конденсированный; ~ **milk** сгущённое молоко

condenser /kən'densər/ n. (elec.) конденсатор

condescend /ˌkɒndə'send/ v. снисходить impf., снизойти pf.

condescending /ˌkɒndə'sendiŋ/ adj. снисходительный

condescension /ˌkɒndə'senʃən/ n. снисхождение

condiment /'kɒndəmənt/ n. приправа

condition /kən'diʃən/ **1.** n. положение; условие **2.** v. обусловливать impf., обусловить pf.

conditional /kən'diʃənl/ adj. условный

condolence /kən'douləns/ n. соболезнование; сочувствие

condom /'kɒndəm/ n. презерватив

condone /kən'doun/ v. прощать impf.

conducive /kən'dusɪv/ adj. способствующий

conduct /n. 'kɒndʌkt; v. kən'dʌkt/ **1.** n. поведение **2.** v. вести impf.; (mus.) дирижировать impf.

conductor /kən'dʌktər/ n. проводник; (bus) кондуктор; (mus.) дирижёр

conduit /'kɒndwɪt/ n. водопроводная труба

cone /koun/ n. конус; (bot.) шишка

confectioner /kən'fekʃənər/ n. кондитер

confectionery /kən'fekʃə,neri/ n. кондитерская

confederation /kən,fedə'reiʃən/ n. конфедерация

confer /kən'fɜr/ v. присуждать impf., присудить pf.; v.i. совещаться impf.

conference /'kɒnfərəns/ n. конференция

confess /kən'fes/ v. признаваться impf., признаться pf.

confession /kən'feʃən/ n. признание

confessor /kən'fesər/ n. исповедник

confidant, confidante /'kɒnfɪ,dænt/ n. доверенное лицо

confide /kən'faid/ v. доверять impf., доверить pf.

confident /'kɒnfɪdənt/ adj. уверенный

confidential /ˌkɒnfɪ'denʃəl/ adj. секретный; конфиденциальный

confine /kən'fain/ v. ограничивать impf., ограничить pf.; (in prison) заключать impf.

confinement /kən'fainmənt/ n. заключение

confirm /kən'fɜrm/ v. подтверждать impf., подтвердить pf.

confirmation /ˌkɒnfər'meiʃən/ n. утверждение; подтверждение; (eccles.) конфирмация

confirmed /kən'fɜrmd/ adj. давний; закоренелый

confiscate /'kɒnfə,skeit/ v. конфисковать impf. & pf.

confiscation /ˌkɒnfə'skeiʃən/ n. конфискация

conflict /n. 'kɒnflıkt; v. kən'flıkt/ **1.** n. конфликт **2.** v. противоречить (+ D) impf.

conform /kən'fɔrm/ v. соответствовать (+ D) impf.

conformity /kən'fɔrmɪti/ n. соответствие

confound /kən'faund/ v. спутывать impf., спутать pf.

confounded /kɒn'faundid/ adj. смущённый

confront /kən'frʌnt/ v. стоять лицом к лицу impf.

confrontation /ˌkɒnfrən'teiʃən/ n. конфронтация

confuse /kən'fyuz/ v. смущать; сбивать с толку impf.

confusion /kən'fyuʒən/ n. беспорядок; смущение

congeal /kən'dʒil/ v. замораживать impf., заморозить pf.

congenial /kən'dʒinyəl/ adj. дружеский; благоприятный

congenital /kən'dʒenɪtl/ adj. прирождённый; врождённый

congested /kən'dʒestid/ adj. перенаселённый; тесный

congestion /kən'dʒestʃən/ n.

перенаселённость; (traffic) затор

congratulate /kən'grætʃə,leit/ v. поздравля́ть *impf.*, поздра́вить *pf.*

congratulation /kən,grætʃə'leiʃən/ n. поздравле́ние

congress /'kɒŋgrɪs/ n. съезд

Congressman /'kɒŋgrɪsmən/ n. конгрессме́н

conic /'kɒnɪk/ adj. кони́ческий

conifer /'kounəfər/ n. хво́йное де́рево

coniferous /kou'nɪfərəs/ adj. хво́йный

conjecture /kən'dʒektʃər/ **1.** n. предположе́ние **2.** v. предполага́ть *impf.*, предположи́ть *pf.*

conjugal /'kɒndʒəgəl/ adj. бра́чный; супру́жеский

conjugate /'kɒndʒə,geit/ v. спряга́ть *impf.*, про-- *pf.*

conjugation /,kɒndʒə'geiʃən/ n. спряже́ние

conjunction /kən'dʒʌŋkʃən/ n. соедине́ние; (gram.) сою́з

conjuncture /kən'dʒʌŋktʃər/ n. стече́ние обстоя́тельств

conjure /'kʌndʒər/ v. заклина́ть; вызыва́ть в воображе́нии *impf*

conjuror /'kʌndʒərər/ n. фо́кусник

connect /kə'nekt/ v. соединя́ть *impf.*, соедини́ть *pf.*

connected /kə'nektɪd/ adj. соединённый; свя́занный

connection /kə'nekʃən/ n. связь *f.*; отноше́ние; (train) переса́дка

connivance /kə'naivəns/ n. попусти́тельство

connive /kə'naiv/ v. потво́рствовать *impf*

connoisseur /,kɒnə'sɜr/ n. знато́к

connotation /,kɒnə'teiʃən/ n. дополни́тельное значе́ние

conquer /'kɒŋkər/ v. завоёвывать *impf.*, завоева́ть *pf.*; побежда́ть *impf.*, победи́ть *pf.*; **—or** n. завоева́тель, победи́тель

conquest /'kɒŋkwest/ n. завоева́ние

conscience /'kɒnʃəns/ n. со́весть *f.*

conscientious /,kɒnʃi'enʃəs/ adj. совестли́вый; добросо́вестный

conscious /'kɒnʃəs/ adj. созна́тельный; **be ~ of** сознава́ть (+ A) *impf*

consciousness /'kɒnʃəsnɪs/ n. созна́ние

conscription /kən'skrɪpʃən/ n. во́инская пови́нность

consecrate /'kɒnsɪ,kreit/ v. посвяща́ть *impf.*, посвяти́ть *pf.*

consecration /,kɒnsɪ'kreiʃən/ n. посвяще́ние

consecutive /kən'sekyətɪv/ adj. после́довательный

consensus /kən'sensəs/ n. о́бщее согла́сие

consent /kən'sent/ **1.** n. согла́сие **2.** v. соглаша́ться *impf.*, -си́ться *pf.*

consequence /'kɒnsɪ,kwens/ n. после́дствие; (importance) значе́ние; **in ~ of** prep. всле́дствие (+ G)

consequential /,kɒnsɪ'kwenʃəl/ adj. ва́жный, значи́тельный

consequently /'kɒnsɪ,kwentli/ adv. сле́довательно

conservation /,kɒnsər'veiʃən/ n. сохране́ние; охра́на приро́ды

conservative /kən'sɜrvətɪv/ **1.** adj. консервати́вный **2.** n. консерва́тор

conservatory /kən'sɜrvə,tɔri/ n. консервато́рия

conserve /kən'sɜrv/ v. сохраня́ть; сберега́ть *impf*

consider /kən'sɪdər/ v. (regard as) счита́ть *impf.*, счесть *pf.*; (think about) рассма́тривать *impf.*, рассмотре́ть *pf.*; (take into account) принима́ть во внима́ние *impf*

considerable /kən'sɪdərəbəl/ adj. значи́тельный

considerate /kən'sɪdərɪt/ adj. внима́тельный к други́м

consideration /kən,sɪdə'reiʃən/ n. рассмотре́ние; внима́ние

consign /kən'sain/ v. поруча́ть *impf.*; (com.) отправля́ть *impf*

consignment /kən'sainmənt/ n. отпра́вка; (batch) па́ртия

consist /kən'sist/ v. состоя́ть (из + G) *impf*

consistency /kən'sistənsi/ n. (logic) после́довательность

consistent /kən'sistənt/ adj. после́довательный

consolation /,kɒnsə'leiʃən/ n. утеше́ние

console¹ /kən'soul/ v. утеша́ть *impf.*, уте́шить *pf.*

console² /'kɒnsoul/ n. (control panel) пульт

consolidate /kən'sɒlɪ,deɪt/ v. укрепля́ть impf., -пи́ть pf.

consolidation /kən,sɒlɪ'deɪʃən/ n. укрепле́ние; объедине́ние

consonant /'kɒnsənənt/ n. согла́сный

conspicuous /kən'spɪkyuəs/ adj. ви́дный, заме́тный

conspiracy /kən'spɪrəsi/ n. за́говор

conspirator /kən'spɪrətər/ n. загово́рщик, -щица

conspiratorial /kən,spɪrə'tɔrɪəl/ adj. конспирато́рский

conspire /kən'spaɪᵊr/ v. устра́ивать за́говор impf.

constancy /'kɒnstənsi/ n. постоя́нство

constant /'kɒnstənt/ adj. постоя́нный

constellation /,kɒnstə'leɪʃən/ n. созве́здие

consternation /,kɒnstər'neɪʃən/ n. оцепене́ние; у́жас

constipation /,kɒnstə'peɪʃən/ n. запо́р

constituency /kən'stɪtʃuənsi/ n. избира́тельный о́круг

constituent /kən'stɪtʃuənt/ n. (part) составна́я часть f.; (elector) избира́тель; (math.) конститу́энт

constitute /'kɒnstɪ,tut/ v. составля́ть impf.

constitution /,kɒnstɪ'tuʃən/ n. конститу́ция; **—al** adj. конституцио́нный

constrain /kən'streɪn/ v. принужда́ть impf.

constrained /kən'streɪnd/ adj. (forced) принуждённый; (cramped) стеснённый

constraint /kən'streɪnt/ n. принужде́ние, принуждённость

constrict /kən'strɪkt/ v. сжима́ть impf., сжать pf.; су́живать impf., су́зить pf.

constriction /kən'strɪkʃən/ n. сжа́тие; суже́ние

construct /kən'strʌkt/ v. стро́ить impf., по- pf.; **—ion** n. строи́тельство; (site) стро́йка

constructive /kən'strʌktɪv/ adj. конструкти́вный; строи́тельный

construe /kən'stru/ v. толкова́ть impf.

consul /'kɒnsəl/ n. ко́нсул

consulate /'kɒnsəlɪt/ n. ко́нсульство

consult /kən'sʌlt/ v. сове́товаться (с + I) impf., по- pf.

consultant /kən'sʌltnt/ n. консульта́нт

consultation /,kɒnsəl'teɪʃən/ n. консульта́ция

consume /kən'sum/ v. потребля́ть impf., потреби́ть pf.

consumer /kən'sumər/ n. потреби́тель

consummate /'kɒnsə,meɪt/ v. заверша́ть; соверше́нствовать impf.

consummation /,kɒnsə'meɪʃən/ n. заверше́ние; (of marriage) осуществле́ние

consumption /kən'sʌmpʃən/ n. потребле́ние; (med.) чахо́тка

contact /'kɒntækt/ **1.** n. конта́кт; (person) связь f. **2.** v. связыва́ться (с + I) impf.

contagious /kən'teɪdʒəs/ adj. зара́зный; Fig. зарази́тельный

contain /kən'teɪn/ v. содержа́ть impf.; ~ **oneself** сде́рживаться impf.

container /kən'teɪnər/ n. сосу́д; (for shipping) конте́йнер

contaminate /kən'tæmə,neɪt/ v. заража́ть; загрязня́ть impf.

contamination /kən,tæmə'neɪʃən/ n. загрязне́ние

contemplate /'kɒntəm,pleɪt/ v. созерца́ть impf.

contemplative /kən'templətɪv/ adj. созерца́тельный

contemporary /kən'tempə,rɛri/ **1.** adj. совреме́нный **2.** n. совреме́нник

contempt /kən'tempt/ n. презре́ние; **—ible** adj. презре́нный

contemptuous /kən'temptʃuəs/ adj. презри́тельный

contend /kən'tend/ v. (assert) утвержда́ть impf., утверди́ть pf.; (compete) состяза́ться impf.

content¹ /kən'tent/ adj. дово́льный

content² /'kɒntent/ n. содержа́ние

contention /kən'tenʃən/ n. (dispute) спор; (claim) утвержде́ние

contentious /kən'tenʃəs/ adj. сварли́вый; спо́рный

contest /'kɒntest/ v. kən'test/ **1.** n. ко́нкурс **2.** v. спо́рить impf.

contestant /kən'testənt/ n. уча́стник, -ница соревнова́ния

context /'kɒntekst/ n. конте́кст

continent /'kɒntɪnənt/ *n.* матери́к

continental /ˌkɒntɪn'entl/ *adj.* материко́вый, континента́льный

contingency /kən'tɪndʒənsɪ/ *n.* случа́йность

contingent /kən'tɪndʒənt/ **1.** *adj.* возмо́жный; **be ~ on** зави́сеть (от + G) *impf.* **2.** *n.* контингéнт

continuation /kənˌtɪnyu'eɪʃən/ *n.* продолже́ние

continue /kən'tɪnyu/ *v.* продолжа́ть *impf.*, продо́лжить *pf.*

continuity /ˌkɒntɪn'uɪtɪ/ *n.* непреры́вность

continuous /kən'tɪnyuəs/ *adj.* непреры́вный

contort /kən'tɔrt/ *v.* искривля́ть *impf.*; —**ion** *n.* искривле́ние

contour /'kɒntur/ *n.* ко́нтур

contraband /'kɒntrəˌbænd/ *n.* контраба́нда

contraception /ˌkɒntrə'sepʃən/ *n.* примене́ние противозача́точных мер

contraceptive /ˌkɒntrə'septɪv/ *adj.* противозача́точный

contract /*n.* 'kɒntrækt; *v.* kən'trækt/ **1.** *n.* догово́р, контра́кт **2.** *v.* заключа́ть догово́р *impf.*; (*reduce*) сжима́ться *impf.*, сжа́ться *pf.*; —**ion** *n.* сжа́тие; сокраще́ние; —**or** *n.* подря́дчик

contradict /ˌkɒntrə'dɪkt/ *v.* противоре́чить *impf.*; —**ion** *n.* противоре́чие; —**ory** *adj.* противоречи́вый

contraindication /ˌkɒntrəˌɪndɪ'keɪʃən/ *n.* противопоказа́ние

contralto /kən'træltou/ *n.* контра́льто *neut. indecl.*

contraption /kən'træpʃən/ *n.* устро́йство

contrary /'kɒntrerɪ/ *adj.* противополо́жный; **~ to** вопреки́ (+ D); **on the ~** наоборо́т

contrast /*n.* 'kɒntræst; *v.* kən'træst/ **1.** *n.* контра́ст **2.** *v.* противопоставля́ть *impf.*, -поста́вить *pf.*

contravene /ˌkɒntrə'vin/ *v.* наруша́ть *impf.*, нару́шить *pf.*

contravention /ˌkɒntrə'venʃən/ *n.* наруше́ние

contribute /kən'trɪbyut/ *v.* же́ртвовать *impf.*, по- *pf.*

contribution /ˌkɒntrə'byuʃən/ *n.* поже́ртвование; вклад

contributor /kən'trɪbyətər/ *n.* сотру́дник; же́ртвователь

contrite /kən'traɪt/ *adj.* ка́ющийся

contrivance /kən'traɪvəns/ *n.* приспособле́ние

contrive /kən'traɪv/ *v.* приду́мывать *impf.*, приду́мать *pf.*

control /kən'troul/ **1.** *n.* прове́рка, контро́ль *m.*; (*direction*) управле́ние **2.** *v.* контроли́ровать *impf.*, про- *pf.*; (*regulate*) управля́ть *impf.*; —**ler** *n.* контролёр

controversial /ˌkɒntrə'vɜrʃəl/ *adj.* спо́рный

controversy /'kɒntrəˌvɜrsɪ/ *n.* спор, поле́мика

convalesce /ˌkɒnvə'les/ *v.* выздора́вливать *impf.*, вы́здороветь *pf.*

convalescence /ˌkɒnvə'lesəns/ *n.* выздоравливание

convene /kən'vin/ *v.* собира́ться *impf.*, собра́ться *pf.*

convenience /kən'vinyəns/ *n.* удо́бство

convenient /kən'vinyənt/ *adj.* удо́бный

convent /'kɒnvent/ *n.* же́нский монасты́рь *m.*

convention /kən'venʃən/ *n.* съезд; (*custom*) обы́чай

conventional /kən'venʃənl/ *adj.* усло́вный; обы́чный

converge /kən'vɜrdʒ/ *v.* сходи́ться *impf.*, сойти́сь *pf.*

conversation /ˌkɒnvər'seɪʃən/ *n.* разгово́р

conversational /ˌkɒnvər'seɪʃənl/ *adj.* разгово́рный

converse[1] /kən'vɜrs/ *v.* бесе́довать *impf.*

converse[2] /kən'vɜrs/ *adj.* противополо́жный

conversely /kən'vɜrslɪ/ *adv.* наоборо́т

conversion /kən'vɜrʒən/ *n.* перево́д; (*relig.*) перехо́д

convert /kən'vɜrt/ *v.* превраща́ть *impf.*, -ти́ть *pf.*; (*relig.*) обраща́ть *impf.*

convertible /kən'vɜrtəbəl/ *adj.* обрати́мый, изменя́мый

convex /kɒn'veks/ *adj.* вы́пуклый

convey /kən'vei/ *v.* перевози́ть *impf.*, перевезти́ *pf.*; передава́ть *impf.*, переда́ть *pf.*; **—ance** *n.* перево́зка

conveyor belt /kən'veiər/ *n.* ле́нточный конве́йер

convict /'kɒnvɪkt/ *n.* осуждённый

conviction /kən'vɪkʃən/ *n.* осужде́ние; (*belief*) убежде́ние

convince /kən'vɪns/ *v.* убежда́ть *impf.*, убеди́ть *pf.*

convincing /kən'vɪnsɪŋ/ *adj.* убеди́тельный

convivial /kən'vɪvɪəl/ *adj.* весёлый

convocation /ˌkɒnvə'keiʃən/ *n.* созы́в; собра́ние

convoluted /'kɒnvəˌlutɪd/ *adj.* изви́листый; запу́танный

convoy /'kɒnvɔi/ *n.* конво́й

convulsion /kən'vʌlʃən/ *n.* су́дороги *pl.*; конву́льсия

cook /kʊk/ **1.** *n.* по́вар, куха́рка **2.** *v.* гото́вить *impf.*, при- *pf.*

cookie /'kʊki/ *n.* пече́нье

cooking /'kʊkɪŋ/ *n.* ку́хня

cool /kul/ **1.** *adj.* прохла́дный **2.** *v.* охлажда́ть *impf.*, охлади́ть *pf.*; **~ off** остыва́ть *impf.*; **—ness** *n.* прохла́да; (*of person*) хладнокро́вие

coop /kup/ *n.* куря́тник

cooperate /kou'ɒpəˌreit/ *v.* сотру́дничать *impf.*

cooperative /kou'ɒpərətɪv/ *adj.* совме́стный, коопера́тив

coordinate /kou'ɔrdnˌeit/ *v.* координи́ровать *impf.* & *pf.*

coordination /kouˌɔrdn'eiʃən/ *n.* координа́ция

cop /kɒp/ *n.* *Colloq.* полице́йский

cope /koup/ *v.* справля́ться (c + I) *impf.*

copier /'kɒpiər/ *n.* копирова́льная маши́на

copious /'koupiəs/ *adj.* оби́льный

copper /'kɒpər/ *n.* медь *f.*

copse /kɒps/ *n.* ро́щица

copulate /'kɒpyəˌleit/ *v.* спа́риваться, совокупля́ться *impf.*

copy /'kɒpi/ **1.** *n.* экземпля́р, ко́пия **2.** *v.* копи́ровать *impf.*; (*transcribe*) перепи́сывать *impf.*

copyright /'kɒpiˌrait/ *n.* а́вторское пра́во

coral /'kɒrəl/ *n.* кора́лл

cord /kɔrd/ *n.* верёвка; (*elec.*) шнур; **vocal —s** голосовы́е свя́зки *pl.*

cordial /'kɔrdʒəl/ *adj.* серде́чный

corduroy /'kɔrdəˌrɔi/ *n.* рубча́тый плис; *pl.* пли́совые штаны́ *pl.*

core /kɔr/ *n.* сердцеви́на; *Fig.* суть *f.*

cork /kɔrk/ *n.* про́бка

corkscrew /'kɔrkˌskru/ *n.* што́пор

corn¹ /kɔrn/ *n.* кукуру́за, зерно́

corn² /kɔrn/ *n.* (*med.*) мозо́ль *f.*

cornea /'kɔrniə/ *n.* рогови́ца

corned beef /kɔrnd/ *n.* солони́на

corner /'kɔrnər/ *n.* у́гол

cornerstone /'kɔrnərˌstoun/ *n.* углово́й ка́мень *m.*

cornet /kɔr'net/ *n.* корне́т

cornflower /'kɔrnˌflauər/ *n.* василёк

cornice /'kɔrnis/ *n.* карни́з

coronary /'kɔrəˌneri/ *adj.* вене́чный

coronation /ˌkɔrə'neiʃən/ *n.* корона́ция

coroner /'kɔrənər/ *n.* патолого-ана́том

corporal¹ /'kɔrpərəl/ *n.* капра́л

corporal² /'kɔrpərəl/ *adj.* теле́сный

corporate /'kɔrpərit/ *adj.* корпорати́вный

corporation /ˌkɔrpə'reiʃən/ *n.* корпора́ция

corporeal /kɔr'pɔriəl/ *adj.* теле́сный; физи́ческий

corps /kɔr/ *n.* ко́рпус

corpse /kɔrps/ *n.* труп

corpulent /'kɔrpyələnt/ *adj.* доро́дный

corpuscle /'kɔrpəsəl/ *n.* кровяно́й ша́рик

correct /kə'rekt/ **1.** *adj.* пра́вильный **2.** *v.* поправля́ть; исправля́ть *impf.*, испра́вить *pf.*; **—ion** *n.* попра́вка

correlation /ˌkɔrə'leiʃən/ *n.* соотноше́ние, корреля́ция

correspond /ˌkɔrə'spɒnd/ *v.* (*by letter*) перепи́сываться *impf.*; (*conform*) соотве́тствовать *impf.*; **—ence** *n.* корреспонде́нция, перепи́ска; (*conformity*) соотве́тствие; **—ent** *n.* корреспонде́нт; **—ing** *adj.* соотве́тствующий

corridor /'kɔridər/ *n.* коридо́р

corroborate /kə'rɒbəˌreit/ *v.* подтвержда́ть *impf.*, -тверди́ть *pf.*

corrode /kə'roud/ v. разъеда́ть *impf.*, разъе́сть *pf.*

corrosion /kə'rouʒən/ n. корро́зия

corrosive /kə'rousiv/ n. е́дкий

corrugated /'kɔrə,geitid/ adj. гофри́рованный; рифлёный

corrupt /kə'rʌpt/ 1. adj. прода́жный 2. v. развраща́ть *impf.*, -ти́ть *pf.*

corruptible /kə'rʌptəbəl/ adj. подку́пный

corruption /kə'rʌpʃən/ n. развраще́ние

corset /'kɔrsit/ n. корсе́т

cortege /kɔr'teʒ/ n. корте́ж

cortex /'kɔrteks/ n. кора́

cosmetic /kɒz'metik/ 1. adj. космети́ческий 2. n.pl. косме́тика

cosmic /'kɒzmik/ adj. косми́ческий

cosmonaut /'kɒzmə,nɔt/ n. космона́вт

cosmopolitan /,kɒzmə'pɒlitn/ adj. космополити́ческий

cosmos /'kɒzmous/ n. ко́смос, вселе́нная

Cossack /'kɒsæk/ 1. adj. каза́цкий 2. n. каза́к, каза́чка

cost /kɔst/ 1. n. сто́имость, цена́ 2. v. сто́ить *impf.*

cost-effective adj. рента́бельный

costly /'kɔstli/ adv. дорого́й

costume /'kɒstum/ n. костю́м

cot /kɒt/ n. раскладу́шка

cottage /'kɒtidʒ/ n. да́ча

cotton /'kɒtn/ 1. adj. хлопчато-бума́жный 2. n. хло́пок; **ab-sorbent** ~ ва́та

couch /kautʃ/ n. дива́н

cough /kɔf/ 1. n. ка́шель m. 2. v. ка́шлять *impf.*; ~ **drop** табле́тка от ка́шля

council /'kaunsəl/ n. сове́т; **—or** n. член сове́та

counsel /'kaunsəl/ 1. n. сове́т; (*law*) адвока́т 2. v. сове́товать *impf.*, по- *pf.*; **—or** n. консульта́нт

count¹ /kaunt/ 1. n. счёт 2. v. счита́ть *impf.*, со- *pf.*

count² /kaunt/ n. граф

countdown /'kaunt,daun/ n. отсчёт вре́мени

countenance /'kauntənəns/ n. лицо́; выраже́ние лица́

counter /'kauntər/ n. счётчик

counteract /,kauntər'ækt/ v. противоде́йствовать (+ D) *impf.*

counterattack /'kauntərə,tæk/ n. контрата́ка

counterbalance /'kauntər,bæləns/ n. противове́с

counterclockwise /,kauntər'klɒk,waiz/ adv. про́тив часово́й стре́лки

counterfeit /'kauntər,fit/ 1. adj. подде́льный 2. v. подде́лывать *impf.*, подде́лать *pf.*; **—er** n. фальшивомоне́тчик

counterpart /'kauntər,part/ n. собра́т

counterpoint /'kauntər,pɔint/ n. контрапу́нкт

counterproductive /,kauntərprə'dʌktiv/ adj. нецелесообра́зный

counterrevolution /'kauntər,revə'luʃən/ n. контрреволю́ция

countess /'kauntis/ n. графи́ня

countless /'kauntlis/ adj. бесчи́сленный

country /'kʌntri/ 1. n. дереве́нский 2. n. страна́; (*native*) ро́дина; (*rural districts*) дере́вня

countryman /'kʌntrimən/ n. соооте́чественник

countryside /'kʌntri,said/ n. се́льская ме́стность

county /'kaunti/ n. о́круг

coup /ku/ n. (*polit.*) переворо́т

couple /'kʌpəl/ 1. n. па́ра 2. v. сцепля́ть *impf.*, -пи́ть *pf.*

coupon /'kupɒn/ n. купо́н

courage /'kɜridʒ/ n. сме́лость

courageous /kə'reidʒəs/ adj. му́жественный, сме́лый

courier /'kɜriər/ n. курье́р

course /kɔrs/ n. курс; ход; (*meal*) блю́до; **of** ~ коне́чно

court /kɔrt/ n. двор; (*law*) суд; (*sports*) корт

courteous /'kɜrtiəs/ adj. ве́жливый

courtesy /'kɜrtəsi/ n. ве́жливость

courtier /'kɔrtiər/ n. придво́рный

courting /'kɔrtiŋ/ n. уха́живание

courtyard /'kɔrt,yard/ n. двор

cousin /'kʌzən/ n. двою́родный брат, двою́родная сестра́

cove /kouv/ n. бу́хточка

covenant /'kʌvənənt/ n. соглаше́ние, догово́р; (*relig.*) заве́т

cover /ˈkʌvər/ **1.** n. (lid) крышка; чехол; (bed) одеяло; (book) переплёт; (protection) прикрытие **2.** v. покрывать impf., покрыть pf.

coverage /ˈkʌvərɪdʒ/ n. (press) освещение; охват

covert /ˈkouvərt/ adj. скрытный

covet /ˈkʌvɪt/ v. жаждать (+ G) impf.

cow /kau/ n. корова

coward /ˈkauərd/ n. трус; **—ly** adj. трусливый

cowardice /ˈkauərdɪs/ n. трусость

cowboy /ˈkau‚bɔɪ/ n. ковбой

cower /ˈkauər/ v. съёживаться impf.

cowl /kaul/ n. капюшон

coy /kɔɪ/ adj. застенчивый

cozy /ˈkouzi/ adj. уютный

crab /kræb/ n. краб

crack /kræk/ **1.** n. трещина, (noise) треск **2.** v. колоть impf., рас- pf.; v.i. трескаться

cracker /ˈkrækər/ n. сухое печенье

crackle /ˈkrækəl/ n. потрескивание, треск; (snow) хруст

cradle /ˈkreidl/ n. колыбель f.

craftiness /ˈkræftinis/ n. хитрость

craftsman /ˈkræftsmən/ n. ремесленник

crafty /ˈkræfti/ adj. хитрый

crag /kræg/ n. скала, утёс

craggy /ˈkrægi/ adj. скалистый

cram /kræm/ v. набивать impf., набить pf.; (study) зубрить impf.

cramp /kræmp/ n. судорога

cramped /kræmpt/ adj. (restricted) стеснённый; (writing) сжатый

cranberry /ˈkræn‚beri/ n. клюква

crane /krein/ n. (bird) журавль m.; (mech.) подъёмный кран

crank /kræŋk/ n. рукоятка

crankshaft /ˈkræŋk‚ʃæft/ n. коленчатый вал

cranky /ˈkræŋki/ adj. (eccentric) чудаковатый, причудливый

cranny /ˈkræni/ n. щель f.

crash /kræʃ/ **1.** n. грохот, треск; **disk ~** (comput.) крах or авария диска **2.** v. разбиться pf.

crash-land v. совершать аварийную посадку impf.

crass /kræs/ adj. (coarse) грубый

crate /kreit/ n. ящик

crater /ˈkreitər/ n. кратер

crave /kreiv/ v. жаждать impf.

craving /ˈkreivɪŋ/ n. страстное желание

crawl /krɔl/ v. ползать indet., ползти det.

crayfish /ˈkrei‚fiʃ/ n. рак

crayon /ˈkreiən/ n. цветной карандаш

craze /kreiz/ n. мания

crazy /ˈkreizi/ adj. сумасшедший

creaky /ˈkriki/ adj. скрипучий

cream /krim/ n. сливки pl.; (cosmetic) крем

creamy /ˈkrimi/ adj. сливочный

crease /kris/ **1.** n. складка; (paper) фальц **2.** v. мять(ся) impf.

create /kriˈeit/ v. творить impf., co- pf.; создавать impf.

creation /kriˈeiʃən/ n. создание

creative /kriˈeitiv/ adj. творческий

creator /kriˈeitər/ n. создатель

creature /ˈkritʃər/ n. существо

crèche /kreʃ/ n. детские ясли pl.

credence /ˈkridns/ n. вера; доверие

credentials /krɪˈdenʃəlz/ n. мандат; верительные грамоты pl.

credibility /‚kredəˈbiliti/ n. правдоподобие

credible /ˈkredəbəl/ adj. вероятный; правдоподобный

credit /ˈkredit/ **1.** n. кредит **2.** v. кредитовать impf. & pf.

creditor /ˈkreditər/ n. кредитор

credulous /ˈkredʒələs/ adj. легковерный

creed /krid/ n. вероучение

creeper /ˈkripər/ n. ползучее растение

creepy /ˈkripi/ adj. жуткий

cremate /ˈkrimeit/ v. кремировать impf. & pf.

crematorium /‚kriməˈtɔriəm/ n. крематорий

crepe /kreip/ n. креп

crescendo /krɪˈʃendou/ n. & adv. крещендо neut. indecl.

crescent /ˈkresənt/ n. полумесяц

crest /krest/ n. гребень m.

crestfallen /ˈkrest‚fɔlən/ adj. удручённый

crevasse /krəˈvæs/ n. расселина

crevice /ˈkrevis/ n. щель f.

crew /kru/ n. экипаж, команда

crib /krib/ n. детская кроватка

cricket /ˈkrikit/ n. сверчок

crime /kraim/ *n.* преступле́ние

Crimea /krai'miə/ *n.* Крым

criminal /'krimənl/ **1.** *adj.* престу́пный **2.** *n.* престу́пник

crimson /'krimzən/ *adj.* багро́вый, мали́новый

cringe /krindʒ/ *v.* раболе́пствовать; съёживаться *impf.*

cripple /'kripəl/ **1.** *n.* кале́ка *m. & f.* **2.** *v.* кале́чить *impf.*, ис- *pf.*

crisis /'kraisis/ *n.* кри́зис; перело́м

crisp /krisp/ *adj.* хрустя́щий

criterion /krai'tiəriən/ *n.* крите́рий

critic /'kritik/ *n.* кри́тик; —al *adj.* крити́ческий

criticism /'kritə,sizəm/ *n.* кри́тика

criticize /'kritə,saiz/ *v.* критикова́ть *impf.*

croak /krouk/ *v.* ква́кать *impf.*

crockery /'krokəri/ *n.* посу́да

crocodile /'krokə,dail/ *n.* крокоди́л

crocus /'kroukəs/ *n.* кро́кус

crony /'krouni/ *n.* закады́чный друг

crook /kruk/ *n.* (*hook*) крюк

crooked /'krukid/ *adj.* криво́й; (*dishonest*) нече́стный

crop /krop/ *n.* урожа́й

croquet /krou'kei/ *n.* кроке́т

cross /kros/ **1.** *adj.* перекре́стный; (*angry*) серди́тый **2.** *n.* крест; (*hybrid*) по́месь *f.* **3.** *v.t.* (*biol.*) скре́щивать *impf.*, скрести́ть *pf.*; (*traverse*) переходи́ть *impf.*, перейти́ *pf.*; *v.i.* пересека́ться *impf.*

crossbeam /'kros,bim/ *n.* кресто-ви́на

crossbreed /'kros,brid/ *n.* гибри́д

cross-examination *n.* перекре́стный допро́с

cross-eyed *adj.* косогла́зый

crossfire /'kros,faiᵊr/ *n.* перекре́стный ого́нь *m.*

crossing /'krosiŋ/ *n.* пересече́ние; (*crossroads*) перекрёсток

cross-legged *adv.* положи́в но́гу на́ ногу

cross-reference *n.* перекре́стная ссы́лка

cross section *n.* попере́чное сече́ние

crossword puzzle /'kros,wərd/ *n.* кроссво́рд

crotch /krotʃ/ *n.* проме́жность

crouch /krautʃ/ *v.* приседа́ть *impf.*; согну́ться *pf.*

crouton /'kruton/ *n.* гре́нок

crow /krou/ *n.* воро́на

crowbar /'krou,bar/ *n.* лом

crowd /kraud/ **1.** *n.* толпа́ **2.** *v.* тесни́ть(ся); толпи́ться *impf.*

crowded /kraudid/ *adj.* те́сный

crown /kraun/ **1.** *n.* коро́на; (*tooth*) коро́нка; (*head*) маку́шка **2.** *v.* коронова́ть *impf. & pf.*

crucial /'kruʃəl/ *adj.* реша́ющий

crucifix /'krusə,fiks/, **crucifixion** /,krusə'fikʃən/ *n.* распя́тие

crucify /'krusə,fai/ *v.* распина́ть *impf.*, распя́ть *pf.*

crude /krud/ *adj.* сыро́й; (*rude*) гру́бый; необрабо́танный

crudeness /'krudnis/ *n.* гру́бость

cruel /'kruəl/ *adj.* жесто́кий

cruelty /'kruəlti/ *n.* жесто́кость

cruise /kruz/ *v.* круи́з

cruiser /'kruzər/ *n.* кре́йсер

crumb /krʌm/ *n.* кро́шка; —ly *adj.* рассы́пчатый

crumble /'krʌmbəl/ *v.* кроши́ться *impf.*

crumple /'krʌmpəl/ *v.* мять(ся) *impf.*, по- *pf.*

crunch /krʌntʃ/ *n.* хруст

crusade /kru'seid/ *n.* кампа́ния; (*hist.*) кресто́вый похо́д

crush /krʌʃ/ *v.* дави́ть; подавля́ть *impf.*, подави́ть *pf.*

crust /krʌst/ *n.* ко́рка; кора́

crutch /krʌtʃ/ *n.* косты́ль *m.*

crux /krʌks/ *n.* суть *f.*

cry /krai/ **1.** *n.* крик, плач **2.** *v.* пла́кать; крича́ть *impf.*

crypt /kript/ *n.* склеп

cryptic /'kriptik/ *adj.* зага́дочный

crystal /'kristl/ **1.** *n.* хруста́ль *m.* **2.** *adj.* хруста́льный

crystallize /'kristl,aiz/ *v.* кристаллизова́ть(ся) *impf. & pf.*

cub /kʌb/ *n.* детёныш

cube /kyub/ *n.* куб

cubic /'kyubik/ *adj.* куби́ческий

cubicle /'kyubikəl/ *n.* каби́нка

cuckold /'kʌkəld/ *n.* рогоно́сец

cuckoo /'kuku/ *n.* куку́шка

cucumber /'kyukʌmbər/ *n.* огуре́ц

cud /kʌd/ *n.* жва́чка

cuddle /'kʌdl/ **1.** *n.* объя́тия *pl.* **2.** *v.* обнима́ть(ся) *impf.*

cudgel /'kʌdʒəl/ *n.* дуби́на

cue[1] /kyu/ *n.* намёк

cue² /kyu/ *n.* (*billiards*) кий

cuff /kʌf/ *n.* манжета

cuff link *n.* запонка

culinary /'kyulə,nɛri/ *adj.* кулинарный

cull /kʌl/ *v.* отбирать *impf.*

culmination /,kʌlmə'neiʃən/ *n.* кульминационный пункт

culpability /,kʌlpə'bɪliti/ *n.* виновность

culpable /'kʌlpəbəl/ *adj.* виновный, преступный

cult /kʌlt/ *n.* культ

cultivate /'kʌltə,veit/ *v.* обрабатывать *impf.*, обработать *pf.*; культивировать *impf. & pf.*

culture /'kʌltʃər/ *n.* культура; —d *adj.* культурный

cumbersome /'kʌmbərsəm/ *adj.* громоздкий

cumulative /'kyumyəlɛtɪv/ *adj.* совокупный, кумулятивный

cunning /'kʌnɪŋ/ **1.** *n.* ловкость, хитрость **2.** *adj.* ловкий, хитрый

cup /kʌp/ *n.* чашка

cupola /'kyupələ/ *n.* купол

curable /'kyurəbəl/ *adj.* излечимый

curative /'kyurətɪv/ *adj.* лечебный

curator /kyu'reitər/ *n.* хранитель

curb /kɜrb/ **1.** *n.* обочина; край тротуара **2.** *v.* обуздывать *impf.*

curd /kɜrd/ *n.* творог

curdle /'kɜrdl/ *v.* свёртываться *impf.*, свернуться *pf.*

cure /kyur/ **1.** *n.* средство **2.** *v.* лечить *impf.*, вылечить *pf.*

curfew /'kɜrfyu/ *n.* комендантский час

curiosity /,kyuri'ɒsiti/ *n.* любопытство

curious /'kyuriəs/ *adj.* любопытный

curl /kɜrl/ **1.** *n.* локон, завиток **2.** *v.t.* завивать *impf.*, завить *pf.*

curler /'kɜrlər/ *n.* бигуди *pl.*

curly /'kɜrli/ *adj.* вьющийся

currant /'kɜrənt/ *n.* смородина

currency /'kɜrənsi/ *n.* (*money*) валюта; (*prevalence*) хождение

current /'kɜrənt/ **1.** *adj.* текущий **2.** *n.* (*flow*) течение; (*elec.*) ток

curriculum /kə'rɪkyələm/ *n.* учебный план; программа

curry¹ /'kɜri/ *n.* кэрри *neut. indecl.*

curry² /'kɜri/ *v.:* ~ favor with заискивать (перед + I) *impf.*

curse /kɜrs/ **1.** *n.* проклятие **2.** *v.* ругаться; проклинать *impf.*

cursor /'kɜrsər/ *n.* (*on slide rule*) движок; (*on screen*) зайчик

cursory /'kɜrsəri/ *adj.* беглый

curt /kɜrt/ *adj.* отрывистый

curtail /kər'teil/ *v.* сокращать *impf.*, -тить *pf.*

curtain /'kɜrtn/ *n.* занавеска; (*theat.*) занавес

curtsy /'kɜrtsi/ *n.* реверанс

curve /kɜrv/ **1.** *n.* изгиб; (*math.*) кривая **2.** *v.* изгибать(ся) *impf.*, изогнуть(ся) *pf.*

cushion /'kuʃən/ *n.* подушка

custard /'kʌstərd/ *n.* заварной крем

custodian /kʌ'stoudiən/ *n.* хранитель, опекун

custody /'kʌstədi/ *n.* охрана, опека; (*police*) арест

custom /'kʌstəm/ *n.* обычай

customary /'kʌstə,mɛri/ *adj.* обычный

customer /'kʌstəmər/ *n.* покупатель, клиент

customs /'kʌstəmz/ **1.** *adj.* таможенный **2.** *n.* таможня

cut /kʌt/ **1.** *n.* порез; снижение **2.** *v.* резать *impf.*, по-, с- *pf.*; (*hair*) стричь *impf.*; (*prices, etc.*) снижать *impf.*; ~ oneself порезаться *pf.*

cutback /'kʌt,bæk/ *n.* сокращение

cute /kyut/ *adj.* милый

cuticle /'kyutikəl/ *n.* заусеница

cutlery /'kʌtləri/ *n.* столовые приборы *pl.*

cutting /'kʌtɪŋ/ *n.* резание, вырезка; (*from plant*) черенок

cyanide /'saiə,naid/ *n.* цианид

cybernetics /,saibər'nɛtɪks/ *n.* кибернетика

cyberspace /'saibər,speis/ *n.* киберпространство

cycle /'saikəl/ **1.** *n.* цикл **2.** *v.* ездить на велосипеде *impf.*

cyclical /'saiklɪkəl, 'sɪklɪ-/ *adj.* циклический

cyclist /'saiklɪst/ *n.* велосипедист

cylinder /'sɪlɪndər/ *n.* цилиндр

cylindrical /sɪ'lɪndrɪkəl/ *adj.* цилиндрический

cymbal /'sɪmbəl/ *n.* тарелка

cynic /'sɪnɪk/ *n.* циник

cynical /'sɪnɪkəl/ *adj.* циничный

cynicism /'sɪnə,sɪzəm/ *n.* цинизм

cypress /'saiprəs/ *n.* кипарис

Cyrillic /'sɪ'rɪlɪk/ *n.* кириллица

cyst /sɪst/ *n.* киста

czar /zɑr, tsɑr/ *n.* царь *m.*

czarina /zɑ'rinə, tsɑ-/ *n.* царица

Czech /tʃek/ **1.** *adj.* чешский **2.** *n.* чех, чешка; **~ Republic** Чешская Республика

— D —

dab /dæb/ **1.** *n.* тычок; мазок **2.** *v.* легко касаться; тыкать *impf.*

dabbler /'dæblər/ *n.* дилетант

dachshund /'dɑks,hʊnt/ *n.* такса

dad /dæd/ *n.* папа, отец

daffodil /'dæfədɪl/ *n.* нарцисс

dagger /'dægər/ *n.* кинжал

dahlia /'dælyə/ *n.* георгин

daily /'deili/ *adj.* ежедневный

dairy /'deəri/ *n.* (*shop*) молочная

dais /'deiɪs/ *n.* помост

daisy /'deizi/ *n.* маргаритка

dale /deil/ *n.* долина

dally /'dæli/ *v.* слоняться, болтаться *impf.*

dam /dæm/ *n.* дамба, плотина

damage /'dæmɪdʒ/ **1.** *n.* ущерб **2.** *v.* повреждать *impf.*, повредить *pf.*

damn /dæm/ *v.* проклинать *impf.*, проклясть *pf.*

damnation /dæm'neiʃən/ *n.* проклятие

damned /dæmd/ *adj.* проклятый

damp /dæmp/ *adj.* сырой; **—ness** *n.* сырость, влажность

dance /dæns/ **1.** *n.* танец **2.** *v.* танцевать *impf.*; **~ band** эстрадный оркестр; **~ hall** танцевальный зал

dancer /'dænsər/ *n.* танцовщик

dandelion /'dændl,aiən/ *n.* одуванчик

dandified /'dændəfaid/ *adj.* щегольской, фатоватый

dandruff /'dændrəf/ *n.* перхоть *f.*

dandy /'dændi/ *n.* денди *m. indecl.*, щёголь *m.*

Dane /dein/ *n.* датчанин, -чанка

danger /'deindʒər/ *n.* опасность

dangerous /'deindʒərəs/ *adj.* опасный; рискованный

dangle /'dæŋgəl/ *v.* покачивать *impf.*

Danish /'deiniʃ/ *adj.* датский

dapper /'dæpər/ *adj.* опрятный

dare /deər/ *v.* осмеливаться *impf.*, осмелиться *pf.*

daredevil /'deər,devəl/ *n.* смельчак

daring /'deəriŋ/ **1.** *n.* отвага **2.** *adj.* отважный, смелый

dark /dɑrk/ *adj.* тёмный; **—en** *v.* затемнять *impf.*, -нить *pf.*

darkness /'dɑrknɪs/ *n.* темнота

darling /'dɑrlɪŋ/ *n.* дорогой, дорогая; любимец, любимка

darn /dɑrn/ *v.* штопать *impf.*, за- *pf.*

dart /dɑrt/ *n.* стрела

dash /dæʃ/ **1.** *n.* рывок; (*hyphen*) тире *neut. indecl.* **2.** *v.* ринуться *pf.*

dashboard /'dæʃ,bɔrd/ *n.* передний щиток

dashing /'dæʃɪŋ/ *adj.* лихой

data /'deitə/ *n.* данные *pl.*

database /'deitəbeis/ *n.* база данных

date[1] /deit/ *n.* дата, число; (*engagement*) свидание

date[2] /deit/ *n.* (*fruit*) финик

dative /'deitiv/ *n.* дательный падеж

daub /dɔb/ *n.* мазня; мазок

daughter /'dɔtər/ *n.* дочь *f.*

daughter-in-law /'dɔtər/ *n.* сноха

dauntless /'dɔntlɪs/ *adj.* бесстрашный

dawdle /'dɔdl/ *v.* мешкать *impf.*

dawn /dɔn/ **1.** *n.* заря **2.** *v.* рассветать *impf.*

day /dei/ *n.* день *m.*; **~ by ~** изо дня в день; **by ~** днём; **every other ~** через день; **in a ~ or two** на днях; **the ~ after tomorrow** послезавтра; **the ~ before** накануне; **the ~ before yesterday** позавчера

daybreak /'dei,breik/ *n.* рассвет

daydream /'dei,drim/ *n.* мечта

daylight /'dei,lait/ *n.* дневной свет

daytime /'dei,taim/ *n.* дневное время *neut.*; **in the ~** днём

dazzle /'dæzəl/ *v.* ослеплять *impf.*

deacon /'dikən/ *n.* дьякон

dead /ded/ *adj.* мёртвый

deaden /'dedn/ *v.* заглушать *impf.*

dead end *n.* тупик

deadline /'dɛd,lain/ *n.*
предѐльный срок

deadlock /'dɛd,lɒk/ *n.* тупѝк

deadly /'dɛdli/ *adj.* смертѐльный

deaf /dɛf/ *adj.* глухѝй

deafen /'dɛfən/ *v.* оглушáть
impf., -шѝть *pf.*

deaf-mute *n.* глухонемѝй

deafness /'dɛfnis/ *n.* глухотá

deal /dil/ **1.** *n.* (*agreement*)
слѐлка; (*cards*) сдáча **2.** *v.*
обходѝться; торговáть (+ *I*)
impf.; (*cards*) раздавáть *impf.*

dealer /'dilər/ *n.* торгѝвец

dean /din/ *n.* декáн

dear /dɪər/ *adj.* дорогѝй

dearth /dɜrθ/ *n.* недостáток

death /dɛθ/ *n.* смерть *f.*

deathly /'dɛθli/ *adj.* смертѐльный

debar /dɪ'bɑr/ *v.* исключáть
impf.

debase /dɪ'beis/ *v.* унижáть
impf., унѝзить; понѝзить *pf.*

debatable /dɪ'beitəbəl/ *adj.*
спѝрный

debate /dɪ'beit/ **1.** *n.* прѐния;
спор **2.** *v.* спѝрить *impf.*

debauchery /dɪ'bɔtʃəri/ *n.* раз-
врáт

debilitate /dɪ'bili,teit/ *v.*
ослаблять *impf.*; ослáбить *pf.*

debility /dɪ'biliti/ *n.* слáбость

debit /'dɛbit/ *n.* дѐбет

debris /də'bri/ *n.* оскѝлки *pl.*

debt /dɛt/ *n.* долг

debtor /'dɛtər/ *n.* должнѝк

debut /dei'byu/ *n.* дебют

decade /'dɛkeid/ *n.* десятилѐтие

decadence /'dɛkədəns/ *n.*
упáдок; декадѐнство

decadent /'dɛkədənt/ *adj.* дека-
дѐнтский, упáдочный

decaffeinated /dɪ'kæfineitid/
adj. без кофеѝна

decanter /dɪ'kæntər/ *n.* графѝн

decapitate /dɪ'kæpi,teit/ *v.*
обезглáвливать *impf.*,
обезглáвить *pf.*

decay /dɪ'kei/ **1.** *n.* гниѐние; раз-
рушѐние **2.** *v.* гнить *impf.*, с- *pf.*

decease /dɪ'sis/ *n.* кончѝна; **—d**
adj. покѝйный

deceit /dɪ'sit/ *n.* обмáн; **—ful**
adj. обмáнчивый; лжѝвый

deceive /dɪ'siv/ *v.* обмáнывать
impf., обманýть *pf.*

deceleration /di,sɛlə'reiʃən/ *n.*
замедлѐние, торможѐние

December /dɪ'sɛmbər/ **1.** *n.*
декáбрь *m.* **2.** *adj.* декáбрьский

decency /'disənsi/ *n.* прилѝчие

decent /'disənt/ *adj.* прилѝчный

decentralize /di'sɛntrə,laiz/ *v.*
децентрализовáть *impf.*

deception /dɪ'sɛpʃən/ *n.* обмáн

deceptive /dɪ'sɛptiv/ *adj.*
обмáнчивый

decibel /'dɛsə,bɛl/ *n.* децибѐл

decide /dɪ'said/ *v.t.* решáть
impf., решѝть *pf.*; **—d** *adj.*
решѝтельный

deciduous /dɪ'sidʒuəs/ *adj.*
лѝственный

decimal /'dɛsəməl/ *n.*
десятѝчная дробь *f.*

decipher /dɪ'saifər/ *v.* расшиф-
рѝвывать *impf.*, расшифровáть
pf.

decision /dɪ'siʒən/ *n.* решѐние

decisive /dɪ'saisiv/ *adj.*
решѝтельный

deck /dɛk/ *n.* пáлуба; (*cards*)
колѝда; **~ chair** шезлѝнг

declaim /dɪ'kleim/ *v.* деклами-
ровáть *impf.*

declaration /,dɛklə'reiʃən/ *n.*
деклáрация; объявлѐние

declare /dɪ'klɛər/ *v.* объявлять
impf., -вѝть *pf.*, заявлять *impf.*,
-вѝть *pf.*

declension /dɪ'klɛnʃən/ *n.* скло-
нѐние

decline /dɪ'klain/ **1.** *n.* умень-
шѐние; (*slope*) склон **2.** *v.t.* отказáться *pf.*; (*gram.*) склонять
impf., про- *pf.*; *v.i.* уменьшáться
impf. умѐньшить *pf.*

decode /di'koud/ *v.* расшифрѝ-
вывать *impf.*

decompose /,dikəm'pouz/ *v.*
разлагáть(ся) *impf.*, раз-
ложѝть(ся) *pf.*

decongestant /,dikən'dʒɛstənt/
n. противозастѝйное (срѐдство)

décor /dei'kɔr/ *n.* декѝр

decorate /'dɛkə,reit/ *v.* укра-
шáть *impf.*, укрáсить *pf.*; (*reward*) награждáть *impf.*, награ-
дѝть *pf.*

decoration /,dɛkə'reiʃən/ *n.*
украшѐние; декорáция; нагрáда

decorous /'dɛkərəs/ *adj.*
прилѝчный, пристѝйный

decorum /dɪ'kɔrəm/ *n.* прилѝчие

decoy /'dikɔi/ *n.* примáнка

decrease / *v.* dɪ'kris; *n.* 'dikris/
1. *v.* уменьшáть(ся) *impf.*,

уме́ньшить(ся) *pf.* **2.** *n.* уменьше́ние

decree /dɪˈkriː/ *n.* декре́т, ука́з

decrepit /dɪˈkrepɪt/ *adj.* дря́хлый

dedicate /ˈdedɪˌkeɪt/ *v.* посвяща́ть *impf.*, -ти́ть *pf.*

dedication /ˌdedɪˈkeɪʃən/ *n.* посвяще́ние

deduce /dɪˈdus/ *v.* выводи́ть *impf.*

deduct /dɪˈdʌkt/ *v.* вычита́ть *impf.*, вы́честь *pf.*; **—ion** *n.* вычита́ние; вы́вод

deed /did/ *n.* посту́пок, де́йствие

deem /dim/ *v.* счита́ть (+ *I*) *impf.*

deep /dip/ *adj.* глубо́кий

deepen /ˈdipən/ *v.* углубля́ть(ся) *impf.*, -би́ть(ся) *pf.*

deep-freeze *v.* замора́живать *impf.*

deer /dɪər/ *n.* оле́нь *m.*

deface /dɪˈfeɪs/ *v.* обезобра́живать *impf.*, обезобра́зить *pf.*

defamation /ˌdefəˈmeɪʃən/ *n.* клевета́

defamatory /dɪˈfæməˌtɔri/ *adj.* клеветни́ческий, позоря́щий

default /dɪˈfɔlt/ *n.* безде́йствие; невыполне́ние; нея́вка; непла́тёж

defeat /dɪˈfit/ **1.** *n.* разгро́м **2.** *v.* побежда́ть *impf.*, победи́ть *pf.*

defeatist /dɪˈfitɪst/ *n.* пораже́нец

defecate /ˈdefɪˌkeɪt/ *v.* испражня́ться *impf.*

defect /ˈdifekt/ *n.* недоста́ток

defection /dɪˈfekʃən/ *n.* дезерти́рство; бе́гство

defective /dɪˈfektɪv/ *adj.* повреждённый, дефе́ктный

defend /dɪˈfend/ *v.* защища́ть *impf.*, -ти́ть *pf.*

defendant /dɪˈfendənt/ *n.* подсуди́мый, обвиня́емый

defender /dɪˈfendər/ *n.* защи́тник

defense /dɪˈfens/ *n.* защи́та

defenseless /dɪˈfenslɪs/ *adj.* беззащи́тный

defensive /dɪˈfensɪv/ *adj.* оборони́тельный

defer /dɪˈfɜr/ *v.* откла́дывать *impf.*, отложи́ть *pf.*

deference /ˈdefərəns/ *n.* уваже́ние

defiance /dɪˈfaɪəns/ *n.* неповинове́ние; **in ~ of** вопреки́ (+ *D*)

defiant /dɪˈfaɪənt/ *adj.* вызыва́ющий

deficiency /dɪˈfɪʃənsi/ *n.* недоста́ток

deficient /dɪˈfɪʃənt/ *adj.* недоста́точный

deficit /ˈdefəsɪt/ *n.* дефици́т

defile /dɪˈfaɪl/ *v.* загрязня́ть *impf.*; **—ment** *n.* оскверне́ние

define /dɪˈfaɪn/ *v.* определя́ть *impf.*, -ли́ть *pf.*

definite /ˈdefənɪt/ *adj.* определённый

definitely /ˈdefənɪtli/ *adv.* без вся́кого сомне́ния; непреме́нно

definition /ˌdefəˈnɪʃən/ *n.* определе́ние

definitive /dɪˈfɪnɪtɪv/ *adj.* оконча́тельный

deflect /dɪˈflekt/ *v.* отклоня́ть *impf.*, -ни́ть *pf.*

deforestation /diˌfɔrɪˈsteɪʃn/ *n.* обезле́сение

deformity /dɪˈfɔrmɪti/ *n.* безобра́зие

defraud /dɪˈfrɔd/ *v.* выма́нивать *impf.*, вы́манить *pf.*

defray /dɪˈfreɪ/ *v.* опла́чивать *impf.*, оплати́ть *pf.*

defrost /dɪˈfrɔst/ *v.* размора́живать *impf.*, -моро́зить *pf.*

deft /deft/ *adj.* ло́вкий, иску́сный

defunct /dɪˈfʌŋkt/ *adj.* уме́рший

defy /dɪˈfaɪ/ *v.* ослуша́ться *pf.*

degenerate /dɪˈdʒenəˌreɪt/ *v.* вырожда́ться *impf.*, вы́родиться *pf.*

degradation /ˌdegrəˈdeɪʃən/ *n.* деграда́ция

degrading /dɪˈgreɪdɪŋ/ *adj.* унизи́тельный

degree /dɪˈgri/ *n.* гра́дус; сте́пень *f.*; (*education*) учёная сте́пень *f.*

dehydrate /dɪˈhaɪdreɪt/ *v.* обезво́живать(ся) *impf.*

dehydration /ˌdihaɪˈdreɪʃən/ *n.* обезво́живание

deity /ˈdiɪti/ *n.* божество́

dejected /dɪˈdʒektɪd/ *adj.* удручённый

delay /dɪˈleɪ/ **1.** *n.* заде́ржка **2.** *v.* откла́дывать *impf.*, отложи́ть *pf.*

delegate / *n.* ˈdelɪgɪt; *v.* -ˌgeɪt/ **1.** *n.* делега́т **2.** *v.* делеги́ровать *impf. & pf.*

delegation /ˌdelɪˈgeɪʃən/ *n.* делега́ция

delete /dɪ'lit/ v. вычёркивать *impf.*, вы́черкнуть *pf.*

deliberate /dɪ'lɪbərɪt/ *adj.* v. -ə,reit/ 1. *adj.* умы́шленный 2. v. совеща́ться *impf.*

deliberately /dɪ'lɪbərɪtli/ *adv.* наро́чно

deliberation /dɪ,lɪbə'reɪʃən/ n. обсужде́ние, обду́мывание

delicacy /'delɪkəsɪ/ n. то́нкость; делика́тность; не́жность

delicate /'delɪkɪt/ *adj.* делика́тный

delicatessen /,delɪkə'tesən/ n. (store) гастроно́м

delicious /dɪ'lɪʃəs/ *adj.* о́чень вку́сный

delight /dɪ'laɪt/ 1. n. восто́рг 2. v. восхища́ть *impf.*, -ти́ть *pf.*

delightful /dɪ'laɪtfəl/ *adj.* восхити́тельный

delinquency /dɪ'lɪŋkwənsɪ/ n. правонаруше́ние

delinquent /dɪ'lɪŋkwənt/ n. правонаруши́тель, -ница

delirious /dɪ'lɪərɪəs/ *adj.* бре́дящий

delirium /dɪ'lɪərɪəm/ n. бред

deliver /dɪ'lɪvər/ v. доставля́ть *impf.*, доста́вить *impf.*; освобожда́ть *impf.*, освободи́ть *pf.*; (*lecture*) чита́ть *impf.*, про- *pf.*;
—**ance** n. избавле́ние

delivery /dɪ'lɪvərɪ/ n. доста́вка, переда́ча; (*birth*) ро́ды pl.

delta /'deltə/ n. де́льта

delude /dɪ'lud/ v. обма́нывать *impf.*, обману́ть *pf.*

deluge /'delɪudʒ/ n. (*flood*) пото́п; (*downpour*) ли́вень m.

delusion /dɪ'luʒən/ n. заблужде́ние

deluxe /də'lʌks/ *adj.* (*in compounds*) -люкс

delve /delv/ v. ры́ться *impf.*

demand /dɪ'mænd/ 1. n. тре́бование; запро́с; **be in ~** по́льзоваться спро́сом *impf.* 2. v. тре́бовать *impf.*, по- *pf.*

demanding /dɪ'mændɪŋ/ *adj.* тре́бовательный

demarcation /,dimɑr'keɪʃən/ n. разграниче́ние

demean /dɪ'min/ v. унижа́ться *impf.*, уни́зиться *pf.*

demeanor /dɪ'minər/ n. поведе́ние; мане́ра держа́ться

demented /dɪ'mentɪd/ *adj.* сумасше́дший

demise /dɪ'maɪz/ n. кончи́на

demobilize /di'moubə,laɪz/ v. демобилизова́ть *impf.* & *pf.*

democracy /dɪ'mɒkrəsɪ/ n. демокра́тия

democrat /'demə,kræt/ n. демокра́т; —**ic** *adj.* демократи́ческий

demolish /dɪ'mɒlɪʃ/ v. разруша́ть *impf.*, разру́шить *pf.*

demolition /,demə'lɪʃən/ n. снос

demon /'dimən/ n. де́мон, дья́вол

demonstrable /dɪ'mɒnstrəbəl/ *adj.* доказу́емый, я́вный

demonstrate /'demən,streɪt/ v. демонстри́ровать *impf.* & *pf.*; уча́ствовать в демонстра́ции *impf.*

demonstration /,demən'streɪʃən/ n. демонстра́ция

demonstrative /də'mɒnstrətɪv/ *adj.* (*gram.*) указа́тельный

demoralize /dɪ'mɔrə,laɪz/ v. деморализова́ть *impf.* & *pf.*

demote /dɪ'mout/ v. понижа́ть в до́лжности *impf.*, пони́зить *pf.*

demure /dɪ'myʊr/ *adj.* серьёзный; сде́ржанный

den /den/ n. ло́говище

denial /dɪ'naɪəl/ n. отрица́ние

denigrate /'denɪ,greɪt/ v. поро́чить, черни́ть *impf.*, о- *pf.*

Denmark /'denmɑrk/ n. Да́ния

denominate /dɪ'nɒmə,neɪt/ v. называ́ть

denote /dɪ'nout/ v. означа́ть; обознача́ть *impf.*, обозна́чить *pf.*

denounce /dɪ'naʊns/ v. осужда́ть *impf.*, осуди́ть *pf.*

dense /dens/ *adj.* густо́й

density /'densɪtɪ/ n. пло́тность

dent /dent/ 1. n. вы́емка 2. v. вда́вливать *impf.*, вдави́ть *pf.*; —**ed** *adj.* с вмя́тиной

dental /'dentl/ *adj.* зубно́й

dentist /'dentɪst/ n. зубно́й врач

dentures /'dentʃərz/ n. вставны́е зу́бы pl.

denunciation /dɪ,nʌnsɪ'eɪʃən/ n. осужде́ние, доно́с

deny /dɪ'naɪ/ v. отрица́ть *impf.*

deodorant /di'oudərənt/ n. дезодора́нт

depart /dɪ'pɑrt/ v. уходи́ть *impf.*, уйти́ *pf.*; уезжа́ть *impf.*, уе́хать *pf.*

department /dɪ'pɑrtmənt/ n. отде́л, отделе́ние; (*university*) ка́федра

department store n. универма́г

departure /dɪ'pɑrtʃər/ n. отбы́тие

depend /dɪ'pɛnd/ v. зави́сеть (от + G) impf.; **—able** adj. надёжный

dependence /dɪ'pɛndəns/ n. зави́симость

dependent /dɪ'pɛndənt/ **1.** adj. зави́симый **2.** n. иждиве́нец

depict /dɪ'pɪkt/ v. изобража́ть impf., -зи́ть pf.; **—ion** n. изображе́ние

deplete /dɪ'plit/ v. истоща́ть, исчерпывать impf.

deplorable /dɪ'plɔrəbəl/ adj. плаче́вный

deplore /dɪ'plɔr/ v. сожале́ть (о + P); порица́ть impf.

deployment /dɪ'plɔɪmənt/ n. развёртывание

deport /dɪ'pɔrt/ v. высыла́ть impf., вы́слать pf.; **—ation** n. вы́сылка

deportment /dɪ'pɔrtmənt/ n. поведе́ние

depose /dɪ'pouz/ v. сверга́ть impf., све́ргнуть pf.

deposit /dɪ'pɒzɪt/ **1.** n. (payment) взнос, зада́ток; (sediment) оса́док **2.** v. положи́ть (в банк) pf.; **—or** n. вкла́дчик

depository /dɪ'pɒzɪ,tɔri/ n. храни́лище; склад; Fig. кла́д

depot /'dipou/ n. депо́ neut. indecl.

deprave /dɪ'preɪv/ v. развраща́ть impf.; **—d** adj. развращённый

deprecatory /'dɛprɪkə,tɔri/ adj. неодобри́тельный

depreciate /dɪ'priʃi,eɪt/ v. обесце́нивать impf., обесце́нить pf.

depreciation /dɪ,priʃi'eɪʃən/ n. обесце́нивание

depress /dɪ'prɛs/ v. подавля́ть impf., -ви́ть pf.; **—ed** adj. пода́вленный, уны́лый

depressing /dɪ'prɛsɪŋ/ adj. уны́лый; угнета́ющий

depression /dɪ'prɛʃən/ n. депре́ссия

deprivation /,dɛprə'veɪʃən/ n. лише́ние

deprive /dɪ'praɪv/ v. лиша́ть impf., лиши́ть (его + G) pf.

deprived /dɪ'praɪvd/ adj. бе́дный

depth /dɛpθ/ n. глубина́

deputation /,dɛpyə'teɪʃən/ n. депута́ция, делега́ция

deputy /'dɛpyəti/ n. депута́т

derailment /dɪ'reɪlmənt/ n. сход с ре́льсов

derangement /dɪ'reɪndʒmənt/ n. психи́ческое расстро́йство

derelict /'dɛrəlɪkt/ adj. поки́нутый, бро́шенный; **—ion** n. забро́шенность

deride /dɪ'raɪd/ v. высме́ивать impf., вы́смеять pf.

derision /dɪ'rɪʒən/ n. высме́ивание

derisive /dɪ'raɪsɪv/ adj. насме́шливый, издева́тельский

derivation /,dɛrə'veɪʃən/ n. происхожде́ние

derivative /dɪ'rɪvətɪv/ adj. произво́дный

derogatory /dɪ'rɒgə,tɔri/ adj. унизи́тельный

descend /dɪ'sɛnd/ v. сходи́ть impf., сойти́ (с) pf.; происходи́ть impf., произойти́ pf.

descendant /dɪ'sɛndənt/ n. пото́мок

descent /dɪ'sɛnt/ n. спуск; происхожде́ние

describe /dɪ'skraɪb/ v. опи́сывать impf., описа́ть pf.

description /dɪ'skrɪpʃən/ n. описа́ние

desecrate /'dɛsɪ,kreɪt/ v. оскверня́ть impf., -ни́ть pf.

desecration /,dɛsɪ'kreɪʃən/ n. оскверне́ние, профана́ция

desegregation /,disɛgrɪ'geɪʃən/ n. десегрега́ция

desert[1] /'dɛzərt/ n. пусты́ня

desert[2] /dɪ'zɜrt/ v. покида́ть impf., поки́нуть pf.; v.i. дезерти́ровать impf. & pf.; **—er** n. дезерти́р

deserve /dɪ'zɜrv/ v. заслу́живать impf., заслужи́ть pf.

deserving /dɪ'zɜrvɪŋ/ adj. досто́йный (+ G)

design /dɪ'zaɪn/ **1.** n. прое́кт; (drawing) узо́р **2.** v. проекти́ровать impf., за-, с- pf.

designate /'dɛzɪg,neɪt/ v. назнача́ть impf., назна́чить pf.

designer /dɪ'zaɪnər/ n. дизайне́р

desirable /dɪ'zaɪərəbəl/ adj. жела́тельный

desire /dɪ'zaɪər/ **1.** n. жела́ние **2.** v. жела́ть impf., по- pf.

desist /dɪ'sɪst/ v. прекраща́ть impf.

desk /dɛsk/ n. пи́сьменный стол

desktop /'dɛsk,tɒp/ n.

настольный; **~ publishing** n. настольное издательство

desolate /ˈdesəlɪt/ adj. необитаемый; заброшенный; покинутый

desolation /ˌdesəˈleɪʃən/ n. опустошение

despair /dɪˈspeər/ n. отчаяние

desperate /ˈdespərɪt/ adj. отчаянный

desperation /ˌdespəˈreɪʃən/ n. отчаяние

despicable /ˈdespɪkəbəl/ adj. подлый

despise /dɪˈspaɪz/ v. презирать impf., презреть pf.

despite /dɪˈspaɪt/ prep. вопреки (+ D), несмотря на (+ A)

despondency /dɪˈspɒndənsɪ/ n. уныние

despondent /dɪˈspɒndənt/ adj. подавленный

despot /ˈdespɒt/ n. деспот, тиран

dessert /dɪˈzɜrt/ n. десерт

destination /ˌdestɪˈneɪʃən/ n. назначение, предназначение

destiny /ˈdestɪnɪ/ n. судьба

destitution /ˌdestɪˈtuʃən/ n. нищета

destroy /dɪˈstrɔɪ/ v. уничтожать impf., уничтожить pf.; разрушать impf., разрушить pf.

destruction /dɪˈstrʌkʃən/ n. разрушение, уничтожение

destructive /dɪˈstrʌktɪv/ adj. разрушительный

detach /dɪˈtætʃ/ v. отделять impf., -лить pf.; **—ed** adj. отдельный

detachment /dɪˈtætʃmənt/ n. отряд

detail /ˈditeɪl/ n. подробность, деталь f.

detailed /dɪˈteɪld/ adj. подробный

detain /dɪˈteɪn/ v. задерживать impf., задержать pf.

detect /dɪˈtekt/ v. открывать impf., открыть pf.; **—ion** n. обнаружение

detective /dɪˈtektɪv/ n. сыщик

detector /dɪˈtektər/ n. детектор

detention /dɪˈtenʃən/ n. задержание

deter /dɪˈtɜr/ v. удерживать impf., удержать pf.

detergent /dɪˈtɜrdʒənt/ n. стиральный порошок

deteriorate /dɪˈtɪərɪəˌreɪt/ v.

deterioration /dɪˌtɪərɪəˈreɪʃən/ n. ухудшение

determination /dɪˌtɜrməˈneɪʃən/ n. решимость

determine /dɪˈtɜrmɪn/ v. определять impf., -лить pf.; **—d** adj. решительный

deterrence /dɪˈtɜrəns/ n. устрашение

detest /dɪˈtest/ v. ненавидеть impf.; **—able** adj. отвратительный

detonation /ˌdetnˈeɪʃən/ n. взрыв

detour /ˈditur/ n. окольный путь m.

detoxify /diˈtɒksəfaɪ/ v. обезвреживать impf.

detract /dɪˈtrækt/ v. умалять; уменьшать impf.

detriment /ˈdetrəmənt/ n. ущерб; **—al** adj. вредный

devaluate /diˈvæljuˌeɪt/ v. обесценивать impf.

devaluation /diˌvæljuˈeɪʃən/ n. девальвация

devastate /ˈdevəˌsteɪt/ v. опустошать, разорять impf.

devastating /ˈdevəˌsteɪtɪŋ/ adj. опустошительный

develop /dɪˈveləp/ v. развиваться(ся) impf., развить(ся) pf.

developer /dɪˈveləpər/ n. (photog.) проявитель; (builder) строитель

development /dɪˈveləpmənt/ n. развитие

deviate /ˈdiviˌeɪt/ v. отклоняться, уклоняться (от + G) impf.

deviation /ˌdiviˈeɪʃən/ n. отклонение

device /dɪˈvaɪs/ n. прибор; приём

devil /ˈdevəl/ n. чёрт, дьявол

devoid /dɪˈvɔɪd/ adj. лишённый (+ G)

devote /dɪˈvout/ v. посвящать impf., -тить pf.; **—d** adj. преданный

devotee /ˌdevəˈti/ n. поклонник

devotion /dɪˈvouʃən/ n. преданность

devour /dɪˈvaur/ v. пожирать impf., пожрать pf.

devout /dɪˈvaut/ adj. набожный

dew /du/ n. роса

dexterity /dekˈsterɪtɪ/ n. проворство, ловкость

dexterous /'dɛkstrəs/ adj.
проворный, ловкий

di- pref. дву-, двух-

diabetes /ˌdaɪə'biːtɪs/ n. диабет

diabetic /ˌdaɪə'betɪk/ **1.** n.
диабетик **2.** adj. диабетический

diabolic /ˌdaɪə'bɒlɪk/ adj.
дьявольский

diadem /'daɪədɛm/ n. диадема

diagnose /'daɪəgˌnoʊs/ v.
ставить диагноз impf.

diagnosis /ˌdaɪəg'noʊsɪs/ n.
диагноз

diagonal /daɪ'ægənl/ **1.** adj. диагональный **2.** n. диагональ f.

diagram /'daɪəˌgræm/ n. диаграмма

dial /'daɪəl/ **1.** n. циферблат,
шкала **2.** v. набирать impf.

dialect /'daɪəˌlɛkt/ n. диалект

dialogue /'daɪəˌlɒg/ n. диалог

diameter /daɪ'æmɪtər/ n.
диаметр

diamond /'daɪmənd/ n. алмаз;
(polished) бриллиант

diaper /'daɪpər/ n. пелёнка

diaphragm /'daɪəˌfræm/ n. диафрагма

diarrhea /ˌdaɪə'riə/ n. понос

diary /'daɪəri/ n. дневник

diatribe /'daɪəˌtraɪb/ n. брань f.

dice /daɪs/ n. игральные кости
pl.

dictate /'dɪkteɪt/ v. диктовать
impf., про- pf.

dictation /dɪk'teɪʃən/ n. диктант

dictator /'dɪkteɪtər/ n. диктатор

dictatorial /ˌdɪktə'tɔriəl/ adj.
диктаторский; повелительный

dictatorship /dɪk'teɪtərˌʃɪp/ n.
диктатура

diction /'dɪkʃən/ n. дикция

dictionary /'dɪkʃəˌnɛri/ n.
словарь m.

didactic /daɪ'dæktɪk/ adj. дидактический; наставительный

die /daɪ/ v. умирать impf.,
умереть pf.; ~ **out** вымирать
impf., вымереть pf.

diesel /'dizəl/ n. дизель m.

diet /'daɪət/ n. диета; пища

dietary /'daɪəˌteri/ adj.
диетический

differ /'dɪfər/ v. различаться
impf.

difference /'dɪfərəns/ n. разница

different /'dɪfərənt/ adj.
различный, разный

differentiate /ˌdɪfə'rɛnʃiˌeɪt/ v.
различать impf., различить pf.

differently /ˌdɪfərəntli/ adv.
иначе; (variously) по-разному

difficult /'dɪfɪˌkʌlt/ adj. трудный

difficulty /'dɪfɪˌkʌlti/ n.
трудность

diffidence /'dɪfɪdəns/ n.
неуверенность в себе

diffident /'dɪfɪdənt/ adj.
неуверенный в себе

diffuse /adj. dɪ'fjus; v. dɪ'fjuz/
1. adj. расплывчатый **2.** v.
(light) рассеивать impf.; (knowledge) распространять impf.

diffused /dɪ'fjuzd/ adj.
рассеянный

dig /dɪg/ v. копать; рыть impf.

digest /dɪ'dʒɛst/ v. переваривать
impf., -варить pf.

digestible /dɪ'dʒɛstəbəl/ adj.
удобоваримый

digestion /dɪ'dʒɛstʃən/ n. пищеварение

digit /'dɪdʒɪt/ n. (numeral)
цифра

digital /'dɪdʒɪtl/ adj. пальцевой

dignified /'dɪgnəˌfaɪd/ adj.
достойный, важный

dignitary /'dɪgnɪˌteri/ n. высокопоставленное лицо

dignity /'dɪgnɪti/ n. достоинство

digress /dɪ'grɛs/ v. отступать
impf., -пить pf.; —**ion** n. отступление

dike /daɪk/ n. дамба, плотина

dilapidated /dɪ'læpɪˌdeɪtɪd/ adj.
ветхий; обветшалый

dilate /daɪ'leɪt/ v. расширять(ся)
impf., расширить(ся) pf.

dilemma /dɪ'lɛmə/ n. дилемма

dilettante /'dɪlɪˌtɑnt/ n. дилетант, любитель, —ница

diligence /'dɪlɪdʒəns/ n. прилежание, усердие

diligent /'dɪlɪdʒənt/ adj.
прилежный

dill /dɪl/ n. укроп

dilute /dɪ'lut/ v. разбавлять
impf., разбавить pf.

diluted adj. разбавленный

dim /dɪm/ **1.** adj. тусклый **2.** v.
делать тусклым impf.

dime /daɪm/ n. (монета в)
десять центов

dimension /dɪ'mɛnʒən/ n.
(math.) измерение; pl. размеры
m.

diminish /dɪ'mɪnɪʃ/ v. уменьшать(ся) impf., уменьшить(ся)
pf.

diminutive /dɪˈmɪnyʊtɪv/ adj. (gram.) уменьши́тельный

dimmer /ˈdɪmər/ n. (elec.) затемни́тель

dimness /ˈdɪmnɪs/ n. ту́склость

dimple /ˈdɪmpəl/ n. я́мочка

din /dɪn/ n. гро́хот, шум

dine /daɪn/ v. обе́дать impf., по- pf.

diner /ˈdaɪnər/ n. ваго́н-рестора́н

dinghy /ˈdɪŋgi/ n. я́лик

dingy /ˈdɪndʒi/ adj. ту́склый

dining car /ˈdaɪnɪŋ/ n. ваго́н-рестора́н

dining room n. столо́вая

dinner /ˈdɪnər/ n. обе́д

dinosaur /ˈdaɪnəˌsɔr/ n. диноза́вр

diocese /ˈdaɪəsɪs/ n. епа́рхия

dip /dɪp/ v. погружа́ть(ся), окуна́ть(ся) (в + A); обма́кивать impf.

diphtheria /dɪfˈθɪəriə, dɪp-/ n. дифтери́я, дифтери́т

diphthong /ˈdɪfθɔŋ/ n. дифто́нг

diploma /dɪˈploumə/ n. дипло́м

diplomacy /dɪˈplouməsi/ n. диплома́тия

diplomat /ˈdɪpləˌmæt/ n. диплома́т

diplomatic /ˌdɪpləˈmætɪk/ adj. дипломати́ческий

dire /daɪər/ adj. ужа́сный

direct /dɪˈrɛkt/ **1.** adj. прямо́й **2.** v. направля́ть impf., напра́вить pf.; руководи́ть impf.; ~ current постоя́нный ток

direction /dɪˈrɛkʃən/ n. направле́ние; (management) руково́дство

directive /dɪˈrɛktɪv/ n. директи́ва

directly /dɪˈrɛktli/ adv. пря́мо

directness /dɪˈrɛktnɪs/ n. прямота́; непосре́дственность

director /dɪˈrɛktər/ n. дире́ктор; (theat., film) режиссёр

directory /dɪˈrɛktəri/ n. спра́вочник; **file** ~ (comput.) фа́йловый катало́г

dirigible /ˈdɪrɪdʒəbəl/ n. дирижа́бль m.

dirt /dɜrt/ n. грязь f.

dirty /ˈdɜrti/ adj. гря́зный

disability /ˌdɪsəˈbɪlɪti/ n. инвали́дность

disadvantage /ˌdɪsədˈvæntɪdʒ/ n. невы́года, невы́годное положе́ние

disadvantageous /dɪsˌædvənˈteɪdʒəs/ adj. невы́годный

disagree /ˌdɪsəˈgri/ v. не соглаша́ться impf., -си́ться pf.

disagreeable /ˌdɪsəˈgriəbəl/ adj. неприя́тный

disagreement /ˌdɪsəˈgrimənt/ n. расхожде́ние во мне́ниях

disappear /ˌdɪsəˈpɪər/ v. исчеза́ть impf., исче́знуть pf.

disappearance /ˌdɪsəˈpɪərəns/ n. исчезнове́ние

disappoint /ˌdɪsəˈpɔɪnt/ v. разочаро́вывать impf., разочарова́ть pf.; **—ment** n. разочарова́ние

disapproval /ˌdɪsəˈpruvəl/ n. неодобре́ние

disapprove /ˌdɪsəˈpruv/ v. не одобря́ть impf.

disapproving /ˌdɪsəˈpruvɪŋ/ adj. неодобри́тельный

disarm /dɪsˈɑrm/ v. разоружа́ть(ся) impf., -жи́ть(ся) pf.

disarmament /dɪsˈɑrməmənt/ n. разоруже́ние

disarray /ˌdɪsəˈreɪ/ n. беспоря́док

disaster /dɪˈzæstər/ n. бе́дствие

disastrous /dɪˈzæstrəs/ adj. бе́дственный, ги́бельный

disband /dɪsˈbænd/ v. распуска́ть impf.

disbelief /ˌdɪsbɪˈlif/ n. неве́рие

disbursement /dɪsˈbɜrsmənt/ n. вы́плата

discard /dɪˈskɑrd/ v. сбра́сывать impf., сбро́сить pf.

discern /dɪˈsɜrn/ v. различа́ть impf., -чи́ть pf.; **—ible** adj. различи́мый

discerning /dɪˈsɜrnɪŋ/ adj. проница́тельный

discharge /dɪsˈtʃɑrdʒ/ v. выпи́сывать impf., вы́писать pf.; выполня́ть impf., вы́полнить pf.

disciple /dɪˈsaɪpəl/ n. учени́к

disciplinary /ˈdɪsəpləˌnɛri/ adj. исправи́тельный

discipline /ˈdɪsəplɪn/ n. дисципли́на

disclaim /dɪsˈkleɪm/ v. отрека́ться impf., отре́чься pf.

disclose /dɪsˈklouz/ v. обнару́живать impf., обнару́жить pf.

disclosure /dɪsˈklouʒər/ n. откры́тие, обнаруже́ние

disco /ˈdɪskou/ n. дискоте́ка

discolor /dɪsˈkʌlər/ v. изменя́ть цвет impf.

discomfit /dɪsˈkʌmfɪt/ v. (confuse) расстра́ивать; смуща́ть impf.

discomfort /dɪsˈkʌmfərt/ n. неудо́бство

disconcert /ˌdɪskənˈsɜrt/ v. смуща́ть impf., -ти́ть pf.

disconnect /ˌdɪskəˈnekt/ v. разъедини́ть impf., -ни́ть pf.; —ed adj. бессвя́зный

disconsolate /dɪsˈkɒnsəlɪt/ adj. неутёшный

discontent /ˌdɪskənˈtent/ n. недово́льство

discontented /ˌdɪskənˈtentɪd/ adj. недово́льный

discontinue /ˌdɪskənˈtɪnyu/ v. прерыва́ть impf., прерва́ть pf.

discord /ˈdɪskɔrd/ n. разногла́сие; (mus.) диссона́нс

discotheque /ˈdɪskəˌtek/ n. дискоте́ка

discount /ˈdɪskaʊnt/ n. ски́дка

discourage /dɪˈskɜrɪdʒ/ v. обескура́живать impf., обескура́жить pf.; —ment n. обескура́женность

discourse /ˈdɪskɔrs/ n. речь f.

discourteous /dɪsˈkɜrtiəs/ adj. неве́жливый, неучти́вый

discover /dɪˈskʌvər/ v. открыва́ть impf., откры́ть pf.; —y n. откры́тие

discredit /dɪsˈkredɪt/ 1. n. позо́р 2. v. дискредити́ровать impf.

discreet /dɪˈskrit/ adj. осмотри́тельный

discrepancy /dɪˈskrepənsi/ n. расхожде́ние, несхо́дство

discriminate /dɪˈskrɪmˌəneɪt/ v. дискримини́ровать impf. & pf.

discrimination /dɪˌskrɪməˈneɪʃən/ n. дискримина́ция

discuss /dɪˈskʌs/ v. обсужда́ть impf., обсуди́ть pf.; —ion n. диску́ссия, обсужде́ние

disdain /dɪsˈdeɪn/ n. (contempt) презре́ние (к + D); —ful adj. презри́тельный

disease /dɪˈziz/ n. боле́знь f.

diseased /dɪˈzizd/ adj. больно́й

disenchant /ˌdɪsənˈtʃænt/ v. разочаро́вывать impf.

disengage /ˌdɪsənˈgeɪdʒ/ v. освобожда́ть(ся) impf.; —ment n. освобожде́ние

disentangle /ˌdɪsənˈtæŋgəl/ v. распу́тывать(ся) impf.

disfavor /dɪsˈfeɪvər/ n. неодобре́ние

disfigure /dɪsˈfɪgyər/ v. уро́довать impf., из- pf.

disgrace /dɪsˈgreɪs/ 1. v. позо́р 2. v. позо́рить impf.; —ful adj. позо́рный

disgruntled /dɪsˈgrʌntld/ adj. недово́льный

disguise /dɪsˈgaɪz/ 1. n. маскиро́вка 2. v. маскирова́ть impf., за- pf.

disgust /dɪsˈgʌst/ 1. n. отвраще́ние 2. v. внуша́ть отвраще́ние impf.; —ing adj. отврати́тельный, гну́сный

dish /dɪʃ/ n. посу́да; (food) блю́до

disharmony /dɪsˈhɑrməni/ n. дисгармо́ния

dishearten /dɪsˈhɑrtn/ v. приводи́ть в уны́ние impf.

disheveled /dɪˈʃevəld/ adj. взъеро́шенный; растрёпанный

dishonest /dɪsˈɒnɪst/ adj. нече́стный; —y n. нече́стность

dishonor /dɪsˈɒnər/ v. бесче́стить impf., о- pf.; —able adj. бесче́стный

dishwasher /ˈdɪʃˌwɒʃər/ n. судомо́йка; посудомо́ечная маши́на

disillusion /ˌdɪsɪˈluʒən/ v. разочаро́вывать impf., разочарова́ть pf.

disinclination /dɪsˌɪnkləˈneɪʃən/ n. неохо́та

disinfect /ˌdɪsɪnˈfekt/ v. дезинфици́ровать impf. & pf.; —ant n. дезинфици́рующее сре́дство

disintegrate /dɪsˈɪntəˌgreɪt/ v. распада́ться, разруша́ться impf.

disinterested /dɪsˈɪntəˌrestɪd/ adj. бескоры́стный

disjointed /dɪsˈdʒɔɪntɪd/ adj. несвя́зный; беспоря́дочный

disjunction /dɪsˈdʒʌŋkʃən/ n. разъедине́ние

disk /dɪsk/ n. диск; ~ **drive** ди́сковый накопи́тель

diskette /dɪsˈket/ n. диске́та

dislike /dɪsˈlaɪk/ 1. n. нелюбо́вь f. 2. v. не люби́ть impf.

dislocate /ˈdɪsloʊˌkeɪt/ v. вы́вихнуть pf.

dislodge /dɪsˈlɒdʒ/ v. смеща́ть; сдвига́ть с ме́ста impf.

disloyal /dɪsˈlɔɪəl/ adj. неве́рный; —ty n. неве́рность, вероло́мство

dismal /ˈdɪzməl/ adj. мра́чный

dismantle /dɪs'mæntl/ v. разбирать (на части) impf.

dismay /dɪs'mei/ n. смущение

dismiss /dɪs'mis/ v. увольнять impf., уволить pf.; **—al** n. увольнение

disobedience /ˌdɪsə'biːdiəns/ n. неповиновение, непослушание

disobedient /ˌdɪsə'biːdiənt/ adj. непослушный

disobey /ˌdɪsə'bei/ v. не слушаться impf.

disorder /dɪs'ɔːrdər/ n. беспорядок; **—ly** adj. беспорядочный

disorient /dɪs'ɔːriˌent/ v. дезориентировать; сбивать с толку impf.

disparage /dɪs'pærɪdʒ/ v. умалять impf.; **—ment** n. умаление

disparity /dɪs'pærɪti/ n. разница

dispassionate /dɪs'pæʃənɪt/ adj. бесстрастный

dispatch /dɪs'pætʃ/ 1. n. отправка 2. v. посылать impf., послать pf.

dispel /dɪs'pel/ v. разгонять impf., разогнать pf.

dispensable /dɪs'pensəbəl/ adj. необязательный

dispense /dɪs'pens/ v. раздавать; распределять impf.

dispersal /dɪs'pɜːrsəl/ n. рассеивание; распространение

disperse /dɪs'pɜːrs/ v. рассеивать(ся) impf.; рассеять(ся) pf.

dispirited /dɪs'pɪrɪtɪd/ adj. унылый, удручённый

displaced /dɪs'pleist/ adj. смещённый; не на своём месте

displacement /dɪs'pleismənt/ n. перемещение, перестановка

display /dɪs'plei/ 1. v. выставлять impf., выставить pf. 2. n. показ

displeasing /dɪs'pliːzɪŋ/ adj. неприятный; непривлекательный

displeasure /dɪs'pleʒər/ n. неудовольствие

disposable /dɪs'poʊzəbəl/ adj. (одно-)разовый

disposal /dɪs'poʊzəl/ n. распоряжение

disposition /ˌdɪspə'zɪʃən/ n. расположение

disproportionate /ˌdɪsprə'pɔːrʃənɪt/ adj. непропорциональный

disprove /dɪs'pruːv/ v. опровергать impf., опровергнуть pf.

dispute /dɪs'pjuːt/ 1. n. спор 2. v. оспаривать impf.

disqualify /dɪs'kwɑːləˌfai/ v. дисквалифицировать impf. & pf.

disquieting /dɪs'kwaiɪtɪŋ/ adj. тревожный

disregard /ˌdɪsrɪ'gɑːrd/ 1. n. невнимание 2. v. игнорировать impf.

disrepair /ˌdɪsrɪ'peər/ n. ветхость

disreputable /dɪs'repjətəbəl/ adj. пользующийся дурной славой

disrepute /ˌdɪsrɪ'pjuːt/ n. плохая репутация

disrespect /ˌdɪsrɪ'spekt/ n. неуважение; **—ful** adj. непочтительный

disrupt /dɪs'rʌpt/ v. нарушать impf., нарушить pf.

disruptive /dɪs'rʌptɪv/ adj. подрывной

dissatisfaction /dɪsˌætɪs'fækʃən/ n. неудовлетворение

dissatisfied /dɪs'sætɪsˌfaid/ adj. недовольный (+ I)

dissect /dɪ'sekt/ v. вскрывать impf., вскрыть pf.; **—ion** n. вскрытие

disseminate /dɪ'seməˌneit/ v. распространять impf., -нить pf.

dissemination /dɪˌsemə'neiʃən/ n. разброс; распространение

dissension /dɪ'senʃən/ n. раздор

dissent /dɪ'sent/ v. расходиться во мнениях impf.

dissertation /ˌdɪsər'teiʃən/ n. диссертация

dissident /'dɪsɪdənt/ 1. n. диссидент 2. adj. диссидентский

dissimilar /dɪ'sɪmələr/ adj. несходный

dissipate /'dɪsəˌpeit/ v. расточать impf., -чить pf.; **—d** adj. беспутный

dissociate /dɪ'soʊʃiˌeit/ v. разъединять; разобщать impf.

dissolute /'dɪsəˌluːt/ adj. распущенный

dissolve /dɪ'zɒlv/ v. растворять(ся) impf., -рить(ся) pf.

dissonance /'dɪsənəns/ n. (mus.) диссонанс

dissonant /'dɪsənənt/ adj. диссонирующий, нестройный

dissuade /dɪ'sweɪd/ v. отговáривать impf., отговорúть pf.

distance /'dɪstəns/ n. расстоя́ние; **in the ~** вдалú

distant /'dɪstənt/ adj. дáльний

distaste /dɪs'teɪst/ n. отвращéние

distend /dɪ'stend/ v. надувáть(ся), раздувáть(ся) impf.

distill /dɪ'stɪl/ v. дистиллúровать impf. & pf.

distillation /,dɪstɪ'leɪʃən/ n. дистилля́ция; перегóнка

distillery /dɪ'stɪləri/ n. винокýренный завóд

distinct /dɪ'stɪŋkt/ adj. отчётливый; **—ion** n. отлúчие, различúе

distinctive /dɪ'stɪŋktɪv/ adj. отличúтельный

distinctly /dɪ'stɪŋktli/ adv. я́сно

distinguish /dɪ'stɪŋgwɪʃ/ v. различáть; отличáть impf., -чúть pf.

distinguished /dɪ'stɪŋgwɪʃt/ adj. выдаю́щийся

distort /dɪ'stɔrt/ v. искажáть impf., -зúть pf.; **—ion** n. искажéние

distract /dɪ'strækt/ v. отвлекáть impf., отвлéчь pf.; **—ion** n. отвлечéние; развлечéние

distraught /dɪ'strɔt/ обезýмевший

distress /dɪ'stres/ **1.** n. гóре **2.** v. огорчáть impf., -чúть pf.

distressed /dɪ'strest/ adj. расстрóенный

distribute /dɪ'strɪbyut/ v. раздавáть impf., раздáть pf.

distribution /,dɪstrɪ'byuʃən/ n. распределéние

distributor /dɪ'strɪbyətər/ n. распределúтель зажигáния

district /'dɪstrɪkt/ n. райóн

distrust /dɪs'trʌst/ **1.** n. недовéрие **2.** v. не доверя́ть impf.; **—ful** adj. недовéрчивый

disturb /dɪ'stɜrb/ v. волновáть impf., вз- pf.; беспокóить impf.

disturbance /dɪ'stɜrbəns/ n. беспокóйство; волнéние

disuse /dɪs'yus/ n.: **fall into ~** вы́йти из употреблéния impf.

ditch /dɪtʃ/ n. канáва, ров

dive /daɪv/ **1.** n. ныря́ние **2.** v. ныря́ть impf.; нырнýть pf.

diver /'daɪvər/ n. ныря́льщик

diverge /dɪ'vɜrdʒ/ v. расходúться; отклоня́ться, уклоня́ться impf.

divergence /dɪ'vɜrdʒəns/ n. расхождéние, отклонéние

diverse /dɪ'vɜrs/ adj. рáзный

diversification /dɪ,vɜrsəfɪ'keɪʃən/ n. разнообрáзность; расширéние

diversify /dɪ'vɜrsə,faɪ/ v. разнообрáзить; расширя́ть impf.

diversion /dɪ'vɜrʒən/ n. отклонéние; отвлечéние

diversity /dɪ'vɜrsɪti/ n. разнообрáзие; несхóдство

divert /dɪ'vɜrt/ v. отклоня́ть impf., -нúть pf.; отвлекáть impf.

divest /dɪ'vest/ v. лишáть impf.

divide /dɪ'vaɪd/ v. делúть impf., по-, раз- pf.

divination /,dɪvə'neɪʃən/ n. гадáние; предсказáние

divine /dɪ'vaɪn/ adj. божéственный

diving /'daɪvɪŋ/ n. ныря́ние; (sport) прыжкú в вóду pl.

diving suit n. скафáндр

divinity /dɪ'vɪnɪti/ n. божéственность; (god) божествó

divisible /dɪ'vɪzəbəl/ adj. делúмый

division /dɪ'vɪʒən/ n. разделéние; делéние; (department) отдéл

divorce /dɪ'vɔrs/ **1.** n. развóд **2.** v. разводúться impf., развестúсь pf.; **—d** adj. разведённый

divulge /dɪ'vʌldʒ/ v. разглашáть impf., разгласúть pf.

dizziness /'dɪzɪnɪs/ n. головокружéние

dizzy /'dɪzi/ adj. головокружúтельный

DNA n. (abbr. of deoxyribonucleic acid) ДНК (abbr. of дезоксирибонуклеúновая кислотá)

do /du/ v. дéлать impf., с- pf.; **~ without** обходúться без impf.

docile /'dɒsəl/ adj. покóрный

docility /dɒ'sɪlɪti/ n. покóрность

dock /dɒk/ **1.** n. док, верфь f. **2.** v. стáвить сýдно в док impf.

docket /'dɒkɪt/ n. реéстр

dockyard /'dɒk,yard/ n. верфь f.

doctor /'dɒktər/ n. врач, дóктор

doctorate /'dɒktərɪt/ n. дóкторская стéпень f.

doctrine /'dɒktrɪn/ n. доктрúна

document / n. 'dɒkyəmənt; v. -,ment/ **1.** n. докуме́нт, свиде́тельство **2.** v. докумети́ровать impf. & pf.

documentary /,dɒkyə'mɛntəri/ adj. документа́льный

documentation /,dɒkyəmɛn'teiʃən/ n. документа́ция

dodge /dɒdʒ/ v. уклоня́ться; увили́вать (от + G) impf.

doe /dou/ n. оле́нуха

dog /dɒg/ n. соба́ка

dog collar n. оше́йник

dogged /'dɒgid/ adj. упря́мый

doghouse /'dɒg,haus/ n. соба́чья конура́

dog lover n. соба́чник

dogma /'dɒgmə/ n. до́гма

dogmatic /dɒg'mætik/ adj. догмати́ческий

dogmatize /'dɒgmə,taiz/ v. догматизи́ровать impf.

do-it-yourself adj. самоде́льный

doleful /'doulfəl/ adj. печа́льный

doll /dɒl/ n. ку́кла

dollar /'dɒlər/ n. до́ллар

dolly /'dɒli/ n. (cart) теле́жка

dolphin /'dɒlfin/ n. дельфи́н

domain /dou'mein/ n. име́ние, владе́ние; (field) о́бласть f.

dome /doum/ n. ку́пол

domesticate /də'mɛsti,keit/ v. прируча́ть impf., -чи́ть pf.; —d adj. ручно́й

domesticity /,doumɛ'stisiti/ n. семе́йная (дома́шняя) жизнь f.

domicile /'dɒmə,sail/ n. местожи́тельство

dominance /'dɒmənəns/ n. госпо́дство; преоблада́ние

dominant /'dɒmənənt/ adj. госпо́дствующий, преоблада́ющий

dominate /'dɒmə,neit/ v. преоблада́ть; госпо́дствовать impf.

domination /,dɒmə'neiʃən/ n. преоблада́ние; госпо́дство

dominion /də'minyən/ n. влады́чество

domino /'dɒmə,nou/ n. домино́ neut. indecl.

don /dɒn/ v. надева́ть impf.

donate /'douneit/ v. дари́ть; же́ртвовать (+ D) impf.

donation /dou'neiʃən/ n. дар, поже́ртвование

donkey /'dɒŋki/ n. осёл

donor /'dounər/ n. же́ртвователь

doom /dum/ **1.** n. ги́бель f. **2.** v. обрека́ть impf., обре́чь pf.

doomed /dumd/ adj. обречённый

door /dɔr/ n. дверь f.

doorbell /'dɔr,bɛl/ n. звоно́к

doorman /'dɔr,mæn/ n. швейца́р

doormat /'dɔr,mæt/ n. полови́к

doorstep /'dɔr,stɛp/ n. поро́г

doorway /'dɔr,wei/ n. вход

dope /doup/ n. (drug) нарко́тик

dormant /'dɔrmənt/ adj. дре́млющий, безде́йствующий

dormitory /'dɔrmi,tori/ n. общежи́тие

dorsal /'dɔrsəl/ adj. спи́нный

dosage /'dousidʒ/ n. дозиро́вка

dose /dous/ n. до́за

dossier /'dɒsi,ei/ n. досье́ neut. indecl.

dot /dɒt/ n. то́чка

dote /dout/ v.: ~ on носи́ть на рука́х impf.

double /'dʌbəl/ **1.** adj. двойно́й, двойственный **2.** n. двойни́к **3.** v. удва́ивать impf., удво́ить pf.

double- двух-, дву-

double-bass /,dʌbəl'beis/ n. контраба́с

double-breasted adj. двубо́ртный

double-dealer n. двуру́шник

double-decker n. двухэта́жный авто́бус

double-spaced adj. напеча́танный че́рез стро́чку

doubling /'dʌbliŋ/ n. удвое́ние

doubly /'dʌbli/ adv. вдвойне́

doubt /daut/ **1.** n. сомне́ние **2.** v. сомнева́ться (в + P) impf.; **—ful** adj. сомни́тельный; **—less** adj. несомне́нный

douche /duʃ/ **1.** n. подмыва́ние **2.** v. подмыва́ть(ся) impf.

dough /dou/ n. те́сто

doughnut /'dounət/ n. по́нчик

dour /dur, dauər/ adj. угрю́мый

douse /daus/ v. обл(ив)а́ть водо́й; окуна́ть в во́ду impf.

dove /dʌv/ n. го́лубь m.

dowel /'dauəl/ n. штырь m.

down[1] /daun/ n. пух

down[2] /daun/ adv. (dir.) вниз; (loc.) внизу́

downcast /'daun,kæst/ adj. пода́вленный, уны́лый

downhill /'daun'hil/ adv. вниз, (dir.) под го́ру; (loc.) под горо́й

downloading /'daun,loudiŋ/ n. (comput.) загру́зка "вниз"

downright /'daun,rait/ *adj.*
прямо́й; соверше́нный

downstream /'daun'strim/ *adv.*
вниз по тече́нию

downtown /'daun'taun/ *n.* делово́й центр (го́рода)

downtrodden /'daun,trɒdn/ *adj.*
расто́птанный; угнетённый

downy /'dauni/ *adj.* пуши́стый

dowry /'dauri/ *n.* прида́ное

doze /douz/ *v.* дрема́ть *impf.*

dozen /'dʌzən/ *n.* дю́жина

drab /dræb/ *adj.* ску́чный

draft /dræft/ **1.** *n.* черновик; эски́з; (*air*) сквозня́к; (*mil.*) призы́в в а́рмию **2.** *v.* составля́ть план *impf.*; **it is —y here** здесь сквозня́т

drag /dræg/ *v.* тащи́ть(ся) *impf.*; *v.i.* тяну́ться *impf.*

dragon /'drægən/ *n.* драко́н

dragonfly /'drægən,flai/ *n.* стреко́за

drain /drein/ **1.** *n.* дрена́жная труба́ **2.** *v.* дрени́ровать *impf.* & *pf.*; **—age** *n.* дрена́ж, осуше́ние

drainpipe /'drein,paip/ *n.* водосто́чная труба́

drake /dreik/ *n.* се́лезень *m.*

drama /'dramə/ *n.* дра́ма

dramatic /drə'mætik/ *adj.* драмати́ческий

dramatist /'dræmətist/ *n.* драмату́рг

dramatization /,dræmətə'zeiʃən/ *n.* драматиза́ция; инсцениро́вка

drape /dreip/ *n.* за́навес

drastic /'dræstik/ *adj.*
реши́тельный; **—ally** *adv.* ре́зко

draw /drɔ/ *v.t.* черпа́ть *impf.*; (*sketch*) рисова́ть *impf.*, на- *pf.*

drawback /'drɔ,bæk/ *n.*
недоста́ток

drawbridge /'drɔ,bridʒ/ *n.* подъёмный мост

drawer /drɔr/ *n.* я́щик

drawing /'drɔiŋ/ *n.* рису́нок

drawing room *n.* гости́ная

dread /dred/ **1.** *n.* страх **2.** *v.* боя́ться (+ *G*) *impf.*

dreadful /'dredfəl/ *adj.* ужа́сный

dream /drim/ **1.** *n.* мечта́ **2.** *v.* мечта́ть *impf.*; ви́деть сон *impf.*

dreamer /'drimər/ *n.* мечта́тель

dreary /'driəri/ *adj.* мра́чный; ску́чный

dredge /dredʒ/ **1.** *n.* дра́га **2.** *v.* драги́ровать *impf.* & *pf.*

dregs /dregz/ *n.* оса́док

drench /drentʃ/ *v.* промока́ть *impf.*; промокну́ть *pf.*

dress /dres/ **1.** *n.* пла́тье, (*attire*) оде́жда **2.** *v.* одева́ть(ся) *impf.*, оде́ть(ся) *pf.*; **~ up** наряжа́ть(ся) *impf.*, -ди́ть(ся) *pf.*

dresser /'dresər/ *n.* комо́д

dressing /'dresiŋ/ *n.* (*med.*) перевя́зка; (*cul.*) припра́ва

dressing gown *n.* хала́т

dressing room *n.* griме́рная

dressmaker /'dres,meikər/ *n.* портни́ха

dribble /'dribəl/ *v.* пуска́ть слю́ни *impf.*; пусти́ть *pf.*

dried /draid/ *adj.* сушёный

drift /drift/ **1.** *n.* тече́ние; (*ocean*) дрейф **2.** *v.* плыть по тече́нию *impf.*

driftwood /'drift,wud/ *n.* пла́вник

drill /dril/ **1.** *n.* (*exercise*) упражне́ние, трениро́вка; (*tool*) сверло́ **2.** *v.* (*train*) трениро́вать *impf.*; (*mech.*) сверли́ть *impf.*

drink /driŋk/ **1.** *n.* питьё, напи́ток **2.** *v.* пить *impf.*, вы- *pf.*

drinking fountain *n.* питьево́й фонта́нчик

drinking water *n.* питьева́я вода́

drip /drip/ *v.* ка́пать *impf.*

drip-dry *adj.* быстросо́хнущий

drive /draiv/ **1.** *n.* ката́нье, прогу́лка; (*urge*) побужде́ние **2.** *v.* е́здить *indet.*, е́хать *det.*, пое́хать *pf.*; вести́ автомоби́ль; **~ out** выгоня́ть *impf.*, вы́гнать *pf.*; **~ up** подъезжа́ть *impf.*

drive-in *adj.* с подъездны́м око́шком

driver /'draivər/ *n.* води́тель

driveway /'draiv,wei/ *n.* подъезд

drizzle /'drizəl/ *n.* ме́лкий дождь, моро́сящий дождь *m.*

dromedary /'drɒmi,deri/ *adj.*
дромаде́р, одного́рбый верблю́д

drone /droun/ **1.** *n.* (*bee; Fig.*) тру́тень *m.*; (*sound*) жужжа́ние; гул **2.** *v.* (*buzz*) жужжа́ть; (*of engine*) гуде́ть *impf.*

drool /drul/ *v.* пуска́ть слю́ни *impf.*

droop /drup/ *v.* поника́ть *impf.*

drop /drɒp/ **1.** *n.* (*liquid*) ка́пля; (*reduction*) пониже́ние **2.** *v.* опуска́ть(ся) *impf.*, опусти́ть(ся) *pf.*; (*price*) снижа́ть(ся) *impf.*; *v.i.* (*fall*) па́дать *impf.*, упа́сть *pf*; *v.t.* (*let fall*) поня́ть *impf.*, поня́ть *pf.*

droppings /'drɒpɪŋz/ *n.* помёт

drought /draut/ *n.* за́суха

drown /draun/ *v.t.* топи́ть *impf.*, у- *pf.*; *v.i.* тону́ть *impf.*, у- *pf.*

drowsy /'drauzi/ *adj.* со́нный

drudgery /'drʌdʒəri/ *n.* тяжёлая рабо́та, ну́дная рабо́та

drug /drʌg/ *n.* лека́рство; (*narcotic*) нарко́тик

drugstore /'drʌg,stɔr/ *n.* апте́ка

drum /drʌm/ *n.* бараба́н

drummer /'drʌmər/ *n.* бараба́нщик

drumstick /'drʌm,stɪk/ *n.* (*of bird*) но́жка

drunk /drʌŋk/ *adj.* пья́ный

drunkard /'drʌŋkərd/ *n.* пья́ница *m.* & *f.*

dry /drai/ **1.** *adj.* сухо́й **2.** *v.* суши́ть *impf.*, вы́сушить *pf.*; со́хнуть *impf.*, вы́- *pf.*

dry cleaner *n.* хими́чистка

dryer /'draiər/ *n.* суши́лка

dryness /'drainɪs/ *n.* су́хость

dual /'duəl/ *adj.* дво́йственный

dub /dʌb/ *v.* (*film*) дубли́ровать *impf.* & *pf.*

dubbing /'dʌbɪŋ/ *n.* (*film*) дубля́ж, дубли́рование

dubious /'dubiəs/ *adj.* сомни́тельный

duchess /'dʌtʃɪs/ *n.* герцоги́ня

duchy /'dʌtʃi/ *n.* ге́рцогство

duck[1] /dʌk/ *n.* (*bird*) у́тка

duck[2] /dʌk/ *v.* окуна́ть(ся) *impf.*, окуну́ть(ся) *pf.*

duckling /'dʌklɪŋ/ *n.* утёнок

duct /dʌkt/ *n.* прото́к

dud /dʌd/ *n.* (*shell*) неразорва́вшийся снаря́д; (*useless thing*) брак

due /du/ **1.** *adj.* до́лжный; надлежа́щий **2.** *n.* до́лжное **3.** ~ **to** *prep.* из-за (+ *G*), благодаря́ (+ *D*)

duel /'duəl/ *n.* поеди́нок, дуэ́ль *f.*

dues /duz/ *n.* сбо́ры, взно́сы *pl.*

duet /du'et/ *n.* дуэ́т

duke /duk/ *n.* ге́рцог

dull /dʌl/ *adj.* тупо́й; (*boring*) ску́чный; (*weather*) па́смурный

duly /'duli/ *adv.* до́лжным о́бразом; своевре́менно

dumb /dʌm/ *adj.* (*mute*) немо́й; (*stupid*) глу́пый

dumbbell /'dʌm,bel/ *n.* ги́ри *pl.*

dummy /'dʌmi/ *n.* манеке́н; (*cards; stupid person*) болва́н

dump /dʌmp/ **1.** *v.* сва́ливать *impf.* **2.** *n.* сва́лка

dumping /'dʌmpɪŋ/ *n.* разгру́зка

dumpling /'dʌmplɪŋ/ *n.* клёцка

dunce /dʌns/ *n.* тупи́ца *m.* & *f.*

dune /dun/ *n.* дю́на

dung /dʌŋ/ *n.* наво́з

dungeon /'dʌndʒən/ *n.* темни́ца

dunk /dʌŋk/ *v.* окуна́ть *impf.*

dupe /dup/ *v.* обма́нывать *impf.*, обману́ть *pf.*

duplicate /*adj.* *n.* 'duplɪkɪt; *v.* -,keit/ **1.** *adj.* двойно́й **2.** *n.* ко́пия **3.** *v.* де́лать ко́пию *impf.*, с- *pf.*

duplicity /du'plɪsɪti/ *n.* дво́йственность, двули́чность

durability /,durə'bɪlɪti/ *n.* про́чность

durable /'durəbəl/ *adj.* про́чный

duration /du'reiʃən/ *n.* продолжи́тельность

duress /du'res/ *n.* принужде́ние

during /'durɪŋ/ *prep.* в тече́ние; во вре́мя (+ *G*)

dusk /dʌsk/ *n.* су́мерки *pl.*

dust /dʌst/ **1.** *n.* пыль *f.* **2.** *v.* стира́ть пыль *impf.*

dustpan /'dʌst,pæn/ *n.* сово́к

dusty /'dʌsti/ *adj.* пы́льный

Dutch /dʌtʃ/ *adj.* голла́ндский; **—man** *n.* голла́ндец; **—woman** *n.* голла́ндка

dutiful /'dutəfəl/ *adj.* послу́шный

duty /'duti/ *n.* обя́занность; (*customs*) по́шлина; **be on ~** дежу́рить *impf.*

duty-free *adj.* беспо́шлинный

dwarf /dwɔrf/ *n.* ка́рлик

dwell /dwel/ *v.* жить, обита́ть *impf.*; ~ **on** остана́вливаться (на + *P*)

dwelling /'dwelɪŋ/ *n.* жило́й дом

dwindle /'dwɪndl/ *v.* уменьша́ться *impf.*, уме́ньшиться *pf.*

dye /dai/ **1.** *n.* кра́ска **2.** *v.* кра́сить *impf.*, по- *pf.*

dying /'daiɪŋ/ *adj.* умира́ющий

dynamic /dai'næmɪk/ *adj.* динами́ческий

dynamite /'dainə,mait/ *n.* динами́т

dynamo /'dainə,mou/ *n.* дина́мо *neut. indecl.*

dynasty /'dainəsti/ *n.* дина́стия

dysentery /'dɪsən,teri/ *n.* дизентерия

dysfunction /dɪs'fʌŋkʃən/ *n.* дисфу́нкция

dyslexia /dɪs'leksiə/ *n.* дисле́ксия

dystrophy /'dɪstrəfi/ *n.*: **muscular ~** мы́шечная дистрофи́я

E

each /itʃ/ *adj., pron.* ка́ждый; ~ **other** друг дру́га

eager /'igər/ *adj.* усе́рдный; **—ness** *n.* усе́рдие

eagerly /'igərli/ *adv.* охо́тно

eagle /'igəl/ *n.* орёл

ear[1] /ɪər/ *n.* у́хо

ear[2] /ɪər/ *n.* (corn) ко́лос

earache /'ɪər,eik/ *n.* боль в у́хе *f.*

eardrum /'ɪər,drʌm/ *n.* бараба́нная перепо́нка

earl /ɜrl/ *n.* граф

early /'ɜrli/ **1.** *adj.* ра́нний **2.** *adv.* ра́но

earmark /'ɪər,mɑrk/ *v.* предназнача́ть; выделя́ть *impf.*

earn /ɜrn/ *v.* зараба́тывать *impf.,* зарабо́тать *pf.;* (deserve) заслу́живать *impf.,* заслужи́ть *pf.*

earnest /'ɜrnɪst/ *adj.* серьёзный

earnings /'ɜrnɪŋz/ *n.* за́работок

earphone /'ɪər,foun/ *n.* нау́шник

earring /'ɪər,rɪŋ/ *n.* серьга́

earshot /'ɪər,ʃɒt/ *n.*: **within ~/ out of ~** *adv.* в преде́лах/вне преде́лов слы́шимости

earth /ɜrθ/ *n.* земля́

earthenware /'ɜrθən,weər/ *n.* гли́няная посу́да

earthly /'ɜrθli/ *adj.* земно́й

earthquake /'ɜrθ,kweik/ *n.* землетрясе́ние

earthy /'ɜrθi/ *adj.* земляно́й

ease /iz/ **1.** *n.* лёгкость **2.** *v.* облегча́ть *impf.,* -чи́ть *pf.*

easel /'izəl/ *n.* мольбе́рт

east /ist/ *n.* восто́к

Easter /'istər/ *n.* Па́сха

eastern /'istərn/ *adj.* восто́чный

eastward /'istwərd/ *adv.* к восто́ку, на восто́к

easy /'izi/ *adj.* лёгкий

easy chair *n.* кре́сло

easygoing /'izi'gouɪŋ/ *adj.* беспе́чный, беззабо́тный

eat /it/ *v.* есть *impf.,* съ- *pf.;* ку́шать *impf.*

eaves /ivz/ *n.* стреха́

eavesdrop /'ivz,drɒp/ *v.* подслу́шивать *impf.*

ebb /eb/ *n.* отли́в, упа́док

ebony /'ebəni/ *n.* чёрное де́рево

ebullient /ɪ'bʌlyənt/ *adj.* кипу́чий

eccentric /ɪk'sentrɪk/ **1.** *adj.* эксцентри́чный **2.** *n.* чуда́к

ecclesiastical /ɪ,klizi'æstɪkəl/ *adj.* церко́вный

echo /'ekou/ **1.** *n.* э́хо **2.** *v.i.* отража́ться *impf.,* -зи́ться *pf.*

eclipse /ɪ'klɪps/ **1.** *n.* затме́ние. **2.** *v.* затмева́ть *impf.,* затми́ть *pf.*

ecological /,ekə'lɒdʒɪkəl/ *adj.* экологи́ческий

ecology /i'kɒlədʒi/ *n.* эколо́гия

economic /,ekə'nɒmɪk/ *adj.* экономи́ческий; **—al** *adj.* эконо́мный

economics /,ekə'nɒmɪks/ *n.* эконо́мика

economize /ɪ'kɒnə,maiz/ *v.* эконо́мить *impf.,* с- *pf.*

economy /i'kɒnəmi/ *n.* эконо́мика, хозя́йство

ecstasy /'ekstəsi/ *n.* экста́з

ecstatic /ek'stætɪk/ *adj.* экстати́ческий

eddy /'edi/ *n.* (in water) воро́нка; (in air) завихре́ние

edge /edʒ/ *n.* край; (of blade) ле́звие

edging /'edʒɪŋ/ *n.* кайма́

edgy /'edʒi/ *adj.* не́рвный

edible /'edəbəl/ *adj.* съедо́бный

edict /'idɪkt/ *n.* эди́кт, указ

edification /,edəfɪ'keiʃən/ *n.* наставле́ние, назида́ние

edifice /'edəfɪs/ *n.* зда́ние

edify /'edəfai/ *v.* наставля́ть *impf.*

edit /'edɪt/ *v.* редакти́ровать *impf.,* от- *pf.;* **—or** *n.* реда́ктор

edition /ɪ'dɪʃən/ *n.* изда́ние

editorial /,edɪ'tɔriəl/ *n.* передова́я статья́

educate /'edʒu,keit/ *v.* дава́ть образова́ние; воспи́тывать *impf.*

educated /'edʒu,keitɪd/ *adj.* образо́ванный

education /,edʒu'keiʃən/ *n.* образова́ние, воспита́ние

educational /ˌedʒʊˈkeɪʃənl/ adj. образова́тельный, уче́бный

educator /ˈedʒʊˌkeɪtər/ n. педаго́г

eel /il/ n. у́горь m.

eerie /ˈɪəri/ adj. жу́ткий

efface /ɪˈfeɪs/ v. стира́ть impf.

effect /ɪˈfekt/ 1. n. сле́дствие; эффе́кт 2. v.: take ~ вступа́ть в си́лу impf.; -пить pf.

effective /ɪˈfektɪv/ adj. эффекти́вный; эффе́ктный

effeminate /ɪˈfemɪnɪt/ adj. женоподо́бный, изне́женный

effervescent /ˌefərˈvesənt/ adj. шипу́чий; Fig. кипу́чий

efficacious /ˌefɪˈkeɪʃəs/ adj. эффекти́вный; де́йственный

efficiency /ɪˈfɪʃənsi/ n. эффекти́вность; рента́бельность

efficient /ɪˈfɪʃənt/ adj. эффекти́вный, производи́тельный

effigy /ˈefɪdʒi/ n. чу́чело

effort /ˈefərt/ n. уси́лие

effrontery /ɪˈfrʌntəri/ n. на́глость, наха́льство

effusive /ɪˈfjusɪv/ adj. экспанси́вный, демонстрати́вный

egalitarian /ɪˌgælɪˈteəriən/ adj. эгалита́рный

egg /eg/ n. яйцо́

eggplant /ˈegˌplænt/ n. баклажа́н

eggshell /ˈegˌʃel/ n. яи́чная скорлупа́; ~ china то́нкий фарфо́р

egocentric /ˌigoʊˈsentrɪk/ adj. эгоцентри́ческий

egoism /ˈigoʊˌɪzəm/ n. эгои́зм

egoist /ˈigoʊɪst/ n. эго́ист; -ic adj. эгоисти́чный

Egypt /ˈidʒɪpt/ n. Еги́пет

Egyptian /ɪˈdʒɪpʃən/ n. египтя́нин, египтя́нка

eiderdown /ˈaɪdərˌdaʊn/ n. гага́чий пух; (comforter) пери́на

eight /eɪt/ 1. adj., n. во́семь 2. n. (cards) восьмёрка

eighteen /ˈeɪˈtin/ adj., n. восемна́дцать; -th adj. восемна́дцатый

eighth /eɪtθ, eɪθ/ adj. восьмо́й

eighty /ˈeɪti/ adj., n. во́семьдесят

either /ˈiðər/ 1. pron., adj. и тот и друго́й; любо́й 2. conj. ~... or... и́ли... и́ли.

eject /ɪˈdʒekt/ v. выбра́сывать impf., вы́бросить pf.; изверга́ть impf., изве́ргнуть pf.

eke out /ik/ v. (a living) перебива́ться кое-как impf.

elaborate /adj. ɪˈlæbərɪt; v. -əˌreɪt/ 1. adj. разрабо́танный, сло́жный 2. v. разраба́тывать; уточня́ть impf.

elapse /ɪˈlæps/ v. проходи́ть impf., пройти́ pf.

elastic /ɪˈlæstɪk/ 1. adj. эласти́чный 2. n. рези́нка

elated /ɪˈleɪtɪd/ adj. в восто́рге

elation /ɪˈleɪʃən/ n. восто́рг

elbow /ˈelboʊ/ 1. n. ло́коть m. 2. v. толка́ться impf.

elder¹ /ˈeldər/ 1. adj. ста́рший 2. n. ста́рец

elder² /ˈeldər/ n. (tree) бузина́

elderly /ˈeldərli/ adj. пожило́й

eldest /ˈeldɪst/ adj. ста́рший

elect /ɪˈlekt/ v. избира́ть impf., избра́ть pf.; —ion n. вы́боры pl.

electoral /ɪˈlektərəl/ adj. избира́тельный

electorate /ɪˈlektərɪt/ n. избира́тели pl.

electrical /ɪˈlektrɪkəl/ adj. электри́ческий

electrician /ɪlekˈtrɪʃən/ n. эле́ктрик

electricity /ɪlekˈtrɪsɪti/ n. электри́чество

electrify /ɪˈlektrəˌfaɪ/ v. электризова́ть impf.; (provide electricity) электрифици́ровать impf. & pf.

electrocute /ɪˈlektrəˌkjut/ v. убива́ть электри́ческим то́ком impf.

electronic /ɪlekˈtrɒnɪk/ adj. электро́нный

electronics /ɪlekˈtrɒnɪks/ n. электро́ника

elegance /ˈelɪgəns/ n. элега́нтность

elegant /ˈelɪgənt/ adj. элега́нтный

elegy /ˈelɪdʒi/ n. эле́гия

element /ˈeləmənt/ n. элеме́нт; be in one's ~ быть в свое́й стихи́и

elemental /ˌeləˈment̬l/ adj. стихи́йный; основно́й

elementary /ˌeləˈmentəri/ adj. элемента́рный, первонача́льный; ~ school нача́льная шко́ла

elephant /ˈeləfənt/ n. слон

elevate /ˈeləˌveɪt/ v. возвыша́ть impf., возвы́сить pf.

elevated /ˈeləˌveɪtɪd/ adj. возвы́шенный; надзе́мный

elevator /ˈeləˌveitər/ n. лифт

eleven /ɪˈlevən/ adj. n. одиннадцать; **—th** adj. одиннадцатый

elf /ɛlf/ n. эльф

elicit /ɪˈlɪsɪt/ v. выявлять impf.

eligible /ˈelɪdʒəbəl/ adj. имеющий возможность, имеющий право

eliminate /ɪˈlɪməˌneit/ v. устранять; исключать impf., -чить pf.

elite /ɪˈlit/ n. элита

ellipse /ɪˈlɪps/ n. эллипс

elliptical /ɪˈlɪptɪkəl/ adj. эллиптический

elm /ɛlm/ n. вяз, ильм

elopement /ɪˈloupmənt/ n. тайное бегство

eloquence /ˈeləkwəns/ n. красноречие

eloquent /ˈeləkwənt/ adj. красноречивый

else /els/ **1.** adj. другой **2.** adv. ещё; **or ~** иначе; **what ~?** что ещё?

elsewhere /ˈelsˌweər/ adv. (loc.) в другом месте; (dir.) в другое место

elusive /ɪˈlusɪv/ adj. неуловимый

emaciate /ɪˈmeiʃiˌeit/ v. истощать(ся) impf.

e-mail /ˈiˌmeil/ n. электронная почта

emanate /ˈeməˌneit/ v. исходить impf.

emancipate /ɪˈmænsəˌpeit/ v. освобождать impf., -бодить pf.

emancipation /ɪˌmænsəˈpeiʃən/ n. эмансипация; освобождение

embalming /emˈbɑmɪŋ/ n. бальзамирование

embankment /emˈbæŋkmənt/ n. набережная; (street) насыпь f.

embargo /emˈbɑrgou/ n. эмбарго neut. indecl.

embark /emˈbɑrk/ v. садиться на корабль impf.; ~ **upon** браться за (+ A) impf.

embarkation /ˌembɑrˈkeiʃən/ n. посадка; (freight) погрузка

embarrass /emˈbærəs/ v. смущать impf., -тить pf.

embarrassing /emˈbærəsɪŋ/ adj. пикантный

embarrassment /emˈbærəsmənt/ n. замешательство; смущение

embassy /ˈembəsi/ n. посольство

embellish /emˈbelɪʃ/ v. укра-

шать; приукрашивать impf.; **—ment** n. украшение

embezzle /emˈbezəl/ v. (незаконно) растратить pf.; **—ment** n. растрата

embitter /emˈbɪtər/ v. озлоблять; ожесточать impf., -чить pf.

emblem /ˈembləm/ n. эмблема

embodiment /emˈbɑdimənt/ n. воплощение, олицетворение

embody /emˈbɑdi/ v. воплощать impf., -тить pf.

emboss /emˈbɔs/ v. чеканить impf.

embrace /emˈbreis/ **1.** n. объятия pl. **2.** v. обнимать(ся) impf., обнять(ся) pf.

embroider /emˈbrɔidər/ v. вышивать impf., вышить pf.

embroil /emˈbrɔil/ v. впутывать (в + A) impf.

embryo /ˈembriˌou/ n. зародыш, эмбрион

emerald /ˈemərəld/ n. изумруд

emerge /ɪˈmɜrdʒ/ v. всплывать impf., всплыть pf.; **—nce** n. появление

emergency /ɪˈmɜrdʒənsi/ **1.** adj. запасной; аварийный **2.** n. крайняя необходимость

emigrant /ˈemigrənt/ n. эмигрант, —ка

emigrate /ˈemiˌgreit/ v. эмигрировать impf. & pf.

emigration /ˌemiˈgreiʃən/ n. эмиграция

eminence /ˈemənəns/ n. знаменитость; возвышенность

eminent /ˈemənənt/ adj. выдающийся, замечательный

emit /ɪˈmɪt/ v. испускать impf., -стить pf.

emotion /ɪˈmouʃən/ n. чувство; эмоция; **—al** adj. эмоциональный

empathize /ˈempəˌθaiz/ v. сопереживать impf.

emperor /ˈempərər/ n. император

emphasis /ˈemfəsɪs/ n. ударение

emphasize /ˈemfəˌsaiz/ v. делать ударение; подчёркивать impf., подчеркнуть pf.

emphatic /emˈfætɪk/ adj. выразительный, эмфатический

empire /ˈempaɪr/ n. империя

empirical /emˈpɪrɪkəl/ adj. эмпирический

employ /emˈplɔi/ v. употреблять

impf., -би́ть *pf.;* (*hire*) нанима́ть *impf.,* -ня́ть *pf.*

employee /ˈemplɔiiː/ *n.* служащий

employer /emˈplɔiər/ *n.* нанима́тель, работода́тель

employment /emˈplɔimənt/ *n.* слу́жба; (*use*) примене́ние

emporium /emˈpɔriəm/ *n.* универма́г; това́рная ба́за

empower /emˈpauər/ *v.* уполномо́чивать *impf.;* уполномо́чить *pf.*

empress /ˈemprɪs/ *n.* императри́ца

emptiness /ˈemptinɪs/ *n.* пустота́

empty /ˈempti/ **1.** *adj.* пусто́й **2.** *v.* опорожня́ть

emulate /ˈemyəˌleit/ *v.* подража́ть (+ *D*) *impf.*

emulsion /iˈmʌlʃən/ *n.* эму́льсия

enable /enˈeibəl/ *v.* дава́ть возмо́жность *impf.,* дать *pf.*

enact /enˈækt/ *v.* постанови́ть *pf.*

enactment /enˈæktmənt/ *n.* введе́ние зако́на в си́лу

enamel /iˈnæməl/ *n.* эма́ль *f.;* —**ed** *adj.* эмали́рованный

encampment /enˈkæmpmənt/ *n.* расположе́ние ла́герем; ла́герь *m.*

enchant /enˈtʃænt/ *v.* очаро́вывать *impf.,* очарова́ть *pf.;* —**ing** *adj.* очарова́тельный; —**ment** *n.* очарова́ние

encircle /enˈsɜːrkəl/ *v.* окружа́ть *impf.,* -жи́ть *pf.*

enclave /ˈenkleiv/ *n.* анкла́в

enclose /enˈklouz/ *v.* прикла́дывать *impf.,* приложи́ть *pf.*

enclosure /enˈklouʒər/ *n.* огоро́женное ме́сто; приложе́ние

encode /enˈkoud/ *v.* шифрова́ть *impf.*

encompass /enˈkʌmpəs/ *v.* окружа́ть *impf.,* -жи́ть *pf.;* заключа́ть *impf.,* -чи́ть *pf.*

encore /ˈɑŋkɔr/ *interj.* бис

encounter /enˈkauntər/ **1.** *n.* встре́ча **2.** *v.* встре́тить *pf.;* ста́лкиваться *impf.,* столкну́ться *pf.*

encourage /enˈkɜːridʒ/ *v.* ободря́ть *impf.,* -ри́ть *pf.;* —**ment** *n.* ободре́ние; поощре́ние

encouraging /enˈkɜːridʒiŋ/ *adj.* ободря́ющий; поощри́тельный

encroach /enˈkroutʃ/ *v.* посяга́ть (на + *A*) *impf.;* —**ment** *n.* посяга́тельство

encumber /enˈkʌmbər/ *v.* загромозжда́ть; обременя́ть *impf.*

encyclopedia /enˌsaikləˈpidiə/ *n.* энциклопе́дия

encyclopedic /enˌsaikləˈpidik/ *adj.* энциклопеди́ческий

end /end/ **1.** *n.* коне́ц; (*purpose*) цель *f.* **2.** *v.* конча́ть(ся) *impf.,* ко́нчить(ся) *pf.;* прекраща́ть *impf.,* -ти́ть *pf.*

endanger /enˈdeindʒər/ *v.* подверга́ть опа́сности *impf.*

endearing /enˈdiəriŋ/ *adj.* привлека́тельный, подкупа́ющий

endeavor /enˈdevər/ **1.** *n.* попы́тка **2.** *v.* пыта́ться, стара́ться *impf.*

ending /ˈendiŋ/ *n.* оконча́ние

endless /ˈendlis/ *adj.* бесконе́чный

endorse /enˈdɔrs/ *v.* подде́рживать *impf.,* -держа́ть *pf.;* —**ment** *n.* подде́ржка

endow /enˈdau/ *v.* обеспе́чивать; одаря́ть *impf.,* -и́ть *pf.*

endowment /enˈdaumənt/ *n.* поже́ртвование; дарова́ние

endurable /enˈdurəbəl/ *adj.* терпи́мый

endurance /enˈdurəns/ *n.* выно́сливость

endure /enˈdur/ *v.* терпе́ть *impf.*

enema /ˈenəmə/ *n.* кли́зма

enemy /ˈenəmi/ *n.* враг

energetic /ˌenərˈdʒetik/ *adj.* энерги́чный

energy /ˈenərdʒi/ *n.* эне́ргия

enforce /enˈfɔrs/ *v.* обеспе́чивать соблюде́ние *impf.;* —**ment** *n.* принужде́ние

enfranchise /enˈfræntʃaiz/ *v.* предоставля́ть избира́тельные права́ (+ *D*) *impf.*

engage /enˈgeidʒ/ *v.* (*occupy*) занима́ть *impf.,* заня́ть *pf.;* (*hire*) нанима́ть *impf.,* наня́ть *pf.*

engaged /enˈgeidʒd/ *adj.* (*busy*) за́нятый (+ *I*); обру́ченный

engagement /enˈgeidʒmənt/ *n.* (*meeting*) свида́ние; (*betrothal*) обруче́ние; (*mil.*) бой, сти́чка; ~ **ring** обруча́льное кольцо́

engaging /enˈgeidʒiŋ/ *adj.* обая́тельный; привлека́тельный

engender /enˈdʒendər/ *v.* порожда́ть *impf.*

engine /'ɛndʒɪn/ *n.* мото́р; ~ **driver** машини́ст

engineer /ˌɛndʒə'nɪər/ *n.* инжене́р

England /'ɪŋglɪnd/ *n.* А́нглия

English /'ɪŋglɪʃ/ *adj.* англи́йский; ~ **Channel** Ла-Ма́нш проли́в

Englishman /'ɪŋglɪʃmən/ *n.* англича́нин

Englishwoman /'ɪŋglɪʃˌwʊmən/ *n.* англича́нка

engrave /ɛn'greiv/ *v.* гравирова́ть *impf.*, вы- *pf.*; **—r** *n.* гравёр

engraving /ɛn'greivɪŋ/ *n.* гравиро́вание; (*etching*) гравю́ра

engross /ɛn'grous/ *v.* поглоща́ть *impf.*; **be —ed in** быть поглощённым (+ *I*) *impf.*

engulf /ɛn'gʌlf/ *v.* поглоща́ть *impf.*

enigma /ə'nɪgmə/ *n.* зага́дка

enjoy /ɛn'dʒɔɪ/ *v.* наслажда́ться *impf.*; **—able** *adj.* прия́тный; **—ment** *n.* удово́льствие

enlarge /ɛn'lɑːrdʒ/ *v.* увели́чивать *impf.*, увели́чить *pf.*

enlighten /ɛn'laɪtn/ *v.* просвеща́ть *impf.*, -ти́ть *pf.*; **—ment** *n.* просвеще́ние

enlist /ɛn'lɪst/ *v.t.* вербова́ть *impf.*, за- *pf.*; *v.i.* поступа́ть на вое́нную слу́жбу *impf.*

enliven /ɛn'laɪvən/ *v.* оживля́ть *impf.*, -ви́ть *pf.*

enmity /'ɛnmɪti/ *n.* вражда́

enormity /ɪ'nɔrmɪti/ *n.* огро́мность

enormous /ɪ'nɔrməs/ *adj.* огро́мный; **—ly** *adv.* чрезвыча́йно

enough /ɪ'nʌf/ *adj.*, *adv.* дово́льно, доста́точно

enrage /ɛn'reidʒ/ *v.* беси́ть *impf.*, вз-

enrapture /ɛn'ræptʃər/ *v.* восхища́ть *impf.*, -ти́ть *pf.*; **—d** *adj.* (быть) в восто́рге

enrich /ɛn'rɪtʃ/ *v.* обогаща́ть *impf.*, обога-

enroll /ɛn'roul/ *v.* зачисля́ть(ся); регистри́ровать *impf.*; **—ment** *n.* регистра́ция

ensemble /ɑn'sɑmbəl/ *n.* анса́мбль *m.*

ensign /'ɛnsən/ *n.* зна́мя; флаг

enslave /ɛn'sleiv/ *v.* порабоща́ть *impf.*, -ти́ть *pf.*

ensnare /ɛn'snɛər/ *v.* пойма́ть в лову́шку *impf.*

ensue /ɛn'su/ *v.* сле́довать *impf.*

ensuing /ɛn'suɪŋ/ *adj.* после́дующий

ensure /ɛn'ʃʊr/ *v.* обеспе́чивать; гаранти́ровать *impf.*

entail /ɛn'teɪl/ *v.* влечь за собо́й; вызыва́ть; зна́чить *impf.*

entangle /ɛn'tæŋgəl/ *v.* запу́тывать *impf.*, запу́тать *pf.*

enter /'ɛntər/ *v.* (*on foot*) входи́ть *impf.*, войти́ *pf.*; (*by vehicle*) въезжа́ть *impf.*, въе́хать *pf.*; (*join*) вступа́ть *impf.*, -пи́ть *pf.*

enterprise /'ɛntərˌpraiz/ *n.* предприя́тие; (*spirit*) предприи́мчивость

enterprising /'ɛntərˌpraizɪŋ/ *adj.* предприи́мчивый

entertain /ˌɛntər'tein/ *v.* развлека́ть *impf.*, развле́чь *pf.*; принима́ть госте́й *impf.*, приня́ть *pf.*; **—er** *n.* (эстра́дный) арти́ст; **—ing** *adj.* заба́вный; развлека́тельный; **—ment** *n.* развлече́ние; представле́ние

enthrall /ɛn'θrɔl/ *v.* увлека́ть *impf.*

enthusiasm /ɛn'θuziˌæzəm/ *n.* энтузиа́зм

enthusiastic /ɛnˌθuzi'æstɪk/ *adj.* по́лный энтузиа́зма

entice /ɛn'tais/ *v.* зама́нивать *impf.*, замани́ть *pf.*; **—ment** *n.* собла́зн

enticing /ɛn'taisɪŋ/ *adj.* зама́нчивый, привлека́тельный

entire /ɛn'taɪər/ *adj.* це́лый; весь

entirely /ɛn'taɪrli/ *adv.* вполне́

entitle /ɛn'taitl/ *v.* дава́ть пра́во *impf.*; (*book*) озагла́вить *pf.*; **be —d to** име́ть пра́во на (+ *A*) *impf.*

entity /'ɛntiti/ *n.* вещь *f.*, объе́кт

entombment /ɛn'tummənt/ *n.* погребе́ние

entourage /ˌɑntu'rɑʒ/ *n.* сви́та

entrails /'ɛntreilz/ *n.* вну́тренности, кишки́ *pl.*

entrance¹ /'ɛntrəns/ **1.** *adj.* входно́й; вступи́тельныйн **2.** *n.* вход

entrance² /ɛn'træns/ *v.* зачаро́вывать *impf.*

entrancing /ɛn'trænsɪŋ/ *adj.* очарова́тельный

entreat /ɛn'trit/ *v.* умоля́ть *impf.*

entreaty /ɛn'triti/ *n.* мольба́

entrée /'ɑntrei/ *n.* второ́е блю́до

entrepreneur /ˌɑntrəprəˈnɜːr/ n. предпринима́тель

entrust /enˈtrʌst/ v. вверя́ть impf., вве́рить pf.; поруча́ть impf., -чи́ть pf.

entry /ˈentri/ n. вход, вступле́ние

enumerate /ɪˈnuːməˌreit/ v. перечисля́ть impf., перечи́слить pf.

enunciate /ɪˈnʌnsiˌeit/ v. произноси́ть impf., произнести́ pf.

envelope /ˈenvəˌloup/ n. конве́рт

enviable /ˈenviəbəl/ adj. зави́дный

envious /ˈenviəs/ adj. зави́стливый

environment /enˈvairənmənt/ n. окруже́ние; среда́; —alist n. защи́тник приро́ды

environs /enˈvairənz/ n. окре́стности pl.

envisage /enˈvizidʒ/ v. предусма́тривать impf., -смотре́ть pf.

envoy /ˈenvoi/ n. посла́нник

envy /ˈenvi/ 1. n. за́висть 2. v. зави́довать impf.

ephemera /ɪˈfemərə/ n. однодне́вки pl.

ephemeral /ɪˈfemərəl/ adj. эфеме́рный

epic /ˈepik/ 1. adj. эпи́ческий 2. n. эпи́ческая поэ́ма

epidemic /ˌepiˈdemik/ 1. adj. эпидеми́ческий 2. n. эпиде́мия

epilepsy /ˈepəˌlepsi/ n. эпиле́псия

epileptic /ˌepəˈleptik/ 1. adj. эпилепти́ческий 2. n. эпиле́птик

epilogue /ˈepəˌlɒg/ n. эпило́г

Epiphany /ɪˈpifəni/ n. Богоявле́ние; Креще́ние

episode /ˈepəˌsoud/ n. эпизо́д

epitaph /ˈepiˌtæf/ n. эпита́фия

epithet /ˈepəˌθet/ n. эпи́тет

epitome /ɪˈpitəmi/ n. конспе́кт

epitomize /ɪˈpitəˌmaiz/ v. воплоща́ть; конспекти́ровать impf.

epoch /ˈepək/ n. эпо́ха

epoch-making adj. эпоха́льный, истори́ческий

equal /ˈiːkwəl/ 1. adj. ра́вный 2. v. равня́ться impf.; —ity n. ра́венство

equalize /ˈiːkwəˌlaiz/ v. ура́внивать impf., уравня́ть pf.

equally /ˈiːkwəli/ adv. одина́ково, в ра́вной сте́пени; равно́

equanimity /ˌiːkwəˈnimiti/ n. самооблада́ние

equation /ɪˈkweiʒən/ n. уравне́ние

equator /ɪˈkweitər/ n. эква́тор

equestrian /ɪˈkwestriən/ 1. adj. ко́нный 2. n. вса́дник, -ница

equilibrium /ˌiːkwəˈlibriəm/ n. равнове́сие

equinox /ˈiːkwəˌnɒks/ n. равноде́нствие

equip /ɪˈkwip/ v. обору́довать impf. & pf.; снабжа́ть impf., снабди́ть pf.; —ment n. обору́дование

equitable /ˈekwitəbəl/ adj. справедли́вый

equity /ˈekwiti/ n. справедли́вость; pl. (econ.) акти́вы pl.

equivalent /ɪˈkwivələnt/ 1. adj. эквивале́нтный 2. n. эквивале́нт

equivocal /ɪˈkwivəkəl/ adj. двусмы́сленный; нея́сный

era /ˈiərə, ˈerə/ n. э́ра

eradicate /ɪˈrædiˌkeit/ v. искореня́ть impf., -ни́ть pf.

erase /ɪˈreis/ v. стира́ть impf., стере́ть pf.; вычёркивать impf.

eraser /ɪˈreisər/ n. рези́нка

erect /ɪˈrekt/ 1. adj. прямо́й 2. v. воздвига́ть impf., воздви́гнуть pf.

erection /ɪˈrekʃən/ n. сооруже́ние; (physiol.) эре́кция

ermine /ˈɜːrmin/ n. горноста́й

erode /ɪˈroud/ v. разъеда́ть impf., разъе́сть pf.

erosion /ɪˈrouʒən/ n. разъеда́ние, эро́зия

erotic /ɪˈrɒtik/ adj. эроти́ческий

err /ɜːr, er/ v. ошиба́ться impf., -би́ться pf.

errand /ˈerənd/ n. поруче́ние; ~ boy ма́льчик на побегу́шках

erratic /ɪˈrætik/ adj. неусто́йчивый

erratum /ɪˈrɑːtəm/ n. (in writing) опи́ска; (in print) опеча́тка

erroneous /əˈrouniəs/ adj. оши́бочный

error /ˈerər/ n. оши́бка

erudite /ˈeryʊˌdait/ adj. учёный

erudition /ˌeryʊˈdiʃən/ n. эруди́ция

erupt /ɪˈrʌpt/ v. взрыва́ться impf.; (volcano) изверга́ться impf.

escalate /ˈeskəˌleit/ v. разраста́ться impf.

escalation /ˌeskəˈleɪʃən/ n. расстание, эскалация

escalator /ˈeskəˌleɪtər/ n. эскалатор

escapade /ˈeskəˌpeɪd/ n. выходка

escape /ɪˈskeɪp/ **1.** n. бегство; (from danger) спасение; (gas) утечка **2.** v. убегать impf., убежать pf.; (save oneself) спасаться impf.

escort / n. ˈeskɔrt; v. ɪˈskɔrt/ **1.** n. эскорт, конвой **2.** v. сопровождать impf., эскортировать impf. & pf.

Eskimo /ˈeskəˌmou/ n. эскимос; —ка

especially /ɪˈspeʃəli/ adv. особенно

espionage /ˈespiəˌnɑʒ/ **1.** adj. шпионский **2.** n. шпионаж

espouse /ɪˈspauz/ v. поддерживать impf.; -держать impf.

essay /ˈeseɪ/ n. очерк, этюд

essence /ˈesəns/ n. сущность f.; (extract) эссенция

essential /ɪˈsenʃəl/ adj. необходимый; существенный

essentially /ɪˈsenʃəli/ adv. по существу; в основном

establish /ɪˈstæblɪʃ/ v. основывать impf., основать impf.; устанавливать impf., установить pf.

establishment /ɪˈstæblɪʃmənt/ n. учреждение; установление

estate /ɪˈsteɪt/ n. имение; (class) сословие

esteem /ɪˈstim/ **1.** n. уважение; почёт **2.** v. уважать impf.

estimate /v. ˈestəˌmeɪt; n. -mɪt/ **1.** v. оценивать impf., оценить pf. **2.** n. оценка

estimation /ˌestəˈmeɪʃən/ n. суждение, мнение

estrange /ɪˈstreɪndʒ/ v. отчуждать impf.; —ment n. отчуждение

estuary /ˈestʃuˌeri/ n. устье реки

etc. abbr. и т. д.

et cetera /et ˈsetərə/ adv. и так далее

etch /etʃ/ v. вытравливать impf.

etching /ˈetʃɪŋ/ n. гравюра

eternal /ɪˈtɜrnəl/ adj. вечный

eternity /ɪˈtɜrnɪti/ n. вечность

ethanol /ˈeθəˌnɔl/ n. этиловый спирт

ether /ˈiθər/ n. эфир

ethereal /ɪˈθɪriəl/ adj. эфирный

ethical /ˈeθɪkəl/ adj. этичный, этический

ethnic /ˈeθnɪk/ adj. этнический

ethnographer /eθˈnɒɡrəfər/ n. этнограф

ethos /ˈiθɒs/ n. дух

ethylene /ˈeθəˌlin/ n. этилен

etiquette /ˈetɪkɪt/ n. этикет; правила поведения pl.

etymology /ˌetəˈmɒlədʒi/ n. этимология

eucalyptus /ˌyukəˈlɪptəs/ n. эвкалипт

Eucharist /ˈyukərɪst/ n. причастие; евхаристия

eulogy /ˈyulədʒi/ n. похвала

euphemism /ˈyufəˌmɪzəm/ n. эвфемизм

euphemistic /ˌyufəˈmɪstɪk/ adj. эвфемистический

euphoria /yuˈfɔriə/ n. эйфория; Colloq. кайф

Europe /ˈyurəp/ n. Европа

European /ˌyurəˈpiən/ **1.** adj. европейский **2.** n. европеец, -пейка; ~ Union Европейское Союз

evacuate /ɪˈvækyuˌeɪt/ v. эвакуировать impf. & pf.

evacuation /ɪˌvækyuˈeɪʃən/ n. эвакуация

evade /ɪˈveɪd/ v. уклоняться (от + G); избегать impf.

evaluate /ɪˈvælyuˌeɪt/ v. оценивать impf., оценить pf.

evaluation /ɪˌvælyuˈeɪʃən/ n. оценка

evangelical /ˌivænˈdʒelɪkəl/ adj. евангельский; евангелический

evangelist /ɪˈvændʒəlɪst/ n. евангелист

evangelize /ɪˈvændʒəˌlaɪz/ v. проповедовать impf.

evaporate /ɪˈvæpəˌreɪt/ v. испаряться(ся) impf., испарить(ся) pf.; —d milk сгущённое молоко

evaporation /ɪˌvæpəˈreɪʃən/ n. испарение

evasion /ɪˈveɪʒən/ n. уклонение

evasive /ɪˈveɪsɪv/ adj. уклончивый

eve /iv/ n. канун; on the ~ of накануне

even /ˈivən/ **1.** adj. ровный; (number) чётный **2.** adv. даже

evening /ˈivnɪŋ/ n. вечер; in the ~ вечером

evenly /ˈivənli/ adv. ровно

event /ɪˈvent/ n. событие

eventful /ɪ'vɛntfəl/ *adj.* по́лный собы́тий

eventual /ɪ'vɛntʃuəl/ *adj.* коне́чный; **—ity** *n.* возмо́жность

ever /'ɛvər/ *adv.* когда́-либо, когда́-нибудь; (*always*) всегда́; **~ since** с тех пор (как)

evergreen /'ɛvər,grin/ *n.* вечнозелёное расте́ние

everlasting /,ɛvər'læstɪŋ/ *adj.* ве́чный

evermore /,ɛvər'mɔr/ *adv.* наве́ки

every /'ɛvri/ *adj.* ка́ждый, вся́кий

everybody /'ɛvri,bɒdi/ *pron.* ка́ждый, вся́кий; все *pl.*

everyday /'ɛvri,deɪ/ *adj.* повседне́вный; ежедне́вный

everyone /'ɛvri,wʌn/ *pron.* ка́ждый, вся́кий; все *pl.*

everything /'ɛvri,θɪŋ/ *pron.* всё

everywhere /'ɛvri,wɛər/ *adv.* всю́ду, везде́

evict /ɪ'vɪkt/ *v.* выселя́ть *impf.*, вы́селить *pf.*; **—ion** *n.* выселе́ние

evidence /'ɛvidəns/ *n.* свиде́тельство; доказа́тельство

evident /'ɛvidənt/ *adj.* очеви́дный

evil /'ivəl/ **1.** *adj.* злой **2.** *n.* зло

evocative /ɪ'vɒkətɪv/ *adj.* напомина́ющий

evoke /ɪ'vouk/ *v.* вызыва́ть *impf.*, вы́звать *pf.*

evolution /,ɛvə'luʃən/ *n.* разви́тие, эволю́ция; **—ary** *adj.* эволюцио́нный

evolve /ɪ'vɒlv/ *v.* развива́ть(ся) *impf.*, разви́ть(ся) *pf.*

ewe /yu/ *n.* овца́

exacerbate /ɪg'zæsər,beit/ *v.* обостря́ть *impf.*, -стри́ть *pf.*

exact /ɪg'zækt/ **1.** *adj.* то́чный, аккура́тный **2.** *v.* взы́скивать

exacting /ɪg'zæktɪŋ/ *adj.* тре́бовательный

exactly /ɪg'zæktli/ *adv.* то́чно; как раз; и́менно

exactness /ɪg'zæktnɪs/ *n.* то́чность

exaggerate /ɪg'zædʒə,reit/ *v.* преувели́чивать *impf.*, -величи́ть *pf.*

exaggeration /ɪg,zædʒə'reiʃən/ *n.* преувеличе́ние

exalt /ɪg'zɔlt/ *v.* возвыша́ть *impf.*

exaltation /,ɛgzɔl'teiʃən/ *n.* возвыше́ние; возвеличе́ние; восто́рг

examination /ɪg,zæmə'neiʃən/ *n.* экза́мен; осмо́тр

examine /ɪg'zæmɪn/ *v.* осма́тривать; рассма́тривать *impf.*, -смотре́ть *pf.*: экзамено́вать *impf.*, про-- *pf.*

examiner /ɪg'zæmənər/ *n.* экзамена́тор; контролёр

example /ɪg'zæmpəl/ *n.* приме́р; **for ~** наприме́р

exasperate /ɪg'zæspə,reit/ *v.* раздража́ть *impf.*, -жи́ть *pf.*

exasperation /ɪg,zæspə'reiʃən/ *n.* раздраже́ние

excavate /'ɛkskə,veit/ *v.* раска́пывать *impf.*, раскопа́ть *pf.*

excavation /,ɛkskə'veiʃən/ *n.* раско́пки *pl.*

exceed /ɪk'sid/ *v.* превыша́ть *impf.*, превы́сить *pf.*

exceedingly /ɪk'sidɪŋli/ *adv.* чрезвыча́йно

excel /ɪk'sɛl/ *v.* превосходи́ть *impf.*, превзойти́ *pf.*

excellence /'ɛksələns/ *n.* превосхо́дство

excellency /'ɛksələnsi/ *n.* (*title*) превосходи́тельство

excellent /'ɛksələnt/ *adj.* отли́чный, превосхо́дный

except /ɪk'sɛpt/ *prep.* кро́ме (+ G)

exception /ɪk'sɛpʃən/ *n.* исключе́ние

exceptional /ɪk'sɛpʃənl/ *adj.* исключи́тельный, необы́чный

excerpt /'ɛksɜrpt/ *n.* отры́вок

excess /ɪk'sɛs, 'ɛksɛs/ *n.* изли́шек, избы́ток

excessive /ɪk'sɛsɪv/ *adj.* чрезме́рный, изли́шний

exchange /ɪks'tʃeindʒ/ **1.** *n.* обме́н, заме́н **2.** *v.* обме́нивать(ся) *impf.*, обменя́ть(ся) *pf.*

exchequer /ɪks'tʃɛkər/ *n.* казна́, казначе́йство

excise[1] /ɪk'saiz/ *v.* выреза́ть *impf.*

excise[2] /'ɛksaiz/ *n.* акци́з

excitable /ɪk'saitəbəl/ *adj.* (легко́) возбуди́мый

excite /ɪk'sait/ *v.* волнова́ть *impf.*, вз- *pf.*; возбужда́ть *impf.*, -ди́ть *pf.*; **—ment** *n.* возбужде́ние; волне́ние

exclaim /ɪk'skleɪm/ v. восклицать impf., воскликнуть pf.

exclamation /ˌekskləˈmeɪʃən/ n. восклицание; ~ point восклицательный знак

exclude /ɪk'sklud/ v. исключать impf., -чить pf.

exclusion /ɪk'skluʒən/ n. исключение

exclusive /ɪk'sklusɪv/ adj. исключительный

excommunicate /ˌekskəˈmjunɪˌkeɪt/ v. отлучать от церкви impf., -чить pf.

excrement /ˈekskrəmənt/ n. экскременты pl.

excrete /ɪk'skrit/ v. выделять impf.

excretion /ɪk'skriʃən/ n. выделение

excruciating /ɪk'skruʃiˌeɪtɪŋ/ adj. мучительный; убийственный

excursion /ɪk'skɜrʒən/ n. экскурсия

excusable /ɪk'skyuzəbəl/ adj. простительный

excuse /ɪk'skyus; v. ɪk'skyuz/ **1.** n. оправдание; (pretext) предлог **2.** v. извинять impf., -нить pf.; (release) освобождать impf.

execute /ˈeksɪˌkyut/ v. исполнять impf., исполнить pf.; (kill legally) казнить impf. & pf.

execution /ˌeksɪˈkyuʃən/ n. исполнение; казнь f., экзекуция

executioner /ˌeksɪˈkyuʃənər/ n. палач

executive /ɪg'zekyətɪv/ **1.** adj. исполнительный **2.** n. директор

exemplary /ɪg'zempləri/ adj. образцовый

exemplify /ɪg'zempləˌfaɪ/ v. служить примером impf., по-

exempt /ɪg'zempt/ **1.** adj. освобождённый **2.** v. освобождать impf., освободить pf.

exemption /ɪg'zempʃən/ n. освобождение

exercise /ˈeksərˌsaɪz/ **1.** n. упражнение **2.** v. упражнять impf.; (duties) исполнять impf.

exert /ɪg'zɜrt/ v. напрягать(ся) impf., напрячь(ся) pf.; оказывать impf.; **—ion** n. напряжение

exhale /eks'heɪl/ v. выдыхать impf., выдохнуть pf.

exhaust /ɪg'zɔst/ **1.** n. выхлоп **2.** v. истощать impf., -щить pf.;

исчерпывать impf., исчерпать pf.

exhausted /ɪg'zɔstɪd/ adj. измученный, изнеможённый

exhausting /ɪg'zɔstɪŋ/ adj. утомительный, изнурительный

exhaustion /ɪg'zɔstʃən/ n. истощение, изнеможение

exhaustive /ɪg'zɔstɪv/ adj. истощающий, исчерпывающий

exhaust pipe n. выхлопная труба

exhibit /ɪg'zɪbɪt/ **1.** n. экспонат **2.** v. выставлять impf., выставить pf.; проявлять impf., -вить pf.

exhibition /ˌeksəˈbɪʃən/ n. показ; выставка

exhibitor /ɪg'zɪbɪtər/ n. экспонент

exhilarate /ɪg'zɪləˌreɪt/ v. оживлять impf.

exhilaration /ɪgˌzɪləˈreɪʃən/ n. весёлость; (thrill) восхищение

exhort /ɪg'zɔrt/ v. увещевать impf.; **—ation** n. увещевание

exhume /ɪg'zum/ v. выкапывать impf., выкопать pf.

exile /ˈegzaɪl/ **1.** n. ссылка; (person) изгнанник **2.** v. ссылать impf., сослать pf.

exist /ɪg'zɪst/ v. существовать impf.; **—ence** n. существование

exit /ˈegzɪt/ **1.** n. выход **2.** v. уходить impf., уйти pf.

exonerate /ɪg'zɒnəˌreɪt/ v. оправдывать impf., оправдать pf.

exorbitant /ɪg'zɔrbɪtənt/ adj. непомерный

exorcise /ˈeksərˌsaɪz/ v. изгонять impf., изгнать pf.

exotic /ɪg'zɒtɪk/ adj. экзотический

expand /ɪk'spænd/ v. расширять(ся) impf., расширить(ся) pf.

expanse /ɪk'spæns/ n. протяжение, пространство

expansion /ɪk'spænʃən/ n. расширение; экспансия

expatriate /eks'peɪtriɪt/ n. экспатриант, —а

expect /ɪk'spekt/ v. ожидать (+ G) impf.; **—ant** adj. ожидающий

expectation /ˌekspekˈteɪʃən/ n. ожидание

expedient /ɪk'spidiənt/ **1.** n.

приём, сре́дство 2. *adj.* целесообра́зный

expedite /'ekspɪˌdaɪt/ *v.* ускоря́ть *impf.*, уско́рить *pf.*

expedition /ˌekspɪ'dɪʃən/ *n.* экспеди́ция

expel /ɪk'spel/ *v.* выгоня́ть *impf.*, вы́гнать *pf.*

expend /ɪk'spend/ *v.* тра́тить *impf.*, ис-, по- *pf.*

expense /ɪk'spens/ *n.* расхо́д; **at the ~ of** за счёт (+ G)

expensive /ɪk'spensɪv/ *adj.* дорого́й

experience /ɪk'spɪərɪəns/ 1. *n.* о́пыт 2. *v.* испы́тывать *impf.*, испыта́ть *pf.*; **—d** *adj.* о́пытный

experiment / *n.* ɪk'sperəmənt; *v.* -,ment/ 1. *n.* экспериме́нт 2. *v.* эксперименти́ровать *impf.*

experimental /ɪkˌsperə'mentl/ *adj.* эксперимента́льный

expert /'ekspɜːrt/ 1. *adj.* о́пытный 2. *n.* экспе́рт

expertise /ˌekspər'tiːz/ *n.* специа́льные зна́ния *pl.*

expiration /ˌekspə'reɪʃən/ *n.* истече́ние; (*air*) выдыха́ние

expire /ɪk'spaɪr/ *v.* истека́ть *impf.*, исте́чь *pf.*

explain /ɪk'spleɪn/ *v.* объясня́ть *impf.*, -ни́ть *pf.*

explanation /ˌeksplə'neɪʃən/ *n.* объясне́ние

expletive /'eksplɪtɪv/ *n.* бра́нное сло́во; (*gram.*) вста́вное сло́во

explicit /ɪk'splɪsɪt/ *adj.* то́чный

explode /ɪk'sploʊd/ *v.* взрыва́ть(ся) *impf.*, взорва́ть(ся) *pf.*

exploit / *n.* 'eksplɔɪt; *v.* ɪk'splɔɪt/ 1. *n.* по́двиг 2. *v.* эксплуати́ровать *impf.*

exploitation /ˌeksplɔɪ'teɪʃən/ *n.* эксплуата́ция

exploration /ˌeksplə'reɪʃən/ *n.* иссле́дование

exploratory /ɪk'splɔːrəˌtɔːri/ *adj.* иссле́довательский

explore /ɪk'splɔːr/ *v.* иссле́довать *impf. & pf.*

explorer /ɪk'splɔːrər/ *n.* иссле́дователь

explosion /ɪk'sploʊʒən/ *n.* взрыв

explosive /ɪk'sploʊsɪv/ *n.* взры́вчатое вещество́

export / *n.* 'ekspɔːrt; *v.* ɪk'spɔːrt/ 1. *n.* э́кспорт 2. *v.* экспорти́ровать *impf. & pf.*

expose /ɪk'spoʊz/ *v.* раскрыва́ть

impf., раскры́ть *pf.*; разоблача́ть *impf.*, -чи́ть *pf.*

exposition /ˌekspə'zɪʃən/ *n.* изложе́ние; (*exhibit*) вы́ставка

exposure /ɪk'spoʊʒər/ *n.* вы́ставление; разоблаче́ние

expound /ɪk'spaund/ *v.* излага́ть; толкова́ть *impf.*

express /ɪk'spres/ 1. *adj.* (*rapid*) сро́чный; (*definite*) то́чный 2. *n.* экспре́сс 3. *v.* выража́ть *impf.*, вы́разить *pf.*

expression /ɪk'spreʃən/ *n.* выраже́ние

expressive /ɪk'spresɪv/ *adj.* вырази́тельный

expressly /ɪk'spresli/ *adv.* (*on purpose*) специа́льно

expressway /ɪk'spreswei/ *n.* автостра́да

expropriate /eks'proʊprɪˌeɪt/ *v.* экспроприи́ровать *impf. & pf.*

expulsion /ɪk'spʌlʃən/ *n.* изгна́ние; исключе́ние

expurgation /ˌekspər'geɪʃən/ *n.* вычёркивание

exquisite /ɪk'skwɪzɪt/ *adj.* изы́сканный, преле́стный

extant /'ekstənt/ *adj.* сохрани́вшийся

extend /ɪk'stend/ *v.t.* протя́гивать *impf.*, протяну́ть *pf.*; *v.i.* тяну́ться *impf.*; **—ed** *adj.* обши́рный

extension /ɪk'stenʃən/ *n.* расшире́ние; продле́ние

extensive /ɪk'stensɪv/ *adj.* обши́рный; экстенси́вный

extent /ɪk'stent/ *n.* сте́пень *f.*

extenuating circumstances /ɪk'stenyuˌeɪtɪŋ/ *n.* смягча́ющие обстоя́тельства *pl.*

exterior /ɪk'stɪərɪər/ 1. *adj.* вне́шний 2. *n.* вне́шность

exterminate /ɪk'stɜːrməˌneɪt/ *v.* истребля́ть *impf.*, -би́ть *pf.*

extermination /ɪkˌstɜːrmə'neɪʃən/ *n.* истребле́ние

external /ɪk'stɜːrnl/ *adj.* вне́шний

extinct /ɪk'stɪŋkt/ *adj.* вы́мерший

extinction /ɪk'stɪŋkʃən/ *n.* вымира́ние; (*volcano*) потуха́ние

extinguish /ɪk'stɪŋgwɪʃ/ *v.* гаси́ть *impf.*, по- *pf.*

extol /ɪk'stoul/ *v.* превозноси́ть *impf.*

extort /ɪk'stɔːrt/ *v.* вымога́ть *impf.*; **—ion** *n.* вымога́тельство

extra /'ekstrə/ *adj.* дополни́тель-
ный; ли́шний
extract /n.'ekstrækt; *v.*
ık'strækt/ **1.** *n.* экстра́кт **2.** *v.*
извлека́ть *impf.*, извле́чь *pf.*
extraction /ık'strækʃən/ *n.* из-
влече́ние, экстра́кция
extradite /'ekstrə,dait/ *v.* вы-
дава́ть *impf.*, вы́дать *pf.*
extramarital /,ekstrə'mærıtl/
adj. внебра́чный
extraneous /ık'streiniəs/ *adj.*
посторо́нний; вне́шний
extraordinary /ık'strɔrdn̩,eri/
adj. чрезвыча́йный
extraterrestrial /,ekstrətə-
'restriəl/ *adj.* внеземно́й
extravagance /ık'strævəgəns/ *n.*
экстравага́нтность; расточи́-
тельство
extravagant /ık'strævəgənt/ *adj.*
непоме́рный; расточи́тельный
extreme /ık'strim/ **1.** *adj.*
кра́йний **2.** *n.* кра́йность
extremity /ık'stremıti/ *n.*
кра́йность; *pl.* коне́чности *pl.*

extricate /'ekstrı,keit/ *v.*
выпу́тывать *impf.*, вы́путать *pf.*
exuberance /ıg'zubərəns/ *n.*
жизнера́достность
exuberant /ıg'zubərənt/ *adj.*
оби́льный; жизнера́достный
exude /ıg'zud/ *v.* выделя́ть(ся)
impf., вы́делить(ся) *pf.*
exult /ıg'zʌlt/ *v.* ликова́ть *impf.*
exultation /,egzʌl'teiʃən/ *n.* ли-
кова́ние; торжество́
eye /ai/ **1.** *n.* глазно́й **2.** *n.*
глаз; (*of needle*) ушко́ **3.** *v.*
наблюда́ть; всма́триваться
impf.
eyeball /'ai,bɔl/ *n.* глазно́е
я́блоко
eyebrow /'ai,brau/ *n.* бровь *f.*
eyeglasses /'ai,glæsız/ *n.* очки́
pl.
eyelash /'ai,læʃ/ *n.* ресни́ца
eyelid /'ai,lıd/ *n.* ве́ко
eyeshadow /'ai,ʃædou/ *n.* ка-
ранда́ш для век
eyesight /'ai,sait/ *n.* зре́ние
eyewitness /'ai,witnıs/ *n.*
очеви́дец, свиде́тель, —ница

F

fable /'feibəl/ *n.* ба́сня; вы́думка
fabric /'fæbrık/ *n.* ткань *f.*,
мате́рия; (*structure*) структу́ра
fabricate /'fæbrı,keit/ *v.* выду́-
мывать *impf.*, вы́думать *pf.*
fabrication /,fæbrı'keiʃən/ *n.*
вы́думка; (*forgery*) подде́лка
fabulous /'fæbyələs/ *adj.*
ска́зочный; легенда́рный
façade /fə'sad/ *n.* фаса́д
face /feis/ **1.** *n.* лицо́; (*expression*) выраже́ние; (*grimace*)
грима́са **2.** *v.* стоя́ть лицо́м к
(+ *D*) *impf.*
facet /'fæsıt/ *n.* грань *f.*
facetious /fə'siʃəs/ *adj.*
шутли́вый; —ness *n.*
шутли́вость
facial /'feiʃəl/ *adj.* лицево́й
facile /'fæsıl/ *adj.* лёгкий; (*superficial*) пове́рхностный
facilitate /fə'sılı,teit/ *v.*
облегча́ть *impf.*, -чи́ть *pf.*
facility /fə'sılıti/ *n.* (*ease*) лёгкость; *pl.* удо́бства, сре́дства *pl.*
facing /'feisıŋ/ *n.* облицо́вка
facsimile /fæk'sıməli/ *n.*
факси́миле *neut. indecl.*
fact /fækt/ *n.* факт; **in ~**
факти́чески; на са́мом де́ле

faction /'fækʃən/ *n.* фра́кция
factor /'fæktər/ *n.* фа́ктор
factory /'fæktəri/ *n.* заво́д
factual /'fæktʃuəl/ *adj.*
факти́ческий
faculty /'fækəlti/ *n.*
спосо́бность, дарова́ние; (*department*) факульте́т
fad /fæd/ *n.* причу́да
fade /feid/ *v.* вя́нуть *impf.*, за-
pf.; (*color*) выцвета́ть *impf.*
fading /'feidıŋ/ *n.* увяда́ние
Fahrenheit /'færən,hait/ *n.*: **60
degrees** ~ 60 гра́дусов по Фа-
ренге́йту
fail /feil/ **1.** *v.* не удава́ться (*impers.* + *D*) *impf.*; (*exam*) про-
вали́ть(ся); обанкро́титься *pf.*
2. *n.*: **without** ~ непреме́нно
failing /'feilıŋ/ **1.** *adj.* (*health*)
сла́бый **2.** *n.* недоста́ток
failure /'feilyər/ *n.* неуда́ча;
банкро́тство; (*person*)
неуда́чник
faint /feint/ **1.** *adj.* сла́бый **2.** *n.*
о́бморок **3.** *v.* па́дать в о́бмо-
рок *impf.*
fainthearted /feint'hartıd/ *adj.*
малоду́шный
faintly /'feintli/ *adv.* едва́

fair¹ /feər/ *adj.* справедли́вый; (*hair*) све́тлый; (*weather*) я́сный

fair² /feər/ *n.* я́рмарка

fairly /'feərli/ *adv.* дово́льно

fairness /'feərnɪs/ *n.* че́стность; справедли́вость

fairy /'feəri/ *n.* фе́я

fairy tale *n.* (волше́бная) ска́зка

faith /feɪθ/ *n.* ве́ра; дове́рие

faithful /'feɪθfəl/ *adj.* ве́рный

faithfulness /'feɪθfəlnɪs/ *n.* ве́рность

fake /feɪk/ **1.** *n.* подде́лка **2.** *v.* подде́лывать *impf.*, подде́лать *pf.*

falcon /'fɔlkən/ *n.* со́кол

fall /fɔl/ **1.** *n.* паде́ние; (*season*) о́сень *f.*; **in the ~** о́сенью **2.** *v.* па́дать *impf.*, (у)па́сть *pf.*; **~ asleep** засыпа́ть *impf.*

fallacy /'fæləsi/ *n.* оши́бка

fallible /'fæləbəl/ *adj.* подве́рженный оши́бкам

fallout /'fɔl,aut/ *n.* выпаде́ние

fallow /'fælou/ *adj.*: **lie ~** остава́ться под па́ром

false /fɔls/ *adj.* ло́жный; фальши́вый

falsehood /'fɔlshud/ *n.* ложь *f.*

falsification /,fɔlsəfɪ'keɪʃən/ *n.* фальсифика́ция

falsify /'fɔlsəfaɪ/ *v.* фальсифи́цировать *impf.* & *pf.*

falsity /'fɔlsɪti/ *n.* лжи́вость

falter /'fɔltər/ *v.* спотыка́ться *impf.*, споткну́ться *pf.*

fame /feɪm/ *n.* сла́ва

famed /feɪmd/ *adj.* изве́стный

familiar /fə'mɪlyər/ *adj.* знако́мый; фамилья́рный

familiarity /fə,mɪli'ærɪti/ *n.* знако́мство; фамилья́рность

familiarize /fə'mɪlyə,raɪz/ *v.* ознакомля́ть *impf.*; ознако́мить (с + *I*) *pf.*

family /'fæməli/ **1.** *n.* семья́; семе́йство **2.** *adj.* семе́йный

famine /'fæmɪn/ *n.* го́лод

famished /'fæmɪʃt/ *adj.* голо́дный; **I am ~** я о́чень го́лоден (-дна́)

famous /'feɪməs/ *adj.* знамени́тый

fan¹ /fæn/ *n.* (*sports*) боле́льщик

fan² /fæn/ **1.** *n.* ве́ер, вентиля́тор **2.** *v.* (*fire*) раздува́ть *impf.*

fanatic /fə'nætɪk/ *n.* фана́тик

fanatical /fə'nætɪkəl/ *adj.* фанати́ческий

fanciful /'fænsɪfəl/ *adj.* причу́дливый; фантасти́ческий

fancy /'fænsi/ **1.** *adj.* причу́дливый **2.** *n.* фанта́зия; (*whim*) причу́да **3.** *v.* представля́ть себе́ *impf.*

fanfare /'fænfeər/ *n.* фанфа́ра

fang /fæŋ/ *n.* клык; ядови́тый зуб

fantastic /fæn'tæstɪk/ *adj.* фантасти́ческий

fantasy /'fæntəsi/ *n.* фанта́зия; воображе́ние

far /fɑr/ *adj. pred.* далеко́; *attrib.* далёкий, да́льний; **as ~ as** *conj.* наско́лько

farce /fɑrs/ *n.* фарс

farcical /'fɑrsɪkəl/ *adj.* смешно́й

fare /feər/ *n.* сто́имость прое́зда

farewell /,feər'wel/ **1.** *n.* проща́ние; **bid ~** *v.* проща́ться *impf.* & *pf.* *attrib.* проща́льный

far-fetched *adj.* наду́манный

farm /fɑrm/ *n.* фе́рма

farmer /'fɑrmər/ *n.* фе́рмер

farming /'fɑrmɪŋ/ *n.* се́льское хозя́йство

farsighted /'fɑr'saɪtɪd/ *adj.* дальнови́дный; (*vision*) дальнозо́ркий

fart /fɑrt/ **1.** *n. Slang* пук **2.** *v.* пу́кать *impf.*, пу́кнуть *pf.*

fascinate /'fæsə,neɪt/ *v.* очаро́вывать *impf.*, очарова́ть *pf.*

fascinating /'fæsə,neɪtɪŋ/ *adj.* увлека́тельный, очарова́тельный

fascination /,fæsə'neɪʃən/ *n.* очарова́ние

fascism /'fæʃɪzəm/ *n.* фаши́зм

Fascist /'fæʃɪst/ **1.** *n.* фаши́ст, —ка **2.** *adj.* фаши́стский

fashion /'fæʃən/ *n.* мо́да, фасо́н

fashionable /'fæʃənəbəl/ *adj.* мо́дный

fast¹ /fæst/ **1.** *adj.* бы́стрый, ско́рый **2.** *adv.* бы́стро, ско́ро

fast² /fæst/ **1.** *n.* пост **2.** *v.* пости́ться *impf.*

fasten /'fæsən/ *v.* прикрепля́ть; привя́зывать *impf.*, привяза́ть *pf.*

fastener /'fæsənər/ *n.* застёжка

fastidious /fæ'stɪdiəs/ *adj.* разбо́рчивый

fat /fæt/ **1.** *adj.* жи́рный; то́лстый **2.** *n.* жир, са́ло

fatal /'feɪtl/ *adj.* смерте́льный

fatality /feɪ'tælɪti/ *n.* смерте́льный слу́чай

fate /feit/ *n.* судьба́, рок
fateful /'feitfəl/ *adj.* роково́й
father /'faðər/ *n.* оте́ц
fatherhood /'faðər,hud/ *n.* отцо́вство
father-in-law *n.* (husband's father) свёкор; (wife's father) тесть *m.*
fatherland /'faðər,lænd/ *n.* оте́чество, отчи́зна
fatherly /'faðərli/ *adj.* оте́ческий
fatigue /fə'tig/ **1.** *n.* уста́лость **2.** *v.* утомля́ть *impf.*, утоми́ть *pf.*
fatiguing /fə'tigiŋ/ *adj.* утоми́тельный
fatten /'fætn/ *v.* отка́рмливать *impf.*, откорми́ть *pf.*
fatty /'fæti/ *adj.* жи́рный
fatuous /'fætʃuəs/ *adj.* глу́пый
faucet /'fɔsɪt/ *n.* кран
fault /fɔlt/ *n.* вина́; недоста́ток
faultless /'fɔltlɪs/ *adj.* безупре́чный
faulty /'fɔlti/ *adj.* оши́бочный
fauna /'fɔnə/ *n.* фа́уна
favor /'feivər/ **1.** *n.* одолже́ние; **in someone's** ~ в по́льзу (+ G) **2.** *v.* отдава́ть предпочте́ние *impf.*
favorable /'feivərəbəl/ *adj.* благоприя́тный
favorite /'feivərɪt/ **1.** *adj.* люби́мый **2.** *n.* люби́мец, -мица
fawn[1] /fɔn/ *n.* молодо́й оле́нь *m.*
fawn[2] /fɔn/ *v.* подли́зываться *impf.*, подлиза́ться *pf.*
fax /fæks/ **1.** *n.* факс **2.** *v.* посыла́ть по фа́ксу *impf.*
fear /fɪər/ **1.** *n.* боя́знь *f.*, страх **2.** *v.* боя́ться *impf.*; **—ful** *adj.* стра́шный; **—less** *adj.* бесстра́шный
feasibility /,fizə'bɪlɪti/ *n.* возмо́жность осуществле́ния
feasible /'fizəbəl/ *adj.* возмо́жный
feast /fist/ **1.** *n.* пра́здник, (meal) пир **2.** *v.* пирова́ть *impf.*
feat /fit/ *n.* по́двиг
feather /'feðər/ *n.* перо́
feature /'fitʃər/ *n.* черта́, осо́бенность *n.*; *pl.* черты́ лица́ *pl.*
February /'febru,eri/ **1.** *n.* февра́ль *m.* **2.** *adj.* февра́льский
feces /'fisiz/ *n.* кал
fecund /'fikʌnd/ *adj.* плодоро́дный

federal /'fedərəl/ *adj.* федера́льный
federation /,fedə'reiʃən/ *n.* федера́ция
fee /fi/ *n.* пла́та, гонора́р; взнос
feeble /'fibəl/ *adj.* сла́бый
feed /fid/ **1.** *n.* корм **2.** *v.* пита́ть(ся), корми́ть(ся) *impf.*
feel /fil/ *v.* чу́вствовать *impf.* по-, *pf.*; чу́вствовать себя́ *impf.*; ~ **like** хоте́ться (impers., + D) *impf.*
feeling /'filiŋ/ *n.* чу́вство; ощуще́ние; эмо́ция
feign /fein/ *v.* притворя́ться *impf.*
feigned /feind/ *adj.* притво́рный
feint /feint/ *n.* ло́жная ата́ка
felicitous /fɪ'lɪsɪtəs/ *adj.* уда́чный
feline /'filain/ *adj.* коша́чий
fell /fel/ *v.* руби́ть, вали́ть *impf.*
fellow /'felou/ *n.* па́рень *m.*; (colleague) собра́т; ~ **countryman** соотече́ственник
fellowship /'felou,ʃip/ *n.* това́рищество; (grant) стипе́ндия
fellow traveler *n.* попу́тчик
felon /'felən/ *n.* престу́пник
felony /'feləni/ *n.* преступле́ние
felt /felt/ *n.* фетр; во́йлок
female /'fimeil/ **1.** *adj.* же́нский **2.** *n.* же́нщина; (animal) са́мка
feminine /'femənin/ *adj.* же́нский, же́нственный; (gram.) же́нского ро́да
femininity /,femə'ninɪti/ *n.* же́нственность
feminism /'femə,nizəm/ *n.* фемини́зм
feminist /'femənɪst/ **1.** *n.* фемини́ст, —ка **2.** *adj.* фемини́стический
fence /fens/ **1.** *n.* забо́р **2.** *v.i.* (sport) фехтова́ть *impf.*; ~ **in** *v.* огора́живать *impf.*, огороди́ть *pf.*
fend /fend/ *v.:* ~ **for oneself** забо́титься о себе́ *impf.*
fender /'fendər/ *n.* крыло́
ferment **1.** *n.* /'fɜrment/ заква́ска; *Fig.* броже́ние **2.** *v.* /fər'ment/ броди́ть *impf.*
fern /fɜrn/ *n.* па́поротник
ferocious /fə'rouʃəs/ *adj.* свире́пый
ferocity /fə'rɒsɪti/ *n.* свире́пость
ferret /'ferɪt/ *n.* хорёк

ferry /ˈfɛri/ **1.** *n.* паро́м **2.** *v.* перевози́ть; переправля́ть *impf.*

fertile /ˈfɜːtl/ *adj.* плодоро́дный

fertilize /ˈfɜːtɪˌaiz/ *v.* удобря́ть *impf.*, удо́брить *pf.*

fertilizer /ˈfɜːtlˌaizər/ *n.* удобре́ние

fervent /ˈfɜːrvənt/ *adj.* горя́чий

fervor /ˈfɜːrvər/ *n.* пыл

fester /ˈfɛstər/ *v.* гнои́ться *impf.*

festival /ˈfɛstəvəl/ *n.* фестива́ль *m.*

festive /ˈfɛstɪv/ *adj.* пра́здничный

festivity /fɛˈstɪvɪti/ *n.* торжество́

fetch /fɛtʃ/ *v.* (*thing*) приноси́ть *impf.*; (*person*) приводи́ть *impf.*; (*by vehicle*) привози́ть *impf.*

fetid /ˈfɛtɪd/ *adj.* злово́нный

fetish /ˈfɛtɪʃ/ *n.* фети́ш

fetter /ˈfɛtər/ *n.* *Fig.* око́вы *pl.*

fetus /ˈfiːtəs/ *n.* заро́дыш

feud /fjuːd/ *n.* вражда́

feudal /ˈfjuːdl/ *adj.* феода́льный

fever /ˈfiːvər/ *n.* жар, лихора́дка; **—ish** *adj.* лихора́дочный

few /fjuː/ *adj.*, *pron.* немно́гие; немно́го, ма́ло (+ *G*); **a ~** не́сколько (+ *G*)

fewer /ˈfjuːər/ *adv.* ме́ньше (+ *G*)

fiancé /ˌfiːɑːnˈsei/ *n.* жени́х

fiancée /ˌfiːɑːnˈsei/ *n.* неве́ста

fiasco /fiˈæskoʊ/ *n.* прова́л

fib /fɪb/ *n.* вы́думка

fiber /ˈfaibər/ *n.* волокно́

fibrous /ˈfaibrəs/ *adj.* волокни́стый

fickle /ˈfɪkəl/ *adj.* изме́нчивый

fiction /ˈfɪkʃən/ *n.* вы́мысел; (*lit.*) худо́жественная литерату́ра

fictional /ˈfɪkʃən/ *adj.* беллетристи́ческий; вы́мышленный

fictitious /fɪkˈtɪʃəs/ *adj.* фикти́вный, вы́мышленный

fiddle /ˈfɪdl/ *n.* скри́пка

fiddler /ˈfɪdlər/ *n.* скрипа́ч

fidelity /fɪˈdɛlɪti/ *n.* ве́рность

fidget /ˈfɪdʒɪt/ *v.* ёрзать *impf.*

fidgety /ˈfɪdʒɪti/ *adj.* неугомо́нный

field /fiːld/ *n.* по́ле; (*interest*) о́бласть *f.*; (*sport*) площа́дка

fiend /fiːnd/ *n.* дья́вол, бес; **—ish** *adj.* дья́вольский

fierce /fiərs/ *adj.* жесто́кий

fiery /ˈfaiəri/ *adj.* о́гненный

fifteen /ˈfɪfˈtiːn/ *adj.*, *n.*

пятна́дцать; **—th** *adj.*, *n.* пятна́дцатый

fifth /fɪfθ/ *adj.*, *n.* пя́тый

fiftieth /ˈfɪftiiθ/ *adj.*, *n.* пятидеся́тый

fifty /ˈfɪfti/ *adj.*, *n.* пятьдеся́т

fig /fɪg/ *n.* инжи́р

fight /fait/ **1.** *n.* борьба́; дра́ка **2.** *v.* боро́ться; дра́ться *impf.*

fighter /ˈfaitər/ *n.* боре́ц; (*plane*) истреби́тель

figment /ˈfɪgmənt/ *n.* вы́думка

figurative /ˈfɪgjʊrətɪv/ *adj.* перено́сный

figure /ˈfɪgjər/ **1.** *n.* фигу́ра; (*number*) ци́фра; (*form*) о́браз **2.** *v.* **~ out** вычисля́ть *impf.*, вы́числить *pf.*

figurehead /ˈfɪgjərˌhɛd/ *n.* *Fig.* подставно́е лицо́

filament /ˈfɪləmənt/ *n.* волокно́

file[1] /fail/ *n.* (*card file*) картоте́ка; (*folder*) па́пка; (*record*) де́ло; (*comput.*) файл **2.** *v.* регистри́ровать *impf.*, за- *pf.*; (*file application*) подава́ть заявле́ние *impf.*

file[2] /fail/ **1.** *n.* (*tool*) напи́льник **2.** *v.* подпи́ливать *impf.*, подпили́ть *pf.*

filigree /ˈfɪlɪˌgriː/ *adj.* филигра́нный

fill /fɪl/ *v.* наполня́ть *impf.*, напо́лнить *pf.*; заполня́ть *impf.*; (*occupy*) занима́ть *impf.*; (*satiate*) насыща́ть *impf.*

filling /ˈfɪlɪŋ/ **1.** *n.* (*dental*) пло́мба; (*cul.*) начи́нка **2.** *adj.* (*food*) сы́тный

filly /ˈfɪli/ *n.* кобы́лка

film /fɪlm/ **1.** *n.* фильм; плёнка **2.** *v.* снима́ть фильм *impf.*

filming /ˈfɪlmɪŋ/ *n.* съёмка

film star *n.* кинозвезда́

filter /ˈfɪltər/ **1.** *n.* фильтр **2.** *v.* фильтрова́ть; проце́живать *impf.*

filth /fɪlθ/ *n.* грязь *f.*

filthy /ˈfɪlθi/ *adj.* гря́зный

fin /fɪn/ *n.* плавни́к

final /ˈfainl/ **1.** *adj.* после́дний; оконча́тельный **2.** *n.* фина́л

finale /fɪˈnæli/ *n.* заключе́ние

finalist /ˈfainlɪst/ *n.* финали́ст

finally /ˈfainli/ *adv.* наконе́ц

finance /ˈfainæns/ **1.** *n.* фина́нсы *pl.* **2.** *v.* финанси́ровать *impf.* & *pf.*

financial /fɪˈnænʃəl/ *adj.* фина́нсовый

financier /ˌfɪnənˈsɪər/ n. финансист

find /faɪnd/ **1.** v. находить impf., найти pf.; ~ **out** узнавать impf., узнать pf. **2.** n. находка

finding /ˈfaɪndɪŋ/ n. (law) решение; pl. выводы

fine¹ /faɪn/ **1.** adj. хороший; (thin) тонкий **2.** adv. хорошо

fine² /faɪn/ **1.** n. штраф **2.** v. штрафовать impf., о- pf.

finesse /fɪˈnes/ n. тактичность

finger /ˈfɪŋɡər/ n. палец

fingernail /ˈfɪŋɡərˌneɪl/ n. ноготь m.

fingerprint /ˈfɪŋɡərˌprɪnt/ n. отпечаток пальца

fingertip /ˈfɪŋɡərˌtɪp/ n. кончик пальца

finicky /ˈfɪnɪki/ adj. привередливый; брезгливый

finish /ˈfɪnɪʃ/ **1.** n. конец; финиш; (polish) полировка **2.** v. кончать(ся) impf., кончить(ся) pf.

finished /ˈfɪnɪʃt/ adj. готовый; ~ **manners** изысканные манеры pl.

finishing /ˈfɪnɪʃɪŋ/ n. отделка

finite /ˈfaɪnaɪt/ adj. конечный

fink /fɪŋk/ n. (spy) стукач; (strikebreaker) штрейкбрехер

Finland /ˈfɪnlənd/ n. Финляндия

Finn /fɪn/ n. финн, финка

Finnish /ˈfɪnɪʃ/ adj. финский

fir /fɜr/ n. пихта, ель f.

fire¹ /faɪər/ **1.** n. огонь m.; пожар; (campfire) костёр **2.** v. (shoot) стрелять impf., выстрелить pf.; (dismiss) увольнять impf.; **catch** ~ загореться pf.; **set on** ~ поджигать impf., поджечь pf.

fire alarm n. пожарная тревога

firearm /ˈfaɪərˌɑrm/ n. огнестрельное оружие

fire brigade n. пожарная команда

fire drill n. учебная пожарная тревога

fire engine n. пожарная машина

fire escape n. пожарная лестница

fire extinguisher n. огнетушитель

firefighter /ˈfaɪərˌfaɪtər/ n. пожарник

firefly /ˈfaɪərˌflaɪ/ n. светлячок

fire hydrant n. пожарный кран

fireplace /ˈfaɪərˌpleɪs/ n. камин

fire station n. пожарное депо neut. indecl.

firewood /ˈfaɪərˌwʊd/ n. дрова pl.

fireworks /ˈfaɪərˌwɜrks/ n.pl. фейерверк

firing /ˈfaɪərɪŋ/ n. (of gun) стрельба; (layoff) увольнение

firm¹ /fɜrm/ adj. твёрдый

firm² /fɜrm/ n. фирма

firmness /ˈfɜrmnɪs/ n. твёрдость

first /fɜrst/ **1.** adj. первый **2.** adv. сперва, сначала; впервые; ~ **of all** прежде всего

first aid n. скорая помощь f.

firstborn /ˈfɜrstˌbɔrn/ n. первенец

first-class adj. первоклассный

firsthand /ˈfɜrstˈhænd/ adv. из первых рук

first name n. имя neut.

fiscal /ˈfɪskəl/ adj. финансовый

fish /fɪʃ/ **1.** n. рыба **2.** adj. рыбный **3.** v. ловить рыбу impf.

fisherman /ˈfɪʃərmən/ n. рыбак

fishery /ˈfɪʃəri/ n. рыбный промысел, рыболовство

fishing /ˈfɪʃɪŋ/ **1.** n. рыбалка **2.** adj. рыболовный; ~ **line** леса; ~ **rod** удочка

fishy /ˈfɪʃi/ adj. рыбный; рыбий; Colloq. сомнительный

fissure /ˈfɪʃər/ n. трещина

fist /fɪst/ n. кулак

fit¹ /fɪt/ **1.** adj. годный, подходящий; (healthy) здоровый **2.** v. годиться (+ D; на + A); подходить (+ D) impf.; (adjust) прилаживать impf., приладить pf.

fit² /fɪt/ n. (impulse) порыв

fitful /ˈfɪtfəl/ adj. порывистый

five /faɪv/ adj., n. пять

fix /fɪks/ **1.** n. затруднительное положение **2.** v. чинить impf., по- pf.; (fasten) укреплять impf.; (set) назначать impf.

fixation /fɪkˈseɪʃən/ n. фиксация

fixed /fɪkst/ adj. неподвижный; назначенный

fixture /ˈfɪkstʃər/ n. приспособление; прибор

fizz /fɪz/ n. шипение

fizzle /ˈfɪzəl/ v. шипеть impf.

flabbergast /ˈflæbərˌɡæst/ v. ошеломлять impf.

flabby /ˈflæbi/ adj. дряблый

flaccid /ˈflæksɪd/ adj. вялый

flag /flæg/ *n.* флаг, знáмя *neut.*

flagellate /'flædʒə,leit/ *v.* бичевáть *impf.*

flagging /'flægɪŋ/ *n.* пол из плит

flagpole /'flæg,poul/ *n.* флагштóк

flagrant /'fleigrənt/ *adj.* вопиющий

flagship /'flæg,ʃɪp/ *n.* флáгман

flair /fleər/ *n.* чутьё (на + *A*)

flake /fleik/ **1.** *n.* хлóпья *pl.* **2.** *v.* слойться *impf.*

flaky /'fleiki/ *adj.* слойстый

flamboyant /flæm'bɔiənt/ *adj.* экспансивный; цветистый

flame /fleim/ *n.* плáмя *neut.*; огóнь *m.*; (passion) пыл

flank /flæŋk/ *n.* бок; (mil.) фланг

flannel /'flænl/ *adj.* фланéлевый

flap /flæp/ **1.** *n.* клáпан; полá **2.** *v.* взмáхивать (+ *I*) *impf.*

flapjack /'flæp,dʒæk/ *n.* блин; олáдья

flare /fleər/ **1.** *n.* вспышка **2.** *v.* вспыхивать *impf.*, вспыхнуть *pf.*

flash /flæʃ/ **1.** *n.* вспышка; (instant) миг **2.** *v.* сверкнуть *pf.*

flashback /'flæʃ,bæk/ *n.* (cinema) ретроспективная сцéна

flash bulb *n.* лáмпа-вспышка

flashlight /'flæʃ,lait/ *n.* фонáрь *m.*

flashy /'flæʃi/ *adj.* крикливый

flask /flæsk/ *n.* фляга, фляжка

flat¹ /flæt/ **1.** *adj.* плóский; Fig. скучный **2.** *n.* (mus.) бемóль *m.*; (tire) спущенная шина

flat² /flæt/ *n.* (apartment) квартира

flatfish /'flæt,fiʃ/ *n.* кáмбала

flatly /'flætli/ *adv.* категорично

flatten /'flætn/ *v.* вырáвнивать(ся) *impf.*, выровнять(ся) *pf.*

flatter /'flætər/ *v.* льстить *impf.*; —ing *adj.* лéстный; —y *n.* лесть *f.*

flaunt /flɔnt/ *v.* щеголять *impf.*

flavor /'fleivər/ *n.* аромáт; привкус *v.* приправлять *impf.*, приправить *pf.*; —ing *n.* приправа; —less *adj.* безвкусный

flaw /flɔ/ *n.* недостáток, порóк

flax /flæks/ *n.* лён

flay /flei/ *v.* сдирáть кóжу (+ *G*) *impf.*

flea /fli/ *n.* блохá

fleck /flek/ *n.* крáпинка

fledgling /'fledʒlɪŋ/ *n.* птенéц

flee /fli/ *v.* бежáть *impf.*

fleece /flis/ **1.** *n.* руно **2.** *v.* Fig. обдирáть *impf.*, ободрáть *pf.*

fleet /flit/ *n.* флот; (bus) парк

fleeting /'flitɪŋ/ *adj.* мимолётный

flesh /fleʃ/ *n.* мясо; (body) плоть *f.*; —y *adj.* мясистый

flex /fleks/ *v.* сгибáть(ся) *impf.*, согнуть(ся) *pf.*

flexibility /,fleksə'bilɪti/ *n.* гибкость; эластичность

flexible /'fleksəbəl/ *adj.* гибкий

flick /flɪk/ **1.** *v.* щёлкать *impf.* **2.** *n.* щелчóк

flicker /'flɪkər/ **1.** *n.* мерцáние **2.** *v.* мерцáть *impf.*

flier /'flaiər/ *n.* лётчик; (circular) реклáмный листóк

flight¹ /flait/ *n.* (escape) бéгство

flight² /flait/ *n.* полёт; рейс

flighty /'flaiti/ *adj.* капризный

flimsy /'flɪmzi/ *adj.* слáбый

flinch /flɪntʃ/ *v.* вздрáгивать *impf.*

fling /flɪŋ/ *v.t.* швырять *impf.*; ~ oneself бросáться *impf.*

flint /flɪnt/ *n.* кремéнь *m.*

flip /flɪp/ *v.* подбрáсывать *impf.*

flippant /'flɪpənt/ *adj.* непочтительный; дéрзкий

flipper /'flɪpər/ *n.* плавник, ласт

flirt /flɜrt/ **1.** *n.* кокéтка **2.** *v.* флиртовáть *impf.*

flirtation /flɜr'teiʃən/ *n.* флирт

flirtatious /flɜr'teiʃəs/ *adj.* кокéтливый

flit /flɪt/ *v.* порхáть *impf.*

float /flout/ **1.** *v.* плáвать *indet.*, плыть *det.* **2.** *n.* поплавóк

flock /flɒk/ **1.** *n.* стáдо, стáя **2.** *v.* толпиться *impf.*

flog /flɒg/ *v.* сечь; порóть *impf.*

flood /flʌd/ **1.** *n.* наводнéние; потóк **2.** *v.* заливáть *impf.*, залить *pf.*

floodlight /'flʌd,lait/ *n.* прожéктор

floor /flɔr/ *n.* пол; (story) этáж

floorboard /'flɔr,bɔrd/ *n.* половица

flop /flɒp/ **1.** *n.* фиáско *neut. indecl.* **2.** *v.* плóхнуться (в, на + *A*) *pf.*

floppy /'flɒpi/ *adj.* висящий

floppy disk *n.* (comput.) дискéта

floral /'flɔrəl/ *adj.* цветóчный

florid /'florɪd/ adj. цветистый

florist /'florɪst/ n. торговец цветами

flounce¹ /flauns/ n. (frill) оборка

flounce² /flauns/ v. бросаться impf.

flounder¹ /'flaundər/ n. камбала

flounder² /'flaundər/ v. барахтаться impf.

flour /flauᵊr/ n. мука

flourish /'flʌrɪʃ/ 1. n. росчерк 2. v. процветать impf.

flow /flou/ 1. n. течение, струя; поток 2. v. течь; литься impf.

flow chart n. блок-схема

flower /'flauər/ 1. n. цветок 2. v. цвести impf.

flowerbed /'flauər‚bed/ n. клумба

flowerpot /'flauər‚pɒt/ n. цветочный горшок

flowery /'flauərɪ/ adj. цветущий

flu /flu/ n. грипп

fluctuate /'flʌktʃu‚eit/ v. колебаться impf.

fluctuation /‚flʌktʃu'eiʃən/ n. колебание

flue /flu/ n. дымоход

fluent /'fluənt/ adj. беглый

fluff /flʌf/ n. пух

fluffy /'flʌfɪ/ adj. пушистый

fluid /'fluɪd/ 1. adj. жидкий; текучий 2. n. жидкость

fluke /fluk/ n. случайность

flunky /'flʌŋkɪ/ n. лакей

fluorescent light /flu'resənt/ n. люминесцентная лампа

fluoride /'floraid/ n. фторид

flurry /'flʌrɪ/ n. (burst) порыв; (agitation) волнение

flush¹ /flʌʃ/ adj. вровень (с + I)

flush² /flʌʃ/ 1. n. румянец 2. v. (rinse) промывать impf., промыть pf.; (blush) краснеть impf.

flute /flut/ n. флейта

flutist /'flutɪst/ n. флейтист

flutter /'flʌtər/ 1. n. порхание 2. v. развеваться; трепетать impf.

flux /flʌks/ n. поток; (change) постоянные изменения pl.

fly¹ /flai/ n. (insect) муха

fly² /flai/ v. летать indet.; лететь det., полететь pf.

flying /'flaiɪŋ/ adj. летучий

flying saucer n. летающая тарелка

foal /foul/ n. жеребёнок

foam /foum/ 1. n. пена 2. v. пениться impf.

focal /'foukəl/ adj. фокусный

focus /'foukəs/ 1. n. фокус 2. v. сосредоточивать impf., -точить pf.

fodder /'fɒdər/ n. фураж, корм

foe /fou/ n. враг

fog /fɒg/ n. туман

foggy /'fɒgɪ/ adj. туманный

foible /'foibəl/ n. слабость

foil¹ /foil/ n. (metal) фольга

foil² /foil/ n. (fencing) рапира

foil³ /foil/ v. расстраивать impf., расстроить pf.; срывать impf.

foist /foist/ v. навязать (+ D) pf.

fold /fould/ 1. n. складка, сгиб 2. v. складывать impf., сложить pf.

folder /'fouldər/ n. папка

folding /'fouldɪŋ/ adj. складной; (back) откидной

foliage /'foulɪdʒ/ n. листва

folk /fouk/ 1. n. (people) люди pl.; народ 2. adj. attrib. народный

folklore /'fouk‚lor/ n. фольклор

follow /'fɒlou/ v. следовать (за + I) impf., по- pf.; **—er** n. последователь, приверженец; **—ing** adj. следующий

folly /'fɒlɪ/ n. глупость

foment /fou'ment/ v. подстрекать; разжигать impf., разжечь pf.

fond /fɒnd/ adj. любящий; нежный; **be ~ of** любить impf.

fondle /'fɒndl/ v. ласкать impf.

font¹ /fɒnt/ n. (typog.) шрифт

font² /fɒnt/ n. (eccles.) купель f.

food /fud/ n. пища; еда

fool /ful/ 1. n. дурак, глупец 2. v. (joke) шутить impf., по- pf.

foolhardy /'ful‚hardɪ/ adj. безрассудно храбрый; безрассудный

foolish /'fulɪʃ/ adj. глупый

foolishness /'fulɪʃnɪs/ n. глупость

foolproof /'ful‚pruf/ adj. надёжный

foot /fut/ n. нога, ступня; (measure) фут; **on ~** пешком

footage /'futɪdʒ/ n. метраж

football /'fut‚bɒl/ n. (American) американский футбол; (soccer) футбол; (ball) футбольный мяч

foothill /'fut‚hɪl/ n. предгорье

foothold /'fut‚hould/ n. точка опоры

footlights /'fut‚laits/ n.pl. рампа

footnote /'fut‚nout/ n. сноска

footpath /'fut,pæθ/ *n.* тропи́нка

footprint /'fut,prɪnt/ *n.* след

footrest /'fut,rest/ *n.* подно́жка

footstep /'fut,step/ *n.* шаг

footwear /'fut,weər/ *n.* о́бувь *f.*

foppish /'fopɪʃ/ *adj.* щегольско́й

for /fɔr/ *prep.* для, ра́ди (+ *G*); (*time*) на (+ *A*), в тече́ние (+ *G*); (*direction*) в (+ *A*), к (+ *D*); (*in place of*) за (+ *A*)

foray /'fɔreɪ/ *n.* набе́г

forbearance /fɔr'beərəns/ *n.* вы́держка

forbid /fɔr'bɪd/ *v.* запреща́ть *impf.*, -ти́ть *pf.*

force /fɔrs/ **1.** *n.* си́ла **2.** *v.* заставля́ть *impf.*, заста́вить *pf.*

forceful /'fɔrsfəl/ *adj.* си́льный

forceps /'fɔrseps/ *n.* щипцы́ *pl.*

forcible /'fɔrsəbəl/ *adj.* наси́льственный

ford /fɔrd/ **1.** *n.* брод **2.** *v.* переходи́ть брод *impf.*, перейти́ *pf.*

forearm /'fɔr,ɑrm/ *n.* предплечье

foreboding /fɔr'boudɪŋ/ *n.* предчу́вствие

forecast /'fɔr,kæst/ **1.** *n.* предсказа́ние, прогно́з **2.** *v.* предска́зывать *impf.*, предсказа́ть *pf.*

foreclose /fɔr'klouz/ *v.* исключа́ть; предреша́ть *impf.*

forefather /'fɔr,faðər/ *n.* пре́док

forefinger /'fɔr,fɪŋgər/ *n.* указа́тельный па́лец

forefront /'fɔr,frʌnt/ *n.* аванга́рд

foregone /fɔr'gɔn/ *adj.* предрешённый

foreground /'fɔr,graund/ *n.* пере́дний план

forehead /'fɔrɪd/ *n.* лоб

foreign /'fɔrɪn/ *adj.* иностра́нный; **—er** *n.* иностра́нец, -нка

forelock /'fɔr,lɔk/ *n.* чуб

foremost /'fɔr,moust/ *adj.* гла́вный; выдаю́щийся

forerunner /'fɔr,rʌnər/ *n.* предше́ственник; предве́стник

foresee /fɔr'si/ *v.* предви́деть *impf.*

foreshadow /fɔr'ʃædou/ *v.* предзнамено́вать *impf.*

foresight /'fɔr,saɪt/ *n.* предусмотри́тельность

forest /'fɔrɪst/ *n.* лес

forestall /fɔr'stɔl/ *v.* предупрежда́ть *impf.*, -преди́ть *pf.*

forester /'fɔrəstər/ *n.* лесни́чий

forest ranger *n.* лесни́к

forestry /'fɔrəstri/ *n.* лесово́дство

foretaste /'fɔr,teɪst/ *n.* предвкуше́ние

foretell /fɔr'tel/ *v.* предска́зывать *impf.*, предсказа́ть *pf.*

forethought /'fɔr,θɔt/ *n.* предусмотри́тельность

forever /fɔr'evər/ *adv.* навсегда́

forewarn /fɔr'wɔrn/ *v.* предостерега́ть *impf.*, -сте́речь *pf.*

foreword /'fɔr,wɜrd/ *n.* предисло́вие

forfeit /'fɔrfɪt/ **1.** *n.* (*game*) фант **2.** *v.* лиши́ться (+ *G*) *pf.*

forge /fɔrdʒ/ **1.** *n.* горн **2.** *v.* кова́ть *impf.*; (*counterfeit*) подде́лывать *impf.*, -де́лать *pf.*

forgery /'fɔrdʒəri/ *n.* подде́лка

forget /fɔr'get/ *v.* забыва́ть *impf.*, забы́ть *pf.*; **—ful** *adj.* забы́вчивый

forgive /fɔr'gɪv/ *v.* проща́ть *impf.*, прости́ть *pf.*; **—ness** *n.* проще́ние

forgo /fɔr'gou/ *v.* отка́зываться (от + *G*) *impf.*, отказа́ться *pf.*

fork /fɔrk/ **1.** *n.* ви́лка; (*road*) развили́на **2.** *v.* разветвля́ться *impf.*, разветви́ться *pf.*

forlorn /fɔr'lɔrn/ *adj.* поки́нутый

form /fɔrm/ **1.** *n.* фо́рма; (*document*) бланк; анке́та **2.** *v.* формирова́ть(ся) *impf.*, с- *pf.*; образо́вывать(ся) *impf.*, образова́ть(ся) *pf.*

formal /'fɔrməl/ *adj.* форма́льный; (*official*) официа́льный

formality /fɔr'mælɪti/ *n.* форма́льность

format /'fɔrmæt/ *n.* форма́т

formation /fɔr'meɪʃən/ *n.* (*geol.*) образова́ние; форма́ция

former /'fɔrmər/ *adj.* пре́жний

formidable /'fɔrmɪdəbəl/ *adj.* гро́зный; тру́дный

formless /'fɔrmlɪs/ *adj.* бесфо́рменный

formula /'fɔrmyələ/ *n.* фо́рмула

formulate /'fɔrmyə,leɪt/ *v.* формули́ровать *impf.*, с- *pf.*

formulation /,fɔrmyə'leɪʃən/ *n.* формулиро́вка

forsake /fɔr'seɪk/ *v.* покида́ть *impf.*, поки́нуть *pf.*; отка́зываться *impf.*

forswear /fɔr'sweər/ *v.* отрека́ться (от + *G*) *impf.*

fort /fɔrt/ *n.* форт

forth /fɔrθ/ *adv.* вперёд, впредь; **back and ~** взад и вперёд

forthcoming /ˈfɔrθˈkʌmɪŋ/ *adj.* предстоящий

forthright /ˈfɔrθˌrait/ *adj.* откровенный

fortieth /ˈfɔrtiiθ/ *adj.* сороковой

fortified /ˈfɔrtəˌfaid/ *adj.* укреплённый; (*enriched*) обогащённый

fortify /ˈfɔrtəˌfai/ *v.* укреплять *impf.*, -пить *pf.*

fortitude /ˈfɔrtiˌtud/ *n.* стойкость

fortnight /ˈfɔrtˌnait/ *n.* две недели *pl.*

fortress /ˈfɔrtrɪs/ *n.* крепость *f.*

fortuitous /fɔrˈtuitəs/ *adj.* случайный

fortunate /ˈfɔrtʃənit/ *adj.* счастливый; **—ly** *adv.* к счастью

fortune /ˈfɔrtʃən/ *n.* судьба; (*luck*) счастье; (*wealth*) состояние

fortuneteller /ˈfɔrtʃənˌtɛlər/ *n.* гадальщик, гадалка

forty /ˈfɔrti/ *adj.*, *n.* сорок

forward /ˈfɔrwərd/ **1.** *adj.* передний, передовой **2.** *adv.* вперёд **3.** *v.* пересылать *impf.*

fossil /ˈfɒsəl/ *n.* ископаемое

fossilize /ˈfɒsəˌlaiz/ *v.* окаменевать *impf.*

foster /ˈfɔstər/ *v.* (*bring up*) воспитывать *impf.*, воспитать *pf.*

foster child *n.* приёмыш

foul /faul/ *adj.* гадкий; отвратительный, вонючий

foul-up *n.* неразбериха

found /faund/ *v.* учреждать *impf.*, учредить *pf.*

foundation /faunˈdeiʃən/ *n.* основание, основа; (*building*) фундамент; (*fund*) фонд

fountain /ˈfauntn/ *n.* фонтан

fountain pen *n.* авторучка

four /fɔr/ *adj.*, *n.* четыре

fourteen /ˈfɔrˈtin/ *adj.*, *n.* четырнадцать; **—th** *adj.* четырнадцатый

fowl /faul/ *n.* домашняя птица

fox /fɒks/ *n.* лисица

fox cub *n.* лисёнок

fox trot *n.* фокстрот

foxy /ˈfɒksi/ *adj.* лисий, хитрый

foyer /ˈfɔiər/ *n.* фойе *neut. indecl.*

fraction /ˈfrækʃən/ *n.* дробь *f.*

fractious /ˈfrækʃəs/ *adj.* раздражительный

fracture /ˈfræktʃər/ **1.** *n.* перелом **2.** *v.* ломать(ся) *impf.*, c- *pf.*

fragile /ˈfrædʒəl/ *adj.* хрупкий

fragment /ˈfrægmənt/ **1.** *n.* обломок, отрывок **2.** *v.* дробить *impf.*; **—ary** *adj.* отрывочный; **—ation** *n.* дробление

fragrance /ˈfreigrəns/ *n.* аромат

fragrant /ˈfreigrənt/ *adj.* ароматный, душистый

frail /freil/ *adj.* хрупкий, хилый

frame /freim/ **1.** *n.* рама; рамка; (*for glasses*) оправа; (*build*) сложение; (*film*) кадр **2.** *v.* обрамлять *impf.*, -мить *pf.*

framework /ˈfreimˌwɜrk/ *n.* структура; остов; рамки *pl.*

France /fræns/ *n.* Франция

franchise /ˈfræntʃaiz/ *n.* право голоса; (*econ.*) привилегия

frank /fræŋk/ *adj.* искренний

frankfurter /ˈfræŋkfərtər/ *n.* сосиска

frankincense /ˈfræŋkɪnˌsens/ *n.* ладан

frantic /ˈfræntɪk/ *adj.* неистовый

fraternal /frəˈtɜrnl/ *adj.* братский

fraternity /frəˈtɜrniti/ *n.* братство

fraud /frɔd/ *n.* мошенничество, обман; (*person*) обманщик

fraudulent /ˈfrɔdʒələnt/ *adj.* мошеннический, обманный

fraught with /frɔt/ *adj.* полный (+ *G*), чреватый (+ *I*)

fray[1] /frei/ *n.* драка

fray[2] /frei/ *v.* изнашивать(ся) *impf.*

freak /frik/ *n.* чудак; урод

freckle /ˈfrekəl/ *n.* веснушка; **—d** *adj.* веснушчатый

free /fri/ **1.** *adj.* свободный; (*gratis*) бесплатный **2.** *v.* освобождать(ся) *impf.*, освободить(ся) *pf.*

freedom /ˈfridəm/ *n.* свобода

freelance /ˈfriˌlæns/ *adj.* внештатный

freethinker /ˈfriˈθiŋkər/ *n.* вольнодумец

freeze /friz/ *v.* замерзать *impf.*, замёрзнуть *pf.*; (*food*) замораживать *impf.*

freezer /ˈfrizər/ *n.* морозилка

freezing /ˈfriːzɪŋ/ **1.** *adj.* морозный **2.** *n.* замерзание

freight /freit/ *n.* фрахт, груз

freighter /ˈfreitər/ *n.* (*ship*) грузовое судно

French /frentʃ/ *adj.* французский

Frenchman /ˈfrentʃmən/ *n.* француз

Frenchwoman /ˈfrentʃˌwumən/ *n.* француженка

frenetic /frɪˈnetɪk/ *adj.* неистовый

frenzied /ˈfrenzid/ *adj.* бешеный

frenzy /ˈfrenzi/ *n.* бешенство

frequency /ˈfriːkwənsi/ *n.* частота

frequent /ˈfriːkwənt/ *adj.* частый

fresco /ˈfreskou/ *n.* фреска

fresh /freʃ/ *adj.* свежий; (*water*) пресный; **—en** *v.* освежать *impf.*, -жить *pf.*

freshman /ˈfreʃmən/ *n.* первокурсник

freshness /ˈfreʃnɪs/ *n.* свежесть

fret /fret/ *v.* разъедать *impf.*; (*worry*) волноваться *impf.*

fretful /ˈfretfəl/ *adj.* раздражительный

friable /ˈfraiəbəl/ *adj.* рыхлый

friar /ˈfraiər/ *n.* монах

friction /ˈfrɪkʃən/ *n.* трение

Friday /ˈfraidei/ *n.* пятница

fried /fraid/ *adj.* жареный

friend /frend/ *n.* друг, подруга; приятель; приятельница

friendly /ˈfrendli/ *adj.* дружеский

friendship /ˈfrendʃɪp/ *n.* дружба

frieze /friːz/ *n.* (*archit.*) фриз

frigate /ˈfrɪɡɪt/ *n.* фрегат

fright /frait/ *n.* испуг

frighten /ˈfraitn/ *v.* пугать *impf.*, испугать *pf.*; **—ed** *adj.* испуганный; **frightful** *adj.* страшный

frigid /ˈfrɪdʒɪd/ *adj.* холодный

frill /frɪl/ *n.* оборка

fringe /frɪndʒ/ *n.* бахрома; край

frisk /frɪsk/ *v.* резвиться *impf.*; (*search*) обыскивать *impf.*

frisky /ˈfrɪski/ *adj.* резвый

fritter[1] /ˈfrɪtər/ *n.* (*cul.*) оладья

fritter[2] /ˈfrɪtər/ *v.*: **~ away** растрачивать по мелочам *impf.*

frivolous /ˈfrɪvələs/ *adj.* легкомысленный, пустой

frizzy /ˈfrɪzi/ *adj.* (*curly*) вьющийся; (*curled*) завитой

fro /frou/ *adv.*: **to and ~** взад и вперёд, туда и сюда

frog /frɒɡ/ *n.* лягушка

frolic /ˈfrɒlɪk/ *n.* веселье

from /frʌm/ *prep.* из, от, с; из-за (+ G)

front /frʌnt/ **1.** *n.* фасад; (*mil.*) фронт **2.** *adj.* передний **3.** *adv.*: **in ~** впереди **4.** *prep.*: **in ~ of** перед (+ I)

frontal /ˈfrʌntl/ *adj.* (*mil.*) лобовой; фронтальный

frontier /frʌnˈtɪər/ *n.* граница

frost /frɒst/ *n.* мороз

frostbite /ˈfrɒstˌbait/ *n.* отморожение; обморожение

frostbitten /ˈfrɒstˌbitn/ *adj.* отмороженный; обмороженный

frosting /ˈfrɒstɪŋ/ *n.* глазурь *f.*

frosty /ˈfrɒsti/ *adj.* морозный

froth /frɒθ/ **1.** *n.* пена **2.** *v.* пениться *impf.*, вс- *pf.*

frown /fraun/ **1.** *n.* хмурый взгляд **2.** *v.* хмуриться *impf.*

frugal /ˈfruːɡəl/ *adj.* бережливый; (*meager*) скудный

fruit /fruːt/ **1.** *n.* фрукт; (*benefits*) плод **2.** *adj.* фруктовый

fruitcake /ˈfruːtˌkeik/ *n.* кекс

fruitful /ˈfruːtfəl/ *adj.* плодотворный

fruition /fruːˈɪʃən/ *n.*: **come to ~** осуществляться *impf.*

fruitless /ˈfruːtlɪs/ *adj.* бесплодный

frustrate /ˈfrʌstreit/ *v.* расстраивать *impf.*, расстроить *pf.*

frustration /frʌˈstreiʃən/ *n.* расстройство; фрустрация

fry[1] /frai/ *n.*: **small ~** малёк *pl.*

fry[2] /frai/ *v.* жарить(ся) *impf.*, из-, за- *pf.*

frying pan *n.* сковорода

fudge /fʌdʒ/ *n.* шоколадная конфета

fuel /ˈfjuːəl/ *n.* топливо

fugitive /ˈfjuːdʒɪtiv/ **1.** *n.* беглец, беженец, дезертир **2.** *adj.* беглый

fugue /fjuːɡ/ *n.* фуга

fulfill /fulˈfɪl/ *v.* выполнять *impf.*, выполнить *pf.*; исполнять *impf.*

fulfillment /fulˈfɪlmənt/ *n.* выполнение, осуществление

full /ful/ *adj.* полный; (*sated*) сытый; **in ~** в полностью

fullness /ˈfulnɪs/ *n.* полнота

full-time *adj.* штатный

fully /ˈfuli/ *adv.* вполне

fumble /ˈfʌmbəl/ *v.* неловко обращаться (с + I) *impf.*

fume /fjuːm/ *n.* чад

fumigate /'fyumɪ,geɪt/ v. окуривать impf., окурить pf.

fun /fʌn/ n. забава; потеха; **have ~** v. хорошо проводить время impf.; **make ~ of** v. шутить над (+ I) impf.

function /'fʌŋkʃən/ **1.** n. функция; pl. обязанности pl. **2.** v. функционировать impf.

functional /'fʌŋkʃənl/ adj. функциональный

fundamentally /,fʌndə'mentlɪ/ adv. по существу

funding /'fʌndɪŋ/ n. финансирование

fund-raising /fʌnd,reɪzɪŋ/ n. сбор средств

funeral /'fyunərəl/ n. похороны pl.

fungus /'fʌŋgəs/ n. грибок

funnel /'fʌnl/ n. воронка

funny /'fʌnɪ/ adj. забавный

fur /fɜr/ n. мех

furious /'fyʊriəs/ adj. яростный

furlough /'fɜrloʊ/ n. отпуск

furnace /'fɜrnɪs/ n. печь f.; горн

furnish /'fɜrnɪʃ/ v. снабжать impf., снабдить pf.; (house)

fundamental /,fʌndə'mentl/ adj. основной; коренной

fund /fʌnd/ n. фонд; запас

меблировать impf. & pf.; **—ing** n. меблировка

furniture /'fɜrnɪtʃər/ **1.** n. мебель f. **2.** adj. мебельный

furor /'fyʊrɔr/ n. фурор

furrow /'fɜroʊ/ n. борозда

furry /'fɜri/ adj. пушистый

further /'fɜrðər/ **1.** adj. дальнейший **2.** adv. дальше **3.** v. продвигать impf., продвинуть pf.

furthermore /'fɜrðər,mɔr/ adv. кроме того; к тому же

furtive /'fɜrtɪv/ adj. вороватый

fury /'fyʊri/ n. ярость

fuse¹ /fyuz/ n. (in bomb) взрыватель

fuse² /fyuz/ **1.** n. (elec.) пробка **2.** v. сплавлять(ся) impf.

fuselage /'fyusə,lɑʒ/ n. фюзеляж

fusible /'fyuzəbəl/ adj. плавкий

fusion /'fyuʒən/ n. плавка; слияние; сплавление; (phys.) синтез

fuss /fʌs/ **1.** n. суета, суматоха **2.** v. суетиться impf.

fussy /'fʌsi/ adj. суетливый; требовательный

futile /'fyutl/ adj. тщетный

future /'fyutʃər/ **1.** adj. будущий **2.** n. будущее

fuzzy /'fʌzi/ adj. пушистый; ворсистый; (vague) смутный

G

gab /gæb/ v. болтать impf.

gable /'geɪbəl/ n. щипец

gadget /'gædʒɪt/ n. приспособление

gaiety /'geɪɪti/ n. весёлость

gain /geɪn/ **1.** n. прибыль f.; доходы pl. **2.** v. получать; добиваться impf.

gait /geɪt/ n. походка

gale /geɪl/ n. сильный ветер

gall /gɔl/ n. (bile) жёлчь f.; (impudence) нахальство

gallant /'gælənt/ adj. храбрый

gallery /'gæləri/ n. галерея

gallon /'gælən/ n. галлон

gallop /'gæləp/ n. галоп

gallows /'gæloʊz/ n.pl. виселица

galvanize /'gælvə,naɪz/ v. гальванизировать impf.

gamble /'gæmbəl/ **1.** n. рискованное предприятие **2.** v. рисковать impf.; **—r** n. игрок

gambling /'gæmblɪŋ/ n. азартные игры pl.

game /geɪm/ n. игра; (single) партия; (hunting) дичь f.

gamut /'gæmət/ n. диапазон

gang /gæŋ/ n. банда; бригада

gangrene /'gæŋgrin/ n. гангрена

gangster /'gæŋstər/ n. гангстер

gangway /'gæŋ,weɪ/ n. проход; сходни pl.

gap /gæp/ n. брешь f.; пробел

gape /geɪp/ v. разевать рот impf.; (chasm) зиять impf.

garage /gə'rɑʒ/ n. гараж

garbage /'gɑrbɪdʒ/ n. мусор

garbage can n. мусорный ящик

garble /'gɑrbəl/ v. искажать impf.

garden /'gɑrdn/ n. сад; (vegetable) огород; **—er** n. садовник; **—ing** n. садоводство

gargle /'gɑrgəl/ v. полоскать горло impf.

garish /'gɛərɪʃ/ adj. кричащий

garland /'gɑrlənd/ n. гирлянда

garlic /'gɑrlɪk/ n. чеснок

garment /ˈgɑrmənt/ n. одежда

garnish /ˈgɑrnɪʃ/ n. гарнир

garret /ˈgærɪt/ n. чердак

garrison /ˈgærəsən/ n. гарнизон

garrulous /ˈgærələs/ adj. болтливый; —ness n. болтливость

gas /gæs/ 1. n. газ; (gasoline) бензин 2. adj. газовый

gash /gæʃ/ n. порез

gasket /ˈgæskɪt/ n. прокладка

gas meter n. газовый счётчик

gasoline /ˌgæsəˈlin/ n. бензин

gasp /gæsp/ 1. v. задыхаться impf. 2. n. вздох

gas range n. газовая плита

gas station n. заправка, бензоколонка

gastric /ˈgæstrɪk/ adj. желудочный

gasworks /ˈgæsˌwɜrks/ n. газовый завод

gate /geit/ n. ворота pl.

gateway /ˈgeitˌwei/ n. ворота pl.

gather /ˈgæðər/ v. собирать(ся) impf., собрать(ся) pf.; —ing n. собрание

gaudy /ˈgɔdi/ adj. кричащий

gauge /geidʒ/ 1. n. измерительный прибор 2. v. измерять impf., измерить pf.

gaunt /gɔnt/ adj. тощий

gauze /gɔz/ n. марля

gavel /ˈgævəl/ n. молоток

gay /gei/ adj. (happy) весёлый

gaze /geiz/ 1. n. пристальный взгляд 2. v. пристально смотреть impf.

gazelle /gəˈzɛl/ n. газель f.

gear /gɪər/ n. (car) передача; (device) устройство

gearbox /ˈgɪərˌbɒks/ n. коробка скоростей

gearshift /ˈgɪərˌʃɪft/ n. переключение передач

gel /dʒɛl/ n. гель m.

gelatin /ˈdʒɛlətn/ n. желатин

gelding /ˈgɛldɪŋ/ n. (horse) мерин

gem /dʒɛm/ n. драгоценный камень m.

gender /ˈdʒɛndər/ n. род

gene /dʒin/ n. ген

genealogy /ˌdʒiniˈɒlədʒi/ n. генеалогия

gene pool n. генофонд

general /ˈdʒɛnərəl/ 1. adj. общий; всеобщий 2. n. генерал 3. adv. in ~ вообще

generalization /ˌdʒɛnərələˈzeiʃən/ n. обобщение

generalize /ˈdʒɛnərəˌlaiz/ v. обобщать impf., —щить pf.

generally /ˈdʒɛnərəli/ adv. вообще; обычно; как правило

general-purpose adj. многоцелевой

generate /ˈdʒɛnəˌreit/ v. порождать impf.

generation /ˌdʒɛnəˈreiʃən/ n. поколение

generic /dʒəˈnɛrɪk/ adj. родовой; (general) общий

generosity /ˌdʒɛnəˈrɒsɪti/ n. великодушие, щедрость

generous /ˈdʒɛnərəs/ adj. великодушный, щедрый

genetic /dʒəˈnɛtɪk/ 1. adj. генетический; 2. n. —s генетика

genial /ˈdʒinyəl/ adj. добродушный, сердечный

genital /ˈdʒɛnɪtl/ 1. adj. половой 2. n.pl. половые органы

genitive /ˈdʒɛnɪtɪv/ n. родительный падеж

genius /ˈdʒinyəs/ n. гений; (ability) гениальность

genocide /ˈdʒɛnəˌsaid/ n. геноцид

genre /ˈʒɑnrə/ n. жанр

genteel /dʒɛnˈtil/ adj. благовоспитанный; вежливый

gentle /ˈdʒɛntl/ adj. кроткий; мягкий; лёгкий

gentleman /ˈdʒɛntlˌmən/ n. джентльмен

gentleness /ˈdʒɛntlˌnɪs/ n. мягкость

gentry /ˈdʒɛntri/ n. дворянство

genuine /ˈdʒɛnyuin/ adj. подлинный; (sincere) искренний

genus /ˈdʒinəs/ n. род; вид

geographical /ˌdʒiəˈgræfɪkəl/ adj. географический

geography /dʒiˈɒgrəfi/ n. география

geological /ˌdʒiəˈlɒdʒɪkəl/ adj. геологический

geology /dʒiˈɒlədʒi/ n. геология

geometric /ˌdʒiəˈmɛtrɪk/ adj. геометрический

geometry /dʒiˈɒmɪtri/ n. геометрия

Georgia /ˈdʒɔrdʒə/ n. Грузия

Georgian /ˈdʒɔrdʒən/ 1. adj. грузинский 2. n. грузин, —ка

geranium /dʒɪˈreiniəm/ n. герань f.

gerbil /ˈdʒɜrbəl/ n. песчанка

geriatric /ˌdʒeri'ætrik/ *adj.* гериатри́ческий

germ /dʒɜrm/ *n.* микро́б

German /'dʒɜrmən/ **1.** *adj.* неме́цкий **2.** *n.* не́мец, не́мка; **—у** *n.* Герма́ния

germane /dʒɜr'mein/ *adj.* уме́стный

germinate /'dʒɜrmə,neit/ *v.* прораста́ть *impf.*, прорасти́ *pf.* (*receive*)

gesticulate /dʒe'stikyə,leit/ *v.* жестикули́ровать *impf.*

gesture /'dʒestʃər/ *n.* жест

get /get/ *v.* (*obtain*) достава́ть *impf.*, доста́ть *pf.*; (*receive*) получа́ть *impf.*, -чи́ть *pf.* (*become*) станови́ться *impf.*, стать *pf.*; **~ off** сойти́ *pf.*; **~ up** встава́ть *impf.*, встать *pf.*; **~ well** поправля́ться *impf.*, попра́виться *pf.*

get-together *n.* сбо́рище; ту́совка

geyser /'gaizər/ *n.* ге́йзер

ghastly /'gæstli/ *adj.* ужа́сный

ghetto /'getou/ *n.* ге́тто *neut. indecl.*

ghost /goust/ *n.* привиде́ние; **—ly** *adj.* при́зрачный

ghoul /gul/ *n.* вурдала́к, вампи́р

giant /'dʒaiənt/ *n.* велика́н

gibberish /'dʒibəriʃ/ *n.* тарабáрщина

gibe /dʒaib/ *v.* насмеха́ться (над + I) *impf.*

giblets /'dʒiblits/ *n.* потроха́ *pl.*

giddiness /'gidinis/ *n.* головокруже́ние; (*frivolity*) легкомы́слие

gift /gift/ *n.* пода́рок, дар

gifted /'giftid/ *adj.* тала́нтливый

gigantic /dʒai'gæntik/ *adj.* гига́нтский

giggle /'gigəl/ *v.* хихи́кать *impf.*

gild /gild/ *v.* золоти́ть *impf.*, по-*pf.*

gill /gil/ *n.* (*fish*) жа́бра

gilt /gilt/ *adj.* позоло́ченный

gimmick /'gimik/ *n.* фо́кус, трюк

gin /dʒin/ *n.* джин

ginger /'dʒindʒər/ *n.* имби́рь *m.*

gingerbread /'dʒindʒər,bred/ *n.* (имби́рный) пря́ник

gingerly /'dʒindʒərli/ *adv.* осторо́жно

gingivitis /ˌdʒindʒə'vaitis/ *n.* воспале́ние дёсен

giraffe /dʒə'ræf/ *n.* жира́ф

girder /'gɜrdər/ *n.* ба́лка

girdle /'gɜrdl/ *n.* корсе́т; по́яс

girl /gɜrl/ *n.* (*little*) де́вочка; (*grown-up*) де́вушка

girlfriend /'gɜrl,frend/ *n.* подру́га

girlish /'gɜrliʃ/ *adj.* деви́чий

girth /gɜrθ/ *n.* обхва́т

gist /dʒist/ *n.* суть *f.*; су́щность

give /giv/ **1.** *v.* дава́ть *impf.*, дать *pf.*; **~ back** возвраща́ть *impf.*, -ти́ть *pf.*; **~ in** уступа́ть *impf.*, -пи́ть *pf.*; **~ oneself up** сдава́ться *impf.*, сда́ться *pf.* **2.** *n.* упру́гость

glacier /'gleiʃər/ *n.* ледни́к

glad /glæd/ **1.** *adj.* ра́достный; *pred.* рад **2.** *v.* **be ~** ра́доваться *impf.*, об- *pf.*; **—den** *v.* ра́довать *impf.*

glade /gleid/ *n.* поля́на

gladly /'glædli/ *adv.* охо́тно

glamor /'glæmər/ *n.* обая́ние; **—ous** *adj.* обая́тельный

glance /glæns/ **1.** *n.* бе́глый взгляд **2.** *v.* взгляну́ть *pf.*

gland /glænd/ *n.* железа́

glandular /'glændʒələr/ *adj.* желе́зистый

glare /gleər/ **1.** *n.* блеск **2.** *v.* сверка́ть *impf.*

glaring /'gleəriŋ/ *adj.* ослепи́тельный

glass /glæs/ **1.** *n.* стекло́; (*container*) стака́н **2.** *adj.* стекля́нный; **—у** *adj.* стекля́нный

glasses /'glæsiz/ *n.* очки́ *pl.*

glaucoma /glɔ'koumə/ *n.* глауко́ма

glaze /gleiz/ *n.* глазу́рь *f.*

glazier /'gleiʒər/ *n.* стеко́льщик

gleam /glim/ **1.** *n.* про́блеск **2.** *v.* свети́ться *impf.*

glean /glin/ *v.* подбира́ть *impf.*

glee /gli/ *n.* весе́лье

gleeful /'glifəl/ *adj.* лику́ющий

glen /glen/ *n.* го́рная доли́на

glib /glib/ *adj.* бо́йкий на язы́к

glide /glaid/ *v.* скользи́ть *impf.*; (*aero.*) плани́ровать *impf.*

glider /'glaidər/ *n.* пла́нёр

glimmer /'glimər/ **1.** *n.* мерца́ние; про́блеск **2.** *v.* мерца́ть *impf.*

glimpse /glimps/ *v.* взгляну́ть ме́льком *pf.*

glint /glint/ *n.* сверка́нье, блеск

glisten /'glisən/ *v.* блесте́ть *impf.*

gloat /glout/ *v.* злора́дствовать *impf.*; **—ing** *adj.* злора́дный

global /'gloubəl/ *adj.* глоба́льный; мирово́й

globe /gloub/ *n.* земно́й шар; (*map*) гло́бус; (*sphere*) шар

gloom /glum/ *n.* мрак

gloomy /'glumi/ *adj.* мра́чный

glorify /'glɔrə‚fai/ *v.* прославля́ть *impf.*, просла́вить *pf.*

glorious /'glɔriəs/ *adj.* сла́вный

glory /'glɔri/ *adj.* сла́ва

gloss[1] /glɔs/ *n.* блеск, лоск

gloss[2] /glɔs/ *n.* (*comment*) гло́сса

glossary /'glɔsəri/ *n.* слова́рь *f.*

glossy /'glɔsi/ *adj.* гля́нцевитый

glove /glʌv/ *n.* перча́тка

glow /glou/ 1. *n.* за́рево; (*of cheeks*) румя́нец 2. *v.* сия́ть *impf.*

glowing /'glouiŋ/ *adj.* (*burning*) тле́ющий; (*healthy*) румя́ный

glowworm /'glou‚wɜrm/ *n.* светля́чок

glucose /'glukous/ *n.* глюко́за

glue /glu/ 1. *n.* клей 2. *v.* кле́ить; прикле́ивать *impf.*

glum /glʌm/ *adj.* угрю́мый

glut /glʌt/ *n.* избы́ток

glutton /'glʌtn/ *n.* обжо́ра; —**ous** *adj.* прожо́рливый

gluttony /'glʌtni/ *n.* обжо́рство

gnarl /narl/ *n.* нарост

gnash /næʃ/ *v.* скрежета́ть *impf.*

gnat /næt/ *n.* мо́шка

gnaw /nɔ/ *v.* грызть *impf.*

gnome /noum/ *n.* гном

go /gou/ *v.* ходи́ть *indet.*, идти́ *det.*, пойти́ *pf.*; (*by vehicle*) е́здить *indet.*, е́хать *det.*, пое́хать *pf.*; ~ **away** уходи́ть *impf.*, уйти́ *pf.*; ~ **back** верну́ться *pf.*; ~ **in** входи́ть *impf.*, войти́ *pf.*; ~ **on** продолжа́ть(ся) *impf.*; ~ **out** выходи́ть *impf.*, вы́йти *pf.*

goad /goud/ *v.* (*cattle*) подгоня́ть; (*incite*) подстрека́ть *impf.*

goal /goul/ *n.* цель *f.*; (*sports*) гол

goalkeeper /'goul‚kipər/ *n.* врата́рь *m.*

goat /gout/ *n.* коза́; козёл

gobble /'gɒbəl/ *v.* жрать *impf.*

go-between /'gou‚bitwin/ *n.* посре́дник

goblet /'gɒblit/ *n.* бока́л; ку́бок

God /gɒd/ *n.* Бог, бо́жество

godchild /'gɒd‚tʃaild/ *n.* крёстник, крёстница

goddess /'gɒdis/ *n.* боги́ня

godfather /'gɒd‚faðər/ *n.* крёстный оте́ц

God-fearing /'gɒd‚fiəriŋ/ *adj.* богобоя́зненный; на́божный

godforsaken /'gɒdfər‚seikən/ *adj.* захолу́стный

godless /'gɒdlis/ *adj.* безбо́жный

godly /'gɒdli/ *adj.* на́божный

godmother /'gɒd‚mʌðər/ *n.* крёстная мать

godparent /'gɒd‚peərənt/ *n.* крёстный, крёстная

godsend /'gɒd‚send/ *n.* дар Бо́жий

go-getter /'gou‚getər/ *n.* пробивно́й

goggle /'gɒgəl/ 1. *v.* тара́щиться глаза́ *impf.*; 2. *n.pl.* защи́тные очки́

going /'gouiŋ/ *n.* (*departure*) ухо́д

goings-on *n.* дела́; происше́ствия *pl.*

gold /gould/ 1. *adj.* золото́й 2. *n.* зо́лото

golden /'gouldən/ *adj.* золото́й

goldfinch /'gould‚fintʃ/ *n.* щего́л

goldfish /'gould‚fiʃ/ *n.* золота́я ры́бка

gold-plated *adj.* золочёный, позоло́ченный

goldsmith /'gould‚smiθ/ *n.* золоты́х дел ма́стер

golf /gɒlf/ *n.* гольф

gondola /'gɒndələ/ *n.* гондо́ла

gong /gɒŋ/ *n.* гонг

gonorrhea /‚gɒnə'riə/ *n.* гоноре́я

good /gud/ 1. *adj.* хоро́ший, до́брый 2. *n.* добро́; по́льза

good-bye /‚gud'bai/ 1. *interj.* до свида́ния!; проща́й(те)! 2. *n.* проща́ние; **say** ~ *v.* проща́ться *impf.*, по- *pf.*

good-looking *adj.* краси́вый, интере́сный

good-natured *adj.* доброду́шный

goodness /'gudnis/ *n.* доброта́

goods /gudz/ *n.* това́ры *pl.*

gooey /'gui/ *adj.* сла́щавый

goof /guf/ *n.* тупи́ца *m.* & *f.*

goose /gus/ 1. *n.* гусь *m.* 2. *adj.* гуси́ный

gooseberry /'gus‚beri/ *n.* крыжо́вник

gopher /'goufər/ *n.* су́слик

gore /gɔr/ *v.* бода́ть *impf.*

gorge /gɔrdʒ/ 1. *n.* уще́лье 2. *v.* глота́ть *impf.*

gorgeous /'gɔrdʒəs/ *adj.* великоле́пный; пы́шный

gorilla /gə'rilə/ *n.* гори́лла

gory /'gɔri/ *adj.* окрова́вленный

goshawk /'gɒs,hɔk/ *n.* я́стреб

Gospel /'gɒspəl/ *n.* Ева́нгелие

gossip /'gɒsəp/ **1.** *n.* спле́тня; (*person*) спле́тник, -ница **2.** *v.* спле́тничать *impf.*

Gothic /'gɒθik/ *adj.* готи́ческий

gouge /gaudʒ/ *v.* выда́лбливать *impf.*, вы́долбить *pf.*

gourmet /gur'mei/ *n.* гурма́н

gout /gaut/ *n.* пода́гра

govern /'gʌvərn/ *v.* управля́ть (+ I) *impf.*

government /'gʌvərnmənt/ *n.* прави́тельство; управле́ние; —**al** *adj.* прави́тельственный

governor /'gʌvərnər/ *n.* губерна́тор; (*mech.*) регуля́тор

gown /gaun/ *n.* пла́тье; ма́нтия

grab /græb/ *v.* хвата́ть *impf.*, схвати́ть *pf.*

grace /greis/ *n.* гра́ция; (*favor*) ми́лость; —**ful** *adj.* грацио́зный

gracious /'greiʃəs/ *adj.* ми́лостивый

gradation /grei'deiʃən/ *n.* града́ция

grade /greid/ **1.** *n.* сте́пень *f.*; (*type*) сорт; (*school*) класс; (*mark*) оце́нка **2.** *v.* сортирова́ть *impf.*

gradual /'grædʒuəl/ *adj.* постепе́нный

graduate /*n.* 'grædʒuit/; *v.* -,eit/ **1.** *n.* выпускни́к **2.** *v.* конча́ть уче́бное заведе́ние *impf.*

graduation /,grædʒu'eiʃən/ *n.* оконча́ние университе́та

graffiti /grə'fiti/ *n.* граффи́ти *pl. indecl.*

grain /grein/ *n.* зерно́; хлеб

gram /græm/ *n.* грамм

grammar /'græmər/ *n.* грамма́тика

grammatical /grə'mætikəl/ *adj.* граммати́ческий

granary /'greinəri/ *n.* амба́р

grand /grænd/ *adj.* великоле́пный, грандио́зный

granddaughter /'græn,dɔtər/ *n.* вну́чка

grandeur /'grændʒər/ *n.* вели́чие

grandfather /'græn,fɑðər/ *n.* де́душка, дед

grandiose /'grændi,ous/ *adj.* грандио́зный

grand master *n.* (*chess*) гроссме́йстер

grandmother /'græn,mʌðər/ *n.* ба́бушка

grandparents /'grænd,peərənts/ *n.* де́душка с ба́бушкой *pl.*

grandson /'græn,sʌn/ *n.* внук

grandstand /'græn,stænd/ *n.* трибу́на

granite /'grænit/ *n.* грани́т

grant /grænt/ **1.** *n.* дар; дота́ция **2.** *v.* предоставля́ть *impf.*; дарова́ть *impf. & pf.*

granulated sugar /'grænyə-,leitid/ *n.* са́харный песо́к

granule /'grænyul/ *n.* зёрнышко

grape /greip/ *n.* виногра́д

grapefruit /'greip,frut/ *n.* гре́йпфру́т

graph /græf/ *n.* гра́фик

graphic /'græfik/ *adj.* графи́ческий; ~ **arts** гра́фика

graphite /'græfait/ *n.* графи́т

grapnel /'græpnl/ *n.* ко́шка

grapple /'græpəl/ *v.* (*fight*) схва́тываться (с + I) *impf.*

grasp /græsp/ **1.** *n.* хва́тка; (*comprehension*) понима́ние **2.** *v.* хвата́ть *impf.*, схвати́ть *pf.*; ула́вливать *impf.*, улови́ть *pf.*

grass /græs/ *n.* трава́

grasshopper /'græs,hɒpər/ *n.* кузне́чик

grassy /'græsi/ *adj.* травяно́й

grate¹ /greit/ *n.* решётка

grate² /greit/ *v.t.* тере́ть *impf.*; *v.i.* скрежета́ть *impf.*

grateful /'greitfəl/ *adj.* благода́рный; —**ness** *n.* благода́рность

grater /'greitər/ *n.* тёрка

gratify /'grætə,fai/ *v.* удовлетворя́ть *impf.*, -ри́ть *pf.*; —**ing** *adj.* ле́стный

grating /'greitiŋ/ *n.* решётка

gratis /'grætis/ *adv.* беспла́тно

gratitude /'græti,tud/ *n.* благода́рность

gratuitous /grə'tuitəs/ *adj.* неуме́стный; (*free*) даро́вой

gratuity /grə'tuiti/ *n.* чаевы́е *pl.*

grave¹ /greiv/ *n.* моги́ла

grave² /greiv/ *adj.* серьёзный

gravedigger /'greiv,digər/ *n.* моги́льщик

gravel /'grævəl/ *n.* гра́вий

gravestone /'greiv,stoun/ *n.* надгро́бный ка́мень *m.*

graveyard /'greiv,yard/ *n.* кла́дбище

gravitate /ˈgrævɪˌteit/ v. тяготе́ть impf.

gravitation /ˌgrævɪˈteiʃən/ n. тяготе́ние

gravity /ˈgræviti/ n. серьёзность; (phys.) тя́жесть

gravy /ˈgreivi/ n. подли́вка, со́ус

gray /grei/ adj. (hair) седо́й; **turn** ~ v. седе́ть impf.

graze¹ /greiz/ v. (touch) заде́вать impf., заде́ть pf.

graze² /greiz/ v. (pasture) пасти́(сь) impf.

grease /gris/ **1.** n. жир; (lubricant) сма́зка **2.** v. сма́зывать impf., сма́зать pf.

greasy /ˈgrisi/ adj. жи́рный

great /greit/ adj. вели́кий, большо́й, огро́мный

great-aunt n. двою́родная ба́бушка

Great Britain n. Великобрита́ния

great-granddaughter n. пра́внучка

great-grandfather n. пра́дед

great-grandmother n. прабабка

great-grandson n. пра́внук

greatly /ˈgreitli/ adv. о́чень

Greece /gris/ n. Гре́ция

greed /grid/ n. жа́дность

greedy /ˈgridi/ adj. жа́дный

Greek /grik/ **1.** adj. гре́ческий **2.** n. грек, греча́нка

green /grin/ adj. зелёный

greenery /ˈgrinəri/ n. зе́лень f.

greengrocer /ˈgrinˌgrousər/ n. зеленщи́к

greenhouse /ˈgrinˌhaus/ n. тепли́ца; ~ **effect** парнико́вый эффе́кт

greet /grit/ v. здоро́ваться (c + I) impf., по- pf.; **-ing** n. приве́тствие; pl. приве́т

gregarious /grɪˈgɛəriəs/ adj. обши́тельный

grenade /grɪˈneid/ n. грана́та

greyhound /ˈgreiˌhaund/ n. грейха́унд

grid /grid/ n. решётка; се́тка

griddle /ˈgridl/ n. сковоро́дка

grief /grif/ n. го́ре

grievance /ˈgrivəns/ n. жа́лоба; оби́да

grieve /griv/ v. скорбе́ть impf.

grievous /ˈgrivəs/ adj. тя́жкий

grill /gril/ **1.** v. жа́рить impf., из- pf.; (interrogate) допра́шивать impf. **2.** n. ра́шпер

grille /gril/ n. решётка

grim /grim/ adj. суро́вый

grimace /ˈgriməs/ **1.** n. грима́са **2.** v. грима́сничать impf.

grime /graim/ n. грязь f.; са́жа

grimy /ˈgraimi/ adj. гря́зный

grin /grin/ **1.** n. усме́шка **2.** v. усмеха́ться impf., усмехну́ться pf.

grind /graind/ v. моло́ть impf., c- pf.; (ax) точи́ть impf., на- pf.

grip /grip/ **1.** n. сжа́тие **2.** v. схва́тывать impf., схвати́ть pf.

gripping /ˈgripɪŋ/ adj. увлека́тельный

grisly /ˈgrizli/ adj. стра́шный

groan /groun/ **1.** n. стон **2.** v. стона́ть impf.

groats /grouts/ n. крупа́

grocer /ˈgrousər/ n. бакале́йщик

groceries /ˈgrousəriz/ n.pl. бакале́я

grocery /ˈgrousəri/ n. бакале́йная ла́вка

groggy /ˈgrogi/ adj. ша́ткий

groin /grɔin/ n. пах

groom /grum/ **1.** n. (bridegroom) жени́х **2.** v. (horse) чи́стить impf.

groove /gruv/ n. желобо́к

grope /group/ v. идти́ о́щупью impf.

gross /grous/ **1.** adj. гру́бый; (total) валово́й; (fat) ту́чный; бру́тто **2.** n. гросс

grotesque /grouˈtɛsk/ adj. гроте́скный

grotto /ˈgrotou/ n. грот

grouch /grautʃ/ n. брюзга́ m. & f.; **-y** adj. ворчли́вый

ground¹ /graund/ n. земля́, по́чва; (sports) площа́дка; pl. основа́ние

ground² /graund/ adj. мо́лотый

ground floor n. пе́рвый эта́ж

groundless /ˈgraundlis/ adj. необосно́ванный

groundwork /ˈgraundˌwɜrk/ n. фунда́мент

group /grup/ **1.** n. гру́ппа **2.** adj. группово́й **3.** v. группирова́ть(ся) impf., c- pf.

grouse /graus/ n. (bird) те́терев; тетёрка

grove /grouv/ n. ро́ща

grovel /ˈgravəl/ v. пресмыка́ться, унижа́ться (перед + I) impf.

grow /grou/ v.i. расти́ impf.; (become) станови́ться impf., стать pf.; v.t. выра́щивать impf.

growl /graul/ 1. *n.* рыча́ние 2. *v.* рыча́ть *impf.*, про- *pf.*

grownup /'groun,ʌp/ *n.* взро́слый

growth /grouθ/ *n.* рост; (*med.*) о́пухоль *f.*

grub /grʌb/ 1. *n.* личи́нка; *Slang* харчи́ *pl.* 2. *v.* ры́ться *impf.*

grubby /'grʌbi/ *adj.* гря́зный

grudge /grʌdʒ/ *n.* недово́льство; **bear a ~** име́ть зуб (на + *A*) *impf.*

grudgingly /'grʌdʒɪŋli/ *adv.* неохо́тно

gruel /'gruəl/ *n.* похлёбка

grueling /'gruəlɪŋ/ *adj.* изнури́тельный

gruesome /'grusəm/ *adj.* ужа́сный; жу́ткий

gruff /grʌf/ *adj.* ре́зкий

grumble /'grʌmbəl/ *v.* ворча́ть *impf.*; **—r** *n.* ворчу́н

grumpy /'grʌmpi/ *adj.* сварли́вый, раздражи́тельный

grunt /grʌnt/ 1. *v.* хрю́кать *impf.*, хрю́кнуть *pf.* 2. *n.* хрю́канье

guarantee /,gærən'ti/ 1. *n.* гара́нтия, поручи́тельство, зало́г 2. *v.* гаранти́ровать *impf.* & *pf.*

guarantor /'gærən,tɔr/ *n.* поручи́тель, гара́нт

guard /gard/ 1. *n.* сто́рож; (*unit*) охра́на 2. *v.* охраня́ть *impf.*, -ни́ть *pf.*

guardian /'gardiən/ *n.* опеку́н; **—ship** *n.* опе́ка

guerilla /gə'rɪlə/ 1. *n.* партиза́н 2. *adj.* партиза́нский

guess /ges/ 1. *n.* дога́дка 2. *v.* уга́дывать *impf.*, угада́ть *pf.*

guesswork /'ges,wɜrk/ *n.* дога́дки *pl.*

guest /gest/ *n.* гость *m.*

guffaw /gʌ'fɔ/ *n.* го́гот *impf.*

guidance /'gaidns/ *n.* руково́дство

guide /gaid/ 1. *n.* гид; проводни́к 2. *v.* руководи́ть *impf.*

guidebook /'gaid,buk/ *n.* путеводи́тель

guideline /'gaid,lain/ *n.* директи́ва

guild /gɪld/ *n.* ги́льдия; цех

guile /gaɪl/ *n.* кова́рство; **—less** *adj.* бесхи́тростный

guillotine /'gɪlə,tin/ *n.* гильоти́на

guilt /gɪlt/ *n.* вино́вность; вина́

guilty /'gɪlti/ *adj.* винова́тый; вино́вный (в + *P*)

guinea pig /'gɪni/ *n.* морска́я сви́нка

guise /gaiz/ *n.* вид; о́блик

guitar /gɪ'tar/ *n.* гита́ра

guitarist /gɪ'tarɪst/ *n.* гитари́ст

gulag /'gulag/ *n.* гула́г

gulf /gʌlf/ *n.* (*geog.*) зали́в; (*chasm*) про́пасть *f.*

gull /gʌl/ *n.* ча́йка

gullet /'gʌlɪt/ *n.* пищево́д, (*throat*) гло́тка

gullible /'gʌləbəl/ *adj.* легкове́рный

gully /'gʌli/ *n.* овра́г

gulp /gʌlp/ 1. *n.* глото́к 2. *v.* глота́ть *impf.*

gum /gʌm/ 1. *n.* гу́мми *neut. indecl.*; (*for chewing*) жва́чка

gum² *n.* (*anat.*) десна́

gun /gʌn/ *n.* ружьё, револьве́р

gunfire /'gʌn,faiər/ *n.* оруди́йный ого́нь *m.*

gunman /'gʌnmən/ *n.* вооружённый банди́т

gunner /'gʌnər/ *n.* артиллери́ст

gunpowder /'gʌn,paudər/ *n.* по́рох

gunshot /'gʌn,ʃɒt/ *n.* вы́стрел

gunsmith /'gʌn,smɪθ/ *n.* ору́жейный ма́стер

gurgle /'gɜrgəl/ *v.* бу́лькать *impf.*

gush /gʌʃ/ *v.* хлы́нуть *pf.*

gust /gʌst/ *n.* поры́в

gusto /'gʌstou/ *n.* смак

gusty /'gʌsti/ *adj.* поры́вистый

gut /gʌt/ *n.* кишка́; *pl. Colloq.* (*courage*) му́жество

gutter /'gʌtər/ *n.* (*road*) кана́вка; (*roof*) жёлоб

guy /gai/ *n. Colloq.* па́рень *m.*

guys /gaiz/ *n. Colloq.* ребя́та *pl.*

guzzle /'gʌzəl/ *v.* жлеба́ть *impf.*

gym /dʒim/ *n.* спортза́л

gymnast /'dʒimnæst/ *n.* гимна́ст, —ка; **—ic** *adj.* гимнасти́ческий; **—ics** *n.* гимна́стика

gynecologist /,gainɪ'kɒlədʒist/ *n.* гинеко́лог

gynecology /,gainɪ'kɒlədʒi/ *n.* гинеколо́гия

gypsy /'dʒipsi/ 1. *adj.* цыга́нский 2. *n.* цыга́н, —ка

gyrate /'dʒaireit/ *v.* враща́ться *impf.*

H

haberdashery /'hæbər,dæʃəri/ *n.*
галантерея

habit /'hæbɪt/ *n.* привычка;
(*monk's*) ряса

habitable /'hæbɪtəbəl/ *adj.*
годный для жилья

habitat /'hæbɪ,tæt/ *n.* среда

habitual /hə'bɪtʃuəl/ *adj.*
привычный; обычный

hack¹ /hæk/ *v.* рубить; дробить
impf.

hack² /hæk/ *n.* (*jade*) кляча;
(*writer*) писака *m. & f.*

hacker /'hækər/ *n. Slang* (*comput.*) хэкер

hackneyed /'hæknɪd/ *adj.*
банальный

hacksaw /'hæk,sɔ/ *n.* ножовка

haddock /'hædək/ *n.* пикша

hag /hæg/ *n.* карга, ведьма

haggard /'hægərd/ *adj.* изможденный

haggle /'hægəl/ *v.* торговаться
impf.

hail¹ /heɪl/ **1.** *n.* град **2.** *v.*
осыпать *impf.*, осыпать *pf.*; **it is
~ing** идёт град

hail² /heɪl/ *v.* подзывать *pf.*

hailstorm /'heɪl,stɔrm/ *n.* гроза с
градом

hair /heər/ *n.* волос; (*animal*)
шерсть *f.*

hairbrush /'heər,brʌʃ/ *n.* щётка
для волос

haircut /'heər,kʌt/ *n.* стрижка

hairdo /'heər,du/ *n.* причёска

hairdresser /'heər,dresər/ *n.* па-
рикмахер

hairdryer /'heər,draɪər/ *n.* фен

hairpin /'heər,pɪn/ *n.* шпилька;
заколка

hair-raising *adj.* ужасающий

hair spray *n.* лак для волос

hair style *n.* причёска

hairy /'heəri/ *adj.* волосатый

half /hæf/ **1.** *adj.* половинный **2.**
n. половина; **in ~** пополам; **one
and a ~** полтора; **~ an hour**
полчаса

halfhearted /'hæf'hɑrtɪd/ *adj.*
нерешительный

half-mast: *n.:* **at ~** *adv.* приспущенный

half sister *n.* сводная сестра

halftime /'hæf,taɪm/ *adj.* на полставки

halfway /'hæf'weɪ/ *adv.* на полпути

half-witted *adj.* слабоумный;
дурацкий

halibut /'hæləbət/ *n.* палтус

hall /hɔl/ *n.* зал; (*entrance*) холл

hallelujah /,hælə'luyə/ *interj.*
аллилуйя

hallmark /'hɔl,mɑrk/ *n.* проба;
Fig. признак

hallucination /hə,lusə'neɪʃən/ *n.*
галлюцинация

hallway /'hɔl,weɪ/ *n.* передняя

halo /'heɪlou/ *n.* сияние; нимб

halt /hɔlt/ **1.** *n.* остановка; (*cessation*) прекращение **2.** *v.* оста-
навливать(ся) *impf.*, остано-
вить(ся) *pf.*

haltingly /'hɔltɪŋli/ *adv.* запи-
наясь

halve /hæv/ *v.* делить пополам
impf., раз- *pf.*

ham /hæm/ *n.* ветчина

hamburger /'hæm,bɜrgər/ *n.*
гамбургер; рубленый шницель

hamlet /'hæmlɪt/ *n.* деревушка

hammer /'hæmər/ *n.* молоток

hammock /'hæmək/ *n.* гамак

hamper¹ /'hæmpər/ *n.* корзина

hamper² /'hæmpər/ *v.* мешать
impf.

hamster /'hæmstər/ *n.* хомяк

hand /hænd/ **1.** *n.* рука; (*of
clock*) стрелка **2.** *v.* подавать
impf., подать *pf.*

handbag /'hænd,bæg/ *n.* сумка

handbook /'hænd,buk/ *n.*
справочник, указатель

handcuff /'hænd,kʌf/ **1.** *n.*
наручник **2.** *v.* надевать
наручники *impf.*

handful /'hændful/ *n.* горсть *f.*

handicap /'hændi,kæp/ *n.*
недостаток; (*hindrance*) помеха

handicapped /'hændi,kæpt/ *adj.*
с физическими недостатками

handicraft /'hændi,kræft/ *n.*
ремесло

handiwork /'hændi,wɜrk/ *n.* ру-
коделие

handkerchief /'hæŋkərtʃɪf/ *n.*
носовой платок

handle /'hændl/ **1.** *n.* ручка,
рукоять *f.* **2.** *v.* (*touch*) трогать
impf.; (*manage*) управлять
(+ *I*) *impf.*; (*treat*) обращаться
(с + *I*) *impf.*

handlebar /'hændl̩ˌbɑr/ *n.* руль *f.*

handler /'hændlər/ *n.* дрессиро́вщик

handmade /'hænd'meid/ *adj.* ручно́й рабо́ты

handout /'hændˌaut/ *n.* листо́к

handrail /'hændˌreil/ *n.* пери́ла *pl.*

handshake /'hændˌʃeik/ *n.* рукопожа́тие

handsome /'hænsəm/ *adj.* краси́вый

handwriting /'hændˌraitɪŋ/ *n.* по́черк

handy /'hændi/ *adj.* ло́вкий; (*convenient*) удо́бный

hang /hæŋ/ *v.t.* ве́шать *impf.*, пове́сить *pf.*, *v.i.* висе́ть *impf.*

hangar /'hæŋər/ *n.* анга́р

hanger /'hæŋər/ *n.* ве́шалка

hangman /'hæŋmən/ *n.* пала́ч

hangnail /'hæŋˌneil/ *n.* заусе́ница

hangover /'hæŋˌouvər/ *n.* (*after drinking*) похме́лье

hanker /'hæŋkər/ *v.* скуча́ть *impf.*

haphazard /'hæp'hæzərd/ *adj.* случа́йный

happen /'hæpən/ *v.* случа́ться *impf.*, -чи́ться *pf.*; происходи́ть *impf.*, произойти́ *pf.*

happiness /'hæpinis/ *n.* сча́стье

happy /'hæpi/ *adj.* счастли́вый

happy-go-lucky /'hæpi/ *adj.* беспе́чный, беззабо́тный

harass /hə'ræs, 'hærəs/ *v.* беспоко́ить; пресле́довать *impf.*; **—ment** *n.* пресле́дование

harbinger /'hɑrbɪndʒər/ *n.* предве́стник

harbor /'hɑrbər/ **1.** *n.* га́вань *f.* **2.** *v.* укрыва́ть *impf.*, укры́ть *pf.*

hard /hɑrd/ *adj.* твёрдый; (*difficult*) тру́дный; тяжёлый

hard-boiled egg *n.* яйцо́ вкруту́ю

hard-core *adj.* непримири́мый, непрекло́нный

hard currency *n.* валю́та

harden /'hɑrdn̩/ *v.i.* тверде́ть; затвердева́ть *impf.*

hardhearted /'hɑrd'hɑrtid/ *adj.* жестокосе́рдный

hardly /'hɑrdli/ *adj.* едва́ (ли)

hardship /'hɑrdʃip/ *n.* нужда́

hardware /'hɑrdˌweər/ *n.* скобяно́й това́р

hardy /'hɑrdi/ *adj.* выно́сливый, сто́йкий

hare /heər/ *n.* за́яц

harem /'heərəm/ *n.* гаре́м

harlequin /'hɑrləkwɪn/ *n.* арлеки́н

harm /hɑrm/ **1.** *n.* вред; уще́рб **2.** *v.* вреди́ть *impf.*, по- *pf.*; **—ful** *adj.* вре́дный; **—less** *adj.* безвре́дный

harmonic /hɑr'mɒnɪk/ **1.** *adj.* гармони́ческий **2.** *n.* оберто́н

harmonica /hɑr'mɒnɪkə/ *n.* губна́я гармо́шка

harmonious /hɑr'mouniəs/ *adj.* гармони́чный; дру́жный

harmony /'hɑrməni/ *n.* гармо́ния

harness /'hɑrnis/ **1.** *n.* у́пряжь *f.* **2.** *v.* запряга́ть *impf.*, *Fig.* испо́льзовать *impf.*

harp /hɑrp/ *n.* а́рфа

harpoon /hɑr'pun/ *n.* гарпу́н

harpsichord /'hɑrpsiˌkɔrd/ *n.* клавеси́н

harrow /'hærou/ *n.* борона́

harsh /hɑrʃ/ *adj.* ре́зкий; суро́вый

harvest /'hɑrvist/ **1.** *n.* жа́тва; (*yield*) урожа́й **2.** *v.* собира́ть (урожа́й) *impf.*

hasp /hæsp/ *n.* (*on door*) запо́р

hassle /'hæsəl/ **1.** *n.* перебра́нка **2.** *v.* пристава́ть *impf.*

haste /heist/ *n.* спе́шка

hasten /'heisən/ *v.* торопи́ть(ся) *impf.*, по- *pf.*; спеши́ть *impf.*, по- *pf.*

hasty /'heisti/ *adj.* поспе́шный

hat /hæt/ *n.* шля́па; ша́пка

hatch¹ /hætʃ/ *v.t.* выси́живать *impf.*; (*eggs*) наси́живать *impf.*

hatch² /hætʃ/ *n.* люк

hatchet /'hætʃit/ *n.* топо́рик

hate /heit/ **1.** *n.* не́нависть *f.* **2.** *v.* ненави́деть *impf.*; **—ful** *adj.* ненави́стный

hatred /'heitrid/ *n.* не́нависть *f.*

haughty /'hɔti/ *adj.* надме́нный

haul /hɔl/ **1.** *v.* тяну́ть *impf.*, по-; тащи́ть *impf.*, по-; перевози́ть *impf.* **2.** *n.* добы́ча

haunt /hɔnt/ *v.* пресле́довать *impf.*; **—ed** *adj.* заколдо́ванный; **—ing** *adj.* навя́зчивый

have /hæv/ *v.* име́ть *impf.*; *impers.* быть *v.* (+ *G*): **I have** у меня́ (есть)

haven /'heivən/ *n.* убе́жище

havoc /'hævək/ *n.* разо́р

hawk /hɔk/ n. я́стреб

hawker /'hɔkər/ n. у́личный торго́вец

hawthorn /'hɔ,θɔrn/ n. боя́рышник

hay /hei/ n. се́но; ~ **fever** сенна́я лихора́дка

hayloft /'hei,lɔft/ n. сенова́л

haystack /'hei,stæk/ n. стог се́на

hazard /'hæzərd/ **1.** n. риск **2.** v. рискова́ть impf., рискну́ть pf.; **—ous** adj. риско́ванный; опа́сный

haze /heiz/ n. тума́н

hazel /'heizəl/ **1.** adj. све́тло-кори́чневый **2.** n. (tree) оре́шник

hazelnut /'heizəl,nʌt/ n. лесно́й оре́х

hazy /'heizi/ adj. тума́нный, сму́тный

he /hi/ pron. он

head /hed/ **1.** n. голова́; (leader) глава́, (mind) ум **2.** v.t. (lead) возглавля́ть impf., возгла́вить pf. **3.** adj. гла́вный

headache /'hed,eik/ n. головна́я боль f.

head cold n. на́сморк

headdress /'hed,dres/ n. головно́й убо́р

heading /'hediŋ/ n. ру́брика

headland /'hedlənd/ n. мыс

headlight /'hed,lait/ n. фа́ра

headline /'hed,lain/ n. заголо́вок

headlong /'hed,lɔŋ/ adv. стремгла́в; о́прометью

head-on adj. фронта́льный, лобово́й

headphone /'hed,foun/ n. нау́шник

headquarters /'hed,kwɔrtərz/ n. штаб-кварти́ра

headscarf /'hed,skɑrf/ n. коси́нка

headstrong /'hed,strɔŋ/ adj. своево́льный

headway /'hed,wei/ n. продвиже́ние вперёд

heady /'hedi/ adj. пьяня́щий

heal /hil/ v.i. зажива́ть impf.; v.t. излечива́ть impf., излечи́ть pf.

healing /'hiliŋ/ **1.** n. лече́ние **2.** adj. целе́бный

health /helθ/ n. здоро́вье

health resort n. куро́рт

healthy /'helθi/ adj. здоро́вый; (beneficial) поле́зный

heap /hip/ **1.** n. гру́да, ку́ча **2.** v. нагроможда́ть impf.

hear /hiər/ v. слы́шать impf.; (listen to) слу́шать impf.; ~ **out** выслу́шивать impf.

hearing /'hiəriŋ/ n. (sense) слух; (law) слу́шание

hearing aid n. слухово́й аппара́т

hearsay /'hiər,sei/ n. слу́хи pl.

hearse /hɜrs/ n. катафа́лк

heart /hɑrt/ **1.** n. се́рдце; (center) центр; (essence) суть f.; **by ~** наизу́сть **2.** adj. серде́чный

heart attack n. серде́чный при́ступ, инфа́ркт

heartbeat /'hɑrt,bit/ n. сердцебие́ние

heartbreaking /'hɑrt,breikiŋ/ adj. душераздира́ющий

heartburn /'hɑrt,bɜrn/ n. изжо́га

hearten /'hɑrtn/ v. ободря́ть impf.

heartfelt /'hɑrt,felt/ adj. и́скренний, серде́чный

hearth /hɑrθ/ n. оча́г

heartless /'hɑrtlɪs/ adj. бессерде́чный

heartrending /'hɑrt,rendiŋ/ adj. душераздира́ющий

heart-to-heart adj. заду́шевный

hearty /'hɑrti/ adj. кре́пкий, здоро́вый; (meal) оби́льный

heat /hit/ **1.** n. жара́; жар; (phys.) теплота́ **2.** v. нагрева́ть(ся) impf., нагре́ть(ся) pf.; (house) топи́ть impf.

heated /'hitɪd/ adj. горя́чий

heater /'hitər/ n. нагрева́тель

heath /hiθ/ n. пу́стошь f.

heathen /'hiðən/ **1.** n. язы́чник **2.** adj. язы́ческий

heather /'heðər/ n. ве́реск

heave /hiv/ v. (lift) поднима́ть impf.; (throw) броса́ть impf., бро́сить pf.

heaven /'hevən/ n. не́бо; рай

heavenly /'hevənli/ adj. небе́сный; боже́ственный

heavy /'hevi/ adj. тяжёлый; тру́дный; (strong) си́льный

heavy-duty adj. мо́щный

heavyweight /'hevi,weit/ adj. тяжелове́сный

Hebrew /'hibru/ **1.** adj. (древне)евре́йский **2.** n. (language) иври́т

heckle /'hekəl/ v. прерыва́ть вы́криками impf.

hectic /ˈhɛktɪk/ adj. лихора́дочный

hedge /hɛdʒ/ n. (живая) и́згородь f.; (barrier) прегра́да

hedgehog /ˈhɛdʒˌhɒg/ n. ёж

heed /hid/ v. обраща́ть внима́ние (на + A) impf., -ти́ть pf.

heedless /ˈhidlɪs/ adj. невнима́тельный, неосторо́жный

heel /hil/ n. (of foot) пята́; пя́тка; (shoe) каблу́к

hefty /ˈhɛfti/ adj. изря́дный

heifer /ˈhɛfər/ n. тёлка

height /hait/ n. высота́, рост

heighten /ˈhaitn/ v. уси́ливать impf., уси́лить pf.

heinous /ˈheinəs/ adj. отврати́тельный

heir /ɛər/ n. насле́дник

heiress /ˈɛərɪs/ n. насле́дница

heirloom /ˈɛərˌlum/ n. фами́льная вещь f.

helicopter /ˈhɛlɪˌkɒptər/ n. вертолёт

helium /ˈhiliəm/ n. ге́лий

hell /hɛl/ n. ад; (in) а́дский

hello /hɛˈlou/ interj. алло́!; (good day) приве́т

helm /hɛlm/ n. руль f.

helmet /ˈhɛlmɪt/ n. ка́ска; шлем

help /hɛlp/ 1. n. по́мощь f. 2. interj. на по́мощь! 3. v. помога́ть (+ D) impf., помо́чь pf.

helper /ˈhɛlpər/ n. помо́щник, -ница

helpful /ˈhɛlpfəl/ adj. поле́зный

helping /ˈhɛlpɪŋ/ n. по́рция

helpless /ˈhɛlplɪs/ adj. беспомо́щный; бесси́льный

helter-skelter /ˈhɛltərˈskɛltər/ adj. как попа́ло

hem /hɛm/ n. рубе́ц, кайма́

hemisphere /ˈhɛmɪˌsfɪər/ n. полуша́рие

hemophilia /ˌhiməˈfɪliə/ n. гемофили́я, кровоточи́вость

hemorrhage /ˈhɛmərɪdʒ/ n. кровоизлия́ние; кровотече́ние

hemorrhoid /ˈhɛməˌrɔid/ n. usu. pl. геморро́й

hemp /hɛmp/ n. (plant) конопля́; (fiber) пенька́

hen /hɛn/ n. ку́рица

hence /hɛns/ adv. сле́довательно

henceforth /ˈhɛnsˈfɔrθ/ adv. отны́не

henchman /ˈhɛntʃmən/ n. приспе́шник

hepatitis /ˌhɛpəˈtaitɪs/ n. гепати́т

her /hɜr/ 1. pron. её, ей 2. adj. её; свой

herald /ˈhɛrəld/ n. ве́стник

herb /ɜrb/ n. трава́

herbal /ˈɜrbəl/ adj. травяно́й

herd /hɜrd/ 1. n. ста́до 2. v. пасти́; гнать impf.

here /hiər/ adv. (dir.) сюда́; (loc.) здесь, тут; ~ and there там и сям

hereafter /hiərˈæftər/ adv. в бу́дущем

hereby /hiərˈbai/ adv. э́тим

hereditary /həˈrɛdiˌtɛri/ adj. насле́дственный

heresy /ˈhɛrəsi/ n. е́ресь f.

heretic /ˈhɛrɪtɪk/ n. ерети́к

heretical /həˈrɛtɪkəl/ adj. ерети́ческий

herewith /hiərˈwiθ/ adv. при э́том

heritage /ˈhɛrɪtɪdʒ/ n. насле́дство, насле́дие

hermit /ˈhɜrmɪt/ n. отше́льник

hernia /ˈhɜrniə/ n. гры́жа

hero /ˈhiərou/ n. геро́й

heroic /hiˈrouɪk/ adj. герои́ческий

heroin /ˈhɛrouɪn/ n. герои́н

heroine /ˈhɛrouɪn/ n. герои́ня

heroism /ˈhɛrouˌɪzəm/ n. герои́зм

heron /ˈhɛrən/ n. ца́пля

hero worship n. культ ли́чности

herpes /ˈhɜrpiz/ n. ге́рпес

herring /ˈhɛrɪŋ/ n. сельдь f.; селёдка

hers /hɜrz/ pron. её; свой

herself /hərˈsɛlf/ pron. (она́) сама́

hesitant /ˈhɛzɪtənt/ adj. колеблющийся; сомневаю́щийся

hesitate /ˈhɛzɪˌteit/ v. колеба́ться impf., по- pf.

hesitation /ˌhɛzɪˈteiʃən/ n. колеба́ние, нереши́тельность

heterogeneous /ˌhɛtərəˈdʒiniəs/ adj. разноро́дный

heterosexuality /ˌhɛtərəˌsɛkʃuˈælɪti/ n. гетеросексуа́льность

hew /hyu/ v. руби́ть; теса́ть impf.

hexagon /ˈhɛksəˌgɒn/ n. шестиуго́льник

heyday /ˈheiˌdei/ n. расцве́т

hi /hai/ interj. приве́т!

hiatus /haiˈeitəs/ n. переры́в

hibernate /'haibər,neit/ v. зимова́ть impf., пере- pf.

hibernation /,haibər'neiʃən/ n. спя́чка; зимо́вка

hiccup /'hikʌp/ 1. n. ико́та 2. v. ика́ть impf.

hide[1] /haid/ n. (skin) шку́ра

hide[2] /haid/ v. пря́тать(ся); скрыва́ть(ся) impf., скрыть(ся) pf.

hideous /'hidiəs/ adj. отврати́тельный

hideout /'haid,aut/ n. укры́тие

hierarchy /'haiə,rɑrki/ n. иера́рхия

hieroglyph /'hairə,glif/ n. иеро́глиф

high /hai/ adj. высо́кий; (strong) си́льный

highbrow /'hai,brau/ adj. интеллектуа́льный

highchair /'hai,tʃeər/ n. высо́кий де́тский сту́льчик

high-class adj. высокока́чественный

higher /'haiər/ adj. вы́сший; ~ education вы́сшее образова́ние

high fidelity adj. с высо́кой то́чностью воспроизведе́ния

high-frequency adj. высокочасто́тный

highlands /'hailəndz/ n. наго́рье

highly /'haili/ adv. о́чень, весьма́

high-minded adj. благоро́дный

Highness /'hainis/ n. Высо́чество

high-pitched adj. пронзи́тельный

high-rise n. высо́тный дом

high school n. сре́дняя шко́ла

highway /'hai,wei/ n. магистра́ль f.

hijacker /'hai,dʒækər/ n. уго́нщик

hijacking /'hai,dʒækiŋ/ n. похище́ние

hike /haik/ n. похо́д

hilarious /hi'leəriəs/ adj. весё́лый

hill /hil/ n. холм

hillock /'hilək/ n. хо́лмик, буго́р

hillside /'hil,said/ n. склон холма́

hilly /'hili/ adj. холми́стый

hilt /hilt/ n. рукоя́тка

him /him/ pron. его́, ему́

himself /him'self/ pron. (он) сам

hind /haind/ adj. за́дний

hinder /'hindər/ v. меша́ть impf.

hindrance /'hindrəns/ n. поме́ха

hindsight /'haind,sait/ n. ретроспе́кция

Hinduism /'hindu,izəm/ n. индуи́зм

hinge /hindʒ/ 1. n. шарни́р 2. v.i. Fig. зави́сеть (on + G) impf.

hint /hint/ 1. n. намёк 2. v. намека́ть impf., намекну́ть pf.

hip /hip/ n. бедро́

hippie /'hipi/ n. хи́ппи m. indecl.

hippopotamus /,hipə'pɒtəməs/ n. гиппопота́м

hire /haiər/ 1. n. наём; прока́т 2. v. нанима́ть impf., наня́ть pf.

hired /haiərd/ adj. наёмный

his /hiz/ adj. его́; свой

hiss /his/ 1. v. шипе́ть; свисте́ть impf. 2. n. шипе́ние; свист

historian /hi'stɔriən/ n. исто́рик

historic /hi'stɔrik/, **historical** /hi'stɔrikəl/ adj. истори́ческий

history /'histəri/ n. исто́рия

histrionic /,histri'ɒnik/ adj. театра́льный

hit /hit/ 1. n. уда́р; (on target) попада́ние; (success) успе́х 2. v. ударя́ть impf., уда́рить pf.; попада́ть (в + A) impf.; ~ oneself ударя́ться impf., уда́риться pf.

hitch /hitʃ/ 1. n. (tug) рыво́к 2. v. (pull up) подтя́гивать impf.

hitchhike /'hitʃ,haik/ v. е́хать автосто́пом impf.

hitherto /'hiðər,tu/ adv. до сих пор

hive /haiv/ n. у́лей

hoard /hɔrd/ 1. n. запа́с 2. v. запаса́ть impf., запасти́ pf.

hoarding /'hɔrdiŋ/ n. накопле́ние

hoarfrost /'hɔr,frɔst/ n. и́ней

hoarse /hɔrs/ adj. хри́плый

hoax /houks/ n. обма́н

hobble /'hɒbəl/ v. ковыля́ть impf.

hobby /'hɒbi/ n. хо́бби neut. indecl.

hobnob /'hɒb,nɒb/ 1. n. бесе́да 2. v. обща́ться impf.

hobo /'houbou/ n. бродя́га m.

hockey /'hɒki/ n. хокке́й

hodgepodge /'hɒdʒ,pɒdʒ/ n. вся́кая вся́чина; смесь f.

hoe /hou/ 1. n. моты́га 2. v. моты́жить impf.

hog /hɒg/ n. свинья́

hoist /hɔist/ 1. n. подъёмник 2. v. поднима́ть impf., подня́ть pf.

hold /hould/ 1. n. хва́тка; (control) влия́ние 2. *v.* держа́ть(ся) *impf.*

holdings /'houldɪŋz/ *n.* (*property*) иму́щество; (*finance*) вклад

holdup /'hould,ʌp/ *n.* налёт

hole /houl/ *n.* дыра́; (*animal's*) нора́

holiday /'hɒlɪ,deɪ/ *n.* пра́здник; (*school vacation*) кани́кулы *pl.*; (*vacation*) о́тпуск

holiness /'houlɪnɪs/ *n.* свя́тость

Holland /'hɒlənd/ *n.* Голла́ндия

hollow /'hɒlou/ 1. *adj.* пусто́й; (*sound*) глухо́й 2. *n.* впа́дина

holly /'hɒli/ *n.* остроли́ст

holocaust /'hɒlə,kɔst/ *n.* ма́ссовое уничтоже́ние

holster /'houlstər/ *n.* кобура́

holy /'houli/ *adj.* свято́й; свяще́нный

homage /'hɒmɪdʒ/ *n.* почте́ние, уваже́ние

home /houm/ 1. *n.* дом 2. *adj.* дома́шний; **at ~** до́ма; **go ~** идти́ домо́й *impf.*

homeland /'houm,lænd/ *n.* ро́дина

homeless /'houmlɪs/ *adj.* бездо́мный

homely /'houmli/ *adj.* просто́й

homemade /'houm'meɪd/ *adj.* дома́шний; самоде́льный

homeopathic /,houmiə'pæθɪk/ *adj.* гомеопати́ческий

homeowner /'houm,ounər/ *n.* домовладе́лец, -лица

homesickness /'houm,sɪknɪs/ *n.* тоска́ по до́му (по ро́дине)

homeward /'houmwərd/ *adv.* домо́й, к до́му

homework /'houm,wɜrk/ *n.* уро́к (на́ дом); дома́шнее зада́ние

homicide /'hɒmə,saɪd/ *n.* (*act*) уби́йство; (*person*) уби́йца *m. & f.*

homily /'hɒməli/ *n.* про́поведь *f.*

homogeneous /,houmə'dʒiniəs/ *adj.* одноро́дный

homogenize /hə'mɒdʒə,naɪz/ *v.* гомогенизи́ровать *impf. & pf.*

homonym /'hɒmənɪm/ *n.* омо́ним

homosexual /,houmə'sɛkʃuəl/ 1. *n.* гомосексуали́ст 2. *adj.* гомосексуа́льный

hone /houn/ *v.* точи́ть *impf.*

honest /'ɒnɪst/ *adj.* че́стный

honesty /'ɒnəsti/ *n.* че́стность *f.*

honey /'hʌni/ *n.* мёд

honeymoon /'hʌni,mun/ *n.* медо́вый ме́сяц

honeysuckle /'hʌni,sʌkəl/ *n.* жи́молость *f.*

honk /hɒŋk/ *n.* (*car*) гудо́к

honor /'ɒnər/ 1. *n.* честь *f.* 2. *v.* ока́зывать честь *impf.*; оказа́ть *pf.*; **—able** *adj.* че́стный; (*respected*) почётный

honorarium /,ɒnə'rɛəriəm/ *n.* гонора́р

honorary /'ɒnə,rɛri/ *adj.* почётный

hood /hʊd/ *n.* капюшо́н; (*tech.*) капо́т

hoodwink /'hʊd,wɪŋk/ *v.* обма́нывать *impf.*

hoof /huf/ *n.* копы́то

hook /hʊk/ 1. *n.* крючо́к 2. *v.* зацепля́ть; застёгивать(ся) *impf.*

hookup /'hʊkʌp/ *n.* связь *f.*

hooligan /'huligən/ *n.* хулига́н

hoop /hup/ *n.* о́бруч

hoot /hut/ *v.* у́хать *impf.*

hop¹ /hɒp/ 1. *n.* прыжо́к 2. *v.* пры́гать *impf.*, пры́гнуть *pf.*

hop² /hɒp/ *n.* (*bot.*) хмель *m.*

hope /houp/ 1. *n.* наде́жда 2. *v.* наде́яться *impf.*; **—ful** *adj.* наде́ющийся

hopeless /'houplɪs/ *adj.* безнадёжный

horde /hɔrd/ *n.* орда́

horizon /hə'raɪzən/ *n.* горизо́нт

horizontal /,hɔrə'zɒntl/ *adj.* горизонта́льный

hormone /'hɔrmoun/ *n.* гормо́н

horn /hɔrn/ *n.* рог; (*car*) гудо́к

hornet /'hɔrnɪt/ *n.* ше́ршень *m.*

horoscope /'hɔrə,skoup/ *n.* гороско́п

horrible /'hɔrəbəl/ *adj.* ужа́сный

horrid /'hɔrɪd/ *adj.* ужа́сный; проти́вный

horrify /'hɔrə,faɪ/ *v.* ужаса́ть *impf.*

horror /'hɔrər/ *n.* у́жас

hors d'oeuvre /'ɔr dɜrv/ *n.* заку́ска

horse /hɔrs/ *n.* ло́шадь *f.*

horseback /'hɔrs,bæk/ *n.*: **on ~** верхо́м

horsefly /'hɔrs,flaɪ/ *n.* слепе́нь *m.*

horseman /'hɔrsmən/ *n.* вса́дник

horseradish /'hɔrs,rædɪʃ/ *n.* хрен

horseshoe /'hɔrs,ʃu/ *n.* подко́ва

horticulture /'hɔrtɪ,kʌltʃər/ n. садоводство

hose /houz/ n. (garden) шланг

hosiery /'houʒəri/ n. чулки; чулочные изделия pl.

hospitable /'hɒspɪtəbəl/ adj. гостеприимный

hospital /'hɒspɪtl/ n. больница

hospitality /,hɒspɪ'tælɪti/ n. гостеприимство

hospitalize /'hɒspɪt,aiz/ v. госпитализировать impf. & pf.

host[1] /houst/ n. хозяин

host[2] /houst/ n. (multitude) множество

hostage /'hɒstɪdʒ/ n. заложник

hostel /'hɒstl/ n. турбаза

hostess /'houstɪs/ n. хозяйка

hostile /'hɒstl/ adj. враждебный

hostility /hɒ'stɪlɪti/ n. враждебность

hot /hɒt/ adj. (weather) жаркий; (liquid) горячий; (spicy) острый

hotel /hou'tel/ n. гостиница

hotheaded /'hɒt'hedɪd/ adj. горячий, опрометчивый

hothouse /'hɒt,haus/ n. теплица

hot-tempered /'hɒt'tempərd/ adj. вспыльчивый

hot-water bottle n. грелка

hound /haund/ 1. n. охотничья собака 2. v. травить impf.

hour /au³r/ n. час

hourglass /'au³r,glæs/ n. песочные часы pl.

hourly /'au³rli/ adj. ежечасный

house / n., adj. haus; v. hauz/ 1. n. дом 2. adj. домашний 3. v. помещать impf., -стить pf.

housebreaker /'haus,breikər/ n. взломщик

housecoat /'haus,kout/ n. халат

household /'haus,hould/ n. семья; (establishment) домашнее хозяйство

housekeeper /'haus,kipər/ n. экономка

housewarming /'haus,wɔrmɪŋ/ n. новоселье

housewife /'haus,waif/ n. домашняя хозяйка

housework /'haus,wɜrk/ n. работа по хозяйству

hovel /'hʌvəl/ n. лачуга

hover /'hʌvər/ v. (bird) парить impf.; (waver) колебаться impf.

how /hau/ adv. как; каким образом; ~ many, ~ much сколько (+ G)

however /hau'evər/ 1. adv. как

бы ни 2. conj. однако; тем не менее

howl /haul/ 1. n. вой 2. v. выть impf., за- pf.

hub /hʌb/ n. (of wheel) ступица; Fig. центр

hubbub /'hʌbʌb/ n. гул, шум

huddle /'hʌdl/ v. ёжиться impf.

hue /hyu/ n. оттенок

huff /hʌf/ n. вспышка гнева

hug /hʌg/ 1. n. объятие 2. v. обнимать impf., обнять pf.

huge /hyudʒ/ adj. огромный

hulk /hʌlk/ n. громадина

hull[1] /hʌl/ n. (husk) шелуха

hull[2] /hʌl/ n. (of ship) корпус

hum /hʌm/ 1. n. жужжание 2. v. жужжать impf.

human /'hyumən/ 1. n. человек 2. adj. человеческий; людской

humane /hyu'mein/ adj. человечный, гуманный

humanitarian /hyu,mænɪ'teəriən/ adj. гуманитарный

humanity /hyu'mænɪti/ n. человечество; (humaneness) гуманность; pl. гуманитарные науки pl.

humanize /'hyumə,naiz/ v. очеловечивать impf.

humble /'hʌmbəl/ 1. adj. смиренный; (modest) скромный 2. v. унижать impf.

humdrum /'hʌm,drʌm/ adj. скучный

humid /'hyumɪd/ adj. влажный

humidifier /hyu'mɪdə,faiər/ n. увлажнитель

humidity /hyu'mɪdɪti/ n. влажность

humiliate /hyu'mɪli,eit/ v. унижать impf., унизить pf.

humiliation /hyu,mɪli'eiʃən/ n. унижение

humility /hyu'mɪlɪti/ n. смирение

humor /'hyumər/ 1. n. юмор; (mood) настроение 2. v. потакать impf.; —ous adj. забавный; юмористический

hump /hʌmp/ n. горб

humus /'hyuməs/ n. чернозём

hunch /hʌntʃ/ 1. n. предчувствие 2. v. горбиться impf.

hunchbacked /'hʌntʃ,bækt/ adj. горбатый

hundred /'hʌndrɪd/ adj., n. сто; —th adj. сотый

Hungarian /hʌŋ'geəriən/ 1. adj.

венгерский 2. *n.* венгр,
венгерка
Hungary /'hʌŋgərɪ/ *n.* Венгрия
hunger /'hʌŋgər/ *n.* голод
hungry /'hʌŋgrɪ/ *adj.* голодный
hunk /hʌŋk/ *n.* ломоть *m.*;
кусок
hunt /hʌnt/ **1.** *n.* охота; (*search*)
поиски *pl.* 2. *v.* охотиться (на
+ *A*) *impf.*; —**er** *n.* охотник
hurdle /'hɜːdl/ *n.* препятствие
hurl /hɜːl/ *v.* бросать *impf.*,
бросить *pf.*
hurrah /hə'rɑː/ *interj.* ура!
hurricane /'hʌrɪˌkeɪn/ *n.* ураган
hurried /'hʌrɪd/ *adj.* торопливый
hurry /'hʌrɪ/ **1.** *n.* спешка 2. *v.*
спешить *impf.*, по- *pf.*
hurt /hɜːt/ **1.** *n.* ущерб 2. *v.t.*
вредить *impf.*, по- *pf.*; *v.i.*
болеть (*y* + *G*) *impf.*
hurtle /'hɜːtl/ *v.* нестись *impf.*
husband /'hʌzbənd/ *n.* муж
hush /hʌʃ/ **1.** *n.* тишина 2. *v.t.*
(*suppress*) замалчивать *impf.*
husk /hʌsk/ *n.* шелуха
huskiness /'hʌskɪnɪs/ *n.* хрипота
hustle /'hʌsəl/ *v.* суетиться;
(*hurry*) спешить *impf.*
hustler /'hʌslər/ *n.* пробивной
человек
hut /hʌt/ *n.* хижина
hybrid /'haɪbrɪd/ *n.* гибрид
hydrant /'haɪdrənt/ *n.* гидрант
hydraulic /haɪ'drɔːlɪk/ *adj.* гид-
равлический
hydrochloric acid /ˌhaɪdrə'klɔːrɪk/
n. соляная кислота
hydroelectric /ˌhaɪdrouɪ'lektrɪk/
adj. гидроэлектрический
hydrofoil /'haɪdrəˌfɔɪl/ *n.* (*vessel*)
судно на подводных крыльях

hydrogen /'haɪdrədʒən/ **1.** *n.* во-
дород 2. *adj.* водородный
hyena /haɪ'iːnə/ *n.* гиена
hygiene /'haɪdʒiːn/ *n.* гигиена
hygienic /ˌhaɪdʒi'enɪk/ *adj.* гиги-
енический
hymen /'haɪmən/ *n.* девственная
плева
hymn /hɪm/ *n.* гимн
hype /haɪp/ *n. Colloq.* очковти-
рательство
hyperbole /haɪ'pɜːbəlɪ/ *n.*
гипербола, преувеличение
hypertension /ˌhaɪpər'tenʃən/ *n.*
гипертония
hyphen /'haɪfən/ *n.* дефис
hyphenate /'haɪfəˌneɪt/ *v.*
писать через дефис *impf.*
hypnosis /hɪp'nousɪs/ *n.* гипноз
hypnotist /'hɪpnətɪst/ *n.* гипно-
тизёр
hypnotize /'hɪpnəˌtaɪz/ *v.* гипно-
тизировать *impf.*, за- *pf.*
hypochondria /ˌhaɪpə'kɒndrɪə/
n. ипохондрия
hypocrisy /hɪ'pɒkrəsɪ/ *n.* лице-
мерие
hypocrite /'hɪpəkrɪt/ *n.* лицемер
hypocritical /ˌhɪpə'krɪtɪkəl/ *adj.*
лицемерный
hypodermic /ˌhaɪpə'dɜːmɪk/ *adj.*
подкожный
hypothesis /haɪ'pɒθəsɪs/ *n.*
гипотеза
hypothetical /ˌhaɪpə'θetɪkəl/ *adj.*
предположительный
hysterectomy /ˌhɪstə'rektəmɪ/ *n.*
удаление матки
hysteria /hɪ'stɪərɪə/ *n.* истерия
hysterical /hɪ'sterɪkəl/ *adj.* исте-
рический
hysterics /hɪ'sterɪks/ *n.* истерика

I

I /aɪ/ *pron.* я
ice /aɪs/ **1.** *n.* лёд 2. *adj.* ледяной
ice axe *n.* ледоруб
iceberg /'aɪsbɜːg/ *n.* айсберг
ice cream *n.* мороженое
ice hockey *n.* хоккей на льду
ice skates *n.* коньки *pl.*
icicle /'aɪsɪkəl/ *n.* сосулька
icing /'aɪsɪŋ/ *n.* (*cake*) глазурь *f.*
icon /'aɪkɒn/ *n.* икона
iconographic /aɪˌkɒnə'græfɪk/
adj. иконографический
icy /'aɪsɪ/ *adj.* ледяной

ID *abbr.* удостоверение личности
idea /aɪ'dɪə/ *n.* идея, мысль *f.*
ideal /aɪ'dɪəl/ **1.** *n.* идеал 2. *adj.*
идеальный
idealism /aɪ'dɪəˌlɪzəm/ *n.* иде-
ализм
idealize /aɪ'dɪəˌlaɪz/ *v.* идеали-
зировать *impf. & pf.*
identical /aɪ'dentɪkəl/ *adj.*
тождественный; одинаковый
identification /aɪˌdentɪfɪ'keɪʃən/
n. опознание; установление
личности

identify /aɪ'dɛntə,faɪ/ v. опознавáть; отождествлять *impf*.

identity /aɪ'dɛntɪti/ n. лѝчность

ideological /,aɪdɪə'lɒdʒɪkəl/ adj. идеологѝческий

ideology /,aɪdɪ'ɒlədʒi/ n. идеолóгия

idiom /'ɪdɪəm/ n. идиóма

idiomatic /,ɪdɪə'mætɪk/ adj. идиоматѝческий

idiosyncrasy /,ɪdɪə'sɪŋkrəsi/ n. характéрная чертá

idiot /'ɪdɪət/ n. идиóт

idiotic /,ɪdɪ'ɒtɪk/ adj. идиóтский

idle /'aɪdl/ **1.** adj. прáздный **2.** v. бездéльничать *impf*.

idleness /'aɪdlnɪs/ n. прáздность

idol /'aɪdl/ n. йдол

idolatry /aɪ'dɒlətri/ n. идолопоклóнство

idolize /'aɪdl,aɪz/ v. боготворѝть *impf*.

idyll /'aɪdl/ n. идѝллия

idyllic /aɪ'dɪlɪk/ adj. идиллѝческий

i.e. abbr. то есть, т.е.

if /ɪf/ conj. éсли; (whether) ли; **as ~** как бýдто; **even ~** дáже éсли

ignite /ɪg'naɪt/ v. зажигáть *impf*., зажéчь *pf*.

ignition /ɪg'nɪʃən/ n. зажигáние

ignominious /,ɪgnə'mɪnɪəs/ adj. позóрный

ignoramus /,ɪgnə'reɪməs/ n. невéжда m. & f.

ignorance /'ɪgnərəns/ n. невéжество

ignorant /'ɪgnərənt/ adj. невéжественный; (uninformed) несвéдущий

ignore /ɪg'nɔr/ v. игнорѝровать *impf*. & *pf*.

ill /ɪl/ **1.** adj. больнóй; **be ~** болéть *impf*.; **become ~** заболéть *pf*. **2.** adv. дýрно **3.** n. зло; вред

ill-advised adj. неблагоразýмный

illegal /ɪ'ligəl/ adj. нелегáльный

illegality /,ɪli'gælɪti/ n. незакóнность

illegible /ɪ'lɛdʒəbəl/ adj. неразбóрчивый, нечёткий

illegitimacy /,ɪlɪ'dʒɪtəməsi/ n. незакóнность

illegitimate /,ɪlɪ'dʒɪtəmɪt/ adj. незаконноρождённый; незакóнный

ill-fated adj. злополýчный, злосчáстный

illicit /ɪ'lɪsɪt/ adj. незакóнный

illiteracy /ɪ'lɪtərəsi/ n. негрáмотность

illiterate /ɪ'lɪtərɪt/ adj., n. негрáмотный

ill-mannered adj. невоспѝтанный, грýбый

illness /'ɪlnɪs/ n. болéзнь f.

illogical /ɪ'lɒdʒɪkəl/ adj. нелогѝчный

illuminate /ɪ'lumə,neɪt/ v. освещáть *impf*., -тѝть *pf*.

illuminating /ɪ'lumə,neɪtɪŋ/ adj. Fig. поучѝтельный

illumination /ɪ,lumə'neɪʃən/ n. освещéние, иллюминáция

illusion /ɪ'luʒən/ n. иллю́зия

illusory /ɪ'lusəri/, **illusive** /-sɪv/ adj. иллюзóрный, обмáнчивый

illustrate /'ɪlə,streɪt/ v. иллюстрѝровать *impf*. & *pf*.

illustration /,ɪlə'streɪʃən/ n. иллюстрáция

illustrative /ɪ'lʌstrətɪv/ adj. иллюстратѝвный

illustrious /ɪ'lʌstrɪəs/ adj. прослáвленный

ill will n. неприя́знь f.

image /'ɪmɪdʒ/ n. óбраз, изображéние; **—ry** n. óбразность

imaginable /ɪ'mædʒənəbəl/ adj. вообразѝмый

imaginary /ɪ'mædʒə,nɛri/ adj. воображáемый; мнѝмый

imagination /ɪ,mædʒə'neɪʃən/ n. воображéние

imagine /ɪ'mædʒɪn/ v. воображáть *impf*., -зѝть *pf*.; представля́ть себé *impf*., -стáвить *pf*.

imbalance /ɪm'bæləns/ n. неустóйчивость

imbecile /'ɪmbəsɪl/ n. слабоýмный; идиóт

imbibe /ɪm'baɪb/ v. пить *impf*.; (absorb) впѝтывать *impf*.

imbue /ɪm'byu/ v. (saturate) пропѝтывать *impf*.; (instill) внушáть *impf*., -шѝть *pf*.

imitate /'ɪmɪ,teɪt/ v. подражáть; имитѝровать *impf*.

imitation /,ɪmɪ'teɪʃən/ n. имитáция, подражáние

immaculate /ɪ'mækyəlɪt/ adj. безупрéчный

immaterial /,ɪmə'tɪərɪəl/ adj. невещéственный; безразлѝчный

immature /ˌɪmə'tʃʊr/ *adj.* незрелый

immeasurable /ɪ'meʒərəbəl/ *adj.* неизмеримый; безмерный

immediate /ɪ'midɪt/ *adj.* немедленный; непосредственный; **—ly** *adv.* сразу же, немедленно

immemorial /ˌɪmə'mɔrɪəl/ *adj.* незапамятный

immense /ɪ'mens/ *adj.* огромный

immerse /ɪ'mɜrs/ *v.* погружать *impf.*; -зить *pf.*

immersion /ɪ'mɜrʒən/ *n.* погружение

immigrant /'ɪmɪgrənt/ *n.* иммигрант, —ка

immigrate /'ɪmɪˌgreɪt/ *v.* иммигрировать *impf. & pf.*

immigration /ˌɪmɪ'greɪʃən/ *n.* иммиграция

imminent /'ɪmənənt/ *adj.* грозящий; неминуемый

immobile /ɪ'moubəl/ *adj.* неподвижный, недвижимый

immobilize /ɪ'moubəˌlaɪz/ *v.* парализовать *impf. & pf.*

immoderate /ɪ'mɒdərɪt/ *adj.* неумеренный

immodest /ɪ'mɒdɪst/ *adj.* нескромный; неприличный

immoral /ɪ'mɔrəl/ *adj.* безнравственный

immorality /ˌɪmə'rælɪti/ *n.* безнравственность

immortal /ɪ'mɔrtl/ *adj.* бессмертный

immortality /ˌɪmɔr'tælɪti/ *n.* бессмертие

immortalize /ɪ'mɔrtlˌaɪz/ *v.* обессмертить *pf.*

immovable /ɪ'muvəbəl/ *adj.* неподвижный, недвижимый

immune /ɪ'myun/ *adj.* невосприимчивый

immunity /ɪ'myunɪti/ *n.* иммунитет

immunize /'ɪmyəˌnaɪz/ *v.* иммунизировать *impf. & pf.*

imp /ɪmp/ *n.* чертёнок, бесёнок

impact /'ɪmpækt/ *n.* удар, столкновение; (*influence*) влияние

impair /ɪm'peər/ *v.* вредить *impf.*, по- *pf.*

impalpable /ɪm'pælpəbəl/ *adj.* неощутимый

impart /ɪm'pɑrt/ *v.* придавать; делиться (с + *I*) *impf.*

impartial /ɪm'pɑrʃəl/ *adj.* беспристрастный

impassable /ɪm'pæsəbəl/ *adj.* непроходимый

impasse /'ɪmpæs/ *n.* тупик

impatience /ɪm'peɪʃəns/ *n.* нетерпение

impatient /ɪm'peɪʃənt/ *adj.* нетерпеливый

impeach /ɪm'pitʃ/ *v.* обвинять *impf.*, -нить *pf.*; **—ment** *n.* импичмент

impeccable /ɪm'pekəbəl/ *adj.* безупречный, безукоризненный

impecunious /ˌɪmpɪ'kyuniəs/ *adj.* безденежный

impede /ɪm'pid/ *v.* препятствовать *impf.*, вос- *pf.*

impediment /ɪm'pedəmənt/ *n.* препятствие; (*defect*) дефект

impel /ɪm'pel/ *v.* побуждать *impf.*

impending /ɪm'pendɪŋ/ *adj.* надвигающийся, предстоящий

impenetrable /ɪm'penɪtrəbəl/ *adj.* непроницаемый

impenitent /ɪm'penɪtənt/ *adj.* нераскаявшийся

imperative /ɪm'perətɪv/ **1.** *adj.* необходимый **2.** *n.* (*gram.*) повелительное наклонение

imperceptible /ˌɪmpər'septəbəl/ *adj.* незаметный

imperfect /ɪm'pɜrfɪkt/ *adj.* несовершённый

imperfection /ˌɪmpər'fekʃən/ *n.* несовершенство; (*fault*) недостаток

imperfective /ˌɪmpər'fektɪv/ *adj.* (*gram.*) несовершённый вид

imperial /ɪm'pɪərɪəl/ *adj.* имперский; царственный

imperialism /ɪm'pɪərɪəˌlɪzəm/ *n.* империализм

imperil /ɪm'perəl/ *v.* подвергать опасности *impf.*

imperious /ɪm'pɪərɪəs/ *adj.* властный, повелительный

impermeable /ɪm'pɜrmiəbəl/ *adj.* непроницаемый

impersonal /ɪm'pɜrsənl/ *adj.* безличный

impersonate /ɪm'pɜrsəˌneɪt/ *v.* олицетворять *impf.*, -рить *pf.*

impertinence /ɪm'pɜrtnəns/ *n.* дерзость

impertinent /ɪm'pɜrtnənt/ *adj.* дерзкий, наглый, нахальный

imperturbable /ˌɪmpər'tɜrbəbəl/ *adj.* невозмутимый

impervious /ɪm'pɜrvɪəs/ *adj.* непроницаемый

impetuous /ɪm'petʃuəs/ *adj.* стремительный

impetus /'ɪmpɪtəs/ *n.* ѝмпульс

impinge /ɪm'pɪndʒ/ *v.* покушаться (на + A) *impf.*

impious /'ɪmpɪəs/ *adj.* нечестивый

implacable /ɪm'plækəbəl/ *adj.* неумолимый

implant /ɪm'plænt/ *v.* насаждать *impf.*

implausible /ɪm'plɔzəbəl/ *adj.* невероятный, неправдоподобный

implementation /,ɪmpləmən'teɪʃən/ *n.* выполнение, осуществление

implicate /'ɪmplɪ,keɪt/ *v.* впутывать *impf.*, впутать *pf.*

implication /,ɪmplɪ'keɪʃən/ *n.* вовлечение; (*significance*) значение

implicit /ɪm'plɪsɪt/ *adj.* подразумеваемый; (*absolute*) безоговорочный

implore /ɪm'plɔr/ *v.* умолять *impf.*

imply /ɪm'plaɪ/ *v.* подразумевать; намекать *impf.*

impolite /,ɪmpə'laɪt/ *adj.* невежливый

imponderable /ɪm'pɒndərəbəl/ *adj.* неопределимый

import /*n.* 'ɪmpɔrt; *v.* ɪm'pɔrt/ **1.** *n.* ѝмпорт; (*significance*) значение **2.** *v.* импортировать *impf.* & *pf.*

importance /ɪm'pɔrtns/ *n.* важность

important /ɪm'pɔrtnt/ *adj.* важный

imported /ɪm'pɔrtɪd/ *adj.* ѝмпортный, ввозной

importer /ɪm'pɔrtər/ *n.* импортёр

importunate /ɪm'pɔrtʃənɪt/ *adj.* назойливый, докучливый

impose /ɪm'pouz/ *v.* налагать; облагать *impf.*, -ложить *pf.*

imposing /ɪm'pouzɪŋ/ *adj.* впечатляющий, импозантный

imposition /,ɪmpə'zɪʃən/ *n.* обложение; наложение

impossibility /ɪm,pɒsə'bɪlɪti/ *n.* невозможность

impossible /ɪm'pɒsəbəl/ *adj.* невозможный

impostor /ɪm'pɒstər/ *n.* самозванец, самозванка

impotence /'ɪmpətəns/ *n.* бессилие; импотенция

impotent /'ɪmpətənt/ *adj.* бессильный; импотентный

impound /ɪm'paund/ *v.* (*confiscate*) конфисковать *impf.* & *pf.*

impoverish /ɪm'pɒvərɪʃ/ *v.* разорять; истощать *impf.*

impractical /ɪm'præktɪkəl/ *adj.* непрактичный; нереалистичный

imprecise /,ɪmprɪ'saɪs/ *adj.* неточный

impregnate /ɪm'pregneɪt/ *v.* оплодотворять *impf.*, -рить *pf.*; (*saturate*) пропитывать *impf.*

impresario /,ɪmprə'sɑri,ou/ *n.* импресарио *m. indecl.*

impress /ɪm'pres/ *v.* производить впечатление (на + A) *impf.*; произвести *pf.*

impression /ɪm'preʃən/ *n.* впечатление

impressive /ɪm'presɪv/ *adj.* поразительный; впечатляющий

imprint /'ɪmprɪnt/ **1.** *n.* отпечаток **2.** *v.* отпечатать *pf.*

imprison /ɪm'prɪzən/ *v.* заключать (в тюрьму) *impf.*, -чить *pf.*; **—ment** *n.* (тюремное) заключение

improbable /ɪm'prɒbəbəl/ *adj.* неправдоподобный

impromptu /ɪm'prɒmptu/ **1.** *adj.* импровизированный **2.** *adv.* экспромтом

improper /ɪm'prɒpər/ *adj.* неправильный; неприличный

improve /ɪm'pruv/ *v.* улучшать(ся) *impf.*, улучшить(ся) *pf.*; **—ment** *n.* улучшение

improvisation /ɪm,prɒvə'zeɪʃən/ *n.* импровизация

improvise /'ɪmprə,vaɪz/ *v.* импровизировать *impf.*

imprudent /ɪm'prudnt/ *adj.* неблагоразумный

impudence /'ɪmpyədəns/ *n.* дерзость, наглость

impudent /'ɪmpyədənt/ *adj.* бесстыдный; дерзкий

impulse /'ɪmpʌls/ *n.* толчок; ѝмпульс; порыв

impulsive /ɪm'pʌlsɪv/ *adj.* побуждающий, импульсивный

impunity /ɪm'pyunɪti/ *n.* безнаказанность

impure /ɪm'pyʊr/ *adj.* нечистый

impute /ɪm'pyut/ v. припи́сывать (+ D) impf., -писа́ть pf.

in /ɪn/ **1.** prep. в (во) (+ A, P), на (+ A, P) **2.** adv. (loc.) внутри́, (dir.) внутрь

inability /ɪnə'bɪlɪtɪ/ n. неспосо́бность; неуме́ние

inaccessible /ˌɪnək'sɛsəbəl/ adj. недосту́пный; непристу́пный

inaccurate /ɪn'ækyərɪt/ adj. нето́чный

inaction /ɪn'ækʃən/ n. безде́йствие

inactivity /ˌɪnæk'tɪvɪtɪ/ n. безде́ятельность

inadequate /ɪn'ædɪkwɪt/ adj. недоста́точный

inadmissible /ˌɪnəd'mɪsəbəl/ adj. недопусти́мый

inadvertent /ˌɪnəd'vɜrtnt/ adj. невнима́тельный; ненаме́ренный

inadvisable /ˌɪnəd'vaizəbəl/ adj. нецелесообра́зный

inalienable /ɪn'eilyənəbəl/ adj. неотъе́млемый

inane /ɪ'nein/ adj. пусто́й; глу́пый

inanimate /ɪn'ænɪmɪt/ adj. неодушевлённый, неживо́й

inanity /ɪ'nænɪtɪ/ n. глу́пость; бессмы́сленность

inapplicable /ɪn'æplɪkəbəl/ adj. неприме́нимый; неуме́стный

inappropriate /ˌɪnə'prouprɪɪt/ adj. неподходя́щий

inarticulate /ˌɪnar'tɪkyəlɪt/ adj. невня́тный, нечленоразде́льный

inasmuch as /ˌɪnəz'mʌtʃ əz/ conj. поско́льку, так как

inattentive /ˌɪnə'tɛntɪv/ adj. невнима́тельный

inaudible /ɪn'ɔdəbəl/ adj. неслы́шный, неслы́шимый

inaugural /ɪn'ɔgyərəl/ adj. вступи́тельный

inauguration /ɪnˌɔgyə'reiʃən/ n. торже́ственное откры́тие

inauspicious /ˌɪnɔ'spɪʃəs/ adj. неблагоприя́тный

inborn /'ɪn'bɔrn/, **inbred** /-'brɛd/ adj. врождённый

incalculable /ɪn'kælkyələbəl/ adj. неисчисли́мый

incandescent /ˌɪnkən'dɛsənt/ adj. накалённый белы́м

incantation /ˌɪnkæn'teiʃən/ n. заклина́ние, заговор

incapable /ɪn'keipəbəl/ adj. неспосо́бный

incapacitated /ˌɪnkə'pæsɪˌteitɪd/ adj. недееспосо́бный

incapacity /ˌɪnkə'pæsɪtɪ/ n. неспосо́бность

incarcerate /ɪn'karsəˌreit/ v. заключа́ть в тюрьму́ impf.

incarceration /ɪnˌkarsə'reiʃən/ n. заточе́ние

incarnate /ɪn'karnɪt/ adj. воплощённый

incarnation /ˌɪnkar'neiʃən/ n. воплоще́ние

incendiary /ɪn'sɛndiˌɛrɪ/ adj. зажига́тельный

incense[1] /'ɪnsɛns/ n. ла́дан

incense[2] /ɪn'sɛns/ v. разгнева́ть pf.

incentive /ɪn'sɛntɪv/ n. сти́мул

inception /ɪn'sɛpʃən/ n. нача́ло

incessant /ɪn'sɛsənt/ adj. непреры́вный

incest /'ɪnsɛst/ n. кровосмеше́ние

inch /ɪntʃ/ n. дюйм

incidence /'ɪnsɪdəns/ n. распростране́ние; (phys.) паде́ние

incident /'ɪnsɪdənt/ n. происше́ствие, инциде́нт, слу́чай

incidental /ˌɪnsɪ'dɛntl/ adj. случа́йный; **—ly** adv. ме́жду про́чим; случа́йно

incinerate /ɪn'sɪnəˌreit/ v. сжига́ть (дотла́) impf.

incinerator /ɪn'sɪnəˌreitər/ n. мусоросжига́тельная печь f.

incision /ɪn'sɪʒən/ n. надре́з

incisive /ɪn'saisɪv/ adj. то́нкий

incite /ɪn'sait/ v. побужда́ть impf., побуди́ть pf.; подстрека́ть (+ D) impf.; **—ment** n. подстрека́тельство

inclement /ɪn'klɛmənt/ adj. суро́вый; нена́стный

inclination /ˌɪnklə'neiʃən/ n. скло́нность; (slope) накло́н

incline /ɪn'ɪnklain/ v. ɪn'klain/ **1.** n. накло́н **2.** v. склоня́ть(ся) impf., -ни́ть(ся) pf.

inclined /ɪn'klaind/ adj. скло́нный, располо́женный

include /ɪn'klud/ v. включа́ть impf., -чи́ть pf.

including /ɪn'kludɪŋ/ prep. включа́я (+ A)

inclusion /ɪn'kluʒən/ n. включе́ние

inclusive /ɪn'klusɪv/ **1.** adj. включа́ющий (в себе́) **2.** adv. включи́тельно

incognito /,ɪnkɒg'niːtou/ adv. инкóгнито

incoherent /,ɪnkou'hɪərənt/ adj. несвязный; бессвязный

income /'ɪnkʌm/ n. дохóд

income tax n. подохóдный налóг

incoming /'ɪn,kʌmɪŋ/ adj. входящий; вступающий

incommensurate /,ɪnkə'mensərɪt/ adj. несоразмéрный

incommunicative /,ɪnkə'mjuːnɪkətɪv/ adj. неразговóрчивый

incomparable /ɪn'kɒmpərəbəl/ adj. несравнимый; (matchless) несравнéнный

incompatible /,ɪnkəm'pætəbəl/ adj. несовместимый

incompetent /ɪn'kɒmpɪtənt/ adj. неспосóбный; некомпетéнтный

incomplete /,ɪnkəm'pliːt/ adj. непóлный, незакóнченный

incomprehensible /,ɪnkɒmprɪ'hensəbəl/ adj. непонятный

inconceivable /,ɪnkən'siːvəbəl/ adj. невообразимый

inconclusive /,ɪnkən'kluːsɪv/ adj. недоказáтельный

incongruous /ɪn'kɒŋgruəs/ adj. несообрáзный

inconsiderable /,ɪnkən'sɪdərəbəl/ adj. незначительный

inconsiderate /,ɪnkən'sɪdərɪt/ adj. невнимáтельный

inconsistency /,ɪnkən'sɪstənsi/ n. непослéдовательность

inconsistent /,ɪnkən'sɪstənt/ adj. непослéдовательный

inconsolable /,ɪnkən'souləbəl/ adj. безутéшный, неутéшный

inconspicuous /,ɪnkən'spɪkyuəs/ adj. незамéтный

incontestable /,ɪnkən'testəbəl/ adj. неоспоримый

incontinence /ɪn'kɒntɪnəns/ n. недержáние

inconvenience /,ɪnkən'viːnyəns/ 1. n. неудóбство 2. v. причинять неудóбство impf.

inconvenient /,ɪnkən'viːnyənt/ adj. неудóбный

incorporate /ɪn'kɔːrpə,reɪt/ v. объединять(ся) impf.

incorporation /ɪn,kɔːrpə'reɪʃən/ n. объединéние; инкорпорáция

incorrect /,ɪnkə'rekt/ adj. непрáвильный

incorrigible /ɪn'kɒrɪdʒəbəl/ adj. неисправимый

incorruptible /,ɪnkə'rʌptəbəl/ adj. (not bribable) неподкýпный

increase /n. 'ɪnkriːs; v. ɪn'kriːs/ **1.** n. увеличéние, рост; повышéние **2.** v. увеличивать(ся) impf., увеличить(ся) pf.

incredible /ɪn'kredəbəl/ adj. невероятный

incredulous /ɪn'kredʒələs/ adj. недовéрчивый

increment /'ɪnkrəmənt/ n. прирóст; (profit) прибыль f.

incriminate /ɪn'krɪmə,neɪt/ v. инкриминировать impf. & pf.

incriminatory /ɪn'krɪmɪnə,tɔːri/ adj. обвинительный

incubate /'ɪnkyə,beɪt/ v. (bacteria) вырáщивать impf.

incubator /'ɪnkyə,beɪtər/ n. инкубáтор

inculcate /ɪn'kʌlkeɪt/ v. внушáть, внедрять impf., -рять pf.

incur /ɪn'kɜːr/ v. навлекáть на себя impf., навлéчь pf.

incurable /ɪn'kyurəbəl/ adj. неизлечимый

incursion /ɪn'kɜːrʒən/ n. вторжéние; набéг

indebted /ɪn'detɪd/ adj. обязан (+ D); в долгý (у + G); —ness n. задóлженность

indecency /ɪn'diːsənsi/ n. неприличие

indecent /ɪn'diːsənt/ adj. неприличный; непристóйный

indecision /,ɪndɪ'sɪʒən/ n. нерешительность

indecisive /,ɪndɪ'saɪsɪv/ adj. нерешительный

indeclinable /,ɪndɪ'klaɪnəbəl/ adj. (gram.) несклоняемый

indeed /ɪn'diːd/ adv. действительно; intertrop. неужéли?

indefatigable /,ɪndɪ'fætɪgəbəl/ adj. неутомимый; неустáнный

indefensible /,ɪndɪ'fensəbəl/ adj. непростительный

indefinite /ɪn'defənɪt/ adj. неопределённый

indelible /ɪn'deləbəl/ adj. несмывáемый

indemnity /ɪn'demnɪti/ n. (compensation) компенсáция; (protection) гарáнтия

indent /ɪn'dent/ v. дéлать абзáц; дéлать óтступ impf.

indentation /,ɪnden'teɪʃən/ n. (typog.) óтступ, абзáц

independence /ˌɪndɪˈpɛndəns/ n. независимость

independent /ˌɪndɪˈpɛndənt/ adj. самостоятельный, независимый

indescribable /ˌɪndɪˈskraɪbəbəl/ adj. неописуемый

indestructible /ˌɪndɪˈstrʌktəbəl/ adj. неразрушимый, нерушимый

indeterminate /ˌɪndɪˈtɜrmənət/ adj. неопределённый; неясный

index /ˈɪndɛks/ n. указатель, индекс

India /ˈɪndɪə/ n. Индия

Indian /ˈɪndɪən/ **1.** adj. (U.S.) индийский; (Asia) индийский **2.** n. (U.S.) индеец, индианка; (Asia) индиец, индианка

indicate /ˈɪndɪˌkeɪt/ v. указывать impf., указать pf.

indication /ˌɪndɪˈkeɪʃən/ n. указание; признак

indicative /ɪnˈdɪkətɪv/ adj. показательный, указывающий; (gram.) изъявительный

indict /ɪnˈdaɪt/ v. предъявлять обвинение impf.

indifference /ɪnˈdɪfərəns/ n. равнодушие

indifferent /ɪnˈdɪfərənt/ adj. равнодушный; (mediocre) посредственный

indigenous /ɪnˈdɪdʒənəs/ adj. (native) туземный; (local) местный

indigent /ˈɪndɪdʒənt/ adj. нищий

indigestible /ˌɪndɪˈdʒɛstəbəl/ adj. неудобоваримый

indigestion /ˌɪndɪˈdʒɛstʃən/ n. расстройство желудка

indignant /ɪnˈdɪɡnənt/ adj. негодующий

indignation /ˌɪndɪɡˈneɪʃən/ n. негодование

indignity /ɪnˈdɪɡnɪti/ n. оскорбление; унижение

indirect /ˌɪndəˈrɛkt/ adj. непрямой; косвенный

indiscreet /ˌɪndɪˈskrit/ adj. нескромный; неосторожный

indiscretion /ˌɪndɪˈskrɛʃən/ n. нескромность; бестактность

indiscriminate /ˌɪndɪˈskrɪmənət/ adj. неразборчивый; огульный

indiscriminately /ˌɪndɪˈskrɪmənɪtli/ adv. без разбора

indispensable /ˌɪndɪˈspɛnsəbəl/ adj. необходимый

indisposed /ˌɪndɪˈspoʊzd/ adj. нездоровый

indisputable /ˌɪndɪˈspyutəbəl/ adj. неоспоримый, бесспорный

indistinct /ˌɪndɪˈstɪŋkt/ adj. неясный, неотчётливый

indistinguishable /ˌɪndɪˈstɪŋɡwɪʃəbəl/ adj. неразличимый

individual /ˌɪndəˈvɪdʒuəl/ **1.** adj. индивидуальный **2.** n. личность

individualism /ˌɪndəˈvɪdʒuəˌlɪzəm/ n. индивидуализм

individuality /ˌɪndəˌvɪdʒuˈælɪti/ n. индивидуальность

indivisible /ˌɪndəˈvɪzəbəl/ adj. неделимый

indoctrinate /ɪnˈdɒktrəˌneɪt/ v. внушать impf., -шить pf.

indoctrination /ɪnˌdɒktrəˈneɪʃən/ n. обработка

indolence /ˈɪndləns/ n. леность

indolent /ˈɪndlənt/ adj. ленивый

indomitable /ɪnˈdɒmɪtəbəl/ adj. неукротимый

Indonesia /ˌɪndəˈniʒə/ n. Индонезия

indoors /ɪnˈdɔrz/ adv. в закрытом помещении

induce /ɪnˈdus/ v. склонять impf., -нить pf.; (bring about) вызывать impf.; **—ment** n. стимул

induct /ɪnˈdʌkt/ v. вводить в должность impf.; **—ion** n. индукция

indulge /ɪnˈdʌldʒ/ v.i. предаваться (+ D) impf., предаться pf.; **—nce** n. потворство; снисхождение

indulgent /ɪnˈdʌldʒənt/ adj. снисходительный; потворствующий

industrial /ɪnˈdʌstriəl/ adj. индустриальный, промышленный; **—ist** n. промышленник

industrious /ɪnˈdʌstriəs/ adj. трудолюбивый, прилежный

industry /ˈɪndəstri/ n. индустрия, промышленность

inedible /ɪnˈɛdəbəl/ adj. несъедобный

ineffable /ɪnˈɛfəbəl/ adj. невыразимый; несказанный

ineffective /ɪnɪˈfɛktɪv/, **ineffectual** /-ˈfɛktʃuəl/ adj. неэффективный; бесплодный

inefficiency /ˌɪnɪˈfɪʃənsi/ n. неспособность; неэффективность

inefficient /ˌɪnɪˈfɪʃənt/ adj. неспособный; неэффективный

ineligible /ɪnˈelɪdʒəbəl/ adj. не имеющий права (на + A)

inept /ɪnˈept/ adj. неумелый

inequality /ˌɪnɪˈkwɒlɪtɪ/ n. неравенство

inequitable /ɪnˈekwɪtəbəl/ adj. несправедливый

inert /ɪnˈɜːt/ adj. инертный

inertia /ɪnˈɜːʃə/ n. инерция

inescapable /ˌɪnəˈskeɪpəbəl/ adj. неизбежный

inevitability /ɪnˌevɪtəˈbɪlɪtɪ/ n. неизбежность

inevitable /ɪnˈevɪtəbəl/ adj. неизбежный

inexcusable /ˌɪnɪkˈskjuːzəbəl/ adj. непростительный

inexhaustible /ˌɪnɪgˈzɔːstəbəl/ adj. неисчерпаемый; неистощимый

inexpensive /ˌɪnɪkˈspensɪv/ adj. недорогой, дешёвый

inexperience /ˌɪnɪkˈspɪərɪəns/ n. неопытность

inexperienced /ˌɪnɪkˈspɪərɪənst/ adj. неопытный

inexplicable /ˌɪnɪkˈsplɪkəbəl/ adj. необъяснимый

infallible /ɪnˈfæləbəl/ adj. безошибочный; непогрешимый

infamous /ˈɪnfəməs/ adj. позорный; гнусный

infamy /ˈɪnfəmɪ/ n. позор

infancy /ˈɪnfənsɪ/ n. раннее детство, младенчество

infant /ˈɪnfənt/ n. младенец

infantile /ˈɪnfənˌtaɪl/ adj. детский; (immature) инфантильный

infantry /ˈɪnfəntrɪ/ n. пехота

infatuate /ɪnˈfætʃʊˌeɪt/ v. вскружить голову (+ D)

infatuation /ɪnˌfætʃʊˈeɪʃən/ n. сильное увлечение

infect /ɪnˈfekt/ v. заражать impf., -зить pf.; **—ion** n. зараза; инфекция

infectious /ɪnˈfekʃəs/ adj. Fig. заразительный; (med.) заразный

infer /ɪnˈfɜː/ v. заключать impf.; **—ence** n. вывод; заключение

inferior /ɪnˈfɪərɪə/ 1. adj. низший; (quality) худший 2. n. подчинённый

inferiority /ɪnˌfɪərɪˈɒrɪtɪ/ n. низкое положение; ~ complex комплекс неполноценности

infernal /ɪnˈfɜːnl/ adj. адский

inferno /ɪnˈfɜːnəʊ/ n. ад

infertile /ɪnˈfɜːtl/ adj. неплодородный

infertility /ˌɪnfɜːˈtɪlɪtɪ/ n. бесплодие

infestation /ˌɪnfeˈsteɪʃən/ n. (med., biol.) инвазия

infidelity /ˌɪnfɪˈdelɪtɪ/ n. неверность

infiltrate /ˈɪnfɪlˌtreɪt/ v. проникать (в + A) impf., проникнуть pf.

infinite /ˈɪnfɪnɪt/ adj. бесконечный; безграничный

infinitesimal /ˌɪnfɪnɪˈtesəməl/ adj. мельчайший

infinitive /ɪnˈfɪnɪtɪv/ n. инфинитив

infinity /ɪnˈfɪnɪtɪ/ n. бесконечность

infirm /ɪnˈfɜːm/ adj. немощный; **—ary** n. медпункт; **—ity** n. слабость; немощь f.

inflamed /ɪnˈfleɪmd/ adj. воспалённый

inflammable /ɪnˈflæməbəl/ adj. огнеопасный, воспламеняемый

inflammation /ˌɪnfləˈmeɪʃən/ n. (med.) воспаление

inflammatory /ɪnˈflæməˌtɒrɪ/ adj. возбуждающий; (med.) воспалительный

inflate /ɪnˈfleɪt/ v. надувать impf., надуть pf.; **—d** adj. (econ.) дутый

inflation /ɪnˈfleɪʃən/ n. инфляция

inflection /ɪnˈflekʃən/ n. флексия

inflexible /ɪnˈfleksəbəl/ adj. негибкий, несгибаемый

inflict /ɪnˈflɪkt/ v. наносить impf., нанести pf.

inflow /ˈɪnˌfləʊ/ n. приток

influence /ˈɪnflʊəns/ 1. n. влияние 2. v. влиять (на + A) impf., по- pf.

influential /ˌɪnflʊˈenʃəl/ adj. влиятельный

influenza /ˌɪnflʊˈenzə/ n. грипп

influx /ˈɪnˌflʌks/ n. наплыв

inform /ɪnˈfɔːm/ v.t. сообщать impf., -щить pf.; v.i. доносить (на + A) impf.

informal /ɪnˈfɔːməl/ adj. неофициальный, неформальный

informality /ˌɪnfɔːˈmælɪtɪ/ n. непринуждённость

informant /ɪn'fɔrmənt/ n. осведомитель

information /,ɪnfər'meɪʃən/ **1.** n. информация **2.** adj. справочный

informative /ɪn'fɔrmətɪv/ adj. содержательный

informer /ɪn'fɔrmər/ n. доносчик

infrared /ˌɪnfrə'red/ adj. инфракрасный

infrastructure /'ɪnfrə,strʌktʃər/ n. инфраструктура

infrequent /ɪn'frikwənt/ adj. редкий

infringe /ɪn'frɪndʒ/ v.t. нарушать impf.; v.i. посягать (на + A) impf.; —ment n. нарушение

infuriate /ɪn'fyʊri,eɪt/ v. бесить impf.; разъярять impf., -рить pf.

infuse /ɪn'fyuz/ v.t. вливать impf.

infusion /ɪn'fyuʒən/ n. внушение; (extract) настой

ingenious /ɪn'dʒinyəs/ adj. остроумный; изобретательный

ingenuity /ˌɪndʒə'nuɪti/ n. изобретательность

ingenuous /ɪn'dʒenyuəs/ adj. бесхитростный; наивный

ingest /ɪn'dʒest/ v. проглатывать impf.

ingot /'ɪŋgət/ n. слиток

ingrained /ɪn'greind/ adj. въевшийся; укоренившийся

ingrate /'ɪngreit/ n. неблагодарный человек

ingratiate /ɪn'greiʃi,eɪt/ v. заискивать (перед + I) impf.

ingratitude /ɪn'græti,tud/ n. неблагодарность

ingredient /ɪn'gridiənt/ n. составная часть f., ингредиент

inhabit /ɪn'hæbɪt/ v. жить; обитать impf.; —able adj. обитаемый; —ant n. житель, обитатель

inhalation /ˌɪnhə'leiʃən/ n. вдыхание

inhale /ɪn'heil/ v. вдыхать impf., вдохнуть pf.

inherent /ɪn'hɪərənt/ adj. присущий (+ D)

inherit /ɪn'herɪt/ v. наследовать impf., y- pf.; —ance n. наследство

inhibit /ɪn'hɪbɪt/ v. сдерживать impf., сдержать pf.; (hinder) препятствовать; —ed adj. замкнутый

inhibition /ˌɪnɪ'bɪʃən/ n. сдерживание; препятствие

inhospitable /ɪn'hɒspɪtəbəl/ adj. негостеприимный; неприветливый

inhuman /ɪn'hyumən/ adj. бесчеловечный

inhumane /ˌɪnhyu'mein/ adj. негуманный, жестокий

inimical /ɪ'nɪmɪkəl/ adj. враждебный

iniquity /ɪ'nɪkwɪti/ n. несправедливость

initial /ɪ'nɪʃəl/ **1.** adj. (перво)начальный **2.** n. инициал **3.** v. подписывать инициалами impf.

initially /ɪ'nɪʃəli/ adv. вначале

initiate /ɪ'nɪʃi,eɪt/ v. начинать impf., начать pf.; (admit) посвящать (в + A) impf.

initiation /ɪ,nɪʃi'eiʃən/ n. посвящение; принятие

initiative /ɪ'nɪʃiətɪv/ n. инициатива

inject /ɪn'dʒekt/ v. впрыскивать impf., впрыснуть pf.

injection /ɪn'dʒekʃən/ n. укол

injunction /ɪn'dʒʌŋkʃən/ n. предписание; (law) судебный запрет

injure /'ɪndʒər/ v. повреждать impf., повредить pf.

injury /'ɪndʒəri/ n. рана

injustice /ɪn'dʒʌstɪs/ n. несправедливость

ink /ɪŋk/ n. чернила pl.

ink-jet printer n. струйный принтер

inland /'ɪn,lænd/ adv. в пределах страны

in-law n. родственник

inlay /ɪn,lei/ v. инкрустация

inlet /'ɪnlet/ n. залив, бухточка

inmate /'ɪn,meit/ n. (prison) заключённый; (asylum) больной

inn /ɪn/ n. гостиница

innards /'ɪnərdz/ n. внутренности pl.

innate /ɪ'neit/ adj. врождённый

inner /'ɪnər/ adj. внутренний

innocence /'ɪnəsəns/ n. невинность; невиновность

innocent /'ɪnəsənt/ adj. невинный; невиновный

innocuous /ɪ'nɒkyuəs/ adj. безобидный, безвредный

innovation /ˌɪnə'veiʃən/ n. нововведение

innovative /'ɪnə,veitɪv/ adj. новаторский

innuendo /ˌɪnyuˈɛndou/ *n.* инсинуа́ция

innumerable /ɪˈnumərəbəl/ *adj.* бесчи́сленный

inoculate /ɪˈnɒkyəˌleɪt/ *v.* привива́ть *impf.*, приви́ть *pf.*

inoculation /ɪˌnɒkyəˈleɪʃən/ *n.* приви́вка

inoffensive /ˌɪnəˈfɛnsɪv/ *adj.* безоби́дный; необи́дный

inopportune /ɪnˌɒpərˈtun/ *adj.* несвоевре́менный

inordinate /ɪnˈɔrdɪnɪt/ *adj.* чрезме́рный

inorganic /ˌɪnɔrˈgænɪk/ *adj.* неоргани́ческий

inpatient /ˈɪnˌpeɪʃənt/ *n.* стациона́рный больно́й

input /ˈɪnˌpʊt/ *n.* пода́ча; ввод

inquest /ˈɪnkwɛst/ *n.* дозна́ние

inquire /ɪnˈkwaɪər/ *v.* спра́шивать *impf.*, спроси́ть *pf.*; (*investigate*) рассле́довать *impf. & pf.*

inquiry /ɪnˈkwaɪri/ *n.* запро́с; спра́вка; (*investigation*) рассле́дование

inquisitive /ɪnˈkwɪzɪtɪv/ *adj.* пытли́вый, любозна́тельный

inroad /ˈɪnˌroud/ *n.* набе́г

insane /ɪnˈseɪn/ *adj.* сумасше́дший; безу́мный

insanity /ɪnˈsænɪti/ *n.* безу́мие

insatiable /ɪnˈseɪʃəbəl/ *adj.* ненасы́тный, жа́дный

inscribe /ɪnˈskraɪb/ *v.* надпи́сывать, впи́сывать *impf.*, -писа́ть *pf.*

inscription /ɪnˈskrɪpʃən/ *n.* на́дпись *f.*; посвяще́ние

inscrutable /ɪnˈskrutəbəl/ *adj.* непостижи́мый

insect /ˈɪnsɛkt/ *n.* насеко́мое

insecticide /ɪnˈsɛktəˌsaɪd/ *n.* инсектици́д

insecure /ˌɪnsɪˈkyur/ *adj.* небезопа́сный; (*lacking confidence*) неуве́ренный в себе́

insemination /ɪnˌsɛməˈneɪʃən/ *n.* оплодотворе́ние

insensitive /ɪnˈsɛnsɪtɪv/ *adj.* нечувстви́тельный

insensitivity /ɪnˌsɛnsɪˈtɪvɪti/ *n.* нечувстви́тельность

inseparable /ɪnˈsɛpərəbəl/ *adj.* неотдели́мый; (*of people*) неразлу́чный

insert /*v.* ɪnˈsɜrt; *n.* ˈɪnsɜrt/ **1.** *v.* вставля́ть *impf.*, вста́вить *pf.* **2.** *n.* вста́вка; вкла́дыш

insertion /ɪnˈsɜrʃən/ *n.* вставле́ние; введе́ние; вста́вка

inside /*prep., adv., adj.* ˌɪnˈsaɪd; *n.* ˈɪnˈsaɪd/ **1.** *prep.* в (+ *A*, *P*), внутри́, внутры́ (+ *G*) **2.** *adv.* внутри́ **3.** *adj.* вну́тренний **4.** *n.* вну́тренность; ~ **out** *adv.* наизна́нку

insidious /ɪnˈsɪdiəs/ *adj.* кова́рный

insight /ˈɪnˌsaɪt/ *n.* проница́тельность

insignia /ɪnˈsɪgniə/ *n.* (*mil.*) зна́ки разли́чия *pl.*

insignificant /ˌɪnsɪgˈnɪfɪkənt/ *adj.* незначи́тельный

insincere /ˌɪnsɪnˈsɪər/ *adj.* нейскренний

insinuate /ɪnˈsɪnyuˌeɪt/ *v.* намека́ть (на + *A*) *impf.*, намекну́ть *pf.*

insinuation /ɪnˌsɪnyuˈeɪʃən/ *n.* намёк; инсинуа́ция

insipid /ɪnˈsɪpɪd/ *adj.* безвку́сный

insist /ɪnˈsɪst/ *v.* наста́ивать *impf.*; —**ence** *n.* насто́йчивость; —**ent** *adj.* насто́йчивый

insole /ˈɪnˌsoul/ *n.* стелька

insolent /ˈɪnsələnt/ *adj.* на́глый

insoluble /ɪnˈsɒlyəbəl/ *adj.* нераствори́мый; неразреши́мый

insolvent /ɪnˈsɒlvənt/ *adj.* несостоя́тельный

insomnia /ɪnˈsɒmniə/ *n.* бессо́нница

inspect /ɪnˈspɛkt/ *v.* осма́тривать *impf.*, осмотре́ть *pf.*; —**ion** *n.* осмо́тр; инспе́кция; —**or** *n.* инспе́ктор

inspiration /ˌɪnspəˈreɪʃən/ *n.* вдохнове́ние

inspire /ɪnˈspaɪər/ *v.* вдохновля́ть *impf.*, -ви́ть *pf.*; —**d** *adj.* вдохнове́нный

instability /ˌɪnstəˈbɪlɪti/ *n.* неусто́йчивость

install /ɪnˈstɔl/ *v.* устана́вливать, ста́вить *impf.*, по- *pf.*

installation /ˌɪnstəˈleɪʃən/ *n.* устано́вка; (*mil.*) ба́за

installment /ɪnˈstɔlmənt/ *n.* взнос; (*publication*) вы́пуск

instance /ˈɪnstəns/ *n.* приме́р; слу́чай; (*law*) инста́нция; **for ~** наприме́р

instant /ˈɪnstənt/ **1.** *adj.* неме́дленный; (*coffee*) раствори́мый **2.** *n.* мгнове́ние; миг

instantaneous /ˌɪnstənˈteɪniəs/ *adj.* мгнове́нный

instantly /'ɪnstəntli/ adv. сра́зу же; неме́дленно; то́тчас

instead /ɪn'sted/ adv. взаме́н, вме́сто (+ G)

instigate /'ɪnstɪ,geɪt/ v. подстрека́ть impf., подстрекну́ть pf.

instigation /,ɪnstɪ'geɪʃən/ n. подстрека́тельство

instill /ɪn'stɪl/ v. внуша́ть impf., -ши́ть pf.

instinct /'ɪnstɪŋkt/ n. инсти́нкт

instinctive /ɪn'stɪŋktɪv/ adj. инстинкти́вный

institute /'ɪnstɪ,tut/ 1. n. институ́т 2. v. учрежда́ть impf., -ди́ть pf.

institution /,ɪnstɪ'tuʃən/ n. учрежде́ние; заведе́ние

instruct /ɪn'strʌkt/ v. обуча́ть impf., -чи́ть pf.; (direct) поруча́ть impf.; **—ion** n. обуче́ние, инстру́кция; **—ive** adj. поучи́тельный; **—or** n. инстру́ктор

instrument /'ɪnstrəmənt/ n. инструме́нт; прибо́р; ору́дие

instrumental /,ɪnstrə'mentl/ adj. инструмента́льный; (gram.) твори́тельный

instrumentation /,ɪnstrəmən'teɪʃən/ n. инструменто́вка

insubordinate /,ɪnsə'bɔrdnɪt/ adj. непослу́шный; непоко́рный

insubstantial /,ɪnsəb'stænʃəl/ adj. непро́чный; неоснова́тельный

insufferable /ɪn'sʌfərəbəl/ adj. невыноси́мый; несно́сный

insufficient /,ɪnsə'fɪʃənt/ adj. недоста́точный

insulate /'ɪnsə,leɪt/ v. изоли́ровать impf. & pf.

insulation /,ɪnsə'leɪʃən/ n. изоля́ция

insulin /'ɪnsəlɪn/ n. инсули́н

insult /n. 'ɪnsʌlt; v. ɪn'sʌlt/ 1. n. оскорбле́ние 2. v. оскорбля́ть impf., -би́ть pf.; **—ing** adj. оскорби́тельный

insurance /ɪn'ʃʊrəns/ 1. n. страхова́ние 2. adj. страхово́й

insure /ɪn'ʃʊr/ v. страхова́ть impf., за- pf.

insurgent /ɪn'sɜrdʒənt/ 1. adj. восста́вший 2. n. повста́нец

insurmountable /,ɪnsər'maʊntəbəl/ adj. непреодоли́мый

insurrection /,ɪnsə'rekʃən/ n. восста́ние; мяте́ж

intact /ɪn'tækt/ adj. неповреждённый; це́лый

intake /'ɪn,teɪk/ n. приём; (quantity) потребле́ние

intangible /ɪn'tændʒəbəl/ adj. неосяза́емый

integral /'ɪntɪgrəl/ adj. неотдели́мый

integrate /'ɪntɪ,greɪt/ v. интегри́ровать impf. & pf.

integration /,ɪntɪ'greɪʃən/ n. интегра́ция; интегри́рование

integrity /ɪn'tegrɪti/ n. це́лость; (honesty) че́стность

intellect /'ɪntl,ekt/ n. интелле́кт

intellectual /,ɪntl'ektʃuəl/ 1. adj. у́мственный; интеллектуа́льный 2. n. интеллиге́нт

intelligence /ɪn'telɪdʒəns/ n. ум; (information) разве́дка

intelligent /ɪn'telɪdʒənt/ adj. у́мный; интеллиге́нтный

intelligentsia /ɪn,telɪ'dʒentsiə/ n. интеллиге́нция

intelligible /ɪn'telɪdʒəbəl/ adj. поня́тный

intemperate /ɪn'tempərɪt/ adj. неуме́ренный; невозде́ржанный

intend /ɪn'tend/ v. собира́ться impf.; (designed for) предназнача́ть (для + G) impf.

intense /ɪn'tens/ adj. напряжённый; си́льный

intensify /ɪn'tensə,faɪ/ v. уси́ливать(ся) impf.

intensity /ɪn'tensɪti/ n. напряжённость; си́ла; интенси́вность

intensive /ɪn'tensɪv/ adj. интенси́вный

intention /ɪn'tenʃən/ n. наме́рение; **—al** adj. наме́ренный; умы́шленный

intently /ɪn'tentli/ adv. внима́тельно

inter /ɪn'tɜr/ v. погреба́ть impf.

interact /,ɪntər'ækt/ v. взаимоде́йствовать impf.; **—ion** n. взаимоде́йствие

intercede /,ɪntər'sid/ v. хода́тайствовать impf., по- pf.

intercept /,ɪntər'sept/ v. перехва́тывать impf., перехвати́ть pf.; **—ion** n. перехва́т

intercession /,ɪntər'seʃən/ n. хода́тайство, засту́пничество

interchange /n. 'ɪntər,tʃeɪndʒ; v. ,ɪntər'tʃeɪndʒ/ 1. n. обме́н, заме́на 2. v. обме́ниваться (+ I) impf.; **—able** adj. взаимозаменя́емость

intercity /ˌɪntərˈsɪti/ adj. междугородный

intercom /ˈɪntərˌkɒm/ n. внутреннее переговорное устройство

interconnect /ˌɪntərkəˈnekt/ v.t. взаимосвязывать impf.; **—ion** n. взаимосвязь f.

intercontinental /ˌɪntərˌkɒntɪˈnentl/ adj. межконтинентальный

intercourse /ˈɪntərˌkɔrs/ n. общение; (sexual) половая связь f.

interdepartmental /ˌɪntərˌdɪpɑrtˈmentl/ adj. межведомственный

interdependent /ˌɪntərdɪˈpendənt/ adj. взаимозависимый

interest /ˈɪntrɪst/ **1.** n. интерес; (econ.) проценты pl. **2.** v. интересовать (+ I) impf., за- pf.; **be —ed** интересоваться (+ I) impf.

interesting /ˈɪntərəstɪŋ/ adj. интересный

interfere /ˌɪntərˈfɪər/ v. вмешиваться impf., вмешаться pf.; **—nce** n. вмешательство; (radio) помехи pl.

interim /ˈɪntərɪm/ adj. промежуточный; временный

interior /ɪnˈtɪəriər/ **1.** adj. внутренний **2.** n. внутренность

interlock /ˌɪntərˈlɒk/ v. сцеплять(ся) impf.

interlope /ˌɪntərˈloup/ v. вмешиваться в чужие дела impf.

interlude /ˈɪntərˌlud/ n. промежуточный эпизод; интерлюдия

intermediary /ˌɪntərˈmidiˌeri/ n. посредник

intermediate /ˌɪntərˈmidiɪt/ adj. промежуточный; средний

interminable /ɪnˈtɜrmɪnəbəl/ adj. бесконечный

intermingle /ˌɪntərˈmɪŋgəl/ v. смешивать(ся) impf.

intermission /ˌɪntərˈmɪʃən/ n. перерыв; (theat.) антракт

intermittent /ˌɪntərˈmɪtnt/ adj. перемежающийся; прерывистый

intern /ˈɪntɜrn/ n. (med.) интерн

internal /ɪnˈtɜrnl/ adj. внутренний

international /ˌɪntərˈnæʃənl/ adj. международный

Internet /ˈɪntərˌnet/ n. Интернет

internist /ˈɪntɜrnɪst/ n. терапевт

interplay /ˈɪntərˌplei/ n. взаимодействие

interpret /ɪnˈtɜrprɪt/ v. (translate) переводить impf., перевести pf.; (explain) толковать impf.

interpretation /ɪnˌtɜrprɪˈteiʃən/ n. перевод; интерпретация

interpreter /ɪnˈtɜrprɪtər/ n. переводчик; -чица

interrelate /ˌɪntərrɪˈleit/ v. взаимосвязывать impf.

interrogate /ɪnˈterəˌgeit/ v. допрашивать impf.

interrogation /ɪnˌterəˈgeiʃən/ n. допрос

interrogative /ˌɪntəˈrɒgətɪv/ adj. вопросительный

interrupt /ˌɪntəˈrʌpt/ v. перебивать; прерывать impf., прервать pf.; **—ion** n. перерыв

intersect /ˌɪntərˈsekt/ v. пересекать, пересечь pf.; **—ion** n. пересечения

intersperse /ˌɪntərˈspɜrs/ v. пересыпать; рассыпать impf.

interval /ˈɪntərvəl/ n. интервал

intervene /ˌɪntərˈvin/ v. вмешиваться impf., вмешаться pf.

intervention /ˌɪntərˈvenʃən/ n. вмешательство; интервенция

interview /ˈɪntərˌvyu/ **1.** n. интервью neut. indecl. **2.** v. интервьюировать impf. & pf.

interviewer /ˈɪntərˌvyuər/ n. интервьюер

interweave /ˌɪntərˈwiv/ v. переплетать(ся) impf.

intestine /ɪnˈtestɪn/ n. кишка

intimacy /ˈɪntəməsi/ n. близость

intimate[1] /ˈɪntəmɪt/ adj. интимный; близкий

intimate[2] /ˈɪntəˌmeit/ v. намекать impf., намекнуть pf.

intimidate /ɪnˈtɪmɪˌdeit/ v. запугивать impf., запугать pf.

into /ˈɪntu/ prep. в (во) (+ A); на (+ A)

intolerable /ɪnˈtɒlərəbəl/ adj. невыносимый; нестерпимый

intolerance /ɪnˈtɒlərəns/ n. нетерпимость

intolerant /ɪnˈtɒlərənt/ adj. нетерпимый

intoxicate /ɪnˈtɒksɪˌkeit/ v. опьянять impf., опьянить pf.

intoxicated /ɪnˈtɒksɪˌkeitɪd/ adj. пьяный

intractable /ɪnˈtræktəbəl/ adj. упрямый; неподатливый

intransigent /ın'trænsıdʒənt/ *adj.* непримиримый, непреклонный

intransitive /ın'trænsıtıv/ *adj.* непереходный

intravenous /,ıntrə'vinəs/ *adj.* внутривенный

intrepid /ın'trepıd/ *adj.* бесстрашный

intricate /'ıntrıkıt/ *adj.* сложный, запутанный

intrigue /ın'trig/ **1.** *n.* интрига **2.** *v.* интриговать *impf.*, за- *pf.*

intrinsic /ın'trınsık/ *adj.* присущий; существенный; свойственный

introduce /,ıntrə'dus/ *v.* вводить *impf.*, ввести *pf.*; (*present*) представлять *impf.*, -ставить *pf.*

introduction /,ıntrə'dʌkʃən/ *n.* введение; представление

introductory /,ıntrə'dʌktərı/ *adj.* вступительный

intrude /ın'trud/ *v.* вторгаться *impf.*, вторгнуться *pf.*

intruder /ın'trudər/ *n.* (*housebreaker*) взломщик

intrusion /ın'truʒən/ *n.* вторжение

intuition /,ıntu'ıʃən/ *n.* интуиция

intuitive /ın'tuıtıv/ *adj.* интуитивный

inundate /'ınən,deıt/ *v.* наводнять *impf.*, -нить *pf.*

invade /ın'veıd/ *v.* вторгаться (в + A) *impf.*, вторгнуться *pf.*

invader /ın'veıdər/ *n.* захватчик

invalid /ın'vælıd/ *adj.* недействительный

invalid² /'ınvəlıd/ *n.* инвалид; больной

invalidate /ın'vælı,deıt/ *v.* делать недействительным *impf.*

invaluable /ın'vælyuəbəl/ *adj.* неоценимый, бесценный

invariable /ın'veərıəbəl/ *adj.* неизменный

invasion /ın'veıʒən/ *n.* нашествие; вторжение

invective /ın'vektıv/ *n.* брань *f.*

invent /ın'vent/ *v.* изобретать *impf.*, изобрести *pf.*; (*fabricate*) выдумывать *impf.*; —ion *n.* изобретение; выдумка; *f.*; —ive *adj.* изобретательный; —or *n.* изобретатель

inventory /'ınvən,tɔrı/ *n.* инвентарь *m.*

inverse /ın'vɜrs/ **1.** *n.* противоположность **2.** *adj.* обратный

invert /ın'vɜrt/ *v.* переставлять *impf.*

invertebrate /ın'vɜrtəbrıt/ *adj.* беспозвоночный

inverted /ın'vɜrtıd/ *adj.* опрокинутый; (*reverse*) обратный

invest /ın'vest/ *v.* вкладывать *impf.*, вложить *pf.*

investigate /ın'vestı,geıt/ *v.* исследовать; расследовать *impf. & pf.*

investigation /ın,vestı'geıʃən/ *n.* исследование; расследование

investment /ın'vestmənt/ *n.* вклад; инвестиция

investor /ın'vestər/ *n.* вкладчик

inveterate /ın'vetərıt/ *adj.* закоренелый; укоренившийся

invidious /ın'vıdıəs/ *adj.* оскорбительный; гнусный

invigorate /ın'vıgə,reıt/ *v.* подбадривать; оживлять *impf.*

invincible /ın'vınsəbəl/ *adj.* непобедимый

inviolable /ın'vaıələbəl/ *adj.* нерушимый; неприкосновенный

invisible /ın'vızəbəl/ *adj.* невидимый

invitation /,ınvı'teıʃən/ *n.* приглашение

invite /ın'vaıt/ *v.* приглашать *impf.*, -сить *pf.*

inviting /ın'vaıtıŋ/ *adj.* привлекательный; заманчивый

invoice /'ınvɔıs/ *n.* наряд расчёта

invoke /ın'vouk/ *v.* призывать *impf.*

involuntary /ın'vɒlən,terı/ *adj.* непроизвольный; невольный

involve /ın'vɒlv/ *v.* вовлекать *impf.*, вовлечь *pf.*; —d *adj.* сложный

invulnerable /ın'vʌlnərəbəl/ *adj.* неуязвимый

inward /'ınwərd/ *adv.* внутрь

iodine /'aıə,daın/ *n.* йод

Iran /ı'ræn/ *n.* Иран

Iranian /ı'reınıən/ **1.** *adj.* иранский **2.** *n.* иранец, иранка

Iraq /ı'ræk/ *n.* Ирак

Iraqi /ı'ræki/ **1.** *adj.* иракский **2.** *n.* иракец

irascible /ı'ræsəbəl/ *adj.* вспыльчивый; раздражительный

irate /aı'reıt/ *adj.* гневный

Ireland /'aıərlənd/ *n.* Ирландия

iridescent /ˌɪrɪ'dɛsənt/ adj. ра́дужный; переливчатый

iris /'aɪrɪs/ n. (eye) ра́дужная оболо́чка; (flower) и́рис

Irish /'aɪrɪʃ/ adj. ирла́ндский

Irishman /'aɪrɪʃmən/ n. ирла́ндец

Irishwoman /'aɪrɪʃˌwʊmən/ n. ирла́ндка

irksome /'ɜːksəm/ adj. надоедли́вый; раздража́ющий

iron /'aɪərn/ **1.** adj. желе́зный **2.** n. желе́зо; (appliance) утю́г **3.** v. гла́дить impf., вы́- pf.

ironical /aɪ'rɒnɪkəl/ adj. ирони́ческий

irony /'aɪrənɪ/ n. иро́ния

irradiate /ɪ'reɪdɪˌeɪt/ v. освеща́ть impf.; (expose to radiation) облуча́ть impf.

irradiation /ɪˌreɪdɪ'eɪʃən/ n. облуче́ние; иррадиа́ция

irrational /ɪ'ræʃənl/ adj. неразу́мный; иррациона́льный

irreconcilable /ɪ'rɛkənˌsaɪləbəl/ adj. непримири́мый

irredeemable /ɪrɪ'diːməbəl/ adj. неисправи́мый

irrefutable /ɪ'rɛfjʊtəbəl/ adj. неопровержи́мый

irregular /ɪ'rɛɡjʊlər/ adj. непра́вильный; нерегуля́рный

irrelevant /ɪ'rɛləvənt/ adj. неуме́стный

irreparable /ɪ'rɛpərəbəl/ adj. непоправи́мый

irreproachable /ˌɪrɪ'prəʊtʃəbəl/ adj. безупре́чный

irresistible /ˌɪrɪ'zɪstəbəl/ adj. неотрази́мый

irresolute /ɪ'rɛzəˌluːt/ adj. нереши́тельный

irrespective /ˌɪrɪ'spɛktɪv/ adj.: ~ **of** незави́симо от (+ G)

irresponsible /ˌɪrɪ'spɒnsəbəl/ adj. безотве́тственный

irretrievable /ˌɪrɪ'triːvəbəl/ adj. невозвра́тный

irreverent /ɪ'rɛvərənt/ adj. непочти́тельный

irreversible /ˌɪrɪ'vɜːsəbəl/ adj. необрати́мый

irrevocable /ɪ'rɛvəkəbəl/ adj. безвозвра́тный

irrigate /'ɪrɪˌɡeɪt/ v. ороша́ть impf., -си́ть pf.

irrigation /ˌɪrɪ'ɡeɪʃən/ n. ороше́ние

irritable /'ɪrɪtəbəl/ adj. раздражи́тельный

irritate /'ɪrɪˌteɪt/ v. раздража́ть impf., -жи́ть pf.

irritation /ˌɪrɪ'teɪʃən/ n. раздраже́ние

Islam /ɪs'lɑːm/ n. Исла́м; —**ic** adj. мусульма́нский

island /'aɪlənd/ n. о́стров; —**er** n. островитя́нин

isle /aɪl/ n. о́стров

isolate /'aɪsəˌleɪt/ v. изоли́ровать impf. & pf.; обособля́ть impf.; —**d** adj. изоли́рованный; отдалённый

isolation /ˌaɪsə'leɪʃən/ n. изоля́ция

Israel /'ɪzrɪəl/ n. Изра́иль m.

Israeli /ɪz'reɪlɪ/ adj. изра́ильский

issue /'ɪʃuː/ **1.** n. изда́ние; (question) вопро́с; (of book) вы́пуск **2.** v.t. выпуска́ть impf., вы́пустить pf.

isthmus /'ɪsməs/ n. переше́ек

it /ɪt/ pron. он, она́, оно́; э́то

Italian /ɪ'tæljən/ **1.** adj. италья́нский **2.** n. италья́нец, -я́нка

italicize /ɪ'tælɪˌsaɪz/ v. вы́делить курси́вом pf.

italics /ɪ'tælɪks/ n. курси́в

Italy /'ɪtlɪ/ n. Ита́лия

itch /ɪtʃ/ **1.** n. зуд **2.** v. чеса́ться impf.

item /'aɪtəm/ n. предме́т; пункт

itemize /'aɪtəˌmaɪz/ v. перечисля́ть по пу́нктам impf.

itinerary /aɪ'tɪnəˌrerɪ/ n. маршру́т

its /ɪts/ poss. pron. его́; её; свой

itself /ɪt'sɛlf/ pron. сам, сама́, само́; себя́

ivory /'aɪvərɪ/ n. слоно́вая кость m.

ivy /'aɪvɪ/ n. плющ

J

jab /dʒæb/ **1.** n. толчок **2.** v. толкать impf., толкнуть pf.

jabber /'dʒæbər/ v. тараторить impf.

jack /dʒæk/ n. (mech.) домкрат; (cards) валет

jackdaw /'dʒæk,dɔ/ n. галка

jacket /'dʒækɪt/ n. жакет, куртка

jackhammer /'dʒæk,hæmər/ n. отбойный молот

jackknife /'dʒæk,naɪf/ n. большой складной нож

jackpot /'dʒæk,pɒt/ n. (at cards) банк; (prize) выигрыш

jade¹ /dʒeɪd/ n. нефрит

jade² /dʒeɪd/ n. (old horse) кляча

jaded /'dʒeɪdɪd/ adj. изнурённый

jagged /'dʒægɪd/ adj. зубчатый

jaguar /'dʒægwɑr/ n. ягуар

jail /dʒeɪl/ **1.** n. тюрьма **2.** v. посадить в тюрьму pf.; **—er** n. тюремщик

jalopy /dʒə'lɒpi/ n. колымага

jam¹ /dʒæm/ n. варенье, джем

jam² /dʒæm/ **1.** n. (traffic) пробка **2.** v. загромождать impf., -дить pf.

jangle /'dʒæŋgəl/ n. бряцание

janitor /'dʒænɪtər/ n. уборщик

January /'dʒænyu,ɛri/ n. январь m. adj. январский

Japan /dʒə'pæn/ n. Япония

Japanese /,dʒæpə'niz/ **1.** adj. японский **2.** n. японец, -нка

jar¹ /dʒɑr/ n. (container) банка

jar² /dʒɑr/ **1.** n. (jolt) потрясение, шок **2.** v. дребезжать impf.

jargon /'dʒɑrgən/ n. жаргон

jasmine /'dʒæzmɪn/ n. жасмин

jaundice /'dʒɔndɪs/ n. желтуха

jaunt /'dʒɔnt/ n. прогулка

javelin /'dʒævlɪn/ n. копьё

jaw /dʒɔ/ n. челюсть f.

jay /dʒeɪ/ n. (bird) сойка

jazz /dʒæz/ n. джаз

jealous /'dʒɛləs/ adj. ревнивый, завистливый; **be ~** v. ревновать impf.; **—y** n. ревность, зависть f.

jeans /dʒɪnz/ n. джинсы pl.

jeep /dʒip/ n. джип, вездеход

jeer /dʒɪər/ **1.** n. насмешка **2.** v. насмехаться (над + I) impf.

jell /dʒɛl/ v. застывать impf.

jelly /'dʒɛli/ n. желе neut. indecl.

jellyfish /'dʒɛli,fɪʃ/ n. медуза

jeopardize /'dʒɛpər,daɪz/ v. подвергать опасности impf.

jeopardy /'dʒɛpərdi/ n. опасность

jerk /dʒɜrk/ **1.** n. рывок; Slang сволочь f. **2.** v. дёргать(ся) impf.

jerky /'dʒɜrki/ adj. судорожный

jersey /'dʒɜrzi/ n. фуфайка; (fabric) джерси neut. indecl.

jest /dʒɛst/ **1.** n. шутка **2.** v. шутить impf., по- pf.; **—er** n. шутник

Jesus /'dʒizəs/ n. Иисус

jet /dʒɛt/ n. струя

jet-black adj. чёрный как смоль

jettison /'dʒɛtəsən/ v. выбрасывать за борт impf.

jetty /'dʒɛti/ n. пирс, пристань f.

Jew /dʒu/ n. еврей, —ка

jewel /'dʒuəl/ n. драгоценный камень m.; **—er** n. ювелир; **—ry** n. драгоценности; ювелирные изделия pl.

Jewish /'dʒuɪʃ/ adj. еврейский

jiffy /'dʒɪfi/ n. Colloq. мгновение

jig /dʒɪg/ n. (template) направляющий шаблон

jilt /dʒɪlt/ v. бросать impf.

jingle /'dʒɪŋgəl/ **1.** n. звякание **2.** v. звякать impf.

jinx /dʒɪŋks/ v. сглазить impf.

jittery /'dʒɪtəri/ adj. нервный

job /dʒɒb/ n. работа, служба

jobber /'dʒɒbər/ n. оптовик

jobless /'dʒɒblɪs/ adj. безработный

jockey /'dʒɒki/ n. жокей

jocular /'dʒɒkyələr/ adj. шутливый

jog /dʒɒg/ **1.** n. (nudge) толчок **2.** v. толкать impf.; (run) бегать impf.

jogging /'dʒɒgɪŋ/ n. джоггинг

join /dʒɔɪn/ v. соединять(ся) impf., -нить(ся) pf.; присоединяться impf., -ниться pf.

joiner /'dʒɔɪnər/ n. столяр

joint /dʒɔɪnt/ **1.** n. (anat.) сустав; (tech.) стык **2.** adj. совместный; общий; ~ **stock** акционерный капитал; ~ **venture** совместное предприятие (abbr. СП)

joist /dʒɔɪst/ n. балка

joke /dʒouk/ **1.** n. шутка **2.** v. шутить impf., по- pf.

joker /'dʒoukər/ *n.* шутник; (*cards*) джокер

jolly /'dʒɒli/ *adj.* весёлый

jolt /dʒoult/ **1.** *n.* тряска **2.** *v.* трясти(ся) *impf.*, тряхнуть(ся) *pf.*

jostle /'dʒɒsəl/ *n.* толкать(ся) *impf.*

jot /dʒɒt/ **1.** *n.* йота **2.** *v.* (*note*) записывать *impf.*

journal /'dʒɜrnl/ *n.* журнал; (*diary*) дневник

journalism /'dʒɜrnlˌizəm/ *n.* журналистика

journalist /'dʒɜrnlist/ *n.* журналист

journey /'dʒɜrni/ **1.** *n.* путешествие **2.** *v.* путешествовать *impf.*

jovial /'dʒouviəl/ *adj.* весёлый

joy /dʒɔi/ *n.* радость; **—ful**, **—ous** *adj.* радостный; **—less** *adj.* безрадостный

joystick /'dʒɔiˌstik/ *n.* ручка управления

jubilant /'dʒubələnt/ *adj.* ликующий

jubilation /ˌdʒubə'leiʃən/ *n.* ликование

jubilee /'dʒubəˌli/ *n.* юбилей

judge /dʒʌdʒ/ **1.** *n.* судья *m.* **2.** *v.* судить *impf.*

judgment /'dʒʌdʒmənt/ *n.* суждение; решение; приговор

judicial /dʒu'diʃəl/ *adj.* судебный

judicious /dʒu'diʃəs/ *adj.* рассудительный

judo /'dʒudou/ *n.* дзюдо *neut. indecl.*

jug /dʒʌg/ *n.* кувшин

juggle /'dʒʌgəl/ *v.* жонглировать *impf.*

juggler /'dʒʌglər/ *n.* жонглёр

jugular /'dʒʌgyələr/ *adj.* яремный

juice /dʒus/ *n.* сок

juicy /'dʒusi/ *adj.* сочный

jukebox /'dʒuk,bɒks/ *n.* проигрыватель-автомат

July /dʒə'lai/ **1.** *n.* июль *m.* **2.** *adj.* июльский

jumble /'dʒʌmbəl/ **1.** *n.* беспорядок **2.** *v.* перепутывать *impf.*, перепутать *pf.*

jump /dʒʌmp/ **1.** *n.* прыжок; скачок **2.** *v.* прыгать *impf.*, прыгнуть *pf.*; скакать *impf.*

jump rope *n.* скакалка

jumpsuit /'dʒʌmp,sut/ *n.* комбинезон

jumpy /'dʒʌmpi/ *adj.* нервный

junction /'dʒʌŋkʃən/ *n.* соединение; узел; перекрёсток

juncture /'dʒʌŋktʃər/ *n.* стечение обстоятельств

June /dʒun/ **1.** *n.* июнь *m.* **2.** *adj.* июньский

jungle /'dʒʌŋgəl/ *n.* джунгли *pl.*

junior /'dʒunyər/ *adj.* младший

juniper /'dʒunəpər/ *n.* можжевельник

junk /dʒʌŋk/ *n.* барахло, хлам

junkie /'dʒʌŋki/ *n. Colloq.* наркоман

jurisdiction /ˌdʒuris'dikʃən/ *n.* юрисдикция

jurisprudence /ˌdʒuris'prudns/ *n.* юриспруденция

juror /'dʒurər/ *n.* присяжный

jury /'dʒuri/ *n.* жюри *neut. indecl.*, присяжные *pl.*

just /dʒʌst/ **1.** *adj.* справедливый; (*deserved*) заслуженный **2.** *adv.* именно, как раз; (*just now*) только что

justice /'dʒʌstis/ *n.* справедливость; юстиция

justifiable /ˌdʒʌstə,faiəbəl/ *adj.* простительный

justification /ˌdʒʌstəfi'keiʃən/ *n.* оправдание

juvenile /'dʒuvənl/ **1.** *adj.* юный, юношеский **2.** *n.* юноша *m.*

juxtapose /ˌdʒʌkstə,pouz/ *v.* сопоставлять *impf.*, -ставить *pf.*

juxtaposition /ˌdʒʌkstəpə'ziʃən/ *n.* сопоставление

K

kaleidoscope /kə'laidə,skoup/ *n.* калейдоскоп

kangaroo /,kæŋgə'ru/ *n.* кенгуру *m. indecl.*

karate /kə'rati/ *n.* карате *neut. indecl.*

Kazakh /kə'zɑk/ *n.* казах, казашка

Kazakhstan /,kazak'stan/ *n.* Казахстан

keel /kil/ **1.** *n.* киль *m.* **2.** *v.:* ~ **over** опрокидывать(ся) *impf.*

keen /kin/ *adj.* острый; пронзительный; **be ~ on** увлекаться *impf.*

keep /kip/ *v.* держать; хранить; сохранять *impf.*, -нить *pf.*

keepsake /'kip,seik/ *n.* подарок на память

keg /keg/ *n.* бочонок

kelp /kelp/ *n.* морская капуста

kennel /'kɛnl/ *n.* конура

kerchief /'kɜrtʃif/ *n.* платок

kernel /'kɜrnl/ *n.* (grain) зерно; (nut) ядро

kerosene /'kerə,sin/ *n.* керосин

ketchup /'ketʃəp/ *n.* кетчуп

kettle /'kɛtl/ *n.* чайник

key /ki/ **1.** *n.* ключ; (piano) клавиша **2.** *adj.* ключевой

keyboard /'ki,bɔrd/ *n.* клавиатура

keyhole /'ki,houl/ *n.* замочная скважина

keystone /'ki,stoun/ *n.* Fig. краеугольный камень *m.*

khaki /'kæki/ *n.* хаки *neut. indecl.*

khan /kɑn/ *n.* хан

kick /kik/ **1.** *n.* пинок; (sports) удар **2.** *v.* пинать *impf.*, пнуть *pf.*; (of horse) брыкать(ся) *impf.*

kickoff /'kik,ɔf/ *n.* Fig. начало

kid[1] /kid/ *n.* (goat) козлёнок; Colloq. (child) ребёнок

kid[2] /kid/ *v.* Colloq. высмеивать *impf.*

kidnap /'kidnæp/ *v.* похищать *impf.*, похитить *pf.*; **—ping** *n.* похищение

kidnapper /'kidnæpər/ *n.* похититель

kidney /'kidni/ *n.* почка

kidney bean *n.* фасоль *f.*

kill /kil/ *v.* убивать *impf.*, убить *pf.*; **—er** *n.* убийца *m. & f.*

killing /'kiliŋ/ **1.** *n.* убийство **2.** *adj.* убийственный

kiln /kiln/ *n.* печь для обжига *f.*

kilo- *pref.* кило-

kilogram /'kilə,græm/ *n.* килограмм

kilometer /ki'lɒmitər/ *n.* километр

kilowatt /'kilə,wɒt/ *n.* киловатт

kilt /kilt/ *n.* шотландская юбка

kimono /kə'mounə/ *n.* кимоно *neut. indecl.*

kin /kin/ *n.* родня; родственники *pl.*

kind[1] /kaind/ *adj.* добрый

kind[2] /kaind/ *n.* вид; род; сорт

kindergarten /'kindər,gɑrdn/ *n.* детский сад

kindhearted /'kaind'hɑrtid/ *adj.* добросердечный

kindle /'kindl/ *v.t.* зажигать *impf.*, зажечь *pf.*

kindness /'kaindnis/ *n.* доброта

kindred /'kindrid/ *adj.* родной

king /kiŋ/ *n.* король *m.*

kingdom /'kiŋdəm/ *n.* царство

kingfisher /'kiŋ,fiʃər/ *n.* зимородок

kink /kiŋk/ *n.* узел; перегиб

kinship /'kinʃip/ *n.* родство

kinsman /'kinzmən/ *n.* родственник

kinswoman /'kinz,wumən/ *n.* родственница

kiosk /'kiɒsk/ *n.* киоск

kipper /'kipər/ *n.* копчёная сельдь *f.*

Kirghiz /'kir'giz/ *n.* киргиз, —ка

kiss /kis/ **1.** *n.* поцелуй **2.** *v.* целовать(ся) *impf.*, по-

kit /kit/ *n.* набор; комплект

kitchen /'kitʃən/ **1.** *n.* кухня **2.** *adj.* кухонный

kite /kait/ *n.* воздушный змей

kitten /'kitn/ *n.* котёнок

knack /næk/ *n.* умение, сноровка

knapsack /'næp,sæk/ *n.* рюкзак

knead /nid/ *v.* месить *impf.*

knee /ni/ *n.* колено

kneecap /'ni,kæp/ *n.* коленная чашечка

kneel /nil/ *v.* стоять на коленях *impf.*

kneepad /'ni,pæd/ *n.* наколенник

knickers /'nikərz/ *n.* бриджи *pl.*

knickknack /'nɪk,næk/ *n.*
безделушка

knife /naɪf/ *n.* нож

knight /naɪt/ *n.* рыцарь *m.*;
(*chess*) конь *m.*

knit /nɪt/ *v.* вязать *impf.*, с- *pf.*

knitted /'nɪtɪd/ *adj.* трикотажный

knitting /'nɪtɪŋ/ *n.* вязание

knob /nɒb/ *n.* шишка; (*handle*)
ручка; **—by** *adj.* шишковатый

knock /nɒk/ **1.** *n.* стук; (*blow*)
удар **2.** *v.* стучать (в + A)
impf., по- *pf.*; (*strike*) ударять
impf.

knockout /'nɒk,aʊt/ *n.* нокаут

knoll /noʊl/ *n.* холмик, бугор

knot /nɒt/ **1.** *n.* узел; (*in wood*)
сучок **2.** *v.* завязывать узлом
impf.; завязать *pf.*

knotty /'nɒti/ *adj.* узловатый;
(*problem*) запутанный

knout /naʊt/ *n.* кнут

know /noʊ/ *v.* знать *impf.*; **~
how** уметь *impf.*, с- *pf.*

know-how *n.* умение

knowing /'noʊɪŋ/ *adj.* (*cunning*)
хитрый; (*astute*) знающий

know-it-all *n.* всезнайка *m. & f.*

knowledge /'nɒlɪdʒ/ *n.* знание

knowledgeable /'nɒlɪdʒəbəl/
adj. знающий, осведомлённый

knuckle /'nʌkəl/ *n.* сустав пальца

kopeck /'koʊpɛk/ *n.* копейка

Korea /kə'riə/ *n.* Корея

Korean /kə'riən/ *n.* кореец,
кореянка

kosher /'koʊʃər/ *adj.* кошерный

Kremlin /'krɛmlɪn/ *n.* Кремль *m.*

Kyrgyzstan /,kɪrgə'stɑn/ *n.* Киргизстан

L

label /'leɪbəl/ **1.** *n.* ярлык,
этикетка **2.** *v.* наклеить ярлык
pf.

labor /'leɪbər/ **1.** *n.* труд; (*childbirth*) роды *pl.* **2.** *adj.* трудовой
3. *v.* трудиться *impf.*

laboratory /'læbrə,tɔri/ *n.*
лаборатория

labor camp *n.* лагерь *m.*

labored /'leɪbərd/ *adj.*
вымученный

laborer /'leɪbərər/ *n.* рабочий

labor pains *n.* родовые схватки
pl.

labor union *n.* профсоюз

labyrinth /'læbərɪnθ/ *n.*
лабиринт

lace /leɪs/ **1.** *n.* кружево; (*shoe*)
шнурок **2.** *v.* шнуровать *impf.*

laceration /,læsə'reɪʃən/ *n.*
разрыв; рваная рана

lack /læk/ **1.** *n.* недостаток;
отсутствие **2.** *v.* не хватать (*impers.* + D) *impf.*

lackadaisical /,lækə'deɪzɪkəl/ *adj.*
тёмный; нерадивый

lackey /'læki/ *n.* лакей

lackluster /'læk,lʌstər/ *adj.*
тусклый

laconic /lə'kɒnɪk/ *adj.* лаконичный

lacquer /'lækər/ **1.** *n.* лак **2.** *v.*
лакировать *impf.*, от- *pf.*

lad /læd/ *n.* (*boy*) мальчик;
(*young fellow*) парень *m.*

ladder /'lædər/ *n.* лестница

lade /leɪd/ *v.* нагружать *impf.*

laden /'leɪdn/ *adj.* нагруженный

ladle /'leɪdl/ **1.** *n.* черпак,
половник **2.** *v.* черпать *impf.*

lady /'leɪdi/ *n.* дама; леди *f. indecl.*

ladybug /'leɪdi,bʌg/ *n.* божья
коровка

lag /læg/ *v.* отставать (от + G)
impf., отстать *pf.*

lager /'lɑgər/ *n.* лёгкое пиво

lagoon /lə'gun/ *n.* лагуна

lair /lɛər/ *n.* логовище; (*bear*)
берлога; нора

laity /'leɪti/ *n.* миряне *pl.*

lake /leɪk/ *n.* озеро

lamb /læm/ *n.* ягнёнок; (*meat*)
баранина

lambaste /læm'beɪst/ *v.* Colloq.
лупить *impf.*

lame /leɪm/ *adj.* хромой

lament /lə'mɛnt/ **1.** *n.* плач **2.** *v.*
оплакивать *impf.*; **—able** *adj.*
прискорбный

laminated /'læmə,neɪtɪd/ *adj.*
слоистый, ламинированный

lamp /læmp/ *n.* лампа; фонарь
m.

lampoon /læm'pun/ *n.* пасквиль
m.

lamppost /'læmp,poʊst/ *n.*
фонарный столб

lampshade /'læmp,ʃeɪd/ *n.*
абажур

lance /læns/ *n.* пи́ка, копьё

land /lænd/ **1.** *n.* земля́; (*country*) страна́ **2.** *v.* (*aero.*) приземля́ть(ся) *impf.*, -ли́ться *pf.*; (*passengers*) выса́живать(ся) *impf.*, вы́садить(ся) *pf.*

landing /'lændɪŋ/ *n.* (*stairs*) площа́дка; (*ship*) вы́садка; (*plane*) поса́дка

landing strip *n.* взлётно-поса́дочная полоса́

landlady /'lænd,leidi/ *n.* хозя́йка

landlord /'lænd,lord/ *n.* хозя́ин

landmark /'lænd,mark/ *n.* ориенти́р

landowner /'lænd,ounər/ *n.* землевладе́лец, -лица

landscape /'lænd,skeip/ *n.* пейза́ж

lane /lein/ *n.* доро́жка; (*sports*) бегова́я доро́жка; (*highway*) полоса́

language /'læŋgwɪdʒ/ *n.* язы́к; речь *f.*

languid /'læŋgwid/ *adj.* вя́лый

languish /'læŋgwɪʃ/ *v.* вя́нуть, ча́хнуть *impf.*; —**ing** *adj.* то́мный

lanky /'læŋki/ *adj.* долговя́зый

lanolin /'lænlɪn/ *n.* ланоли́н

lantern /'læntərn/ *n.* фона́рь *m.*

lap /læp/ *n.* коле́ни *pl.*; ло́но; (*sports*) эта́п, круг

lapel /lə'pel/ *n.* ла́цкан

lapse /læps/ **1.** *n.* недосмо́тр, ля́псус; (*interval*) промежу́ток **2.** *v.* истека́ть *impf.*, исте́чь *pf.*

laptop computer /'læp,top/ *n.* ла́птоп; доро́жный компью́тер

larceny /'larsəni/ *n.* воровство́

lard /lard/ *n.* са́ло

larder /'lardər/ *n.* кладова́я

large /lardʒ/ *adj.* кру́пный, большо́й; **at ~** на свобо́де

large-scale *adj.* крупномасшта́бный

largess /lar'dʒes/ *n.* ще́дрость

lark¹ /lark/ *n.* (*bird*) жа́воронок

lark² /lark/ *n.* (*prank*) прока́за

larva /'larvə/ *n.* личи́нка

laryngitis /,lærən'dʒaitis/ *n.* ларинги́т

larynx /'lærɪŋks/ *n.* горта́нь *f.*

lascivious /lə'sɪvɪəs/ *adj.* похотли́вый

laser /'leizər/ *n.* ла́зер; **~ printer** ла́зерный при́нтер

lash /læʃ/ **1.** *n.* уда́р пле́тью; (*eyelash*) ресни́ца **2.** *v.* хлеста́ть *impf.*; —**ing** *n.* по́рка

lassitude /'læsɪ,tud/ *n.* вя́лость

lasso /'læsou/ *n.* арка́н

last¹ /læst/ **1.** *adj.* после́дний; про́шлый **2.** *adv.* по́сле всех; **at ~** наконе́ц

last² /læst/ *v.* продолжа́ться *impf.*, продо́лжиться *pf.*

lasting /'læstɪŋ/ *adj.* дли́тельный; (*durable*) про́чный

latch /lætʃ/ *n.* задви́жка, запо́р

late /leit/ **1.** *adj.* по́здний; (*deceased*) поко́йный **2.** *adv.* по́здно; **be ~** опа́здывать *impf.*, опозда́ть *pf.*

lately /'leitli/ *adv.* за (*or* в) после́днее вре́мя

latent /'leitnt/ *adj.* скры́тый

later /'leitər/ *adv.* пото́м

lateral /'lætərəl/ *adj.* боково́й

latex /'leitɛks/ *n.* ла́текс

lathe /leið/ *n.* тока́рный стано́к

lather /'læðər/ **1.** *n.* мы́льная пе́на **2.** *v.* намы́ливать *impf.*, намы́лить *pf.*

Latin /'lætn/ **1.** *n.* лати́нский язы́к **2.** *adj.* лати́нский

latitude /'lætɪ,tud/ *n.* широта́

latrine /lə'trin/ *n.* отхо́жее ме́сто

latter /'lætər/ *adj.* после́дний

lattice /'lætɪs/ *n.* решётка

Latvia /'lætvɪə/ *n.* Ла́твия

Latvian /'lætvɪən/ **1.** *adj.* латви́йский **2.** *n.* латви́ец, -и́йка

laud /lɔd/ *v.* хвали́ть *impf.*, по-; —**able** *adj.* похва́льный

laugh /læf/ **1.** *n.* смех **2.** *v.* смея́ться (над + I) *impf.*; —**able** *adj.* смешно́й

laughingstock /'læfɪŋ,stok/ *n.* посме́шище

laughter /'læftər/ *n.* смех

launch¹ /lɔntʃ/ *n.* (*boat*) ка́тер

launch² /lɔntʃ/ **1.** *n.* за́пуск **2.** *v.t.* спуска́ть на́ воду; (*rocket*) де́лать за́пуск *impf.*

launcher /'lɔntʃər/ *n.* (*for missiles*) пускова́я устано́вка

launder /'lɔndər/ *v.* стира́ть *impf.*, вы́-

Laundromat /'lɔndrə,mæt/ *n.* сти́рка самообслу́живания

laundry /'lɔndri/ *n.* (*place*) пра́чечная; (*articles*) бельё

laurel /'lɔrəl/ *n.* лавр

lava /'lavə/ *n.* ла́ва

lavatory /'lævə,tɔri/ *n.* убо́рная

lavender /'lævəndər/ *n.* лава́нда

lavish /'lævɪʃ/ **1.** *adj.* ще́дрый **2.** *v.* расточа́ть (+ D) *impf.*, -чи́ть *pf.*

law /lɔ/ n. закон; право
law-abiding adj. законопослушный
lawbreaker /'lɔ,breikər/ n. правонарушитель
law court n. суд; здание суда
lawful /'lɔfəl/ adj. законный
lawless /'lɔlis/ adj. беззаконный
lawn /lɔn/ n. газон
lawn mower n. косилка
lawsuit /'lɔ,sut/ n. судебный процесс
lawyer /'lɔyər/ n. адвокат, юрист
lax /læks/ adj. слабый, вялый
laxative /'læksətiv/ n. слабительное средство
laxity /'læksiti/ n. небрежность
lay[1] /lei/ adj. (secular) светский
lay[2] /lei/ v. класть impf., положить pf.
layer /'leiər/ n. 1. слой, пласт 2. v. наслаивать impf.
layman /'leimən/ n. мирянин; (nonexpert) непрофессионал
layoff /'lei,ɔf/ n. увольнение
layout /'lei,aut/ n. оформление
laze /leiz/ v. бездельничать impf.
lazy /'leizi/ adj. ленивый
lead[1] /led/ n. (metal) свинец
lead[2] /lid/ 1. n. (example) пример; (leadership) руководство; (first place) первое место; (theat.) главная роль f. 2. v. (guide) водить indet., вести det., по- pf.
leaded fuel n. этилированное топливо
leaden /'ledn/ adj. свинцовый
leader /'lidər/ n. руководитель, —ница; лидер; **—ship** n. руководство
leading /'lidiŋ/ adj. ведущий; выдающийся
leaf /lif/ n. лист
leaflet /'liflit/ n. листовка
league /lig/ n. лига; союз
leak /lik/ 1. n. утечка 2. v. течь impf.
lean[1] /lin/ adj. худой; (meat) постный
lean[2] /lin/ v. наклоняться impf., -нуться pf.
leaning /'liniŋ/ n. склонность
leap /lip/ 1. n. прыжок, скачок 2. v. прыгать impf., прыгнуть pf.
leapfrog /'lip,frɔg/ n. чехарда
leap year n. високосный год

learn /lɜrn/ v. учиться impf.
learned /'lɜrnid/ adj. учёный
learner /'lɜrnər/ n. учащийся
learning /'lɜrniŋ/ n. учёность; учение
lease[1] /lis/ n. аренда, сдача в аренду
leaseholder /'lis,houldər/ n. арендатор
leash /liʃ/ n. поводок
least /list/ 1. adj. наименьший 2. adv. меньше всего; **at ~** по крайней мере; **not in the ~** ничуть
leather /'leðər/ 1. n. кожа 2. adj. кожаный
leave[1] /liv/ n. (absence) отпуск; (permission) разрешение
leave[2] /liv/ v.i. уходить; уезжать impf.; v.t. оставлять impf., оставить pf.
leave-taking n. прощание
lecherous /'letʃərəs/ adj. развратный, распутный
lectern /'lektərn/ n. (church) аналой; (speaker's) пюпитр
lecture /'lektʃər/ 1. n. лекция 2. v. читать лекцию impf.
lecturer /'lektʃərər/ n. лектор
ledge /ledʒ/ n. выступ
ledger /'ledʒər/ n. гроссбух
leech /litʃ/ n. пиявка
leek /lik/ n. лук-порей
leer /liər/ 1. n. косой взгляд 2. v. смотреть искоса impf.
leeward /'liwərd/ n. подветренная сторона
leeway /'li,wei/ n. Fig. свобода действий
left /left/ 1. adj. левый 2. adv. налево; слева
left-handed person n. левша m. & f.
leftover /'left,ouvər/ n. остаток
left-wing adj. левый
leg /leg/ n. нога; (of furniture) ножка; (of trip) этап
legacy /'legəsi/ n. наследство
legal /'ligəl/ adj. законный; юридический; судебный
legality /li'gæliti/ n. легальность
legalize /'ligə,laiz/ v. легализировать impf. & pf.
legend /'ledʒənd/ n. легенда; **—ary** adj. легендарный
leggings /'legiŋz/ n. рейтузы pl.
legible /'ledʒəbəl/ adj. разборчивый, чёткий
legion /'lidʒən/ n. легион

legislate /'lɛdʒɪs,leit/ v. издавать законы impf.

legislation /,lɛdʒɪs'leiʃən/ n. законодательство

legislative /'lɛdʒɪs,leitɪv/ adj. законодательный

legislator /'lɛdʒɪs,leitər/ n. законодатель

legitimate /lɪ'dʒɪtəmit/ adj. законный

legitimize /lɪ'dʒɪtə,maiz/ v. узаконивать impf., -конить pf.

leisure /'liʒər/ n. досуг; свободное время neut.; **—ly** adj. неторопливый; спокойный

lemon /'lɛmən/ **1.** n. лимон, цитрон **2.** adj. лимонный

lemonade /,lɛmə'neid/ n. лимонад

lend /lɛnd/ v. давать взаймы; одалживать impf., одолжить pf.

length /lɛŋkθ/ n. длина; продолжительность

lengthen /'lɛŋkθən/ v. удлинять(ся) impf., удлинить(ся) pf.

lengthwise /'lɛŋkθ,waiz/ adv. в длину

lengthy /'lɛŋkθi/ adj. растянутый

leniency /'liniənsi/ n. снисходительность

lenient /'liniənt/ adj. снисходительный

lens /lɛnz/ n. линза; (photog.) объектив; (anat.) хрусталик

Lent /lɛnt/ n. Великий Пост

lentil /'lɛntil/ n. чечевица

leopard /'lɛpərd/ n. леопард

leotard /'liə,tɑrd/ n. трико neut. indecl.

leprosy /'lɛprəsi/ n. проказа

lesbian /'lɛzbiən/ **1.** n. лесбиянка **2.** adj. лесбийский

lesion /'liʒən/ n. повреждение

less /lɛs/ **1.** adj. меньший **2.** adv. меньше; менее **3.** prep. без (+ G)

lessee /lɛ'si/ n. съёмщик

lessen /'lɛsən/ v. уменьшать(ся) impf., уменьшиться pf.

lesser /'lɛsər/ adj. меньший

lesson /'lɛsən/ n. урок

let /lɛt/ v. позволять impf., позволить pf.; ~ **be** оставлять в покое impf.; ~ **know** давать знать impf.

lethal /'liθəl/ adj. смертельный

lethargic /lə'θɑrdʒik/ adj. летаргический

letter /'lɛtər/ n. письмо; (alphabet) буква

letterhead /'lɛtər,hɛd/ n. фирменная бумага

lettering /'lɛtərɪŋ/ n. шрифт

lettuce /'lɛtis/ n. салат, латук

letup /'lɛt,ʌp/ n. передышка; прекращение

leukemia /lu'kimiə/ n. лейкемия

level /'lɛvəl/ **1.** adj. ровный **2.** n. уровень m. **3.** v. уравнивать impf., уравнять pf.

levelheaded /'lɛvəl'hɛdid/ adj. уравновешенный

lever /'lɛvər/ n. рычаг

leverage /'lɛvərɪdʒ/ n. действие рычага; Fig. влияние

levity /'lɛviti/ n. легкомыслие

levy /'lɛvi/ **1.** n. сбор **2.** v. облагать налогом impf.

lewd /lud/ adj. похотливый

lexicon /'lɛksi,kɒn/ n. словарь m.

liability /,laiə'bɪliti/ n. ответственность; **assets and ~s** активы и пассив

liable /'laiəbəl/ adj. ответственный; подверженный (+ D)

liaison /li'eizɒn/ n. связь f.

liar /'laiər/ n. лгун, лгунья

libel /'laibəl/ **1.** n. клевета **2.** v. клеветать (на + A) impf., на- pf.; **—ous** adj. клеветнический

liberal /'lɪbərəl/ adj. щедрый; (polit.) либеральный; (education) гуманитарный

liberate /'lɪbə,reit/ v. освобождать impf., освободить pf.

liberation /,lɪbə'reiʃən/ n. освобождение

libertine /'lɪbər,tin/ n. распутник

liberty /'lɪbərti/ n. свобода

librarian /lai'brɛəriən/ n. библиотекарь m.

library /'lai,brɛri/ n. библиотека

libretto /lɪ'brɛtou/ n. либретто neut. indecl.

license /'laisəns/ n. разрешение; лицензия; **driver's ~** водительские права pl.

licensed /'laisənst/ adj. законный

license plate n. номерной знак

licentious /lai'sɛnʃəs/ adj. распущенный

lichen /'laikən/ n. лишайник

lick /lɪk/ v. лизать impf., лизнуть pf.

licorice /'lɪkərɪʃ, -rɪs/ n. лакрица

lid /lɪd/ n. крышка; (eye) веко

lie¹ /laɪ/ **1.** n. ложь f. **2.** v. (*tell untruths*) лгать impf., co- pf.

lie² /laɪ/ v. (*recline*) лежа́ть impf.; ~ **down** ложи́ться impf.; лечь pf.

lien /lɪn/ n. пра́во удержа́ния

lieu /lu/ n.: **in ~ of** prep. вме́сто (+ G)

lieutenant /luˈtɛnənt/ n. лейтена́нт

life /laɪf/ n. жизнь f.

life belt n. спаса́тельный по́яс

lifeboat /ˈlaɪf.bout/ n. спаса́тельная ло́дка

life buoy n. спаса́тельный круг

lifeguard /ˈlaɪf.gɑrd/ n. спаса́тель

life insurance n. страхова́ние жи́зни

life jacket n. спаса́тельный жиле́т

lifeless /ˈlaɪflɪs/ adj. безжи́зненный

lifelike /ˈlaɪf.laɪk/ adj. сло́вно живо́й

lifelong /ˈlaɪf.lɔŋ/ adj. пожи́зненный

lifesaver /ˈlaɪf.seɪvər/ n. спаси́тель, —ница

life-size adj. в натура́льную величину́

lifestyle /ˈlaɪf.staɪl/ n. о́браз жи́зни

lift /lɪft/ v. поднима́ть(ся) impf., подня́ть(ся) pf.; (*remove*) снима́ть impf.

liftoff /ˈlɪft.ɔf/ n. (*rocket*) пуск

ligament /ˈlɪgəmənt/ n. свя́зка

light¹ /laɪt/ adj. лёгкий

light² /laɪt/ **1.** adj. (*color*) све́тлый **2.** n. свет, освеще́ние **3.** v. (*illuminate*) освеща́ть impf., -ти́ть pf.; (*ignite*) зажига́ть(ся) impf., заже́чь(ся) pf.

lighten /ˈlaɪtn/ v. облегча́ть(ся) impf., облегчи́ть(ся) pf.

lighter /ˈlaɪtər/ n. зажига́лка

lighthearted /ˈlaɪtˈhɑrtɪd/ adj. беззабо́тный, беспе́чный

lighthouse /ˈlaɪt.haus/ n. мая́к

lighting /ˈlaɪtɪŋ/ n. освеще́ние

lightning /ˈlaɪtnɪŋ/ n. мо́лния

lightweight /ˈlaɪt.weɪt/ **1.** adj. легкове́с **2.** adj. легкове́сный

light-year n. светово́й год

like¹ /laɪk/ adj. похо́жий

like² /laɪk/ v. нра́виться (*impers.* + D); люби́ть impf.

likelihood /ˈlaɪkli.hud/ n. вероя́тность

likely /ˈlaɪkli/ adj. вероя́тно

liken /ˈlaɪkən/ v. сра́внивать (с + I) impf.

likeness /ˈlaɪknɪs/ n. схо́дство; ко́пия

likewise /ˈlaɪk.waɪz/ adv. та́кже

liking /ˈlaɪkɪŋ/ n. симпа́тия; вкус

lilac /ˈlaɪlək/ n. сире́нь f.

lily /ˈlɪli/ n. ли́лия

limb /lɪm/ n. член

lime¹ /laɪm/ n. и́звесть f.

lime² /laɪm/ n. (*fruit*) лайм

limestone /ˈlaɪm.stoun/ n. известня́к

limit /ˈlɪmɪt/ **1.** n. преде́л; грани́ца **2.** v. ограни́чивать impf., ограни́чить pf.

limitation /ˌlɪmɪˈteɪʃən/ n. ограниче́ние

limitless /ˈlɪmɪtlɪs/ adj. безграни́чный

limousine /ˈlɪməˌzin/ n. лимузи́н

limp¹ /lɪmp/ adj. (*soft*) вя́лый

limp² /lɪmp/ **1.** n. хромота́ **2.** v. хрома́ть impf.

limpid /ˈlɪmpɪd/ adj. прозра́чный

linchpin /ˈlɪntʃˌpɪn/ n. чека́

line /laɪn/ **1.** n. ли́ния; (*print*) строка́; (*queue*) о́чередь f.; (*limit*) грани́ца; (*row*) ряд **2.** v. линова́ть impf.

lineage /ˈlɪniɪdʒ/ n. родосло́вная

linear /ˈlɪniər/ adj. лине́йный

lined /laɪnd/ adj. линёванный; (*face*) морщи́нистый

linen /ˈlɪnən/ n. полотно́; (*bedding*) (посте́льное) бельё

liner /ˈlaɪnər/ n. пассажи́рский парохо́д

lineup /ˈlaɪnˌʌp/ n. расстано́вка

linger /ˈlɪŋgər/ v. заде́рживаться impf., задержа́ться pf.

lingerie /ˌlɑnʒəˈreɪ/ n. же́нское бельё

lingering /ˈlɪŋgərɪŋ/ adj. медли́тельный; затяжно́й

lingo /ˈlɪŋgou/ n. жарго́н

linguist /ˈlɪŋgwɪst/ n. лингви́ст

linguistics /lɪŋˈgwɪstɪks/ n. лингви́стика; языкозна́ние

lining /ˈlaɪnɪŋ/ n. подкла́дка

link /lɪŋk/ **1.** n. звено́; связь f. **2.** v. соединя́ть(ся) impf., -ни́ть(ся) pf.

linoleum /lɪˈnouliəm/ n. лино́леум

lintel /ˈlɪntl/ n. перемы́чка

lion /ˈlaɪən/ **1.** n. лев **2.** adj. льви́ный; **—ess** n. льви́ца

lionize /'laɪə,naɪz/ *v.* чéствовать *impf.*

lip /lɪp/ *n.* губá

lipstick /'lɪp,stɪk/ *n.* губнáя помáда

liquefy /'lɪkwə,faɪ/ *v.* сжижáть(ся); разжижáть(ся) *impf.*

liqueur /lɪ'kзr/ *n.* ликёр

liquid /'lɪkwɪd/ *n.* жидкость 2. *adj.* жидкий; (*econ.*) ликвидный

liquidate /'lɪkwɪ,deɪt/ *adj.* ликвидировать *impf.* & *pf.*

liquidation /,lɪkwɪ'deɪʃən/ *n.* ликвидáция

liquor /'lɪkər/ *n.* спиртнóй напиток

lisp /lɪsp/ *v.* шепелявить *impf.*

list¹ /lɪst/ *n.* список 2. *v.* составлять список *impf.*

list² /lɪst/ *v.* крениться *impf.*

listen /'lɪsən/ *v.* слушать *impf.*

listener /'lɪsənər/ *n.* слушатель

listless /'lɪstlɪs/ *adj.* апатичный

litany /'lɪtni/ *n.* литáния

liter /'litər/ *n.* литр

literacy /'lɪtərəsi/ *n.* грáмотность

literal /'lɪtərəl/ *adj.* буквáльный

literary /'lɪtə,rɛri/ *adj.* литерату́рный

literate /'lɪtərɪt/ *adj.* грáмотный

literature /'lɪtərətʃər/ *n.* литератýра

lithe /laɪð/ *adj.* гибкий

lithograph /'lɪθə,græf/ *n.* литогрáфия

Lithuania /,lɪθu'einiə/ *n.* Литвá

Lithuanian /,lɪθu'einiən/ *n.* литóвский; *n.* литóвец, -вка

litigant /'lɪtɪgənt/ *n.* судя́щийся

litigate /'lɪtɪ,geɪt/ *v.* судиться *impf.*

litigation /,lɪtɪ'geɪʃən/ *n.* судéбное дéло; иск; процéсс

litmus /'lɪtməs/ *n.* лáкмус

litter /'lɪtər/ *n.* 1. (*stretcher*) носилки *pl.*; (*disorder*) беспоря́док; (*animals*) помёт 2. *v.* (*scatter*) разбрáсывать *impf.*, разбросáть *pf.*

little /'lɪtl/ *adj.* 1. мáленький; (*quantity*) мáло (+ *G*) 2. *adv.* мáло; немнóго

liturgy /'lɪtərdʒi/ *n.* литургия

live¹ /lɪv/ *v.* жить *impf.*

live² /laɪv/, **lively** /'laɪvli/ *adj.* живóй

livelihood /'laɪvli,hud/ *n.* срéдства к жизни *pl.*

liveliness /'laɪvlinɪs/ *n.* живость

liven /'laɪvən/ *v.* оживля́ть(ся) *impf.*, -вить(ся) *pf.*

liver /'lɪvər/ *n.* пéчень *f.*; (*cul.*) печёнка

livery /'lɪvəri/ *n.* ливрéя

livestock /'laɪv,stɒk/ *n.* скот

livid /'lɪvɪd/ *adj.* (*angry*) разъярённый

living /'lɪvɪŋ/ 1. *adj.* живóй 2. *n.* срéдства к жизни *pl.*; ~ quarters жильё; ~ room гостиная

lizard /'lɪzərd/ *n.* я́щерица

load /loud/ 1. *n.* груз; тя́жесть 2. *v.* грузить *impf.*, на-, по- *pf.*; (*gun*) заряжáть *impf.*

loaf¹ /louf/ *n.* бухáнка, каравáй

loaf² /louf/ *n.* бездéльничать *impf.*; —er *n.* бездéльник

loan /loun/ 1. *n.* заём 2. *v.* давáть взаймы́ *impf.*

loath /louθ/ *adj.*: be ~ to *v.* не хотéть *impf.*

loathe /louð/ *v.* ненавидеть *impf.*; —ing *n.* отвращéние; —some *adj.* отвратительный

lobby /'lɒbi/ *n.* прихóжая

lobbyist /'lɒbiɪst/ *n.* лоббист

lobe /loub/ *n.* (*ear*) мóчка (ухá)

lobster /'lɒbstər/ *n.* омáр

local /'loukəl/ *adj.* мéстный

locality /lou'kælɪti/ *n.* мéстность

localize /'loukə,laɪz/ *v.* локализовáть *impf.* and *pf.*

locate /'loukeɪt/ *v.* определя́ть местонахождéние *impf.*; be ~d находиться *impf.*

location /lou'keɪʃən/ *n.* местонахождéние

lock¹ /lɒk/ 1. *n.* замóк 2. *v.* запирáть(ся) *impf.*, запере́ть(ся) *pf.*

lock² /lɒk/ *n.* (*of hair*) лóкон

locker /'lɒkər/ *n.* шкáфчик

locket /'lɒkɪt/ *n.* медальóн

locksmith /'lɒk,smɪθ/ *n.* слéсарь *f.*

locomotion /,loukə'mouʃən/ *n.* передвижéние

locust /'loukəst/ *n.* саранчá

lodge /lɒdʒ/ 1. *n.* дóмик; сторóжка 2. *v.* помещáть *impf.*, -стить *pf.*; (*complaint*) подавáть *impf.*, подáть *pf.*

lodger /'lɒdʒər/ *n.* жилéц, -лица

lodging /'lɒdʒɪŋ/ *n.* помещéние

loft /lɒft/ *n.* чердáк

lofty /'lɒfti/ *adj.* возвы́шенный

log /lɒg/ n. бревно́, чурба́н

logarithm /'lɒgə,rɪðəm/ n. логари́фм

logbook /'lɒg,bʊk/ n. (aero.) бортово́й журна́л; (registration) формуля́р

log cabin n. сруб

logic /'lɒdʒɪk/ n. ло́гика; **—al** adj. логи́ческий

login /'lɒg,ɪn/ n. (comput.) вход в сеть

logout /'lɒg,aʊt/ n. (comput.) вы́ход из сети́

loin /lɔɪn/ n. поясни́ца; (cul.) филе́йная часть f.

loiter /'lɔɪtər/ v. слоня́ться impf.

lollipop /'lɒli,pɒp/ n. леденец на па́лочке

lone /loʊn/ adj. одино́кий

loneliness /'loʊnlɪnɪs/ n. одино́чество

long¹ /lɒŋ/ 1. adj. до́лгий; дли́нный 2. adv. до́лго

long² /lɒŋ/ v. (miss) тоскова́ть (по + D)

long-distance adj. на да́льнее расстоя́ние; (intercity; international) междугоро́дный; междунаро́дный

longevity /lɒn'dʒevɪti/ n. долгове́чность

longing /'lɒŋɪŋ/ n. тоска́; стра́стное жела́ние

longitude /'lɒndʒɪ,tud/ n. долгота́

longstanding /lɒŋ'stændɪŋ/ adj. да́вний; долголе́тний

long-term adj. долгосро́чный

look /lʊk/ 1. n. (glance) взгляд; (appearance) вид 2. v. смотре́ть impf., по- pf.; (appear) вы́глядеть impf.

lookout /'lʊk,aʊt/ n.: **be on the ~** быть насторо́же impf.

loom¹ /lum/ n. тка́цкий стано́к

loom² /lum/ v. надвига́ться impf.

loop /lup/ n. петля́

loophole /'lup,hoʊl/ n. лазе́йка

loose /lus/ adj. свобо́дный; не натя́нутый; сла́бый

looseleaf binder /'lus,lif/ n. скоросшива́тель

loosen /'lusən/ v. развя́зывать impf., развяза́ть pf.

loot /lut/ 1. n. добы́ча 2. v. гра́бить impf., о- pf.

lopsided /'lɒp'saɪdɪd/ adj. (crooked) криво́й, кривобо́кий

loquacious /loʊ'kweɪʃəs/ adj. болтли́вый, говорли́вый

lord /lɔrd/ n. госпо́дин; (rank) лорд; cap. (eccles.) Госпо́дь m.

lore /lɔr/ n. зна́ния pl.

lose /luz/ v. теря́ть impf., по- pf.; (game, etc.) прои́грывать impf., проигра́ть pf.

loss /lɒs/ n. убы́ток, поте́ря; (in game) про́игрыш

lot /lɒt/ n. (fate) жре́бий, у́часть f.; (land) уча́сток; **a ~ of** мно́го (+ G)

lotion /'loʊʃən/ n. лосьо́н

lottery /'lɒtəri/ n. лотере́я

loud /laʊd/ adj. гро́мкий

loudmouthed /'laʊd,maʊðd/ adj. крикли́вый

loudspeaker /'laʊd,spikər/ n. громкоговори́тель; дина́мик

lounge /laʊndʒ/ 1. n. (hotel) вести́бюль m. 2. v. слоня́ться; безде́льничать impf.

lounger /'laʊndʒər/ n. ло́дырь m.

louse /laʊs/ n. вошь f.

lousy /'laʊzi/ adj. вши́вый; Colloq. проти́вный, отврати́тельный

lout /laʊt/ n. грубия́н; хам

lovable /'lʌvəbəl/ adj. ми́лый

love /lʌv/ 1. n. любо́вь f.; **in ~** adj. влюблённый; **fall in ~** влюби́ться (в + A) pf. & люби́ть impf.; **~ affair** рома́н

lovely /'lʌvli/ adj. преле́стный

lovemaking /'lʌv,meɪkɪŋ/ n. половы́е сноше́ния

lover /'lʌvər/ n. любо́вник, -ница; (enthusiast) люби́тель

low /loʊ/ adj. ни́зкий; (quiet) ти́хий

lower /'loʊər/ 1. v. снижа́ть; понижа́ть impf., -ни́зить pf. 2. adj. ни́жний

lowland /'loʊlənd/ n. ни́зменность, низи́на

low-pitched adj. ни́зкий

loyal /'lɔɪəl/ adj. ве́рный; **—ty** n. ве́рность

lozenge /'lɒzɪndʒ/ n. лепёшка

lubricant /'lubrɪkənt/ n. сма́зка

lubricate /'lubri,keɪt/ v. сма́зывать impf., сма́зать pf.

lubrication /,lubri'keɪʃən/ n. сма́зка

lucid /'lusɪd/ adj. я́сный

luck /lʌk/ n. сча́стье; уда́ча

luckily /'lʌkəli/ adv. к сча́стью

lucky /'lʌki/ adj. счастли́вый

lucrative /'lukrətɪv/ adj. прибыльный

ludicrous /'ludɪkrəs/ adj. смешной

lug /lʌg/ v. волочить impf.

luggage /'lʌgɪdʒ/ n. багаж

lugubrious /lu'gubrɪəs/ adj. печальный, мрачный

lukewarm /'luk'wɔrm/ adj. тепловатый

lull /lʌl/ **1.** n. затишье **2.** v. убаюкивать impf., убаюкать pf.

lullaby /'lʌlə,baɪ/ n. колыбельная песня

lumber /'lʌmbər/ n. лесоматериал

lumberjack /'lʌmbər,dʒæk/ n. лесоруб

lumberyard /'lʌmbər,yard/ n. лесной склад

luminary /'lumə,nɛri/ n. светило

luminous /'lumənəs/ adj. светлый, светящийся

lump /lʌmp/ n. ком; (of sugar) кусок; (swelling) шишка

lunacy /'lunəsi/ n. помешательство

lunar /'lunər/ adj. лунный

lunatic /'lunətɪk/ n. сумасшедший

lunch /lʌntʃ/ **1.** n. обед **2.** v. обедать impf., по- pf.; ~ hour обеденный перерыв

lung /lʌŋ/ n. лёгкое

lunge /lʌndʒ/ **1.** n. выпад **2.** v. делать выпад impf., с- pf

lure /lur/ **1.** n. приманка **2.** v. приманивать impf., приманить pf.

lurid /'lurɪd/ adj. жуткий

lurk /lɜrk/ v. скрываться impf.

luscious /'lʌʃəs/ adj. сочный

lush /lʌʃ/ adj. пышный

lust /lʌst/ n. похоть f.; —ful adj. похотливый

lustrous /'lʌstrəs/ adj. глянцевитый; блестящий

lute /lut/ n. лютня

luxuriant /lʌg'ʒurɪənt/ adj. буйный, пышный

luxurious /lʌg'ʒurɪəs/ adj. роскошный

luxury /'lʌkʃəri/ n. роскошь f.

lying /'laɪɪŋ/ n. враньё

lymph /lɪmf/ n. лимфа

lynch /lɪntʃ/ v. линчевать impf. & pf.

lynx /lɪŋks/ n. рысь f.

lyric /'lɪrɪk/ n. лирика f.; pl. текст (песни); —al adj. лирический

M

macabre /mə'kabrə/ adj. жуткий

macaroni /,mækə'rouni/ n. макароны pl.

mace /meis/ n. (weapon) булава; (staff of office) жезл

machinations /,mækɪ'neiʃənz/ n. козни; махинации pl.

machine /mə'ʃin/ **1.** n. машина, механизм **2.** adj. машинный

machine gun n. автомат; пулемёт

machinery /mə'ʃinəri/ n. машины, механизмы pl.

machinist /mə'ʃinɪst/ n. машинист; станочник

mackerel /'mækərəl/ n. макрель f.

mackintosh /'mækɪn,tɒʃ/ n. непромокаемое пальто neut. indecl.

mad /mæd/ adj. сумасшедший

madam /'mædəm/ n. мадам f. indecl., госпожа

madden /'mædn/ v. бесить impf., вз- pf.

maddening /'mædnɪŋ/ adj. невыносимый

madhouse /'mæd,haus/ n. сумасшедший дом

madman /'mæd,mæn/ n. сумасшедший

madness /'mædnɪs/ n. сумасшествие

maestro /'maistrou/ n. маэстро m. indecl.

magazine /,mægə'zin/ **1.** n. журнал **2.** adj. журнальный

maggot /'mægət/ n. личинка

magic /'mædʒɪk/ **1.** n. волшебство **2.** adj. волшебный

magician /mə'dʒɪʃən/ n. волшебник; (entertainer) фокусник

magistrate /'mædʒə,streit/ n. судья m.

magnanimity /,mægnə'nimiti/ n. великодушие

magnanimous /mæg'nænəməs/ adj. великодушный

magnesium /mæg'niziəm/ n. магний

magnet /'mægnɪt/ n. магнит; —ic adj. магнитный

magnetize /'mægnɪ,taiz/ v. намагни́чивать impf., -ни́тить pf.

magnification /,mægnəfɪ'keiʃən/ n. увеличе́ние; усиле́ние

magnificence /mæg'nɪfəsəns/ n. великоле́пие

magnificent /mæg'nɪfəsənt/ adj. великоле́пный

magnify /'mægnə,fai/ v. увели́чивать impf., увели́чить pf.; —**ing glass** n. лу́па

magnitude /'mægnɪ,tud/ n. величина́; ва́жность

magpie /'mæg,pai/ n. (bird) соро́ка

mahatma /mə'hɑtmə/ n. маха́тма

mahogany /mə'hɒgəni/ n. кра́сное де́рево

maid /meid/ n. прислу́га, го́рничная

maiden /'meidn/ adj. (unmarried) незаму́жняя; (first) пе́рвый; ~ **name** де́вичья фами́лия

mail /meil/ 1. n. по́чта 2. adj. почто́вый 3. v. посыла́ть по́чтой impf., посла́ть pf.

mailbox /'meil,bɒks/ n. почто́вый я́щик

mailman /'meil,mæn/ n. почтальо́н

mail order n. почто́вый зака́з

maim /meim/ v. кале́чить impf., ис- pf.

main /mein/ adj. гла́вный; осно́вно́й; (road) магистра́льный; —**ly** adv. гла́вным о́бразом

mainframe /'mein,freim/ n. (comput.) се́рвер

mainland /'mein,lænd/ n. матери́к

main line /'mein,lain/ n. (railroad) магистра́ль f.

mainstay /'mein,stei/ n. Fig. гла́вная опо́ра

maintain /mein'tein/ v. подде́рживать impf., -держа́ть pf.; (assert) утвержда́ть impf.

maintenance /'meintənəns/ n. подде́ржка; содержа́ние; (tech.) обслу́живание

maize /meiz/ n. ма́ис, кукуру́за

majestic /mə'dʒestɪk/ adj. вели́чественный

majesty /'mædʒəsti/ n. вели́чественность; (title) вели́чество

major /'meidʒər/ **1.** adj. бо́льший; гла́вный; (mus.)

мажо́рный **2.** n. (mil.) майо́р; (mus.) мажо́р **3.** v. (college) специализи́роваться impf.

majority /mə'dʒɔriti/ n. большинство́

make /meik/ **1.** v. де́лать impf., с- pf.; производи́ть impf., -вести́ pf.; (earn) зараба́тывать impf., зарабо́тать pf. **2.** n. ма́рка

make-believe n. притво́рство; вы́думка

makeshift /'meik,ʃift/ adj. вре́менный; самоде́льный

makeup /'meik,ʌp/ n. косме́тика; (theat.) грим; (composition) соста́в; сбор

maladjusted /,mælə'dʒʌstid/ adj. неприспосо́бленный

malady /'mælədi/ n. боле́знь f.

malaise /mæ'leiz/ n. недомога́ние

malaria /mə'leəriə/ n. маляри́я

male /meil/ **1.** adj. мужско́й **2.** n. мужчи́на m.; (zool.) саме́ц

malevolence /mə'levələns/ n. недоброжела́тельство

malevolent /mə'levələnt/ adj. недоброжела́тельный

malfunction /mæl'fʌŋkʃən/ n. отка́з

malice /'mælis/ n. зло́ба

malicious /mə'liʃəs/ adj. злой; зло́бный

malign /mə'lain/ v. клевета́ть (на + A) impf., на- pf.

malignant /mə'lignənt/ adj. (med.) злока́чественный

malingerer /mə'liŋgərər/ n. симуля́нт, —ка

malingering /mə'liŋgəriŋ/ n. симуля́ция

mall /mɔl/ n. алле́я; shopping ~ торго́вый центр

malleable /'mæliəbəl/ adj. ко́вкий

mallet /'mælɪt/ n. деревя́нный молото́к

malnutrition /,mælnu'triʃən/ n. недоеда́ние

malt /mɔlt/ n. со́лод

maltreatment /mæl'tritmənt/ n. плохо́е обраще́ние

mammal /'mæməl/ n. млекопита́ющее

mammoth /'mæməθ/ **1.** n. ма́монт **2.** adj. огро́мный

man /mæn/ n. челове́к; (male) мужчи́на m.

manacles /'mænəkəlz/ n. нару́чники pl.

manage /'mænɪdʒ/ v. управля́ть (+ I) impf.; (cope) справля́ться impf., спра́виться pf.

management /'mænɪdʒmənt/ n. управле́ние; администра́ция

manager /'mænɪdʒər/ n. заве́дующий; дире́ктор; ме́неджер

managerial /ˌmænɪ'dʒɪərɪəl/ adj. администрати́вный

mandate /'mændeit/ n. манда́т

mandatory /'mændəˌtɔri/ adj. обяза́тельный; манда́тный

mane /mein/ n. гри́ва

maneuver /mə'nuvər/ **1.** n. манёвр **2.** v. маневри́ровать impf. & pf.

manganese /'mæŋgəˌnis/ n. ма́рганец

manger /'meindʒər/ n. я́сли pl.

mangy /'meindʒi/ adj. чесо́точный; парши́вый

manhandle /'mæn,hændl/ v. гру́бо обраща́ться impf.

manhood /'mænhud/ n. возмужа́лость; зре́лость

mania /'meiniə/ n. ма́ния

maniac /'meini,æk/ n. манья́к

manicure /'mæni,kyur/ n. маникю́р

manicurist /'mæni,kyurist/ n. маникю́рша

manifest /'mænə,fɛst/ **1.** adj. очеви́дный, я́сный **2.** v. проявля́ть impf., -ви́ть pf.

manifestation /ˌmænəfɛ'steiʃən/ n. проявле́ние

manifold /'mænə,fould/ adj. разнообра́зный

Manila paper /mə'nilə/ n. мани́льская бума́га из пеньки́

manipulate /mə'nɪpyəˌleit/ v. манипули́ровать (+ I) impf.

manipulation /məˌnɪpyə'leiʃən/ n. манипуля́ция

mankind /'mæn'kaind/ n. челове́чество

manly /'mænli/ adj. мужественный

manner /'mænər/ n. о́браз, спо́соб; pl. мане́ры pl.

mannerism /'mænə,rizəm/ n. мане́рность

manor /'mænər/ n. поме́стье

manpower /'mæn,pauər/ n. рабо́чая си́ла

mansion /'mænʃən/ n. особня́к

manslaughter /'mæn,slɔtər/ n. непредумы́шленное уби́йство

manual /'mænyuəl/ **1.** adj. ручно́й **2.** n. спра́вочник; руково́дство

manufacture /ˌmænyə'fæktʃər/ **1.** v. производи́ть impf., -вести́ pf. **2.** n. произво́дство

manufacturer /ˌmænyə-'fæktʃərər/ n. фабрика́нт

manure /mə'nur/ n. наво́з

manuscript /'mænyə,skript/ **1.** n. ру́копись f. **2.** adj. рукопи́сный

many /'mɛni/ adj. мно́го (+ G); мно́гие pl.; **how** ~ ско́лько (+ G)

many-sided adj. многосторо́нний

map /mæp/ n. ка́рта; (of city) план

maple /'meipəl/ n. клён

mar /mar/ v. по́ртить impf., испо́рти pf.

marathon /'mærə,θɒn/ n. марафо́н; марафо́нский бег

marauder /mə'rɔdər/ n. мародёр

marble /'marbəl/ n. мра́мор; (toy) ша́рик **2.** adj. мра́морный

march /martʃ/ **1.** n. марш **2.** v. марширова́ть impf.

March /martʃ/ n. март

mare /meər/ n. кобы́ла

margarine /'mardʒərin/ n. маргари́н

margin /'mardʒɪn/ n. (on page) поля́ pl.; (edge) край

marginal /'mardʒənl/ adj. кра́йний; незначи́тельный

marijuana /ˌmærə'wɑnə/ n. марихуа́на

marinate /'mærəˌneit/ v. маринова́ть impf.

marine /mə'rin/ **1.** adj. морско́й **2.** n. морско́й пехоти́нец; pl. морска́я пехо́та

mariner /'mærənər/ n. моря́к

marital /'mærɪtl/ adj. супру́жеский; ~ **status** n. семе́йное положе́ние

maritime /'mæri,taim/ adj. морско́й; морско́е

mark /mark/ **1.** n. знак; ме́тка; (grade) отме́тка; (aim) цель f. **2.** v. отмеча́ть impf., отме́тить pf.

marked /markt/ adj. заме́тный

marker /'markər/ n. (pen) флома́стер; (sign, tag) знак; ме́тка

market /'markit/ **1.** n. ры́нок **2.** adj. ры́ночный; —**able** adj.

ходово́й; **—ing** n. марке́тинг;
—place n. ры́нок

marksman /ˈmɑrksmən/ n.
(ме́ткий) стрело́к

markup /ˈmɑrkˌʌp/ n. наце́нка

marmalade /ˈmɑrməˌleid/ n.
джем; повидло

maroon /məˈrun/ adj. тёмно-
бордо́вый

marquee /mɑrˈki/ n. наве́с

marquise /mɑrˈkiz/ n. марки́за

marriage /ˈmæridʒ/ 1. n. брак;
(wedding) сва́дьба 2. adj.
бра́чный

married /ˈmærid/ adj. (man)
жена́тый; (woman) заму́жняя

marrow /ˈmærou/ n. ко́стный
мозг

marry /ˈmæri/ v. (man) жени́ться
(на + P) impf. & pf.; (woman)
выходи́ть за́муж (за + A)
impf., вы́йти pf.; (couple)
пожени́ться pf.

marsh /mɑrʃ/ n. боло́то

marshal /ˈmɑrʃəl/ n. ма́ршал

marsupial /mɑrˈsupiəl/ n.
су́мчатое живо́тное

marten /ˈmɑrtn/ n. куни́ца

martial /ˈmɑrʃəl/ adj. вое́нный; ~
law вое́нное положе́ние

martyr /ˈmɑrtər/ n. му́ченик,
-ница; **—dom** n. му́ченичество

marvel /ˈmɑrvəl/ 1. n. чу́до 2. v.
удивля́ться impf., -ви́ться pf.,
—ous adj. чуде́сный

Marxist /ˈmɑrksɪst/ 1. n.
маркси́ст 2. adj. маркси́стский

mascara /mæˈskærə/ n. тушь f.

mascot /ˈmæskɒt/ n. талисма́н

masculine /ˈmæskyəlɪn/ adj.
мужско́й; мужеподо́бный;
(gram.) мужско́го ро́да

mash /mæʃ/ v. размина́ть impf.,
размя́ть pf.

mask /mæsk/ 1. n. ма́ска 2. v.
маскирова́ть impf., за- pf.

masochism /ˈmæsəˌkɪzəm/ n.
мазохи́зм

mason /ˈmeisən/ n. ка́менщик;
cap. (Freemason) масо́н; **—ry** n.
ка́менная кла́дка

Mass /mæs/ n. обе́дня

mass /mæs/ 1. n. ма́сса 2. adj.
ма́ссовый; ~ **media** сре́дства
ма́ссовой информа́ции pl.

massacre /ˈmæsəkər/ 1. n. резня́
2. v. производи́ть резню́ impf.

massage /məˈsɑʒ/ 1. n. масса́ж
2. v. масси́ровать pf. & impf.

masseur /məˈsɜr/, **masseuse**
/məˈsus/ n. массажи́ст, —ка

massive /ˈmæsiv/ adj.
масси́вный

mass production n. ма́ссовое
произво́дство

mast /mæst/ n. ма́чта

master /ˈmæstər/ 1. n. хозя́ин;
ма́стер; (of ship) капита́н; **—'s
degree** сте́пень маги́стра f. 2. v.
овладева́ть (+ I) impf., овла-
де́ть pf.; **—ful** adj. вла́стный

master key n. отмы́чка

masterpiece /ˈmæstərˌpis/ n.
шеде́вр

mastery /ˈmæstəri/ n. ма́стер-
ство́; владе́ние

masturbation /ˌmæstərˈbeiʃən/
n. мастурба́ция, онани́зм

mat /mæt/ n. мат, цино́вка

match[1] /mætʃ/ n. спи́чка

match[2] /mætʃ/ 1. n. (sports) со-
стяза́ние, матч 2. v. (select)
подбира́ть (под + A) impf.

matchbox /ˈmætʃˌbɒks/ n.
спи́чечный коробо́к

matchmaker /ˈmætʃˌmeikər/ n.
сва́ха

mate[1] /meit/ 1. n. (buddy)
това́рищ; (spouse) супру́г,
супру́га 2. v. спа́риватъ(ся)
impf.

mate[2] /meit/ n. (chess) мат

material /məˈtiəriəl/ 1. n. мате-
риа́л, мате́рия; принадле́жности
pl. 2. adj. материа́льный

materialize /məˈtiəriəˌlaiz/ v.
осуществля́ться impf., -ви́ться
pf.

maternal /məˈtɜrnl/ adj. мате-
ри́нский

maternity /məˈtɜrniti/ n. мате-
ри́нство ~ **leave** декре́тный
о́тпуск

mathematical /ˌmæθəˈmætikəl/
adj. математи́ческий

mathematics /ˌmæθəˈmætiks/ n.
матема́тика

matriarchal /ˌmeitriˈɑrkəl/ adj.
матриарха́льный

matriculation /məˌtrikyəˈleiʃən/
n. зачисле́ние в вуз

matrimonial /ˌmætrəˈmouniəl/
adj. бра́чный; супру́жеский

matrimony /ˈmætrəˌmouni/ n.
супру́жество; брак

matrix /ˈmeitriks/ n. шабло́н

matte /mæt/ adj. ма́товый

matter /ˈmætər/ 1. n. вещество́;
мате́рия; (affair; question) де́ло,

вопрос; **what's the ~?** в чём
дело? **2.** *v.* имёть значёние
impf.

matter-of-fact *adj.* факти́ческий;
прозаи́чный

mattress /'mætrıs/ *n.* матра́с

mature /mə'tʃur/ **1.** *adj.* зрёлый
2. *v.* созревáть *impf.*, созрёть
pf.

maturity /mə'tʃurıti/ *n.* зрёлость

mausoleum /,mɔsə'liəm/ *n.* мав-
золёй

maxim /'mæksım/ *n.* сентёнция

maximum /'mæksəməm/ **1.** *adj.*
максимáльный **2.** *n.* мáксимум

may /mei/ *v. aux.* мочь *impf.*, с-
pf.; возмóжно, что...

May /mei/ **1.** *n.* май **2.** *adj.*
мáйский

maybe /'meibi/ *adv.* мóжет быть

mayhem /'meihem/ *n.* хáос

mayonnaise /,meiə'neiz/ *n.* май-
онéз

mayor /'meiər/ *n.* мэр

maze /meiz/ *n.* лабири́нт

me /mi/ *pron.* меня́; мне; мнóю

meadow /'medou/ *n.* луг

meager /'migər/ *adj.* скýдный

meal¹ /mil/ *n.* (*food*) едá; **—time**
n. врéмя еды́ *neut.*

meal² /mil/ *n.* (*flour*) мукá

mean¹ /min/ *adj.* (*base*) пóдлый;
(*stingy*) скупóй

mean² /min/ **1.** *adj.* (*average*)
срéдний **2.** *n.* середи́на

mean³ /min/ *v.* (*signify*) знáчить
impf.; (*intend*) имéть в виду́
impf.

meandering /mi'ændəriŋ/ *adj.*
изви́листый

meaning /'miniŋ/ *n.* значéние;
—ful *adj.* многозначи́тельный;
—less *adj.* бессмы́сленный

means /minz/ *n.* срéдство,
срéдства *pl.*

meantime /'min,taim/ *n.*: **in the
meantime, meanwhile**
/'min,wail/ *adv.* тем врéменем;
мéжду тем

measles /'mizəlz/ *n.* корь *f.*

measurable /'meʒərəbəl/ *adj.*
измери́мый

measure /'meʒər/ **1.** *n.* мéра;
(*mus.*) такт **2.** *v.* измеря́ть
impf., измéрить *pf.*; **—ment**
(*act*) измерéние; *pl.* (*size*)
размéры *pl.*

meat /mit/ **1.** *n.* мя́со **2.** *adj.*
мяснóй

meatball /'mit,bɔl/ *n.* тефтéля

meaty /'miti/ *adj.* мяси́стый

mechanic /mə'kænık/ *n.*
механик; **—al** *adj.* механи́-
ческий; *Fig.* маши́нáльный; **—s**
n. механика

mechanism /'mekə,nızəm/ *n.*
механи́зм

mechanize /'mekə,naiz/ *v.*
механизи́ровать *impf.* & *pf.*

medal /'medl/ *n.* медáль *f.*

meddle /'medl/ *v.* вмéшиваться
impf., вмешáться *pf.*

media /'midiə/ *n.* срéдства
мáссовой информáции *pl.*

mediate /'midi,eit/ *v.*
посрéдничать *impf.*

mediator /'midi,eitər/ *n.*
посрéдник

medical /'medıkəl/ *adj.* меди-
ци́нский; **~ student** студéнт-
мéдик

medication /,medı'keiʃən/ *n.*
лекáрство, медикамéнт

medicinal /mə'dısənl/ *adj.*
лекáрственный; целéбный

medicine /'medəsın/ *n.* меди-
ци́на; (*remedy*) лекáрство

medieval /,midi'ivəl/ *adj.* срéдне-
векóвый

mediocre /,midi'oukər/ *adj.*
посрéдственный

meditate /'medı,teit/ *v.* раз-
мышля́ть *impf.*

meditation /,medı'teiʃən/ *n.* размышлéние; медитáция

medium /'midiəm/ **1.** *adj.*
срéдний **2.** *n.* (*means*) срéдство

medley /'medli/ *n.* мешани́на

meek /mik/ *adj.* крóткий

meet /mit/ *v.* встречáть(ся)
impf., встрéтить(ся) *pf.*; (*make
acquaintance*) знакóмиться (с
+ I) *impf.* no- *pf.*; **—ing** *n.*
ми́тинг, собрáние; (*encounter*)
встрéча

megaphone /'megə,foun/ *n.*
ру́пор, мегафóн

melancholic /,melən'kɒlık/ *adj.*
меланхоли́ческий

melancholy /'melən,kɒli/ **1.** *adj.*
гру́стный **2.** *n.* грусть *f.*

mellow /'melou/ *adj.* мя́гкий;
(*ripe*) спéлый

melodious /mə'loudiəs/ *adj.* ме-
лоди́чный

melodrama /'melə,dramə/ *n.* ме-
лодрáма

melody /'melədi/ *n.* мелóдия

melon /'melən/ *n.* ды́ня

melt /melt/ *v.* растворя́ть(ся)

impf., -ри́ть(ся) *pf.*; (*thaw*) та́ять *impf.*, рас- *pf.*

melting point /'meltɪŋ/ *n.* то́чка плавле́ния

member /'membər/ *n.* член; **—ship** *n.* чле́нство; коли́чество чле́нов

membrane /'membreɪn/ *n.* перепо́нка, плёнка, оболо́чка

memoir /'memwar/ *n.*: *pl.* воспомина́ния; мемуа́ры *pl.*

memorable /'memərəbəl/ *adj.* (досто)па́мятный

memorandum /,memə'rændəm/ *n.* мемора́ндум

memorial /mə'mɔriəl/ **1.** *adj.* мориа́льный **2.** *n.* па́мятник

memorize /'meməraɪz/ *v.* запомина́ть *impf.*, запо́мнить *pf.*

memory /'meməri/ *n.* па́мять *f.*

menace /'menɪs/ **1.** *n.* угро́за **2.** *v.* угрожа́ть; грози́ть *impf.*

mend /mend/ *v.* чини́ть *impf.*, по- *pf.*

mending /'mendɪŋ/ *n.* што́пка

menial /'miniəl/ *adj.* ни́зкий

meningitis /,menɪn'dʒaɪtɪs/ *n.* менинги́т

menopause /'menə,pɔz/ *n.* кли́макс

Menshevik /'menʃəvɪk/ *n.* меньшеви́к

menstrual /'menstruəl/ *adj.* менструа́льный

menstruation /,menstru'eɪʃən/ *n.* менструа́ция

mental /'mentl/ *adj.* у́мственный; (*sickness*) психи́ческий; **—ly** *adv.* мы́сленно

mentality /men'tæliti/ *n.* ум; склад ума́

mention /'menʃən/ **1.** *n.* упомина́ние **2.** *v.* упомина́ть *impf.*, упомяну́ть *pf.*

mentor /'mentər/ *n.* наста́вник

menu /'menyu/ *n.* меню́ *neut. indecl.*

mercantile /'mɜrkən,til/ *adj.* меркати́льный

mercenary /'mɜrsə,neri/ **1.** *adj.* коры́стный **2.** *n.* наёмник

merchandise /'mɜrtʃən,daɪs/ *n.* това́р; това́ры *pl.*

merchant /'mɜrtʃənt/ *n.* торго́вый 2. *n.* купе́ц; торго́вый

merciful /'mɜrsɪfəl/ *adj.* милосе́рдный

merciless /'mɜrsilɪs/ *adj.* беспоща́дный

mercury /'mɜrkyəri/ *n.* ртуть *f.*

mercy /'mɜrsi/ *n.* милосе́рдие

mere /mɪər/ *adj.* просто́й; **—ly** *adv.* то́лько, про́сто

merge /mɜrdʒ/ *v.* слива́ть(ся) *impf.*, слить(ся) *pf.*; **—r** *n.* объедине́ние

meringue /mə'ræŋ/ *n.* мере́нга

merit /'merɪt/ **1.** *n.* заслу́га; досто́инство **2.** *v.* заслу́живать (+ *G*) *impf.*, заслужи́ть *pf.*

mermaid /'mɜr,meɪd/ *n.* руса́лка

merriment /'merimənt/ *n.* весе́лье

merry /'meri/ *adj.* весёлый

merry-go-round *n.* карусе́ль *f.*

mesh /meʃ/ *n.* сеть *f.*

mesmerize /'mezmə,raɪz/ *v.* гипнотизи́ровать *impf.*, за- *pf.*

mess /mes/ *n.* беспоря́док; (*mil.*) столо́вая *n.*

message /'mesɪdʒ/ *n.* сообще́ние

messenger /'mesəndʒər/ *n.* курье́р, посы́льный

Messianic /,mesi'ænɪk/ *adj.* мессиа́нский

messy /'mesi/ *adj.* гря́зный; беспоря́дочный

metabolism /mə'tæbə,lɪzəm/ *n.* метаболи́зм, обме́н веще́ств

metal /'metl/ **1.** *n.* мета́лл **2.** *adj.* металли́ческий

metallic /mə'tælɪk/ *adj.* металли́ческий

metallurgy /'metl,ɜrdʒi/ *n.* металлурги́я

metamorphosis /,metə'mɔrfəsɪs/ *n.* метаморфо́за; (*biol.*) метаморфо́з

metaphor /'metə,fər/ *n.* мета́фора

metaphysics /,metə'fɪzɪks/ *n.* метафи́зика

meteor /'mitiər/ *n.* метео́р

meteorology /,mitiə'rɒlədʒi/ *n.* метеороло́гия

meter /'mitər/ *n.* (*instrument*) счётчик; (*measure*) метр

method /'meθəd/ *n.* ме́тод, спо́соб, систе́ма

methodical /mə'θɒdɪkəl/ *adj.* методи́ческий

meticulous /mə'tɪkyələs/ *adj.* дета́льный; тща́тельный

metric /'metrɪk/ *adj.* метри́ческий; **—s** *n.* ме́трика

metro /'metrou/ *n.* метро́ *neut. indecl.*

metropolis /mɪ'trɒpəlɪs/ *n.* метропо́лия; столи́ца

metropolitan /,metrə'pɒlɪtn/ **1.**

n. (*eccles.*) митрополи́т **2.** *adj.* столи́чный

Mexican /ˈmɛksɪkən/ **1.** *adj.* мексика́нский **2.** *n.* мексика́нец, -нка

Mexico /ˈmɛksɪˌkoʊ/ *n.* Ме́ксика

mezzanine /ˈmɛzəˌniːn/ *n.* (*theat.*) бельэта́ж

microbe /ˈmaɪkroʊb/ *n.* микро́б

microbiology /ˌmaɪkroʊbaɪˈɒlədʒi/ *n.* микробиоло́гия

microchip /ˈmaɪkroʊˌtʃɪp/ *n.* чип, микросхе́ма

microcomputer /ˈmaɪkroʊkəmˌpjuːtər/ *n.* микрокомпью́тер

microcosm /ˈmaɪkrəˌkɒzəm/ *n.* микроко́см

microfilm /ˈmaɪkrəˌfɪlm/ *n.* микрофи́льм

microphone /ˈmaɪkrəˌfoʊn/ *n.* микрофо́н

microscope /ˈmaɪkrəˌskoʊp/ *n.* микроско́п

microscopic /ˌmaɪkrəˈskɒpɪk/ *adj.* микроскопи́ческий

microwave /ˈmaɪkroʊˌweɪv/ *n.* микроволна́; (*appliance*) микроволно́вая печь *f.*

midday / *n.* ˈmɪdˈdeɪ; *adj.* ˈmɪdˌdeɪ/ **1.** *n.* по́лдень *m.* **2.** *adj.* полуденный

middle /ˈmɪdl/ **1.** *n.* середи́на **2.** *adj.* сре́дний

middle-aged *adj.* сре́дних лет; пожило́й

Middle Ages *n.* средневеко́вье

middleman /ˈmɪdlˌmæn/ *n.* посре́дник; (*com.*) комиссионе́р

midge /mɪdʒ/ *n.* мо́шка

midget /ˈmɪdʒɪt/ *n.* ка́рлик

midnight /ˈmɪdˌnaɪt/ **1.** *n.* по́лночь *f.* **2.** *adj.* полуно́чный

midriff /ˈmɪdrɪf/ *n.* диафра́гма

mid-size *adj.* сре́днего разме́ра

midsummer /ˈmɪdˈsʌmər/ *n.* середи́на ле́та

midway /ˈmɪdˈweɪ/ *adv.* на полпути́; на полдоро́ге

midwife /ˈmɪdˌwaɪf/ *n.* акуше́рка

might /maɪt/ *n.* могу́щество; мощь *f.*; **—y** *adj.* могу́щественный; мо́щный

migraine /ˈmaɪɡreɪn/ *n.* мигре́нь *f.*

migrant /ˈmaɪɡrənt/ **1.** *n.* переселе́нец **2.** *adj.* кочу́ющий

migrate /ˈmaɪɡreɪt/ *v.* переселя́ться *impf.*, -ли́ться *pf.*; мигри́ровать *impf.* & *pf.*

migration /maɪˈɡreɪʃən/ *n.* переселе́ние, мигра́ция

migratory /ˈmaɪɡrəˌtɔːri/ *adj.* (*bird*) перелётный

mike /maɪk/ *n. Colloq.* микрофо́н

mild /maɪld/ *adj.* мя́гкий; лёгкий

mildew /ˈmɪlˌduː/ *n.* пле́сень *f.*

mile /maɪl/ *n.* ми́ля

milieu /mɪlˈjuː/ *n.* среда́

militant /ˈmɪlɪtənt/ **1.** *adj.* вои́нствующий **2.** *n.* активи́ст

military /ˈmɪlɪˌteri/ **1.** *adj.* вои́нский, вое́нный **2.** *n.* вое́нные *pl.*

militia /mɪˈlɪʃə/ *n.* мили́ция

milk /mɪlk/ **1.** *n.* молоко́ **2.** *adj.* моло́чный **3.** *v.* дои́ть *impf.*, по- *pf.*

milk shake *n.* моло́чный кокте́йль *m.*

milky /ˈmɪlki/ *adj.* моло́чный

Milky Way *n.* Мле́чный Путь *m.*

mill /mɪl/ **1.** *n.* ме́льница; (*factory*) фа́брика; заво́д **2.** *v.* моло́ть *impf.*, с- *pf.*

millennium /mɪˈlɛniəm/ *n.* тысячеле́тие

miller /ˈmɪlər/ *n.* ме́льник

millet /ˈmɪlɪt/ *n.* про́со; (*grain*) пшено́

milligram /ˈmɪlɪˌɡræm/ *n.* миллигра́мм

millimeter /ˈmɪləˌmiːtər/ *n.* миллиме́тр

million /ˈmɪljən/ *n.* миллио́н; **—th** *adj.* миллио́нный

millionaire /ˌmɪljəˈnɛər/ *n.* миллионе́р

millstone /ˈmɪlˌstoʊn/ *n.* жёрнов

mimic /ˈmɪmɪk/ **1.** *n.* подража́тель **2.** *v.* имити́ровать *impf.*; **—ry** *n.* ми́мика; подража́ние

minced /mɪnst/ *adj.* ру́бленый

mind /maɪnd/ **1.** *n.* ум **2.** *v.* (*look after*) присма́тривать (за + *I*); (*object*) возража́ть *impf.*, -зи́ть *pf.*; **never ~** *interj.* ничего́!; **—ful** *adj.* по́мнящий, внима́тельный; **—less** *adj.* бессмы́сленный

mine[1] /maɪn/ *poss. pron.* мой, моя́, моё, *pl.* мои́

mine[2] /maɪn/ *n.* ша́хта; (*explosive*) ми́на

minefield /ˈmaɪnˌfiːld/ *n.* ми́нное по́ле

miner /ˈmaɪnər/ *n.* шахтёр

mineral /ˈmɪnərəl/ **1.** *n.* минера́л **2.** *adj.* минера́льный

mineralogy /ˌmɪnəˈrɒlədʒɪ/ n. минералогия

mingle /ˈmɪŋɡəl/ v. смешивать(ся) impf., смешать(ся) pf.

miniature /ˈmɪnɪətʃər/ 1. n. миниатюра 2. adj. миниатюрный

minibus /ˈmɪnɪˌbʌs/ n. микроавтобус

minimal /ˈmɪnɪməl/ adj. минимальный

minimize /ˈmɪnəˌmaɪz/ v. преуменьшать impf., преуменьшить pf.

minimum /ˈmɪnɪməm/ 1. n. минимум 2. adj. минимальный

mining /ˈmaɪnɪŋ/ 1. n. горное дело 2. adj. горный

minister /ˈmɪnɪstər/ n. министр; (eccles.) священник

ministration /ˌmɪnɪˈstreɪʃən/ n. оказание помощи

ministry /ˈmɪnɪstrɪ/ n. министерство; (eccles.) духовенство

mink /mɪŋk/ 1. n. норка 2. adj. норковый

minor /ˈmaɪnər/ 1. adj. незначительный; второстепенный; (mus.) минорный 2. n. (underage) несовершеннолетний; (mus.) минор

minority /maɪˈnɒrɪtɪ/ n. меньшинство

mint[1] /mɪnt/ 1. n. (money) монетный двор 2. v. чеканить impf. 3. adj.: — condition как новый

mint[2] /mɪnt/ 1. n. (plant) мята 2. adj. мятный

minuet /ˌmɪnjuˈet/ n. менуэт

minus /ˈmaɪnəs/ 1. prep. без (+ G) 2. n. минус

minute[1] /ˈmɪnɪt/ 1. adj. минутный 2. n. минута; pl. протокол

minute[2] /maɪˈnjuːt/ adj. мелкий; мельчайший; подробный

miracle /ˈmɪrəkəl/ n. чудо

miraculous /mɪˈrækjələs/ adj. чудесный; чудотворный; —ly adv. (каким-то) чудом

mirror /ˈmɪrər/ n. зеркало

mirth /mɜːrθ/ n. веселье

misadventure /ˌmɪsədˈventʃər/ n. несчастный случай

misapprehend /ˌmɪsæprɪˈhend/ v. недопонимать impf.

misappropriate /ˌmɪsəˈprouprɪˌeɪt/ v. незаконно присваивать impf., присвоить pf.

misbehave /ˌmɪsbɪˈheɪv/ v. дурно вести себя impf.

misbehavior /ˌmɪsbɪˈheɪvjər/ n. плохое (дурное) поведение

miscalculate /mɪsˈkælkjəˌleɪt/ v. просчитываться impf., просчитаться pf.

miscalculation /mɪsˌkælkjəˈleɪʃən/ n. просчёт

miscarriage /ˈmɪsˌkærɪdʒ/ n. (med.) выкидыш

miscellaneous /ˌmɪsəˈleɪnɪəs/ adj. разнообразный; разнородный

mischief /ˈmɪstʃɪf/ n. озорство; (tricks) шалость

mischievous /ˈmɪstʃəvəs/ adj. шаловливый, озорной

misconception /ˌmɪskənˈsepʃən/ n. недоразумение

misconduct /mɪsˈkɒndʌkt/ n. дурное поведение

misdemeanor /ˌmɪsdɪˈmiːnər/ n. проступок

miser /ˈmaɪzər/ n. скупец

miserable /ˈmɪzərəbəl/ adj. жалкий, несчастный; (nasty) скверный

miserly /ˈmaɪzərlɪ/ adj. скупой

misery /ˈmɪzərɪ/ n. невзгода; (poverty) нищета

misfire /ˌmɪsˈfaɪər/ n. (gun) осечка; (engine) перебой

misfortune /mɪsˈfɔːrtʃən/ n. несчастье

misgiving /mɪsˈɡɪvɪŋ/ n. опасение; дурное предчувствие

misguided /mɪsˈɡaɪdɪd/ adj. обманутый

mishap /ˈmɪshæp/ n. неприятность

mishmash /ˈmɪʃˌmæʃ/ n. путаница

misinformation /ˌmɪsɪnfərˈmeɪʃən/ n. дезинформация

misinterpret /ˌmɪsɪnˈtɜːrprɪt/ v. неверно толковать impf.

misjudge /mɪsˈdʒʌdʒ/ v. неправильно оценивать impf.

misleading /mɪsˈliːdɪŋ/ adj. обманчивый

mismanage /mɪsˈmænɪdʒ/ v. плохо управлять impf.; —ment n. бесхозяйственность

misogynist /mɪˈsɒdʒənɪst/ n. женоненавистник

misplaced /mɪsˈpleɪst/ adj. неуместный

misprint /ˈmɪsˌprɪnt/ n. опечатка

misquote /mɪsˈkwoʊt/ v. неточно цитировать impf.

misrepresent /ˌmɪsreprɪˈzent/ v. искажа́ть impf., -зи́ть pf.; **—ation** n. искаже́ние

Miss[1] /mɪs/ n. мисс f. indecl.

miss[2] /mɪs/ **1.** n. про́мах **2.** v. промахну́ться pf.; (long for) скуча́ть (по + D) impf.; (train) опозда́ть (на + A) pf.

missile /ˈmɪsəl/ n. снаря́д

missing /ˈmɪsɪŋ/ adj. отсу́тствующий; (mil.) без ве́сти пропа́вший

mission /ˈmɪʃən/ n. ми́ссия

missionary /ˈmɪʃəˌneri/ n. миссионе́р

mist /mɪst/ n. лёгкий тума́н

mistake /mɪˈsteɪk/ **1.** n. оши́бка; **by ~** по оши́бке **2.** v. (take for) приня́ть (за + A); **make a ~, be —n** ошиба́ться impf., -би́ться pf.; **—n** adj. оши́бочный

mister /ˈmɪstər/ n. господи́н; ми́стер

mistletoe /ˈmɪsəlˌtou/ n. оме́ла

mistreat /mɪsˈtrit/ v. ду́рно обраща́ться impf.

mistress /ˈmɪstrɪs/ n. хозя́йка

mistrust /mɪsˈtrʌst/ **1.** v. не доверя́ть impf. **2.** n. недове́рие; **—ful** adj. недове́рчивый

misty /ˈmɪsti/ adj. тума́нный

misunderstand /ˌmɪsʌndərˈstænd/ v. непра́вильно понима́ть impf., поня́ть pf.; **—ing** n. недоразуме́ние

misuse 2. v. mɪsˈyuz/ n. mɪsˈyus/ **1.** v. злоупотребля́ть impf., -би́ть pf. **2.** n. злоупотребле́ние

mite /maɪt/ n. (parasite) клещ

mitigate /ˈmɪtɪˌgeɪt/ v. смягча́ть impf., -чи́ть pf.

mitigating circumstance /ˈmɪtɪˌgeɪtɪŋ/ n. смягча́ющее обстоя́тельство

mitten /ˈmɪtn/ n. рукави́ца; ва́режка

mix /mɪks/ **1.** n. смесь f. **2.** v. сме́шивать(ся) impf., смеша́ть(ся) pf.

mixer /ˈmɪksər/ n. (machine) меша́лка; (cul.) ми́ксер

mixture /ˈmɪkstʃər/ n. смесь f.

mix-up /ˈ/ n. пу́таница

moan /moun/ **1.** n. стон **2.** v. стона́ть impf., про- pf.

mob /mɒb/ n. толпа́

mobile /ˈmoubəl/ adj. подви́жный; моби́льный; **~ phone** n. моби́льный телефо́н

mobility /mouˈbɪlɪti/ n. подви́жность

mobilize /ˈmoubəˌlaɪz/ v. мобилизова́ть(ся) impf. & pf.

mock /mɒk/ v. высме́ивать impf.; **—ery** n. издева́тельство

modal /ˈmoudl/ adj. мода́льный

mode /moud/ n. о́браз; спо́соб; (fashion) мо́да

model /ˈmɒdl/ **1.** n. моде́ль, f., образе́ц; (artist's) нату́рщик, -щица; (fashion) манеке́нщик, -щица **2.** adj. образцо́вый **3.** v. (shape) модели́ровать impf. & pf.

modem /ˈmoudəm/ n. моде́м

moderate 2. v. /ˈmɒdərɪt/ v. -əˌreɪt/ **1.** adj. уме́ренный **2.** v. умеря́ть(ся) impf., уме́рить(ся) pf.

moderation /ˌmɒdəˈreɪʃən/ n. уме́ренность

moderator /ˈmɒdəˌreɪtər/ n. председа́тель, —ница

modern /ˈmɒdərn/ adj. совреме́нный

modernize /ˈmɒdərˌnaɪz/ v. модернизи́ровать impf. & pf.

modest /ˈmɒdɪst/ adj. скро́мный; **—y** n. скро́мность

modification /ˌmɒdɪfɪˈkeɪʃən/ n. модифика́ция

modify /ˈmɒdəˌfaɪ/ v. модифици́ровать impf. & pf.

modish /ˈmoudɪʃ/ adj. мо́дный

modular /ˈmɒdʒələr/ adj. мо́дульный

modulate /ˈmɒdʒəˌleɪt/ v. модули́ровать impf.

modulation /ˌmɒdʒəˈleɪʃən/ n. модуля́ция

module /ˈmɒdʒul/ n. мо́дуль m.

mohair /ˈmouˌheər/ n. мохе́р

Mohammed /muˈhæmɪd/ n. Магоме́т

Mohammedan /muˈhæmɪdn/ n. магомета́нин, мусульма́нин

moist /mɔɪst/ adj. вла́жный

moisten /ˈmɔɪsən/ v. сма́чивать impf., смочи́ть pf.

moisture /ˈmɔɪstʃər/ n. вла́га

moisturize /ˈmɔɪstʃəˌraɪz/ v. увлажня́ть impf., -ни́ть pf.; **—r** n. увлажни́тель

mold[1] /mould/ n. **1.** n. фо́рма; шабло́н **2.** v. формова́ть impf., с- pf.

mold[2] /mould/ n. (fungus) пле́сень f.; **—y** adj. заплесне́велый

Moldavia /mɒlˈdeɪvɪə/ n. Молда́вия, Молдо́ва; —n n. молдава́нин, -ва́нка

mole[1] /moʊl/ n. (on skin) ро́динка

mole[2] /moʊl/ n. (zool.) крот

molecular /məˈlekjələr/ adj. молекуля́рный

molecule /ˈmɒləˌkjuːl/ n. моле́кула

molest /məˈlest/ v. пристава́ть (к + D) impf., приста́ть pf.

molt /moʊlt/ v. ли́нька

molten /ˈmoʊltn/ adj. распла́вленный

moment /ˈmoʊmənt/ n. моме́нт; миг; —ary adj. мгнове́нный

momentous /moʊˈmentəs/ adj. ва́жный

momentum /moʊˈmentəm/ n. дви́жущая си́ла; коли́чество движе́ния

monarch /ˈmɒnərk/ n. мона́рх; —y n. мона́рхия

monastery /ˈmɒnəˌsteri/ n. монасты́рь n.

monastic /məˈnæstɪk/ adj. мона́шеский

monatomic /ˌmɒnəˈtɒmɪk/ adj. одноа́томный

Monday /ˈmʌndeɪ/ n. понеде́льник

monetary /ˈmɒnɪˌteri/ adj. де́нежный

money /ˈmʌni/ n. де́ньги pl.

moneylender /ˈmʌniˌlendər/ n. ростовщи́к

moneymaker /ˈmʌniˌmeɪkər/ n. вы́годное де́ло

Mongol /ˈmɒŋɡəl/ **1.** adj. монго́льский **2.** n. монго́л, —ка

Mongolia /mɒŋˈɡoʊliə/ n. Монго́лия

monitor /ˈmɒnɪtər/ **1.** n. (tech.) монито́р **2.** v. контроли́ровать impf.

monk /mʌŋk/ n. мона́х

monkey /ˈmʌŋki/ n. обезья́на

monochromatic /ˌmɒnəkroʊˈmætɪk/ adj. одноцве́тный

monogamy /məˈnɒɡəmi/ n. моногáмия

monogram /ˈmɒnəˌɡræm/ n. моногрáмма

monolith /ˈmɒnəlɪθ/ n. моноли́т

monologue /ˈmɒnəˌlɔɡ/ n. моноло́г

monopolize /məˈnɒpəˌlaɪz/ v. монополизи́ровать impf. & pf.

monopoly /məˈnɒpəli/ n. монопо́лия

monosyllabic /ˌmɒnəsɪˈlæbɪk/ adj. односло́жный

monotonous /məˈnɒtənəs/ adj. моното́нный; однообра́зный

monotony /məˈnɒtəni/ n. моното́нность; однообра́зие

monster /ˈmɒnstər/ n. чудо́вище

monstrous /ˈmɒnstrəs/ adj. чудо́вищный; (huge) грома́дный

montage /mɒnˈtɑʒ/ n. монта́ж

month /mʌnθ/ n. ме́сяц; —ly n., adj. ме́сячный; ежеме́сячник

monument /ˈmɒnyəmənt/ n. па́мятник; монуме́нт

monumental /ˌmɒnyəˈmentl/ adj. монумента́льный

moo /mu/ v. мыча́ть impf.

mood[1] /mud/ n. настрое́ние; —y adj. капри́зный

mood[2] /mud/ n. (gram.) накло-не́ние

moon /mun/ n. луна́

moonlight /ˈmunˌlaɪt/ n. лу́нный свет

moonstruck /ˈmunˌstrʌk/ adj. поме́шанный

moor[1] /mʊr/ n. ве́ресковая пу́стошь f.

moor[2] /mʊr/ v. пришварто́-вывать impf., пришвартова́ть pf.

mooring /ˈmʊrɪŋ/ n. (place) прича́л

moose /mus/ n. лось m.

moot /mut/ adj. спо́рный

mop /mɒp/ **1.** n. шва́бра **2.** v. чи́стить шва́брой impf.

mope /moʊp/ v. хандри́ть impf.

moral /ˈmɔrəl/ **1.** adj. мора́льный, нра́вственный **2.** n. мора́ль f.; pl. нра́вственность; нра́вы pl.

morale /məˈræl/ n. мора́льное состоя́ние

moralist /ˈmɔrəlɪst/ n. морали́ст

morality /məˈræləti/ n. нра́вственность; нравоуче́ние

moralize /ˈmɔrəˌlaɪz/ v. морализи́ровать impf.

morass /məˈræs/ n. боло́то

morbid /ˈmɔrbɪd/ adj. боле́зненный, нездоро́вый

more /mɔr/ **1.** adj. бо́льше (+ G); бо́льший **2.** adv. бо́льше, бо́лее; **once ~** ещё раз; **~ or**

less бóлее и́ли мéнее; —**over**
adv. сверх тогó; крóме тогó

morgue /mɔrg/ *n.* морг

morning /'mɔrnɪŋ/ **1.** *n.* у́тро;
good ~ дóброе у́тро; **in the ~**
adv. у́тром **2.** *adj.* у́тренний

morose /mə'rous/ *adj.* угрю́мый

morphine /'mɔrfin/ *n.* мóрфий

Morse code /mɔrs/ *n.* áзбука
Мóрзе

morsel /'mɔrsəl/ *n.* кусóчек

mortal /'mɔrtl/ **1.** *adj.* смéртный;
(*fatal*) смертéльный **2.** *n.*
смéртный

mortar[1] /'mɔrtər/ *n.* (*cement*) из-
весткóвый раствóр

mortar[2] /'mɔrtər/ *n.* (*weapon*)
миномёт; (*for grinding*) сту́пка

mortgage /'mɔrgɪdʒ/ **1.** *n.*
ипотéка; (*deed*) закладнáя **2.** *v.*
закла́дывать *impf.*, заложи́ть
pf.

mortify /'mɔrtə,faɪ/ *v.* унижáть
impf., уни́зить *pf.*

mortuary /'mɔrtʃu,ɛri/ *n.* морг

mosaic /mou'zeɪk/ **1.** *n.*
мозáика **2.** *adj.* мозаи́ческий

Moses /'mouzɪz/ *n.* Моисéй

mosque /mɒsk/ *n.* мечéть *f.*

mosquito /mə'skitou/ *n.* комáр

moss /mɒs/ *n.* мох; —**y** *adj.*
мши́стый

most /moust/ **1.** *adj.*
наибóльший; **2.** *n.* наибóльшее
кол`и́чество **3.** *adv.* бóльше
всегó; **at (the) ~** сáмое
бóльшее; **for the ~ part**, —**ly**
бóльшей чáстью

motel /mou'tɛl/ *n.* мотéль *m.*

moth /mɔθ/ *n.* моль *f.*

mother /'mʌðər/ *n.* мать *f.*

motherhood /'mʌðər,hud/ *n.*
матери́нство

mother-in-law *n.* (*wife's
mother*) тёща, (*husband's
mother*) свекрóвь *f.*

motherly /'mʌðərli/ *adj.* мате-
ри́нский

mother-of-pearl *n.* перламу́тр

motif /mou'tif/ *n.* моти́в

motion /'mouʃən/ **1.** *n.*
движéние; (*gesture*) жест **2.** *v.*
пока́зывать жéстом *impf.*, по-
каза́ть *pf.*; —**less** *adj.* непо-
дви́жный

motion picture *n.* кинó *neut. indecl.*

motivate /'moutə,veɪt/ *v.*
побуждáть *impf.*, побуди́ть *pf.*

motivation /,moutə'veɪʃən/ *n.*
побуждéние

motive /'moutɪv/ *n.* моти́в

motley /'mɒtli/ *adj.* пёстрый

motor /'moutər/ *n.* мотóр;
дви́гатель

motorboat /'moutər,bout/ *n.*
мотóрная лóдка

motorcycle /'moutər,saikəl/ *n.*
мотоци́кл

motorcyclist /'moutər,saiklɪst/ *n.*
мотоцикли́ст

motorist /'moutərɪst/ *n.* автомо-
били́ст

motorized /'moutə,raizd/ *adj.*
моторизóванный

mottled /'mɒtld/ *adj.* пёстрый;
крáпчатый

motto /'mɒtou/ *n.* деви́з

mound /maund/ *n.* холм; (*heap*)
нáсыпь *f.*

mount /maunt/ *v.t.* поднимáться
(на + *A*) *impf.*, подня́ться *pf.*;
(*jewel*) вставля́ть *impf.*,
встáвить *pf.*; (*horse*) сади́ться
(на + *A*) *impf.*, сесть *pf.*

mountain /'mauntn/ **1.** *n.* горá
2. *adj.* гóрный; —**ous** *adj.*
гори́стый

mountaineer /,mauntn'ɪər/ *n.*
альпини́ст, —ка

mourn /mɔrn/ *v.* скорбéть (о
+ *P*) *impf.*; —**ful** *adj.*
скóрбный; печáльный; —**ing** *n.*
тра́ур

mouse /maus/ *n.* мышь *f.*

mousetrap /'maus,træp/ *n.*
мышелóвка

mouth /mauθ/ *n.* рот; (*of river*)
у́стье; —**ful** *n.* глотóк

mouthpiece /'mauθ,pis/ *n.* (*pipe,
instrument, etc.*) мундшту́к

mouthwash /'mauθ,wɒʃ/ *n.* по-
лоскáтель

movable /'muvəbəl/ *adj.* по-
движнóй; (*property*) дви́жимый

move /muv/ **1.** *n.* ход; (*change
residence*) переéзд **2.** *v.*
дви́гать(ся) *impf.*, дви́нуть(ся)
pf.; (*change residence*) пере-
езжáть *impf.*, переéхать *pf.*;
—**ment** *n.* движéние; (*mus.*)
часть *f.*

movie /'muvi/ *n.* фильм

moving /'muvɪŋ/ *adj.* дви́жу-
щийся; *Fig.* трóгательный

mow /mou/ *v.* коси́ть *impf.*, с-
pf.; —**er** *n.* коси́лка; **lawn** —**er**
n. газонокоси́лка

Mr. /ˈmɪstər/ *abbr.* ми́стер; господи́н

Mrs. /ˈmɪsɪz/ *abbr.* ми́ссис; госпожа́

much /mʌtʃ/ 1. *n.*, *adj.* мно́го (+ *G*) 2. *adv.* о́чень; гора́здо; **how ~** ско́лько; **as ~...as...** сто́лько... ско́лько...

muck /mʌk/ *n.* грязь *f.*; наво́з

mucus /ˈmyukəs/ *n.* слизь *f.*

mud /mʌd/ *n.* грязь *f.*; **~ bath** грязева́я ва́нна

muddle /ˈmʌdl/ 1. *n.* пу́таница 2. *v.* пу́тать *impf.*, с- *pf.*

muddy /ˈmʌdi/ *adj.* гря́зный

mudpack /ˈmʌdˌpæk/ *n.* косметическая ма́ска

muff /mʌf/ *n.* му́фта

muffin /ˈmʌfɪn/ *n.* сдо́ба

muffle /ˈmʌfəl/ *v.* (*wrap up*) заку́тывать *impf.*, заку́тать *pf.*; (*sound*) глуши́ть *impf.*, за- *pf.*

muffler /ˈmʌflər/ *n.* глуши́тель

mug /mʌg/ *n.* кру́жка

mugger /ˈmʌgər/ *n.* граби́тель

muggy /ˈmʌgi/ *adj.* ду́шный

mulberry /ˈmʌlˌberi/ *n.* (*tree*) ту́товое де́рево; шелкови́ца

mule /myul/ *n.* мул

multichannel /ˈmʌltiˌtʃænəl/ *adj.* многокана́льный

multicolored /ˈmʌltiˌkʌlərd/ *adj.* многоцве́тный

multidimensional /ˌmʌltɪdɪˈmenʃənl/ *adj.* многоме́рный

multilateral /ˌmʌltiˈlætərəl/ *adj.* многосторо́нний

multimillionaire /ˌmʌltiˌmɪlyəˈneər/ *n.* мультимиллионе́р

multinational /ˌmʌltiˈnæʃənl/ *adj.* многонациона́льный

multiple /ˈmʌltəpəl/ *adj.* многокра́тный; многочи́сленный

multiplication /ˌmʌltəplɪˈkeiʃən/ *n.* умноже́ние

multiplicity /ˌmʌltəˈplɪsɪti/ *n.* многочи́сленность

multiply /ˈmʌltəˌplai/ *v.t.* умножа́ть *impf.*; *v.i.* размножа́ться *impf.*, размно́житься *pf.*

multipurpose /ˌmʌltiˈpɜrpəs/ *adj.* универса́льный; многоцелево́й

multistoried /ˌmʌltiˈstɔrid/ *adj.* многоэта́жный

multitude /ˈmʌltiˌtud/ *n.* мно́жество; ма́сса

mumble /ˈmʌmbəl/ *v.* бормота́ть *impf.*, про- *pf.*

mummy /ˈmʌmi/ *n.* му́мия

mumps /mʌmps/ *n.* сви́нка

munch /mʌntʃ/ *v.* жева́ть *impf.*

mundane /mʌnˈdein/ *adj.* земно́й

municipal /myuˈnɪsəpəl/ *adj.* городско́й; муниципа́льный

municipality /myuˌnɪsəˈpæliti/ *n.* муниципалите́т

munitions /myuˈnɪʃənz/ *n.* вое́нное иму́щество

mural /ˈmyorəl/ 1. *adj.* стенно́й 2. *n.* стенна́я ро́спись *f.*

murder /ˈmɜrdər/ 1. *n.* уби́йство 2. *v.* убива́ть *impf.*, уби́ть *pf.*

murderer /ˈmɜrdərər/, **murderess** /ˈmɜrdərɪs/ *n.* уби́йца *m.* & *f.*; **—ous** *adj.* уби́йственный

murky /ˈmɜrki/ *adj.* мра́чный

murmur /ˈmɜrmər/ 1. *n.* (*water*) журча́ние; (*voices*) шёпот 2. *v.* журча́ть; шепта́ть *impf.*

muscle /ˈmʌsəl/ *n.* мы́шца; му́скул

Muscovite /ˈmʌskəˌvait/ *n.* москви́ч, —а

muscular /ˈmʌskyələr/ *adj.* мы́шечный; (*person*) му́скулистый

muse /myuz/ *v.* размышля́ть *impf.*

museum /myuˈziəm/ *n.* музе́й

mushroom /ˈmʌʃrum/ *n.* гриб

music /ˈmyuzɪk/ *n.* му́зыка; (*score*) но́ты *pl.*; **—al** *adj.* музыка́льный; ~ **comedy** *n.* музыка́льная коме́дия; ~ **hall** мю́зик-холл

musician /myuˈzɪʃən/ *n.* музыка́нт

musk /mʌsk/ *n.* му́скус

musk ox *n.* овцебы́к

muskrat /ˈmʌskˌræt/ *n.* онда́тра

Muslim /ˈmʌzlɪm, ˈmuz-/ 1. *n.* мусульма́нин, -ма́нка 2. *adj.* мусульма́нский

mussel /ˈmʌsəl/ *n.* (*cul.*) ми́дия

must /mʌst/ *v.* до́лжен (+ *infin.*), должна́, должно́, до́лжны; на́до (*impers.* + *D* & *infin.*); **~ not** нельзя́ (*impers.* + *D* & *infin.*)

mustache /ˈmʌstæʃ/ *n.* усы́ *pl.*

mustard /ˈmʌstərd/ *n.* горчи́ца

musty /ˈmʌsti/ *adj.* за́тхлый

mutate /ˈmyuteit/ *v.* видоизменя́ть(ся) *impf.*

mutation /myuˈteiʃən/ *n.* мута́ция

mute /myut/ *adj.* & *n.* немой

muteness /'myutnɪs/ *n.* немота

mutilate /'myut‚leit/ *v.* увечить *impf.,* из- *pf.;* калечить *impf.,* ис- *pf.*

mutinous /'myutnəs/ *adj.* мятежный

mutiny /'myutnɪ/ **1.** *n.* мятеж; бунт **2.** *v.* бунтовать *impf.*

mutter /'mʌtər/ *v.* бормотать *impf.,* про- *pf.;* —**ing** *n.* бормотание

mutton /'mʌtn/ **1.** *n.* баранина **2.** *adj.* бараний

mutual /'myutʃuəl/ *adj.* взаимный; *(common)* общий

muzzle /'mʌzəl/ *n.* морда; *(on animal)* намордник; *(on gun)* дуло

my /mai/ *adj.* мой, моя, моё, *pl.* мой; свой

myopia /mai'oupiə/ *n.* близорукость

myrtle /'mɜrtl/ *n.* мирт

myself /mai'self/ *pron.* сам, сама; *refl.* себя

mysterious /mɪ'stɪəriəs/ *adj.* таинственный

mystery /'mɪstəri/ *n.* тайна

mystic /'mɪstɪk/ **1.** *adj.* мистический **2.** *n.* мистик

mystify /'mɪstə‚fai/ *v.* озадачивать *impf.*

mystique /mɪ'stik/ *n.* мистика

myth /mɪθ/ *n.* миф; —**ical** *adj.* мифический

mythology /mɪ'θɒlədʒi/ *n.* мифология

N

nag /næg/ *v.* пилить *impf.*

nagging /'nægɪŋ/ *adj.* (*grumbling*) ворчливый; *(pain)* ноющий

nail /neil/ **1.** *n.* гвоздь *m.;* *(anat.)* ноготь *m.* **2.** *v.* прибивать *impf.,* прибить *pf.*

naive /nɑ'iv/ *adj.* найвный

naked /'neikɪd/ *adj.* голый; нагой; —**ness** *n.* нагота

name /neim/ **1.** *n.* *(first)* имя *neut.;* *(last name)* фамилия; *(appellation)* название **2.** *v.* называть *impf.,* назвать *pf.;* *(appoint)* назначать *impf.,* назначить *pf.;* ~ **day** именины *pl.;* —**less** *adj.* безымянный; —**ly** *adv.* а именно

namesake /'neim‚seik/ *n.* тёзка *m.* & *f.*

nanny /'næni/ *n.* няня

nap /næp/ *n.* короткий сон; **take a** ~ вздремнуть *pf.*

nape /neip/ *n.* загривок

napkin /'næpkɪn/ *n.* салфетка

narcissus /nar'sɪsəs/ *n.* нарцисс

narcotic /nar'kɒtɪk/ **1.** *adj.* наркотический **2.** *n.* наркотик

narration /næ'reiʃən/ *n.* повествование; комментарий

narrative /'nærətɪv/ **1.** *adj.* повествовательный **2.** *n.* рассказ

narrator /'næreitər/ *n.* рассказчик

narrow /'nærou/ **1.** *adj.* узкий; тесный **2.** *v.* суживать(ся) *impf.;* —**ness** *n.* узость

narrow-minded *adj.* ограниченный

nasal /'neizəl/ *adj.* носовой

nasty /'næsti/ *adj.* скверный; гадкий

nation /'neiʃən/ *n.* страна; нация

national /'næʃənl/ *adj.* государственный

nationalism /'næʃənl‚izəm/ *n.* национализм

nationality /‚næʃə'næliti/ *n.* национальность; гражданство

nationalize /'næʃənl‚aiz/ *v.* национализировать *impf.* & *pf.*

native /'neitiv/ **1.** *adj.* родной; туземный **2.** *n.* уроженец, -нка

natural /'nætʃərəl/ *adj.* естественный; природный; натуральный; —**ly** *adv.* конечно; естественно

naturalize /'nætʃərə‚laiz/ *v.* натурализовать *impf.* & *pf.*

nature /'neitʃər/ *n.* природа; натура; характер

naughty /'nɔti/ *adj.* непослушный

nausea /'nɔziə/ *n.* тошнота

nauseous /'nɔʃəs/ *adj.:* **I feel** ~ меня тошнит

nautical /'nɔtɪkəl/ *adj.* морской

naval /'neivəl/ *adj.* военно-морской

navel /'neivəl/ *n.* пуп, пупок

navigable /'nævigəbəl/ *adj.* судоходный

navigation /‚nævi'geiʃən/ *n.* навигация; мореплавание

navigator /'nævɪ,geɪtər/ *n.* мореплаватель; штурман

navy /'neɪvi/ *n.* военно-морской флот

near /nɪər/ **1.** *adj.* близкий **2.** *adv.* близко **3.** *prep.* у, около (+ G); недалеко (от + G); —**ly** *adv.* близко, рядом; —**ly** *adv.* почти

nearsighted /'nɪər,saɪtɪd/ *adj.* близорукий

neat /nit/ *adj.* опрятный; аккуратный; —**ness** *n.* опрятность; аккуратность

nebulous /'nebyələs/ *adj.* неясный; туманный

necessary /'nesə,seri/ *adj.* необходимый; нужный

necessity /nə'sesɪti/ *n.* необходимость

neck /nek/ *n.* шея

necklace /'neklɪs/ *n.* ожерелье

necktie /'nek,taɪ/ *n.* галстук

née /neɪ/ *adj.* урождённая

need /nid/ **1.** *n.* нужда; надобность **2.** *v.* нуждаться (в + P) *impf.*

needle /'nidl/ *n.* игла, иголка; (*of instrument*) стрелка

needy /'nidi/ *adj.* нуждающийся

negation /nɪ'geɪʃən/ *n.* отрицание

negative /'negətɪv/ **1.** *adj.* отрицательный **2.** *n.* (*photog.*) негатив

neglect /nɪ'glekt/ **1.** *n.* пренебрежение **2.** *v.* пренебрегать *impf.*, -бречь *pf.*

negligence /'neglɪdʒəns/ *n.* небрежность

negligible /'neglɪdʒəbəl/ *adj.* незначительный

negotiate /nɪ'goʊʃi,eɪt/ *v.* вести переговоры *impf.*; (*arrange*) заключать *impf.*

negotiation /nɪ,goʊʃi'eɪʃən/ *n.* переговоры *pl.*

Negro /'nigroʊ/ **1.** *n.* негр, негритянка **2.** *adj.* негритянский

neighbor /'neɪbər/ *n.* сосед, —ка; —**hood** *n.* соседство; район; —**ing** *adj.* соседний

neither /'niðər/ **1.** *adj.* ни тот, ни другой **2.** *adv.* также не; ~... **nor** ни... ни

neon /'niɒn/ *n.* неон; ~ **light** *n.* неоновый свет

nephew /'nefyu/ *n.* племянник

nepotism /'nepə,tɪzəm/ *n.* кумовство

nerve /nɜrv/ *n.* нерв; *Colloq.* (*impudence*) нахальство

nervous /'nɜrvəs/ *adj.* нервный; **be ~** *v.* нервничать *impf.*

nervousness /'nɜrvəsnɪs/ *n.* нервность; нервозность

nest /nest/ *n.* гнездо

nest egg *n.* сбережения *pl.*

nestle /'nesəl/ *v.* приютиться *pf.*

net¹ /net/ **1.** *adj.* нетто *neut. indecl.*; чистый **2.** *v.* приносить чистый доход *impf.*

net² /net/ *n.* сеть; *f.*; сетка

Netherlands /'neðərləndz/ *n.* **the,** Нидерланды *pl.*

nettle /'netl/ *n.* крапива

network /'net,wɜrk/ *n.* сеть *f.*

neural /'nʊrəl/ *adj.* нервный

neurologist /nʊ'rɒlədʒɪst/ *n.* невропатолог

neurology /nʊ'rɒlədʒi/ *n.* неврология

neurosis /nʊ'roʊsɪs/ *n.* невроз

neuter /'nutər/ **1.** *adj.* (*gram.*) средний, среднего рода **2.** *v.* кастрировать *impf.* & *pf.*

neutral /'nutrəl/ *adj.* нейтральный

neutrality /nu'trælɪti/ *n.* нейтралитет

neutralize /'nutrə,laɪz/ *v.* нейтрализовать *impf.* & *pf.*

neutron /'nutrɒn/ *n.* нейтрон

never /'nevər/ *adv.* никогда; ~ **mind** ничего!

nevertheless /,nevərðə'les/ *adv.* тем не менее

new /nu/ *adj.* новый

newborn /'nu'bɔrn/ *adj.* новорождённый

newcomer /'nu,kʌmər/ *n.* новоприбывший; пришелец

newly /'nuli/ *adv.* недавно

newlyweds /'nuli,wedz/ *n.* новобрачные; молодожёны *pl.*

news /nuz/ *n.* известия; новости; известия *pl.*

newsletter /'nuz,letər/ *n.* информационный бюллетень *m.*

newspaper /'nuz,peɪpər/ **1.** *n.* газета **2.** *adj.* газетный

newsreel /'nuz,ril/ *n.* кинохроника, киножурнал

newsstand /'nuz,stænd/ *n.* газетный киоск

newt /nut/ *n.* тритон

next /nekst/ **1.** *adj.* следующий; ближайший **2.** *adv.* затем, потом; ~ **to** рядом (*c* + *I*); ~ **of kin** *n.* ближний родственник

nib /nɪb/ n. кончик

niche /nɪtʃ/ n. ниша

nick /nɪk/ n. царапина; засечка

nickel /'nɪkəl/ n. никель m.

nickname /'nɪk,neim/ n. прозвище

nicotine /'nɪkə,tin/ n. никотин

niece /nis/ n. племянница

niggardly /'nɪgərdli/ adj. скупой

niggling /'nɪglɪŋ/ adj. мелочный

night /nait/ 1. n. ночь f.: at ~ ночью; good ~! спокойной ночи!; last ~ вчера вечером 2. adj. ночной

nightclub /'nait,klʌb/ n. ночной клуб

nightgown /'nait,gaun/ n. ночная рубашка

nightingale /'naitiŋ,geil/ n. соловей

night-light /nait/ n. ночник

nightly /'naitli/ adj. еженощный

nightmare /'nait,meər/ n. кошмар

night shift n. ночная смена

nil /nɪl/ n. ноль m.; нуль m.

nimble /'nɪmbəl/ adj. гибкий, проворный

nine /nain/ adj., n. девять, девятка

nineteen /'nain'tin/ adj., n. девятнадцать; —th adj. девятнадцатый

ninetieth /'naintiɪθ/ adj. девяностый

ninety /'nainti/ adj., n. девяносто

ninth /nainθ/ adj. девятый

nipple /'nɪpəl/ n. сосок

nippy /'nɪpi/ adj. прохладный

nit /nɪt/ n. гнида

nitpicker /'nɪt,pɪkər/ n. Colloq. придира m. & f.

nitrate /'naitreit/ n. нитрат

nitric acid n. азотная кислота

nitrogen /'naitrədʒən/ n. азот

nitroglycerin /,naitrə'glisərin/ n. нитроглицерин

no /nou/ 1. adj. никакой 2. adv. нет

Nobel prize /'noubəl/ n. Нобелевская премия

nobility /nou'bɪliti/ n. благородство; дворянство

noble /'noubəl/ adj. благородный

nobleman /'noubəlmən/ n. дворянин

nobody /'nou,bɒdi/ 1. pron. никто 2. n. ничтожество

nocturnal /nɒk'tɜrnl/ adj. ночной

nod /nɒd/ 1. n. кивок 2. v. кивать головой impf.

nodule /'nɒdʒul/ n. узелок

noise /nɔiz/ n. шум; —less adj. бесшумный

noisy /'nɔizi/ adj. шумный

nomad /'noumæd/ n. кочевник

nomadic /nou'mædɪk/ adj. кочевой

nomenclature /'noumən,kleitʃər/ n. номенклатура

nominal /'nɒmənl/ adj. номинальный; именной

nominate /'nɒmə,neit/ v. выдвигать кандидатуру impf., выдвинуть pf.

nomination /,nɒmə'neiʃən/ n. выдвижение кандидата; назначение

nominative /'nɒmənətɪv/ adj. (gram.) именительный

nominee /,nɒmə'ni/ n. кандидат

nonalcoholic /,nɒnælkə'hɒlɪk/ adj. безалкогольный

nonappearance /,nɒnə'pɪərəns/ n. неявка

nonchalant /,nɒnʃə'lɑnt/ adj. беззаботный, беспечный

nonclassified /,nɒn'klæsə,faid/ adj. незасекреченный

noncommittal /,nɒnkə'mɪtl/ adj. уклончивый

nonconformity /,nɒnkən'fɔrmiti/ n. неподчинение

nondescript /,nɒndɪ'skrɪpt/ adj. неопределённого вида

none /nɒn/ 1. pron. никто; ничто; ни один 2. adv. нисколько

nonentity /nɒn'entiti/ n. (person) ничтожество

nonessential /,nɒni'senʃəl/ adj. несущественный

nonetheless /,nʌnðə'les/ adv. тем не менее

nonexistent /,nɒnig'zistənt/ adj. несуществующий

nonfiction /nɒn'fɪkʃən/ n. научная и научно-популярная литература

nonpayment /nɒn'peimənt/ n. неплатёж; неуплата

nonplus /nɒn'plʌs/ v. ставить в тупик impf.

nonresistance /,nɒnrɪ'zistəns/ n. несопротивление

nonsense /'nɒnsens/ n. ерунда

nonsensical /nɒn'sɛnsɪkəl/ adj. бессмы́сленный

nonsmoker /nɒn'smoukər/ n. (person) некуря́щий

nonstop /nɒn'stɒp/ adj. безостано́вочный; беспоса́дочный

nonviolent /nɒn'vaiələnt/ adj. ненаси́льственный

noodle /'nudl/ n. лапша́

nook /nuk/ n. уголо́к

noon /nun/ n. по́лдень m.

noose /nus/ n. петля́

nor /nɔr/ conj. и не, та́кже не; **neither**... ~ ни... ни

norm /nɔrm/ n. но́рма; **—al** adj. норма́льный; обы́чный

normalize /'nɔrmə,laiz/ v. нормализова́ть impf. & pf.

north /nɔrθ/ 1. n. се́вер 2. adj. се́верный 3. adv. к се́веру, на се́вер

northeast /,nɔrθ'ist/ n. се́веровосто́к; **—ern** adj. се́веро-восто́чный

northerly /'nɔrðərli/, **northern** /'nɔrðərn/ adj. се́верный

northerner /'nɔrðərnər/ n. северя́нин, северя́нка

northward /'nɔrθwərd/ adv. на се́вер

northwest /,nɔrθ'wɛst/ n. се́веро-за́пад; **—ern** adj. се́веро-за́падный

Norway /'nɔrwei/ n. Норве́гия

Norwegian /nɔr'widʒən/ 1. adj. норве́жский 2. n. норве́жец, -жка

nose /nouz/ n. нос

nosebleed /'nouz,blid/ adj. кровотече́ние из но́са n.

nosedive /'nouz,daiv/ n. (aero.) круто́е пики́рование

nostalgia /nɒ'stældʒə/ n. ностальги́я

nostalgic /nɒ'stældʒik/ adj. ностальги́ческий

nostril /'nɒstrəl/ n. ноздря́

not /nɒt/ adv. не; нет; ~ **at all** совсе́м не (нет)

notable /'noutəbəl/ adj. выдаю́щийся; значи́тельный

notably /'noutəbli/ adv. заме́тно

notary /'noutəri/ n. нота́риус

notation /nou'teiʃən/ n. нота́ция

notch /nɒtʃ/ n. вы́емка; зару́бка

note /nout/ 1. n. запи́ска; заме́тка; (mus.) но́та 2. v. (notice) замеча́ть impf., заме́тить pf.

notebook /'nout,buk/ n. запи́сная кни́жка, тетра́дь f.

noted /'noutid/ adj. знамени́тый

notepad /'nout,pæd/ n. блокно́т

noteworthy /'nout,wɜrði/ adj. заслу́живающий внима́ния

nothing /'nʌθiŋ/ pron. ничто́; ничего́; **for** ~ (in vain) напра́сно; (free) да́ром

notice /'noutis/ 1. n. объявле́ние; (attention) внима́ние 2. v. замеча́ть impf., заме́тить pf.; **—able** adj. заме́тный

notification /,noutəfi'keiʃən/ n. извеще́ние; уведомле́ние

notify /'noutə,fai/ v. извеща́ть (о +P) impf., -сти́ть pf.

notion /'nouʃən/ n. поня́тие

notorious /nou'tɔriəs/ adj. пресло́вутый

notwithstanding /,nɒtwið'stændiŋ/ 1. adv. тем не ме́нее 2. prep. несмотря́ на (+ A)

nougat /'nugət/ n. нуга́

noun /naun/ n. (имя) суще́стви́тельное neut.

nourish /'nɜriʃ/ v. пита́ть impf.; **—ing** adj. пита́тельный; **—ment** n. пита́ние; пи́ща

novel /'nɒvəl/ 1. adj. но́вый 2. n. рома́н; **—ist** n. романи́ст; **—ty** n. новизна́

November /nou'vɛmbər/ 1. n. ноя́брь m. 2. adj. ноя́брьский

novice /'nɒvis/ n. новичо́к; (eccles.) послу́шник

now /nau/ adv. тепе́рь; тотча́с же

nowadays /'nauə,deiz/ adv. в на́ше вре́мя

nowhere /'nou,wɛər/ adj. (dir.) никуда́; (loc.) нигде́

noxious /'nɒkʃəs/ adj. вре́дный

nozzle /'nɒzəl/ n. сопло́

nuance /'nuɑns/ n. нюа́нс

nuclear /'nukliər/ adj. я́дерный

nucleus /'nukliəs/ n. ядро́

nude /nud/ 1. adj. наго́й; го́лый 2. n. обнажённая фигу́ра

nudge /nʌdʒ/ 1. n. толчо́к ло́ктем 2. v. подтолкну́ть ло́ктем pf.

nudity /'nuditi/ n. нагота́

nugget /'nʌgit/ n. саморо́док

nuisance /'nusəns/ n. доса́да; (person) надое́дливый челове́к

null /nʌl/ adj. недействи́тельный

nullify /'nʌlə,fai/ v. аннули́ровать impf. & pf.

numb /nʌm/ adj. онеме́лый

number /'nʌmbər/ **1.** n. число́; (total) коли́чество; (No.) но́мер **2.** v. (assign number) нумерова́ть impf., за- pf.; **—ing** n. нумера́ция; **—less** adj. бесчи́сленный

numbness /'nʌmnɪs/ n. онеме́ние; оцепене́ние; окочене́ние

numeral /'numərəl/ n. ци́фра; (gram.) (и́мя) числи́тельное neut.

numerical /nu'merɪkəl/ adj. числово́й; цифрово́й

numerous /'numərəs/ adj. многочи́сленный; (many) мно́гие pl.

nun /nʌn/ n. мона́хиня

nunnery /'nʌnərɪ/ n. же́нский монасты́рь m.

nurse /nɜrs/ **1.** n. медсестра́, медбра́т; (child's) ня́ня **2.** v.

уха́живать за (+ I) impf.; (suckle) корми́ть impf., на-, по- pf.

nursery /'nɜrsərɪ/ n. де́тская (ко́мната); (day ~) я́сли pl.; (for plants) пито́мник

nursing home n. дом преста́релых

nut /nʌt/ n. оре́х; (mech.) га́йка

nutcracker /'nʌt,krækər/ n. щипцы́ для оре́хов pl.

nutmeg /'nʌtmeg/ n. муска́тный оре́х

nutrition /nu'trɪʃən/ n. пита́ние

nutritious /nu'trɪʃəs/ adj. пита́тельный

nutshell /'nʌt,ʃel/ n. оре́ховая скорлупа́

nylon /'nailən/ **1.** n. нейло́н **2.** adj. нейло́новый

nymph /nimf/ n. ни́мфа

— **O** —

oak /ouk/ **1.** n. дуб **2.** adj. дубо́вый

oar /ɔr/ n. весло́

oarsman /'ɔrzmən/ n. гребе́ц

oasis /ou'eisis/ n. оа́зис

oat /out/ n. ове́с

oath /ouθ/ n. кля́тва; прися́га

oatmeal /'out,mil/ n. овся́нка

obedient /ou'bidiənt/ adj. послу́шный

obese /ou'bis/ adj. ту́чный

obey /ou'bei/ v. слу́шаться (+ G); повинова́ться (+ D) impf.

obituary /ou'bɪtʃu,erɪ/ n. некроло́г

object / n. 'ɒbdʒɪkt; v. əb'dʒekt/ **1.** n. предме́т; (aim) цель f.; (gram.) дополне́ние **2.** v. возража́ть impf., -зи́ть pf.; **—ion** n. возраже́ние

objective /əb'dʒektɪv/ **1.** adj. объекти́вный **2.** n. цель f.

obligation /,ɒblɪ'geiʃən/ n. обяза́тельство

obligatory /ə'blɪgə,tɔrɪ/ adj. обяза́тельный

oblige /ə'blaidʒ/ v. обя́зывать impf., обяза́ть pf.

obliging /ə'blaidʒɪŋ/ adj. услу́жливый

oblique /ə'blik/ adj. косо́й

obliterate /ə'blɪtə,reit/ v. стира́ть impf., стере́ть pf.; (destroy) уничтожа́ть impf.

oblivion /ə'blɪviən/ n. забве́ние

oblong /'ɒb,lɒŋ/ adj. продолго́ватый

obscene /əb'sin/ adj. неприли́чный; непристо́йный

obscenity /əb'senɪtɪ/ n. непристо́йность

obscure /əb'skyur/ **1.** adj. малоизве́стный; (unclear) нея́сный **2.** v. затемня́ть impf., затми́ть pf.

obscurity /əb'skyurɪtɪ/ n. нея́сность; неизве́стность

obsequious /əb'sikwiəs/ adj. подобостра́стный; раболе́пный

observance /əb'zɜrvəns/ n. соблюде́ние; (rite) обря́д

observant /əb'zɜrvənt/ adj. наблюда́тельный

observation /,ɒbzɜr'veiʃən/ n. наблюде́ние; (remark) замеча́ние

observatory /əb'zɜrvə,tɔrɪ/ n. обсервато́рия

observe /əb'zɜrv/ v. наблюда́ть impf.; (comply) соблюда́ть impf.; **—r** n. наблюда́тель

obsession /əb'seʃən/ n. одержи́мость; ма́ния

obsolete /,ɒbsə'lit/ adj. уста́релый

obstacle /'ɒbstəkəl/ n. препя́тствие

obstetrician /,ɒbstɪ'trɪʃən/ n. акуше́р, **—ка**

obstinacy /'ɒbstənəsi/ *n.* упрямство

obstinate /'ɒbstənɪt/ *adj.* упрямый

obstruct /əb'strʌkt/ *v.* препятствовать; заграждать *impf.*, заградить *pf.*; **—ion** *n.* препятствие

obtain /əb'teɪn/ *v.* получать *impf.*, -чить *pf.*; **-able** *adj.* доступный

obvious /'ɒbvɪəs/ *adj.* очевидный

occasion /ə'keɪʒən/ *n.* случай; (*cause*) повод; возможность; **—al** *adj.* случайный; редкий; **-ally** *adv.* иногда; время от времени

occupant /'ɒkyəpənt/ *n.* жилец, -лица

occupation /ˌɒkyə'peɪʃən/ *n.* занятие; (*profession*) профессия; (*mil.*) оккупация

occupy /'ɒkyə,paɪ/ *v.* занимать *impf.*, занять *pf*

occur /ə'kɜr/ *v.* случаться *impf.*, -читься *pf.*; **—rence** *n.* случай, происшествие

ocean /'ouʃən/ *n.* океан

o'clock /ə'klɒk/ *adv.*: (at) ten ~ (в) десять часов

octave /'ɒktɪv/ *n.* октава

October /ɒk'toubər/ **1.** *n.* октябрь *m.* **2.** *adj.* октябрьский

octopus /'ɒktəpəs/ *n.* осьминог

odd /ɒd/ *adj.* странный; (*math.*) нечётный; **—ity** *n.* странность

odds /ɒdz/ *n.* шансы *pl.*

odious /'oudiəs/ *adj.* отвратительный

odor /'oudər/ *n.* запах

of /ʌv/ *prep.* (*from*) из (+ G); (*about*) о, об (+ P)

off /ɒf/ *prep.* с, со; от (+ G)

offend /ə'fend/ *v.* обижать *impf.*, обидеть *pf.*; **-er** *n.* обидчик; (*law*) правонарушитель

offensive /ə'fensɪv/ **1.** *adj.* обидный; противный; (*mil.*) наступательный **2.** *n.* наступление

offer /'ɒfər/ **1.** *n.* предложение **2.** *v.* предлагать *impf.* -ложить *pf.*

offhand /'ɒf'hænd/ *adv.* экспромтом; без подготовки

office /'ɒfɪs/ *n.* (*room*) кабинет; (*position*) должность; (*place*) бюро *neut. indecl.*; контора; ~ **hours** приёмные часы *pl.*; **—r** *n.*

должностное лицо; (*mil.*) офицер

official /ə'fɪʃəl/ **1.** *adj.* официальный **2.** *n.* служебное лицо

offshoot /'ɒf,ʃut/ *n.* отпрыск

offspring /'ɒf,sprɪŋ/ *n.* потомок

often /'ɒfən/ *adv.* часто

oil /ɔɪl/ **1.** *n.* масло; (*petroleum*) нефть *f.* **2.** *v.* смазывать *impf.*, смазать *pf.*

oilcloth /'ɔɪl,klɒθ/ *n.* клеёнка

oil pipeline *n.* нефтепровод

oilskin /'ɔɪl,skɪn/ *n.* тонкая клеёнка; непромокаемый костюм

oil well *n.* нефтяная скважина

oily /'ɔɪli/ *adj.* маслянистый

ointment /'ɔɪntmənt/ *n.* мазь *f.*

old /ould/ *adj.* старый; ~ **age** *n.* старость

Old Believer *n.* старовер, **—ка**

old-fashioned *adj.* старомодный

old man *n.* старик

Old Testament 1. *n.* Ветхий Завет **2.** *adj.* ветхозаветный

old woman *n.* старуха

olive /'ɒlɪv/ **1.** *n.* олива **2.** *adj.* оливковый

Olympic Games /ə'lɪmpɪk/ *n.* Олимпийские игры *pl.*

omelet /'ɒmlɪt/ *n.* омлет

ominous /'ɒmɪnəs/ *adj.* зловещий

omission /ou'mɪʃən/ *n.* пропуск

omit /ou'mɪt/ *v.* пропускать, упускать *impf.*, -стить *pf.*

omnipotence /ɒm'nɪpətəns/ *n.* всемогущество

omniscient /ɒm'nɪʃənt/ *adj.* всезнающий; всеведущий

on /ɒn/ **1.** *prep.* (*loc.*) на (+ P); (*dir.*) на (+ A); (*about*) о, об, обо (+ P) **2.** *adv.* дальше, вперёд

once /wʌns/ *adv.* (один) раз; однажды

on-duty *adj.* дежурный

one /wʌn/ **1.** *adj.* один; единственный **2.** *n.* один; единица; (*when counting*) раз; ~ **another** друг друга

one-time *adj.* (*single use*) одноразовый; (*former*) бывший

onerous /'ɒnərəs/ *adj.* обременительный; тягостный

oneself /wʌn'self/ *pron.* себя; -ся

onion /'ʌnyən/ *n.* (*coll.*) лук; (*single bulb*) луковица

on-line *adj.* диалоговый; интерактивный

onlooker /'ɒn,lʊkər/ n. наблюдатель

only /'ounli/ **1.** adj. единственный **2.** adv. только; **if ~** если бы только

onset /'ɒn,set/ n. начало

onslaught /'ɒn,slɔt/ n. натиск

onward /'ɒnwərd/ adv. вперёд

ooze /uz/ v. сочиться impf.

opaque /ou'peik/ adj. непрозрачный

open /'oupən/ **1.** adj. открытый; откровенный **2.** v. открывать(ся) impf., открыть(ся) pf.; **—ing** n. открытие; (hole) отверстие; (start) начало; **—ness** n. откровенность

opera /'ɒprə/ **1.** n. опера **2.** adj. оперный; **~ glasses** театральный бинокль m.

operate /'ɒpə,reit/ v. (manage) управлять impf.; (med.) оперировать impf. & pf.; (function) действовать (на + A) impf.

operation /,ɒpə'reiʃən/ n. действие; (med.; econ.; mil.) операция

operator /'ɒpə,reitər/ n. оператор; (telephone) телефонист, —ка

opinion /ə'pinyən/ n. мнение; **in my ~** по-моему

opium /'oupiəm/ n. опиум

opponent /ə'pounənt/ n. противник; оппонент

opportunity /,ɒpər'tuniti/ n. удобный случай; возможность

oppose /ə'pouz/ v. противиться impf., вос-

opposite /'ɒpəzit/ **1.** adj. противоположный; (reverse) обратный **2.** prep. (на)против (+ G) **3.** n. противоположность

opposition /,ɒpə'ziʃən/ n. сопротивление; (polit.) оппозиция

oppress /ə'prɛs/ v. угнетать impf.; **—ion** n. угнетение; adj. гнетущий

optical /'ɒptikəl/ adj. зрительный; оптический

optician /ɒp'tiʃən/ n. оптик

optics /'ɒptiks/ n. оптика

optimistic /,ɒptə'mistik/ adj. оптимистический

option /'ɒpʃən/ n. выбор; **—al** adj. необязательный

or /ɔr/ conj. или; **~ else** иначе

oral /'ɔrəl/ adj. устный

orange /'ɔrindʒ/ **1.** n. апельсин **2.** adj. апельсиновый; (color) оранжевый

orator /'ɔrətər/ n. оратор

orbit /'ɔrbit/ n. орбита

orchard /'ɔrtʃərd/ n. (фруктовый) сад

orchestra /'ɔrkəstrə/ n. оркестр

orchestration /,ɔrkə'streiʃən/ n. оркестровка; инструментовка

orchid /'ɔrkid/ n. орхидея

ordeal /ɔr'dil/ n. тяжёлое испытание

order /'ɔrdər/ **1.** n. порядок; (command) приказ; (business) заказ; **in ~ to** (для того) чтобы **2.** v. (command) приказывать impf., приказать pf.; (goods, etc.) заказывать impf., заказать pf.; **—ly 3.** adj. аккуратный **4.** n. (med.) санитар

ordinance /'ɔrdnəns/ n. декрет

ordinary /'ɔrdn,eri/ adj. обычный; простой

ore /ɔr/ n. руда

organ /'ɔrgən/ **1.** n. орган; (mus.) орган **2.** adj. органный

organic /ɔr'gænik/ adj. органический

organism /'ɔrgə,nizəm/ n. организм

organization /,ɔrgənə'zeiʃən/ n. организация; устройство

organize /'ɔrgə,naiz/ v. организовать impf. & pf.; **—r** n. организатор

Orient /'ɔriənt/ n. восток

orient /'ɔri,ent/ v. ориентировать impf. & pf.

Oriental /,ɔri'entl/ **1.** adj. восточный **2.** n. житель Востока

orientation /,ɔriən'teiʃən/ n. ориентация

origin /'ɔridʒin/ n. происхождение; начало

original /ə'ridʒənl/ **1.** adj. первоначальный; подлинный **2.** n. подлинник

ornament /'ɔrnəmənt/ v. 'ɔrnə,ment/ **1.** n. украшение **2.** v. украшать impf., украсить pf.

ornamental /,ɔrnə'mentl/ adj. декоративный; орнаментальный

orphan /'ɔrfən/ n. сирота m. & f.; **—age** n. детдом

orthodox /'ɔrθə,dɒks/ adj. ортодоксальный; cap. (eccles.) православный

Orthodoxy /'ɔːθə,dɒksi/ *n.* пра-
воcлáвие

ostensible /ɒ'stensəbəl/ *adj.*
мни́мый; очеви́дный

ostentatious /,ɒsten'teiʃəs/ *adj.*
показно́й

ostracize /'ɒstrə,saiz/ *v.* из-
гоня́ть из о́бщества *impf.*

ostrich /'ɒstritʃ/ *n.* стра́ус

other /'ʌðər/ **1.** *adj.* друго́й;
ино́й **2.** *pron.* друго́й

otherwise /'ʌðər,waiz/ *adv.*,
conj. ина́че; а то

otter /'ɒtər/ *n.* вы́дра

ought /ɔːt/ *v.* до́лжен, -жна́,
-жно́, *pl.* -жны́ (бы) (+ *infin.*)

ounce /auns/ *n.* у́нция

our /auər/ *pron.* наш, на́ша,
на́ше, *pl.* на́ши

ourselves /ɑːr'selvz/ *pron.* себя́;
себе́, -ся; (мы) са́ми

oust /aust/ *v.* вытесня́ть *impf.*,
вы́теснить *pf.*

out /aut/ *adv.* нару́жу; вон; **she
is ~** её нет до́ма; **~ of** из, вне
(+ *G*)

outbreak /'aut,breik/ *n.*
вспы́шка; (*of war*) нача́ло

outburst /'aut,bɜːrst/ *n.* взрыв;
вспы́шка

outcast /'aut,kæst/ *n.* изгна́нник

outcome /'aut,kʌm/ *n.* резуль-
та́т

outdated /,aut'deitid/ *adj.* уста-
ре́лый; устаре́вший

outdoors /,aut'dɔːrz/ *adv.* на
откры́том во́здухе; (*dir.*) на
во́здух; на у́лицу

outer /'autər/ *adj.* вне́шний;
нару́жный; (*far*) да́льний

outfit /'aut,fit/ *n.* снаряже́ние

outhouse /'aut,haus/ *n.* нужни́к

outing /'autiŋ/ *n.* экску́рсия

outlaw /'aut,lɔ/ **1.** *n.* челове́к
вне зако́на **2.** *v.* запреща́ть
impf.

outlet /'autlet/ *n.* вы́ход; (*business*) ры́нок сбы́та

outline /'aut,lain/ *n.* очерта́ние
схе́ма

outlive /,aut'liv/ *v.* пережива́ть
impf., пережи́ть *pf.*

outlook /'aut,luk/ *n.* вид; пер-
спекти́ва

outpatient clinic /'aut,peiʃənt/
n. амбулато́рия

output /'aut,put/ *n.* вы́пуск;
производи́тельность; проду́кция

outrageous /aut'reidʒəs/ *adj.*
возмути́тельный

outside / *adj.*, *adv.*, *prep.*
,aut'said; *n.* 'aut'said/ **1.** *adj.*
вне́шний; нару́жный **2.** *adv.*
снару́жи; нару́жу; (*outdoors*) на
у́лице; (*dir.*) на у́лицу **3.** *prep.*
вне́шность **4.** *prep.* вне, за
преде́лами, за преде́лы (+ *G*);
—r *n.* посторо́нний

outskirts /'aut,skɜːrts/ *n.*
окра́ина

outstanding /,aut'stændiŋ/ *adj.*
(*distinguished*) выдаю́щийся;
(*unpaid*) неупла́ченный

outward /'autwərd/ *adj.*
нару́жный; вне́шний; **—ly** *adv.*
вне́шне; **—s** *adv.* нару́жу

outwit /,aut'wit/ *v.* перехитри́ть
impf.

oval /'ouvəl/ **1.** *n.* ова́л **2.** *adj.*
ова́льный

ovary /'ouvəri/ *n.* я́ичник

oven /'ʌvən/ *n.* духо́вка

over /'ouvər/ *prep.* над (+ *I*);
сверх, вы́ше (+ *G*); че́рез
(+ *A*)

overbearing /,ouvər'beəriŋ/ *adj.*
вла́стный

overboard /'ouvər,bɔːrd/ *adv.* за
бо́ртом; (*dir.*) за борт

overcast /'ouvər'kæst/ *adj.*
(*cloudy*) о́блачный; па́смурный

overcoat /'ouvər,kout/ *n.* пальто́
neut. indecl.

overcome /,ouvər'kʌm/ *v.* прео-
долева́ть *impf.*; преодоле́ть *pf.*

overcrowding /,ouvər'kraudiŋ/
n. теснота́; перенаселённость

overdue /,ouvər'du/ *adj.* запоз-
да́лый; просро́ченный

overflow /,ouvər'flou/ *v.* раз-
лива́ться *impf.*

overgrown /,ouvər'groun/ *adj.*
(*with weeds*) заро́сший

overhead / *adv.* ,ouvər'hed; *n.*
'ouvər,hed/ **1.** *adv.* над голово́й
2. *n.* накладны́е расхо́ды *pl.*

overhear /,ouvər'hiər/ *v.* под-
слу́шивать *impf.*

overload /,ouvər'loud/ *n.* пере-
гру́зка

overlook /,ouvər'luk/ *v.t.* (*miss*)
просмотре́ть *pf.*; (*have view*)
выходи́ть на (+ *A*) *impf.*

overnight /'ouvər'nait/ *adv.* на
ночь; за ночь; **stay ~** ночева́ть
impf.

overpower /,ouvər'pauər/ *v.*
одолева́ть *impf.*, одоле́ть *pf.*

overrule /,ouvər'rul/ *v.*
отверга́ть *impf.*, отве́ргнуть *pf.*

overseas /'ouvər'si:z/ *adj.* заморский; заграничный

oversee /,ouvər'si/ *v.* надзирать (за + I)

oversight /'ouvər,sait/ *n.* недосмотр

oversleep /,ouvər'slip/ *v.* просыпать *impf.*

overspend /,ouvər'spend/ *v.* переплачивать; растрачивать *impf.*

overtake /,ouvər'teik/ *v.* обгонять *impf.*, обогнать *pf.*

overthrow /,ouvər'θrou/ *v.* свергать *impf.*, свергнуть *pf.*

overtime /'ouvər,taim/ *n.* сверхурочное (время)

overture /'ouvər'tʃər/ *n.* увертюра; (*initiative*) инициатива

overturn /,ouvər'tɜrn/ *v.* опрокидывать(ся) *impf.*, опрокинуть(ся) *pf.*

overwhelm /,ouvər'welm/ *v.* (*with work*) заваливать *impf.*; (*weigh down*) подавлять *impf.*, -вить *pf.*; **—ing** подавляющий

overwork /,ouvər'wɜrk/ *v.* переутомлять(ся) *impf.*, -мить(ся) *pf.*

owe /ou/ *v.* быть должным; быть обязанным *impf.*

owing to /'ouiŋ/ *prep.* вследствие (+ G); благодаря (+ D)

owl /aul/ *n.* сова

own /oun/ **1.** *adj.* собственный **2.** *v.* владеть (+ I) *impf.*; **—er** *n.* владелец, -лица

ox /ɒks/ *n.* вол

oxide /'ɒksaid/ *n.* окись *f.*

oxygen /'ɒksidʒən/ *n.* кислород **2.** *adj.* кислородный

oyster /'ɔistər/ *n.* устрица

ozone /'ouzoun/ *n.* озон

P

pace /peis/ **1.** *n.* шаг; *Fig.* темп **2.** *v.* шагать *impf.*

pacifier /'pæsə,faiər/ *n.* соска

pacify /'pæsə,fai/ *v.* усмирять *impf.*, -рить *pf.*

pack /pæk/ **1.** *n.* (*of cigarettes*) пачка; (*of wolves*) стая; (*cards*) колода **2.** *v.* упаковывать *impf.*, упаковать *pf.*; (*cram*) набивать *impf.*, набить *pf.*; **—age** *n.* пакет; тюк; **—aging** *n.* упаковка; **~ animal** вьючное животное

packet /'pækit/ *n.* пакет; пачка

pact /pækt/ *n.* пакт; договор

pad /pæd/ *n.* (*cushion*) подушка; (*note* ~) блокнот; **—ding** *n.* набивка

paddle /'pædl/ *n.* весло

paddock /'pædək/ *n.* загон

padlock /'pæd,lɒk/ *n.* висячий замок

pagan /'peigən/ **1.** *adj.* языческий **2.** *n.* язычник, -ница; **—ism** *n.* язычество

page /peidʒ/ *n.* страница

paid /peid/ *adj.* платный; оплаченный

pail /peil/ *n.* ведро

pain /pein/ *n.* боль *f.*; **—ful** *adj.* болезненный

painkiller /'pein,kilər/ *n.* болеутоляющее (средство)

painstaking /'peinz,teikiŋ/ *adj.* старательный

paint /peint/ **1.** *n.* краска **2.** *v.* (*picture*) писать (красками) *impf.*, на- *pf.*; (*wall*) красить *impf.*, по- *pf.*; **—er** *n.* (*artist*) художник; живописец; (*worker*) маляр; **—ing** *n.* картина; (*act*) живопись *f.*

pair /peər/ **1.** *n.* пара **2.** *v.* спаривать *impf.*, спарить *pf.*; **~ off** разделяться на пары *impf.*; **—ed** *adj.* спаренный

pajamas /pə'dʒaməz/ *n.* пижама

Pakistan /,pækə,stæn/ *n.* Пакистан; **—i 1.** *adj.* пакистанский **2.** *n.* пакистанец, -анка

pal /pæl/ *n.* *Colloq.* приятель, —ница

palace /'pælis/ *n.* дворец

palate /'pælit/ *n.* нёбо; *Fig.* вкус

pale /peil/ *adj.* бледный; **turn ~** бледнеть *impf.*, по- *pf.*; **—ness** *n.* бледность

palette /'pælit/ *n.* палитра

pallet /'pælit/ *n.* тюфяк

pallid /'pælid/ *adj.* бледный

pallor /'pælər/ *n.* бледность

palm[1] /pɑm/ *n.* (*anat.*) ладонь *f.*

palm[2] /pɑm/ *n.* **1.** (*tree*) пальма **2.** *adj.* пальмовый

Palm Sunday *n.* Вербное Воскресенье

palpable /'pælpəbəl/ *adj.* ощутимый; (*obvious*) явный

palpitation /,pælpɪ'teiʃən/ *n.* (сильное) сердцебиение

palsy /'pɔlzi/ n. парали́ч

paltry /'pɔltri/ adj. ничто́жный

pamper /'pæmpər/ v. балова́ть impf., из- pf.

pamphlet /'pæmflit/ n. брошю́ра

pan /pæn/ n. сковорода́

pancake /'pæn,keik/ n. блин

pancreas /'pænkriəs/ n. поджелу́дочная железа́

pane /pein/ n. око́нное стекло́

panel /'pænl/ n. пане́ль f.; **control ~** пульт управле́ния

pang /pæŋ/ n. о́страя боль f.

panic /'pænik/ **1.** n. па́ника **2.** v.i. впада́ть в па́нику impf.

panorama /,pænə'ræmə/ n. панора́ма

pansy /'pænzi/ n. аню́тины гла́зки pl.

pant /pænt/ v. задыха́ться impf.

panther /'pænθər/ n. панте́ра

panties /'pæntiz/ n. тру́сики pl.

pantry /'pæntri/ n. кладова́я

pants /pænts/ n. брю́ки; штаны́ pl.

panty hose /'pænti/ n. колго́тки pl.

papal /'peipəl/ adj. па́пский

paper /'peipər/ **1.** adj. бума́га; (newspaper) газе́та; (essay) докла́д **2.** adj. бума́жный

paperback /'peipər,bæk/ n. кни́га в мя́гком переплёте

paper clip n. скре́пка

paperwork /'peipər,wɜrk/ n. канцеля́рская рабо́та

par /pɑr/ n. (econ.) номина́л; **on a ~ with** adv. наравне́ с (+ I)

parable /'pærəbəl/ n. при́тча

parachute /'pærə,ʃut/ n. парашю́т

parachutist /'pærə,ʃutist/ n. парашюти́ст

parade /pə'reid/ n. пара́д

paradise /'pærə,dais/ n. рай

paradox /'pærə,dɒks/ n. парадо́кс

paraffin /'pærəfin/ n. парафи́н

paragon /'pærə,gɒn/ n. образе́ц

paragraph /'pærə,græf/ n. пара́граф; абза́ц

parakeet /'pærə,kit/ n. попуга́й

parallel /'pærə,lel/ **1.** n. паралле́ль f. **2.** adj. паралле́льный

paralysis /pə'ræləsis/ n. парали́ч

paralyze /'pærə,laiz/ v. парализова́ть impf. & pf.

paramilitary /,pærə'mili,teri/ adj. полувое́нный

paramount /'pærə,maunt/ adj. первостепе́нный

paraphrase /'pærə,freiz/ **1.** v. переска́зывать impf., -сказа́ть pf. **2.** n. переска́з

parasite /'pærə,sait/ n. (biol.) парази́т; (person) туне́ядец

parcel /'pɑrsəl/ n. паке́т, посы́лка

pardon /'pɑrdn/ **1.** n. проще́ние **2.** v. проща́ть impf., -сти́ть pf.; (law) поми́ловать pf.

pare /peər/ (fruit) чи́стить impf.

parent /'peərənt/ n. роди́тель

parental /pə'rentl/ adj. роди́тельский

parenthesis /pə'renθəsis/ n. кру́глая ско́бка

parish /'pæriʃ/ n. прихо́д

parishioner /pə'riʃənər/ n. прихожа́нин, -жа́нка

parity /'pæriti/ n. ра́венство; (econ.) парите́т

park /pɑrk/ **1.** n. парк **2.** v. ста́вить (маши́ну) impf., по- pf.; **—ing** n. стоя́нка

parking lot n. автостоя́нка

parliament /'pɑrləmənt/ n. парла́мент

parliamentary /,pɑrlə'mentəri/ adj. парла́ментский

parochial /pə'roukiəl/ adj. (of parish) прихо́дский; (narrow) у́зкий

parody /'pærədi/ **1.** n. паро́дия **2.** v. пароди́ровать impf. & pf.

parrot /'pærət/ n. попуга́й

parry /'pæri/ v. пари́ровать impf. & pf.

parsley /'pɑrsli/ n. петру́шка

part /pɑrt/ **1.** n. часть f.; (role) роль f.; (mus.) па́ртия **2.** v. разлуча́ть(ся) impf., -чи́ть(ся) pf.; **~ with** расстава́ться (с + I) impf., расста́ться pf.

partake /pɑr'teik/ v. принима́ть уча́стие (в + P) impf.

partiality /pɑrʃi'æliti/ n. (bias) пристра́стие (к + D)

participant /pɑr'tisəpənt/ n. уча́стник, -ница

participate /pɑr'tisə,peit/ v. уча́ствовать (в + P) impf.

participle /'pɑrtə,sipəl/ n. прича́стие

particle /'pɑrtikəl/ n. части́ца

particular /pɑr'tikyələr/ **1.** adj. осо́бенный **2.** n. подро́бность

parting /'pɑrtiŋ/ n. расстава́ние; (of hair) пробо́р

partition /pɑr'tɪʃən/ n. разделе́ние; (wall) перегоро́дка
partly /'pɑrtli/ adv. части́чно
partner /'pɑrtnər/ n. партнёр
part-owner n. совладе́лец
partridge /'pɑrtrɪdʒ/ n. куропа́тка
part-time adv. на полста́вки
party /'pɑrti/ **1.** n. ве́чер; вечери́нка; (polit.) па́ртия (group) гру́ппа **2.** adj. парти́йный
pass /pæs/ **1.** n. (permit) про́пуск; (cards; sports) пас; (geog.) перева́л **2.** v. проходи́ть (ми́мо + G) impf., пройти́ pf.; (exam) сдава́ть impf., сдать pf.; (cards; sports) пасова́ть impf.; **~ away** сконча́ться pf.
passage /'pæsɪdʒ/ n. прое́зд, прохо́д; (on ship) рейс; (corridor) коридо́р; (of book) отры́вок
passenger /'pæsəndʒər/ **1.** n. пассажи́р, —ка **2.** adj. пассажи́рский
passerby /'pæsər'baɪ/ n. прохо́жий
passion /'pæʃən/ n. страсть f.
passionate /'pæʃənɪt/ adj. стра́стный
passive /'pæsɪv/ adj. пасси́вный; (gram.) страда́тельный
passkey /'pæs,ki/ n. отмы́чка
Passover /'pæs,ouvər/ n. Па́сха
passport /'pæspɔrt/ n. па́спорт
password /'pæs,wɜrd/ n. паро́ль m.
past /pæst/ **1.** adj. про́шлый; (gram.) проше́дший **2.** n. про́шлое **3.** prep. ми́мо (+ G); по́сле (+ G), за (+ A, I) **4.** adv. ми́мо
pasta /'pɑstə/ n. макаро́ны pl.
paste /peɪst/ **1.** n. па́ста; (glue) клей **2.** v. скле́ивать impf., скле́ить pf.
pastime /'pæs,taɪm/ n. развлече́ние
pastry /'peɪstri/ n. пиро́жное
pasture /'pæstʃər/ n. па́стбище
patch /pætʃ/ **1.** n. запла́та; (of land) уча́сток **2.** v. (mend) лата́ть impf., за- pf.
patchwork /'pætʃ,wɜrk/ n. лоску́тная рабо́та
pâté /pɑ'teɪ/ n. паште́т
patent /'pætnt/ **1.** adj. (obvious) очеви́дный; (patented) патенто́ванный **2.** n. пате́нт **3.** v. патентова́ть impf.

paternal /pə'tɜrnl/ adj. отцо́вский
path /pæθ/ n. тропи́нка; путь m.
pathetic /pə'θetɪk/ adj. жа́лкий
patience /'peɪʃəns/ n. терпе́ние
patient /'peɪʃənt/ **1.** adj. терпели́вый **2.** n. больно́й
patriarchal /,peɪtri'ɑrkəl/ adj. патриарха́льный
patriot /'peɪtriət/ n. патрио́т, —ка
patrol /pə'troul/ **1.** n. патру́ль m. **2.** v. патрули́ровать impf.
patron /'peɪtrən/ n. покрови́тель; (of the arts) мецена́т
patronizing /'peɪtrə,naɪzɪŋ/ adj. снисходи́тельный
pattern /'pætərn/ n. (model) образе́ц; (decoration) узо́р
pauper /'pɔpər/ n. бедня́к; ни́щий
pause /pɔz/ **1.** n. па́уза, переры́в **2.** v. остана́вливаться impf., останови́ться pf.
pave /peɪv/ v. мости́ть impf.; Fig. устила́ть impf., устла́ть pf.
paw /pɔ/ n. ла́па
pawn /pɔn/ **1.** n. (chess) пе́шка **2.** v. закла́дывать impf., заложи́ть pf.
pawnshop /'pɔn,ʃɑp/ n. ломба́рд
pay /peɪ/ **1.** n. зарпла́та **2.** v. плати́ть impf., за-, у- pf.
payload /'peɪ,loud/ n. поле́зная нагру́зка
payment /'peɪmənt/ n. платёж, упла́та
payoff /'peɪ,ɔf/ n. отпла́та; распла́та
payroll /'peɪ,roul/ n. платёжная ве́домость
pea /pi/ **1.** n. горо́шина; pl. горо́х **2.** adj. горо́ховый
peace /pis/ n. мир; **—ful** adj. ми́рный
peach /pitʃ/ n. пе́рсик
peacock /'pi,kɑk/ n. павли́н
peak /pik/ n. пик; верши́на; (cap) козырёк
peal /pil/ n. (bells) звон; (laughter) взрыв; (thunder) раска́т
peanut /'pi,nʌt/ n. ара́хис
pear /pɛər/ n. гру́ша
pearl /pɜrl/ **1.** n. жемчу́жина **2.** adj. жемчу́жный
peasant /'pezənt/ **1.** n. крестья́нин, —я́нка **2.** adj. крестья́нский
peat /pit/ n. торф

pebble /ˈpebəl/ *n.* га́лька

peck /pek/ *v.* клева́ть *impf.*

peculiar /pɪˈkyulyər/ *adj.* осо́бенный; (*strange*) стра́нный

peculiarity /pɪˌkyuliˈærɪti/ *n.* осо́бенность; стра́нность

pedal /ˈpedl/ *n.* педа́ль *f.*

pedestal /ˈpedəst/ *n.* пьедеста́л

pedestrian /pəˈdestriən/ **1.** *n.* пешехо́д **2.** *adj.* пешехо́дный

pediatrician /ˌpidiəˈtrɪʃən/ *n.* педиа́тр

pedicure /ˈpedɪˌkyur/ *n.* педикю́р

pedigree /ˈpedɪˌgri/ *n.* родосло́вная

peel /pil/ **1.** *n.* кожура́; ко́рка **2.** *v.* очища́ть *impf.*, очи́стить *pf.*

peelings /ˈpilɪŋz/ *n.pl.* шелуха́; очи́стки *pl.*

peep /pip/ *v.* взгля́дывать (на + *A*) *impf.*

peephole /ˈpipˌhoul/ *n.* глазо́к

peer /pɪər/ *n.* ро́вня *m.* & *f.*

peg /peg/ *n.* ко́лышек

pejorative /pɪˈdʒɔrətɪv/ *adj.* уничижи́тельный

pelican /ˈpelɪkən/ *n.* пелика́н

pelvis /ˈpelvɪs/ *n.* таз

pen /pen/ *n.* ру́чка; fountain ~, ballpoint ~ авторучка

penalty /ˈpenlti/ *n.* наказа́ние; штраф

penchant /ˈpentʃənt/ *n.* скло́нность (к + *D*)

pencil /ˈpensl/ *n.* каранда́ш

pencil case *n.* пена́л

pendulum /ˈpendʒələm/ *n.* ма́ятник

penetrate /ˈpenɪˌtreit/ *v.* проника́ть *impf.*, прони́кнуть *pf.*

penetrating /ˈpenɪˌtreitɪŋ/ *adj.* пронзи́тельный; проница́тельный

penguin /ˈpeŋgwɪn/ *n.* пингви́н

peninsula /pəˈnɪnsələ/ *n.* полуо́стров

penitent /ˈpenɪtənt/ **1.** *n.* ка́ющийся **2.** *adj.* ка́ющийся

penitentiary /ˌpenɪˈtenʃəri/ **1.** *n.* тюрьма́ **2.** *adj.* пенитенциа́рный

pennant /ˈpenənt/ *n.* вы́мпел

penny /ˈpeni/ *n.* (*Brit.*) пенс, (*U.S.*) пе́нни *neut. indecl.*

pension /ˈpenʃən/ *n.* пе́нсия

pensive /ˈpensɪv/ *adj.* заду́мчивый

penultimate /pɪˈnʌltəmɪt/ *adj.* предпосле́дний

people /ˈpipəl/ **1.** *n.* лю́ди *pl.*;

(*nation*) наро́д **2.** *v.* населя́ть *impf.*, -ли́ть *pf.*

pepper /ˈpepər/ *n.* пе́рец

pepper mill *n.* пе́речница

peppermint /ˈpepərˌmɪnt/ *n.* (*bot.*) мя́та (пе́речная)

per /pər/ *prep.* че́рез (+ *A*), посре́дством (+ *G*); в; на (+ *A*); по (+ *D*); с (+ *G*); за (+ *A*)

perceive /pərˈsiv/ *v.* ощуща́ть *impf.*, ощути́ть *pf.*

percent /pərˈsent/ *n.* проце́нт

percentage /pərˈsentɪdʒ/ *n.* проце́нт; проце́нтное соотноше́ние; (*portion*) часть *f.*

perceptible /pərˈseptəbəl/ *adj.* ощути́мый; заме́тный

perception /pərˈsepʃən/ *n.* восприя́тие; понима́ние

perch[1] /pərtʃ/ *n.* (*roost*) насе́ст

perch[2] /pərtʃ/ *n.* (*fish*) о́кунь *m.*

perfect 1. /ˈpərfɪkt/ *adj.* соверше́нный; по́лный **2.** /pərˈfekt/ *v.* соверше́нствовать *impf.*, у- *pf.*; —**ion** *n.* соверше́нство

perfective /pərˈfektɪv/ *n.* (*gram.*) соверше́нный вид

perform /pərˈfɔrm/ *v.* исполня́ть *impf.*, испо́лнить *pf.*; —**ance** *n.* исполне́ние; (*theat.*) игра́; —**er** *n.* исполни́тель, -ница

perfume /ˈpərfyum/ *n.* духи́ *pl.*

perfunctory /pərˈfʌŋktəri/ *adj.* пове́рхностный; небре́жный

perhaps /pərˈhæps/ *adv.* мо́жет быть

peril /ˈperəl/ *n.* опа́сность; риск

perilous /ˈperələs/ *adj.* опа́сный

period /ˈpɪəriəd/ *n.* пери́од; эпо́ха; (*punctuation*) то́чка

periodical /ˌpɪəriˈɒdɪkəl/ **1.** *n.* периоди́ческий журна́л **2.** *adj.* периоди́ческий; —**ly** *adv.* вре́мя от вре́мени

perish /ˈperɪʃ/ *v.* погиба́ть *impf.*, поги́бнуть *pf.*; —**able** *adj.* скоропортя́щийся

perjury /ˈpərdʒəri/ *n.* клятвопреступле́ние; лжесвиде́тельство

permanence /ˈpərmənəns/ *n.* постоя́нство; неизме́нность

permanent /ˈpərmənənt/ *adj.* постоя́нный, (*n.*) (*hair*) перманэ́нт

permeable /ˈpərmiəbəl/ *adj.* проница́емый

permissible /pərˈmɪsəbəl/ *adj.* позволи́тельный; допусти́мый

permission /pər'mɪʃən/ n. разрешéние

permit / n. 'pɜːrmɪt; v. pər'mɪt/ **1.** n. разрешéние; (pass) прóпуск **2.** v. разрешáть impf., -шить pf.

perpetrate /'pɜːrpɪ,treɪt/ v. совершáть impf., -шить pf.

perpetual /pər'petʃuəl/ adj. вéчный

perpetuate /pər'petʃu,eɪt/ v. увековéчивать impf.

perplex /pər'pleks/ v. озадáчивать impf., озадáчить pf.; **—ing** adj. озадáчивающий; стрáнный

persecute /'pɜːrsɪ,kyut/ v. преслéдовать impf.

persecution /,pɜːrsɪ'kyuʃən/ n. преслéдование

perseverance /,pɜːrsə'vɪərəns/ n. настóйчивость

Persian /'pɜːrʒən/ **1.** adj. персúдский **2.** n. перс, —úянка

persist /pər'sɪst/ v. упóрствовать impf.; **—ence** n. упóрство

person /'pɜːrsən/ n. человéк; осóба; (gram.) лицó; **—age** n. лúчность; (theat.) персонáж

personal /'pɜːrsənl/ adj. лúчный; чáстный; ~ **computer** (abbr. **P.C.**) персонáльный компьютер; ~ **identification number** n. (abbr. **P.I.N.**) персонáльный код

personality /,pɜːrsə'nælɪti/ n. лúчность; индивидуáльность

personification /pər,sɒnəfɪ'keɪʃən/ n. олицетворéние; (embodiment) воплощéние

personnel /,pɜːrsə'nel/ n. персонáл; лúчный состáв

perspective /pər'spektɪv/ n. перспектúва

persuade /pər'sweɪd/ v. убеждáть impf., -дúть pf.; уговáривать impf.

persuasion /pər'sweɪʒən/ n. убеждéние

persuasive /pər'sweɪsɪv/ adj. убедúтельный

pertinent /'pɜːrtnənt/ adj. подходящий; умéстный

pervasive /pər'veɪsɪv/ adj. распространённый

perversion /pər'vɜːrʒən/ n. извращéние

pervert / n. 'pɜːrvɜːrt; v. pər'vɜːrt/ **1.** n. извращённый человéк **2.** v. извращáть impf., -тúть pf.

pessimism /'pesə,mɪzəm/ n. пессимúзм

pest /pest/ n. (insect) вредúтель; зарáза; (person) занýда m. & f.

pet /pet/ n. **1.** n. любúмец, -мица; (animal) домáшнее живóтное **2.** v. ласкáть impf.

petal /'petl/ n. лепестóк

petition /pə'tɪʃən/ **1.** n. петúция **2.** v. обращáться с петúцией; **—er** n. (law) истéц

petrify /'petrə,faɪ/ v. окаменéть pf.

petroleum /pə'troulɪəm/ **1.** n. нефть f. **2.** adj. нефтянóй

petty /'peti/ adj. маловáжный; мéлкий; мéлочный

petulant /'petʃələnt/ adj. раздражúтельный

phalanx /'feɪlæŋks/ n. фалáнга

phantom /'fæntəm/ n. прúзрак

pharmacist /'farməsɪst/ n. аптéкарь m.; фармацéвт

pharmacy /'farməsi/ n. (science) фармацúя; (store) аптéка

phase /feɪz/ n. фáза

pheasant /'fezənt/ n. фазáн

phenomenal /fɪ'nɒmənl/ adj. феноменáльный

phial /'faɪəl/ n. пузырёк; склянка

philharmonic /,fɪlhɑr'mɒnɪk/ adj. филармонúческий

philologist /fɪ'lɒlədʒɪst/ n. филóлог; языковéд

philosopher /fɪ'lɒsəfər/ n. филóсоф

philosophy /fɪ'lɒsəfi/ n. филосóфия

phlegm /flem/ n. мокрóта

phone /foun/ **1.** n. телефóн **2.** v. звонúть impf., по- pf.; ~ **booth** телефóн-автомáт

phonetic /fə'netɪk/ adj. фонетúческий

phonograph /'founə,græf/ n. граммофóн; патефóн

phosphorus /'fɒsfərəs/ n. фóсфор

photo /'foutou/ n. снúмок

photocell /'foutou,sel/ n. фотоэлемéнт

photocopier /'foutə,kɒpiər/ n. ксéрокс

photocopy /'foutə,kɒpi/ **1.** n. ксерокóпия, фотокóпия **2.** v. ксерокопúровать impf. & pf.

photograph /'foutə,græf/ **1.** n. фотогрáфия; снúмок **2.** v. фотографúровать impf., с- pf.

photographer /fə'tɒgrəfər/ n. фотóграф

photography /fə'tɒgrəfi/ n. фотография;

phrase /freiz/ **1.** n. фра́за; выраже́ние **2.** v. формули́ровать impf., c- pf.; ~ **book** n. разгово́рник

physical /'fɪzɪkəl/ adj. физи́ческий

physician /fɪ'zɪʃən/ n. врач

physicist /'fɪzəsɪst/ n. фи́зик

physics /'fɪzɪks/ n. фи́зика

pianist /'pɪənɪst/ n. пиани́ст, —ка

piano /pɪ'ænou/ n. роя́ль m. (upright) пиани́но neut. indecl.

pick /pɪk/ **1.** n. (choice) вы́бор **2.** v. (choose) выбира́ть impf., вы́брать pf.; (gather) собира́ть impf., собра́ть pf.; ~ **up** поднима́ть impf., подня́ть pf.

pickax /'pɪkæks/ n. кирка́

picket /'pɪkɪt/ **1.** n. пике́т **2.** v. пикети́ровать impf.

pickle /'pɪkəl/ **1.** n. солёный огуре́ц **2.** v. маринова́ть impf., за- pf.; ~**d** adj. марино́ванный; солёный

pickpocket /'pɪk,pɒkɪt/ n. карма́нник

picnic /'pɪknɪk/ n. пикни́к

picture /'pɪktʃər/ **1.** n. карти́на; (movie) фильм; (photo) сни́мок **2.** v. вообража́ть impf.; (depict) изобража́ть impf., -зи́ть pf.

picturesque /,pɪktʃə'resk/ adj. живопи́сный

pie /pai/ n. пиро́г

piece /pis/ n. кусо́к; часть f.; —**work** n. сде́льная рабо́та

pier /pɪər/ n. пирс; мол

pierce /pɪərs/ v. пронза́ть impf., -зи́ть pf.

piercing /'pɪərsɪŋ/ adj. пронзи́тельный

piety /'paiti/ n. на́божность

pig /pɪg/ n. свинья́

pigeon /'pɪdʒən/ n. го́лубь m.

piggy bank /'pɪgi/ n. копи́лка

pigtail /'pɪg,teil/ n. коси́чка

pike /paik/ n. (fish) щу́ка

pilaf /pɪ'laf/ n. плов

pile /pail/ **1.** n. ку́ча; гру́да **2.** v. нагроможда́ть impf., -озди́ть pf.

pilgrim /'pɪlgrɪm/ n. пало́мник, -ница; —**age** n. пало́мничество

pill /pɪl/ n. пилю́ля

pillar /'pɪlər/ n. столб

pillow /'pɪlou/ n. поду́шка; —**case** n. на́волочка

pilot /'pailət/ **1.** n. пило́т; лётчик **2.** v. (aero.) пилоти́ровать impf. **3.** adj. о́пытный; про́бный; ~**light** n. контро́льная горе́лка

pimple /'pɪmpəl/ n. прыщик

pin /pɪn/ **1.** n. була́вка; (mech.) па́лец; болт; (badge) значо́к **2.** v. прика́лывать impf., приколо́ть pf.

pincers /'pɪnsərz/ n. пинце́т; (tool) кле́щи pl.

pinch /pɪntʃ/ **1.** n. щипо́к; (of salt) щепо́тка **2.** v. щипа́ть impf., ущипну́ть pf.

pine[1] /pain/ n. (tree) сосна́

pine[2] /pain/ v. ча́хнуть impf.

pineapple /'pai,næpəl/ n. анана́с

ping-pong /'pɪŋ,pɒŋ/ n. пинг-по́нг, насто́льный те́ннис

pink /pɪŋk/ adj. ро́зовый

pinnacle /'pɪnəkəl/ n. верши́на

pint /paint/ n. пи́нта

pioneer /,paiə'nɪər/ **1.** n. пионе́р, —ка **2.** adj. пионе́рский

pious /'paiəs/ adj. на́божный

pipe /paip/ n. труба́; (for smoking) тру́бка

pipeline /'paip,lain/ n. трубопрово́д; (oil) нефтепрово́д

pirate /'pairət/ n. пира́т

pistachio /pɪ'stæʃi,ou/ n. фиста́шка

pistol /'pɪstl/ n. пистоле́т

piston /'pɪstən/ n. по́ршень m.

pit /pɪt/ n. я́ма; (fruit) ко́сточка

pitch /pɪtʃ/ **1.** n. (ship) ка́чка; (mus.) высота́; (degree) сте́пень f. **2.** v. (throw) броса́ть impf.; (tent) разбива́ть impf.

pitch-dark n. кроме́шная тьма

pitcher /'pɪtʃər/ n. (vessel) кувши́н; (baseball) пи́тчер

pitfall /'pɪt,fɔl/ n. лову́шка

pitiful /'pɪtɪfəl/ adj. жа́лкий

pitiless /'pɪtɪlɪs/ adj. безжа́лостный

pity /'pɪti/ **1.** n. жа́лость **2.** v. жале́ть impf., по- pf.; **what a ~!** как жаль!

pivot /'pɪvət/ **1.** n. сте́ржень m.; Fig. центр **2.** v. враща́ться impf.

pizza /'pitsə/ n. пи́цца

placard /'plækard/ n. плака́т

place /pleis/ **1.** n. ме́сто **2.** v. ста́вить impf., по- pf.; помеща́ть impf.; —**ment** n. расстано́вка; расположе́ние

placid /'plæsɪd/ adj. споко́йный

plagiarism /'pleidʒə,rɪzəm/ n. плагиа́т

plague /pleig/ **1.** *n.* чума́ **2.** *v.* досажда́ть *impf.*, досади́ть *pf.*

plaice /pleis/ *n.* камбала́

plain /plein/ **1.** *adj.* я́сный; просто́й **2.** *n.* равни́на

plaintiff /ˈpleintif/ *n.* исте́ц, -тица

plaintive /ˈpleintiv/ *adj.* жа́лобный

plait /pleit/ **1.** *n.* коса́ **2.** *v.* плести́ *impf.*, с- *pf.*

plan /plæn/ **1.** *n.* план; прое́кт **2.** *v.* плани́ровать *impf.*, за- *pf.*; (*intend*) собира́ться *impf.*

plane[1] /plein/ *n.* (*surface*) пло́скость; (*airplane*) самолёт

plane[2] /plein/ *n.* (*tool*) руба́нок **2.** *v.* строга́ть *impf.*

planet /ˈplænit/ *n.* плане́та

plank /plæŋk/ *n.* доска́

plant /plænt/ **1.** *n.* расте́ние; (*factory*) заво́д **2.** *v.* сажа́ть *impf.*, посади́ть *pf.*

plantation /plænˈteiʃən/ *n.* планта́ция

plaque /plæk/ *n.* доще́чка

plaster /ˈplæstər/ **1.** *n.* (*med.*) пла́стырь *m.*; (*wall*) гипс **2.** *v.* штукату́рить *impf.*, о- *pf.*

plastic /ˈplæstik/ **1.** *n.* пласт-ма́сса **2.** *adj.* пластма́ссовый; пласти́ческий; пласти́чный

plate /pleit/ *n.* (*dish*) таре́лка

plateau /ˈplætou/ *n.* плоского́рье

platform /ˈplætform/ *n.* платфо́рма; (*stage*) помо́ст

platinum /ˈplætnəm/ **1.** *n.* пла́тина **2.** *adj.* пла́тиновый

platter /ˈplætər/ *n.* блю́до

plausible /ˈplɔzəbəl/ *adj.* вероя́тный; правдоподо́бный

play /plei/ *n.* игра́; (*theat.*) пье́са **v.** игра́ть *impf.*, сыгра́ть *pf.*; —er *n.* игро́к; —ful *adj.* игри́вый

playground /ˈplei,graund/ *n.* де́тская площа́дка

playwright /ˈplei,rait/ *n.* драмату́рг

plaza /ˈplazə/ *n.* пло́щадь *f.*

plea /pli/ *n.* мольба́; (*law*) заявле́ние

plead /plid/ *v.* умоля́ть *impf.*; ~ a case защища́ть де́ло *impf.*

pleasant /ˈplezənt/ *adj.* прия́тный

please /pliz/ **1.** *v.* нра́виться *impf.*, по- *pf.* **2.** *adv.* пожа́-

луйста!; —d *adj.* дово́льный; *pred.* рад

pleasure /ˈpleʒər/ *n.* удово́льствие

pleat /plit/ *n.* скла́дка

pledge /pledʒ/ **1.** *n.* (*security*) зало́г; (*promise*) обеща́ние **2.** *v.* (*leave as security*) закла́дывать *impf.*, заложи́ть *pf.*; (*vow*) кля́сться (в + P) *impf.*

plentiful /ˈplentifəl/ *adj.* оби́льный

plenty /ˈplenti/ **1.** *n.* изоби́лие **2.** *adj.* *Colloq.* изря́дно

pliable /ˈplaiəbəl/ *adj.* ги́бкий

pliers /ˈplaiərz/ *n.* плоскогу́бцы *pl.*

plight /plait/ *n.* затрудни́тельное положе́ние

plot /plot/ **1.** *n.* (*of land*) уча́сток; (*fiction*) сюже́т; (*conspiracy*) за́говор **2.** *v.* замышля́ть *impf.*, замы́слить *pf.*

plow /plau/ **1.** *n.* плуг **2.** *v.* паха́ть *impf.*, вс- *pf.*

plowshare /ˈplau,ʃeər/ *n.* ле́мех

ploy /ploi/ *n.* уло́вка; приём

plug /plʌg/ **1.** *n.* заты́чка; про́бка; (*elec.*) ви́лка **2.** *v.* затыка́ть *impf.*, заткну́ть *pf.*

plum /plʌm/ **1.** *n.* сли́ва **2.** *adj.* сли́вовый

plumber /ˈplʌmər/ *n.* сле́сарь *m.*

plumbing /ˈplʌmiŋ/ *n.* санте́хника

plump /plʌmp/ *adj.* пу́хлый; по́лный

plunder /ˈplʌndər/ **1.** *n.* грабёж **2.** *v.* гра́бить *impf.*, о- *pf.*

plunge /plʌndʒ/ *v.* погружа́ть(ся) *impf.*, -зи́ть(ся) *pf.*

plural /ˈplurəl/ *n.* мно́жественное число́

plurality /pluˈræliti/ *n.* мно́жественность; большинство́

plus /plʌs/ *prep.* плюс (+ A)

plywood /ˈplai,wud/ *n.* фане́ра

pneumonia /nuˈmounjə/ *n.* воспале́ние лёгких; пневмони́я

poacher /ˈpoutʃər/ *n.* браконье́р

pocket /ˈpokit/ **1.** *n.* карма́н **2.** *adj.* карма́нный **3.** *v.* прикарма́нивать *impf.*, прикарма́нить *pf.*

pocketbook /ˈpokit,buk/ *n.* бума́жник; кошелёк

pocketknife /ˈpokit,naif/ *n.* карма́нный (складно́й) но́ж(ик)

poem /ˈpouəm/ *n.* стихотворе́ние

poet /'pouɪt/ *n.* поэ́т; **—ry** *n.* поэ́зия

pogrom /pə'grʌm/ *n.* погро́м

point /pɔɪnt/ 1. *n.* то́чка; пункт; (*tip*) ко́нчик; ~ **of view** то́чка зре́ния; **that's not the** ~ де́ло не в э́том 2. *v.* пока́зывать; ука́зывать пальцем, -каза́ть *pf.*; **—er** *n.* (*on dial, etc.*) указа́тель; стре́лка; **—less** *adj.* бессмы́сленный

poison /'pɔɪzən/ 1. *n.* яд 2. *v.* отравля́ть *impf.*, -ви́ть *pf.*; **—ous** *adj.* ядови́тый

poke /pouk/ 1. *n.* толчо́к 2. *v.* ты́кать *impf.*, ты́кнуть *pf.*; **—r** *n.* (*rod*) кочерга́; (*cards*) по́кер

Poland /'poulənd/ *n.* По́льша

polar /'poulər/ *adj.* поля́рный

polar fox *n.* песе́ц

polarity /pou'lærɪti/ *n.* поля́рность

Pole /poul/ *n.* поля́к, по́лька

pole /poul/ *n.* шест; столб; (*geog.*) по́люс

polemic /pə'lemɪk/ 1. *n.* поле́мика 2. *adj.* полеми́ческий

police /pə'lis/ 1. *n.* поли́ция 2. *adj.* полице́йский; **—man, of-ficer** *n.* полице́йский

policy /'pɒlɪsi/ *n.* поли́тика; (*in-surance*) по́лис

Polish /'poulɪʃ/ *adj.* по́льский

polish /'pɒlɪʃ/ 1. *n.* полиро́вка; *Fig.* лоск 2. *v.* полирова́ть *impf.*, отполирова́ть *pf.*; **shoe** ~ крем для о́буви

polite /pə'laɪt/ *adj.* ве́жливый; **—ness** *n.* ве́жливость

political /pə'lɪtɪkəl/ *adj.* полити́ческий

politician /ˌpɒlɪ'tɪʃən/ *n.* поли́тик

politics /'pɒlɪtɪks/ *n.* поли́тика

poll /poul/ *n.* баллотиро́вка; (*survey*) опро́с

pollen /'pɒlən/ *n.* пыльца́

pollute /pə'lut/ *v.* загрязня́ть *impf.*, -ни́ть *pf.*

pollution /pə'luʃən/ *n.* загрязне́ние

polytechnic /ˌpɒli'teknɪk/ *n.* политéхникум

pomade /pɒ'meɪd/ *n.* пома́да

pomp /pɒmp/ *n.* пы́шность

pompous /'pɒmpəs/ *adj.* напыщенный

pond /pɒnd/ *n.* пруд

ponder /'pɒndər/ *v.* обду́мывать *impf.*, обду́мать *pf.*; **—ous** *adj.* тяжеловéсный

pool /pul/ *n.* (*puddle*) лу́жа; (*swimming pool*) бассе́йн

poor /pur/ 1. *adj.* бе́дный; (*bad*) плохо́й 2. *n.*: **the** ~ бе́дные *pl.*

Pope /poup/ *n.* Па́па

poplar /'pɒplər/ *n.* то́поль *m.*

poppy /'pɒpi/ *n.* мак

popular /'pɒpyələr/ *adj.* популя́рный; наро́дный

popularity /ˌpɒpyə'lærɪti/ *n.* популя́рность

population /ˌpɒpyə'leɪʃən/ *n.* населе́ние

populous /'pɒpyələs/ *adj.* густонаселённый

porcelain /'pɔrsəlɪn/ *n.* фарфо́р

porch /pɔrtʃ/ *n.* вера́нда

porcupine /'pɔrkyə,paɪn/ *n.* дикобра́з

pore /pɔr/ *n.* по́ра

pork /pɔrk/ 1. *n.* свини́на 2. *adj.* свино́й

porous /'pɔrəs/ *adj.* по́ристый

port[1] /pɔrt/ *n.* (*city*) порт; га́вань *f.*

port[2] /pɔrt/ *n.* (*wine*) портве́йн

portable /'pɔrtəbəl/ *adj.* перено́сный; портати́вный

porter /'pɔrtər/ *n.* носи́льщик

portfolio /pɔrt'fouli,ou/ *n.* портфе́ль *m.*; па́пка

portion /'pɔrʃən/ *n.* часть *f.*; до́ля; (*of food*) по́рция

portrait /'pɔrtrɪt/ *n.* портре́т

portray /pɔr'treɪ/ *v.* изобража́ть *impf.*, -зи́ть *pf.*

Portugal /'pɔrtʃəgəl/ *n.* Португáлия

Portuguese /ˌpɔrtʃə'giz/ 1. *adj.* португáльский 2. *n.* португáлец, -гáлка

pose /pouz/ 1. *n.* по́за 2. *v.* пози́ровать *impf.*; (*put*) ста́вить *impf.*; по- *pf.*; ~ **as** выдава́ть себя́ (за + *A*) *impf.*

position /pə'zɪʃən/ *n.* положе́ние; пози́ция; (*rank*) до́лжность

positive /'pɒzɪtɪv/ *adj.* положи́тельный; **—ly** *adv.* несомне́нно

possess /pə'zes/ *v.* владе́ть; облада́ть (+ *I*) *impf.*; **—ed** *adj.* одержи́мый

possession /pə'zeʃən/ *n.* владе́ние; *pl.* иму́щество

possibility /ˌpɒsə'bɪlɪti/ *n.* возмо́жность

possible /'pɒsəbəl/ *adj.* возмо́жный

post¹ /poust/ **1.** n. (pole) столб **2.** v. вывешивать impf., вывесить pf.

post² /poust/ n. (station) пост; (job) должность; **—age** n. почтовая оплата; **—al** adj. почтовый; **~ card** n. открытка

poster /'poustər/ n. плакат; афиша

posterity /po'steriti/ n. потомство

postgraduate /poust'grædʒuit/ n. аспирант

postman /'poustmən/ n. почтальон

postmark /'poust,mark/ n. почтовый штемпель m.

post office n. почта

postpone /poust'poun/ v. откладывать impf., отложить pf.; отсрочивать impf., отсрочить pf.; **—ment** n. отсрочка

posture /'postfər/ n. поза; положение; (carriage) осанка

pot /pot/ n. кастрюля; (for flowers) горшок

potassium /pə'tæsiəm/ n. калий

potato /pə'teitou/ **1.** n. картофель m. **2.** adj. картофельный

potent /'poutnt/ adj. сильный

potential /pə'tenfəl/ **1.** adj. потенциальный **2.** n. потенциал

pothole /'pot,houl/ n. (in road) рытвина; выбоина

pot roast n. тушёное мясо

potter /'potər/ n. гончар; **—y** n. глиняные изделия pl.

pouch /pautʃ/ n. мешок; сумка

poultry /'poultri/ n. домашняя птица

pounce /pauns/ v. набрасываться; налетать (на + A) impf.

pound¹ /paund/ n. фунт

pound² /paund/ v. (crush) толочь impf., рас- pf.

pour /por/ v. лить(ся) impf.

poverty /'povərti/ n. бедность

powder /'paudər/ **1.** n. порошок; (talcum) пудра; (gun) порох **2.** v. пудрить impf., на- pf.

power /'pauər/ n. сила; мощь; власть f.; **—ful** adj. сильный; мощный; **—less** adj. бессильный; **~ station** n. электростанция

practical /'præktikəl/ adj. практический

practice /'præktis/ **1.** n.

практика; (habit) привычка; (exercise) упражнение **2.** v. (drill) упражняться; практиковаться impf.

praise /preiz/ **1.** n. похвала **2.** v. хвалить impf., по- pf.

prank /præŋk/ n. шалость

prattle /'prætl/ v. лепетать impf.

prawn /prɔn/ n. креветка

pray /prei/ v. молиться impf.

prayer /preər/ n. молитва

preach /pritʃ/ v. проповедовать impf.; **—er** n. проповедник

precaution /pri'kɔʃən/ n. предосторожность

precede /pri'sid/ v. предшествовать impf.

precedent /'presidənt/ n. прецедент

preceding /pri'sidiŋ/ adj. предыдущий; предшествующий

precept /'prisept/ n. наставление

precinct /'prisiŋkt/ n. (police) отделение милиции

precious /'prefəs/ adj. драгоценный

precipice /'presəpis/ n. обрыв

precipitate /pri'sipitit/ n. (hasten) ускорять impf., ускорить pf.

precipitous /pri'sipitəs/ adj. крутой; обрывистый

precise /pri'sais/ adj. точный

precision /pri'siʒən/ n. точность

preconceived /,prikən'sivd/ adj. предвзятый

predator /'predətər/ n. хищник

predecessor /'predə,sesər/ n. предшественник

predicament /pri'dikəmənt/ n. затруднительное положение

predict /pri'dikt/ v. предсказывать impf., предсказать pf.

predisposition /,pri,dispə'ziʃən/ n. предрасположение (к + D)

predominant /pri'domənənt/ adj. преобладающий

prefabricated /pri'fæbri,keitid/ adj. сборный

preface /'prefis/ n. предисловие

prefer /pri'fər/ v. предпочитать impf.

preference /'prefərəns/ n. предпочтение

prefix /'prifiks/ n. приставка

pregnancy /'pregnənsi/ n. беременность

pregnant /'pregnənt/ adj. беременная

prehistoric /ˌpriːhɪˈstɒrɪk/ adj. доисторический

prejudice /ˈpredʒədɪs/ n. предубеждение; (detriment) ущерб; **—d** adj. (against) предубеждённый (прóтив + G)

preliminary /prɪˈlɪmɪˌneri/ adj. предварительный

prelude /ˈprelyud/ n. прелюдия

premature /ˌpriːməˈtʃʊr/ adj. преждевременный

premier /prɪˈmɪr/ n. премьéр-министр

première /prɪˈmɪr/ n. премьéра

premise /ˈpremɪs/ n. предпосылка; pl. (land) помещéние

premium /ˈpriːmiəm/ n. прéмия

preoccupied /priˈɒkyəˌpaɪd/ adj. (anxious) озабóченный

preoccupy /priˈɒkyəˌpaɪ/ v. поглощáть impf.

preparation /ˌprepəˈreɪʃən/ n. приготовлéние; подготóвка

preparatory /prɪˈpærəˌtɔri/ adj. подготовительный

prepare /prɪˈpeər/ v. готовить(ся) (к + D) impf., при- pf.; **—d** adj. готóвый

preposition /ˌprepəˈzɪʃən/ n. предлóг

preposterous /prɪˈpɒstərəs/ adj. абсýрдный

prerequisite /priˈrekwəzɪt/ n. предпосылка

prerogative /prɪˈrɒgətɪv/ n. прерогатива

preschool /ˈpriːˌskul/ adj. дошкóльный

prescribe /prɪˈskraɪb/ v. предписывать impf.; (med.) прописывать impf., -писáть pf.

prescription /prɪˈskrɪpʃən/ n. предписáние; (med.) рецéпт

presence /ˈprezəns/ n. присýтствие

present[1] /adj., n. ˈprezənt/ v. prɪˈzent/ **1.** adj. присýтствующий; (time) настоящий; **be ~** присýтствовать impf. **2.** n. настоящее врéмя neut.; **—ly** adv. сейчáс

present[2] /ˈprezənt/ **1.** n. (gift) подáрок **2.** v. (gift) дарить impf., по- pf.; (introduce) представлять impf., представить pf.

presentable /prɪˈzentəbəl/ adj. приличный

presentation /ˌprezənˈteɪʃən/ n. представлéние

preservation /ˌprezərˈveɪʃən/ n. сохранéние

preservative /prɪˈzɜrvətɪv/ n. консервант

preserve /prɪˈzɜrv/ **1.** n. (for game) заповéдник; pl. (jam) варéнье **2.** v. сохранять impf., -нить pf.; (food) консервировать impf.

preside /prɪˈzaɪd/ v. председáтельствовать impf.

president /ˈprezɪdənt/ n. президéнт; председáтель

press /pres/ **1.** n. (device) пресс; (the press) печáть f.; прéсса **2.** v. нажимáть impf., нажáть pf.; давить impf.

pressure /ˈpreʃər/ n. давлéние

prestige /preˈstiʒ/ n. престиж

presumably /prɪˈzuːməbli/ adv. предположительно

presume /prɪˈzuːm/ v. предполагáть impf., предположить pf.

presumption /prɪˈzʌmpʃən/ n. предположéние

presumptuous /prɪˈzʌmptʃuəs/ adj. самонадéянный

pretend /prɪˈtend/ v. притворяться (+ I), -риться pf.

pretension /prɪˈtenʃən/ n. претéнзия

pretentious /prɪˈtenʃəs/ adj. претенциóзный

pretext /ˈpriːtekst/ n. предлóг

pretty /ˈprɪti/ **1.** adj. хорошéнький; приятный **2.** adv. довóльно

prevailing /prɪˈveɪlɪŋ/ adj. преобладáющий; господствующий

prevent /prɪˈvent/ v. (protect) предохранять impf., -нить pf.; (hinder) препятствовать impf.; **—ion** n. предупреждéние

preventive /prɪˈventɪv/ adj. предупредительный

previous /ˈpriːviəs/ adj. предыдущий; **—ly** adv. рáньше

prewar /ˈpriːˈwɔr/ adj. довоéнный

prey /preɪ/ n. (animal) добыча

price /praɪs/ **1.** n. ценá **2.** v. оцéнивать impf., оценить pf.; **—less** adj. бесцéнный; **~ list** n. прейскурáнт

prick /prɪk/ **1.** n. укóл **2.** v. колóть impf., у-, кольнýть pf.; **—ly** adj. колючий

pride /praɪd/ n. гóрдость

priest /priːst/ n. свящéнник

prim /prɪm/ *adj.* чо́порный

primarily /'praɪ'meərəli/ *adv.* в пе́рвую о́чередь

primary /'praɪmeri/ *adj.* основно́й; **~ school** *n.* нача́льная шко́ла

prime /praɪm/ *adj.* гла́вный; **in one's ~** в расцве́те сил; **~ minister** *n.* премье́р-мини́стр

primitive /'prɪmɪtɪv/ *adj.* примити́вный

primp /prɪmp/ *v.* прихора́шиваться *impf.*

primrose /'prɪm‚rouz/ *n.* при́мула

prince /prɪns/ *n.* князь *m.*; (non-Russian) принц

princess /'prɪnsɪs/ *n.* княги́ня; (daughter) княжна́; (non-Russian) принце́сса

principal /'prɪnsəpəl/ **1.** *adj.* гла́вный **2.** *n.* (of school) дире́ктор

principle /'prɪnsəpəl/ *n.* при́нцип

print /prɪnt/ **1.** *n.* печа́ть *f.*; шрифт; (mark) отпеча́ток; (art) гравю́ра **2.** *v.* печа́тать *impf.*, на~ *pf.*; **—er** *n.* при́нтер; **—ing** *n.* печа́тание

printout /'prɪnt‚aut/ *n.* распеча́тка

prior /'praɪər/ *adj.* пре́жний

priority /praɪ'ɔrɪti/ *n.* приорите́т

prism /'prɪzəm/ *n.* при́зма

prison /'prɪzən/ **1.** *n.* тюрьма́ **2.** *adj.* тюре́мный; **~ camp** *n.* ла́герь *m.*; **—er** *n.* заключённый

privacy /'praɪvəsi/ *n.* уедине́ние

private /'praɪvɪt/ **1.** *adj.* ча́стный; ли́чный **2.** *n.* (mil.) рядово́й

privatize /'praɪvə‚taɪz/ *v.* приватизи́ровать *impf.*

privilege /'prɪvəlɪdʒ/ *n.* привиле́гия; **—d** *adj.* привилегиро́ванный

prize /praɪz/ **1.** *n.* приз **2.** *v.* высоко́ цени́ть *impf.*

prizewinner /'praɪz‚wɪnər/ *n.* призёр

probability /‚prɒbə'bɪlɪti/ *n.* вероя́тность; правдоподо́бие

probable /'prɒbəbəl/ *adj.* возмо́жный; вероя́тный

probation /prou'beɪʃən/ *n.* (law) усло́вный пригово́р; **—ary** *adj.* испыта́тельный

problem /'prɒbləm/ *n.* зада́ча; пробле́ма

procedure /prə'sidʒər/ *n.* процеду́ра

proceed /prə'sid/ *v.* продолжа́ть(ся) *impf.*; **—ings** *n.* (law) судопроизво́дство; (minutes) протоко́л

process /'prɒsɛs/ *n.* проце́сс; **data —ing** *n.* обрабо́тка да́нных

procession /prə'sɛʃən/ *n.* проце́ссия

proclaim /prou'kleɪm/ *v.* провозглаша́ть *impf.*, -си́ть *pf.*

proclamation /‚prɒklə'meɪʃən/ *n.* провозглаше́ние

procure /prou'kyur/ *v.* добыва́ть *impf.*, добы́ть *pf.*

prodigal /'prɒdɪgəl/ *adj.* расточи́тельный

prodigious /prə'dɪdʒəs/ *adj.* огро́мный; изуми́тельный

prodigy /'prɒdɪdʒi/ *n.* одарённый челове́к; (child) вунде́ркинд

produce /prə'dus/ *v.* производи́ть *impf.*, произвести́ *pf.*

product /'prɒdʌkt/ *n.* проду́кт; результа́т

production /prə'dʌkʃən/ *n.* произво́дство

productive /prə'dʌktɪv/ *adj.* производи́тельный; плодови́тый

profanity /prə'fænɪti/ *n.* богоху́льство; руга́тельство

profession /prə'fɛʃən/ *n.* профе́ссия; **—al** *adj.* профессиона́льный *n.* профессиона́л

professor /prə'fɛsər/ *n.* профе́ссор

proficient /prə'fɪʃənt/ *adj.* иску́сный; уме́лый

profile /'proufaɪl/ *n.* про́филь *m.*

profit /'prɒfɪt/ **1.** *n.* при́быль *f.* **2.** *v.* приноси́ть по́льзу *impf.*; **—able** *adj.* при́быльный

profiteer /‚prɒfɪ'tɪər/ *n.* спекуля́нт; **—ing** *n.* спекуля́ция

profound /prə'faund/ *adj.* глубо́кий

profuse /prə'fyus/ *adj.* оби́льный

progeny /'prɒdʒəni/ *n.* пото́мство

prognosis /prɒg'nousɪs/ *n.* прогно́з

program /'prougræm/ **1.** *n.* програ́мма **2.** *v.* программи́ровать *impf.*; **—er** *n.* программи́ст

progress /*n.* 'prɒgrɛs; *v.* prə'grɛs/ **1.** *n.* прогре́сс; успе́хи pl. **2.** v. прогрессировать; **make ~** делать успехи impf.; **—ive** adj. прогрессивный

prohibit /prou'hɪbɪt/ v. запрещать impf., -тить pf.

prohibition /,prouə'bɪʃən/ n. запрещение

project / n. 'prɒdʒɛkt; prə'dʒɛkt/ **1.** n. проект **2.** v. (plan) проектировать impf., -pf.

projection /prə'dʒɛkʃən/ n. проекция

projector /prə'dʒɛktər/ n. кинопроектор

proliferate /prə'lɪfə,reɪt/ v. распространяться impf., -ниться pf.

prolific /prə'lɪfɪk/ adj. плодовитый

prologue /'prɒulɒg/ n. пролог

prolong /prə'lɒŋ/ v. продлевать impf.; продлить pf.

prominent /'prɒmənənt/ adj. выдающийся

promise /'prɒmɪs/ **1.** n. обещание **2.** v. обещать impf., по- pf.

promising /'prɒmɪsɪŋ/ adj. многообещающий

promote /prə'mout/ v. (raise) продвигать impf., продвинуть pf.; (publicize) рекламировать impf.

promotion /prə'mouʃən/ n. продвижение; (com.) реклама

prompt /prɒmpt/ **1.** adj. быстрый **2.** v. побуждать impf., побудить pf.; (theat.) суфлировать impf.

prone /proun/ adj. (inclined to) склонный (к + D)

pronoun /'prou,naun/ n. местоимение

pronounce /prə'nauns/ v. произносить impf., произнести pf.; **—ment** n. объявление; заявление

pronunciation /prə,nʌnsɪ'eɪʃən/ n. произношение

proof /pruf/ n. доказательство

prop¹ /prɒp/ n. (support) опора

prop² /prɒp/ n.pl. (theat.) реквизит

propaganda /,prɒpə'gændə/ n. пропаганда

propagate /'prɒpə,geɪt/ v. распространять impf., -нить pf.

propeller /prə'pɛlər/ n. пропеллер; винт

propensity /prə'pɛnsɪti/ n. склонность

proper /'prɒpər/ adj. приличный; правильный; **—ly** adv. как следует; ~ **name** n. имя собственное neut.

property /'prɒpərti/ n. имущество, собственность

prophecy /'prɒfəsi/ n. пророчество

prophet /'prɒfɪt/ n. пророк

proponent /prə'pounənt/ n. сторонник

proportion /prə'pɔrʃən/ n. пропорция; pl. (size) размеры pl.

proposal /prə'pouzəl/ n. предложение

propose /prə'pouz/ v. предлагать impf.; (propose marriage) делать предложение impf.

proprietor /prə'praɪɪtər/ n. собственник, владелец

prose /prouz/ n. проза

prosecute /'prɒsɪ,kjut/ v. преследовать судебным порядком impf.

prosecution /,prɒsɪ'kjuʃən/ n. судебное преследование; (accusing party) обвинение

prosecutor /'prɒsɪ,kjutər/ n. обвинитель

prospect /'prɒspɛkt/ n. перспектива

prosper /'prɒspər/ v. процветать impf.; **—ous** adj. процветающий; (wealthy) зажиточный

prosperity /prɒ'spɛrɪti/ n. процветание

prostate gland /'prɒsteɪt/ n. простата

prostitute /'prɒstɪ,tut/ n. проститутка

protect /prə'tɛkt/ v. охранять impf., -нить pf.; **—ion** n. охрана; **—ive** adj. защитный; покровительственный

protein /'proutin/ n. протеин

protest / n. 'proutest; prə'tɛst/ **1.** n. протест **2.** v. протестовать impf. & pf.

Protestant /'prɒtəstənt/ **1.** adj. протестантский **2.** n. протестант; **—ка**

protocol /'proutə,kɒl/ n. протокол

prototype /'proutə,taɪp/ n. прототип

protracted /prou'træktɪd/ adj. длительный

protrude /prou'trud/ v. торчать impf.

proud /praud/ adj. го́рдый; **be ~ of** v. горди́ться (+ I) impf.

prove /pruːv/ v.t. дока́зывать impf., доказа́ть pf.

provenance /'prɒvənəns/ n. происхожде́ние

proverb /'prɒvɜːb/ n. посло́вица

provide /prə'vaɪd/ v. обеспе́чивать (+ I) impf.

provided (that) /prə'vaɪdɪd/ conj. при усло́вии, что

provident /'prɒvɪdənt/ adj. предусмотри́тельный

province /'prɒvɪns/ n. прови́нция; о́бласть f.

provision /prə'vɪʒən/ n. обеспе́чение; (stipulation) усло́вие; pl. (supplies) прови́зия; **—al** adj. вре́менный

provocation /,prɒvə'keɪʃən/ n. провока́ция

provoke /prə'vəuk/ v. провоци́ровать impf., с- pf.

proximity /prɒk'sɪmɪtɪ/ n. бли́зость

proxy /'prɒksɪ/ n. полномо́чие

prudence /'pruːdns/ n. благоразу́мие; расчётливость

prudent /'pruːdnt/ adj. благоразу́мный; расчётливый

prune /pruːn/ n. черносли́в

psalm /sɑːm/ n. псало́м

psychiatrist /sɪ'kaɪətrɪst/ n. психиа́тр

psychological /,saɪkə'lɒdʒɪkəl/ adj. психологи́ческий

psychologist /sai'kɒlədʒɪst/ n. психо́лог

psychology /sai'kɒlədʒɪ/ n. психоло́гия

psychotherapy /,saɪkou'θerapi/ n. психотерапи́я

puberty /'pjuːbɜːtɪ/ n. полова́я зре́лость; возмужа́лость

public /'pʌblɪk/ **1.** adj. публи́чный; обще́ственный **2.** n. публика

publication /,pʌblɪ'keɪʃən/ n. изда́ние; публика́ция

publicity /pʌ'blɪsɪtɪ/ n. рекла́ма

publicize /'pʌblɪsaɪz/ v. реклами́ровать impf. & pf.

publish /'pʌblɪʃ/ v. издава́ть impf., изда́ть pf.; публикова́ть impf.; o- pf.; **—er** n. изда́тель; **—ing house** n. изда́тельство

pudding /'pudɪŋ/ n. пу́динг

puddle /'pʌdl/ n. лу́жа

puff /pʌf/ **1.** n. клуб; (air, etc.) дунове́ние **2.** v. пыхте́ть impf.

pug /pʌg/ n. (dog) мопс

pull /pul/ **1.** n. тя́га, натяже́ние **2.** v. тяну́ть impf., по- pf.; тащи́ть impf., по- pf.

pullover /'pul,ouvər/ n. пуло́вер

pulp /pʌlp/ n. пу́льпа; (of fruit) мя́коть f.

pulse /pʌls/ n. пульс

pulverize /'pʌlvə,raɪz/ v. превраща́ть(ся) в порошо́к impf.

pump /pʌmp/ **1.** n. насо́с **2.** v. кача́ть impf.

pumpkin /'pʌmpkɪn/ n. ты́ква

pun /pʌn/ n. каламбу́р; игра́ слов

punch /pʌntʃ/ **1.** n. уда́р кулако́м **2.** v. ударя́ть кулако́м impf.; (make hole) пробива́ть impf., проби́ть pf.

punctual /'pʌŋktʃuəl/ adj. пунктуа́льный

punctuation /,pʌŋktʃu'eɪʃən/ n. пунктуа́ция

puncture /'pʌŋktʃər/ **1.** n. проко́л **2.** v. прока́лывать impf., проколо́ть pf.

pungent /'pʌndʒənt/ adj. е́дкий

punish /'pʌnɪʃ/ v. нака́зывать impf., наказа́ть pf.; **—ment** n. наказа́ние

pupil¹ /'pjuːpəl/ n. учени́к, -ни́ца

pupil² /'pjuːpəl/ n. (eye) зрачо́к

puppet /'pʌpɪt/ **1.** n. ку́кла; марионе́тка **2.** adj. ку́кольный

puppy /'pʌpɪ/ n. щено́к

purchase /'pɜːtʃəs/ **1.** n. поку́пка **2.** v. покупа́ть impf., купи́ть pf.; **—r** n. покупа́тель

pure /pjuər/ adj. чи́стый

purge /pɜːdʒ/ n. чи́стка

purify /'pjuərə,faɪ/ v. очища́ть impf., очи́стить pf.

Puritan /'pjuərɪtn/ adj. пурита́нский

purity /'pjuərɪtɪ/ n. чистота́

purple /'pɜːrpəl/ adj. багря́ный; пурпу́рный

purpose /'pɜːrpəs/ n. цель f.; **—less** adj. бесце́льный; **—ly, on** — adv. наро́чно

purr /pɜːr/ v. мурлы́кать impf.

purse /pɜːrs/ n. су́мка; (for money) кошелёк

pursue /pər'suː/ v. пресле́довать; гна́ться impf.

pursuit /pər'suːt/ n. пого́ня; (occupation) заня́тие

pus /pʌs/ n. гной

push /puʃ/ **1.** n. толчо́к **2.** v. толка́ть impf.; (through)

проталкивать(ся) *impf.*, протолкнуть(ся) *pf.*; — **button** *n.* кнопка; —**y** *adj.* пробивной
put /put/ *v.* класть *impf.*, положить *pf.*; ставить *impf.*, по— *pf.*; ~ **aside** отложить *pf.*; ~ **on** (*clothes*) надевать *impf.*, надеть *pf.*

putrid /'pyutrɪd/ *adj.* гнилой
putter /'pʌtər/ *v.* возиться *impf.*
puzzle /'pʌzəl/ **1.** *n.* загадка **2.** *v.* ставить в тупик *impf.*; —**d** *adj.* озадаченный
Pygmy /'pɪgmi/ *n.* пигмей
pyramid /'pɪrəmɪd/ *n.* пирамида

Q R

quack¹ /kwæk/ **1.** *n.* кряканье **2.** *v.* крякать *impf.*
quack² /kwæk/ *n.* шарлатан
quadrangle /'kwɒd,ræŋgəl/ *n.* четырёхугольник
quail /kweil/ *n.* перепел
quaint /kweint/ *adj.* причудливый
qualification /,kwɒləfɪ'keiʃən/ *n.* квалификация; (*restriction*) оговорка
qualified /'kwɒlə,faid/ *adj.* (*limited*) ограниченный; (*competent*) компетентный
qualify /'kwɒlə,fai/ *v.* квалифицировать(ся) *impf. & pf.*
quality /'kwɒlɪti/ *n.* качество
qualm /kwɑm/ *n. usu. pl.* угрызение совести
quantity /'kwɒntɪti/ *n.* количество; (*math.*) величина
quarantine /'kwɔrən,tin/ *n.* карантин
quarrel /'kwɔrəl/ **1.** *n.* ссора **2.** *v.* ссориться *impf.*, по— *pf.*; —**some** *adj.* сварливый
quarry /'kwɔri/ *n.* каменоломня
quart /kwɔrt/ *n.* (*measure*) кварта
quarter /'kwɔrtər/ *n.* четверть *f.*; (*of year; district*) квартал; *pl.* (*lodgings*) помещение; **a ~ to one** без четверти час; ~**ly** *adv.* квартальный, раз в три месяца
quaver /'kweivər/ *v.* дрожать
quay /ki, kei/ *n.* пристань *f.*
queen /kwin/ *n.* королева; (*cards*) дама; (*chess*) ферзь *m.*
queer /kwɪər/ *adj.* странный
quench /kwɛntʃ/ *v.* гасить *impf.*, по— *pf.*; (*thirst*) утолять *impf.*
quest /kwɛst/ *n.* поиски *pl.*
question /'kwɛstʃən/ **1.** *n.* вопрос **2.** *v.* (*law*) допрашивать *impf.*, допросить *pf.*; —**able** *adj.* сомнительный; —**ing** *n.* допрос; ~ **mark** вопросительный знак

questionnaire /,kwɛstʃə'nɛər/ *n.* анкета
quibble /'kwɪbəl/ *v.* спорить *impf.*
quick /kwɪk/ *adj.* быстрый
quicken /'kwɪkən/ *v.* ускорять *impf.*, ускорить *pf.*
quicksilver /'kwɪk,sɪlvər/ *n.* ртуть *f.*
quick-tempered *adj.* вспыльчивый
quick-witted *adj.* сообразительный
quiet /'kwaiət/ **1.** *adj.* спокойный; тихий **2.** *n.* покой; тишина **3.** *v.* успокаивать *impf.*, успокоить *pf.*
quilt /kwɪlt/ *n.* стёганое одеяло
quince /kwɪns/ *n.* айва
quintet /kwɪn'tɛt/ *n.* квинтет
quirk /kwɜrk/ *n.* причуда
quit /kwɪt/ *v.* (*leave*) покидать *impf.*, покинуть *pf.*; (*give up*) бросать *impf.*, бросить *pf.*
quite /kwait/ *adv.* совсем; довольно; **not ~** не совсем
quiver /'kwɪvər/ **1.** *n.* дрожь *f.*, трепет **2.** *v.* трепетать *impf.*
quiz /kwɪz/ *n.* (*short exam*) контрольная работа; (*contest*) викторина
quota /'kwoutə/ *n.* квота; доля
quotation /kwou'teiʃən/ *n.* цитата; (*price*) расценка; ~ **marks** кавычки *pl.*
quote /kwout/ *v.* цитировать *impf.*, про— *pf.*; сослаться (на + *A*) *pf.*; (*price*) назначать *impf.*, назначить *pf.*
rabbi /'ræbai/ *n.* раввин
rabbit /'ræbɪt/ *n.* кролик
rabble /'ræbəl/ *n.* сброд
rabies /'reibiz/ *n.* бешенство
raccoon /ræ'kun/ *n.* енот
race¹ /reis/ **1.** *n.* (*cars, etc.*) гонка, гонки *pl.*; (*on foot*) бег; (*horse*) скачки *pl.* **2.** *v.* состязаться в скорости *impf.*; —**track** *n.* ипподром; трек

race² /reis/ n. (ethnicity) páca

racial /'reiʃəl/ adj. páсовый

racist /'reisist/ 1. n. расист; —ка 2. adj. расистский

rack /ræk/ n. (shelving) стелла́ж; (for hats, coats) ве́шалка

racket¹ /'rækit/ n. (noise) шум

racket² /'rækit/ n. (sports) раке́тка

radar /'reidɑr/ n. рада́р

radiance /'reidiəns/ n. сия́ние

radiant /'reidiənt/ adj. сия́ющий

radiation /reidi'eiʃən/ n. излуче́ние; радиа́ция

radiator /'reidi,eitər/ n. батаре́я; радиа́тор

radical /'rædikəl/ 1. adj. радика́льный; коренно́й 2. n. радика́л

radio /'reidi,ou/ n. ра́дио neut. indecl.; ~ **operator** радист

radish /'rædiʃ/ n. реди́ска

radius /'reidiəs/ n. ра́диус

raffle /'ræfəl/ n. лотере́я

raft /ræft/ n. плот

rag /ræg/ n. тря́пка

rage /reidʒ/ 1. n. гнев; я́рость 2. v. бе́ситься; бушева́ть impf.

ragged /'rægid/ adj. рва́ный

raid /reid/ 1. n. набе́г; налёт 2. v. (police) устра́ивать обла́ву impf.

rail /reil/ n. (train) рельс; —ing n. пери́ла; (fence) частоко́л

railroad /'reil,roud/ 1. n. желе́зная доро́га 2. adj. железнодоро́жный

rain /rein/ 1. n. дождь m. 2. adj. дождево́й 3. v.: it is —ing идёт дождь

rainbow /'rein,bou/ n. ра́дуга

raincoat /'rein,kout/ n. плащ

rain forest n. джу́нгли pl.

rainy /'reini/ adj. дождли́вый

raise /reiz/ 1. n. повыше́ние 2. v. поднима́ть impf., подня́ть pf.

raisin /'reizin/ n. изю́минка; pl. изю́м

rake /reik/ 1. n. (tool) гра́бли pl. 2. v. грести́ impf.

rally /'ræli/ n. собра́ние; ми́тинг; (motor) (авто)ра́лли neut. indecl.

RAM /ræm/ n. (comput.) операти́вная па́мять f.

ram /ræm/ n. бара́н

ramble /'ræmbəl/ 1. n. прогу́лка 2. v. броди́ть impf.

rambling /'ræmbliŋ/ adj. (speech) бессвя́зный

ramp /ræmp/ n. укло́н; скат

rampage /'ræmpeidʒ/ n. бу́йство

rampart /'ræmpɑrt/ n. вал

ramshackle /'ræm,ʃækəl/ adj. ве́тхий; (rickety) ша́ткий

ranch /ræntʃ/ n. ра́нчо neut. indecl.

rancid /'rænsid/ adj. прого́рклый

random /'rændəm/ adj. случа́йный; **at** ~ науга́д

range /reindʒ/ n. преде́л; разма́х; —r лесни́к; **shooting** ~ тир

rank /ræŋk/ 1. n. (row) ряд; (status) зва́ние; чин; ранг 2. v.t. классифици́ровать impf. & pf.

ransom /'rænsəm/ 1. n. вы́куп 2. v. выкупа́ть impf., вы́купить pf.

rape /reip/ 1. n. изнаси́лование 2. v. наси́ловать impf., из- pf.

rapid /'ræpid/ adj. бы́стрый; ско́рый; —s n.pl. поро́г

rapist /'reipist/ n. наси́льник

rapture /'ræptʃər/ n. восто́рг

rare /reər/ adj. ре́дкий

rarity /'reəriti/ n. ре́дкость

rascal /'ræskəl/ n. моше́нник; (child) озорни́к; шалу́н

rash¹ /ræʃ/ adj. необду́манный; —ness n. опроме́тчивость

rash² /ræʃ/ n. сыпь f.

rasp /ræsp/ n. (file) ра́шпиль

raspberry /'ræz,beri/ 1. n. мали́на 2. adj. мали́новый

rat /ræt/ n. кры́са

rate /reit/ 1. n. но́рма; ста́вка (speed) ско́рость; ~ **of exchange** валю́тный курс 2. v. оце́нивать impf., оцени́ть pf.

rather /'ræðər/ adv. скоре́е; предпочти́тельно; (somewhat) дово́льно

ratification /,rætəfɪ'keiʃən/ n. ратифика́ция

ratify /'rætə,fai/ v. ратифици́ровать impf. & pf.

rating /'reitiŋ/ n. оце́нка; (popularity) ре́йтинг

ratio /'reiʃiou/ n. пропо́рция

ration /'ræʃən/ 1. n. паёк; рацио́н 2. v. норми́ровать impf. & pf.; —al adj. разу́мный

rationality /,ræʃə'næliti/ n. разу́мность; рациона́льность

rationalize /'ræʃənəl,aiz/ v. рационализи́ровать impf. & pf.

rattle /'rætl/ 1. n. треск; (toy) погрему́шка 2. v. греме́ть impf.

rattlesnake /'rætl,sneik/ n. грему́чая змея́

ravage /'rævɪdʒ/ v. опустошáть *impf.*, -шить *pf.*

rave /reiv/ v. брéдить *impf.*

raven /'reivən/ n. вóрон

ravine /rə'vin/ n. оврáг; ущéлье

ravishing /'rævɪʃɪŋ/ adj. восхитительный

raw /rɔ/ adj. сырóй

ray /rei/ n. луч

razor /'reizər/ n. бритва

reach /ritʃ/ 1. n. предéл досягáемости 2. v. (get to) достигáть; доходить (до + G) *impf.*, дойти *pf.*

react /ri'ækt/ v. реагировать *impf.*, от- *pf.*; **—ion** n. реáкция

reactionary /ri'ækʃə,neri/ 1. adj. реакцибнный 2. n. реакционéр

read /rid/ v. читáть *impf.*, про- *pf.*; **—er** n. читáтель, -ница; **—ing** n. чтéние

readily /'redli/ adv. охóтно

readiness /'redinis/ n. готóвность

ready /'redi/ adj. готóвый

ready-made adj. (clothes) готóвый

real /'riəl/ adj. действительный; реáльный; настоящий; ~ estate n. недвижимость

realistic /,riə'lɪstɪk/ adj. реалистический; реáльный

reality /ri'ælɪti/ n. действительность

realization /,riələ'zeiʃən/ n. осознáние; осуществлéние

realize /'riə,laiz/ v.t. (plans, etc.) осуществлять *impf.*, -вить *pf.*; (assets) реализовáть *impf. & pf.*; (apprehend) осознавáть *impf.*

really /'riəli/ adv. действительно

realm /relm/ n. óбласть f.

reap /rip/ v. жать *impf.*, с- *pf.*

rear[1] /riər/ 1. adj. зáдний 2. n. зáдняя часть f.; (mil.) тыл

rear[2] /riər/ v. воспитывать *impf.*, воспитáть *pf.*

rearmament /ri'ɑrməmənt/ n. перевооружéние

reason /'rizən/ 1. n. рáзум; рассýдок; (cause) причина 2. v. рассуждáть *impf.*; **—able** adj. разýмный; умéренный; **—ing** n. рассуждéние

reassure /,riə'ʃur/ v. успокáивать *impf.*, успокóить *pf.*

rebate /'ribeit/ n. скидка

rebel /n. 'rebəl; v. ri'bel/ 1. n. повстáнец; бунтовщик 2. v. восставáть *impf.*, восстáть *pf.*

rebellion /ri'belyən/ n. восстáние

rebuff /ri'bʌf/ 1. n. отпóр 2. v. давáть отпóр *impf.*

rebuke /ri'byuk/ 1. n. упрёк; выговор 2. v. упрекáть *impf.*

recall /ri'kɔl/ v. вспоминáть *impf.*, вспóмнить *pf.*

recede /ri'sid/ v. отступáть *impf.*, -пить *pf.*

receipt /ri'sit/ n. квитáнция

receive /ri'siv/ v. получáть *impf.*, -чить *pf.*; (entertain) принимáть *impf.*; **—r** n. получáтель; (telephone) трýбка; (radio) приёмник

recent /'risənt/ adj. недáвний

reception /ri'sepʃən/ n. приём; (hotel) регистратýра; **—ist** n. регистрáтор; **~ room** приёмная

receptive /ri'septiv/ adj. восприимчивый

recess /ri'ses/ n. перерыв; **—ion** n. (econ.) спад

recipe /'resəpi/ n. рецéпт

recipient /ri'sipiənt/ n. получáтель

reciprocal /ri'siprəkəl/ adj. взаимный

recital /ri'saitl/ n. (mus.) концéрт

recite /ri'sait/ v. декламировать *impf.*

reckless /'reklis/ adj. безрассýдный

reckon /'rekən/ v. считáть *impf.*

reckoning /'rekənɪŋ/ n. счёт

recline /ri'klain/ v. полулежáть *impf.*

recognition /,rekəg'nɪʃən/ n. узнавáние; (acclaim) признáние

recognize /'rekəg,naiz/ v. узнавáть *impf.*, узнáть *pf.*

recoil /ri'kɔil/ v. отскáкивать *impf.*; (of gun) отдавáть *impf.*

recollect /,rekə'lekt/ v. вспоминáть *impf.*, вспóмнить *pf.*; **—ion** n. вспоминáние

recommend /,rekə'mend/ v. рекомендовáть *impf. & pf.*

recommendation /,rekəmen'deiʃən/ n. рекомендáция

recompense /'rekəm,pens/ 1. n. вознаграждéние 2. v. вознаграждáть *impf.*

reconcile /'rekən,sail/ v. примирять *impf.*, -рить *pf.*

reconciliation /,rekən,sili'eiʃən/ n. примирéние; улáживание

reconnaissance /rɪˈkɒnəsəns/ *n.* разведка

reconsider /ˌrikənˈsɪdər/ *v.* пересматривать *impf.*, пересмотреть *pf.*

reconstruction /ˌrikənˈstrʌkʃən/ *n.* перестройка; реконструкция

record / *n. adj.* ˈrekərd, *v.* rɪˈkɔrd/ **1.** *adj.* запись *f.*; (*mus.*) пластинка; (*sports*) рекорд *v.* **2.** *v.* записывать *impf.*, записать *pf.* **3.** *adj.* рекордный; **~ player** *n.* проигрыватель

recorder /rɪˈkɔrdər/ *n.:* **tape ~** *n.* магнитофон

recording /rɪˈkɔrdɪŋ/ *n.* запись *f.*

recover /rɪˈkʌvər/ *v.t.* получить обратно; *v.i.* выздоравливать *impf.*, выздороветь *pf.*; **—y** *n.* возвращение; (*health*) выздоровление

recreation /ˌrekriˈeiʃən/ *n.* отдых; (*amusement*) развлечение

recruit /rɪˈkrut/ **1.** *n.* новобранец **2.** *v.* вербовать *impf.*, за- *pf.*

rectangle /ˈrekˌtæŋgəl/ *n.* прямоугольник

rectify /ˈrektəˌfai/ *v.* исправлять *impf.*, исправить *pf.*

recur /rɪˈkɜr/ *v.* повторяться *impf.*

recurrence /rɪˈkɜrəns/ *n.* повторение

recycle /riˈsaikəl/ *v.* перерабатывать *impf.*, -работать *pf.*

red /red/ *adj.* красный; **—dish** *adj.* красноватый; (*hair*) рыжеватый; **~ tape** *n.* волокита

redeem /rɪˈdim/ *v.* выкупать *impf.*, выкупить *pf.*

redemption /rɪˈdempʃən/ *n.* выкуп; искупление

redo /riˈdu/ *v.* повторять; переделывать *impf.*, -делать *pf.*

redress /ˈridres/ *n.* возмещение

reduce /rɪˈdus/ *v.* уменьшать *impf.*, уменьшить *pf.*; сокращать *impf.*, -тить *pf.*

reduction /rɪˈdʌkʃən/ *n.* уменьшение; сокращение

reed /rid/ *n.* тростник

reef /rif/ *n.* риф

reek /rik/ *v.* вонять (+ *I*) *impf.*

reel[1] /ril/ *n.* катушка; (*film*) бобина

reel[2] /ril/ *v.* (*feel dizzy*) кружиться *impf.*

refer /rɪˈfɜr/ *v.i.* относиться (к

+ *D*) *impf.*; (*cite*) ссылаться (на + *A*) *impf.*, сослаться *pf.*

referee /ˌrefəˈri/ *n.* судья *m.*

reference /ˈrefərəns/ **1.** *n.* ссылка; справка **2.** *adj.* справочный; **~ book** *n.* справочник

referendum /ˌrefəˈrendəm/ *n.* референдум

referral /rɪˈfɜrəl/ *n.* направление

refine /rɪˈfain/ *v.* рафинировать *impf. & pf.*; **—d** *adj.* изысканный; **—ment** *n.* утончённость

reflect /rɪˈflekt/ *v.* отражать *impf.*, -зить *pf.*; **—ion** *n.* отражение; *Fig.* размышление

reflex /ˈrifleks/ *n.* рефлекс

reform /rɪˈfɔrm/ **1.** *n.* реформа **2.** *v.* реформировать *impf. & pf.*

reformation /ˌrefərˈmeiʃən/ *n.* исправление; *cap.* Реформация

refrain[1] /rɪˈfrein/ *n.* (*mus.*) припев

refrain[2] /rɪˈfrein/ *v.* воздерживаться (от + *G*) *impf.*, воздержаться *pf.*

refresh /rɪˈfreʃ/ *v.* освежать *impf.*, -жить *pf.*; **—ing** *adj.* тонизирующий; **—ment** *n.* подкрепление

refrigerator /rɪˈfrɪdʒəˌreitər/ *n.* холодильник

refuel /riˈfyuəl/ *v.* заправлять(ся) топливом *impf.*, -править(ся) *pf.*

refuge /ˈrefyudʒ/ *n.* убежище

refugee /ˌrefyuˈdʒi/ *n.* беженец, беженка

refund / *n.* ˈrifʌnd, *v.* riˈfʌnd/ **1.** *n.* возмещение **2.** *v.* возмещать *impf.*, возместить *pf.*

refusal /rɪˈfyuzəl/ *n.* отказ

refuse[1] /ˈrefyus/ *n.* отбросы *pl.*

refuse[2] /rɪˈfyuz/ *v.* отказываться *impf.*, отказаться *pf.*

refutation /ˌrefyuˈteiʃən/ *n.* опровержение

refute /rɪˈfyut/ *v.* опровергать *impf.*, опровергнуть *pf.*

regard /rɪˈgɑrd/ **1.** *n.* уважение; *pl.* привет; **—ing** *prep.* относительно (+ *G*) **2.** *v.* смотреть (на + *A*); относиться *impf.*; **—less** *adv.* независимо (от + *G*)

regenerate /rɪˈdʒenəˌreit/ *v.* перерождать(ся) *impf.*, -родить(ся) *pf.*

regent /ˈridʒənt/ *n.* регент

regime /rəˈʒim/ *n.* режим

regiment /ˈredʒəmənt/ *n.* полк

region /'riːdʒən/ *n.* райо́н; о́бласть *f.;* —**al** *adj.* региона́льный

register /'redʒəstər/ **1.** *n.* рее́стр; регистр; **cash ~** ка́сса **2.** *v.* регистри́ровать(ся) *impf.*, за- *pf.;* —**ed** *adj.* зарегистри́рованный; —**ed letter** *n.* заказно́е письмо́

registration /,redʒə'streiʃən/ *n.* регистра́ция; за́пись *f.*

regret /ri'gret/ **1.** *n.* сожале́ние **2.** *v.* сожале́ть *impf.*

regular /'regjələr/ *adj.* регуля́рный; пра́вильный; постоя́нный

regulate /'regjə,leit/ *v.* регули́ровать *impf.*

regulation /,regjə'leiʃən/ *n.* регули́рование; *pl.* (*rules*) пра́вила *pl.*, (*mil.*) уста́в

rehabilitate /,rihə'bili,teit/ *v.* реабилити́ровать *impf.* & *pf.*

rehearsal /ri'hɜrsəl/ *n.* репети́ция

rehearse /ri'hɜrs/ *v.* репети́ровать *impf.*

reheat /ri'hit/ *v.* разогрева́ть *impf.*

reign /rein/ **1.** *n.* ца́рствование **2.** *v.* ца́рствовать; цари́ть *impf.*

reimburse /,riim'bɜrs/ *v.* возмеща́ть *impf.*, возмести́ть *pf.*

rein /rein/ *n.* по́вод *m.*

reindeer /'rein,diər/ *n.* се́верный оле́нь *m.*

reinforce /,riin'fɔrs/ *v.* уси́ливать *impf.*, уси́лить *pf.*

reject / *v.* ri'dʒekt; *n.* 'ridʒekt/ **1.** *v.* отверга́ть, отве́ргнуть *pf.* **2.** *n.* брак; —**ion** *n.* отка́з

rejoice /ri'dʒɔis/ *v.* ра́доваться *impf.*, об- *pf.*

relapse /'rilæps/ *n.* рециди́в

relate /ri'leit/ *v.* свя́зывать *impf.*, связа́ть *pf.*, (*tell*) расска́зывать *impf.*, рассказа́ть *pf.*; —**d** *adj.* свя́занный; (*in family*) ро́дственный

relation /ri'leiʃən/ *n.* отноше́ние; связь *f.;* —**ship** *n.* родство́

relative /'relətiv/ **1.** *adj.* относи́тельный; сравни́тельный **2.** *n.* ро́дственник, -ница

relax /ri'læks/ *v.t.* ослабля́ть *impf.*, осла́бить *impf.; v.i.* рассла́бляться *impf.*, рассла́биться *pf.*

relaxation /,rilæk'seiʃən/ *n.* рассла́бле́ние; ослабле́ние; о́тдых

release /ri'lis/ **1.** *n.* освобожде́ние; (*issue*) вы́пуск **2.** *v.*

освобожда́ть *impf.*, -боди́ть *pf.*; выпуска́ть *impf.*, вы́пустить *pf.*

relent /ri'lent/ *v.* смягча́ться *impf.*, -чи́ться *pf.*

relevant /'reləvənt/ *adj.* относя́щийся к де́лу; уме́стный

reliability /ri,laiə'biliti/ *n.* надёжность

reliable /ri'laiəbəl/ *adj.* надёжный

relic /'relik/ *n.* рели́квия

relief[1] /ri'lif/ *n.* облегче́ние

relief[2] /ri'lif/ *n.* (*art; geol.*) рельеф

relieve /ri'liv/ *v.* облегча́ть *impf.*, -чи́ть *pf.*

religion /ri'lidʒən/ *n.* рели́гия

religious /ri'lidʒəs/ *adj.* религио́зный

relinquish /ri'liŋkwiʃ/ *v.* отка́зываться (от + *G*); сдава́ть *impf.*, сдать *pf.*

reluctance /ri'lʌktəns/ *n.* неохо́та; нежела́ние

reluctant /ri'lʌktənt/ *adj.* неохо́тный

rely /ri'lai/ *v.* полага́ться (на + *A*) *impf.*, положи́ться *pf.*

remain /ri'mein/ *v.* остава́ться *impf.*, оста́ться *pf.*; —**der** *n.* оста́ток; —**s** *n.pl.* оста́тки *pl.*

remark /ri'mɑrk/ **1.** *n.* замеча́ние **2.** *v.* замеча́ть *impf.*, заме́тить *pf.*; —**able** *adj.* замеча́тельный

remedy /'remidi/ **1.** *n.* сре́дство (от + *G*) **2.** *v.* исправля́ть *impf.*, испра́вить *pf.*

remember /ri'membər/ *v.* по́мнить, вспомина́ть *impf.*

remembrance /ri'membrəns/ *n.* па́мять *f.;* воспомина́ние

remind /ri'maind/ *v.* напомина́ть *impf.*, напо́мнить *pf.*; —**er** *n.* напомина́ние

remit /ri'mit/ *v.* пересыла́ть *impf.*, пересла́ть *pf.*; —**tance** *n.* перево́д (де́нег)

remnant /'remnənt/ *n.* оста́ток

remorse /ri'mɔrs/ *n.* угрызе́ние со́вести; раска́яние

remote /ri'mout/ *adj.* отдалённый

remote-control *n.* дистанцио́нное управле́ние

remove /ri'muv/ *v.* перемеща́ть *impf.*, -сти́ть *pf.*; (*take away*) удаля́ть *impf.*

remuneration /ri,mjunə'reiʃən/ *n.* опла́та; вознагражде́ние

Renaissance /ˌrenə'sɑns/ n. эпоха Возрождéния

render /'rendər/ v. окáзывать impf., оказáть pf.; (make) дéлать impf., с- pf.

renew /rɪ'nu/ v. возобновлять impf., -вить pf. —al n. возобновлéние

renounce /rɪ'nauns/ v. отказываться (от + G) impf.; отказáться pf

renown /rɪ'naun/ n. слáва

rent /rent/ 1. n. квартирная (арéндная) плáта 2. v. (~ to) сдавáть в арéнду impf.; (~ from) брать в арéнду; снимáть impf.

repair /rɪ'peər/ 1. n. ремóнт 2. v. чинить v.; ремонтировать impf., от- pf.

reparation /ˌrepə'reɪʃən/ n. возмещéние; (polit.) репарáция

repay /rɪ'peɪ/ v. отплáчивать impf., отплатить pf. —ment n. возвращéние (дéнег); отплáта

repeal /rɪ'pil/ v. отменять impf.

repeat /rɪ'pit/ v. повторять impf., -рить pf.; —edly adv. неоднокрáтно

repel /rɪ'pel/ v. отражáть impf., -зить pf.; отталкивать impf.

repent /rɪ'pent/ v. рáскаиваться (в + P) impf., раскáяться pf

repetition /ˌrepɪ'tɪʃən/ n. повторéние

repetitious /ˌrepɪ'tɪʃəs/ adj. повторяющийся

replace /rɪ'pleɪs/ v. (substitute) заменять impf., -нить pf.; —ment n. замéна

replenish /rɪ'plenɪʃ/ v. пополнять impf., пополнить pf.

reply /rɪ'plaɪ/ 1. n. ответ 2. v. отвечáть impf., ответить pf.

report /rɪ'pɔrt/ 1. n. сообщéние; доклáд; отчёт; 2. v. сообщáть impf., -щить pf.; —er n. репортёр

represent /ˌreprɪ'zent/ v. изображáть impf., -зить pf.; представлять impf., -стáвить pf.

representation /ˌreprɪzen'teɪʃən/ n. изображéние; представлéние

representative /ˌreprɪ'zentətɪv/ 1. adj. характéрный; показáтельный 2. n. представитель

repress /rɪ'pres/ v. подавлять impf., -вить pf.; —ion n. подавлéние; репрéссия

reprimand /'reprəˌmænd/ 1. n.

выговор 2. v. дéлать выговор impf.

reproach /rɪ'proutʃ/ 1. n. упрёк 2. v. упрекáть impf. -кнýть pf.; —ful adj. укоризненный

reproduce /ˌriprə'dus/ v. воспроизводить impf., воспроизвести pf.

reproduction /ˌriprə'dʌkʃən/ n. воспроизведéние; репродýкция

reptile /'reptaɪl/ n. пресмыкáющееся; рептилия

republic /rɪ'pʌblɪk/ n. респýблика

republican /rɪ'pʌblɪkən/ 1. adj. республикáнский 2. n. республикáнец, -кáнка

repulsion /rɪ'pʌlʃən/ n. отвращéние; отталкивание

repulsive /rɪ'pʌlsɪv/ adj. омерзительный; отталкивающий

reputation /ˌrepyə'teɪʃən/ n. репутáция; слáва

request /rɪ'kwest/ 1. n. прóсьба 2. v. просить impf., по- pf.

require /rɪ'kwaɪər/ v. трéбовать impf., по- pf.; —d adj. необходимый; —ment n. трéбование

requisition /ˌrekwə'zɪʃən/ n. реквизиция

rescue /'reskyu/ 1. n. спасéние 2. v. спасáть impf., спасти pf.

research /rɪ'sɜrtʃ, 'risɜrtʃ/ 1. n. исслéдование 2. adj. исслéдовательский; —er n. исслéдователь

resemblance /rɪ'zembləns/ n. схóдство

resemble /rɪ'zembəl/ v. быть похóжим (на + A) impf.

resent /rɪ'zent/ v. негодовáть (на + A) impf.; —ful adj. обиженный; (quick to ~) обидчивый

reservation /ˌrezər'veɪʃən/ n. оговóрка; (booking) брóня; (public land) заповéдник; (Indian) резервáция

reserve /rɪ'zɜrv/ 1. n. запáс; (restraint) сдéржанность 2. v. резервировать impf. & pf.; (book) бронировать impf.

reside /rɪ'zaɪd/ v. проживáть impf.

residence /'rezɪdəns/ n. местожительство; (act) проживáние

resident /'rezɪdənt/ n. житель

residue /'rezɪˌdu/ n. остáток

resign /rɪ'zaɪn/ v. уходить в отстáвку impf.

resignation /ˌrezɪg'neɪʃən/ n.

312

отста́вка; (*being resigned*)
поко́рность
resin /'rezɪn/ *n.* смола́
resist /rɪ'zɪst/ *v.* сопротивля́ть-
ся; отбива́ть *impf.*, отби́ть *pf.*;
—ance *n.* сопротивле́ние
resolute /'rezə,lut/ *adj.*
реши́тельный
resolution /,rezə'luʃən/ *n.* раз-
реше́ние; резолю́ция
resolve /rɪ'zɒlv/ *v.* реша́ть *impf.*,
реши́ть *pf.*
resort /rɪ'zɔrt/ **1.** *n.* куро́рт; (*re-
course*) ресу́рс **2.** *v.* прибега́ть
(к + D) *impf.*, прибе́гнуть *pf.*
resounding /rɪ'zaundɪŋ/ *adj.*
зво́нкий; гро́мкий; си́льный
resourceful /rɪ'sɔrsfəl/ *adj.*
нахо́дчивый, изобрета́тельный
resources /'rɪsɔrsəz/ *n.* ресу́рсы;
запа́сы *pl.*; **natural ~**
есте́ственные бога́тства *pl.*
respect /rɪ'spekt/ **1.** *n.* уваже́ние;
(*reference*) отноше́ние **2.** *v.*
уважа́ть *impf.*; **—able** *adj.*
прили́чный; **—ful** *adj.* почти́-
тельный; **—ive** *adj.* соот-
ве́тственный
respiration /,respə'reɪʃən/ *n.*
дыха́ние
respite /'respɪt/ *n.* переды́шка
respond /rɪ'spɒnd/ *v.* отвеча́ть
(на + A) *impf.*, отве́тить *pf.*
response /rɪ'spɒns/ *n.* отве́т;
реа́кция
responsibility /rɪ,spɒnsə'bɪlɪti/
n. отве́тственность; обя́зан-
ность
responsible /rɪ'spɒnsəbəl/ *adj.*
отве́тственный
responsive /rɪ'spɒnsɪv/ *adj.*
отве́тный; отзы́вчивый
rest[1] /rest/ **1.** *n.* о́тдых; поко́й **2.**
v. отдыха́ть *impf.*, отдохну́ть
pf.
rest[2] /rest/ *n.* (*remainder*)
оста́ток; (*people*) остальны́е *pl.*;
—less *adj.* неспоко́йный
restaurant /'restərənt/ *n.* рестора́н
restoration /,restə'reɪʃən/ *n.* рес-
таврация
restore /rɪ'stɔr/ *v.* восстана́в-
ливать *impf.*, восстанови́ть *pf.*;
реставри́ровать *impf. & pf.*
restrain /rɪ'streɪn/ *v.* сде́рживать
impf., сдержа́ть *pf.*; **—t** *n.*
сде́ржанность
restrict /rɪ'strɪkt/ *v.* ограни́-
чивать *impf.*, ограни́чить *pf.*;
—ion *n.* ограниче́ние

rest room *n.* туале́т
result /rɪ'zʌlt/ **1.** *n.* результа́т **2.**
v. сле́довать *impf.* по- *pf.*
resume /rɪ'zum/ *v.* продолжа́ть
impf., продолжи́ть *pf.*
résumé /'rezu,meɪ/ *n.* резюме́
neut. indecl.
resurrection /,rezə'rekʃən/ *n.*
воскресе́ние
retail /'riteɪl/ **1.** *n.* ро́зничная
прода́жа **2.** *adv.* в ро́зницу
retain /rɪ'teɪn/ *v.* сохраня́ть
impf., -ни́ть *pf.*
retaliate /rɪ'tæli,eɪt/ *v.* отпла́чи-
вать тем же *impf.*, отплати́ть
pf.
retaliation /rɪ,tæli'eɪʃən/ *n.*
возме́здие
retarded /rɪ'tɑrdɪd/ *adj.*
отста́лый
retention /rɪ'tenʃən/ *n.*
уде́рживание; удержа́ние
reticent /'retəsənt/ *adj.*
сде́ржанный; молчали́вый
retinue /'retn,u/ *n.* сви́та
retire /rɪ'taɪr/ *v.* уходи́ть в
отста́вку *impf.*; (*sleep*)
ложи́ться спать *impf.*; **—d** *adj.*
на пе́нсию
retreat /rɪ'trit/ **1.** *n.* отступ-
ле́ние; (*haven*) убе́жище **2.** *v.*
отступа́ть *impf.*, -пи́ть *pf.*
retribution /,retrə'byuʃən/ *n.*
возме́здие
return /rɪ'tɜrn/ **1.** *n.* возвра-
ще́ние; (*profit*) при́быль *f.* **2.**
v. обра́тный **3.** *v.* возвра-
ща́ть(ся) *impf.*, возврати́ть(ся)
pf.
reunion /ri'yunyən/ *n.* встре́ча;
воссоедине́ние
reveal /rɪ'vil/ *v.* обнару́живать
impf., -ру́жить *pf.*; **—ing** *adj.*
показа́тельный
revelation /,revə'leɪʃən/ *n.* откро-
ве́ние; откры́тие
revelry /'revəlri/ *n.* весе́лье
revenge /rɪ'vendʒ/ *n.* месть *f.*;
take ~ мстить *impf.*, отом-
сти́ть *pf.*; **—ful** *adj.* мсти́тель-
ный
revenue /'revən,yu/ *n.* дохо́д
reverberate /rɪ'vɜrbə,reɪt/ *v.*
отража́ть(ся) *impf.*
revere /rɪ'vɪər/ *v.* почита́ть *impf.*
reverence /'revərəns/ *n.*
почте́ние
reverent /'revərənt/ *adj.*
почти́тельный; благогове́йный
reverse /rɪ'vɜrs/ **1.** *adj.*

обра́тный 2. *n.* противополо́жное; обра́тное; (*gear*) за́дний ход 3. *v.* (*change*) изменя́ть *impf.*, -ни́ть *pf.*

revert /rɪˈvɜrt/ *v.* возвраща́ться *impf.*, -ти́ться *pf.*

review /rɪˈvyu/ 1. *n.* пересмо́тр; обзо́р; (*criticism*) реце́нзия; (*mil.*) смотр 2. *v.* пересма́тривать *impf.*, (*survey*) обозрева́ть *impf.*, обозре́ть *pf.*

revise /rɪˈvaiz/ *v.* перераба́тывать *impf.*, перерабо́тать *pf.*

revision /rɪˈvɪʒən/ *n.* исправле́ние; пересмо́тр

revival /rɪˈvaivəl/ *n.* возрожде́ние

revive /rɪˈvaiv/ *v.t.* оживля́ть *impf.*, -ви́ть *pf.*; *v.i.* ожива́ть *impf.*, ожи́ть *pf.*

revoke /rɪˈvouk/ *v.* отменя́ть *impf.*, -ни́ть *pf.*

revolt /rɪˈvoult/ 1. *n.* восста́ние 2. *v.* восстава́ть *impf.*, восста́ть *pf.*; **—ing** *adj.* отврати́тельный

revolution /ˌrevəˈluʃən/ *n.* револю́ция; оборо́т; **—ary** *adj.* революцио́нный; *n.* революционе́р

revolve /rɪˈvɒlv/ *v.* верте́ться *impf.*; **—r** револьве́р

revulsion /rɪˈvʌlʃən/ *n.* отвраще́ние

reward /rɪˈwɔrd/ 1. *n.* награ́да 2. *v.* награжда́ть *impf.*, -гради́ть *pf.*

rheumatism /ˈruməˌtɪzəm/ *n.* ревмати́зм

rhinoceros /raiˈnɒsərəs/ *n.* носоро́г

rhyme /raim/ 1. *n.* ри́фма 2. *v.* рифмова́ть(ся) *impf.*

rhythm /ˈrɪðəm/ *n.* ритм

rib /rɪb/ *n.* ребро́

ribbon /ˈrɪbən/ *n.* ле́нта

rice /rais/ 1. *n.* рис 2. *adj.* ри́совый

rich /rɪtʃ/ *adj.* бога́тый; (*food*) жи́рный; **—es** *n.pl.* бога́тство

rid /rɪd/ *v.*: **get ~ of** избавля́ться (от + *G*) *impf.*, изба́виться *pf.*

riddle /ˈrɪdl/ *n.* зага́дка

ride /raid/ 1. *n.* прогу́лка 2. *v.* е́здить *indet.*, е́хать *det.*, пое́хать *pf.*; **—r** *n.* (*horse*) вса́дник

ridge /rɪdʒ/ *n.* хребе́т

ridicule /ˈrɪdɪˌkyul/ 1. *n.* насме́шка 2. *v.* осме́ивать *impf.*, осмея́ть *pf.*

ridiculous /rɪˈdɪkyələs/ *adj.* неле́пый; смешно́й

rifle /ˈraifəl/ *n.* винто́вка

rift /rɪft/ *n.* тре́щина

right /rait/ 1. *adj.* пра́вый; пра́вильный 2. *adv.* пра́вильно; **on** *or* **to the ~** напра́во 3. *n.* пра́во; справедли́вость; (*~ side*) пра́вая сторона́ 4. *v.* исправля́ть *impf.*, испра́вить *pf.*; **~ angle** прямо́й у́гол

righteous /ˈraitʃəs/ *adj.* пра́ведный; справедли́вый

rigid /ˈrɪdʒɪd/ *adj.* неги́бкий

rigorous /ˈrɪgərəs/ *adj.* стро́гий; суро́вый

rim /rɪm/ *n.* край; (*of wheel*) о́бод

rind /raind/ *n.* кожура́; ко́рка

ring¹ /rɪŋ/ *n.* кольцо́; круг

ring² /rɪŋ/ 1. *n.* (*bell*) звон; звоно́к 2. *v.i.* звене́ть *impf.*

rink /rɪŋk/ *n.* (*skating*) като́к

rinse /rɪns/ *v.* полоска́ть *impf.*

riot /ˈraiət/ 1. *n.* бунт; мяте́ж 2. *v.* бунтова́ть *impf.*

rip /rɪp/ 1. *n.* проре́ха 2. *v.* рвать; разрыва́ть *impf.*, разорва́ть *pf.*

ripe /raip/ *adj.* зре́лый; спе́лый; **—n** *v.* зреть; созрева́ть *impf.*, созре́ть *pf.*

ripoff /ˈrɪpˌɔf/ *n. Colloq.* обма́н

ripple /ˈrɪpəl/ *n.* рябь *f.*

rise /raiz/ 1. *n.* повыше́ние; возвыше́ние; восхо́д 2. *v.* подыма́ться *impf.*, подня́ться *pf.*; (*get up*) встава́ть *impf.*, встать *pf.*; (*sun*) восходи́ть *impf.*, взойти́ *pf.*

risk /rɪsk/ 1. *n.* риск 2. *v.* рискова́ть (+ *I*) *impf.*, рискну́ть *pf.*; **—y** *adj.* риско́ванный

rite /rait/ *n.* обря́д

rival /ˈraivəl/ *n.* сопе́рник; **—ry** *n.* сопе́рничество

river /ˈrɪvər/ 1. *n.* река́ 2. *adj.* речно́й

rivet /ˈrɪvɪt/ *n.* заклёпка

roach /routʃ/ *n.* тарака́н

road /roud/ *n.* доро́га

roadblock /ˈroudˌblɒk/ *n.* загражде́ние на доро́ге

roadside /ˈroudˌsaid/ *n.* обо́чина

roam /roum/ *v.* броди́ть *impf.*

roar /rɔr/ 1. *n.* рёв 2. *v.* реве́ть *impf.*

roast /roust/ 1. *n.* жарко́е 2. *adj.* жа́реный 3. *v.* жа́рить(ся) *impf.*, из- *pf.*

rob /rɒb/ v. гра́бить impf., o-pf.; **—ber** n. граби́тель; **—bery** n. грабёж

robe /roub/ n. (bathrobe) хала́т

robin /'rɒbɪn/ n. мали́новка

robot /'roubɒt/ n. ро́бот

robust /rou'bʌst/ adj. здоро́вый; кре́пкий

rock[1] /rɒk/ n. (cliff) скала́; (geog.) го́рная поро́да

rock[2] /rɒk/ v. кача́ть(ся) impf.; **—ing chair** n. кача́лка

rocket /'rɒkɪt/ **1.** n. раке́та **2.** adj. раке́тный

rocky /'rɒki/ adj. скали́стый

rod /rɒd/ n. прут; брус; **fishing ~** у́дочка

rodent /'roudnt/ n. грызу́н

roe[1] /rou/ n. (fish) икра́; (soft) моло́ки pl.

roe[2] /rou/ n. (deer) косу́ля

rogue /roug/ n. моше́нник

role /roul/ n. роль f.

roll /roul/ **1.** n. руло́н; (bread) бу́лочка **2.** v. кати́ть(ся) impf.; **~ up** свёртывать(ся) impf., сверну́ть(ся) pf.

roller /'roulər/ n. ва́лик; ро́лик; **~ coaster** америка́нские го́ры pl.

Rollerblades /'roulər,bleidz/ n.pl. ро́ликовые коньки́; Colloq. ро́лики

roller-skate v. ката́ться на ро́ликах impf.

ROM /rɒm/ n. (comput.) ПЗУ

Roman /'roumən/ **1.** adj. ри́мский **2.** n. ри́млянин, -нка; **~ numeral** ри́мская ци́фра

romance /rou'mæns/ n. (love affair) рома́н

Romania /ru'meiniə/ n. Румы́ния

Romanian /ru'meiniən/ **1.** adj. румы́нский **2.** n. румы́н, —ка

romantic /rou'mæntik/ adj. романти́чный; романти́ческий

roof /ruf/ n. кры́ша

rook[1] /ruk/ n. (bird) грач

rook[2] /ruk/ n. (chess) ладья́, тура́

room /rum/ n. ко́мната; (in hotel) ка́мера; (space) ме́сто; **~ and board** по́лный пансио́н; **—y** adj. просто́рный

rooster /'rustər/ n. пету́х

root /rut/ n. ко́рень m.

rope /roup/ n. кана́т; верёвка

rose /rouz/ **1.** n. ро́за **2.** adj. ро́зовый

rostrum /'rɒstrəm/ n. трибу́на

rosy /'rouzi/ adj. ро́зовый; (cheeks) румя́ный

rot /rɒt/ **1.** n. гние́ние **2.** v. гнить impf.; **—ten** adj. гнило́й; прогни́вший

rotate /'routeit/ v.t. враща́ть(ся) impf.

rotation /rou'teiʃən/ n. враще́ние

rough /rʌf/ adj. гру́бый; (uneven) неро́вный; **~ copy** чернови́к; **—ly** adv. гру́бо; (approximately) приблизи́тельно

round /raund/ **1.** adj. кру́глый **2.** n. круг; (sports) тур; (boxing) раунд **3.** v. округля́ть(ся) impf., -ли́ть(ся) pf.; **~ trip** пое́здка туда́ и обра́тно

round-the-clock adj. круглосу́точный

rouse /rauz/ v. буди́ть impf., раз- pf.; возбужда́ть impf., -буди́ть pf.

route /rut, raut/ n. маршру́т

routine /ru'tin/ **1.** adj. устано́вленный **2.** n. режи́м

rove /rouv/ v. броди́ть impf.

row[1] /rou/ n. (line) ряд

row[2] /rau/ n. (uproar) шум; гвалт

row[3] /rou/ v. грести́ impf.; **—ing** n. гребля́

rowan /'rouən/ n. (tree) ряби́на

rowdy /'raudi/ adj. бу́йный

royal /'rɔiəl/ adj. короле́вский; **—ty** n. чле́ны короле́вской семьи́ pl.; (author) гонора́р

rub /rʌb/ **1.** n. тре́ние; натира́ние **2.** v. тере́ть(ся) impf.; (chafe) натира́ть impf., натере́ть pf.; **~ off** v. стира́ть(ся) impf., стере́ть(ся) pf.

rubber /'rʌbər/ **1.** n. рези́на; pl. гало́ши pl. **2.** adj. рези́новый; **~ band** n. рези́нка

rubbish /'rʌbiʃ/ n. му́сор; (nonsense) чепуха́

rubble /'rʌbəl/ n. разва́лины pl.

ruble /'rubəl/ n. рубль m.

ruby /'rubi/ n. руби́н

rucksack /'rʌk,sæk/ n. рюкза́к

rudder /'rʌdər/ n. руль m.

ruddy /'rʌdi/ adj. кра́сный; румя́ный

rude /rud/ adj. гру́бый

rudeness /'rudnis/ n. гру́бость

rudimentary /,rudə'mentəri/ adj. элемента́рный

rudiments /'rudəmənts/ n. осно́вы pl.

ruffian /'rʌfiən/ n. хулига́н

ruffle /'rʌfəl/ v. ряби́ть impf.; (dishevel) еро́шить impf.

rug /rʌg/ n. ковёр; ко́врик

Rugby /'rʌgbi/ n. ре́гби neut. indecl.

ruin /'ruin/ 1. n. ги́бель f.; pl. руи́ны pl. 2. v. губи́ть; разруша́ть impf., -ру́шить pf.

rule /rul/ 1. n. пра́вило; (government) управле́ние; **as a** ~ как пра́вило 2. v. пра́вить (+ I) impf.; ~ **out** исключа́ть impf., -чи́ть pf.; —**r** n. прави́тель; (measure) лине́йка; —**ing** n. (decision) постановле́ние; adj. госпо́дствующий

rum /rʌm/ n. ром

rumble /'rʌmbəl/ n. гро́хот; гул

ruminate /'rumə,neit/ v. размышля́ть impf.

rummage /'rʌmidʒ/ v. ры́ться (в + P) impf.

rumor /'rumər/ n. слух; молва́

run /rʌn/ 1. n. бег; пробе́г 2. v. бе́гать indet., бежа́ть det., побежа́ть pf.; ~ **away** убега́ть

impf., убежа́ть pf.; —**ner** n. бегу́н, —ья́; (of sled) по́лоз; —**ning** n. бег; (machine) ход; (managing) управле́ние

rung /rʌŋ/ n. ступе́нька

runway /'rʌn,wei/ n. (airport) взлётно-поса́дочная полоса́

rupture /'rʌptʃər/ 1. n. разры́в 2. v. прорыва́ть(ся) impf.

rural /'rurəl/ adj. се́льский

rush /rʌʃ/ 1. n. спе́шка; на́тиск 2. v. торопи́ть(ся); спеши́ть impf.; ~ **hour** n. час пик

Russian /'rʌʃən/ 1. adj. ру́сский; росси́йский 2. n. ру́сский, ру́сская

rust /rʌst/ 1. n. ржа́вчина 2. v. ржаве́ть impf., за- pf.; —**y** adj. ржа́вый

rustic /'rʌstik/ adj. дереве́нский

rustle /'rʌsəl/ 1. n. ше́лест; шо́рох 2. v. шурша́ть impf.

rut /rʌt/ n. коле́я; борозда́

ruthless /'ruθlıs/ adj. безжа́лостный

rye /rai/ 1. n. рожь f. 2. adj. ржано́й

S

sabbatical /sə'bætikəl/ n. годи́чный о́тпуск

sable /'seibəl/ n. со́боль m.

sabotage /'sæbə,taʒ/ 1. n. сабота́ж 2. v. саботи́ровать impf. & pf.

sack[1] /sæk/ n. мешо́к

sack[2] /sæk/ v. (plunder) громи́ть impf.

sackcloth /'sæk,klɔθ/ n. мешкови́на

sacrament /'sækrəmənt/ n. та́инство

sacred /'seikrid/ adj. свяще́нный; свято́й

sacrifice /'sækrə,fais/ 1. n. же́ртва 2. v. же́ртвовать impf., по- pf.

sacrilege /'sækrəlidʒ/ n. святота́тство

sad /sæd/ adj. печа́льный; гру́стный; —**den** v. печа́лить impf., o- pf.; —**ness** n. печа́ль; грусть f.

saddle /'sædl/ 1. n. седло́ 2. v. седла́ть impf., o- pf.

safe /seif/ 1. n. сейф 2. adj. безопа́сный; (unharmed) невреди́мый

safeguard /'seif,gard/ n. гара́нтия

safety /'seifti/ n. безопа́сность; ~ **pin** англи́йская була́вка

sag /sæg/ v. прогиба́ться impf., провиса́ть impf.

sagacious /sə'geiʃəs/ adj. проница́тельный

sage[1] /seidʒ/ n. мудре́ц

sage[2] /seidʒ/ n. (herb) шалфе́й

sail /seil/ 1. n. па́рус 2. v. пла́вать; плыть impf.

sailing /'seiliŋ/ n. пла́вание; (sports) па́русный спорт; ~ **ship** па́русник

sailor /'seilər/ n. матро́с

saint /seint/ n. свято́й; —**ly** adj. свято́й

sake /seik/ n.: **for the** ~ **of** ра́ди (+ G)

salad /'sæləd/ n. сала́т

salary /'sæləri/ n. жа́лованье; зарпла́та

sale /seil/ n. прода́жа; **on** ~ в прода́же; —**able** adj. ходово́й; —**s slip** n. квита́нция

salesperson /'seilz,pərsən/ n. продаве́ц, -вщи́ца

salient /'seiliənt/ adj. заме́тный

saliva /sə'laivə/ n. слюна́

sallow /'sælou/ adj. желтова́тый
salmon /'sæmən/ n. лосо́сь m., (cul.) лососи́на
salt /sɔlt/ 1. n. соль f. 2. v. соли́ть impf., по- pf.; —ed, -ed adj. солёный
salt shaker / n. соло́нка
salutation /,sælyə'teiʃən/ n. приве́тствие
salute /sə'lut/ 1. n. салю́т 2. v. салютова́ть impf., от- pf.
salvage /'sælvidʒ/ 1. n. спасе́ние; спасённое иму́щество 2. v. спаса́ть impf., спасти́ pf.
salvation /sæl'veiʃən/ n. спасе́ние
same /seim/ 1. pron. тот са́мый 2. adj. одно́ и то же; тот же са́мый; (identical) одина́ковый; all the ~ безразли́чно; всё-таки
sample /'sæmpəl/ 1. n. образе́ц; про́ба 2. v. про́бовать impf., по- pf.
sanatorium /,sænə'tɔriəm/ n. санато́рий
sanctify /'sæŋktə,fai/ v. освяща́ть impf., -ти́ть pf.
sanctimonious /,sæŋktə'mouniəs/ adj. ха́нжеский
sanction /'sæŋkʃən/ 1. n. са́нкция 2. v. санкциони́ровать impf. & pf.
sanctuary /'sæŋktʃu,eri/ n. святи́лище; убе́жище
sand /sænd/ n. песо́к
sandal /'sændl/ n. санда́лия
sandbank /'sænd,bæŋk/ n. о́тмель f.
sandpaper /'sænd,peipər/ n. нажда́чная бума́га
sandwich /'sændwitʃ/ n. бутербро́д
sandy /'sændi/ adj. песо́чный; песча́ный
sane /sein/ adj. норма́льный; здравомы́слящий
sanitary /'sæni,teri/ adj. санита́рный; гигиени́ческий; ~ napkin n. гигиени́ческий паке́т
sanity /'sæniti/ n. здравомы́слие
Santa Claus /'sæntə ,klɔz/ n. дед-моро́з
sap /sæp/ 1. n. сок 2. v. истоща́ть impf., -щи́ть pf.
sapling /'sæpliŋ/ n. са́женец
sapphire /'sæfaiər/ n. сапфи́р
sarcastic /sar'kæstik/ adj. сарка́стический
sardine /sar'din/ n. сарди́на

sash¹ /sæʃ/ n. (belt) куша́к; (for medal) ле́нта
sash² /sæʃ/ n. (window) око́нная ра́ма
Satan /'seitn/ n. Сатана́ m.
satellite /'sætl,ait/ n. сателли́т; спу́тник; ~ dish Colloq. таре́лка
satiate /'seiʃi,eit/ v. насыща́ть impf., насы́тить pf.
satin /'sætn/ n. атла́с
satire /'sætaiər/ n. сати́ра
satirize /'sætə,raiz/ v. высмея́ть pf.
satisfaction /,sætis'fækʃən/ n. удовлетворе́ние
satisfactory /,sætis'fæktəri/ adj. удовлетвори́тельный
satisfied /'sætis,faid/ adj. дово́льный (+ I)
satisfy /'sætis,fai/ v. удовлетворя́ть impf., -ри́ть pf.
saturate /'sætʃə,reit/ v. насыща́ть impf., насы́тить pf.
Saturday /'sætər,dei/ 1. n. суббо́та 2. adj. суббо́тний
sauce /sɔs/ n. со́ус
saucepan /'sɔs,pæn/ n. кастрю́ля
saucer /'sɔsər/ n. блю́дце
Saudi Arabia /'saudi ə'reibiə, 'sɔdi/ n. Сау́довская Ара́вия
sauerkraut /'sau³r,kraut/ n. ква́шеная капу́ста
sausage /'sɔsidʒ/ n. колбаса́
savage /'sævidʒ/ 1. adj. ди́кий; свире́пый 2. n. дика́рь m.
save /seiv/ v. спаса́ть impf., спасти́ pf.; бере́чь; эконо́мить impf., с- pf.
savings /'seiviŋz/ n.pl. сбереже́ния pl.; ~ bank сберега́тельная ка́сса, сберка́сса
savior /'seivyər/ n. спаси́тель
savor /'seivər/ n. вкус; при́вкус
saw /sɔ/ 1. n. пила́ 2. v. пили́ть impf.
sawdust /'sɔ,dʌst/ n. опи́лки pl.
say /sei/ v. говори́ть impf., сказа́ть pf.; —ing n. погово́рка
scab /skæb/ n. струп; ко́рка
scaffolding /'skæfəldiŋ/ n. строи́тельные леса́ pl.
scald /skɔld/ v. ошпа́ривать impf., ошпа́рить pf.
scale¹ /skeil/ n. шкала́; (on map) масшта́б; (mus.) га́мма; on a large ~ в больши́х масшта́бах
scale² /skeil/ n. (of fish) чешуя́
scales /skeilz/ n.pl. весы́ pl.

scrape

scallion /'skælyən/ n. зелёный лук

scallop /'skɒləp, 'skæl-/ n. гребешо́к; (pattern) фестон

scalpel /'skælpəl/ n. ска́льпель m.

scan /skæn/ v. скани́ровать impf.

scandal /'skændl/ n. позо́р; скандал; —**ize** v. шоки́ровать impf. & pf.; —**ous** adj. позо́рный; скандальный

scanner /'skænər/ n. ска́нер

scanning /'skænɪŋ/ n. скани́рование

scant /skænt/, —**y** adj. ску́дный

scapegoat /'skeip,gout/ n. козёл отпуще́ния

scar /skɑr/ **1.** n. шрам; рубе́ц **2.** v. обезобра́живать impf.

scarce /skeərs/ adj. ре́дкий; (goods) дефици́тный; —**ly** adv. едва́ (ли)

scarcity /'skeərsiti/ n. недоста́ток; нехва́тка; дефици́т

scare /skeər/ v. пуга́ть impf., испугать pf.

scarecrow /'skeər,krou/ n. пу́гало

scarf /skɑrf/ n. шарф

scarlet /'skɑrlit/ adj. а́лый; ~ **fever** n. скарлати́на

scatter /'skætər/ v. разбра́сывать impf., разбро́сать pf.; рассе́ивать(ся) impf., рассе́ять(ся) pf.

scavenge /'skævɪndʒ/ v. ры́ться в му́соре impf.; —**r** n. (zool.) падальщик

scenario /sɪ'neəri,ou/ n. сцена́рий

scene /sin/ n. сце́на; ме́сто де́йствия; **behind the —s** за кули́сами; —**ry** n. пейза́ж; (theat.) декора́ции pl.

scenic /'sinɪk/ adj. живопи́сный

scent /sɛnt/ n. за́пах; (sense) чутьё; нюх; (trail) след; —**ed** adj. души́стый

scepter /'sɛptər/ n. ски́петр

schedule /'skɛdʒul/ n. расписа́ние; —**d** adj. заплани́рованный; (regular, of trip) ре́йсовый

scheme /skim/ **1.** n. план; прое́кт; (intrigue) махина́ция **2.** v. интригова́ть impf.

schism /'sɪzəm/ n. раско́л

schizophrenia /,skɪtsə'friniə/ n. шизофрени́я

scholar /'skɒlər/ n. учёный; —**ly** adj. учёный; нау́чный

scholarship /'skɒlər,ʃɪp/ n. учёность; (stipend) стипе́ндия

school /skul/ **1.** n. шко́ла; учи́лище **2.** adj. шко́льный; —**ing** n. обуче́ние

schoolbook /'skul,buk/ n. уче́бник

schoolboy /'skul,bɔi/ n. шко́льник

schoolgirl /'skul,gɜrl/ n. шко́льница

schoolmate /'skul,meit/ n. одноклассник

science /'saiəns/ n. нау́ка; ~ **fiction** /'saiən'tɪfɪk/ фанта́стика

scientific /,saiən'tɪfɪk/ adj. нау́чный

scientist /'saiəntɪst/ n. учёный

scissors /'sɪzərz/ n.pl. но́жницы pl.

sclerosis /sklɪ'rousɪs/ n. склеро́з

scold /skould/ v. брани́ть impf.

scone /skoun/ n. лепёшка

scoop /skup/ **1.** n. сово́к; (ladle) черпа́к **2.** v. черпа́ть impf.

scooter /'skutər/ n. (child's) самока́т; **motor** ~ n. мотороллер

scope /skoup/ n. разма́х; (outlook) кругозо́р

scorch /skɔrtʃ/ v. пали́ть impf.

score /skɔr/ **1.** n. ито́г; счёт; (mus.) партиту́ра **2.** v. получа́ть (очки́) impf.; (mus.) оркестрова́ть impf. & pf.

scoreboard /'skɔr,bɔrd/ n. табло́ neut. indecl.

scorn /skɔrn/ **1.** n. презре́ние **2.** v. презира́ть impf.; —**ful** adj. презри́тельный

Scot /skɒt/ n. шотла́ндец, -дка

Scotch /skɒtʃ/ **1.** adj. шотла́ндский **2.** n. шотла́ндское ви́ски; ~ **tape** скотч

Scotland /'skɒtlənd/ n. Шотла́ндия

scoundrel /'skaundrəl/ n. подле́ц

scour /skauər/ v. чи́стить impf., по- pf.

scourge /skɜrdʒ/ n. бич

scout /skaut/ n. разве́дчик; (boy scout) бойска́ут

scowl /skaul/ n. хму́рый взгляд

scrambled eggs /'skræmbəld/ n. pl. яи́чница-болту́нья

scrap /skræp/ **1.** n. клочо́к; утиль m. **2.** v. отдава́ть на слом impf.

scrape /skreip/ v. скрести́(ся) impf.

scratch /skrætʃ/ **1.** n. цара́пина **2.** v. цара́пать impf., о- pf.

scream /skrim/ **1.** n. крик **2.** v. крича́ть impf., кри́кнуть pf.

screech /skritʃ/ n. визг

screen /skrin/ n. ши́рма; (movie, comput.) экра́н

screen-test n. кинопро́ба

screw /skru/ **1.** n. винт **2.** v. приви́нчивать impf., привинти́ть pf.

screwdriver /'skru,draivər/ n. отвёртка

scribble /'skrıbəl/ v. небре́жно (неразбо́рчиво) колеба́ние

script /skrıpt/ n. (of speech, etc.) текст; (film) сцена́рий

Scripture /'skrıptʃər/ n. Свяще́нное Писа́ние

scroll /skroul/ n. сви́ток

scrooge /skrudʒ/ n. скря́га m. & f.

scrub /skrʌb/ v. мыть щёткой impf.

scruple /'skrupəl/ n. угрызе́ние со́вести; (hesitation) колеба́ние

scrupulous /'skrupyələs/ adj. со́вестли́вый; скрупулёзный

scrutinize /'skrutn̩,aiz/ v. рассма́тривать impf.

scrutiny /'skrutn̩i/ n. рассма́тривание

scuba diver /'skubə/ n. аквалангист

scuffle /'skʌfəl/ n. дра́ка; схва́тка

sculptor /'skʌlptər/, **sculptress** n. ску́льптор

sculpture /'skʌlptʃər/ **1.** n. скульпту́ра **2.** v. вая́ть impf., из- pf.

scum /skʌm/ n. на́кипь f.

scurrilous /'skɜrələs/ adj. гру́бый; (indecent) непристо́йный

scurvy /'skɜrvi/ n. цинга́

scythe /saið/ n. коса́

sea /si/ **1.** n. мо́ре; by ~ мо́рским путём **2.** adj. морско́й

seafarer /'si,feərər/ n. морепла́ватель

sea gull n. ча́йка

seal[1] /sil/ **1.** n. печа́ть f. **2.** v. запеча́тывать impf., запеча́тать pf.

seal[2] /sil/ n. (animal) тюле́нь m.; (fur ~) ко́тик

sealing wax n. сургу́ч

seam /sim/ n. шов; —less adj. без шва

seaman /'simən/ n. моря́к

seamstress /'simstrıs/ n. швея́

search /sɜrtʃ/ **1.** n. по́иски pl.; о́быск **2.** v. иска́ть impf.; ~ warrant n. о́рдер на о́быск

searchlight /'sɜrtʃ,lait/ n. проже́ктор

seashore /'si,ʃɔr/ n. побере́жье

seasickness /'si,sıknıs/ n. морска́я боле́знь f.

seaside /'si,said/ adj. примо́рский

season /'sizən/ **1.** n. вре́мя го́да neut.; сезо́н **2.** v. (flavor) приправля́ть impf., припра́вить pf.; —al adj. сезо́нный; ~ ticket n. абонеме́нт; проездно́й биле́т

seasoning /'sizənıŋ/ n. припра́ва

seat /sit/ **1.** n. стул, ме́сто; сиде́нье **2.** v. уса́живать impf., усади́ть pf.; be —ed сади́ться impf., сесть pf.

seat belt n. реме́нь безопа́сности m.

seaweed /'si,wid/ n. морска́я во́доросль f.

secession /sı'sɛʃən/ n. откол

secluded /sı'kludıd/ adj. уединённый

seclusion /sı'kluʒən/ n. уедине́ние

second[1] /'sɛkənd/ adj. второ́й

second[2] /'sɛkənd/ n. секу́нда

secondary /'sɛkən,dɛri/ adj. второстепе́нный; втори́чный

second-class adj. второкла́ссный; второсо́ртный

secondhand /'sɛkənd'hænd/ adj. поде́ржанный

secondly /'sɛkəndli/ adv. во-вторы́х

secrecy /'sikrəsi/ n. секре́тность

secret /'sikrıt/ **1.** n. та́йна; секре́т **2.** adj. та́йный; секре́тный

secretary /'sɛkrı,tɛri/ n. секрета́рь m., секрета́рша

secretion /sı'kriʃən/ n. выделе́ние

secretive /'sikrıtıv/ adj. скры́тный

sect /sɛkt/ n. се́кта

section /'sɛkʃən/ n. се́кция; отде́л

sector /'sɛktər/ n. се́ктор

secular /'sɛkyələr/ adj. све́тский

secure /sı'kyur/ **1.** adj. безопа́сный; надёжный; уве́ренный **2.** v. (ensure) обеспе́чивать impf., обеспе́чить pf.; (get) достава́ть impf., доста́ть pf.

security /sɪ'kyʊrɪti/ n. безопа́сность; (pledge) зало́г

sedative /'sɛdətɪv/ n. успока́ивающее сре́дство

sedentary /'sɛdn̩ˌtɛri/ adj. сидя́чий

sediment /'sɛdəmənt/ n. оса́док

seduce /sɪ'dus/ v. соблазня́ть impf., -ни́ть pf.

seductive /sɪ'dʌktɪv/ adj. соблазни́тельный

see /si/ v. ви́деть impf., у- pf.; (watch) смотре́ть impf., по- pf.; ~ off провожа́ть impf., -ди́ть pf.

seed /sid/ n. се́мя neut.

seedling /'sidlɪŋ/ n. се́янец

seek /sik/ v. иска́ть impf.

seem /sim/ v. каза́ться impf., по- pf.; **—ing** adj. ви́димый; **—ingly** adv. по-ви́димому

seesaw /'siˌsɔ/ n. каче́ли pl.

seethe /sið/ v. кипе́ть impf.

segment /'sɛgmənt/ n. отре́зок

segregate /'sɛgrɪˌgeɪt/ v. отделя́ть impf., -ли́ть pf.

segregation /ˌsɛgrɪ'geɪʃən/ n. сегрега́ция; разделе́ние

seize /siz/ v. хвата́ть impf., схвати́ть pf.

seizure /'siʒər/ n. захва́т; (med.) при́ступ

seldom /'sɛldəm/ adv. ре́дко

select /sɪ'lɛkt/ **1.** adj. отбо́рный **2.** v. выбира́ть impf., вы́брать pf.; **—ion** n. вы́бор; **—ive** adj. разбо́рчивый

self-adjusting adj. саморегули́руемый

self-assurance n. самоуве́ренность

self-centered adj. эгоисти́ческий; эгоисти́чный

self-confidence n. самоуве́ренность

self-confident adj. самоуве́ренный

self-conscious adj. засте́нчивый; стыдли́вый

self-control n. самооблада́ние

self-defense n. самозащи́та; самооборо́на

self-esteem n. самоуваже́ние

self-evident adj. очеви́дный

self-interest n. своекоры́стие

selfish /'sɛlfɪʃ/ adj. эгоисти́чный

selfless /'sɛlflɪs/ adj. самоотве́рженный; бескоры́стный

self-portrait n. автопортре́т

self-reliant adj. самостоя́тельный

self-respect n. самоуваже́ние

self-righteous adj. ха́нжеский; фарисе́йский

self-satisfied adj. самодово́льный

self-service n. самообслу́живание

self-sufficient adj. самостоя́тельный; незави́симый

sell /sɛl/ v. продава́ть(ся) impf., прода́ть(ся) pf.; **—er** n. продаве́ц, -вщи́ца

semblance /'sɛmbləns/ n. подо́бие; (appearance) вид

semester /sɪ'mɛstər/ n. семе́стр

semicircle /'sɛmɪˌsɜrkəl/ n. полукру́г

semicolon /'sɛmɪˌkoʊlən/ n. то́чка с запято́й

semifinal /ˌsɛmɪ'faɪnl/ n. полуфина́л

seminar /'sɛməˌnɑr/ n. семина́р

semiprecious /ˌsɛmɪ'prɛʃəs/ adj.: ~ stone n. самоцве́т

senate /'sɛnɪt/ n. сена́т

senator /'sɛnətər/ n. сена́тор

send /sɛnd/ v. посыла́ть impf., посла́ть pf.; **—er** n. отправи́тель

send-off n. про́воды pl.

senior /'sinyər/ adj., n. ста́рший; ~ citizen n. пенсионе́р, -ка

seniority /sin'yɔrɪti/ n. старшинство́

sensation /sɛn'seɪʃən/ n. ощуще́ние; сенса́ция; **—al** adj. сенсацио́нный

sense /sɛns/ **1.** n. чу́вство; ощуще́ние; (meaning) смысл **2.** v. ощуща́ть impf., -ти́ть pf.; **—less** adj. бессмы́сленный

sensibility /ˌsɛnsə'bɪlɪti/ n. чувстви́тельность

sensible /'sɛnsəbəl/ adj. (благо) разу́мный; здравомы́слящий

sensitive /'sɛnsɪtɪv/ adj. чувстви́тельный

sensitivity /ˌsɛnsɪ'tɪvɪti/ n. чувстви́тельность

sensual /'sɛnʃuəl/, **sensuous** /'sɛnʃuəs/ adj. чу́вственный

sentence /'sɛntns/ **1.** n. (gram.) предложе́ние; (law) пригово́р **2.** v. пригова́ривать impf., приговори́ть pf.

sentimental /ˌsɛntə'mɛntl/ adj. сентимента́льный

sentry /'sɛntri/ n. часово́й

separate /adj. 'sɛpərɪt; v. 'sepə,reit/ **1.** adj. отдельный **2.** v. отделя́ть(ся) impf., отдели́ть(ся) pf.

separation /,sepə'reiʃən/ n. отделе́ние; разделе́ние; разлу́ка

September /sep'tembər/ **1.** n. сентя́брь m. **2.** adj. сентя́брьский

sequel /'sikwəl/ n. продолже́ние; (по)сле́дствие

sequence /'sikwəns/ n. после́довательность; ряд

Serbian /'sɜrbiən/ **1.** adj. се́рбский **2.** n. серб, се́рбка

sergeant /'sɑrdʒənt/ n. сержа́нт

serial /'sɪəriəl/ adj. сери́йный

series /'sɪəriz/ n. се́рия; ряд

serious /'sɪəriəs/ n. серьёзный

sermon /'sɜrmən/ n. про́поведь f.

serpent /'sɜrpənt/ n. змея́

serum /'sɪərəm/ n. сы́воротка

servant /'sɜrvənt/ n. слуга́ m., служа́нка; служащий

serve /sɜrv/ n. служи́ть impf., по- pf.

service /'sɜrvɪs/ n. слу́жба; обслу́живание; **be of** ~ быть поле́зным; ~**able** adj. поле́зный; ~ **station** n. (авто)запра́вочная ста́нция

serviceman /'sɜrvɪsmən/ n. (mil.) военнослу́жащий

serving /'sɜrvɪŋ/ n. по́рция

session /'sɛʃən/ n. се́ссия; заседа́ние

set /set/ **1.** n. набо́р; компле́кт; (television) телеви́зор; (tennis) сет; (theat.) декора́ция **2.** adj. устано́вленный **3.** v. устана́вливать impf., установи́ть pf.; (sun) заходи́ть impf., зайти́ pf.

setback /'set,bæk/ n. неуда́ча; (obstacle) препя́тствие

setting /'setɪŋ/ n. (for jewelry) опра́ва; (of sun) зака́т

settle /'setl/ v.t. (decide) реша́ть impf.; (arrange) ула́живать impf.; v.i. посели́ться impf., -ли́ться pf.; —**ment** n. (colony) поселе́ние; (payment) расчёт; —**r** n. поселе́нец, -ка

seven /'sevən/ n., adj. семь; —**th** adj. седьмо́й; —**tieth** adj. семидеся́тый; —**ty** n., adj. се́мьдесят

seventeen /'sevən'tin/ n., adj. семна́дцать; —**th** adj. семна́дцатый

several /'sevərəl/ pron., adj. не́сколько

severe /sə'vɪər/ adj. стро́гий; суро́вый

sew /sou/ v. шить impf., с- pf.

sewer /'suər/ n. канализацио́нная труба́; —**age** n. канализа́ция

sex /seks/ **1.** n. секс; (gender) пол **2.** adj. полово́й

sexual /'sekʃuəl/ adj. полово́й; сексуа́льный

shabby /'ʃæbi/ adj. потрёпанный; убо́гий

shack /ʃæk/ n. (hut) лачу́га

shackle /'ʃækəl/ n. кандалы́

shade /ʃeid/ **1.** n. тень f. **2.** v. заслоня́ть impf., -ни́ть pf.; затеня́ть impf., -ни́ть pf.

shadow /'ʃædou/ n. тень f.

shady /'ʃeidi/ adj. тени́стый; (dubious) сомни́тельный

shaft /ʃæft/ n. (ray) луч; (tech.) вал; (mine) ша́хта

shaggy /'ʃægi/ adj. лохма́тый

shake /ʃeik/ v. трясти́(сь) impf.; ~ **hands** пожа́ть ру́ку pf.

shaky /'ʃeiki/ adj. ша́ткий

shallow /'ʃælou/ adj. ме́лкий; Fig. пове́рхностный

sham /ʃæm/ n. (pretense) притво́рство; (deception) обма́н

shame /ʃeim/ **1.** n. стыд m., срам **2.** v. стыди́ть impf., при- pf.; —**ful** adj. позо́рный; —**less** adj. бессты́дный

shampoo /ʃæm'pu/ n. шампу́нь m.

shape /ʃeip/ **1.** n. фо́рма; о́браз **2.** v. придава́ть фо́рму impf.; —**less** adj. бесфо́рменный; —**ly** adv. стро́йный

share /ʃeər/ **1.** n. до́ля; (econ.) а́кция **2.** v. дели́ться impf., по- pf.

shark /ʃɑrk/ n. аку́ла

sharp /ʃɑrp/ **1.** adj. о́стрый; ре́зкий **2.** n. (mus.) дие́з

sharpen /'ʃɑrpən/ v. точи́ть impf., на- pf.; заостря́ть impf., -ри́ть pf.

sharpness /'ʃɑrpnɪs/ n. острота́

shatter /'ʃætər/ v. разбива́ть(ся) impf., разби́ть(ся) pf.

shave /ʃeiv/ **1.** n. бритьё **2.** v. брить(ся) impf., по- pf.

shawl /ʃɔl/ n. шаль f.

she /ʃi/ pron. она́

shears /ʃɪrz/ n.pl. но́жницы pl.

sheath /ʃiθ/ n. но́жны pl.

shed[1] /ʃɛd/ *n.* навёс; сарай

shed[2] /ʃɛd/ *v.* проливать *impf.*, пролить *pf.*

sheep /ʃip/ *n.* овца; баран

sheepdog /ʃip,dɔg/ *n.* овчарка

sheet /ʃit/ *n.* (linen) простыня; (paper) лист

shelf /ʃɛlf/ *n.* полка

shell /ʃɛl/ *n.* (egg, nut) скорлупа; (sea) раковина

shellfish /ʃɛl,fiʃ/ *n.* моллюск

shelter /ʃɛltər/ **1.** *n.* приют; убежище **2.** *v.* приютить *pf.*

shelving /ʃɛlvɪŋ/ *n.* стеллаж

shepherd /ʃɛpərd/ *n.* пастух

sherry /ʃɛri/ *n.* херес

shield /ʃild/ **1.** *n.* щит **2.** *v.* заслонять *impf.*, -нить *pf.*

shift /ʃift/ **1.** *n.* перемещение; (work) смена **2.** *v.* перемещать(ся) *impf.*, переместить(ся) *pf.*; —**ing** *adj.* непостоянный; —**y** *adj.* скользкий; ненадёжный

shin /ʃin/ *n.* (anat.) голень *f.*

shine /ʃain/ **1.** *n.* сияние; блеск **2.** *v.i.* сиять *impf.*; *v.t.* полировать *impf.*

shiny /ʃaini/ *adj.* блестящий

ship /ʃip/ **1.** *n.* корабль *m.*; судно **2.** *v.* отправлять *impf.*, отправить *pf.*; —**ment** *n.* отправка

shipwreck /ʃip,rɛk/ *n.* кораблекрушение

shipyard /ʃip,yard/ *n.* верфь *f.*

shirk /ʃɜrk/ *v.* увиливать (от + G) *impf.*

shirt /ʃɜrt/ *n.* рубашка

shiver /ʃivər/ **1.** *n.* дрожь *f.* **2.** *v.* дрожать *impf.*

shock /ʃɔk/ **1.** *n.* удар; потрясение; шок **2.** *v.* потрясать *impf.*, потрясти *pf.*; ~ **absorber** *n.* амортизатор; —**ing** *adj.* ужасный

shoddy /ʃɔdi/ *adj.* дрянной

shoe /ʃu/ **1.** *n.* туфля; ботинок **2.** *adj.* обувной

shoelace /ʃu,leis/ *n.* шнурок

shoemaker /ʃu'meikər/ *n.* сапожник

shoot /ʃut/ **1.** *n.* (bot.) росток; побег **2.** *v.* стрелять *impf.*; (kill) застрелить *pf.*; (execute) расстрелять *pf.*; —**ing** *n.* стрельба

shop /ʃɔp/ **1.** *n.* магазин; (tech.) цех **2.** *v.* делать покупки *impf.*, с- *pf.*

shoplifting /ʃɔp,liftɪŋ/ *n.* магазинная кража

shopper /ʃɔpər/ *n.* покупатель

shopping /ʃɔpɪŋ/ *n.* покупки *pl.*; ~ **center** *n.* торговый центр

shore /ʃɔr/ *n.* берег

short /ʃɔrt/ **1.** *adj.* короткий; краткий; (stature) низкого роста; **in** ~ вкратце **2.** *n.pl.* шорты; трусы *pl.*

shortage /ʃɔrtidʒ/ *n.* недостаток

shortchange /ʃɔrt'tʃeindʒ/ *v.* обсчитывать *impf.*

short circuit *n.* короткое замыкание

shorten /ʃɔrtn/ *v.* сокращать *impf.*, -тить *pf.*

shorthand /ʃɔrt,hænd/ *n.* стенография

shortly /ʃɔrtli/ *adv.* вскоре; ~ **before** незадолго (до + G)

shortness /ʃɔrtnis/ *n.* краткость

shortsighted /ʃɔrt'saitid/ *adj.* близорукий

short story *n.* рассказ

short-term *adj.* краткосрочный

shortwave /ʃɔrt,weiv/ *adj.* (radio) коротковолновый

shot /ʃɔt/ *n.* выстрел; (marksman) стрелок

shoulder /ʃouldər/ *n.* плечо

shout /ʃaut/ **1.** *n.* крик **2.** *v.* кричать *impf.*, крикнуть *pf.*

shove /ʃʌv/ **1.** *n.* толчок **2.** *v.* толкать *impf.*, толкнуть *pf.*

shovel /ʃʌvəl/ *n.* лопата

show /ʃou/ **1.** *n.* (theat.) зрелище; спектакль *m.*; (movie) киносеанс; (display) показ **2.** *v.* показывать *impf.*, показать *pf.*; ~ **business** *n.* шоу-бизнес

showcase /ʃou,keis/ *n.* витрина

shower /ʃauər/ *n.* (rain) дождь; ливень *m.*; (bath) душ; ~ **room** *n.* душевая

shrewd /ʃrud/ *adj.* проницательный; хитрый

shriek /ʃrik/ **1.** *n.* визг **2.** *v.* визжать *impf.*

shrill /ʃril/ *adj.* пронзительный

shrimp /ʃrimp/ *n.* креветка

shrine /ʃrain/ *n.* святыня; рака

shrink /ʃrɪŋk/ *v.* садиться *impf.*; (recoil) уклоняться (от + G) *impf.*; —**age** *n.* усадка

shrivel /ʃrivəl/ *v.* высыхать; (curl up) съёживаться *impf.*

Shrovetide /ʃrouv,taid/ *n.* Масленица

shrub /ʃrʌb/ *n.* куст; кустарник

shrug /ʃrʌg/ v. пожима́ть (плеча́ми) impf.

shudder /'ʃʌdər/ 1. n. содрога́ние 2. v. вздра́гивать impf., вздро́гнуть pf.

shuffle /'ʃʌfl/ v. (feet) ша́ркать (+ I) impf.; (cards) тасова́ть impf.

shun /ʃʌn/ v. избега́ть (+ G) impf.

shut /ʃʌt/ v. закрыва́ть impf., закры́ть pf.

shutter /'ʃʌtər/ n. ста́вень m.; (photog.) затво́р

shuttle /'ʃʌtl/ n. челно́к

shy /ʃai/ adj. засте́нчивый

Siberian /sai'biəriən/ 1. adj. сиби́рский 2. n. сибиря́к, -я́чка

sick /sik/ adj. больно́й; ~ **leave** n. о́тпуск по боле́зни

sickening /'sikənɪŋ/ adj. отврати́тельный; проти́вный

sickle /'sikəl/ n. серп

sickly /'sikli/ adj. боле́зненный

sickness /'siknis/ n. боле́знь f.

side /said/ 1. n. сторона́; бок 2. adj. боково́й 3. v. встава́ть на сто́рону (+ G) impf.

sideboard /'said,bɔrd/ n. буфе́т

sideline /'said,lain/ n. (work) подрабо́тка

sidelong /'said,lɒŋ/ adj. косо́й

sidewalk /'said,wɔk/ n. тротуа́р

siege /sidʒ/ n. оса́да

sieve /siv/ n. си́то

sift /sift/ v. просе́ивать impf., просе́ять pf.

sigh /sai/ 1. n. вздох 2. v. вздыха́ть impf., вздохну́ть pf.

sight /sait/ n. зре́ние; вид; **at first ~** с пе́рвого взгля́да

sightseer /'sait,siər/ n. тури́ст, -ка

sign /sain/ 1. n. (при́)знак; вы́веска 2. v. подпи́сывать(ся) impf., подписа́ть(ся) pf.

signal /'signl/ 1. n. сигна́л 2. v. сигнализи́ровать impf. & pf.

signature /'signətʃər/ n. по́дпись f.

significance /sig'nifikəns/ n. значе́ние; значи́тельность

signify /'signə,fai/ v. зна́чить impf.

signpost /'sain,poust/ n. указа́тельный столб

silence /'sailəns/ n. молча́ние; тишина́

silent /'sailənt/ adj. молчали́вый; ти́хий

silk /silk/ 1. n. шёлк 2. adj. шёлковый; **—y** adj. шелкови́стый

sill /sil/ n. подоко́нник

silly /'sili/ adj. глу́пый

silver /'silvər/ 1. n. серебро́ 2. adj. сере́бряный; **—y** adj. серебри́стый

silverware /'silvər,weər/ n. столо́вое серебро́

similar /'simələr/ adj. подо́бный; похо́жий

similarity /,simə'læriti/ n. схо́дство; подо́бие

simmer /'simər/ v.t. (cul.) кипяти́ть на ме́дленном огне́ impf.

simple /'simpəl/ adj. просто́й

simplicity /sim'plisiti/ n. простота́

simplify /'simplə,fai/ v. упроща́ть impf., упрости́ть pf.

simulate /'simyə,leit/ v. симули́ровать impf. & pf.

simultaneous /,saiməl'teiniəs/ adj. одновреме́нный

sin /sin/ 1. n. грех 2. v. греши́ть impf., co- pf. **—ful** adj. гре́шный

since /sins/ 1. adv. с тех пор 2. prep. с (+ G) 3. conj. с тех пор, как; так как

sincere /sin'siər/ adj. и́скренний

sincerity /sin'seriti/ n. и́скренность

sinew /'sinyu/ n. сухожи́лие

sing /siŋ/ v. петь impf, c- pf.

singe /sindʒ/ v. пали́ть impf., o- pf.

singer /'siŋər/ n. певе́ц, певи́ца

single /'siŋgəl/ adj. оди́н; (unmarried) холосто́й, незаму́жняя

single-minded adj. целеустремлённый

singular /'siŋgyələr/ n. (gram.) еди́нственное число́

sinister /'sinistər/ adj. злове́щий

sink /siŋk/ 1. n. ра́ковина 2. v.t. топи́ть impf., по- pf.; v.i. тону́ть impf., по- pf.

sinner /'sinər/ n. гре́шник, -ница

sip /sip/ n. глото́к

sir /sɜr/ n. сэр

siren /'sairən/ n. сире́на

sirloin /'sɜrlɔin/ n. филе́ neut. in-decl.

sister /'sistər/ n. сестра́

sister-in-law n. (brother's wife) неве́стка; (husband's sister) золо́вка

sit /sit/ v. сиде́ть impf.; ~ **down** v. сади́ться impf., сесть pf.

site /sait/ n. местоположе́ние

situated /'sɪtʃu,eitid/ adj. расположенный

situation /,sɪtʃu'eiʃən/ n. местоположение; положение; состояние

six /sɪks/ n., adj. шесть; **—th** adj. шестой

sixteen /'sɪks'tin/ n., adj. шестнадцать

sixtieth /'sɪkstiθ/ adj. шестидесятый

sixty /'sɪksti/ n., adj. шестьдесят

sizable /'saizəbl/ adj. значительный; изрядный

size /saiz/ n. размер; объём; величина́

skate /skeit/ **1.** n. конёк **2.** v. ката́ться на конька́х impf.

skateboard /'skeit,bɔrd/ n. роликовая доска́

skeleton /'skelɪtn/ n. скелет

skeptic /'skeptɪk/ n. скептик; **—al** adj. скептический

sketch /sketʃ/ **1.** n. эскиз; набро́сок **2.** v. де́лать эскиз impf., с- pf.; **—y** adj. схематичный

sketchy /'sketʃi/ adj. (in outline) схематичный; (scanty) скудный

skewer /'skyuər/ n. ве́ртел

ski /ski/ **1.** v. ходи́ть на лы́жах impf. **2.** n. лы́жа

skid /skid/ v. заноси́ть impf., занести́ pf.

skier /'skiər/ n. лы́жник, -ница

skill /skil/ n. уме́ние; мастерство́; **—ed** adj. квалифицированный; **—ful** adj. иску́сный; ло́вкий

skillet /'skilit/ n. сковорода́

skim milk /skɪm/ n. обезжи́ренное молоко́

skin /skin/ n. ко́жа; шку́ра

skinny /'skini/ adj. то́щий; худо́й

skip /skip/ v. скака́ть; пры́гать impf.; (omit) пропуска́ть impf., -сти́ть pf.

skirmish /'skɜrmiʃ/ n. схва́тка

skirt /skɜrt/ n. ю́бка

skit /skit/ n. скетч

skull /skʌl/ n. че́реп

skunk /skʌŋk/ n. воню́чка; скунс

sky /skai/ n. не́бо

skylark /'skai,lɑrk/ n. жа́воронок

skyline /'skai,lain/ n. горизо́нт

skyscraper /'skai,skreipər/ n. небоскрёб

slab /slæb/ n. плита́

slack /slæk/ adj. сла́бый; вя́лый;

—en v. замедля́ть(ся) impf., заме́длить(ся) pf.

slacks /slæks/ n. брюки pl.

slam /slæm/ v. хло́пнуть pf.

slander /'slændər/ **1.** n. клевета́ **2.** v. клевета́ть impf., o- pf.

slang /slæŋ/ n. жарго́н; сленг

slant /slænt/ **1.** n. склон; укло́н **2.** v. наклоня́ть(ся) impf.; **—ing** adj. накло́нный; косо́й

slap /slæp/ **1.** n. шлепо́к; **a ~ in the face** пощёчина **2.** v. шлёпать impf., шлёпнуть pf.

slash /slæʃ/ **1.** n. уда́р ножо́м **2.** v. поре́зать impf., поре́зать pf.

slate /sleit/ n. сла́нец; ши́фер

slaughter /'slɔtər/ **1.** n. убо́й; Fig. резня́ **2.** v. ре́зать impf., за- pf.

slaughterhouse /'slɔtər,haus/ n. скотобо́йня

Slav /slɑv/ n. славяни́н, славя́нка

slave /sleiv/ n. раб, **—ы́ня**

slavery /'sleivəri/ n. ра́бство

Slavic /'slɑvɪk/ adj. славя́нский

slay /slei/ v. убива́ть impf., уби́ть pf.

sled /sled/ n. са́ни pl.

sleek /slik/ adj. гла́дкий

sleep /slip/ **1.** n. сон **2.** v. спать impf.

sleeping /'slipɪŋ/ adj. спя́щий; **—bag** n. спа́льный мешо́к; **~ car** n. спа́льный ваго́н; **~ pill** n. снотво́рная табле́тка

sleepless /'sliplɪs/ adj. бессо́нный

sleepy /'slipi/ adj. со́нный

sleeve /sliv/ n. рука́в; **—less** adj. безрука́вный

sleigh /slei/ n. са́ни; са́нки pl.

slender /'slendər/ adj. то́нкий; стро́йный

sleuth /sluθ/ n. сы́щик

slice /slais/ **1.** n. ло́мтик; кусо́к **2.** v. ре́зать ло́мтиками impf.

slide /slaid/ **1.** v. скользи́ть impf. **2.** n. (photog.) слайд

slight /slait/ **1.** adj. лёгкий; то́нкий; небольшо́й **2.** v. пренебрега́ть impf.; -бре́чь pf.

slim /slim/ adj. стро́йный; то́нкий

slime /slaim/ n. слизь f.

sling /slɪŋ/ n. (med.) перевя́зь f.

slip /slip/ **1.** n. (skid) скольже́ние; (mistake) оши́бка; (garment) комбина́ция **2.** v. скользи́ть impf.

slip² /slɪp/ *n.* (*paper*) листо́чек

slipper /'slɪpər/ *n.* та́почка

slippery /'slɪpəri/ *adj.* ско́льзкий

slogan /'slougən/ *n.* ло́зунг

slope /sloup/ **1.** *n.* накло́н; склон; скат **2.** *v.* име́ть накло́н *impf.*

sloping /'sloupɪŋ/ *adj.* накло́нный; пока́тый; отло́гий

sloppy /'slɒpi/ *adj.* неря́шливый

slot /slɒt/ *n.* отве́рстие; щёлка

slot machine *n.* игрово́й автома́т

Slovakia /slou'vakiə/ *n.* Слова́кия

Slovenia /slou'viniə/ *n.* Слове́ния

slow /slou/ **1.** *adj.* ме́дленный; be ~ (*timepiece*) отстава́ть *impf.* **2.** *v.:* ~ **down** замедля́ть(ся) *impf.*, заме́длить(ся) *pf.*

slug /slʌg/ *n.* (*zool.*) слизня́к; (*bullet*) пу́ля; (*token*) жето́н

sluggish /'slʌgɪʃ/ *adj.* вя́лый

sluice /slus/ *n.* шлюз

slum /slʌm/ *n.* трущо́ба

slush /slʌʃ/ *n.* сля́коть

sly /slai/ *adj.* хи́трый

small /smɔl/ *adj.* ма́ленький; ме́лкий

small-minded *adj.* ме́лочный

smallpox /'smɔl,pɒks/ *n.* о́спа

smart /smart/ **1.** *adj.* у́мный; (*dress*) элега́нтный **2.** *v.* испы́тывать о́струю боль *impf.*

smash /smæʃ/ *v.* разбива́ть(ся) *impf.*, разби́ть(ся) *pf.*

smear /smɪər/ **1.** *n.* пятно́; (*med.*) мазо́к **2.** *v.* ма́зать *impf.*

smell /smel/ **1.** *n.* за́пах; (*sense*) обоня́ние **2.** *v.t.* чу́ять *impf.*; *v.i.* па́хнуть (+ *I*) *impf.*

smelly /'smeli/ *adj.* злово́нный

smile /smail/ **1.** *n.* улы́бка **2.** *v.* улыба́ться *impf.*, улыбну́ться *pf.*

smith /smɪθ/ *n.* кузне́ц

smock /smɒk/ *n.* хала́т

smoke /smouk/ **1.** *n.* дым **2.** *v.* дыми́ться *impf.*; (*tobacco*) кури́ть *impf.*; (*food*) копти́ть *impf.*; **—d** *adj.* (*cul.*) копчёный; **—r** *n.* куря́щий

smoky /'smouki/ *adj.* ды́мный

smolder /'smouldər/ *v.* тлеть *impf.*

smooth /smuð/ **1.** *adj.* гла́дкий; ро́вный **2.** *v.* прогла́живать *impf.*, прогла́дить *pf.*

smother /'smʌðər/ *v.* души́ть *impf.*, за- *pf.*

smuggle /'smʌgəl/ *v.* занима́ться контраба́ндой *impf.*

snack /snæk/ *n.* заку́ска

snag /snæg/ *n.* *Fig.* загво́здка

snail /sneil/ *n.* ули́тка

snake /sneik/ *n.* змея́

snap /snæp/ **1.** *n.* треск **2.** *v.t.* (*make sound*) щёлкать *impf.*, щёлкнуть *pf.*; *v.i.* (*break*) ло́паться *impf.*, ло́пнуть *pf.*

snapshot /'snæp,ʃɒt/ *n.* сни́мок

snare /snɛər/ *n.* лову́шка

snarl /snarl/ *v.* рыча́ть (на + *A*) *impf.*

snatch /snætʃ/ *v.* хвата́ть *impf.*, схвати́ть *pf.*

sneak /snik/ *v.* кра́сться *impf.*

sneaker /'snikər/ *n.* кроссо́вка

sneer /snɪər/ **1.** *n.* насме́шка **2.** *v.* насмеха́ться (над + *I*) *impf.*

sneeze /sniz/ **1.** *n.* чиха́ние **2.** *v.* чиха́ть *impf.*, чихну́ть *pf.*

snicker /'snɪkər/ *v.* хихи́кать *impf.*

snore /snɔr/ **1.** *n.* храп **2.** *v.* храпе́ть *impf.*

snort /snɔrt/ *v.* фы́ркать *impf.*

snout /snaut/ *n.* мо́рда; ры́ло

snow /snou/ **1.** *n.* снег **2.** *adj.* снежный **3.** *v.i.:* **it —s** идёт снег

snowball /'snou,bɔl/ *n.* снежо́к

snowdrift /'snou,drɪft/ *n.* сугро́б

snowfall /'snou,fɔl/ *n.* снегопа́д

snowflake /'snou,fleik/ *n.* снежи́нка

snowstorm /'snou,stɔrm/ *n.* мете́ль *f.*

snug /snʌg/ *adj.* ую́тный

snuggle /'snʌgəl/ *v.* обнима́ть; прижима́ться (к + *D*) *impf.*

so /sou/ **1.** *adv.* так; таки́м о́бразом; (*also*) та́кже; то́же **2.** *conj.* (*therefore*) поэ́тому; ~ **that** что́бы

soak /souk/ *v.* зама́чивать *impf.*, замочи́ть *pf.*

soap /soup/ **1.** *n.* мы́ло **2.** *adj.* мы́льный **3.** *v.* намы́ливать *impf.*, намы́лить *pf.*; ~ **bubble** *n.* мы́льный пузы́рь *m.*; ~ **dish** мы́льница; ~ **opera** мы́льная о́пера

soar /sɔr/ *v.* пари́ть *impf.*

sob /sɒb/ *v.* рыда́ть *impf.*

sober /'soubər/ *adj.* тре́звый

so-called *adj.* так называ́емый

soccer /'sɒkər/ *n.* футбо́л

sociable /ˈsəʊʃəbəl/ *adj.* общительный; дружеский

social /ˈsəʊʃəl/ *adj.* общественный; **—ism** *n.* социализм; **—ist** *adj.* социалистический; **~ science** *n.* общественные науки *pl.*; **~ security** социальное обеспечение

socialize /ˈsəʊʃəˌlaɪz/ *v. (be sociable)* общаться *impf.*

society /səˈsaɪɪtɪ/ *n.* общество

sociology /ˌsəʊsɪˈɒlədʒɪ/ *n.* социология

sock /sɒk/ *n.* носок

socket /ˈsɒkɪt/ *n. (elec.) (for bulb)* патрон; *(outlet)* розётка

soda /ˈsəʊdə/ *n.* газированная вода; *(chem.)* сода

sodium /ˈsəʊdɪəm/ *n.* натрий

sofa /ˈsəʊfə/ *n.* диван

sofa bed *n.* кушётка, диван-кровать *f.*

soft /sɒft/ *adj.* мягкий; тихий

soft-boiled egg *n.* яйцо всмятку

soften /ˈsɒfən/ *v.* смягчать(ся) *impf.*, смягчить(ся) *pf.*

softness /ˈsɒftnɪs/ *n.* мягкость

software /ˈsɒftˌweər/ *n.* программное обеспечение; набор программ

soil[1] /sɔɪl/ *n.* почва

soil[2] /sɔɪl/ *v.* пачкать *impf.*, за- *pf.*

solace /ˈsɒlɪs/ *n.* утешение

solar /ˈsəʊlər/ *adj.* солнечный

solder /ˈsɒdər/ *v.* паять *impf.*

soldier /ˈsəʊldʒər/ *n.* солдат

sole[1] /səʊl/ *adj.* единственный

sole[2] /səʊl/ *n.* подошва

sole[3] /səʊl/ *v. (fish)* камбала

solemn /ˈsɒləm/ *adj.* торжественный

solemnity /səˈlemnɪtɪ/ *n.* торжественность

solid /ˈsɒlɪd/ *adj.* твёрдый; прочный; солидный

solidarity /ˌsɒlɪˈdærɪtɪ/ *n.* солидарность; общность

solitary /ˈsɒlɪˌterɪ/ *adj.* одинокий

solitude /ˈsɒlɪˌtjuːd/ *n.* одиночество

soloist /ˈsəʊləʊɪst/ *n.* солист, —ка

solstice /ˈsɒlstɪs/ *n.* солнцестояние

soluble /ˈsɒljəbəl/ *adj.* растворимый

solution /səˈluːʃən/ *n.* решение; *(liquid)* раствор

solve /sɒlv/ *v.* (раз)решать *impf.*, -шить *pf.*; **—nt** *n.* растворитель; *adj. (able to pay)* платёжеспособный

somber /ˈsɒmbər/ *adj.* мрачный

some /sʌm/ **1.** *pron.* нёкоторые; одни **2.** *adj.* нёкоторый; какой-то, какой-нибудь

somebody /ˈsʌmˌbɒdɪ/ *pron.* кто-то; кто-нибудь

somehow /ˈsʌmˌhaʊ/ *adv.* как-то, как-нибудь

something /ˈsʌmθɪŋ/ *pron.* что-то; что-нибудь

sometime /ˈsʌmˌtaɪm/ *adv.* когда-нибудь; *(—s)* иногда

somewhat /ˈsʌmˌwʌt/ *adv.* отчасти; немного; несколько

somewhere /ˈsʌmˌweər/ *adv. (loc.)* где-то; где-нибудь; *(dir.)* куда-то; куда-нибудь

son /sʌn/ *n.* сын

song /sɒŋ/ *n.* пёсня

sonic /ˈsɒnɪk/ *adj.* звуковой

son-in-law *n.* зять *m.*

soon /suːn/ *adv.* скоро; вскоре; **as ~ as** как только; **as ~ as possible** как можно быстрее

soot /sʊt/ *n.* сажа

soothe /suːð/ *v.* облегчать *impf.*, -чить *pf.*; **—ing** *adj.* успокоительный

sophisticated /səˈfɪstɪˌkeɪtɪd/ *adj.* искушённый; *(tech.)* сложный

sorcery /ˈsɔːsərɪ/ *n.* колдовство; волшебство

sordid /ˈsɔːdɪd/ *adj.* грязный

sore /sɔːr/ **1.** *n.* болячка; язва **2.** *adj.* больной; воспалённый

sorrow /ˈsɒrəʊ/ *n.* печаль *f.*; гóре; **—ful** *adj.* печальный

sorry /ˈsɒrɪ/ *adj.* жалкий; **I'm ~!** простите!; **be ~** жалеть *impf.*, по- *pf.*; *(regret)* сожалеть *impf.*

sort /sɔːt/ **1.** *n.* род; сорт; вид **2.** *v.* разбирать; сортировать *impf.*

soul /səʊl/ *n.* душа

sound[1] /saʊnd/ *adj.* здоровый; *(logical)* разумный

sound[2] /saʊnd/ **1.** *n.* звук **2.** *adj.* звуковой **3.** *v.* звучать *impf.*, про- *pf.*

sound[3] /saʊnd/ **1.** *n. (med.)* зонд **2.** *v.* измерять глубину *impf.*; *(med., Fig.)* зондировать *impf.*

sound[4] /saʊnd/ *n. (strait)* пролив

soundproof /ˈsaʊndˌpruːf/ *adj.* звуконепроницаемый

soup /sup/ **1.** n. суп **2.** adj. суповой

sour /sauər/ adj. ки́слый; ~ **cream** n. смета́на

source /sɔrs/ n. исто́к; исто́чник

south /sauθ/ **1.** n. юг **2.** adv. на юг; к ю́гу

southeast /,sauθ'ist/ **1.** n. юго-восто́к **2.** adj. юго-восто́чный

southern /'sʌðərn/ adj. ю́жный; —**er** n. южа́нин, южа́нка

southwest /,sauθ'west/ **1.** n. юго-за́пад **2.** adj. юго-за́падный

souvenir /,suvə'nɪər/ n. сувени́р

sovereign /'sɒvrɪn/ **1.** n. госуда́рь m.; суверéн **2.** adj. суверéнный; полновла́стный; —**ty** n. суверените́т

soviet /'souvi,et/ **1.** n. совéт **2.** adj. cap. совéтский

sow[1] /sau/ n. (hog) свинья́

sow[2] /sou/ v. céять impf., по- pf.

soybean /'soi,bin/ **1.** n. со́я; **2.** adj. со́евый боб m., со́евый

space /speis/ **1.** n. простра́нство; промежу́ток; мéсто **2.** adj. косми́ческий

spaceship /'speis,ʃɪp/ n. косми́ческий кора́бль m.

spacious /'speiʃəs/ adj. просто́рный; обши́рный

spade[1] /speid/ n. лопа́та

spade[2] /speid/ n. (cards) пи́ка

Spain /spein/ n. Испа́ния

span /spæn/ n. отрéзок; (of bridge) пролёт; (aero.) разма́х

Spaniard /'spænyərd/ n. испа́нец, испа́нка

Spanish /'spænɪʃ/ adj. испа́нский

spanking /'spæŋkɪŋ/ n. трёпка

spare /spɛər/ **1.** adj. запасно́й; свобо́дный; ли́шний **2.** v. (life) щади́ть impf., по- pf.; ~ **parts** n. запасны́е ча́сти pl.

sparing /'spɛərɪŋ/ adj. ску́дный; эконо́мный; (careful) умéренный

spark /spɑrk/ n. и́скра; ~ **plug** n. свеча́ зажига́ния

sparkle /'spɑrkəl/ v. и́скриться; сверка́ть impf.

sparrow /'spærou/ n. воробéй

spatter /'spætər/ v. забры́згивать impf., забры́згать pf.

speak /spik/ v. говори́ть impf., сказа́ть pf.; —**er** n. докла́дчик, -чица; выступа́ющий; говоря́щий

special /'speʃəl/ adj. специа́льный; осо́бенный; ~ **delivery** n. сро́чная доста́вка; —**ist** n. специали́ст

specialize /'speʃə,laiz/ v. специализи́ровать(ся) impf. & pf.

specialty /,speʃəlti/ n. специа́льность; осо́бенность

specific /spɪ'sɪfɪk/ adj. осо́бенный; специфи́ческий

specify /'speSə,fai/ v. определя́ть impf., -ли́ть pf.

specimen /'spesəmən/ n. образéц; экземпля́р

speck /spek/ n. пя́тнышко; кра́пинка; (in eye) сори́нка

spectacle /'spektəkəl/ n. спекта́кль m.; зрéлище

spectator /'spekteitər/ n. зри́тель

spectrum /'spektrəm/ n. спектр

speculation /,spekyə'leiʃən/ n. предположéние, спекуля́ция

speech /spitʃ/ n. речь f.; —**less** adj. безмо́лвный

speed /spid/ **1.** n. ско́рость **2.** v. мча́ться impf.; ~ **limit** n. дозво́ленная ско́рость

spell[1] /spel/ n. заклина́ние

spell[2] /spel/ n. (time) промежу́ток врéмени

spell[3] /spel/ v. произноси́ть по бу́квам impf.; ~ **checker** n. корре́ктор; —**ing** n. правописа́ние

spend /spend/ v. тра́тить impf., ис- pf.; (time) проводи́ть impf.

sphere /sfɪər/ n. сфéра; шар

spice /spais/ **1.** n. спéция; пря́ность **2.** v. приправля́ть impf., припра́вить pf.

spicy /'spaisi/ adj. о́стрый

spider /'spaidər/ n. пау́к

spider web n. паути́на

spike /spaik/ n. шип; гвоздь m.

spill /spɪl/ v. пролива́ть(ся) impf., проли́ть(ся) pf.

spin /spɪn/ v. крути́ть(ся) impf.

spinach /'spɪnɪtʃ/ n. шпина́т

spinal /'spainəl/ adj. спинно́й

spine /spain/ n. позвоно́чник; (book) корешо́к; —**less** adj. Fig. бесхара́ктерный

spin-off n. побо́чный проду́кт

spiral /'spairəl/ **1.** adj. спира́льный **2.** n. спира́ль f.

spire /spaiər/ n. шпиль m.

spirit /'spɪrɪt/ n. дух; настроéние

spiritual /'spɪrɪtʃuəl/ adj. духо́вный

spit /spɪt/ **1.** n. слюна́ **2.** v. плева́ть impf., плю́нуть pf.

spite /spait/ n. злоба; in ~ of несмотря на (+ A); —ful adj. злобный

spittle /'spitl/ n. слюна

splash /splæʃ/ 1. n. брызги pl.; плеск 2. v. брызгать(ся) impf.

spleen /splin/ n. селезёнка

splendid /'splendid/ adj. великолепный; блестящий

splendor /'splendər/ n. великолепие; блеск

splinter /'splintər/ 1. n. осколок; заноза 2. v. щепать(ся) impf., -пить(ся) pf.

split /split/ 1. n. раскол 2. v. раскалывать(ся) impf., -колоть(ся) pf.

spoil /spɔil/ v. портить(ся) impf., ис- pf.; —ed adj. испорченный; (child, etc.) избалованный

spoke /spouk/ n. спица

spokesman /'spouksmən/ n. представитель, —ница

sponge /spʌndʒ/ n. губка

sponge cake n. бисквитный торт

sponsor /'sponsər/ 1. n. спонсор 2. v. финансировать impf. & pf.

spontaneous /spon'teiniəs/ adj. самопроизвольный; спонтанный

spoon /spun/ n. ложка

sport /spɔrt/ n. спорт; —s adj. спортивный

sportsman /'spɔrtsmən/ n. спортсмен

sportswoman /'spɔrts,wumən/ n. спортсменка

spot /spot/ n. пятно; (place) место 2. v. (see) увидеть pf.; —ted adj. пятнистый

spotlight /'spot,lait/ n. прожектор

spouse /spaus/ n. супруг, супруга

sprain /sprein/ 1. n. растяжение связок 2. v. растягивать связки impf.

sprat /spræt/ n. шпрот; килька

spray /sprei/ 1. n. распылитель 2. v. обрызгивать impf., обрызгать pf.

spread /spred/ 1. n. распространение 2. v. распространять(ся) impf., -нить(ся) pf.

spreadsheet /'spred,ʃit/ n. крупноинформатная электронная таблица (abbr. КЭТ)

spree /spri/ n. кутёж

spring /spriŋ/ 1. n. (device)

пружина; (season) весна; (water) родник; in the ~ adv. весной 2. v. прыгать impf.

springboard /'spriŋ,bɔrd/ n. (sports) трамплин

sprinkle /'spriŋkəl/ v. кропить impf., по- pf.

sprint /sprint/ n. спринт

sprout /spraut/ v. прорастать impf.

spruce¹ /sprus/ n. ель f.

spruce² /sprus/ v.: ~ up приводить в порядок impf.

spur /spər/ n. шпора; Fig. стимул; on the ~ of the moment экспромтом adv.

spurt /spərt/ 1. n. струя 2. v. бить струёй impf.

spy /spai/ 1. n. шпион, —ка 2. v. шпионить (за + I) impf.

squabble /'skwobəl/ 1. n. перебранка 2. v. вздорить impf., по- pf.

squad /skwod/ n. отряд; команда

squalid /'skwolid/ adj. (dirty) грязный; (wretched) убогий

squander /'skwondər/ v. растрачивать impf., растратить pf.

square /skwεər/ 1. adj. квадратный 2. n. (open area) площадь f.; (math.) квадрат

squash¹ /'skwoʃ/ n. кабачок

squash² /'skwoʃ/ v. раздавливать impf., раздавить pf.

squat /skwot/ v. сидеть на корточках impf.

squeak /skwik/ 1. n. скрип; писк 2. v. скрипеть impf.

squeeze /skwiz/ 1. n. (crush) давка 2. v. сжимать impf., сжать pf.; ~ out выжимать impf., выжать pf.

squid /skwid/ n. (zool.) кальмар

squint /skwint/ v. косить impf.

squirrel /'skwərəl/ n. белка

stab /stæb/ 1. n. удар (ножом) 2. v. вонзать impf., вонзить pf.

stability /stə'biliti/ n. стабильность

stable¹ /'steibəl/ n. конюшня

stable² /'steibəl/ adj. стойкий; постоянный; стабильный

stack /stæk/ 1. n. (hay) стог, (heap) стопка 2. v. складывать в стопку impf.

stadium /'steidiəm/ n. стадион

staff /stæf/ 1. n. (stick) посох; жезл; (personnel) персонал; штат 2. adj. штатный

stage /steidʒ/ **1.** n. (*period*) ста́дия; (*platform*) подмо́стки pl.; (*theat.*) сце́на **2.** v. ста́вить impf., по- pf.; организова́ть impf. & pf.

stagger /'stægər/ v.i. шата́ться impf., —**ing** adj. потряса́ющий

stagnant /'stægnənt/ adj. стоя́чий; Fig. засто́йный

stagnation /stæg'neiʃən/ n. засто́й

stain /stein/ **1.** n. пятно́ **2.** v. пятна́ть; па́чкать(ся) impf.; —**less steel** n. нержаве́ющая сталь f.

stair /steər/ n. ступе́нька; pl. ле́стница

staircase /'steər,keis/ n. ле́стница

stake[1] /steik/ n. кол; столб

stake[2] /steik/ **1.** n. (*bet*) ста́вка **2.** v. (*cards*) ста́вить (на + A) impf.

stale /steil/ adj. несве́жий; чёрствый

stalemate /'steil,meit/ n. тупи́к

stalk[1] /stɔk/ n. стебе́ль m.;

stalk[2] /stɔk/ v. высле́живать impf.

stall /stɔl/ **1.** n. сто́йло; (*booth*) ларёк **2.** v.t. заде́рживать impf., задержа́ть pf.; v.i. гло́хнуть impf., за- pf.

stallion /'stælyən/ n. жеребе́ц

stamina /'stæmənə/ n. выно́сливость

stammer /'stæmər/ **1.** n. заика́ние **2.** v. заика́ться impf.

stamp /stæmp/ **1.** n. штéмпель m.; печа́ть f.; (*postage*) почто́вая ма́рка **2.** v. штампова́ть impf.

stand /stænd/ **1.** n. подста́вка; кио́ск; (*position*) пози́ция **2.** v. стоя́ть impf.; ~ **up** встава́ть impf., встать pf.

standard /'stændərd/ **1.** n. станда́рт; но́рма **2.** adj. станда́ртный

standardize /'stændər,daiz/ v. стандартизи́ровать impf. & pf.

standpoint /'stænd,pɔint/ n. то́чка зре́ния

stanza /'stænzə/ n. строфа́

staple[1] /'steipəl/ **1.** n. (*for paper*) ско́бка **2.** v. скрепля́ть (ско́бкой, ско́бками) impf., -пи́ть pf.

staple[2] /'steipəl/ n. (*principal product*) основно́й проду́кт

star /stɑr/ n. звезда́

starch /stɑrtʃ/ **1.** n. крахма́л **2.** v. крахма́лить impf., на- pf.

stare /steər/ v. смотре́ть при́стально (на + A) impf.

stark /stɑrk/ adj. абсолю́тный

starling /'stɑrliŋ/ n. скворе́ц

start /stɑrt/ **1.** n. нача́ло; старт **2.** v. начина́ть(ся) impf., нача́ть(ся) pf.

starvation /stɑr'veiʃən/ n. го́лод; голода́ние

starve /stɑrv/ v. голода́ть impf.

state /steit/ **1.** n. (*condition*) состоя́ние; (*government*) госуда́рство; штат **2.** adj. госуда́рственный **3.** v. излага́ть impf., изложи́ть pf.; —**ly** adj. вели́чественный; —**ment** n. заявле́ние

statesman /'steitsmən/ n. госуда́рственный де́ятель

static /'stætik/ **1.** adj. неподви́жный **2.** n. атмосфе́рные поме́хи pl.

station /'steiʃən/ n. ста́нция; (*terminal*) вокза́л; (*post*) пост

stationary /'steiʃə,neri/ adj. неподви́жный

stationery /'steiʃə,neri/ n. канцеля́рские принадле́жности pl.

statistics /stə'tistiks/ n. стати́стика

statue /'stætʃu/ n. ста́туя

status /'steitəs, 'stætəs/ n. ста́тус; положе́ние

statute /'stætʃut/ n. зако́н

stay /stei/ **1.** n. пребыва́ние **2.** v. оставля́ться impf., оста́ться pf.; гости́ть impf.

steadfast /'sted,fæst/ adj. сто́йкий; непоколеби́мый

steady /'stedi/ **1.** adj. усто́йчивый; равноме́рный; неизме́нный **2.** v. ура́вновесить impf.

steak /steik/ n. бифште́кс

steal /stil/ v. красть impf., у- pf.

stealthy /'stelθi/ adj. скры́тый

steam /stim/ **1.** n. пар **2.** v. па́рить(ся) impf.; —**y** adj. горя́чий

steamship /'stim,ʃip/ n. парохо́д

steel /stil/ **1.** n. сталь f. **2.** adj. стально́й

steelyard /'stil,yɑrd/ n. безме́н

steep /stip/ adj. круто́й

steeple /'stipəl/ n. шпиль m.

steer[1] /stiər/ n. (*ox*) вол

steer[2] /stiər/ v.t. пра́вить; управля́ть (+ I) impf.

steering wheel n. руль m.

stem /stɛm/ *n.* стéбель *m.*; (*linguistics*) оснóва; ~ **from** происходи́ть *impf.*, произойти́ *pf.*

stench /stɛntʃ/ *n.* злово́ние

stenographer /stə'nɒɡrəfər/ *n.* стеногрáфист, —ка

step /stɛp/ 1. *n.* шаг; (*stair*) ступéнька; ~ **by** ~ шаг за шáгом 2. *v.*: ~ **on** наступáть *impf.*, -пи́ть *pf.*

stepfather /'stɛp,fɑðər/ *n.* о́тчим

stepladder /'stɛp,lædər/ *n.* стремя́нка

stepmother /'stɛp,mʌðər/ *n.* мáчеха

steppe /stɛp/ *n.* степь *f.*

stereo /'stɛriou/ *n.* стéрео *neut. indecl.*

stereophonic /,stɛriə'fɒnɪk/ *adj.* стереофони́ческий

sterile /'stɛrɪl/ *adj.* беспло́дный; стери́льный

sterilize /'stɛrə,laɪz/ *v.* стерилизовáть *impf.* & *pf.*

stern[1] /stɜrn/ *n.* кормá

stern[2] /stɜrn/ *adj.* стро́гий

sternum /'stɜrnəm/ *n.* груди́на

stew /stu/ 1. *n.* тушёное мя́со 2. *v.* туши́ть(ся) *impf.*

steward /'stuərd/ *n.* официáнт; стю́ард; **—ess** *n.* стюардéсса

stick[1] /stɪk/ *n.* пáлка; трость *f.*

stick[2] /stɪk/ *v.i.* ли́пнуть (к + *D*) *impf.*; ~ **in** *v.t.* втыкáть *impf.*, воткну́ть *pf.*; **—er** *n.* накléйка; **—y** *adj.* ли́пкий; кléйкий

stiff /stɪf/ *adj.* неги́бкий; жёсткий; (*manners*) чо́порный

stifle /'staɪfəl/ *v.* подавля́ть *impf.*

stigma /'stɪɡmə/ *n.* клеймо́

still /stɪl/ 1. *adj.* ти́хий; неподви́жный 2. *adv.* (всё) ещё; всё-таки; ~ **life** *n.* натюрмóрт

stilted /'stɪltɪd/ *adj.* ходу́льный

stimulant /'stɪmjələnt/ *n.* возбуждáющее срéдство

stimulate /'stɪmjə,leɪt/ *v.* возбуждáть *impf.*, возбуди́ть *pf.*

stimulus /'stɪmjələs/ *n.* сти́мул

sting /stɪŋ/ 1. *n.* жáло; уку́с 2. *v.* жáлить *impf.*, у- *pf.*

stingy /'stɪndʒi/ *adj.* скупо́й

stink /stɪŋk/ 1. *n.* вонь *f.* 2. *v.* воня́ть *impf.*; **—ing** *adj.* воню́чий

stipulate /'stɪpjə,leɪt/ *v.* обусло́вливать *impf.*, обусло́вить *pf.*

stir /stɜr/ 1. *n.* шевелéние 2. *v.t.* (*mix*) размéшивать *impf.*, размешáть *pf.*; (*move*) возбуждáть *impf.*, -буди́ть *pf.*; *v.i.* дви́гаться *impf.*, дви́нуться *pf.*

stitch /stɪtʃ/ 1. *n.* стежóк; (*med.*) шов 2. *v.* шить *impf.*, с- *pf.*

stock /stɒk/ 1. *n.* (*supply*) запáс; инвентáрь *m.*; (*share*) áкция 2. *v.*: **have in** — имéть в продáже *impf.*; ~ **exchange,** ~ **market** *n.* фондовáя би́ржа

stockbroker /'stɒk,broukər/ *n.* (биржевóй) мáклер

stockholder /'stɒk,houldər/ *n.* владéлец áкций; акционéр

stocking /'stɒkɪŋ/ *n.* чулóк

stockpile /'stɒk,paɪl/ *n.* резéрв

stoical /'stouɪkəl/ *adj.* стои́ческий

stoker /'stoukər/ *n.* кочегáр

stomach /'stʌmək/ *n.* желу́док; живóт

stomachache /'stʌmək,eɪk/ *n.* боль в животé *f.*

stomp /stɒmp/ *v.* топтáть *impf.*

stone /stoun/ 1. *n.* кáмень *m.*; (*fruit*) кóсточка 2. *adj.* кáменный

stool /stul/ *n.* табурéтка; скамéечка

stoop /stup/ *v.* наклоня́ться *impf.*, -ни́ться *pf.*; *Fig.* унижáться (до + *G*) *impf.*, уни́зиться *pf.*

stop /stɒp/ 1. *n.* останóвка 2. *v.* останáвливать(ся) *impf.*, останови́ть(ся) *pf.*

stoplight /'stɒp,laɪt/ *n.* светофóр; (*on car*) стоп-сигнáл

stoppage /'stɒpɪdʒ/ *n.* прекращéние

stopper /'stɒpər/ *n.* заты́чка; пробка; (*tech.*) стóпор

storage /'stɔrɪdʒ/ *n.* хранéние; (*place*) храни́лище; склад

store /stɔr/ 1. *n.* магази́н; (*supply*) запáс 2. *v.* запасáть *impf.*, запасти́ *pf.*; отдавáть на хранéние *impf.*; ~ **window** *n.* витри́на

storehouse /'stɔr,haus/ *n.* склад

stork /stɔrk/ *n.* áист

storm /stɔrm/ 1. *n.* бу́ря; грозá 2. *v.* (*mil.*) штурмовáть *impf.*

stormy /'stɔrmi/ *adj.* бу́рный

story[1] /'stɔri/ *n.* (*floor*) эáтж

story[2] /'stɔri/ *n.* (*lit.*) расскáз; новéлла; (*anecdote*) анекдóт

stout /staut/ *adj.* ту́чный

stove /stouv/ *n.* плита́; (*wood stove*) печь *f.*

straight /streit/ **1.** *adj.* прямо́й **2.** *adv.* пря́мо

straighten /'streitn/ *v.* выпрямля́ть(ся) *impf.*, вы́прямить(ся) *pf.*

straightforward /,streit'fɔːrwərd/ *adj.* прямо́й; открове́нный

strain /strein/ **1.** *n.* натяже́ние; напряже́ние **2.** *v.* натя́гивать *impf.*, натяну́ть *pf.*; напряга́ть(ся) *impf.*, напря́чь(ся) *pf.*; **—ed** *adj.* (*forced*) напряжённый; (*sprained*) растя́нутый; **—er** *n.* си́то; си́течко

strait /streit/ *n.* проли́в

straitjacket /'streit,dʒækit/ *n.* смири́тельная руба́шка

strand /strænd/ *n.* (*of hair, etc.*) прядь *f.*; (*thread*) ни́тка

strange /streindʒ/ *adj.* стра́нный; незнако́мый; **—r** *n.* незнако́мец, -мка

strangle /'stræŋgəl/ *v.* души́ть *impf.*, за- *pf.*

strap /stræp/ *n.* реме́нь *m.*

strategic /strə'tiːdʒik/ *adj.* стратеги́ческий

strategy /'strætidʒi/ *n.* страте́гия

straw /strɔː/ **1.** *n.* соло́ма; (*for drinking*) соло́минка **2.** *adj.* соло́менный

strawberry /'strɔː,beri/ *n.* клубни́ка; (*wild*) земляни́ка

stray /strei/ **1.** *n.* (*dog*) дворня́га *m. & f.* **2.** *v.* (*deviate*) сбива́ться *impf.*

streak /striːk/ *n.* потёк; полоса́

stream /striːm/ **1.** *n.* пото́к; (*brook*) руче́й; (*current*) тече́ние **2.** *v.* течь, струи́ться *impf.*

streamlined /'striːm,laind/ *adj.* обтека́емый

street /striːt/ **1.** *n.* у́лица **2.** *adj.* у́личный

streetcar /'striːt,kɑːr/ *n.* трамва́й

strength /streŋkθ/ *n.* си́ла

strengthen /'streŋkθən/ *v.* уси́ливать; укрепля́ть *impf.*

strenuous /'strenjuəs/ *adj.* тяжёлый

stress /stres/ **1.** *n.* напряже́ние; стресс; *v.* (*emphasis*) ударе́ние **2.** *v.* подчёркивать *impf.*

stretch /stretʃ/ **1.** *n.* протяже́ние; (*duration*) срок **2.** *v.* рас-, на-, вы-, тя́гивать(ся) *impf.*; **—er** *n.* носи́лки *pl.*

strew /struː/ *v.* разбра́сывать *impf.*, разброса́ть *pf.*

strict /strikt/ *adj.* стро́гий

stride /straid/ **1.** *n.* большо́й шаг **2.** *v.* шага́ть *impf.*

strike /straik/ **1.** *n.* забасто́вка; (*blow*) уда́р **2.** *v.t.* (*hit*) ударя́ть *impf.*, уда́рить *pf.*; *v.i.* (*labor*) бастова́ть *impf.*, за- *pf.*; **—r** *n.* забасто́вщик; басту́ющий

striking /'straikiŋ/ *adj.* порази́тельный

string /striŋ/ *n.* верёвка; ни́тка; (*mus.*) струна́; (*row*) ряд; **~ bean** стручко́вая фасо́ль *f.*

strip[1] /strip/ *n.* полоса́; поло́ска

strip[2] /strip/ *v.* сдира́ть *impf.*, содра́ть *pf.*

stripe /straip/ *n.* полоса́; (*mil.*) наши́вка; **—d** *adj.* полоса́тый

strive /straiv/ *v.* стреми́ться *impf.*

stroke[1] /strouk/ *n.* (*also med.*) уда́р; (*brush, etc.*) штрих

stroke[2] /strouk/ *v.* (*pet*) гла́дить *impf.*, по- *pf.*

stroll /stroul/ **1.** *n.* прогу́лка **2.** *v.* прогу́ливаться *impf.*, -гуля́ться *pf.*; **—er** *n.* де́тская коля́ска

strong /strɔŋ/ *adj.* си́льный; кре́пкий

stronghold /'strɔŋ,hould/ *n.* кре́пость *f.*; тверды́ня

strong-willed *adj.* волево́й

structure /'strʌktʃər/ *n.* структу́ра

struggle /'strʌgəl/ **1.** *n.* борьба́ **2.** *v.* боро́ться *impf.*

stub /stʌb/ *n.* огры́зок; (*cigarette*) оку́рок

stubble /'stʌbəl/ *n.* (*on field*) жнивьё; (*beard*) щети́на

stubborn /'stʌbərn/ *adj.* упря́мый; упо́рный

stuck /stʌk/ *adj.*: **be ~** застря́ть *pf.*; быть в тупике́ *impf.*

student /'stuːdnt/ **1.** *n.* студе́нт, —ка **2.** *adj.* студе́нческий

studio /'stuːdiou/ *n.* мастерска́я; сту́дия; (*apartment*) одноко́мнатная кварти́ра

studious /'stuːdiəs/ *adj.* приле́жный; усе́рдный

study /'stʌdi/ **1.** *n.* изуче́ние; иссле́дование; (*room*) кабине́т; *pl.* заня́тия *pl.* **2.** *v.* изуча́ть *impf.*, -чи́ть *pf.*; *v.i.* учи́ться *impf.*

stuff /stʌf/ **1.** *n.* материа́л;

sudden

вещество; вéщи pl. 2. v.
набивáть impf., набить pf.;
—ing n. набивáние; (cul.)
начи́нка; —y adj. дýшный; (person) чóпорный

stumble /'stʌmbəl/ v. спотыкáться impf., споткнýться pf.

stump /stʌmp/ n. пень m.; обрýбок

stun /stʌn/ v. ошеломля́ть impf., -ми́ть pf.; —ning adj. ошеломля́ющий; потряса́ющий

stunt /stʌnt/ n. трюк; фóкус

stupendous /stu'pendəs/ adj. изуми́тельный

stupid /'stupɪd/ adj. глýпый

stupidity /stu'pɪdɪti/ n. глýпость

sturdy /'stɜrdi/ adj. стóйкий; твёрдый

sturgeon /'stɜrdʒən/ n. осётр; (cul.) осетри́на

stutter /'stʌtər/ 1. n. заика́ние 2. v. заика́ться impf.

style /stail/ n. стиль m.; мóда

stylish /'stailɪʃ/ adj. мóдный

stylist /'stailɪst/ n. модельéр

subconscious /sʌb'kɒnʃəs/ 1. adj. подсозна́тельный 2. n. подсозна́ние

subdivide /,sʌbdɪ'vaid/ v. подразделя́ть impf. -ли́ть pf.

subdue /səb'du/ v. покоря́ть impf., -ри́ть pf.

subject / n., adj. 'sʌbdʒɪkt; v. səb'dʒɛkt/ 1. n. тéма; предмéт; (polit.) пóдданный; (gram.) подлежа́щее 2. adj. подлежа́щий 3. v. подверга́ть impf., подвéргнуть pf.

subjective /səb'dʒɛktɪv/ adj. субъекти́вный

sublime /sə'blaim/ adj. возвы́шенный; грандиóзный

submachine gun /,sʌbmə'ʃin/ n. автома́т

submarine /,sʌbmə'rin/ 1. n. подвóдная лóдка 2. adj. подвóдный

submerge /səb'mɜrdʒ/ v. погружа́ть(ся) impf., -зи́ть(ся) pf.

submissive /səb'mɪsɪv/ adj. покóрный; смирéнный

submit /səb'mɪt/ v.i. подчиня́ться (+ D) impf.; v.t. представля́ть impf.

subordinate / n. sə'bɔrdnɪt; v. sə'bɔrdn,eit/ 1. adj., n. подчинённый 2. v. подчиня́ть impf., -ни́ть pf.

subscribe /səb'skraib/ v.

подпи́сываться (на + A) impf., -писа́ться pf.

subscription /səb'skrɪpʃən/ n. подпи́ска; абонемéнт

subsequent /'sʌbsɪkwənt/ adj. послéдующий; —ly adv. впослéдствии

subside /səb'said/ v. (recede) убыва́ть impf., убы́ть pf.; (abate) стиха́ть impf.

subsidiary /səb'sɪdi,ɛri/ n. филиа́л

subsidize /'sʌbsɪ,daiz/ v. субсиди́ровать impf. & pf.

subsidy /'sʌbsɪdi/ n. субси́дия

subsist /səb'sɪst/ v. существова́ть impf.; (live) жить (+ I) impf.

substance /'sʌbstəns/ n. вещество́; сýщность; (content) содержа́ние

substantial /səb'stænʃəl/ adj. существенный

substantive /'sʌbstəntɪv/ n. (gram.) и́мя существи́тельное neut.

substitute /'sʌbstɪ,tut/ 1. n. замести́тель; замени́тель 2. v. заменя́ть impf., -ни́ть pf.; замеща́ть impf., -сти́ть pf.

subtitle /'sʌb,taitl/ n. субти́тр

subtle /'sʌtl/ adj. тóнкий; утончённый

subtract /səb'trækt/ v. вычита́ть impf., вы́честь pf.; —ion n. вычита́ние

suburb /'sʌbɜrb/ n. при́город

suburban /sə'bɜrbən/ adj. при́городный

subversive /səb'vɜrsɪv/ adj. подрывнóй

subway /'sʌb,wei/ n. метрó neut. indecl.

succeed /sək'sid/ v. удава́ться (impers., + D) impf.; преуспева́ть impf., преуспéть pf.

success /sək'ses/ n. успéх; —ful adj. успéшный

succession /sək'sɛʃən/ n. послéдовательность

successor /sək'sesər/ n. наслéдник, -ница; преéмник, -ница

succinct /sək'sɪŋkt/ adj. (brief) кра́ткий; (precise) чёткий

such /sʌtʃ/ adj. такóй

suck /sʌk/ v. соса́ть impf.; —le v. корми́ть грýдью impf.

sudden /'sʌdn/ adj. внеза́пный; —ly adv. вдруг; внеза́пно

sue /su/ v. преследовать судебным порядком *impf.*

suede /sweid/ 1. n. замша 2. adj. замшевый

suffer /'safər/ v. страдать *impf.*, по- *pf.*; **—ing** n. страдание

sufficient /sə'fɪʃənt/ adj. достаточный

suffocate /'safə,keit/ v.i. задохнуться *impf.*, задохнуться *pf.*; v.t. душить *impf.*

sugar /'ʃugər/ 1. n. сахар 2. adj. сахарный; **~ bowl** n. сахарница

suggest /səg'dʒest/ v. предлагать *impf.*, предложить *pf.*; **—ion** n. предложение

suicide /'suə,said/ n. самоубийство; (person) самоубийца m. & f.; **commit ~** покончить с собой *pf.*

suit /sut/ 1. n. (outfit) костюм; (law) процесс 2. v. подходить; устраивать *impf.*; **—able** adj. подходящий

suitcase /'sut,keis/ n. чемодан

suitor /'sutər/ n. поклонник

sulfur /'salfər/ n. сера

sulk /salk/ v. дуться *impf.*

sullen /'salən/ adj. угрюмый

sultry /'saltri/ adj. знойный

sum /sam/ 1. n. сумма; итог 2. v.: **~ up** подводить итог *impf.*

summarize /'samə,raiz/ v. суммировать; резюмировать *impf. & pf.*

summary /'saməri/ n. резюме *neut. indecl.*; конспект

summer /'samər/ 1. n. лето; **in the ~** adv. летом 2. adj. летний

summit /'samit/ n. вершина

summon /'samən/ v. вызывать *impf.*, вызвать *pf.*; **—s** n. вызов

sumptuous /'samptʃuəs/ adj. пышный; роскошный

sun /san/ 1. n. солнце 2. adj. солнечный

sunbathe /'san,beið/ v. загорать (на солнце) *impf.*

sunburn /'san,bərn/ n. загар

Sunday /'sandei/ 1. n. воскресенье 2. adj. воскресный

sunflower /'san,flauər/ n. подсолнечник, подсолнух

sunken /'saŋkən/ adj. (hollow) вялый; (ship) затопленный

sunny /'sani/ adj. солнечный

sunrise /'san,raiz/ n. восход солнца

sunscreen /'san,skrin/ n. солнцезащитный крем

sunset /'san,set/ n. закат

sunshine /'san,ʃain/ n. солнечный свет

superb /su'pərb/ adj. великолепный; прекрасный

superficial /,supər'fɪʃəl/ adj. поверхностный

superfluous /su'pərfluəs/ adj. излишний

superintendent /,supərin'tendənt/ n. управляющий; (building) комендант

superior /sə'pɪəriər/ 1. adj. высший; старший 2. n. начальник

superiority /sə,pɪəri'ɔriti/ n. превосходство (над + I)

supermarket /'supər,markit/ n. универсам

supernatural /,supər'nætʃərəl/ adj. сверхъестественный

superpower /'supər,pauər/ n. сверхдержава

supersede /,supər'sid/ v. заменять *impf.*, -нить *pf.*

superstition /,supər'stɪʃən/ n. суеверие

superstitious /,supər'stɪʃəs/ adj. суеверный

supervise /'supər,vaiz/ v. заведовать; руководить (+ I) *impf.*

supervision /,supər'vɪʒən/ n. наблюдение; надзор

supervisor /'supər,vaizər/ n. начальник

supper /'supər/ n. ужин; **have ~** ужинать *impf.*

supple /'sapəl/ adj. гибкий

supplement /n. 'sapləmənt; v. 'saplə,ment/ 1. n. дополнение; приложение 2. v. дополнять *impf.*, дополнить *pf.*

supplementary /,saplə'mentəri/ adj. дополнительный

suppliant /'sapliənt/ n. проситель

supplier /sə'plaiər/ n. поставщик

supply /sə'plai/ 1. n. снабжение; (stock) запас 2. v. снабжать *impf.*, снабдить *pf.*; доставлять *impf.*, доставить *pf.*

support /sə'pɔrt/ 1. n. поддержка; подпорка 2. v. поддерживать *impf.*, -жать *pf.*

supporter /sə'pɔrtər/ n. сторонник, -ница

suppose /sə'pouz/ v. предполагать *impf.*, предположить *pf.*; **—d** adj. предполагаемый; **—dly** adv. якобы

supposition /ˌsʌpəˈzɪʃən/ n. предположение; гипотеза

suppository /səˈpɒzɪˌtɔri/ n. свеча

suppress /səˈpres/ v. подавлять impf., -вить pf. —**ion** n. подавление

supreme /səˈprim/ adj. верховный; высший

surcharge /ˈsɜrˌtʃɑrdʒ/ n. приплата; доплата

sure /ʃʊr/ 1. adj. верный, уверенный; **make ~** убедиться pf. I, pf. 2. adv. конечно

surface /ˈsɜrfɪs/ n. поверхность

surfing /ˈsɜrfɪŋ/ n. сёрфинг

surgeon /ˈsɜrdʒən/ n. хирург

surgery /ˈsɜrdʒəri/ n. хирургия

surmount /sərˈmaʊnt/ v. (overcome) преодолевать impf.

surname /ˈsɜrˌneim/ n. фамилия

surpass /sərˈpæs/ v. превосходить impf., превзойти pf.

surplus /ˈsɜrplʌs/ 1. n. излишек 2. adj. излишний

surprise /sərˈpraiz/ 1. n. удивление; сюрприз; **by ~** неожиданно 2. adj. неожиданный 3. v. удивлять impf., удивить pf.; **be ~d** удивляться impf.

surprising /sərˈpraiziŋ/ adj. удивительный

surrender /səˈrendər/ 1. n. сдача; капитуляция 2. v. сдавать(ся) impf., сдать(ся) pf.

surround /səˈraʊnd/ v. окружать impf., -жить pf. —**ing** adj. окружающий

surveillance /sərˈveiləns/ n. надзор; наблюдение

survey /n. ˈsɜrvei; v. sərˈvei/ 1. n. обозрение; осмотр; (poll) опрос 2. v. обозревать impf., обозреть pf.

survival /sərˈvaivəl/ n. выживание; (relic) пережиток

survive /sərˈvaiv/ v.t. пережить pf.; v.i. уцелеть pf.; выживать impf., выжить pf.

susceptible /səˈseptəbəl/ adj. восприимчивый

suspect /n., adj. ˈsʌspekt; v. səˈspekt/ 1. n. подозреваемый 2. adj. подозрительный 3. v. подозревать impf.

suspend /səˈspend/ v. (hang) вешать impf., повесить pf.; (stop) приостанавливать impf., -остановить pf.; —**ers** n. подтяжки pl.

suspense /səˈspens/ n. ожидание

suspicion /səˈspɪʃən/ n. подозрение

suspicious /səˈspɪʃəs/ adj. подозрительный

sustain /səˈstein/ v. поддерживать impf., поддержать pf.; (suffer) потерпеть pf.

sustenance /ˈsʌstənəns/ n. пища

swaddle /ˈswɒdl/ v. (child) пеленать impf.

swallow[1] /ˈswɒloʊ/ 1. n. глоток 2. v. проглатывать impf., -глотить pf.

swallow[2] /ˈswɒloʊ/ n. (bird) ласточка

swamp /swɒmp/ n. болото

swan /swɒn/ n. лебедь m.; ~ **song** лебединая песня

swap /swɒp/ v. обменивать(ся) impf., обменять(ся) pf.

swarm /swɔrm/ n. рой

swarthy /ˈswɔrði/ adj. смуглый

sway /swei/ v. качать(ся); колебать(ся) impf.; Fig. повлиять impf.

swear /swɛər/ v. (vow) клясться impf., по- pf.; (curse) ругаться impf.

sweat /swet/ 1. n. пот 2. v. потеть impf., вс- pf.

sweater /ˈswetər/ n. свитер

Swede /swid/ n. швед, шведка

Sweden /ˈswidn/ n. Швеция

Swedish /ˈswidiʃ/ adj. шведский

sweep /swip/ v. подметать impf., -мести pf.; —**ing** adj. огульный

sweet /swit/ adj. сладкий; милый

sweetheart /ˈswitˌhɑrt/ n. возлюбленный, возлюбленная

sweetness /ˈswitnis/ n. сладость

swell /swel/ v. опухать impf., опухнуть pf.; —**ing** n. опухоль f.; припухлость

swerve /swɜrv/ v. вилять impf.; (to one side) вильнуть pf.

swift /swift/ adj. быстрый; —**ness** n. быстрота

swim /swim/ v. n. плавать indet., плыть det., поплыть pf.; —**mer** n. пловец, пловчиха; —**ming** n. плавание

swimming pool n. бассейн

swimsuit /ˈswimˌsut/ n. купальник

swindle /ˈswindl/ v. обманывать impf.; —**r** n. жулик

swing /swiŋ/ 1. n. качели pl. 2. v. качать(ся) impf.; качнуть(ся) pf.

Swiss /swɪs/ **1.** *adj.* швейца́рский **2.** *n.* швейца́рец, -ца́рка
switch /swɪtʃ/ **1.** *n.* (*elec.*) выключа́тель; переключа́тель **2.** *v.* переключа́ть *impf.*, -чи́ть *pf.*
switchboard /ˈswɪtʃˌbɔrd/ *n.* распредели́тельный щит
Switzerland /ˈswɪtsərlənd/ *n.* Швейца́рия
swollen /ˈswoulən/ *adj.* взду́тый
sword /sɔrd/ *n.* меч; шпа́га
syllable /ˈsɪləbəl/ *n.* слог
syllabus /ˈsɪləbəs/ *n.* програ́мма обуче́ния
symbol /ˈsɪmbəl/ *n.* си́мвол
symbolize /ˈsɪmbəˌlaɪz/ *v.* символизи́ровать *impf.*
symmetry /ˈsɪmɪtri/ *n.* симме́трия

sympathetic /ˌsɪmpəˈθetɪk/ *adj.* сочу́вственный; симпати́чный
sympathize /ˈsɪmpəˌθaɪz/ *v.* сочу́вствовать (+ D) *impf.*
sympathy /ˈsɪmpəθi/ *n.* сочу́вствие, симпа́тия
symphony /ˈsɪmfəni/ *n.* симфо́ния
symptom /ˈsɪmptəm/ *n.* симпто́м
synagogue /ˈsɪnəˌgɒg/ *n.* синаго́га
syndicate /ˈsɪndɪkɪt/ *n.* синдика́т
synonym /ˈsɪnənɪm/ *n.* сино́ним
synopsis /sɪˈnɒpsɪs/ *n.* конспе́кт
syntax /ˈsɪntæks/ *n.* си́нтаксис
synthetic /sɪnˈθetɪk/ *adj.* синтети́ческий; иску́сственный
syringe /səˈrɪndʒ/ *n.* шприц
syrup /ˈsɪrəp/ *n.* сиро́п; па́тока
system /ˈsɪstəm/ *n.* систе́ма

T

tab /tæb/ *n. Colloq.* (*bill*) счёт
table /ˈteibəl/ *n.* стол; (*chart*) табли́ца; ~ **of contents** оглавле́ние
tablecloth /ˈteibəlˌklɔθ/ *n.* ска́терть *f.*
tablespoon /ˈteibəlˌspun/ *n.* столо́вая ло́жка
tablet /ˈtæblɪt/ *n.* дощечка; (*med.*) табле́тка
tabloid /ˈtæblɔɪd/ *n.* бульва́рная газе́та
tack /tæk/ *n.* кно́пка; гво́здик
tackle /ˈtækəl/ *n.* снасть *f.*; обору́дование
tact /tækt/ *n.* такт; такти́чность; —**ful** *adj.* такти́чный; —**ic, —ics** *n.* та́ктика; —**less** *adj.* бестактный
tadpole /ˈtædpoul/ *n.* голова́стик
taffy /ˈtæfi/ *n.* ири́с; тяну́чка
tag /tæg/ *n.* этике́тка
tail /teil/ *n.* хвост; ~ **coat** *n.* фрак
taillight /ˈteilˌlait/ *n.* (*car*) за́дний фона́рь *m.*
tailor /ˈteilər/ *n.* портно́й; —**ing** *n.* покро́й
tailpipe /ˈteilˌpaip/ *n.* (*car*) выхлопна́я труба́
taint /teint/ *v.* (*spoil*) по́ртить(ся) *impf.*, ис- *pf.*
Taiwan /ˈtaiˈwɑn/ *n.* Тайва́нь *m.*
Tajik /tɑˈdʒɪk/ *n.* таджи́к, -жи́чка

Tajikistan /tɑˈdʒɪkɪˌstæn/ *n.* Таджикиста́н
take /teik/ *v.* брать *impf.*, взять *pf.*; ~ **off** снима́ть *impf.*, снять *pf.*; (*aero.*) взлете́ть *pf.*; ~ **out** вынима́ть *impf.*, вы́нуть *pf.*
takeoff /ˈteikˌɔf/ *n.* (*aero.*) взлёт
talcum powder /ˈtælkəm/ *n.* тальк
tale /teil/ *n.* расска́з; по́весть *f.*; ска́зка
talent /ˈtælənt/ *n.* тала́нт; —**ed** *adj.* тала́нтливый
talk /tɔk/ **1.** *n.* разгово́р; (*chat*) бесе́да; *pl.* перегово́ры *pl.* **2.** *v.* говори́ть; разгова́ривать *impf.*
talkative /ˈtɔkətɪv/ *adj.* разгово́рчивый; болтли́вый
tall /tɔl/ *adj.* высо́кий
tame /teim/ **1.** *adj.* ручно́й; приру́ченный **2.** *v.* прируча́ть *impf.*, -чи́ть *pf.*; —**r** *n.* укроти́тель; дрессиро́вщик
tan /tæn/ **1.** *n.* зага́р **2.** *v.t.* (*cure*) дуби́ть *impf.*, вы́- *pf.*; *v.i.* (*suntan*) загора́ть *impf.*, загоре́ть *pf.*
tangerine /ˌtændʒəˈrin/ *n.* мандари́н
tangible /ˈtændʒəbəl/ *adj.* осяза́емый; материа́льный
tangle /ˈtæŋgəl/ **1.** *n.* пу́таница **2.** *v.* запу́тывать(ся) *impf.*, запу́тать(ся) *pf.*
tangy /ˈtæŋi/ *adj.* о́стрый
tank /tæŋk/ *n.* цисте́рна; бак;

(*mil.*) танк; **—er** *n.* (*ship*) та́нкер

tantalize /'tæntˌaiz/ *v.* дразни́ть *impf.*

tantamount /'tæntəˌmaunt/ *adj.* равноси́льный (+ *D*)

tap /tæp/ **1.** *n.* (*water*) кран; (*rap*) стук **2.** *v.* постуки́вать *impf.*; ~ **dance** *n.* чечётка

tape /teip/ **1.** *n.* ле́нточка; плёнка **2.** *v.* (*seal*) закле́ивать *impf.*; (*record*) запи́сывать на плёнку *impf.*; ~ **deck** *n.* магнитофо́нная де́ка; ~ **measure** ме́рная ле́нта; ~ **recorder** магнитофо́н

tapestry /'tæpəstri/ *n.* гобеле́н

tar /tɑr/ **1.** *n.* смола́; дёготь *m.* **2.** *v.* смоли́ть; ма́зать дёгтем *impf.*

tardy /'tɑrdi/ *adj.* запозда́лый

tare[1] /teər/ *n.* (*com.*) та́ра

tare[2] /teər/ *n.* (*bot.*) ви́ка

target /'tɑrgit/ *n.* цель; мише́нь *f.*

tariff /'tærif/ *n.* тари́ф

tarnish /'tɑrniʃ/ *v.* тускне́ть *impf.*, по- *pf.*

tarpaulin /tɑr'pɔlin/ *n.* брезе́нт

tart[1] /tɑrt/ *n.* пиро́г

tart[2] /tɑrt/ *adj.* те́рпкий; ки́слый

tartar /'tɑrtər/ *n.* зубно́й ка́мень *m.*

task /tæsk/ *n.* зада́ча; зада́ние

tassel /'tæsəl/ *n.* ки́сточка

taste /teist/ **1.** *n.* вкус **2.** *v.t.* про́бовать *impf.*, по- *pf.*; *v.i.* име́ть вкус (+ *G*) *impf.*; **—less** *adj.* безвку́сный; (*behavior*) беста́ктный; **—y** *adj.* вку́сный

Tatar /'tɑtər/ **1.** *adj.* тата́рский **2.** *n.* тата́рин, татарка

Tatarstan /ˌtɑtər'stæn/ *n.* Татарста́н

tattoo /tæ'tu/ *n.* (*on skin*) татуиро́вка

taunt /tɔnt/ *v.* насмеха́ться (над + *I*) *impf.*

taut /tɔt/ *adj.* туго́й; подтя́нутый

tax /tæks/ **1.** *n.* нало́г **2.** *adj.* нало́говый **3.** *v.* облага́ть нало́гом *impf.*

taxation /tæk'seiʃən/ *n.* обложе́ние нало́гом; налогообложе́ние

taxi /'tæksi/, **taxicab** *n.* такси́ *neut. indecl.*; ~ **driver** води́тель такси́

taxpayer /'tæksˌpeiər/ *n.* налогоплате́льщик

TB *n.* туберкулёз

tea /ti/ **1.** *n.* чай **2.** *adj.* ча́йный

teach /titʃ/ *v.* преподава́ть; учи́ть *impf.*, на- *pf.*; **—er** *n.* учи́тель, —ница; **—ing** *n.* преподава́ние; *pl.* уче́ние

teakettle /'tiˌketl/ *n.* ча́йник

team /tim/ *n.* кома́нда

teamster /'timstər/ *n.* води́тель грузовика́

teamwork /'timˌwɜrk/ *n.* сла́женность

tear[1] /teər/ **1.** *n.* проре́ха **2.** *v.* рвать(ся) *impf.*, разорва́ть(ся) *pf.*

tear[2] /tiər/ *n.* (*eye*) слеза́; **—ful** *adj.* слезли́вый

tease /tiz/ *v.* дразни́ть *impf.*

teaspoon /'tiˌspun/ *n.* ча́йная ло́жка

technical /'teknikəl/ *adj.* техни́ческий

technician /tek'niʃən/ *n.* те́хник

technique /tek'nik/ *n.* те́хника

technology /tek'nɒlədʒi/ *n.* техноло́гия; те́хника

teddy bear /'tedi/ *n.* медвежо́нок; ми́шка

tedious /'tidiəs/ *adj.* ску́чный

teem /tim/ *v.* кише́ть (+ *I*) *impf.*

teenage /'tinˌeidʒ/ *adj.* о́троческий; **—r** *n.* подро́сток

telecast /'teliˌkæst/ *n.* телевизио́нная переда́ча

telecommunications /ˌteliˌkəˌmyuni'keiʃənz/ *n.* (теле-)связь *f.*

telegram /'teliˌgræm/ *n.* телегра́мма

telegraph /'teliˌgræf/ **1.** *n.* телегра́ф **2.** *adj.* телегра́фный **3.** *v.* телеграфи́ровать *impf.* & *pf.*

telephone /'teləˌfoun/ **1.** *n.* телефо́н **2.** *adj.* телефо́нный **3.** *v.* телефони́ровать *impf.* and *pf.*; звони́ть по телефо́ну *impf.*

telescope /'teləˌskoup/ *n.* телеско́п

televise /'teləˌvaiz/ *v.* передава́ть по телеви́дению *impf.*

television /'teləˌviʒən/ *n.* телеви́дение; ~ **set** телеви́зор

tell /tel/ *v.* говори́ть *impf.*, сказа́ть *pf.*; (*narrate*) расска́зывать *impf.*, рассказа́ть *pf.*; **—er** *n.* (*bank*) касси́р, —ша; **—ing** *adj.* многозначи́тельный

temper /'tempər/ **1.** *n.* нрав; (*mood*) настрое́ние; (*anger*) гнев **2.** *v.* *Fig.* умеря́ть *impf.*, уме́рить *pf.*

temperament /ˈtɛmpərəmənt/ n. темперáмент

temperate /ˈtɛmpərɪt/ adj. умéренный

temperature /ˈtɛmpərətʃər/ n. температýра

tempest /ˈtɛmpɪst/ n. бýря

template /ˈtɛmplɪt/ n. шаблóн

temple[1] /ˈtɛmpəl/ n. храм

temple[2] /ˈtɛmpəl/ n. (anat.) висóк

tempo /ˈtɛmpoʊ/ n. темп

temporarily /ˌtɛmpəˈrɛərəli/ adv. врéменно; на врéмя

temporary /ˈtɛmpəˌrɛri/ adj. врéменный

tempt /tɛmpt/ v. искушáть impf.

temptation /tɛmpˈteɪʃən/ n. искушéние

ten /tɛn/ n., adj. дéсять

tenacity /təˈnæsɪti/ n. цéпкость

tenant /ˈtɛnənt/ n. нанимáтель; арендáтор

tend[1] /tɛnd/ v. (care for) ухáживать (за + I) impf.

tend[2] /tɛnd/ v.: — **to** (be disposed) склонáться impf.

tendency /ˈtɛndənsi/ n. склóнность; тендéнция

tender /ˈtɛndər/ adj. нéжный; чувствúтельный; —**ness** n. нéжность

tenderloin /ˈtɛndərˌlɔɪn/ n. вырезка

tendon /ˈtɛndən/ n. сухожúлие

tendril /ˈtɛndrɪl/ n. ýсик

tennis /ˈtɛnɪs/ n. тéннис

tenor /ˈtɛnər/ n. тéнор

tense[1] /tɛns/ adj. напряжённый

tense[2] /tɛns/ n. (gram.) врéмя neut.

tension /ˈtɛnʃən/ n. напряжéние

tent /tɛnt/ n. палáтка; шатёр

tentative /ˈtɛntətɪv/ adj. прóбный; предварúтельный

tenth /tɛnθ/ adj. десятый

tenuous /ˈtɛnyuəs/ adj. непрóчный

tepid /ˈtɛpɪd/ adj. тепловáтый

term /tɜrm/ n. срок; (name) тéрмин; (univ.) семéстр; pl. услóвия; отношéния pl.

terminal /ˈtɜrmənəl/ 1. n. (railroad) вокзáл; конéчная стáнция (comput.) терминáл 2. adj. конéчный; (med.) смертéльный

terminate /ˈtɜrməˌneɪt/ v. кончáть(ся) impf., кóнчить(ся) pf.

termination /ˌtɜrməˈneɪʃən/ n. прекращéние

terminus /ˈtɜrmənəs/ n. (railroad) конéчная стáнция

terrace /ˈtɛrəs/ n. террáса

terrain /təˈreɪn/ n. мéстность

terrible /ˈtɛrəbəl/ adj. ужáсный

terrific /təˈrɪfɪk/ adj. колоссáльный; (splendid) великолéпный

terrify /ˈtɛrəˌfaɪ/ v. ужасáть impf.

territory /ˈtɛrəˌtɔri/ n. территóрия

terror /ˈtɛrər/ n. ýжас; террóр; —**ism** n. терроризм; —**ist** 1. adj. террористúческий 2. n. террорúст, —ка

test /tɛst/ n. испытáние; (exam) экзáмен; (med.) анáлиз 2. adj. испытáтельный 3. v. проверя́ть impf., -вéрить pf.

testament /ˈtɛstəmənt/ n. завещáние; **Old, New Testament** Вéтхий, Нóвый Завéт

testicle /ˈtɛstɪkəl/ n. я́ичко

testify /ˈtɛstəˌfaɪ/ v. свидéтельствовать impf.

testimony /ˈtɛstəˌmouni/ n. свидéтельство; (proof) доказáтельство

test tube n. пробúрка

tetanus /ˈtɛtnəs/ n. столбня́к

text /tɛkst/ n. текст

textbook /ˈtɛkstˌbʊk/ n. учéбник

textile /ˈtɛkstaɪl/ 1. adj. текстúльный 2. n. ткань f.; текстúльное издéлие

texture /ˈtɛkstʃər/ n. структýра

than /ðæn/ conj. чем

thank /θæŋk/ v. благодарúть impf., по- pf.; у вас спасúбо; —**s to** благодаря́ (+ D); —**ful** adj. благодáрный; —**less** adj. неблагодáрный

thanks /θæŋks/ n. благодáрность

thanksgiving /ˌθæŋksˈɡɪvɪŋ/ n. благодарéние

that /ðæt/ 1. pron., adj. (э)тот, (э)та, (э)то 2. adv. так; до такóй стéпени 3. conj. что; чтобы

thaw /θɔ/ 1. n. óттепель f. 2. v.i. тáять; оттáивать impf.

the /ði, ðə/ article (no equivalent in Russian): ~..., ~... чем..., тем...

theater /ˈθiətər/ n. теáтр

theft /θɛft/ n. воровствó; крáжа

their /ðɛr/ pron. их; свой, своя́, своё, pl. свой; —**s** их

them /ðɛm/ pron. их; им

theme /θiːm/ n. (also mus.) тéма

themselves /ðəmˈselvz/ pron. себя́, себé; сáми

then /ðen/ adv. тогдá; (afterwards) потóм

theology /θiˈɒlədʒi/ n. богослóвие

theoretical /ˌθiəˈretikəl/ adj. теоретический

theory /ˈθiəri/ n. теóрия

therapeutic /ˌθerəˈpjuːtik/ adj. лечéбный; терапевтический

therapy /ˈθerəpi/ n. терапия

there /ðeər/ adv. (loc.) там; (dir.) тудá; ~ **is, ~ are** есть; имéется; имéются impf.

thereby /ˌðeərˈbai/ adv. таким óбразом

therefore /ˈðeərfɔː/ adv. поэтому

thermal /ˈθɜːməl/ adj. теплово́й

thermometer /θəˈmɒmitər/ n. грáдусник; термóметр

thermonuclear /ˌθɜːmoʊˈnuːkliər/ adj. термоядерный

thermos /ˈθɜːməs/ n. тéрмос

thermostat /ˈθɜːməstæt/ n. термостáт

these /ðiːz/ adj., pron. эти

thesis /ˈθiːsis/ n. тéзис; (dissertation) диссертáция

they /ðei/ pron. они

thick /θik/ adj. тóлстый; густóй

thicken /ˈθikən/ v. сгущáть(ся) impf., сгустить(ся) pf.

thicket /ˈθikit/ n. чáща

thickness /ˈθiknis/ n. толщинá

thickset /ˈθikˈset/ adj. коренáстый

thick-skinned adj. толстокóжий

thief /θiːf/ n. вор

thievery /ˈθiːvəri/ n. воровствó

thigh /θai/ n. бедрó

thimble /ˈθimbəl/ n. напёрсток

thin /θin/ adj. тóнкий; (skinny) худóй; (soup) жидкий

thing /θiŋ/ n. вещь f.; предмéт

think /θiŋk/ v. дýмать impf., поpf.; —**er** n. мыслитель; —**ing** n. размышлéние

third /θɜːd/ **1.** adj. трéтий **2.** n. треть f. —**ly** adv. в-трéтьих; **Third World** n. стрáны трéтьего мира pl.

thirst /θɜːst/ n. жáжда; **be** ~ хотéть пить impf.

thirteen /ˈθɜːˈtiːn/ n., adj. тринáдцать; —**th** adj. тринáдцатый

thirtieth /ˈθɜːtiiθ/ adj. тридцáтый

thirty /ˈθɜːti/ n., adj. тридцать

this /ðis/ **1.** adj. этот, эта, это, pl. эти **2.** pron. это

thistle /ˈθisəl/ n. чертопóлох

thorn /θɔːn/ n. шип; колючка

thorny /ˈθɔːni/ adj. колючий

thorough /ˈθɜːroʊ/ adj. основáтельный; совершéнный

thoroughfare /ˈθɜːroʊˌfeər/ n. проéзд; магистрáль f.

those /ðoʊz/ adj., pron. те; эти

though /ðoʊ/ **1.** adv. однáко **2.** conj. хотя; несмотря на то, что

thought /θɔːt/ n. мысль f.; —**ful** adj. задýмчивый; (considerate) внимáтельный

thousand /ˈθaʊzənd/ n., adj. тысяча; —**th** adj. тысячный

thread /θred/ n. нитка; нить f.; (of screw) резьбá

threadbare /ˈθredˌbeər/ adj. потёртый; (clothes) понóшенный

threat /θret/ n. угрóза

threaten /ˈθretn/ v. грозить impf.; угрожáть impf.

three /θriː/ n., adj. три

three-dimensional adj. трёхмéрный; **3-D film** n. стереофильм

thresh /θreʃ/ v. молотить impf.

threshold /ˈθreʃoʊld/ n. порóг

thrift /θrift/ n. бережливость; —**y** adj. бережливый; домовитый

thrill /θril/ **1.** n. óстрое ощущéние; трéпет **2.** v. захвáтывать impf.; —**ed** adj. в восторге (от + G)

thrive /θraiv/ v. процветáть impf.

throat /θroʊt/ n. гóрло

throb /θrɒb/ v. сильно биться; пульсировать impf.

throne /θroʊn/ n. трон; престóл

throng /θrɒŋ/ n. толпá

throttle /ˈθrɒtl/ **1.** n. (tech.) дрóссель n. **2.** v. (strangle) душить impf.

through /θruː/ **1.** prep. чéрез; сквозь (+ A); по (+ D) **2.** adv. насквóзь **3.** adj. беспересáдочный; прямóй

throughout /θruːˈaʊt/ **1.** adv. повсюду; во всех отношéниях **2.** prep. по всему (+ D)

throw /θroʊ/ v. бросáть impf.; брóсить pf.; ~ **out** выбрáсывать impf., выбросить pf.

thrust /θrʌst/ **1.** n. толчо́к **2.** v. толка́ть(ся); сова́ть impf.

thruway /'θru,wei/ n. автостра́да

thumb /θʌm/ n. большо́й па́лец

thumbtack /'θʌm,tæk/ n. кно́пка

thump /θʌmp/ n. тяжёлый уда́р; глухо́й стук

thunder /'θʌndər/ **1.** n. гром **2.** v. греме́ть impf.; **—ing** n. гро́хот; **—ous** adj. громово́й

thunderclap /'θʌndər,klæp/ n. раска́т гро́ма

thunderstorm /'θʌndər,stɔrm/ n. гроза́

thunderstruck /'θʌndər,strʌk/ adj. ошеломлённый

thurifer /'θʊrəfər/ n. кади́льщик

Thursday /'θɜrzdei/ n. четве́рг

thus /ðʌs/ adv. таки́м о́бразом

thwart /θwɔrt/ v. меша́ть impf.

thy /ðai/ pron. твой

thyroid /'θairɔid/ n. щитови́дная железа́

tick /tɪk/ n. (parasite) клещ

ticket /'tɪkɪt/ n. биле́т; (receipt) квита́нция; (traffic) штраф; **~ punch** компо́стер; **~ office** ка́сса

tickle /'tɪkəl/ v. щекота́ть impf., по- pf.

ticklish /'tɪklɪʃ/ adj. щекотли́вый

tide /taid/ n. прили́в и отли́в

tidiness /'taidinɪs/ n. опря́тность

tidy /'taidi/ adj. опря́тный; аккура́тный

tie /tai/ **1.** n. (bond) связь f.; (pl. ýзы pl.); (necktie) га́лстук; (equal score) ничья́ **2.** v. завя́зывать impf., завяза́ть pf.

tier /tɪər/ n. я́рус

tiger /'taigər/ n. тигр

tight /tait/ adj. пло́тный; те́сный; сжа́тый; туго́й; (stingy) скупо́й

tighten /'taitn/ v. (contract) сжима́ть impf., сжать pf.

tight-fisted /'tait'fistid/ adj. прижи́мистый

tights /taits/ n. трико́ indecl.; колго́тки pl.

tile /tail/ n. (roof) черепи́ца; (decorative) ка́фель m.

till¹ /tɪl/ v. паха́ть impf.

till² /tɪl/ prep. до (+ G)

timber /'tɪmbər/ n. лесоматериа́л

time /taim/ n. вре́мя neut.; (occasion) раз; (period) вре́мя; (mus.) такт; **for a long ~** до́лго; **on ~** во́время; **from ~ to ~**

вре́мя от вре́мени; **what ~ is it?** кото́рый час?; **—less** adj. ве́чный; **~ limit** n. преде́льный срок; **—ly** adj. своевре́менный

timepiece /'taim,pis/ n. часы́ pl.

time sheet n. та́бель m.

timetable /'taim,teibəl/ n. расписа́ние

timid /'tɪmɪd/ adj. ро́бкий

timing /'taimɪŋ/ n. (choice) вы́бор вре́мени

tin /tɪn/ n. о́лово

tincture /'tɪŋktʃər/ n. насто́йка

tinfoil /'tɪn,fɔil/ n. фольга́

tinge /tɪndʒ/ n. (tint) отте́нок; (flavor) при́вкус

tinsel /'tɪnsəl/ n. мишура́

tint /tɪnt/ n. окра́ска; (shade) отте́нок

tiny /'taini/ adj. кро́шечный

tip¹ /tɪp/ n. ко́нчик; наконе́чник

tip² /tɪp/ **1.** n. (gratuity) чаевы́е pl. **2.** v. дава́ть на чай impf.

tip³ /tɪp/ v. (tilt) наклоня́ть(ся) impf., -ни́ть(ся) pf.

tipsy /'tɪpsi/ adj. подвы́пивший

tiptoe /'tɪp,tou/ n.: **on ~s** на цы́почках

tiptop /'tɪp,tɒp/ adj. превосхо́дный; отли́чный

tire¹ /taiᵊr/ n. ши́на

tire² /taiᵊr/ v. утомля́ть(ся); устава́ть impf., уста́ть pf.; **—d** adj. уста́лый; **—less** adj. неутоми́мый; **—some** adj. надое́дливый; утоми́тельный

tiring /'taiᵊrɪŋ/ adj. утоми́тельный

tissue /'tɪʃu/ n. ткань f.; (thin paper) бума́жная салфе́тка

tit /tɪt/ n. (bird) сини́ца

titillate /'tɪtl,eit/ v. (arouse) возбужда́ть impf.

title /'taitl/ **1.** n. загла́вие; назва́ние; (rank) зва́ние; ти́тул **2.** v. называ́ть impf., назва́ть pf.; озагла́вливать impf.

titleholder /'taitl,houldər/ n. чемпио́н

to /tu/ prep. к (+ D); в, на (+ A); (until) до (+ G); **~ and fro** взад и вперёд

toad /toud/ n. жа́ба

toast¹ /toust/ **1.** n. гре́нок **2.** v. поджа́ривать impf., поджа́рить pf.

toast² /toust/ **1.** n. (drink) тост **2.** v. пить тост за impf.

toaster /'toustər/ n. то́стер

toastmaster /'toust,mæstər/ *n.* тамада́

tobacco /tə'bækou/ **1.** *n.* таба́к **2.** *adj.* таба́чный

toboggan /tə'bɒgən/ *n.* са́нки *pl.*

tocsin /'tɒksın/ *n.* (*alarm*) наба́т; (*bell*) наба́тный ко́локол

today /tə'dei/ **1.** *adv.* сего́дня **2.** *n.* сего́дняшний день *m.*

toddler /'tɒdlər/ *n.* малы́ш

toe /tou/ *n.* па́лец на ноге́

together /tə'geðər/ *adv.* вме́сте; ~ **with** вме́сте с (+ *I*)

toil /tɔil/ **1.** *n.* труд; рабо́та **2.** *v.* труди́ться *impf.*

toilet /'tɔilıt/ *n.* туале́т; убо́рная; (*fixture*) унита́з; ~ **paper**, ~ **tissue** туале́тная бума́га; —**ry** туале́тная принадле́жность

token /'toukən/ *n.* знак; сувени́р; (*coin*) жето́н

tolerance /'tɒlərəns/ *n.* терпи́мость

tolerant /'tɒlərənt/ *adj.* терпи́мый

tolerate /'tɒlə,reit/ *v.* терпе́ть *impf.*

toll /toul/ *n.* по́шлина; сбор

tomato /tə'meitou/ **1.** *n.* помидо́р; тома́т **2.** *adj.* тома́тный

tomb /tum/ *n.* моги́ла

tombstone /'tum,stoun/ *n.* моги́льный ка́мень *m.*

tomorrow /tə'mɒrou/ **1.** *adv.* за́втра **2.** *adj.* за́втрашний; **the day after** ~ послеза́втра

ton /tʌn/ *n.* то́нна

tonality /tou'nælıti/ *n.* тона́льность

tone /toun/ *n.* тон

tongs /tɒŋz/ *n.* щипцы́ *pl.*

tongue /tʌŋ/ *n.* язы́к

tonic /'tɒnık/ *n.* тонизи́рующее сре́дство; (*water*) то́ник

tonight /tə'nait/ *adv.* сего́дня ве́чером; сего́дня но́чью

tonsil /'tɒnsəl/ *n.* минда́лина

too /tu/ *adv.* сли́шком; (*also*) та́кже; то́же

tool /tul/ *n.* ору́дие; рабо́чий инструме́нт; (*machine tool*) стано́к

toot /tut/ *v.* гуде́ть *impf.*;

tooth /tuθ/ *n.* зуб; зубе́ц

toothache /'tuθ,eik/ *n.* зубна́я боль *f.*

toothbrush /'tuθ,brʌʃ/ *n.* зубна́я щётка

toothpaste /'tuθ,peist/ *n.* зубна́я па́ста

toothpick /'tuθ,pık/ *n.* зубочи́стка

top /tɒp/ **1.** *n.* верши́на; верх; (*of head*) маку́шка; (*lid*) кры́шка; **from ~ to bottom** све́рху до́низу **2.** *adj.* ве́рхний; (*best*) лу́чший **3.** *v.* (*surpass*) превосходи́ть *impf.*, превзойти́ *pf.*

topcoat /'tɒp,kout/ *n.* пальто́ *neut. indecl.*

top hat *n.* цили́ндр

topic /'tɒpık/ *n.* те́ма; предме́т; —**al** *adj.* актуа́льный; злобо-дне́вный

top-level *adj.* на вы́сшем у́ровне

topple /'tɒpəl/ *v.* опроки́дывать(ся) *impf.*; (*from power*) сверга́ть *impf.*

top-secret *adj.* соверше́нно секре́тный

topsy-turvy /'tɒpsi'tɜrvi/ *adj.* переве́рнутый вверх дном

torch /tɔrtʃ/ *n.* фа́кел; (*for welding*) горе́лка

torment /'tɔrmɛnt/ *n.* тɔr'mɛnt/ **1.** *n.* муче́ние; му́ка **2.** *v.* му́чить *impf.*, из- *pf.*

tormenting /tɔr'mɛntıŋ/ *adj.* мучи́тельный

tornado /tɔr'neidou/ *n.* смерч

torpedo /tɔr'pidou/ *n.* торпе́да

torrent /'tɔrənt/ *n.* пото́к

torrid /'tɔrıd/ *adj.* (*hot*) зно́йный

torso /'tɔrsou/ *n.* ту́ловище; торс

tort /tɔrt/ *n.* дели́кт; граж-да́нское правонаруше́ние

tortoise /'tɔrtəs/ *n.* черепа́ха

tortoiseshell /'tɔrtəs,ʃel/ *adj.* черепа́ховый

tortuous /'tɔrtʃuəs/ *adj.* извили́стый

torture /'tɔrtʃər/ **1.** *n.* пы́тка; му́ка **2.** *v.* пыта́ть; му́чить *impf.*

torturer /'tɔrtʃərər/ *n.* мучи́тель; пала́ч

toss /tɒs/ *v.* броса́ть *impf.*, бро́сить *pf.*; *v.i.* мета́ться *impf.*

total /'toutl/ **1.** *adj.* о́бщий; со-воку́пный, тота́льный **2.** *n.* ито́г; —**ly** *adj.* по́лностью; соверше́нно

totalitarian /tou,tælı'teəriən/ *adj.* тоталита́рный

totality /tou'tælıti/ *n.* совоку́п-ность

totter /'tɒtər/ *v.* шата́ться *impf.*

toucan /'tukæn/ n. тукáн

touch /tʌtʃ/ 1. n. (со)прикоснове́ние 2. v. трóгать impf., тронýть pf.; —ing adj. трóгательный

touchscreen /'tʌtʃ,skrin/ n. сенсóрный экрáн; (pad) сенсóрный планшéт

touch-up n. ретýшь f.

touchy /'tʌtʃi/ adj. обúдчивый

tough /tʌf/ adj. жёсткий; прóчный; (difficult) трýдный; —en v. закалять impf.

toughness /'tʌfnis/ n. закáлка

tour /tur/ 1. n. путешéствие; поéздка; (excursion) экскýрсия 2. v. путешéствовать impf.

tourism /'turizəm/ 1. n. турúзм 2. adj. туристи́ческий

tourist /'turist/ 1. n. турúст, —ка 2. adj. туристúческий

tournament /'turnəmənt/ n. турнúр

tousle /'tauzəl/ v. взъерóшивать impf.

tow /tou/ 1. n. (act) буксирóвка 2. v. буксировáть impf.

toward /tɔrd/ prep. к (+ D)

towed /toud/ adj. прицепнóй

towel /'tauəl/ n. полотéнце

tower /'tauər/ n. бáшня; —ing adj. (high) возвышáющийся

towline /'tou,lain/ n. буксúр

town /taun/ n. гóрод, городóк

township /'taunʃip/ n. муниципалитéт; (small town) посёлок

toxic /'toksik/ adj. ядовúтый

toxin /'toksin/ n. токсúн; яд

toy /tɔi/ 1. n. игрýшка 2. adj. игрýшечный 3. v. игрáть impf.

trace /treis/ 1. n. след 2. v. (draw) черти́ть impf.; (track) выслéживать; Fig. проследи́ть pf.

track /træk/ 1. n. след, дорóжка; (sports) лыжнáя; беговáя дорóжка; (railroad) путь m. 2. v. следи́ть (за + I) impf.; —ing n. прослéживание; выслéживание; ~ suit тренирóвочный костюм

traction /'trækʃən/ n. тяга

tractor /'træktər/ n. трáктор

trade /treid/ 1. n. торгóвля; профéссия 2. adj. торгóвый 3. v. торговáть impf.

trademark /'treid,mark/ n. фабрúчная мáрка

trader /'treidər/, **tradesman** /'treidzmən/ n. торгóвец

trade union n. профсою́з; (U.S. & U.K.) тред-юнио́н

tradition /trə'diʃən/ n. традúция —al adj. традицио́нный

traffic /'træfik/ n. движéние; ~ light светофóр; ~ police дорóжная полúция

tragedy /'trædʒidi/ n. трагéдия

tragic /'trædʒik/ adj. траги́ческий

trail /treil/ 1. n. след; (path) тропá 2. v.t. идти́ по слéду; v.i. (drag) волочи́ться impf.; —er n. прицéп; трéйлер

train /trein/ 1. n. пóезд; (sequence) ход; (of dress) шлейф 2. v. тренировáть(ся) impf.; ~ compartment n. купé neut. indecl.; —ed adj. (person) обýченный; (animal) дрессирóванный

trainee /trei'ni/ n. стажёр; практикáнт

trainer /'treinər/ n. (sports) трéнер; (animals) дрессирóвщик

training /'treiniŋ/ n. подготóвка; обучéние

trait /treit/ n. (харáктерная) чертá; осóбенность

traitor /'treitər/ n. предáтель

tram /træm/ n. трамвáй

tramp /træmp/ n. тóпот; (vagabond) бродя́га m. & f.

trample /'træmpəl/ v. топтáть impf., по-, ис- pf.; подавля́ть impf.

trampoline /,træmpə'lin/ n. батýт

tranquil /'træŋkwil/ adj. спокóйный

tranquilize /'træŋkwə,laiz/ v. успокáивать impf.

tranquilizer /'træŋkwə,laizər/ n. успокáивающее срéдство

transact /træn'sækt/ v. заключáть impf.; —ion n. дéло; сдéлка

transatlantic /,trænsət'læntik/ adj. трансатланти́ческий

transcend /træn'send/ v. превосходи́ть impf. превзойти́ pf.

transcendental /,trænsen'dentl/ adj. трансцендентáльный

transcribe /træn'skraib/ v. (copy) переписывать impf.

transcript /'trænskript/ n. кóпия

transfer /n. 'trænsfər; v. træns'fər/ n. 1. перенóс; перемещéние; (funds) перевóд 2. v. переноси́ть impf., перенести́ pf.; перемещáть impf., -мести́ть pf.

transfiguration /,trænsfigyə'reiʃən/ n. преобразовáние

transform /træns'fɔrm/ v. превраща́ть *impf.*, преврати́ть *pf.*

transformation /ˌtrænsfər'meiʃən/ n. преобразова́ние; изменение

transformer /træns'fɔrmər/ n. трансформа́тор

transfusion /træns'fyuʒən/ n. перелива́ние (кро́ви)

transgress /træns'gres/ v. переступа́ть *impf.*, -пи́ть *pf.*; —ion n. наруше́ние; (sin) грех

transient /'trænziənt/ 1. n. прехо́дящий 2. n. прое́зжий

transistor /træn'zistər/ n. транзи́стор

transit /'trænsit/ 1. n. транзи́т; in ~ в пути́ 2. adj. транзи́тный

transition /træn'ziʃən/ n. перехо́д; —al adj. перехо́дный

transitory /'trænziˌtɔri/ adj. преходя́щий; мимолётный

translate /træns'leit/ v. переводи́ть *impf.*, перевести́ *pf.*

translation /træns'leiʃən/ n. перево́д

translator /træns'leitər/ n. перево́дчик, -чица

transmigration /ˌtrænsmai'greiʃən/ n. переселе́ние

transmission /træns'miʃən/ n. переда́ча

transmit /træns'mit/ v. передава́ть *impf.*, -да́ть *pf.*

transom /'trænsəm/ n. фрамуга

transparency /træns'pɛərənsi/ n. прозра́чность; (slide) диапозити́в

transparent /træns'pɛərənt/ adj. прозра́чный; очеви́дный

transpire /træn'spai̯ər/ v. обнару́живаться *impf.*; (happen) случа́ться, происходи́ть *impf.*

transplant /træns'plænt/ v. переса́живать *impf.*; (med.) де́лать переса́дку *impf.*, с- *pf.*

transport /ˈtrænspɔrt/ n. /trænsˈpɔrt/ v. 1. n. тра́нспорт; перево́зка 2. adj. тра́нспортный 3. v. перевози́ть *impf.*

transportation /ˌtrænspɔr'teiʃən/ n. тра́нспорт; перево́зка; public ~ обще́ственный тра́нспорт

trap /træp/ n. ловушка 2. v. лови́ть (зама́нивать) в лову́шку *impf.*, замани́ть *impf.*; ~ door n. люк

trapeze /træ'piz/ n. трапе́ция

trash /træʃ/ n. му́сор; хлам; ~ can му́сорный я́щик

trauma /'traumə/ n. тра́вма

traumatic /trə'mætik/ adj. травмати́ческий; сокруши́тельный

travel /'trævəl/ 1. n. путеше́ствие 2. adj. доро́жный 3. v. путеше́ствовать *impf.*; — agency n. турагентство

traveler /'trævələr/ n. путеше́ственник, -ница (passenger) пассажи́р

traveler's check n. доро́жный чек

traverse /trə'vɜrs/ v. пересека́ть *impf.*

travesty /'trævəsti/ n. паро́дия

trawler /'trɔlər/ n. тра́улер

tray /trei/ n. подно́с

treacherous /'tretʃərəs/ adj. преда́тельский; (unsafe) опа́сный

treachery /'tretʃəri/ n. преда́тельство

tread /tred/ 1. n. похо́дка; (of tire) проте́ктор 2. v. ступа́ть

treason /'trizən/ n. изме́на

treasure /'treʒər/ n. сокро́вище

treasure house n. сокро́вищница

treasurer /'treʒərər/ n. казначе́й

treasury /'treʒəri/ n. 1. госуда́рственное казначе́йство 2. adj. казначе́йский

treat /trit/ v. (behave) обходи́ться (с + I) *impf.*, обойти́сь *pf.*; (med.) лечи́ть *impf.*; (entertain) угоща́ть *impf.* —ment n. обраще́ние; (med.) лече́ние; ухо́д; (discussion) тракто́вка

treatise /'tritis/ n. тракта́т; моногра́фия

treaty /'triti/ n. догово́р

treble /'trebəl/ 1. n. (mus.) дискант 2. adj. диска́нтовый

tree /tri/ n. де́рево

trek /trek/ n. путь m.; похо́д

tremble /'trembəl/ v. дрожа́ть *impf.*

tremendous /trɪ'mɛndəs/ adj. огро́мный

tremor /'tremər/ n. дрожь f.; (earthquake) толчо́к

trench /trentʃ/ n. (ditch) кана́ва; ров; (mil.) око́п; транше́я

trend /trend/ n. направле́ние; тенде́нция

trepidation /ˌtrepi'deiʃən/ n. трево́га; тре́пет

trespass /'trespəs/ v. нару́шить грани́цу *pf.*; —er n. наруши́тель

triad /ˈtraɪæd/ n. триа́да

trial /ˈtraɪəl/ n. 1. испыта́ние; про́ба; (law) суде́бный проце́сс 2. adj. испыта́тельный; про́бный

triangle /ˈtraɪæŋgəl/ n. треуго́льник

triangular /traɪˈæŋgyələr/ adj. треуго́льный

tribal /ˈtraɪbəl/ adj. племенно́й

tribe /traɪb/ n. пле́мя neut.; род

tribulation /ˌtrɪbyəˈleɪʃən/ n. несча́стье

tribunal /traɪˈbyunl/ n. трибуна́л

tributary /ˈtrɪbyəˌteri/ n. прито́к

tribute /ˈtrɪbyut/ n. дань f.

tricentennial /ˌtraɪsenˈteniəl/ n. трёхсотле́тие

trick /trɪk/ n. 1. обма́н; фо́кус; трюк 2. v. обма́нывать impf., обману́ть pf.

trickle /ˈtrɪkl/ n. 1. стру́йка 2. v. ка́пать; сочи́ться impf.

tricky /ˈtrɪki/ adj. хи́трый; ло́вкий; (complex) сло́жный

trifle /ˈtraɪfəl/ n. пустя́к; ме́лочь f.

trifling /ˈtraɪflɪŋ/ adj. пустяко́вый

trigger /ˈtrɪgər/ n. куро́к; крючо́к

trill /trɪl/ v. залива́ться тре́лью impf.

trilogy /ˈtrɪlədʒi/ n. трило́гия

trim /trɪm/ 1. adj. опря́тный 2. v. подреза́ть impf., подре́зать pf.; (hair) подстрига́ть impf., подстри́чь pf.

Trinity /ˈtrɪniti/ n. Тро́ица

trinket /ˈtrɪŋkɪt/ n. безделу́шка

trip /trɪp/ n. 1. путеше́ствие; пое́здка 2. v.i. (stumble) спотыка́ться impf.; v.t. (cause to stumble) подста́вить но́жку impf.

tripe /traɪp/ n. (cul.) рубе́ц

triple /ˈtrɪpəl/ 1. adj. тройно́й; (tripled) утро́енный 2. v. утра́ивать(ся) impf., утро́ить(ся) pf.

triplet /ˈtrɪplɪt/ n. тройня́

tripod /ˈtraɪpod/ n. трено́жник

trite /traɪt/ adj. бана́льный

triumph /ˈtraɪəmf/ n. 1. побе́да; торжество́ 2. v. побежда́ть impf., -бедить pf.

triumphant /traɪˈʌmfənt/ adj. победоно́сный

trivia /ˈtrɪviə/ n.pl. ме́лочи pl.

trivial /ˈtrɪviəl/ adj. тривиа́льный; незначи́тельный

trolley /ˈtroli/ n. теле́жка; (serving table) сто́лик на колёсиках; ~ **bus** тролле́йбус

troop /trup/ n. отря́д; pl. войска́ pl.; —**er** n. (ко́нный) полице́йский

trophy /ˈtroufi/ n. приз; трофе́й

tropic /ˈtropɪk/ n. тро́пик; —**al** adj. тропи́ческий

trot /trot/ 1. n. рысь f. 2. v. идти́ ры́сью impf.

trouble /ˈtrʌbəl/ n. 1. беда́; забо́та; pl. хло́поты pl. 2. v. беспоко́ить(ся); затрудня́ть(ся) impf., -ни́ть(ся) pf.; —**ed** adj. беспоко́йный; —**some** adj. беспоко́йный; (difficult) тру́дный

troupe /trup/ n. тру́ппа

trousers /ˈtrauzərz/ n. брю́ки; штаны́ pl.

trout /traut/ n. форе́ль f.

truant /ˈtruənt/ n. прогу́льщик

truce /trus/ n. переми́рие

truck /trʌk/ n. грузови́к; (hand truck) теле́жка

trudge /trʌdʒ/ v. плести́сь; тащи́ться impf.

true /tru/ adj. ве́рный; пра́вильный; правди́вый

truffle /ˈtrʌfəl/ n. трю́фель m.

truly /ˈtruli/ adj. (faithfully) ве́рно; (really) действи́тельно

trump /trʌmp/ n. ко́зырь m.

trumpet /ˈtrʌmpɪt/ n. труба́

trumpeter /ˈtrʌmpɪtər/ n. труба́ч

truncate /ˈtrʌŋkeɪt/ v. усека́ть impf. усе́чь pf.

trunk /trʌŋk/ n. (box) сунду́к; (tree) ствол m.; (of elephant) хо́бот; (car) бага́жник

trunks /trʌŋks/ n. трусы́ pl.; (swimming) пла́вки pl.

truss /trʌs/ n. (structural frame) фе́рма; (med.) грыжево́й банда́ж

trust /trʌst/ 1. n. дове́рие; ве́ра; (econ.) трест 2. v. доверя́ть impf., дове́рить pf.; —**ful**, —**ing** adj. дове́рчивый

trustee /trʌˈsti/ n. попечи́тель, -ница

trustworthy /ˈtrʌstˌwзrði/ adj. надёжный

truth /truθ/ n. пра́вда; и́стина

truthful /ˈtruθfəl/ adj. правди́вый

try /traɪ/ 1. n. попы́тка 2. v. про́бовать impf. по- pf.; (law) суди́ть impf.; ~ **on** примеря́ть *impf.*, **примерить** *pf.*; **-ing** *adj.* утомительный

tsar /zɑr, tsɑr/ *n.* царь *m.*

tsarina /zɑ'rinə, tsɑ-/ *n.* царица

T-shirt *n.* футболка; майка

tub /tʌb/ *n.* (*vat*) кадка (*bath*) ванна

tubby /'tʌbi/ *adj.* толстенький

tube /tub/ *n.* труба; трубка; (*of toothpaste, etc.*) тюбик

tuber /'tubər/ *n.* клубень *m.*

tuberculosis /tʊ,bɜrkyə'loʊsɪs/ *n.* туберкулёз

tubular /'tubyələr/ *adj.* трубчатый

tuck /tʌk/ *v.* (*put away*) засовывать *impf.*

Tuesday /'tuzdei/ *n.* вторник

tuft /tʌft/ *n.* пучок

tug /tʌg/ **1.** *n.* рывок; (*boat*) буксир **2.** *v.* дёргать *impf.*, дёрнуть *pf.*

tuition /tu'ɪʃən/ *n.* плата за обучение

tulip /'tulɪp/ *n.* тюльпан

tumble /'tʌmbəl/ **1.** *n.* падение; **2.** *v.* падать *impf.*, упасть *pf.*; (*acrobatics*) кувыркаться *impf.*

tumble-dry *v.* сушить в барабанной сушилке *impf.*

tumbler /'tʌmblər/ *n.* стакан

tumor /'tumər/ *n.* опухоль *f.*

tumult /'tuməlt/ *n.* суматоха; шум

tumultuous /tu'mʌltʃuəs/ *adj.* буйный

tuna /'tunə/ *n.* тунец

tune /tun/ **1.** *n.* мелодия; мотив **2.** *v.* (*instrument*) настраивать *impf.*, настроить *pf.*; (*engine*) регулировать *impf.*

tungsten /'tʌŋstən/ *n.* вольфрам

tunic /'tunɪk/ *n.* туника; (*of uniform*) китель *m.*

tuning fork /'tunɪŋ/ *n.* камертон

tunnel /'tʌnl/ *n.* туннель *m.*

turban /'tɜrbən/ *n.* тюрбан; (*Muslim*) чалма

turbidity /tər'bɪdɪti/ *n.* мутность

turbine /'tɜrbɪn/ *n.* турбина

turbulence /'tɜrbyələns/ *n.* бурность; (*aero.*) турбулентность

turbulent /'tɜrbyələnt/ *adj.* буйный; бурный

turf /tɜrf/ *n.* дёрн

Turk /tɜrk/ *n.* турок, турчанка

turkey /'tɜrki/ *n.* индюк, индейка

Turkey /'tɜrki/ *n.* Турция

Turkish /'tɜrkɪʃ/ *adj.* турецкий

Turkmenistan /,tɜrkmɛnə'stæn/ *n.* Туркменистан

turmoil /'tɜrmɔil/ *n.* суматоха; беспорядок

turn /tɜrn/ **1.** *n.* оборот; поворот; (*in line*) очередь *f.* **2.** *v.* (*reverse*) поворачивать(ся) *impf.*; (*direct*) обращать(ся) *impf.*, обратить(ся) *pf.*; **~ around** оборачиваться *impf.*; обернуться *pf.*; **~ off** выключать *impf.*, выключить *pf.*; **~ on** включать *impf.*, -чить *pf.*

turncoat /'tɜrn,kout/ *n.* ренегат

turner /'tɜrnər/ *n.* токарь *m.*

turning /'tɜrnɪŋ/ *n.* (*rotation*) вращение; **~ point** перелом

turnip /'tɜrnɪp/ *n.* репа

turnover /'tɜrn,ouvər/ *n.* оборот

turnpike /'tɜrn,paik/ *n.* автострада

turnstile /'tɜrn,stail/ *n.* турникет

turpentine /'tɜrpən,tain/ *n.* скипидар

turquoise /'tɜrkɔiz/ **1.** *n.* (*gem*) бирюза **2.** *adj.* бирюзовый

turtle /'tɜrtl/ *n.* черепаха

tusk /tʌsk/ *n.* клык; бивень *m.*

tutor /'tutər/ **1.** *n.* репетитор **2.** *v.* давать частные уроки *impf.*

tuxedo /tʌk'sidou/ *n.* смокинг

TV *n.* телевидение; **TV set** телевизор

tweezers /'twizərz/ *n.pl.* пинцет; щипчики *pl.*

twelfth /twelfθ/ *adj.* двенадцатый

twelve /twelv/ *n.*, *adj.* двенадцать

twentieth /'twentiθ/ *adj.* двадцатый

twenty /'twenti/ *n.*, *adj.* двадцать

twice /twais/ *adv.* дважды

twig /twig/ *n.* веточка

twilight /'twai,lait/ *n.* сумерки *pl.*

twin /twɪn/ *n.* близнец; *pl.* близнецы *pl.*

twine /twain/ *n.* бечёвка; шпагат

twinkle /'twɪŋkəl/ *v.* мерцать; сверкать *impf.*

twinkling /'twɪŋklɪŋ/ *n.* мерцание

twirl /twɜrl/ *v.* вертеть(ся) *impf.*

twist /twist/ *v.* крутить *impf.*, *pf.*; сучить *impf.*

twister /'twɪstər/ n. смерч

twitch /twɪtʃ/ v. дёргать(ся); подёргивать(ся) impf.

twitter /'twɪtər/ n. щебет 2. v. щебетать; чирикать impf.

two /tu/ 1. n., adj. два; две 2. coll. двое

twofold /'tu,fould/ adj. двойной

two-piece suit n. костюм

two-way /'tai'wei/ adj. двусторонний

tycoon /tai'kun/ n. магнат

type /taip/ 1. n. тип; род; (print) шрифт 2. v. печатать (на машинке) impf.; **—d** adj. машинописный

typeset /'taip,set/ v. набирать impf.; **—ting** n. набор

typewriter /'taip,raitər/ n. пишущая машинка

typhus /'taifəs/ n. сыпной тиф

typical /'tipikəl/ adj. типичный

typing /'taipiŋ/ n. машинопись

typist /'taipist/ n. машинистка

typo /'taipou/ n. Colloq. опечатка

tyrannical /ti'rænikəl/ adj. тиранический

tyranny /'tirəni/ n. тирания

tyrant /'tairənt/ n. тиран; деспот

U

ubiquitous /yu'bikwitəs/ adj. вездесущий; повсеместный

udder /'ʌdər/ n. вымя neut.

ugliness /'ʌglinis/ n. уродство

ugly /'ʌgli/ adj. уродливый; некрасивый; безобразный

Ukraine /yu'krein/ n. Украина

Ukrainian /yu'kreiniən/ 1. adj. украинский 2. n. украинец, -нка

ulcer /'ʌlsər/ n. язва

ulterior /ʌl'tiəriər/ adj. скрытый

ultimate /'ʌltəmit/ adj. окончательный; конечный

ultimatum /,ʌltə'meitəm/ n. ультиматум

ultrasound /'ʌltrə,saund/ n. ультразвук

ultraviolet /,ʌltrə'vaiəlit/ adj. ультрафиолетовый

umbilical cord /ʌm'bilikəl/ n. пуповина

umbrage /'ʌmbridʒ/ n.: **take ~** обижаться impf.

umbrella /ʌm'brelə/ n. зонтик

umpire /'ʌmpaiər/ n. судья m.

unabated /,ʌnə'beitid/ adj. неослабевающий

unable /ʌn'eibəl/ adj. неспособный; **be ~ to** не мочь impf.

unabridged /,ʌnə'bridʒd/ adj. несокращённый; полный

unacceptable /,ʌnik'septəbəl/ adj. неприемлемый

unaccompanied /,ʌnə'kʌmpənid/ adj. без сопровождения

unaccountable /,ʌnə'kauntəbəl/ adj. необъяснимый

unaccustomed /,ʌnə'kʌstəmd/ adj. непривыкший (к + D)

unaffected /,ʌnə'fektid/ adj. непринуждённый

unanimous /yu'nænəməs/ adj. единогласный; единодушный

unannounced /,ʌnə'naunst/ adj. без предупреждения

unarmed /ʌn'ɑrmd/ adj. невооружённый; безоружный

unassuming /,ʌnə'sumiŋ/ adj. скромный

unattended /,ʌnə'tendid/ adj. без присмотра

unattractive /,ʌnə'træktiv/ adj. непривлекательный

unauthorized /ʌn'ɔθə'raizd/ adj. неразрешённый; неправомочный

unavailable /,ʌnə'veiləbəl/ adj. не имеющийся в наличии; недоступный

unavoidable /,ʌnə'vɔidəbəl/ adj. неизбежный

unaware /,ʌnə'wɛər/ adj. не подозревающий; **be ~ of** не сознавать impf.

unbalanced /ʌn'bælənst/ adj. неуравновешенный

unbearable /ʌn'bɛərəbəl/ adj. невыносимый

unbelievable /,ʌnbi'livəbəl/ adj. невероятный

unbiased /ʌn'baiəst/ adj. беспристрастный

unbolt /ʌn'boult/ v. отпирать impf.

unbroken /ʌn'broukən/ adj. целый; непрерывный

unburden /ʌn'bɜrdn/ v. облегчать impf., -чить pf.

unbutton /ʌn'bʌtn/ v. расстёгивать impf.

uncalled-for /ʌn'kɔld,fɔr/ adj. ненужный

uncanny /ʌn'kæni/ adj. жуткий

unceasing /ʌnˈsiːsɪŋ/ *adj.* беспрестанный; беспрерывный

uncertain /ʌnˈsɜːrtn/ *adj.* неуверенный; **—ty** *n.* неопределённость

unchanging /ʌnˈtʃeɪndʒɪŋ/ *adj.* неизменный

uncharitable /ʌnˈtʃærɪtəbəl/ *adj.* недобрый; жестокий

uncivilized /ʌnˈsɪvəˌlaɪzd/ *adj.* нецивилизованный

unclaimed /ʌnˈkleɪmd/ *adj.* невостребованный

uncle /ˈʌŋkəl/ *n.* дядя *m.*

unclean /ʌnˈkliːn/ *adj.* нечистый

unclear /ʌnˈklɪər/ *adj.* неясный

uncomfortable /ʌnˈkʌmftəbəl/ *adj.* неудобный

uncommon /ʌnˈkɒmən/ *adj.* необычный; необыкновенный

uncompromising /ʌnˈkɒmprəˌmaɪzɪŋ/ *adj.* бескомпромиссный

unconcerned /ʌnkənˈsɜːrnd/ *adj.* беззаботный

unconditional /ʌnkənˈdɪʃənl/ *adj.* безоговорочный; безусловный

unconscious /ʌnˈkɒnʃəs/ *adj.* бессознательный; **be —** быть без сознания; **—ness** *n.* бессознательное состояние

unconstitutional /ˌʌnkɒnstɪˈtuʃənl/ *adj.* неконституционный

unconstrained /ˌʌnkənˈstreɪnd/ *adj.* непринуждённый

unconventional /ˌʌnkənˈvɛnʃənl/ *adj.* необычный

uncooked /ʌnˈkʊkt/ *adj.* сырой

uncooperative /ˌʌnkoʊˈɒpərətɪv/ *adj.* неуступчивый

uncover /ʌnˈkʌvər/ *v.* открывать *impf.*, открыть *pf.*

undamaged /ʌnˈdæmɪdʒd/ *adj.* неповреждённый

undecided /ˌʌndɪˈsaɪdɪd/ *adj.* нерешённый

undeclared /ˌʌndɪˈklɛərd/ *adj.* необъявленный

undeniable /ˌʌndɪˈnaɪəbəl/ *adj.* неоспоримый

under /ˈʌndər/ **1.** *prep.* под (*loc.*: + I; *dir.*: + A) **2.** *adv.* ниже, вниз; внизу

underage /ˌʌndərˈeɪdʒ/ *adj.* несовершеннолётний

underbrush /ˈʌndərˌbrʌʃ/ *n.* подлесок

undercover /ˌʌndərˈkʌvər/ *adj.* секретный; тайный

undercurrent /ˈʌndərˌkɜːrənt/ *n.* подводное течение; *Fig.* скрытая тенденция

underdeveloped /ˌʌndərdɪˈvɛləpt/ *adj.* недоразвитый

underestimate /ˌʌndərˈɛstəˌmeɪt/ *v.* недооценивать *impf.*, недооценить *pf.*

undergo /ˌʌndərˈɡoʊ/ *v.* подвергаться *impf.*, подвергнуться *pf.*

undergraduate /ˌʌndərˈɡrædʒuɪt/ *n.* студент, **—ка**

underground /ˈʌndərˌɡraʊnd/ **1.** *adj.* подземный; подпольный **2.** *n.* подполье

undergrowth /ˈʌndərˌɡroʊθ/ *n.* подрост; заросли *pl.*

underline /ˌʌndərˈlaɪn/ *v.* подчёркивать *impf.*, подчеркнуть *pf.*

undermine /ˌʌndərˈmaɪn/ *v.* подрывать *impf.*, подорвать *pf.*

underneath /ˌʌndərˈniːθ/ **1.** *adv.* вниз, внизу **2.** *prep.* под (+ I)

undernourished /ˌʌndərˈnɜːrɪʃt/ *adj.* недокормленный

underpants /ˈʌndərˌpænts/ *n.* трусики; трусы *pl.*

underpass /ˈʌndərˌpæs/ *n.* подземный переход

underprivileged /ˌʌndərˈprɪvəlɪdʒd/ *adj.* неимущий

underproduction /ˌʌndərprəˈdʌkʃən/ *n.* недопроизводство

underrate /ˌʌndərˈreɪt/ *v.* недооценивать *impf.*, -ценить *pf.*

underscore /ˈʌndərˌskɔːr/ *v.* подчёркивать *impf.*

undershirt /ˈʌndərˌʃɜːrt/ *n.* нижняя рубашка

understand /ˌʌndərˈstænd/ *v.* понимать *impf.*, понять *pf.*; (*assume*) подразумевать *impf.*; **—ing** *n.* понимание

understate /ˌʌndərˈsteɪt/ *v.* преуменьшать *impf.*

understudy /ˈʌndərˌstʌdi/ *n.* дублёр

undertake /ˌʌndərˈteɪk/ *v.* предпринимать *impf.*, предпринять *pf.*; **—r** *n.* владелец похоронного бюро

undertaking /ˌʌndərˈteɪkɪŋ/ *n.* предприятие

underwater /ˌʌndərˈwɔːtər/ *adj.* подводный

underwear /ˈʌndərˌwɛər/ *n.* нижнее бельё

underworld /ˈʌndərˌwɜːrld/ *n.* (*crime*) преступный мир; (*myth.*) преисподняя

underwrite /ˌʌndərˈraɪt/ v.
(*guarantee*) гаранти́ровать
impf. & pf.; —r *n.* страхо́вщик

undeserved /ˌʌndɪˈzɜːrvd/ *adj.*
незаслу́женный

undeserving /ˌʌndɪˈzɜːrvɪŋ/ *adj.*
недосто́йный

undesirable /ˌʌndɪˈzaɪərəbəl/ *adj.*
нежела́тельный

undeveloped /ˌʌndɪˈveləpt/ *adj.*
нера́звитый

undigested /ˌʌndɪˈdʒestɪd/ *adj.*
неусво́енный

undisciplined /ʌnˈdɪsəplɪnd/ *adj.*
недисциплини́рованный

undisclosed /ˌʌndɪˈsklouzd/ *adj.*
необнаро́дованный

undisputed /ˌʌndɪˈspjuːtɪd/ *adj.*
бесспо́рный

undistinguished
/ˌʌndɪˈstɪŋɡwɪʃt/ *adj.* посре́дственный; зауря́дный

undivided /ˌʌndɪˈvaɪdɪd/ *adj.*
це́лый; безразде́льный

undoubted /ʌnˈdautɪd/ *adj.*
несомне́нный

undress /ʌnˈdres/ v. раздева́ть(ся) *impf.,* разде́ть(ся) *pf.*

undue /ʌnˈduː/ *adj.* чрезме́рный

undulating /ˈʌndʒəˌleɪtɪŋ/ *adj.*
волни́стый; холми́стый

undying /ʌnˈdaɪɪŋ/ *adj.* бессме́ртный; бесконе́чный

uneasiness /ʌnˈiːzinəs/ *n.* беспоко́йство

uneasy /ʌnˈiːzi/ *adj.* нело́вкий;
обеспоко́йный; встрево́женный

uneconomical /ˌʌnekəˈnɒmɪkəl/
adj. неэкономи́чный; нерента́бельный; неэконо́мный

uneducated /ʌnˈedʒuˌkeɪtɪd/ *adj.*
необразо́ванный

unemployed /ˌʌnemˈplɔɪd/ *adj.*
безрабо́тный

unemployment /ˌʌnemˈplɔɪmənt/ *n.* безрабо́тица; ~
benefit посо́бие по безрабо́тице

unending /ʌnˈendɪŋ/ *adj.* ве́чный

unendurable /ˌʌnenˈdʊrəbəl/
adj. невыноси́мый

unenlightened /ˌʌnenˈlaɪtɪnd/
adj. непросвещённый

unequal /ʌnˈiːkwəl/ *adj.*
нера́вный

unequaled /ʌnˈiːkwɒld/ *adj.* несравне́нный

unequivocal /ˌʌnɪˈkwɪvəkəl/ *adj.*
недвусмы́сленный

uneven /ʌnˈiːvən/ *adj.* неро́вный;
(*odd*) нечётный

unexpected /ˌʌnɪkˈspektɪd/ *adj.*
неожи́данный; непредви́денный

unfading /ʌnˈfeɪdɪŋ/ *adj.* неувяда́емый

unfair /ʌnˈfeər/ *adj.* несправедли́вый

unfaithful /ʌnˈfeɪθfəl/ *adj.*
неве́рный

unfamiliar /ˌʌnfəˈmɪljər/ *adj.* незнако́мый; стра́нный

unfasten /ʌnˈfæsən/ v. (*dress*)
расстёгивать *impf.;* (*untie*)
развя́зывать *impf.*

unfavorable /ʌnˈfeɪvərəbəl/ *adj.*
неблагоприя́тный

unfeeling /ʌnˈfiːlɪŋ/ *adj.*
бесчу́вственный

unfinished /ʌnˈfɪnɪʃt/ *adj.*
неоко́нченный

unfit /ʌnˈfɪt/ *adj.* него́дный

unflattering /ʌnˈflætərɪŋ/ *adj.*
неле́стный

unfold /ʌnˈfould/ v. раскрыва́ть(ся) *impf.,* раскры́ть(ся) *pf.*

unforced /ʌnˈfɔːrst/ *adj.* непринуждённый

unforeseen /ˌʌnfɔːrˈsiːn/ *adj.*
непредви́денный

unforgettable /ˌʌnfərˈɡetəbəl/
adj. незабыва́емый

unforgivable /ˌʌnfərˈɡɪvəbəl/
adj. непрости́тельный

unfortunate /ʌnˈfɔːrtʃənɪt/ *adj.*
несча́стный; —ly *adv.* к
сожале́нию; к несча́стью

unfounded /ʌnˈfaundɪd/ *adj.*
необосно́ванный

unfriendly /ʌnˈfrendli/ *adj.*
недру́жеский; неприве́тливый

unfurnished /ʌnˈfɜːrnɪʃt/ *adj.*
немеблиро́ванный

ungainly /ʌnˈɡeɪnli/ *adj.*
нескла́дный

ungifted /ʌnˈɡɪftɪd/ *adj.*
безда́рный

ungovernable /ʌnˈɡʌvərnəbəl/
adj. неуправля́емый

ungrateful /ʌnˈɡreɪtfəl/ *adj.*
неблагода́рный

unguarded /ʌnˈɡɑːrdɪd/ *adj.* неохраня́емый

unhappiness /ʌnˈhæpinɪs/ *n.*
несча́стье

unhappy /ʌnˈhæpi/ *adj.* несча́стливый; несча́стный

unharmed /ʌnˈhɑːrmd/ *adj.* невреди́мый

unhealthy /ʌnˈhelθi/ *adj.* нездоро́вый

unheard-of /ʌn'hɜrd,ʌv/ adj. неслыханный

unhesitating /ʌn'hɛzɪ,teɪtɪŋ/ adj. решительный

unhook /ʌn'hʊk/ v. расстёгивать impf.

unicorn /'yunɪ,kɔrn/ n. единорог

unidentified /,ʌnaɪ'dɛntəfaɪd/ adj. неопознанный

unification /,yunəfɪ'keɪʃən/ n. объединение; унификация

uniform /'yunə,form/ 1. adj. единообразный; форменный 2. n. форма; мундир

uniformity /,yunə'fɔrmɪti/ n. единообразие

unify /'yunə,faɪ/ v. объединять impf., -нить pf.

unilateral /,yunə'lætərəl/ adj. односторонний

unimaginable /,ʌnɪ'mædʒənəbəl/ adj. невообразимый

unimportant /,ʌnɪm'pɔrtn̩t/ adj. неважный; незначительный

uninformed /,ʌnɪn'fɔrmd/ adj. неосведомлённый

uninhabited /,ʌnɪn'hæbɪtɪd/ adj. необитаемый

uninhibited /,ʌnɪn'hɪbɪtɪd/ adj. нестеснённый

uninspired /,ʌnɪn'spaɪərd/ adj. невдохновлённый

uninsured /,ʌnɪn'ʃʊrd/ adj. незастрахованный

unintelligible /,ʌnɪn'tɛlɪdʒəbəl/ adj. невнятный

unintentional /,ʌnɪn'tɛnʃən̩l/ adj. ненамеренный

uninterested /ʌn'ɪntərəstɪd/ adj. равнодушный

uninterrupted /,ʌnɪntə'rʌptɪd/ adj. непрерывный

uninvited /,ʌnɪn'vaɪtɪd/ adj. неприглашённый; незваный

union /'yunyən/ 1. n. союз 2. adj. (of trade union) профсоюзный

unique /yu'nik/ adj. уникальный; единственный в своём роде

unison /'yunəsən/ n. согласие

unit /'yunɪt/ n. единица; (mil.) часть f.

unite /yu'naɪt/ v. соединять(ся) impf., соединить(ся) pf.; **—d** adj. соединённый

United States n.pl. Соединённые Штаты pl.

unity /'yunɪti/ n. единство

universal /,yunə'vɜrsəl/ adj. уни-

версальный; всеобщий; всемирный; **—ly** adv. всюду

universe /'yunə,vɜrs/ n. вселенная; мир

university /,yunə'vɜrsɪti/ **1.** n. университет **2.** adj. университетский

unjust /ʌn'dʒʌst/ adj. несправедливый

unkempt /ʌn'kɛmpt/ adj. нечёсаный

unkind /ʌn'kaɪnd/ adj. недобрый

unknown /ʌn'noun/ adj. неизвестный

unless /ʌn'lɛs/ conj. если... не

unlike /ʌn'laɪk/ adj. непохожий; **—ly** adj. маловероятный

unload /ʌn'loud/ v. разгружать impf., разгрузить pf.

unlock /ʌn'lɒk/ v. отпирать(ся) impf., отпереть(ся) pf.; открывать(ся) impf., открыть(ся) pf.

unlucky /ʌn'lʌki/ adj. неудачный

unmanageable /ʌn'mænɪdʒəbəl/ adj. неуправляемый

unmarried /ʌn'mærɪd/ adj. (man) холостой; неженатый; (woman) незамужняя

unmask /ʌn'mæsk/ v. разоблачать impf., -чить pf.

unmerited /ʌn'mɛrɪtɪd/ adj. незаслуженный

unmistakable /,ʌnmɪ'steɪkəbəl/ adj. безошибочный

unnatural /ʌn'nætʃərəl/ adj. неестественный

unnecessary /ʌn'nɛsə,sɛri/ adj. ненужный; излишний

unnoticed /ʌn'noutɪst/ adj. незамеченный

unobliging /,ʌnə'blaɪdʒɪŋ/ adj. нелюбезный

unobtainable /,ʌnəb'teɪnəbəl/ adj. недоступный

unoccupied /ʌn'ɒkyə,paɪd/ adj. незанятый

unofficial /,ʌnə'fɪʃəl/ adj. неофициальный

unpack /ʌn'pæk/ v. распаковывать impf.

unpaid /ʌn'peɪd/ adj. неоплаченный

unparalleled /ʌn'pærə,lɛld/ adj. беспримерный

unplanned /ʌn'plænd/ adj. незапланированный

unpleasant /ʌn'plɛzənt/ c приятный; **—ness** n. ность

unplug /ʌnˈplʌg/ v. выдернуть вилку; разъединить pf.

unpopular /ʌnˈpɒpjʊlər/ adj. непопулярный

unpractical /ʌnˈpræktɪkəl/ adj. непрактичный

unprecedented /ʌnˈpresɪˌdentɪd/ adj. беспрецедентный

unprepared /ˌʌnprɪˈpeərd/ adj. неподготовленный

unprincipled /ʌnˈprɪnsəpəld/ adj. беспринципный

unproductive /ˌʌnprəˈdʌktɪv/ adj. непродуктивный

unprofessional /ˌʌnprəˈfeʃənl/ adj. непрофессиональный

unprofitable /ʌnˈprɒfɪtəbəl/ adj. неприбыльный; убыточный

unprotected /ˌʌnprəˈtektɪd/ adj. незащищённый

unprovoked /ˌʌnprəˈvoʊkt/ adj. неспровоцированный

unpublished /ʌnˈpʌblɪʃt/ adj. неопубликованный

unqualified /ʌnˈkwɒlɪˌfaɪd/ adj. не имеющий квалификации

unquestionable /ʌnˈkwestʃənəbəl/ adj. несомненный

unravel /ʌnˈrævəl/ v. распутывать(ся) impf.

unreachable /ʌnˈriːtʃəbəl/ adj. недостижимый

unreal /ʌnˈrɪəl/ adj. нереальный

unreasonable /ʌnˈriːzənəbl/ adj. неразумный; неоправданный

unrecognizable /ʌnˈrekəgˌnaɪzəbəl/ adj. неузнаваемый

unrelenting /ˌʌnrɪˈlentɪŋ/ adj. неумолимый

unreliable /ˌʌnrɪˈlaɪəbəl/ adj. ненадёжный

unremarkable /ˌʌnrɪˈmɑːrkəbəl/ adj. заурядный

unrequited /ˌʌnrɪˈkwaɪtɪd/ adj. безответный

unresponsive /ˌʌnrɪˈspɒnsɪv/ adj. неотзывчивый

unrest /ʌnˈrest/ n. волнения pl.

unⸯed /ˌʌnrɪˈstreɪnd/ adj.

unⸯⸯt /ˌʌnrɪˈstrɪktɪd/ adj.

unruly /ʌnˈruːli/ adj. непокорный; непослушный

unsafe /ʌnˈseɪf/ adj. ненадёжный; опасный

unsaleable /ʌnˈseɪləbəl/ adj. неходкий

unsanitary /ʌnˈsænɪˌteri/ adj. негигиеничный; антисанитарный

unsatisfactory /ˌʌnsætɪsˈfæktəri/ adj. неудовлетворительный

unsatisfied /ʌnˈsætɪsˌfaɪd/ adj. неудовлетворённый

unscientific /ˌʌnsaɪənˈtɪfɪk/ adj. ненаучный

unscrew /ʌnˈskruː/ v. отвинчивать(ся) impf.

unscrupulous /ʌnˈskruːpjələs/ adj. бессовестный; беспринципный

unseat /ʌnˈsiːt/ v. (unhorse) сбрасывать с седла impf.; (polit.) лишать должности impf., -шить pf.

unseemly /ʌnˈsiːmli/ adj. неприличный; неподобающий

unselfish /ʌnˈselfɪʃ/ adj. бескорыстный

unserviceable /ʌnˈsɜːrvɪsəbəl/ adj. бесполезный

unsettle /ʌnˈsetl/ v. выбивать из колеи; расстраивать impf.

unsettling /ʌnˈsetlɪŋ/ adj. беспокоящий

unshaven /ʌnˈʃeɪvən/ adj. небритый

unskilled /ʌnˈskɪld/ adj. неквалифицированный

unskillful /ʌnˈskɪlfəl/ adj. неумелый

unsociable /ʌnˈsoʊʃəbəl/ adj. необщительный; нелюдимый

unsolicited /ˌʌnsəˈlɪsɪtɪd/ adj. непрошеный

unsophisticated /ˌʌnsəˈfɪstɪˌkeɪtɪd/ adj. простодушный

unspeakable /ʌnˈspiːkəbəl/ adj. невыразимый

unspecified /ʌnˈspesəˌfaɪd/ adj. неназванный

unspent /ʌnˈspent/ adj. неистраченный

unspoilt /ʌnˈspɔɪlt/ adj. неиспорченный

unstable /ʌnˈsteɪbəl/ adj. неустойчивый

unsteady /ʌnˈstedi/ adj. шаткий

unsubstantial /ˌʌnsəbˈstænʃəl/ adj. несущественный

unsuccessful /ˌʌnsək'sesfəl/ adj. безуспе́шный; неуда́чный

unsuitable /ʌn'sutəbəl/ adj. неподходя́щий

unsuited /ʌn'sutɪd/ adj. неприго́дный

unsure /ʌn'ʃʊr/ adj. неуве́ренный

unsuspecting /ˌʌnsə'spɛktɪŋ/ adj. неподозрева́ющий

unsympathetic /ˌʌnsɪmpə'θɛtɪk/ adj. несочу́вствующий

untalented /ʌn'tæləntɪd/ adj. безда́рный

untangle /ʌn'tæŋgəl/ v. распу́тывать impf.

unthinkable /ʌn'θɪŋkəbəl/ adj. немы́слимый

unthinking /ʌn'θɪŋkɪŋ/ adj. легкомы́сленный

untidy /ʌn'taɪdi/ adj. неопря́тный

untie /ʌn'taɪ/ v. развя́зывать impf., развяза́ть pf.

until /ʌn'tɪl/ 1. prep. до (+ D); **not ~** не ра́ньше (+ G) 2. conj. пока́... не

untiring /ʌn'taɪᵊrɪŋ/ adj. неутоми́мый

untold /ʌn'toʊld/ adj. несме́тный

untrained /ʌn'treɪnd/ adj. необу́ченный

untried /ʌn'traɪd/ adj. неиспы́танный

untroubled /ʌn'trʌbəld/ adj. споко́йный

untrue /ʌn'tru/ adj. неве́рный

untrustworthy /ʌn'trʌst,wɜrði/ adj. не заслу́живающий дове́рия

untruthful /ʌn'truθfəl/ adj. лжи́вый; неправди́вый

unusable /ʌn'yuzəbəl/ adj. неприго́дный

unused /ʌn'yuzd/ adj. (not used) неиспо́льзованный

unusual /ʌn'yuʒʊəl/ adj. необыкнове́нный

unveil /ʌn'veɪl/ v. раскрыва́ть impf.

unwanted /ʌn'wɑntɪd/ adj. нежела́тельный; нену́жный

unwary /ʌn'weᵊri/ adj. неосторо́жный

unwavering /ʌn'weɪvərɪŋ/ adj. непоколеби́мый

unwelcome /ʌn'wɛlkəm/ adj. неприя́тный; нежела́тельный

unwell /ʌn'wɛl/ adj. нездоро́вый

unwieldy /ʌn'wildi/ adj. неуклю́жий

unwilling /ʌn'wɪlɪŋ/ adj. неохо́тный; не жела́ющий

unwind /ʌn'waɪnd/ v. разма́тывать(ся) impf.

unwise /ʌn'waɪz/ adj. неблагоразу́мный

unworkable /ʌn'wɜrkəbəl/ adj. непракти́чный; непримени́мый

unworthy /ʌn'wɜrði/ adj. недосто́йный

unwrap /ʌn'ræp/ v. развора́чивать(ся); развёртывать(ся) impf.

unyielding /ʌn'yildɪŋ/ adj. непода́тливый

unzip /ʌn'zɪp/ v. расстёгивать мо́лнию impf.

up /ʌp/ 1. adv. (dir.) наве́рх; вверх; (loc.) наверху́ 2. prep. вверх по (+ D)

upbraid /ʌp'breɪd/ v. упрека́ть impf.

upbringing /'ʌp,brɪŋɪŋ/ n. воспита́ние

upcoming /'ʌp,kʌmɪŋ/ adj. предстоя́щий

update /ʌp'deɪt/ v. осовреме́нить pf.

upgrade /'ʌp,greɪd/ v. повыша́ть impf.

upheaval /ʌp'hivəl/ n. переворо́т

uphill /'ʌp'hɪl/ adv. в го́ру

uphold /ʌp'hoʊld/ v. подде́рживать impf., поддержа́ть pf.

upholstery /ʌp'hoʊlstəri/ n. оби́вка

upkeep /'ʌp,kip/ n. содержа́ние

uplift /'ʌp,lɪft/ n. подъём

upon /ə'pɑn/ prep. на (dir.: + A; loc.: + P)

upper /'ʌpər/ adj. ве́рхний; вы́сший

uppermost /'ʌpər,moʊst/ adj. са́мый ве́рхний; преоблада́ющий

upright /'ʌp,raɪt/ adv. верти-ка́льно; пря́мо; стоймя́

uprising /'ʌp,raɪzɪŋ/ n. восста́ние

uproar /'ʌp,rɔr/ n. шум; волне́ние

uproot /ʌp'rut/ v. вырыва́ть с ко́рнем impf.; (displace) срыва́ть с ме́ста impf.

upset /ʌp,set; v. ʌp'set/ 1. n. расстро́йство 2. v. опроки́дывать(ся) impf., опроки́нуть

(-ся) *pf.*; (*person*) расстраивать *impf.*

upside down /ˈʌpsaɪd/ *adv.* вверх дном

upstairs /ˈʌpˈsteərz/ *adv.* (*loc.*) наверху́; (*dir.*) наве́рх; вверх по ле́стнице

up-to-date /ˈʌp/ *adj.* совреме́нный

upturned /ˈʌp,tɜrnd/ *adj.* переве́рнутый; вздёрнутый

upward /ˈʌpwərd/ *adv.* вверх; (*more*) бо́льше

uranium /juˈreɪniəm/ *n.* ура́н

urban /ˈɜrbən/ *adj.* городско́й

urge /ɜrdʒ/ **1.** *n.* побужде́ние **2.** *v.* подгоня́ть *impf.*

urgency /ˈɜrdʒənsi/ *n.* сро́чность, необходи́мость

urgent /ˈɜrdʒənt/ *adj.* сро́чный; настоя́тельный; неотло́жный

urinate /ˈjʊrə,neɪt/ *v.* мочи́ться *impf.*, по- *pf.*

urine /ˈjʊrɪn/ *n.* моча́

urn /ɜrn/ *n.* у́рна

urologist /jʊˈrɒlədʒɪst/ *n.* уро́лог

us /ʌs/ *pers. pron.* нас; нам; на́ми

USA *abbr.* США

usage /ˈjusɪdʒ/ *n.* употребле́ние

use / n. yus; v. yuz/ **1.** *n.* упо-

треbléние **2.** *v.* употребля́ть *impf.*, -би́ть *pf.*; по́льзоваться (+ *I*) *impf.*; **—d** *adj.* испо́льзованный; (*secondhand*) поде́ржанный

useful /ˈjusfəl/ *adj.* поле́зный

useless /ˈjuslɪs/ *adj.* бесполе́зный

user /ˈjuzər/ *n.* потреби́тель

usher /ˈʌʃər/ *n.* билетёр, —ша

usual /ˈjuʒuəl/ *adj.* обы́чный; обыкнове́нный; **as ~** *adv.* как обы́чно

utensil /juˈtensəl/ *n.* посу́да; *pl.* у́тварь *f.*

uterus /ˈjutərəs/ *n.* ма́тка

utility /juˈtɪlɪti/ *n.* поле́зность; *pl.* (дома́шние) удо́бства *pl.*

utilize /ˈjut],aɪz/ *v.* применя́ть *impf.*, -ни́ть *pf.*

utmost /ˈʌt,moʊst/ *adj.* кра́йний; велича́йший

utter[1] /ˈʌtər/ *adj.* соверше́нный

utter[2] /ˈʌtər/ *v.* произноси́ть, издава́ть (звук) *impf.*

utterance /ˈʌtərəns/ *n.* выска́зывание

U-turn /ˈ/ *n.* разворо́т

Uzbek /ˈʊzbek/ *n.* узбе́к, узбе́чка

Uzbekistan /ʊzˈbekə,stæn/ *n.* Узбекиста́н

V

vacancy /ˈveɪkənsi/ *n.* вака́нсия

vacant /ˈveɪkənt/ *adj.* пусто́й; свобо́дный; вака́нтный

vacate /ˈveɪkeɪt/ *v.* освобожда́ть *impf.*, -боди́ть *pf.*

vacation /veɪˈkeɪʃən/ *n.* кани́кулы *pl.*; (*leave*) о́тпуск

vaccination /ˌvæksəˈneɪʃən/ *n.* приви́вка

vaccine /vækˈsin/ *n.* вакци́на

vacillate /ˈvæsə,leɪt/ *v.* колеба́ться (ме́жду + *I*) *impf.*

vacuous /ˈvækjuəs/ *adj.* пусто́й

vacuum /ˈvækyum/ *n.* ва́куум

vacuum cleaner *n.* пылесо́с

vagabond /ˈvægə,bɒnd/ *n.* бродя́га *m. & f.*

vagina /vəˈdʒaɪnə/ *n.* влага́лище

vague /veɪg/ *adj.* неопределённый; нея́сный

vain /veɪn/ *adj.* тщесла́вный; (*futile*) тще́тный; **in ~** *adv.* напра́сно; тще́тно

valedictory /ˌvælɪˈdɪktəri/ *n.* проща́льное сло́во

valerian /vəˈlɪəriən/ *n.* валерья́нка

valet /væˈleɪ/ *n.* слуга́ *m.*

valiant /ˈvælyənt/ *adj.* до́блестный

valid /ˈvælɪd/ *adj.* име́ющий си́лу; действи́тельный

validity /vəˈlɪdɪti/ *n.* действи́тельность

valley /ˈvæli/ *n.* доли́на

valor /ˈvælər/ *n.* до́блесть *f.*

valuable /ˈvælyuəbəl/ *adj.* це́нный; **—s** *n. pl.* це́нности *pl.*

value /ˈvælyu/ **1.** *n.* сто́имость; це́нность **2.** *v.* (*treasure*) цени́ть *impf.*; (*appraise*) оце́нивать *impf.*, оцени́ть *pf.*

valve /vælv/ *n.* кла́пан

vampire /ˈvæmpaɪr/ *n.* вампи́р

van /væn/ *n.* фурго́н

vandalism /ˈvænd],ɪzəm/ *n.* вандали́зм

vandalize /ˈvænd],aɪz/ *v.* бессмы́сленно разруша́ть *impf.*

vanguard /'væn,gɑrd/ n.
авангáрд

vanilla /vəˈnɪlə/ n. ванúль f.

vanish /ˈvænɪʃ/ v. исчезáть
impf., исчéзнуть pf.

vanity /ˈvænɪti/ n. тщеслáвие;
суетá

vapor /ˈveɪpər/ n. пар

vaporizer /ˈveɪpəˌraɪzər/ n. ато-
мизáтор

variable /ˈveəriəbəl/ **1.** n.
(math.) перемéнная **2.** adj.
изменчивый; (also math.) перемéнный

variant /ˈveəriənt/ n. вариáнт

variation /ˌveəriˈeɪʃən/ n. изме-
нéние; (also mus.) вариáция

varied /ˈveərid/ adj. рáзный

variety /vəˈraɪti/ n. разнообрáзие

various /ˈveəriəs/ adj. рáзный

varnish /ˈvɑrnɪʃ/ **1.** n. лак **2.** v.
лакировáть impf., от- pf.

vary /ˈveəri/ v. менять(ся); из-
менять(ся), -нúть(ся) pf.;
—ing adj. перемéнный

vase /veɪz, vɑz/ n. вáза

vast /væst/ adj. обшúрный;
огрóмный

vat /væt/ n. чан; бак

vaudeville /ˈvɔdvɪl/ n. водевúль
m.

vault /vɔlt/ n. свод; подвáл;
(burial) склеп; —ed adj.
свóдчатый

VDU n. дисплéй

veal /vil/ **1.** n. теля́тина **2.** adj.
теля́чий

veer /vɪər/ v. менять направ-
лéние impf.; повернýть pf.

vegetable /ˈvedʒtəbəl/ **1.** n.
óвощ **2.** adj. овощнóй;
растúтельный; ~ **garden** n.
огорóд

vegetarian /ˌvedʒɪˈteəriən/ n.
вегетариáнец, -áнка

vegetate /ˈvedʒɪˌteɪt/ v. (be passive) прозябáть impf.

vegetation /ˌvedʒɪˈteɪʃən/ n.
растúтельность

vehemence /ˈviəməns/ n. сúла;
стрáстность

vehement /ˈviəmənt/ adj.
нейстовый

vehicle /ˈviːkəl/ n. (motor vehicle) машúна; перевóзочное
срéдство; Fig. провóдник

veil /veɪl/ **1.** n. вуáль f. **2.** v.
скрывáть impf., скрыть pf.

vein /veɪn/ n. вéна; жúла; жúлка

Velcro /ˈvelkrou/ n. липýчка

velocity /vəˈlɒsɪti/ n. скóрость

velvet /ˈvelvɪt/ **1.** n. бáрхат **2.**
adj. бáрхатный

vending machine n. (торгóвый)
автомáт

vendor /ˈvendər/ n. продавéц;
торгóвец

veneer /vəˈnɪər/ n. фанéра

venerable /ˈvenərəbəl/ adj.
почтéнный; (ancient) дрéвний

venerate /ˈvenəˌreɪt/ благогó-
вéть impf.

venereal disease /vəˈnɪəriəl/ n.
венерúческое заболевáние

venetian blind n. жалюзú neut.
indecl.

vengeance /ˈvendʒəns/ n. месть
f.

vengeful /ˈvendʒfəl/ adj.
мстúтельный

venom /ˈvenəm/ n. яд; Fig.
злóба

vent /vent/ n. отвéрстие; вы́ход

ventilate /ˈventlˌeɪt/ v. провéт-
ривать impf., провéтрить pf.

ventilation /ˌventlˈeɪʃən/ n.
провéтривание

ventilator /ˈventlˌeɪtər/ n. венти-
ля́тор

ventriloquist /venˈtrɪləkwɪst/ n.
чревовещáтель

venture /ˈventʃər/ n.
(рискóванное) предприя́тие

Venus /ˈvinəs/ n. Венéра

veracity /vəˈræsɪti/ n. достовéр-
ность

veranda /vəˈrændə/ n. верáнда

verb /vɜrb/ n. глагóл; —al
adj. ýстный

verbatim /vərˈbeɪtɪm/ adj.
дословный

verbose /vərˈbous/ adj. много-
слóвный

verdant /ˈvɜrdnt/ adj. зелёный

verdict /ˈvɜrdɪkt/ n. приговóр

verge /vɜrdʒ/ n. край

verification /ˌverɪfɪˈkeɪʃən/ n.
провéрка; верификáция

verify /ˈverɪˌfaɪ/ v. проверя́ть
impf., провéрить pf.

verisimilitude /ˌverɪsɪˈmɪlɪˌtud/ n.
правдоподóбие

vermin /ˈvɜrmɪn/ n. паразúты pl.

vermouth /vərˈmuθ/ n. вéрмут

vernacular /vərˈnækyələr/ n.
гóвор; нарéчие; (popular speech)
просторéчие

versatile /'vɜrsətl/ *adj.* многосторонний

verse /vɜrs/ *n.* (*stanza*) строфа́; (*line of poetry*) стих; (*poetry*) стихи́ *pl.;* —**d** *adj.* све́дущий (в + P)

version /'vɜrʒən/ *n.* ве́рсия; вариа́нт

versus /'vɜrsəs/ *prep.* про́тив (+ G)

vertical /'vɜrtɪkəl/ *adj.* вертика́льный

vertigo /'vɜrtɪ,gou/ *n.* головокруже́ние

very /'veri/ **1.** *adj.* тот са́мый **2.** *adv.* о́чень

vespers /'vespərz/ *n.* Вече́рня

vessel /'vesəl/ *n.* (*also anat.*) сосу́д; (*ship*) су́дно

vest /vest/ *n.* жиле́т

vestibule /'vestə,byul/ *n.* пере́дняя; вестибю́ль *m.*

vestige /'vestɪdʒ/ *n.* след

veteran /'vetərən/ *n.* ветера́н

veterinarian /,vetərə'neəriən/ *n.* ветерина́р

veto /'vitou/ **1.** *n.* ве́то *neut. indecl.* **2.** *v.* налага́ть ве́то (на + A) *impf.*

vex /veks/ *v.* раздража́ть *impf.*, -жи́ть *pf.*

vexation /vek'seiʃən/ *n.* доса́да

via /'vaɪə, 'viə/ *prep.* че́рез (+ A)

viable /'vaɪəbəl/ *adj.* жизнеспосо́бный

vial /'vaɪəl/ *n.* пузырёк

vibrant /'vaɪbrənt/ *adj.* живо́й

vibrate /'vaɪbreit/ *v.* вибри́ровать *impf.*

vibration /vai'breiʃən/ *n.* вибра́ция

vice /vais/ *n.* поро́к

vice president *n.* ви́це-президе́нт

vice versa /'vais vɜrsə/ *adv.* наоборо́т

vicinity /vɪ'sɪnɪti/ *n.* окре́стности *pl.*

vicious /'vɪʃəs/ *adj.* поро́чный; злой; —**ness** *n.* жесто́кость

victim /'vɪktɪm/ *n.* же́ртва

victimize /'vɪktə,maiz/ *v.* пресле́довать *impf.*

victor /'vɪktər/ *n.* победи́тель

victorious /vɪk'tɔriəs/ *adj.* победоно́сный

victory /'vɪktəri/ *n.* побе́да

video /'vɪdi,ou/ *n.* ви́део *neut. indecl.*

video game *n.* игра́-аттракцио́н

videotape /'vɪdiou,teip/ *n.* видеоокассе́та; ~ **recorder** видеомагнитофо́н

vie /vai/ *v.* сопе́рничать (с + I) *impf.*

Vienna /vi'enə/ *n.* Ве́на

Vietnam /vi,et'nam/ *n.* Вьетна́м

view /vyu/ **1.** *n.* вид; (*opinion*) взгляд; **in ~ of** вви́ду (+ G) **2.** *v.* осма́тривать; рассма́тривать *impf.*

viewpoint /'vyu,pɔint/ *n.* то́чка зре́ния

vigilant /'vɪdʒələnt/ *adj.* бди́тельный

vigor /'vɪgər/ *n.* эне́ргия; си́ла; —**ous** *adj.* энерги́чный; си́льный

vile /vail/ *adj.* по́длый

vilify /'vɪlə,fai/ *v.* клевета́ть *impf.*

villa /'vɪlə/ *n.* ви́лла

village /'vɪlɪdʒ/ *n.* дере́вня; село́; —**r** *n.* дереве́нский жи́тель

villain /'vɪlən/ *n.* негодя́й; злоде́й

vindicate /'vɪndɪ,keit/ *v.* опра́вдывать *impf.*, оправда́ть *pf.*

vindication /,vɪndɪ'keiʃən/ *n.* оправда́ние

vindictive /vɪn'dɪktɪv/ *adj.* мсти́тельный

vine /vain/ *n.* виногра́дная лоза́

vinegar /'vɪnɪgər/ *n.* у́ксус

vineyard /'vɪnyərd/ *n.* виногра́дник

vintage /'vɪntɪdʒ/ *n.* урожа́й (виногра́да)

viola[1] /vi'oulə/ *n.* (*bot.*) фиа́лка

viola[2] /vi'oulə/ *n.* (*mus.*) альт

violate /'vaiə,leit/ *v.* наруша́ть *impf.*, нару́шить *pf.*

violation /,vaiə'leiʃən/ *n.* наруше́ние

violence /'vaiələns/ *n.* наси́лие; нейство́

violent /'vaiələnt/ *adj.* нейстовый; наси́льственный

violet /'vaiəlit/ *n.* **1.** (*bot.*) фиа́лка **2.** *adj.* фиоле́товый

violin /,vaiə'lin/ *n.* скри́пка; —**ist** *n.* скрипа́ч, —ка

violoncello /,vaiələn'tʃelou/ *n.* виолонче́ль *f.*

viper /'vaipər/ *n.* гадю́ка; змея́

virgin /'vɜrdʒin/ *n.* **1.** де́вственник, -ница **2.** *adj.* де́вственный

virile /'vɪrəl/ *adj.* возмужа́лый; му́жественный

virtual /'vɜrtʃuəl/ *adj.* действи́тельный; факти́ческий

virtue /'vɜrtʃu/ *n.* доброде́тель *f.*

virtuosity /ˌvɜrtʃu'ɒsɪti/ *n.* виртуо́зность

virtuous /'vɜrtʃuəs/ *adj.* доброде́тельный

virus /'vaɪrəs/ *n.* ви́рус

visa /'vizə/ *n.* ви́за

viscose /'vɪskous/ *n.* виско́за

viscous /'vɪskəs/ *adj.* вя́зкий

vise /vais/ *n.* тиски́ *pl.*

visibility /ˌvɪzə'bɪliti/ *n.* ви́димость

visible /'vɪzəbəl/ *adj.* ви́димый; я́вный

vision /'vɪʒən/ *n.* зре́ние; (*insight*) проница́тельность

visit /'vɪzɪt/ **1.** *n.* посеще́ние; визи́т **2.** *v.* посеща́ть *impf.*, -ти́ть *pf.*; **—or** *n.* посети́тель, —ница *f.*; (*guest*) гость *m.*

visor /'vaɪzər/ *n.* козырёк

visual /'vɪʒuəl/ *adj.* зри́тельный; нагля́дный

visualize /'vɪʒuˌlaɪz/ *v.* вообража́ть *impf.*, -зи́ть *pf.*

vital /'vaɪtl/ *adj.* жи́зненный

vitality /vaɪ'tælɪti/ *n.* жи́зненность

vitamin /'vaɪtəmɪn/ *n.* витами́н

vivacious /vɪ'veɪʃəs/ *adj.* оживлённый; живо́й

vivacity /vɪ'væsɪti/ *n.* оживлённость

vivid /'vɪvɪd/ *adj.* я́ркий; живо́й; пы́лкий; **—ness** *n.* жи́вость; я́ркость

vocabulary /vou'kæbjəˌleri/ *n.* запа́с слов; слова́рь *m.*

vocal /'voukəl/ *adj.* голосово́й; вока́льный; **~ cords** *n.* голосовы́е свя́зки *pl.*

vocalist /'voukəlɪst/ *n.* певе́ц, певи́ца

vocation /vou'keɪʃən/ *n.* призва́ние; профе́ссия; **—al** *adj.* профессиона́льный

vogue /voug/ *n.* мо́да

voice /vɔɪs/ **1.** *n.* го́лос; (*gram.*) зало́г **2.** *v.* выража́ть *impf.*,

výrazit *pf.*; **—less** *adj.* безмо́лвный; (*ling.*) глухо́й

void /vɔɪd/ **1.** *adj.* недействи́тельный; (*empty*) пусто́й **2.** *n.* пустота́; **~ of** лишённый (*+ G*)

volatile /'vɒlətl/ *adj.* неусто́йчивый

volcano /vɒl'keɪnou/ *n.* вулка́н

volition /vou'lɪʃən/ *n.* во́ля

volley /'vɒli/ *v.* (*sports*) ударя́ть с лёта *impf.*

volleyball /'vɒliˌbɒl/ *n.* волейбо́л

volt /voult/ *n.* вольт

voltage /'voultɪdʒ/ *n.* напряже́ние

volume /'vɒlyum/ *n.* объём; ёмкость; (*book*) том; (*sound*) гро́мкость

voluminous /və'lumənəs/ *adj.* многото́мный; объёмистый

voluntary /'vɒlənˌteri/ *adj.* доброво́льный

volunteer /ˌvɒlən'tɪər/ **1.** *n.* доброво́лец **2.** *v.* вызыва́ться *pf.*

voluptuous /və'lʌptʃuəs/ *adj.* сластолюби́вый; чу́вственный

vomit /'vɒmɪt/ **1.** *n.* рво́та **2.** *v.* рвать *impers.* (*+ I*) *impf.*, вы́- *pf.*

voracious /vɔ'reɪʃəs/ *adj.* жа́дный; ненасы́тный

vortex /'vɔrteks/ *n.* вихрь *m.*; водоворо́т

vote /vout/ **1.** *n.* (*act*) голосова́ние; (*opinion*) го́лос **2.** *v.* голосова́ть *impf.*, про- *pf.*; **—r** *n.* избира́тель

vouch /vautʃ/ *v.*: **~ for** руча́ться (за *+ A*) *impf.*; **—er** *n.* тало́н; ва́учер

vow /vau/ **1.** *n.* кля́тва **2.** *v.* кля́сться (в *+ P*) *impf.*

vowel /'vauəl/ *n.* гла́сный (звук)

voyage /'vɔɪdʒ/ *n.* (*by sea*) пла́вание; путеше́ствие

vulgar /'vʌlgər/ *adj.* гру́бый; вульга́рный

vulgarity /vʌl'gærɪti/ *n.* вульга́рность

vulnerable /'vʌlnərəbəl/ *adj.* уязви́мый; рани́мый

vulture /'vʌltʃər/ *n.* гриф

WXYZ

wad /wɒd/ n. комо́к; па́чка

wade /weid/ v. (river) перехо́дить вброд impf., перейти́ pf.

wafer /weifər/ n. ва́фля; (eccles.) обла́тка

waffle¹ /wɒfəl/ n. ва́фля

waffle² /wɒfəl/ v. увили́вать от прямо́го отве́та impf.

wag /wæg/ v. маха́ть impf., махну́ть pf.

wage /weidʒ/ **1.** n. usu. pl. зарабо́тная пла́та **2.** v.: ~ **war** вести́ войну́ impf.

wager /weidʒər/ **1.** n. пари́ neut. indecl. **2.** v. держа́ть пари́ impf.

wagon /wægən/ n. коля́ска; теле́жка; пово́зка

wail /weil/ **1.** n. вопль m. **2.** v. вопи́ть impf.

waist /weist/ n. та́лия

waistcoat /weskət/ n. жиле́т

waistline /weist,lain/ n. та́лия

wait /weit/ **1.** n. ожида́ние **2.** v. ждать impf., подо- pf.; ~ **on** обслу́живать impf.; **—er** n. официа́нт

waiting /weitɪŋ/ n. ожида́ние; ~ **list** о́чередь f.; ~ **room** зал ожида́ния

waitress /weitris/ n. официа́нтка

waive /weiv/ v. отка́зываться (от + G) impf.; **—r** n. докуме́нт об отка́зе

wake /weik/ v.t. буди́ть impf., раз- pf.; v.i. просыпа́ться impf., проснуться pf.; **—ful** adj. бди́тельный

walk /wɔk/ **1.** n. прогу́лка; ходьба́ **2.** v. ходи́ть indet., идти́ det.; **—er** n. ходо́к; **—ing** n. ходьба́

walkie-talkie /wɔki 'tɔki/ n. ра́ция

walkout /wɔk,aut/ n. забасто́вка

wall /wɔl/ n. стена́

wallet /wɒlit/ n. бума́жник

wallow /wɒlou/ v. валя́ться impf.

wallpaper /wɔl,peipər/ n. обо́и pl.

walnut /wɔl,nʌt/ n. гре́цкий оре́х

walrus /wɔlrəs/ n. морж

waltz /wɔlts/ n. вальс

wander /wɒndər/ v. броди́ть; блужда́ть impf.

wane /wein/ v. убыва́ть impf.

want /wɒnt/ **1.** n. (need) потре́бность; (lack) недоста́ток **2.** v. хоте́ть impf.; **—ed** adj. ну́жный; необходи́мый; **—ing** adj.: be ~ недостава́ть (impers. + G)

war /wɔr/ **1.** n. война́ **2.** adj. вое́нный

warbler /wɔrblər/ n. сла́вка

ward /wɔrd/ n. (hospital) пала́та; (prison) ка́мера; (child) подопе́чный

warden /wɔrdn/ n. нача́льник тюрьмы́; смотри́тель

wardrobe /wɔrdroub/ n. гардеро́б

ware /wɛər/ n. usu. pl. изде́лия pl.; това́р

warehouse /wɛər,haus/ n. склад

warfare /wɔr,fɛər/ n. война́

warm /wɔrm/ **1.** adj. тёплый; серде́чный **2.** v. греть(ся); согрева́ть(ся) impf., согре́ть(ся) pf.

warmth /wɔrmθ/ n. теплота́; тепло́; Fig. серде́чность

warn /wɔrn/ v. предостерега́ть impf., предостере́чь pf.; **—ing** n. предупрежде́ние

warp /wɔrp/ v. коро́бить(ся) impf., по- pf.

warrant /wɔrənt/ **1.** n. о́рдер **2.** v. опра́вдывать impf.

warranty /wɔrənti/ n. гара́нтия

warrior /wɔriər/ n. во́ин

wart /wɔrt/ n. борода́вка

wary /wɛəri/ adj. осмотри́тельный

wash /wɒʃ/ **1.** v. мыть(ся); умыва́ть(ся); (clothes) стира́ть impf. **2.** n. сти́рка; **—ing ma-chine** стира́льная маши́на

washbowl /wɒʃ,boul/, **washba-sin** /-,beisin/ n. умыва́льник

washer /wɒʃər/ n. (mech.) прокла́дка

wasp /wɒsp/ n. оса́

waste /weist/ **1.** n. (рас)тра́та; отбро́сы pl. **2.** v. тра́тить impf., по-, ис- pf.; (time) теря́ть impf., по- pf.; **—ful** adj. неэконо́мный

wastebasket /weist,bæskit/ n. корзи́на для бума́г

wasteland /'weist,lænd/ n. пустыня

wastepaper /'weist,peipər/ n. макулатура

watch /wɒtʃ/ 1. n. стража; дозор; (timepiece) часы pl. 2. v. смотреть; наблюдать; следить impf.; **~ out** остерегаться impf.

watchband /'wɒtʃ,bænd/ n. ремешок для часов

watchdog /'wɒtʃ,dɒg/ n. сторожевая собака

watchful /'wɒtʃfəl/ adj. бдительный

watchmaker /'wɒtʃ,meikər/ n. часовщик

watchman /'wɒtʃmən/ n. сторож

water /'wɔtər/ 1. n. вода 2. adj. водяной; водный 3. v. (flowers, etc.) поливать impf., полить pf.

watercolor /'wɔtər,kʌlər/ 1. n. акварель f. 2. adj. акварельный

waterfall /'wɔtər,fɔl/ n. водопад

water main n. водопроводная магистраль f.

watermelon /'wɔtər,melən/ n. арбуз

water pipe n. водопроводная труба

waterproof /'wɔtər,pruf/ adj. непромокаемый; водонепроницаемый

watershed /'wɔtər,ʃed/ n. водораздел; Fig. перелом

water-skiing n. воднолыжный спорт

water-soluble adj. водорастворимый

waterworks /'wɔtər,wɜrks/ n. водопроводная станция

watery /'wɔtəri/ adj. водяной

watt /wɒt/ n. ватт

wave /weiv/ 1. n. волна; (in hair) завивка 2. v.t. (hand, etc.) махать impf.; (hair) завивать; (flag, etc.) размахивать impf.; v.i. развеваться impf.

waver /'weivər/ v. колыхаться impf.

wax /wæks/ 1. n. воск; (ear) сера 2. n. восковой

wax paper n. вощёная бумага

way /wei/ n. путь m.; дорога; **by the ~** между прочим; **on the ~** по дороге, по пути

wayside /'wei,said/ n. обочина

wayward /'weiwərd/ adj. своенравный

we /wi/ pron. мы

weak /wik/ adj. слабый; **—ly** adv. хилый

weaken /'wikən/ v.t. ослаблять impf., ослабить pf.; v.i. слабеть impf., о- pf.

weakness /'wiknɪs/ n. слабость

wealth /welθ/ n. богатство

wealthy /'welθi/ adj. богатый

weapon /'wepən/ n. оружие; **—ry** n. вооружение

wear /wer/ 1. n. ношение; износ 2. v. носить(ся) impf.; **~ out** изнашивать(ся) impf., износить(ся) pf.; **~ and tear** износ

weariness /'wiərinɪs/ n. усталость

wearing /'weəriŋ/, **wearisome** /'wiərisəm/ adj. утомительный

weary /'wiəri/ adj. уставший, утомлённый

weasel /'wizəl/ n. ласка

weather /'weðər/ n. погода

weathercock /'weðər,kɒk/, **weather vane** n. флюгер

weatherman /'weðər,mæn/ n. синоптик

weave /wiv/ v. ткать impf., со- pf.; —r n. ткач, -иха

web /web/ n. (spider) паутина; Fig. сплетение

Web site n. станция Web; узел Web; сайт

wedding /'wedɪŋ/ 1. n. свадьба 2. adj. свадебный

wedge /wedʒ/ 1. n. клин 2. v. заклинивать(ся) impf.

wedlock /'wed,lɒk/ n. брак

Wednesday /'wenzdei/ n. среда

weed /wid/ 1. n. сорняк 2. v. полоть impf., вы- pf.

week /wik/ n. неделя

weekday /'wik,dei/ n. будний день m.

weekend /'wik,end/ n. выходные дни pl.

weekly /'wikli/ 1. adj. еженедельный 2. n. еженедельник

weep /wip/ v. плакать impf.

weigh /wei/ v.t. взвешивать impf., взвесить pf.; v.i. весить impf.

weight /weit/ n. вес; (sports) штанга; **—less** adj. невесомый; **—y** adj. веский

weightlifter /'weit,lɪftər/ n. штангист

weir /wiər/ n. плотина; запруда

weird /wiərd/ adj. странный

welcome /'welkəm/ 1. adj. желанный 2. n. приём;

приветствие 3. *v.* приветствовать *impf.* 4. *interj.* Добро пожаловать!; you're ~! пожалуйста!

weld /weld/ *v.* сваривать *impf.;* —er *n.* сварщик; —ing *n.* сварка

welfare /ˈwelˌfeər/ *n.* благосостояние

well[1] /wel/ 1. *adj.* хороший; здоровый 2. *adv.* хорошо; ~ done! молодец!

well[2] /wel/ *n.* колодец; родник

well-aimed *adj.* меткий

well-balanced *adj.* уравновешенный

well-behaved *adj.* воспитанный

well-being *n.* благополучие

well-bred /ˈwelˈbred/ *adj.* воспитанный; культурный

well-disposed *adj.* благожелательный

well-fed /ˈwelˈfed/ *adj.* откормленный

well-informed *adj.* сведущий

well-known *adj.* известный

well-meaning *adj.* благонамеренный

well-off *adj.* состоятельный; зажиточный

well-paid /ˈwelˈpeid/ *adj.* хорошо оплачиваемый

well-read /ˈwelˈred/ *adj.* начитанный

well-timed *adj.* своевременный

well-to-do *adj.* зажиточный

welt /welt/ *n.* рубец

wen /wen/ *n.* жировик

wend /wend/ *v.:* ~ one's way направлять путь *impf.*

werewolf /ˈweərˌwulf/ *n.* оборотень *m.*

west /west/ 1. *n.* запад 2. *adj.* западный 3. *adv.* к западу; на запад

western /ˈwestərn/ *adj.* западный

westward /ˈwestwərd/ 1. *adj.* направленный к западу 2. *adv.* на запад

wet /wet/ 1. *adj.* мокрый 2. *v.* мочить; смачивать *impf.,* смочить *pf.;* get ~ промокать *impf.,* промокнуть *pf.*

wetness /ˈwetnis/ *n.* влажность

whack /wæk/ *n.* звонкий удар

whale /weil/ 1. *n.* кит 2. *adj.* китовый

wharf /wɔrf/ *n.* пристань *f.*

what /wʌt/ *pron.* какой; что; ~ is the matter? в чём дело?

whatever /wʌtˈevər/ 1. *adj.* любой; какой бы ни 2. *pron.* всё что; что бы ни

wheat /wit/ 1. *n.* пшеница 2. *adj.* пшеничный

wheel /wil/ *n.* колесо; колёсико; (steering wheel) руль *m.*

wheelbarrow /ˈwil,bærou/ *n.* тачка

wheelchair /ˈwil,tʃeər/ *n.* инвалидная коляска

wheeze /wiz/ *n.* хрип

wheezy /ˈwizi/ *adj.* хриплый

whelp /welp/ *n.* щенок

when /wen/ *adv.,* *conj.* когда

whenever /wenˈevər/ *conj.* когда; всякий раз когда

where /weər/ *adv.,* *conj.* (dir.) куда; (loc.) где; (from where) откуда; (to where) туда; куда

whereabouts /ˈweərə,bauts/ *pl.* местонахождение

whereas /weərˈæz/ *conj.* тогда как; поскольку

wherever /weərˈevər/ *adv.* куда бы ни; где бы ни

wherewithal /ˈweərwið,ɔl/ *n.* средства *pl.*

whet /wet/ *v.* точить *impf.*

whether /ˈweðər/ *conj.* ли

whey /wei/ *n.* сыворотка

which /witʃ/ *pron.,* *adj.* который; какой; кто

whichever /witʃˈevər/ *pron.,* *adj.* какой; какой бы ни; любой

whiff /wif/ *n.* дуновение

while /wail/ 1. *conj.* пока; в то время как; (although) хотя 2. *n.* некоторое время *neut.;* a long ~ долго; a short ~ недолго; for a ~ на время; once in a ~ время от времени

whim /wim/ *n.* каприз; прихоть *f.*

whimper /ˈwimpər/ *v.* хныкать *impf.*

whimsical /ˈwimzikəl/ *adj.* затейливый

whine /wain/ *n.* скулёж

whip /wip/ 1. *n.* кнут; хлыст 2. *v.* хлестать *impf.;* (food) сбивать *impf.,* сбить *pf.;* —ping *n.* порка

whirl /wɜrl/ *v.* кружить(ся) *impf.*

whirlpool /ˈwɜrl,pul/ *n.* водоворот

whirlwind /ˈwɜrl,wind/ *n.* вихрь *m.*

whisk /wisk/ *v.t.* помáхивать; сбивáть *impf.*

whisker /'wiskər/ *n. usu. pl.* бакенбáрд; (*of animal*) усы *pl.*

whiskey /'wiski/ *n.* вúски *neut. indecl.*

whisper /'wispər/ **1.** *n.* шёпот; **in a ~** *adv.* шёпотом **2.** *v.* шептáть *impf.*, шепнýть *pf.*

whistle /'wisl/ **1.** *n.* свист; (*instrument*) свистóк **2.** *v.* свистéть *impf.*, свúстнуть *pf.*

whistling /'wisliŋ/ *n.* свист

white /wait/ **1.** *adj.* бéлый **2.** *n.* бéлый цвет; (*of egg*) белóк

white-collar *adj.* *n.* слýжащий

white-haired *adj.* седóй

whiten /'waitn/ *v.t.* белúть *impf.*, по- *pf.*; *v.i.* белéть *impf.*, по- *pf.*

whiteness /'waitnis/ *n.* белизнá

whitewashing /'wait,wɒʃiŋ/ *n.* побéлка

whittle /'witl/ *v.* обстрýгивать *impf.*; **~ down** уменьшáть *impf.*

whiz /wiz/ *n.* свист

who /hu/ *pron.* кто; котóрый

whodunit /hu'dʌnit/ *n. Colloq.* детектúв

whoever /hu'evər/ *pron.* кто бы ни

whole /houl/ **1.** *adj.* цéлый; весь **2.** *n.* цéлое; итóг

wholehearted /'houl'hɑrtid/ *adj.* úскренний; **—ly** *adv.* от всегó сéрдца

wholesale /'houl,seil/ **1.** *n.* оптóвая торгóвля **2.** *adj.* оптóвый **3.** *adj.* óптом; **—r** *n.* оптóвый торгóвец; оптовúк

wholesome /'houlsəm/ *adj.* здорóвый; благотвóрный

wholly /'houli/ *adv.* пóлностью; целикóм

whom /hum/ *pron.* когó; котóрого

whooping cough /'hupiŋ/ *n.* кóклюш

whopper /'wɒpər/ *n. Colloq.* громáдина

whopping /'wɒpiŋ/ *adj. Colloq.* здоровéнный

whore /hɔr/ *n.* проститýтка

whose /huz/ *pron.* чей, чья, чьё, *pl.* чьи

why /wai/ *adv.* почемý

wick /wik/ *n.* фитúль *m.*

wicked /'wikid/ *adj.* злой; пóдлый; **—ness** *n.* злóбность; злой постýпок

wicker /'wikər/ *adj.* плетёный

wicket /'wikit/ *n.* калúтка

wide /waid/ *adj.* ширóкий

wide-awake /'waid/ *adj.* бóдрствующий

widen /'waidn/ *v.* расширять(ся) *impf.*, расшúрить(ся) *pf.*

widespread /'waid'spred/ *adj.* ширóко распространённый

widow /'widou/ *n.* вдовá

widowed /'widoud/ *adj.* вдóвый

widower /'widouər/ *n.* вдовéц

width /widθ/ *n.* ширинá; широтá

wield /wild/ *v.* владéть (+ *I*) *impf.*

wiener /'winər/ *n.* сосúска

wife /waif/ *n.* женá

wig /wig/ *n.* парúк

wiggle /'wigəl/ *v.* шевелúть(ся) *impf.*; (*wag*) вилять (+ *I*) *impf.*

wiggly /'wigli/ *adj.* волнúстый

wild /waild/ *adj.* дúкий; бéшеный

wilderness /'wildərnis/ *n.* дúкая мéстность

wildfire /'waild,faiᵊr/ *n.* леснóй пожáр

wildflower /'waild,flauər/ *n.* полевóй цветóк

wildlife /'waild,laif/ *n.* живáя прирóда

wile /wail/ *n.* хúтрость

will /wil/ **1.** *n.* вóля; сúла вóли; (*law*) завещáние **2.** *v.* заставлять *impf.*, застáвить *pf.*; (*law*) завещáть *impf. & pf.*; **—ful** *adj.* предумы́шленный

willing /'wiliŋ/ *adj.* готóвый; **—ly** *adv.* охóтно; добровóльно; **—ness** *n.* готóвность

willow /'wilou/ *n.* úва

willy-nilly /'wili'nili/ *adv.* волей-нево́лей

wilt /wilt/ *v.* вянуть *impf.*, за- *pf.*

wily /'waili/ *adj.* хúтрый

wimp /wimp/ *n. Fig.* тряпка *m. & f.*

win /win/ *v.* выúгрывать *impf.*, вы́играть *pf.*

wince /wins/ *n.* вздрáгивание

wind¹ /wind/ *n.* вéтер

wind² /waind/ *v.t.* мотáть *impf.*; (*watch*) заводúть *impf.*, завестú *pf.*; *v.i.* вúться *impf.*, извúваться *impf.*

windbag /'wind,bæg/ *n.* болтýн

windbreaker /'wind,breikər/ *n.* анорáк; штормóвка

winded /'wɪndɪd/ adj. запыха́вшийся

winding /'waɪndɪŋ/ adj. изви́листый; (twisted) вито́й

wind instrument /wɪnd/ n. духово́й инструме́нт

windmill /'wɪnd,mɪl/ n. ветряна́я ме́льница

window /'wɪndou/ 1. n. окно́; (shop) витри́на 2. adj. око́нный; ~ ledge, ~ sill n. подоко́нник

windowpane /'wɪndou,peɪn/ n. око́нное стекло́

windpipe /'wɪnd,paɪp/ n. дыха́тельное го́рло; трахе́я

windshield /'wɪnd,ʃild/ n. лобово́е стекло́; ~ wiper дво́рник

windy /'wɪndɪ/ adj. ве́треный

wine /waɪn/ 1. n. вино́ 2. adj. ви́нный; ~ list n. ка́рта вин

wineglass /'waɪn,glæs/ n. бока́л; фуже́р

winery /'waɪnərɪ/ n. ви́нный заво́д

wing /wɪŋ/ n. крыло́; (theat.) кули́са; —ed adj. крыла́тый

wink /wɪŋk/ 1. n. морга́ние; мига́ние 2. v. моргну́ть impf., моргну́ть pf.

winner /'wɪnər/ n. победи́тель, —ница

winning /'wɪnɪŋ/ n. вы́игрыш

winter /'wɪntər/ 1. n. зима́; in the ~ adv. зимо́й 2. adj. зи́мний

wintry /'wɪntrɪ/ adj. зи́мний

wipe /waɪp/ v. вы́тирать impf., вы́тереть pf.; ~ out стира́ть impf., стере́ть pf.

wire /waɪər/ 1. n. про́волока; про́вод 2. adj. про́волочный 3. v. протя́гивать провода́ impf.; —less adj. беспро́волочный

wiretap /'waɪər,tæp/ n. (phone) подслу́шивание телефо́нных разгово́ров

wiring /'waɪərɪŋ/ n. электропрово́дка

wiry /'waɪərɪ/ adj. жи́листый

wisdom /'wɪzdəm/ n. му́дрость

wise /waɪz/ adj. му́дрый; ~ guy n. Colloq. всезна́йка m. & f.

wisecrack /'waɪz,kræk/ 1. n. остро́та 2. v. остри́ть impf.

wish /wɪʃ/ 1. n. (по)жела́ние 2. v. хоте́ть; жела́ть impf., по- pf.

wishy-washy /'wɪʃɪ,wɒʃɪ/ adj. бесхара́ктерный

wistful /'wɪstfəl/ adj. заду́мчивый

wit /wɪt/ n.pl. остроу́мие; ум

witch /wɪtʃ/ n. ве́дьма

witchcraft /'wɪtʃ,kræft/ n. колдовство́

with /wɪθ/ prep. с, со (+ I)

withdraw /wɪθ'drɔ/ v.t. отдёргивать impf., отдёрнуть pf.; v.i. удаля́ться impf., -ли́ться pf.; (from bank) брать impf., взять pf.

withdrawal /wɪθ'drɔəl/ n. (mil.) вы́вод; отхо́д; (bank) сня́тие

withdrawn /wɪθ'drɔn/ adj. за́мкнутый

wither /'wɪðər/ v. со́хнуть impf.

withers /'wɪðərz/ n. хо́лка

withhold /wɪθ'hould/ v. уде́рживать impf., удержа́ть pf.

within /wɪð'ɪn/ 1. adv. внутри́ 2. prep. в (+ P), в преде́лах; внутри́ (+ G)

without /wɪð'aut/ 1. adv. вне; снару́жи 2. prep. без(о) (+ G)

withstand /wɪθ'stænd/ v. выде́рживать; противостоя́ть (+ D) impf.

witness /'wɪtnɪs/ 1. n. свиде́тель, —ница 2. v. быть свиде́телем

witticism /'wɪtə,sɪzəm/ n. остро́та

witty /'wɪtɪ/ adj. остроу́мный

wizard /'wɪzərd/ n. чароде́й

wizened /'wɪzənd/ adj. высо́хший

wobbly /'wɒblɪ/ adj. ша́ткий

woe /wou/ n. го́ре; —ful adj. го́рестный

wolf /wulf/ n. волк

wolfhound /'wulf,haund/ n. волкода́в

woman /'wumən/ 1. n. же́нщина 2. adj. же́нский; —ly adj. же́нственный

womb /wum/ n. ма́тка

wonder /'wʌndər/ 1. n. чу́до; удивле́ние; изумле́ние; no ~ adv. неудиви́тельно 2. v. удивля́ться (+ D) impf., -ви́ться pf.; —ful adj. замеча́тельный

woo /wu/ v. уха́живать (за + I) impf.

wood /wud/ n. лес; (material) де́рево; (for fire) дрова́ pl.; —ed adj. леси́стый; —en adj. деревя́нный; ~ engraving n. ксилогра́фия

woodcut /'wud,kʌt/ n. гравю́ра на де́реве

woodpecker /'wʊd,pɛkər/ n. дятел

woodwork /'wʊd,wɜrk/ n. деревянное строение

woody /'wʊdɪ/ adj. лесистый

wool /wʊl/ n. шерсть f.; **—en** adj. шерстяной

woolgather /'wʊl,gæðər/ v. погружаться в размышления impf.

woolly /'wʊlɪ/ adj. шерстистый; мохнатый

word /wɜrd/ **1.** n. слово; ~ **for** ~ слово в слово; **in a** ~ одним словом **2.** v. выражать словами impf.; **—ing** n. выбор слов; **—less** adj. молчаливый; **—y** adj. многословный

word processing n. текстообработка

word processor n. процессор (для обработки текстов)

work /wɜrk/ **1.** n. работа; (creation) произведение; сочинение; (toil) труд **2.** v. работать impf.

workable /'wɜrkəbəl/ adj. осуществимый; применимый

workbench /'wɜrk,bentʃ/ n. верстак

workday /'wɜrk,deɪ/ n. будний день; рабочий день m.

worker /'wɜrkər/ n. работник; рабочий

work force n. рабочая сила

working /'wɜrkɪŋ/ adj. рабочий

workload /'wɜrk,loʊd/ n. нагрузка

workman /'wɜrkmən/ n. работник

workmanship /'wɜrkmən,ʃɪp/ n. мастерство

workout /'wɜrk,aʊt/ n. разминка; тренировка

workplace /'wɜrk'pleɪs/ n. место работы

workshop /'wɜrk,ʃɒp/ n. (small) мастерская; (in factory) цех

work station n. автоматизированное рабочее место (abbr. APM)

world /wɜrld/ **1.** n. мир **2.** adj. мировой; **—ly** adj. светский

worldwide /'wɜrld'waɪd/ adj. всемирный

World Wide Web n. (abbr. WWW) всемирная паутина

worm /wɜrm/ n. червяк; червь m.

worm-eaten adj. червивый

wormwood /'wɜrm,wʊd/ n. полынь m.

worn /wɔrn/ adj. поношенный

worn-out adj. (clothes) изношенный

worrisome /'wɜrɪsəm/ adj. беспокойный

worry /'wɜrɪ/ **1.** n. забота; беспокойство **2.** v. беспокоить(ся) impf.; **—ing** adj. беспокоящий

worse /wɜrs/ **1.** adj. худший **2.** adv. хуже **3.** v.: **get** ~, **worsen** ухудшаться impf., ухудшиться pf.

worship /'wɜrʃɪp/ **1.** n. поклонение **2.** v. поклоняться impf.; **—er** n. поклонник, -ница

worst /wɜrst/ **1.** adj. самый плохой; наихудший **2.** adv. хуже всего

worth /wɜrθ/ n. стоимость; ценность; **be** ~ стоить impf.; **—less** adj. ничего не стоящий

worthwhile /'wɜrθ'waɪl/ adj. стоящий, полезный

worthy /'wɜrðɪ/ adj. достойный

would-be adj. воображающий себя

wound /wund/ **1.** n. рана; ранение **2.** v. ранить impf. & pf.; **—ed** adj. раненый

woven /'woʊvən/ adj. тканый

wrangle /'ræŋgəl/ n. пререкание

wrap /ræp/ v. завёртывать impf., завернуть pf.; **—per**, **—ping** n. обёртка

wrath /ræθ/ n. гнев

wreak /rik/ v.: ~ **havoc** разорять impf.

wreath /riθ/ n. венок

wreck /rɛk/ **1.** n. крушение; (car) разбитая машина **2.** v. разрушать impf., разрушить pf.

wreckage /'rɛkɪdʒ/ n. обломки pl.

wrench /rɛntʃ/ n. (sprain) вывих; (tool) гаечный ключ

wrest /rɛst/ v. вырывать impf.

wrestle /'rɛsəl/ v. бороться impf.

wrestler /'rɛslər/ n. борец

wrestling /'rɛslɪŋ/ n. борьба

wretched /'rɛtʃɪd/ adj. жалкий

wriggle /'rɪgəl/ v. извиваться impf., извиться pf.

wring /rɪŋ/ v. выжимать impf., выжать pf.

wrinkle /'rɪŋkəl/ **1.** n. морщина **2.** v. морщить(ся) impf., с- pf.

wrist /rɪst/ n. запя́стье; ~ **watch** n. нару́чные часы́ pl.

wristband /ˈrɪst,bænd/ n. манже́та

writ /rɪt/ n. (law) суде́бный прика́з

write /raɪt/ v. писа́ть impf., na-pf.; ~ **down** запи́сывать impf., записа́ть pf.

write-off n. (econ.) спи́санные со счёта су́ммы pl.

writer /ˈraɪtər/ n. писа́тель, —ница

write-up n. описа́ние

writhe /raɪð/ v. ко́рчиться impf.

writing /ˈraɪtɪŋ/ n. (act) писа́ние; (works) сочине́ния

written /ˈrɪtn/ adj. пи́сьменный

wrong /rɒŋ/ 1. adj. непра́вильный; оши́бочный; не тот 2. n. зло; несправедли́вость 3. v. вреди́ть impf., по- pf.; **—ful** adj. несправедли́вый; (unlawful) незако́нный; **—ly** adv. непра́вильно; несправедли́во

wrought iron /rɔt/ n. сва́рочное желе́зо

wry /raɪ/ adj. криво́й

xenophobia /ˌzenəˈfoubiə/ n. ксенофо́бия

xerox /ˈzɪərɒks/ v. ксерокопи́ровать impf., от- pf.; ~ **copy** n. ксероко́пия

x-ray /ˈeks,reɪ/ 1. n. рентге́новский сни́мок; pl. рентге́новы лучи́ pl. 2. adj. рентге́новский 3. v. де́лать рентге́н impf., с- pf.

xylophone /ˈzaɪlə,foun/ n. ксилофо́н

yacht /jɒt/ n. я́хта; **—ing** n. па́русный спорт

yachtsman /ˈyɒtsmən/ n. яхтсме́н; спортсме́н-па́русник

Yakut /yəˈkut/ n. яку́т, я́кутка

yam /yæm/ n. ямс; бата́т

yank /yæŋk/ v. дёргать impf.

yap /yæp/ v. тя́вкать impf.

yard[1] /yɑrd/ n. двор

yard[2] /yɑrd/ n. (measure) ярд

yardstick /ˈyɑrd,stɪk/ n. (measure) ме́рка; Fig. мери́ло

yarn /yɑrn/ n. пря́жа

yawn /yɔn/ v. зево́к m. зева́ть impf., зевну́ть pf.

yea /yeɪ/ adv. да

year /yɪər/ n. год; **this** ~ в э́том году́; **—ly** adj. ежего́дный

yearbook /ˈyɪər,buk/ n. ежего́дник

yearn /yɜrn/ v. тоскова́ть (по + D) impf.; **—ing** n. тоска́

yeast /yist/ n. дро́жжи pl.

yell /yel/ 1. n. пронзи́тельный крик 2. v. крича́ть impf., кри́кнуть pf.

yellow /ˈyelou/ adj. жёлтый

yellowish /ˈyelouɪʃ/ adj. желтова́тый

yelp /yelp/ 1. n. визг 2. v. визжа́ть impf.

yes /yes/ adv. да

yesterday /ˈyestər,deɪ/ 1. adv. вчера́; **the day before** ~ adv. позавчера́ 2. n. ~'s adj. вчера́шний

yet /yet/ 1. adv. всё (ещё) 2. conj. одна́ко; **not** ~ ещё не(т)

Yiddish /ˈyɪdɪʃ/ n. и́диш

yield /yild/ 1. v. дава́ть impf., дать pf.; (surrender) уступа́ть impf., -пи́ть pf. 2. n. (econ.) дохо́д; **—ing** adj. усту́пчивый

yoga /ˈyougə/ n. йо́га

yogurt /ˈyougərt/ n. йо́гурт

yoke /youk/ n. ярмо́; и́го

yolk /youk/ n. желто́к

you /yu/ pron. ты; вы

young /yʌŋ/ adj. молодо́й

younger /ˈyʌŋgər/ adj. мла́дший; pred. моло́же

youngest /ˈyʌŋgɪst/ adj. (са́мый) мла́дший

your /yur/ adj. твой; ваш

yourself /yurˈself/ pron. ты сам(а́); вы са́ми; (refl.) себя́

youth /yuθ/ n. ю́ность; мо́лодость; (man) ю́ноша m.; coll. молодёжь f.

youthful /ˈyuθfəl/ adj. ю́ношеский

Yugoslav /ˈyougou,slɑv/ 1. adj. югосла́вский 2. n. югосла́в, —ка

Yugoslavia /ˌyougouˈslɑviə/ n. Югосла́вия

yuletide /ˈyul,taɪd/ 1. n. Свя́тки pl. 2. adj. свя́точный

zany /ˈzeɪni/ adj. чудно́й

zeal /zil/ n. усе́рдие; рве́ние

zealot /ˈzelət/ n. фана́тик; ревни́тель

zealous /ˈzeləs/ adj. усе́рдный

zebra /ˈzibrə/ n. зе́бра

Zen /zen/ n. Дзен-будди́зм

zenith /ˈzinɪθ/ n. зени́т

zeppelin /ˈzepəlɪn/ n. цеппели́н

zero /ˈzɪərou/ 1. n. ноль; нуль m. 2. adj. нулево́й

zest /zest/ n. пика́нтность

zestful /'zɛstfəl/ adj. живо́й

zigzag /'zɪg,zæg/ n. зигза́г

zinc /zɪŋk/ **1.** n. цинк **2.** adj. ци́нковый

Zionism /'zaɪə,nɪzəm/ n. сиони́зм

zip /zɪp/ v. застёгивать(ся) (на мо́лнию) impf., застегну́ть(ся) pf.; **~ code** n. почто́вый и́ндекс

zipper /'zɪpər/ n. (застёжка-) мо́лния

zither /'zɪθər/ n. ци́тра

zodiac /'zoudɪ,æk/ n. зодиа́к

zombie /'zɒmbi/ n. ожи́вший поко́йник

zone /zoun/ n. зо́на; (geog.) по́яс

zoning /'zounɪŋ/ n. райони́рование; зони́рование

zoological /,zouə'lɒdʒɪkəl/ adj. зоологи́ческий

zoology /zou'ɒlədʒi/ n. зооло́гия

zoo /zu/ n. зоопа́рк

Useful Words and Expressions
Слова́рь пе́рвой необходи́мости

Hello	Здра́вствуйте
Hi!	Приве́т!
Good morning	До́брое у́тро
Good afternoon	До́брый де́нь
Good evening	До́брый ве́чер
Allow me to introduce (myself)	Позво́льте предста́вить(ся) . . .
My name is . . .	Меня́ зову́т . . .
What is your name?	Как Вас зову́т?
I'm pleased to meet you!	О́чень рад (ра́да) с Ва́ми познако́миться!
How are you?	Как дела́?
I come from New York	Я из Нью-Йо́рка
(Chicago, Washington,	(Чика́го, Вашингто́на,
California, Florida)	Калифо́рнии, Фло́риды)
Thank you	Спаси́бо/Благодарю́ Вас
Thank you very much	Большо́е спаси́бо
Excuse me	Извини́те
Please	Пожа́луйста
Yes	Да
No	Нет
All right	Хорошо́
Very good	О́чень хорошо́
O.K.	Хорошо́!/Всё в поря́дке!
You're welcome	Рад (ра́да) помо́чь/Пожа́луйста
Please help me	Пожа́луйста, помоги́те мне
Where is the hotel?	Где нахо́дится гости́ница?
How much is this?	Ско́лько э́то сто́ит?
What time is it?	Кото́рый час?/Ско́лько вре́мени?
With pleasure!	С удово́льствием!
Congratulations!	Поздравля́ю!
Happy holiday!	Поздравля́ю с пра́здником!
Happy birthday!	Поздравля́ю с Днём Рожде́ния!
Do you speak English?	Вы говори́те по-англи́йски?

I don't speak Russian	Я не говорю́ по-ру́сски
I (we) need an interpreter	Мне (нам) ну́жен перево́дчик
I didn't understand	Я не по́нял (не поняла́)
I don't know	Я не зна́ю
Please speak slowly	Говори́те, пожа́луйста, ме́дленнее
Please repeat it	Повтори́те, пожа́луйста, ещё раз
What is this?	Что э́то тако́е?
What do you call this in Russian?	Как э́то называ́ется по-ру́сски?
What does this word mean?	Что означа́ет э́то сло́во?
As you please	Как Вам уго́дно
Could you tell me please how to get to (the subway, the . . . street, building No.) . . .	Скажи́те, пожа́луйста, как пройти́ (в метро́, на у́лицу . . . , к до́му но́мер . . .) . . .
I have to get to the subway stop . . .	Мне (нам) нужна́ ста́нция метро́ . . .
Good luck!	Всего́ хоро́шего (до́брого)!
Good night	Споко́йной но́чи
Bon voyage!	Счастли́вого пути́!
Give my regards to . . .	Переда́йте приве́т . . .
Goodbye	До свида́ния
Welcome!	Добро́ пожа́ловать!
Entrance	Вход
Staff Only	Служе́бный вход
Exit	Вы́ход
Emergency Exit	Запа́сный (Авари́йный) вы́ход
Transfer	Перехо́д
No smoking!	Не кури́ть!
Don't litter!	Не сори́ть!
Attention!	Внима́ние!
Danger!	Опа́сно!
Carefully!	Осторо́жно!
Man/Men	Мужчи́на
Woman/Women	Же́нщина
Left Luggage	Ка́мера хране́ния
Lost and Found	Стол нахо́док
Information	Спра́вочное бюро́
Open	Откры́то

Closed	Закры́то
Dead End	Тупи́к
No Throughway	Прохо́д закры́т

Menu Меню́

Cold Appetizers	**Холо́дные заку́ски:**
Salad	Сала́т
Beet Salad	Винегре́т
Aspic	Холоде́ц
Eggs	Я́йца
Sauerkraut	Капу́ста ква́шеная
Sandwich	Бутербро́д
Cheese	Сыр
Bread	Хлеб

First Course	**Пе́рвые блю́да:**
Cabbage soup	Щи
Beet Soup	Борщ
Fish Soup	Уха́
Broth	Бульо́н
Vegetable soup (Vegetarian)	Суп овощно́й (вегетариа́нский)
Noodle Soup	Суп с лапшо́й
Mushroom Soup	Суп грибно́й

Entrées	**Вторы́е блю́да:**
Burger	Котле́ты
Steak	Бифште́кс
Meatballs	Фрикаде́льки
Schnitzel	Шни́цель
Beef Stroganoff	Бефстро́ганов
Beef	Говя́дина
Pork	Свини́на
Mutton	Бара́нина
Chicken	Ку́рица
Liver	Печёнка
Sausage	Колбаса́
Knockwurst	Сарде́льки
Hot Dogs	Соси́ски
Fish	Ры́ба
Shrimp	Креве́тки

Crabs	**Кра́бы**
Crayfish	**Ра́ки**
Dumplings	**Пельме́ни**
Omelet	**Яи́чница**

Side Dishes	**Гарни́ры:**
French Fries	**Карто́фель-фри**
Mashed Potatoes	**Карто́фель-пюре́**
Pasta	**Макаро́ны**
Rice	**Рис**

Sauces and Seasonings	**Со́усы и припра́вы:**
Sauce	**Со́ус**
Gravy	**Подли́ва**
Horseradish	**Хрен**
Mustard	**Горчи́ца**
Garlic	**Чесно́к**
Salt	**Соль**
Pepper	**Пе́рец**

Desserts	**Десе́рты:**
Candy	**Конфе́ты**
Cookies	**Пече́нье**
Raisin Cake/Raisin Muffin	**Кекс**
Chocolate	**Шокола́д**
Pastry	**Пиро́жное**
Cake	**Торт**
Fruit Jelly	**Мармела́д**
Ice Cream	**Моро́женое**
Apples	**Я́блоки**
Oranges	**Апельси́ны**
Grapes	**Виногра́д**
Watermelon	**Арбу́з**
Cantaloupe	**Ды́ня**

Hot Beverages	**Горя́чие напи́тки:**
Coffee	**Ко́фе**
Tea	**Чай**
Hot Chocolate	**Кака́о**

Cold Beverages	**Холо́дные напи́тки:**
(Mineral) Water	**(Минера́льная) вода́**
Juice	**Сок**

Stewed Fruit	**Компо́т**
Lemonade	**Лимона́д**
Coke	**Ко́ла**

Alcoholic Beverages **Алкого́льные напи́тки:**

Vodka	**Во́дка**
Wine	**Вино́**
Beer	**Пи́во**
Cognac	**Конья́к**
Cocktail	**Кокте́йль**
Champagne	**Шампа́нское**

Days of the Week

Дни неде́ли

Sunday	воскресе́нье
Monday	понеде́льник
Tuesday	вто́рник
Wednesday	среда́
Thursday	четве́рг
Friday	пя́тница
Saturday	суббо́та

Months of the Year

Ме́сяцы го́да

January	янва́рь
February	февра́ль
March	март
April	апре́ль
May	май
June	ию́нь
July	ию́ль
August	а́вгуст
September	сентя́брь
October	октя́брь
November	ноя́брь
December	дека́брь

Numerals

Имена́ числи́тельные

one	оди́н
two	два
three	три
four	четы́ре
five	пять
six	шесть
seven	семь
eight	во́семь
nine	де́вять
ten	де́сять
eleven	оди́ннадцать
twelve	двена́дцать
thirteen	трина́дцать
fourteen	четы́рнадцать
fifteen	пятна́дцать
sixteen	шестна́дцать
seventeen	семна́дцать

eighteen	восемна́дцать
nineteen	девятна́дцать
twenty	два́дцать
thirty	три́дцать
forty	со́рок
fifty	пятьдеся́т
sixty	шестьдеся́т
seventy	се́мьдесят
eighty	во́семьдесят
ninety	девяно́сто
one hundred	сто
two hundred	две́сти
three hundred	три́ста
four hundred	четы́реста
five hundred	пятьсо́т
six hundred	шестьсо́т
seven hundred	семьсо́т
eight hundred	восемьсо́т
nine hundred	девятьсо́т
one thousand	ты́сяча
one million	миллио́н

Comparative Table of Temperatures

Celsius		Fahrenheit	
−40°	37.8°	−40°	100°
−35°	40°	−31°	104°
−25°	100° (Water boils)	−13°	212°
−15°		5°	
−10°		14°	
−5°		23°	
0° (Water freezes)		32°	
4°		39.2°	
8°		46.4°	
12°		53.6°	
16°		60.8°	
20°		68°	
24°		75.2°	
28°		82.4°	
32°		89.6°	
36°		96.8°	
37° (Body temperature)		98.6°	

English Irregular Verbs

Указатель английских нерегулярных глаголов

Present	Past Tense	Past Participle
arise	arose	arisen
awake	awoke*	awoken*
be	was/were	been
bear	bore	borne, born
beat	beat	beaten
become	became	become
begin	began	begun
bend	bent	bent
bereave	bereft*	bereft*
bid	bade, bid	bidden, bid
bind	bound	bound
bite	bit	bitten
bleed	bled	bled
blow	blew	blown
break	broke	broken
breed	bred	bred
bring	brought	brought
build	built	built
burn	burnt*	burnt*
burst	burst	burst
buy	bought	bought
cast	cast	cast
choose	chose	chosen
cleave	cleft, clove	cleft, cloven
cling	clung	clung
come	came	come
cost	cost	cost
creep	crept	crept
cut	cut	cut
deal	dealt	dealt
dig	dug	dug
do	did	done
draw	drew	drawn
dream	dreamt*	dreamt*
drink	drank	drunk
drive	drove	driven

Verbs marked * are more commonly conjugated in the regular weak form.

Present	Past Tense	Past Participle
dwell	dwelt*	dwelt*
eat	ate	eaten
fall	fell	fallen
feed	fed	fed
feel	felt	felt
fight	fought	fought
find	found	found
flee	fled	fled
fling	flung	flung
fly	flew	flown
forbid	forbade	forbidden
foretell	foretold	foretold
forget	forgot	forgotten
forgive	forgave	forgiven
forsake	forsook	forsaken
freeze	froze	frozen
get	got	got, gotten
give	gave	given
go	went	gone
grind	ground	ground
grow	grew	grown
hang	hung*	hung*
have	had	had
hear	heard	heard
heave	hove*	hove*
hide	hid	hidden, hid
hit	hit	hit
hold	held	held
hurt	hurt	hurt
keep	kept	kept
kneel	knelt*	knelt*
knit	knit	knit
know	knew	known
lay	laid	laid
lead	led	led
leap	leapt*	leapt*
leave	left	left
lend	lent	lent
let	let	let

Verbs marked * are more commonly conjugated in the regular weak form.

Present	Past Tense	Past Participle
lie (лежáть)	lay	lain
light	lit*	lit*
lose	lost	lost
make	made	made
mean	meant	meant
meet	met	met
pay	paid	paid
prove	proved	proven
put	put	put
read	read	read
rid	rid, ridded	rid, ridded
ride	rode	ridden
ring	rang	rung
rise	rose	risen
run	ran	run
say	said	said
see	saw	seen
seek	sought	sought
sell	sold	sold
send	sent	sent
set	set	set
sew	sewed	sewn*
shake	shook	shaken
shed	shed	shed
shine	shone	shone
shoot	shot	shot
show	showed	shown*
shrink	shrunk, shrank	shrunk
shut	shut	shut
sing	sang	sung
sink	sank, sunk	sunk
sit	sat	sat
sleep	slept	slept
slide	slid	slid
sling	slung	slung
slit	slit	slit
speak	spoke	spoken
speed	sped*	sped*
spend	spent	spent

Verbs marked * are more commonly conjugated in the regular weak form.

Present	Past Tense	Past Participle
spin	spun	spun
spit	spit, spat	spit, spat
split	split	split
spread	spread	spread
spring	sprung, sprang	sprung
stand	stood	stood
steal	stole	stolen
stick	stuck	stuck
sting	stung	stung
stink	stank, stunk	stunk
strike	struck	struck (stricken)
string	strung	strung
strive	strove	striven
swear	swore	sworn
sweep	swept	swept
swell	swelled	swollen*
swim	swam	swum
swing	swung	swung
take	took	taken
teach	taught	taught
tear	tore	torn
tell	told	told
think	thought	thought
throw	threw	thrown
thrust	thrust	thrust
tread	trod	trod, trodden
wake	woke, waked	waked, woke[n]
wear	wore	worn
weave	wove	woven
weep	wept	wept
wet	wet, wetted	wet, wetted
win	won	won
wind	wound	wound
wring	wrung	wrung
write	wrote	written

Verbs marked * are more commonly conjugated in the regular weak form.